Lith. Chs. Shober & Co. Chicago, Ill.

Ant'y Wayne

HISTORY

OF

FORT WAYNE,

FROM

THE EARLIEST KNOWN ACCOUNTS

OF

THIS POINT,

TO THE PRESENT PERIOD.

EMBRACING AN EXTENDED VIEW OF THE ABORIGINAL TRIBES OF THE NORTHWEST, INCLUDING, MORE ESPECIALLY, THE MIAMIES, OF THIS LOCALITY—THEIR HABITS, CUSTOMS, ETC.—TOGETHER WITH A COMPREHENSIVE SUMMARY OF THE GENERAL RELATIONS OF THE NORTHWEST, FROM THE LATTER PART OF THE SEVENTEENTH CENTURY, TO THE STRUGGLES OF 1812-14;

WITH A SKETCH OF THE

LIFE OF GENERAL ANTHONY WAYNE;

INCLUDING ALSO A LENGTHY

BIOGRAPHY OF THE LATE HON. SAMUEL HANNA,

TOGETHER WITH SHORT

SKETCHES OF SEVERAL OF THE EARLY PIONEER SETTLERS OF FORT WAYNE.

ALSO AN ACCOUNT OF THE

MANUFACTURING, MERCANTILE, AND RAILROAD INTERESTS

OF FORT WAYNE AND VICINITY.

——o——

BY WALLACE A. BRICE.

——o——

WITH ILLUSTRATIONS.

——o——

FORT WAYNE, IND:

D. W. JONES & SON, STEAM BOOK AND JOB PRINTERS.

1868.

TO THE CITIZENS

OF THE

CITY OF FORT WAYNE AND VICINITY,

AND

Farmers of Allen County,

AS AN HUMBLE TRIBUTE OF ESTEEM,

This Volume is most Kindly dedicated,

BY THE AUTHOR.

PREFATORY REMARKS.

When I first thought to gather together and arrange the material with which to form the HISTORY OF FORT WAYNE, I had little comprehended the magnitude and extent of the field or matter thereof; and after receiving the ready and liberal assurances and aid of a large mass of the citizens of Fort Wayne in substantial subscriptions thereto, and made known my intention to issue the work, I soon found myself encompassed on all sides by a vast store of information and facts, from which to draw and form the material for the work.

Though, from an early day, widely known as a point of great interest and importance, both as to its aboriginal renown, throughout the northwest, for many consecutive years; and the whites, for nearly a century before the war of 1812, yet, aside from a few short, hastily-written, and very incomplete sketches of the place and adjacent localities, no one had ever ventured or been sufficiently aroused to the importance and value of such a volume, to write and arrange the history of this old carrying-place, and former center of Indian life, in view of which, the French, the English, and the American soldiers had so long successively stood guard.

Having procured many valuable documents, old and rare, from which to draw much of interest for the work, and received also much important information from those of the Pioneer fathers and mothers among us, who still survive to tell the story of

> "the early times out west,
> * * * * * *
> In the days when THEY were Pioneers,
> Fifty years ago,"

I readily saw that, to do justice to so extended a body of matter, time would not only be required to put it into readable form, but much care needed in the sifting and selection of the material; and so, with large perseverance and a determination not to slight or overlook any important feature of the work, during the latter part of May and first of June last, I began industriously to devote myself to the task of writing and arranging the matter for the volume, often, during the warm months of summer, repairing to the woods in the vicinity, writing much of the work upon the ground, where, in former years, were to be seen many Indian lodges, and also contiguous to points where the early skirmishes between the Indians and whites had occurred.

Thus pushing forward, filling several hundred pages of paper, by the latter part of September, I found my task about complete, and the MSS. in the hands of the printer.

In my efforts to obtain information, I am pleased to say that many not only freely told me all the important facts they could call to mind, but kindly extended to me the use of valuable books, papers, &c. Among these I may name Chas. B.

Lasselle, Esq., of Logansport, Ind., John P. Hedges, Esq., Hon. J. W. Borden, Louis Peltier, T. N. Hood, Dr. J. B. Brown, J. L. Williams, Esq., Mr. J. J. Comparet, Mrs. Griswold, Mrs. Laura Suttenfield, and others.

Among the historical works referred to, and drawn from, I have been particularly careful to "keep good company," and have used the material of those volumes only which have well sustained a reputation for accuracy, some of which have long since gone out of print. Among these, I may mention "The History of the Late War in the Western Country," by Col. Robt. B. M'Afee, who was here with the army during much of the war of 1812 and '14—(this volume is now fifty years old); Butler's "History of Kentucky"—1836; Drake's "Life of Black Hawk"—1833; "The Hesperian, or Western Monthly Magazine"—1838; "The American Pioneer;" "Wau-Bun, the 'Early Day' in the Northwest;" "Western Annals;" Sparks' "American Biography," "States and Territories of the Great West;" Parkman's "History of the Conspiracy of Pontiac;" Dillon's "History of Indiana;" Judge Law's "Address"—1839; etc., etc., together with a number of papers containing interesting and valuable sketches.

Much more might have been added to the work; but the price charged for it would not well admit of an enlargement beyond the number of pages presented. In actual amount of matter, however, the pages being "solid," it will not fall far short of many works of a similar character, which, though containing a less number of lines on each page, are yet much more bulky and voluminous. Indeed, so extensive were many of the facts and matter generally from which the work has been drawn, that, in some instances, I have been compelled to leave out and cut short much matter that I should liked to have presented in the present issue. But all will "keep," very well, subject to a further call by the public.

In the latter part of this volume, the reader will find, together with some other matter of interest, several sketches of early settlers of Fort Wayne, conspicuous among which will be found a very lengthy Biography of our late most beloved and lamented fellow-citizen, Hon. Samuel Hanna, from the able pen of his old friend and companion, one of Fort Wayne's most worthy and respected citizens, G. W. Wood, Esq. A short sketch of the father of Charles B. Lasselle, Esq., "the first white man born at Ke-ki-ong-a," will be found in this part of the work; one also of Mr H. Rudisill, father of our county Auditor. But all will be read with equal care and interest by the reader. Thanking the citizens generally, of Fort Wayne and Allen county, including especially the publishers of each of our city papers, for the interest manifested in behalf of the work, and the liberal aid extended to it, in the form of subscriptions, I trust, in return, the volume may not only prove a source of much interest and value to all, but be successful in rescuing from a comparative oblivion the historic importance to which Fort Wayne is so justly entitled.

WALLACE A. BRICE.

FORT WAYNE, IND., Dec., 1867.

BIOGRAPHY OF GEN. ANTHONY WAYNE.

SKETCH OF THE LIFE

OF

GENERAL ANTHONY WAYNE.

—o—

"Lives of TRUE men all remind us
We can make our lives sublime,
And, departing, leave behind us
Foot-prints on the sands of time."

—o—

ANTHONY WAYNE was not alone a valiant officer and soldier. He was a moral hero. His frontal brain was large, and the crown of his head well expanded. Largely intuitive, ever thoughtful, sagacious, and resolute of will; his soul was imbued with a large feeling of benificence as well as determination—a high admiration of the beautiful and picturesque in nature. While clinging to the sword, as a means of safety, he was disposed to invite his antagonist to join in a council of peace. Always on the look-out—cautious and most prudent in his movements—bold, intrepid, and fearless, when called to the field of battle, his opponents were sure, sooner or later, to come to defeat. He was, by nature and organization, a soldier, a tactician, a hero. Somewhat scholarly, he wrote not only a fair hand, but an agreeable diction; and was noted for his laconicism.* Born with the great spirit of true Freedom deeply impressed upon him, at an early age he became imbued with the importance of freeing his country, and making it an asylum for the out-growth, establishment, and perpetuation of unsullied liberty, free institutions, and good government. Thus actuated and impelled, the name of ANTHONY WAYNE is found among the first to lead the way at the commencement of the American Revolution; and when, a few years after the long struggle for Independence, the West called for the services of one equal to the emergency of the time, he was soon sent to her relief; and the country, after the lapse of a few months, subsequent to his movement thither, was made to rejoice under a new reign of peace and safety.†

The grand-father of Wayne was an Englishman by birth, who left his native country during 1681, and removed to Ireland, where he devoted

*At the capture of Stony Point, he addressed the following to Gen. Washington :

STONY POINT, 16TH JULY, 1776, 2 O'clock, A. M.

DEAR GENERAL:—The fort and garrison with Col. Johnson are ours. Our officers and men behaved like men who are determined to be free. Yours most sincerely

Gen. Washington. ANT'Y WAYNE.

†See Chapter XII of this volume.

himself to agriculture for a period of several years. Entering the army of William of Orange, against King James, the exile, in 1690, he fought at the battle of the Boyne, and took part in the siege of Limerick, making himself quite servicable to the state, for which he seems never to have been duly rewarded, and becoming eventually much dissatisfied with the general relations of his adopted country, at the age of sixty-three he left Ireland, and ventured upon a voyage across the Ocean, reaching Pennsylvania in 1722. With the new country he was much pleased, and soon purchased a farm and settled in Chester county of that state; and it was here that his grand-son and name-sake, the subject of this sketch, was born, on the 1st of January, 1745.

But little is known of the early life of Wayne, further than he was accounted a "pretty wild boy," and from his youth seemed to have had a greater fondness for the art and peril of war than any thing his mind could be called to. For this pass-time and amusement, he forsook school, school-books, and gave little heed to much earnest advice. His uncle, Gilbert Wayne, to whom Anthony was sent as a pupil to acquire the common rudiments of an education, wrote to his father as follows concerning his nephew:

"I really suspect," said he, "that parental affection blinds you; and that you have mistaken your son's capacity. What he may be best qualified for, I know not; but one thing I am certain of, that he will never make a scholar. He may make a soldier; he has already distracted the brains of two-thirds of the boys under my direction, by rehersals of battles, and sieges &c. They exhibit more the appearance of Indians and harlequins than of students; this one, decorated with a cap of many colors; and others, habited in coats as variegated as Joseph's of old; some, laid up with broken heads, and others with black eyes. During noon, instead of the usual games and amusements, he has the boys employed in throwing up redoubts, skirmishing, &c. I must be candid with you, brother Isaac; unless Anthony pays more attention to his books, I shall be under the painful necessity of dismissing him from the school."

The result of this was a severe lecture from his father, who threatened, likewise, to withdraw him from school and place him upon the farm at hard work, if failing to conduct himself differently, in the future, and give over his sham battling, erection of redoubts, military rehearsals, and building of mud forts. The earnest, resolute words of his father, for whom he entertained a strong affection and regard, were deeply impressed upon him; and he resolved to return to his uncle, devote himself to his studies, and forsake all that had given rise to former complaint against him. Thus acting and applying himself diligently to his studies for a period of eighteen months, his uncle was compelled to admit that he had not only "acquired all that his master could teach," but that "he merited the means of higher and more general instruction," which induced his father at once to send him to the Philadelphia Academy, where, at the age of eighteen years, he had acquired an extended knowledge of Astronomy and Mathematics. Returning again to his native county, he now entered upon the business of land surveying.

It was about this period that the peace between the powers of Great Britain and France was terminated, which placed Nova Scotia in the possession of the former, and the British government at once bethought to colonize her newly acquired territory; and associations soon began to be formed in some of the older provinces with a view to colonizing these newly acquired regions. Prominent among these was a company of merchants and others, from Pennsylvania, embracing among their number Benjamin Franklin, and through the recomendation of Franklin, young WAYNE, then in his twenty-first year, was readily chosen special agent to visit the newly-acquired territory, to examine the soil best adapted to agricultural pursuits, and to gain information as to "the means of commercial facilities connected with it." Upon this important mission young Wayne not only soon embarked and performed the duties thereof most satisfactorily to all concerned, but was continued in the trust till the year 1767, when the difficulties, then assuming a serious attitude between the mother country and the colonial settlements of America, had the effect to break up the enterprise and call the attention of the colonists to matters of self-defense directly within the colonial settlements.

Returning again to Pennsylvania, young Wayne, in 1767, was united in wedlock to the daughter of a distinguished merchant in Philadelphia, of the name of Benjamin Penrose, whither he soon returned to Chester county, and again embarked in the occupation of surveying, engaging also in agricultural pursuits when a short cessation or pause in his profession occurred; and in this latter vocation he is said to have "found much to gratify his taste."

Continuing to menace the colonies, and insist upon her policy of taxation, up to the period of 1774-5—to which time we find Wayne still engaged in the business of surveying and farming—Great Britain was at length met with a formidable front by the colonists, who had determined to resist the further aggressions of the king and Parliament of the British government, even to the sword.. Indeed, matters had now assumed such a shape as to leave no room or hope for escape on the part of the colonial settlements; and WAYNE was among the first to step forward and declare for a positive stand against the further encroachment of the British Crown.

The events now surely leading to a long and severe struggle against the mother country, in which he was to take so active a part, had years before, when but a boy, been foreshadowed in his ardent love of military sports—his fondness for the erection of redoubts and mud forts, of which his uncle so earnestly complained; and seeing largely the importance of *readiness* for such a campaign, Wayne began at once to withdraw himself from all political assemblies of the country, and devote himself to the organization and instruction of military bodies. In this he was not only wise, but successful; for, within the period of six weeks, he was able to bring together and form a company of volunteers, "having," says the account,* from which the foregoing was principally drawn, "more the appearance of a veteran than of a military regiment."

The energy and capacity of WAYNE had now begun to attract public attention; and during the early part of January, 1776, the Continental Congress readily conferred upon him the title of Colonel, and gave him the command of "one of the four regiments required from Pennsylvania, in reinforcement of the northern army." In his new capacity, he was ever

*Prepared by his son, Isaac Wayne, and first published in a work printed in Philadelphia some years ago, called "THE CASKET."

noted for his diligence and activity, and his efforts were always attended with marked success.

The regiment under his command having been speedily raised and equiped, he soon took up his line of march for Canada; whither he arrived about the latter part of June, ('76,) and formed a part of Thompson's brigade, at the mouth of the river Sorel. Major-General Sullivan, then in command of the northern army, arrived at this point about the same period of Wayne's arrival, and learning that the British commander had sent a detachment of some six hundred light infantry to the westward, as far as the village of Trois Rivieres, unattended by any relief corps, a plan was at once agreed upon for the capture of the detachment and post, and establishing there a formidable battery, "which, if not sufficient entirely to prevent the ascent of the British armed vessels and transports to Montreal, might, for a time so embarrass the navigation, as greatly to retard their progress thither."*

Accordingly, on the 3rd of July, with St. Clair's, Wayne's and Irvine's regiments, Major Sullivan dispatched Thompson to a little village on the south side of the St. Lawrence, called Niccolete, which stood nearly opposite to the village of Trois Rivieres.

Learning "that a place called the White-house (still nearer to the assailants than Trois Rivieres) was occupied by an advanced guard," and Thompson, a tactician of the old school, being of the opinion that "troops acting offensively should leave no hostile post in their rear," began to move in the direction of the supposed position of the enemy, but soon found that the point was unoccupied.

After the loss of much time and the encounter of many perplexities, besides placing his men in a fair position for a surprise and capture, Thompson now directed the troops to return to the place of their landing. Having, for some hours previous, been shielded by the night, the dawn now began to appear, and the enemy caught sight of the detachment, and were soon driving it from point to point, until, at length, the troops under Thompson were compelled to seek safety in a considerable morass, "from which he had just extricated himself," where "he and a few others," were soon captured; and Col. St. Clair, second in command, having, about the same time, been disabled in one of his feet, the further direction of the forces remaining fell upon Col. Wayne; and though badly wounded, so successful was he in the conduct of the movement, that he soon gained the western side of the river Des Loups, and rapidly made his "way along the northern bank of the St. Lawrence, to the village of Berthier," gaining the American camp at the mouth of the river Sorel in safety.

Late in June, General Sullivan began to perceive, from the movements of the British, that his position was no longer a safe one; and immediately issued an order for the evacuation of the fort of the Sorel, and a retreat upon Lake Champlain.

In this movement Wayne and the Pennsylvania regiments were directed to cover the rear. So close was the enemy, in this move, "that the boats latest getting into motion were not beyond the reach of musket shot, when the head of the enemy's column entered the fort." Without further molestation or alarm, the army, on the 17th of July, succeeded in reaching Ticonderoga.

*St. Clair's narrative.

Thus we see, in the very out-set of the struggle for Independence, how our hero, step by step, made himself most serviceable to his country and, laid the foundation for lasting renown.

The command of the northern troops, now devolving upon Gen. Gates, who, learning of the perilous condition of Washington, "with eight regiments," marched "to the aid of the Commander-in-chief," leaving the post of Ticonderoga in the command of Col. Wayne, with a force of two thousand five hundred men—an arrangement that not only proved most pleasing to the troops under him, but highly agreeable to Congress, which body, in order the better to encourage and sustain the appointment, soon conferred upon Wayne the title of Brigadier-General, continuing him in command of Ticonderoga until the following spring, at which period he was called to the ranks of the main army under Gen. Washington, reaching headquarters on the 15th of May, 1777, where he was at once placed at the head of a brigade "which," said Washington, "could not fail under his direction to be soon and greatly distinguished."

We now find Wayne connected with nearly every important movement of the Revolution; and though, as on occasions already referred to, closely pursued or surrounded, he yet, sooner or later, was ever the successful leader or actor in every engagement.

After the retreat of the British from Philadelphia, in June, 1777, we find the corps under Wayne, with those of Sullivan, Maxwell, and Morgan, sent in pursuit, of which, two alone (Wayne's and Morgan's) were enabled to follow up the retreat, of whom Washington, in his report to Congress, said: "They displayed great bravery and good conduct; constantly advancing on an enemy far superior to themselves in numbers, and well secured by redoubts."

At the battle of Brandywine "Wayne was assigned the post of honor, that of leading the American attack; a service he performed with a gallantry now become habitual to himself and the division he commanded."*

At the famous engagement of Stoney Point, Wayne's own escapes are stated as "of the hair-breadth kind."† Shortly after capturing and entering the fortification of the enemy, he was struck by a musket-ball on the head, which caused his fall; but he immediately rallied, crying out, "march on, carry me into the fort; for should tho wound be mortal, I will die at the head of the column."

This engagement, considered "the most brilliant of the war," is said to have "covered the commanding general (Wayne) with laurels;" of whom Washington, referring to this occasion, said in his report to Congress: "To the encoumiums he (Wayne) has deservedly bestowed on the officers and men under his command, it gives me pleasure to add that his own conduct throughout the whole of this arduous enterprise merits the warmest approbation of Congress. He improved on the plan recommended by me, and executed it in a manner that does honor to his judgement and bravery;" and Congress tendered him a vote of thanks for his valiant efforts on the occasion in question. In addition to these, Wayne was the recipient also of many complimentary letters from men of distinction at the time, one of which, from Gen. Charles Lee, will serve as illustrative,

*Sparks' Biography, vol. 4.

†So intrepid and daring was he, that early in the campaign of the Revolution he received the appellation of MAD ANTHONY, and ever afterward retained the title, by which he is still familiarly known and called.

perhaps, of their general tenor. Said Mr. Lee: "what I am going to say you will not I hope consider as paying my court in this your hour of glory; for, as it is at least my present intention to leave this continent, I can have no interest in paying my court to any individual. What I shall say therefore is dictated by the genuine feelings of my heart. I do most sincerely declare that your assault of Stony Point is not only the most brilliant in my opinion, throughout the whole course of the war on either side, but that it is the most brilliant I am acquainted with in history; the assault of Schweidnitz by Marshal Loudon, I think inferior to it. I wish you, therefore, most sincerely, joy of the laurels you have deservedly acquired, and that you may long live to wear them. With respect and no small admiration, I remain, &c."

If a mutinous spirit arose among the troops at any time there were none better able to quell it than Wayne. Universally beloved and admired by all the privates under him, he readily exerted a salutary influence over them. This power of Wayne was strikingly illustrated during the fore part of January, 1781, soon after the distribution of the army for winter quarters. Shortly after the ordinary festivies of the day, "the whole division, with a few exceptions, was found in a state of open and decided insurrection, disclaiming all further obedience, and boldly avowing an intention of immediately abandoning the post, and of seeking, with arms in their hands, a redress of their grievances."* The affair proved a serious one. Every attempt to quell the movement seemed to have been met by blows—"wounds were inflicted and lives lost." The grievances complained of, were "clothing generally bad in quality, and always deficient in quantity; wages irregularly paid, and in a currency far below its nominal value; and, lastly, service greatly prolonged beyond the legal term of enlistment."

The conflict closed about half-past eleven o'clock; and being no longer obstructed, the insurgents began a march toward Princeton; and Wayne, then stationed in the neighborhood of Morristown, at some risk, determined to follow them and endeavor to bring them again to order. In a conciliatory and dignified manner, overtaking the main body at Vealtown, he at once began to open negotiations with some of the non-commissioned officers in whom he placed most confidence; and it was not long before he succeeded in convincing them that, in order to succeed in their demands, a change in their course and demeanor would be of the first necessity—that without such a course of order on the part of the agrieved, nothing whatever could be effected—urging the necessity of organizing a board or appointing a committee among them to set forth the grievances, and by "a full and clear statement of their demands"—pledging himself to become a zealous advocate in their behalf, in "so far as the claims made should be founded in justice or equity."

These suggestions had the desired effect; the committee was duly appointed, and the march towards Princeton was again begun, but in a manner much more orderly than before.

Such was the power and force of character of the good man and valiant soldier after whom our thriving city is named; and may it ever emulate his example.

As early as 1777-8, the British government having determined to direct

*Hazard's "Register of Pennsylvania."

some formidable operations against the industrial relations of the South, in the early part of April, 1781, Washington despatched Lafayette, "with twelve hundred regular infantry to Virginia; and not long after, gave to the remains of the Pennsylvania line (about eleven hundred, commanded by Wayne,) a similar destination." We find Gen. Wayne engaging the British at Green Spring, driving the enemy's pickets, and advancing in person to within some "fifty yards of the whole British army drawn up in order of battle, and already pushing forward flank-corps to envelope him." Determining to make up in boldness what he seemed to have lost or was about to lose in a too near approach to the enemy's lines, he made a bold and sudden move upon the enemy, and then retreated, which gave the British commandant to infer that it was an effort to draw his forces into ambush, which made so decided an impression in this direction, "that all pursuit of the American corps was forbidden."

By some this movement was deemed rash; but Washington, in a letter to the General, said: "I received, with the greatest pleasure, the account of the action at Green Spring." Gen. Greene said: "the Marquis gives you great glory for your conduct in the action at Jamestown; and I am sensible that you merit it. O that I had but had you with me a few days ago! Your glory and the public good might have been greatly advanced."

On the first day of January following this movement, by order of Gen. Greene, Gen. Wayne was sent "to reinstate, as far as might be possible, the authority of the Union within the limits of Georgia, with one hundred regular dragoons, three hundred undisciplined Georgia militia, and about the same number of State cavalry."

Though greatly inadequate to the end desired, yet Wayne is said to have uttered no complaint or objection, but resolutely moved forward on his mission, bringing to bear his usual boldness and wisdom, sufficient, with this small force, to push "the enemy from all his interior posts," and to "cut off Indian detachments marching to his aid;" intercepted the forays of the enemy's main body, and on the land side, penned him up, in a great degree, within the narrow limits of the town of Savannah; and all in the "short space of five weeks."

In a letter to Gen. Greene, bearing date Feb. 28, 1782, Wayne said: "The duty we have done in Georgia was more difficult than that imposed upon the children of Isreal; they had only to make bricks with straw, but we have had provision, forage, and almost every other aparatus of war, to procure without money; boats, bridges, &c., to build without material, except those taken from the stump; and, what was more difficult than all, to make *whigs* out of *tories*. But this we have effected, and wrested the country out of the hands of the enemy, with the exception only of the town of Savannah. How to keep it without some additional force, is a matter worthy of consideration."*

The British troops having evacuated Savannah about the 12th of July, Wayne, by order of General Greene, with the troops under his command, was recalled to South Carolina. In the letter, addressed to General Wayne, recalling him from Georgia, Greene thus wrote: "I am happy at the approaching deliverance of that unfortunate country; and what adds to my happiness,

*In a letter to a friend the General said: "In the five weeks we have been here, not an officer or soldier with me has once undressed, except for the purpose of changing his linen. The actual force of the enemy at this moment is more than three times that of mine. What we have been able to do has been done by maneuve ng rather than by force."

is, that it will reflect no small honor upon you. I wish you to be persuaded, that I shall do you ample justice in my public accounts to Congress and the Commander-in-chief. I think you have conducted your command with great prudence and with astonishing perseverance ; and, in so doing, you have fully answered the high expectations I ever entertained of your military abilities, from our earliest acquaintance."

Soon after the evacuation of Savannah, Charleston was given up by the British, which, after a treaty of peace, and an absence of seven years from his family, Wayne again returned to his homestead in Chester county, Pennsylvania, truly one of the most remarkable men of his day, crowned, as he well deserved, with the blessings of a whole nation of free men, and noble women.

But his well known abilities, and the high esteem in which he was held by his fellow-citizens, soon brought him before the public again, but in another capacity from that of a soldier. He was now elected a member of the Council of Censors ; and soon after this event he was honered with a seat in the Convention "called to revise and amend the Constitution of the State ;" in the discharge of which duties he acquitted himself with marked ability, and much to the satisfaction of the people.

At the close of these duties, declining any further services of a civil or political nature, prefering to lead a life of retirement rather than one of public distinction of any kind ; and thus, principally employed in the pursuits of agriculture, was his time passed until, by the wish of Washington and the voice of the people, in the early part of 1792, Wayne was again called to the service of his country, and "appointed to the command of the legion and army of the West," the result of causes which the reader will find detailed in Chapters X, XI, and XII, of this volume.

At the close of his labors in the west, returning to the east, "plaudits and thanks, public and private," were showered upon him ; and "Congress, then in session, unanimously adopted resolutions highly complimentary to the General and the whole army."

The year following the treaty of Greenville, (1796), being appointed sole commissioner to treat with the northwestern Indians, and also "receiver of the military posts given up by the British government, General Wayne again returned to the west ; and, after a prompt and faithful discharge of the duties attached to these new functions, while descending Lake Erie from Detroit, he was attacked by the gout," where he soon after died ; and, at his own request, (having previously been removed to the block-house) he was buried at the foot of the flag-staff of the garrison, with the simple inscription of "A. W." upon the stone that served to remind the inmates and the stranger of the burial place of the patriot, the hero, the soldier, and the man of true courage and remarkable foresight, ANTHONY WAYNE.

For thirteen years the remains of Wayne continued to repose beneath this simple head-stone, at the foot of the old flag-staff of Erie, when, in 1809, his son, Col. Isaac Wayne, desiring to remove the bones of his valiant father to the family burial place, in the cemetery of St. David's Church, in Chester county, Pennsylvania, the body was disinterred, still in a fine state of preservation, and removed as above, where a monument was raised to his memory by the "Pennsylvania State Society of the Cincinnati," on which the visitant may still read on the north and south front thereof, the following inscription ;

"NORTH FRONT:—Major-general ANTHONY WAYNE was born at Waynesborough, in Chester county, State of Pennsylvania, A. D., 1745. After a life of honor and usefulness, he died in December, 1796, at a military post on the shore of Lake Erie, Commander-in-chief of the Army of the United States. His military achievements are consecrated in the history of his country, and in the hearts of his countrymen. His remains are here deposited.

"SOUTH FRONT:—In honor of the distinguished military services of MAJOR-GENERAL ANTHONY WAYNE, and as an affectionate tribute of respect to his memory, this stone was erected by his companions in arms, the Pennsylvania State Society of the Cincinnati, July 4th, A. D., 1809, thirty-fourth anniversary of the Independence of the United States; an event which constitutes the most appropriate eulogium of an American soldier and patriot."

The accompanying portrait of General Wayne is from an old painting of him, and is doubtless very accurate, and will no doubt be highly prized by every citizen of Fort Wayne and lover of his country into whose hands it should chance to fall.

Why a monument has not long ago been erected, on the site of the old fort, to the memory of this heroic and worthy man, including also Major Hamtramck, and the valiant soldiery under their command, I know not; but feel that, though so long forgotten or neglected, the work will yet be performed by the people of the city of Fort Wayne and county of Allen; thus enabling the stranger visiting the historic scenes of our city and adjacent localities to behold, instead of the old garrison,—whose only remains among us consists in a few plainly-wrought canes, in the possession of a few of our citizens, preserved as mementoes of the fort so long over-looking the confluence of the St. Mary and St. Joseph,—a substantial and appropriate monument to the memory of ANTHONY WAYNE and the brave men who dared to follow him to this ancient stronghold, that the then infant and enfeebled settlements of the west might enjoy peace and safety, and our beautiful country be enabled to march steadily on, as she has, to her present condition of growth and prosperity.

Lith. Chas. Shober & Co. Chicago, Ill.

CITY of FORT WAYNE from the Fort Wayne College.

HISTORY OF FORT WAYNE,

From the Earliest Known Accounts of this Point to the Present Period.

> "I watch the circle of the eternal years,
> And read forever in the storied page
> One lengthened roll of blood and wrong and tears—
> One onward step of Truth from age to age."

> "The eternal surge
> Of Time and tide rolls on, and bears afar
> Our bubbles; and the old burst—new emerge,
> Lashed from the foam of ages; while the graves
> Of empires heave but like some passing waves."

CHAPTER I.—PRELIMINARY.

Primitive traces—Situation, general appearance of the City, and quality of the Soil in the region—The "glorious gate"—Its early advantages both to the Indians and the Whites—The Key to the Northwest—Early occupation by the French, English, and Americans—For centuries doubtless the home of the Red Man—Its prominence and early discovery by the French—The best route to the Mississippi—First Settlement at Vincennes—This point evidently visited before Vincennes—La Salle's journey afoot—His journal to Frontenac—Best route—D'Aubry's expedition—Early settlements—Appearance in 1794—English and French Settlements—Early missionaries—Efforts of the French—La Salle's voyage—New France—French trading posts—First Mission among the Miamies—Their territory—Indian liberality—Hennepin—The missionaries and Miamies—La Barre's remonstr[illegible]nce—Illinois Indians—Feuds of the Iroquois, Miami, and Illinois tribes—T[illegible]raders and squaws—Kaskaskia—Trade and traffic—Best points—French Vo[illegible]yageurs and Ouiatenons—French militia arrive here—French fort—Capt. d'[illegible] [illegible]incennes—The English fort—Traced by Wayne in 1794—A Note—Conclus[illegible] [illegible]ve evidence.

TO WRITE of the pa[illegible]—to preserve the historic records of a former age—to [illegible]ll the good and the true of any time—to render green [illegible] again the memories and relations of early days, even thro[illegible]gh blood and carnage had marked the fields and the foot-prints of the periods gone with gory redness, and made the rivers and rivulets to run crimson with the blood of the slain—is but to perform a common duty to a common humanity!

The primitive traces and early evidences of barbaric and civilized life in this part of the State of Indiana are many and various; and the present site of the City of Fort Wayne, with contiguous localities, is fully and fairly entitled to HISTORIC GROUND!

Situated upon a point of land, the most elevated in the State, Fort Wayne is very appropriately called the SUMMIT CITY. The general face of the country surrounding is rolling and somewhat uneven, with here and there a considerable promontory, overlooking the beautiful streams and valleys in the region. With strong impregnations of iron and sulphur, the soil is variously composed of the most valuable elements, admirably adapted both for farming and building purposes,—consisting of the loamy, sandy, clayey qualities. Embodying much of the romantic and picturesque in nature, the surrounding aspects and scenery of the place never fail to awaken the liveliest admiration and curiosity of the stranger; while the general appearance of the city, itself, at the present period, with its numerous fruit and shade trees, handsome dwellings and yards—beautiful shrubbery, and well cultivated gardens, in seasons of verdure and flowers, is ever one of exceeding pleasantness and beauty, alike to the *habitant* and the momentary sojourner.

From a very early period, with the Indians, it was a "glorious gate" "through which all the good words of" their "chiefs had to pass from the north to the south, and from the east to the west."* At a later period in the history of events in America—in the struggle between barbarism and civilization—it became at once the pivotal point upon which the most important relations of the country turned, both for the advancing civilization of the time and the barbaric force against which it had to contend—THE KEY, IN FACT, TO THE GREAT NORTHWEST!

Early occupied as a military point of great importance, alike to the French, the English and our own Government, each, in turn, establishing and maintaining a military post here, as a means by which to attain and exercise an extended control over the destinies and resources of the new world, "questions of infinite reach, involving dominion, race, language, law and religion, have hung upon the petty display of military power at the junction of these rivers."†

Here the red man had lived, doubtless, for centuries before the first civilized settlement in America had begun,—his squaws cultivating the maze and performing the common hardships of life, while he hunted the buffalo and wild game of the forest and prairie;

* Little Turtle. † Jesse L. Williams, Esq.

NOTE: Judge Law, in his interesting Address, "The Colonial History of Vincennes," (Ind.) page 10, says; "It is a singular fact, yet no less true, that the Wabash was known and navigated by the whites long before the Ohio was known to exist. Indeed, all the maps—and I have seen two before the year 1730—call the Ohio at its confluence with the Mississippi, 'Ouabache.' The reason is obvious, when one reflects for a single instant, that the whole course of travel to the Mississippi was either by the Illinois or the Wabash. The only communication with the Mississippi WAS BY THE FRENCH in the latter part of the 17th and early in the 18th century, and was from the Lakes. The priest and the soldier were the only travelers. They ascended the Maumee, crossed the Portage, and descended the Wabash to this Post."

speared the fish in the beautiful streams gliding by; leisurely basked in the sunshine; devoted himself to plays and games; huddled about the wigwam and the camp-fire; or went forth to secure the trophies and honors of war.

Being situated at the head and terminus of two considerable streams, (the St. Joseph and Maumee), the one flowing from the region of Lake Michigan and the other into Lake Erie, direct from and into points near to and from which the early *voyageurs*, missionaries, and traders sought so earnestly to extend their efforts and discoveries—together with the fact, at an early period, of a strong relationship * and doubtless frequent intercourse between, the tribes along those lakes and the Miamies of this part of their extended territory,—it is not probable that this point could have long escaped their attention. And, as will be seen in subsequent pages, there exists the strongest evidence that the early French missionaries, explorers and traders, from Canada, had visited the junction of these rivers as early as 1680 to 1682–'3—and the probability is very strong that they were here at a much earlier period.

Judge Law, in his able Address, concerning the first settlement of Vincennes by the French, concludes it to have been about the year 1710 or 1711; and thinks it most probable in the first of the two years mentioned, "inasmuch," says he, "as the *Fort* must have been built and garrisoned before an application was made for a missionary." Now, the advantages of navigation, the nearness of this point to the Lakes, the extensive openings of this region,† and the fame it seems to have so long enjoyed as a "glorious gate," give to it a claim *priori* to that of the establishment of a Post and Mission at Vincennes. And it is not improbable, that a temporary mission was established here before or soon after the eventful year of 1682.

In the early part of 1680, LaSalle, having penetrated the west to a point, which is now known as Peoria, Ill., where he built a fort, which he called *Crevecœur*, (Broken Heart,) because of his former misfortunes, and soon finding himself without supplies and necessary materials for the completion of a vessel he had then begun at the foot of Lake Peoria, in the month of March, of that year, determining upon a plan to hasten the needed supplies, with but three attendants, he set out a-foot towards Lake Erie, "following along the water-shed, or divide, which seperates the streams that flow into the Ohio river from those which flow into Lake Erie," and reached

*The Mascoutens, says Gallatin, dwelling about Lake Michigan were a branch of the Miamies.

†The following, from the "daily journal of Wayne's campaign," will show the appearance of this point, on the arrival of the army here, in 1794:

"Camp Miami Villages, 17th September, 1794.—The army halted on this ground at 5 o'clock, p. m., being 47 miles from Fort Defiance and 14 from our last encampment: there are nearly 500 acres of cleared land lying in one body on the rivers St. Joseph, St. Mary's and the Miami; there are fine points of land contiguous to those rivers adjoining the cleared land. The rivers are navigable for small crafts in the summer, and in the winter there is water sufficient for large boats, the land adjacent fertile and well timbered, and from every appearance it has been one of the largest settlements made by the Indians in this country."

his destination in safety;* which makes it quite evident, together with the fact of his having spent the Autumn of 1679 in the erection of a fort at the mouth of the St. Joseph's river, sounding the channel of that stream, and establihsing there "a depot for supplies and goods," that he was by no means unacquainted, at an early period of his efforts, with this region of the north-west.

The reputed rival as well as co-laborer of La Salle, Louis Hennepin, a Franciscan friar, of the Recollect variety, and said to have been very ambitious as a discoverer, as also daring, hardy, energetic, with other peculiarities closely allied thereto, as early as 1663-4 speaks of the "Hohio," and of a route from the Lakes (northern) to the Mississippi by the Wabash, the account of which he had heard, and which was explored in 1676. In Hennepin's volume of 1698, is a journal, says the best accounts, said to be that sent by La Salle to Count Frontenac, in 1682 or 1683, which mentions *the route by the Maumee and Wabash as the most direct to the great western river*, (Mississippi;)† which makes it quite evident that this region was not only early visited, but that the route leading through this immediate vicinity, was often very early traversed by explorers, missionaries and fur-traders. And, in view of the navigable streams concentrating at this point; the vast amount of fur that must annually have been accummulated here; the great number of Indians dwelling at this locality, and in the region, —that these adventurous and zealous spirits should have early selected this as a favorable and most advantageous site, not only for the prosecution of the labors of the missionary and the accumulation of fur by the trader, but for the early establishment of a military post, seems most reasonable indeed, and requires but little conjecture to arrive at a somewhat definite conclusion as to the truthfulness of the question considered.

Not only did the earliest of the French *voyageurs* and explorers consider this the most direct route to the great western river, Mississippi, but those of a later period seem to have universally regarded the route by the Miami or *Omee* villages, at this point, as the best. Says J. W. Dawson, Esq., in his researches: "By reference to early history, we find that, in 1716, among the routes of travel established by the French, was one from the head of Lake Erie, (now Manhattan, or its more successful rival, Toledo,) up the Maumee river to the site of Fort Wayne, thence by portage to the head of Little River, across the marsh now crossed by the Toledo, Wabash and Western railroad; thence by Little River to the Wabash, about nine miles below Huntington; thence down the Wabash to the Ohio; and thence to the Mississippi." And as late as 1759 the same route is favored. Says the same researches: "The next interesting reference to Fort Wayne, is in 1759, and advises us of a most distinguished expedition fitted out by M. d'Aubry, commandant at Illinois. The

*"Western Annals," pages 62 and 63.

†"States and Territories of the Great West," pages 68 and 69.

French having exhausted their supplies in Pennsylvania, and unable to withstand the British, it was conceived by M. d'Aubry to reinforce his brethern. Accordingly, a levey of 400 men, and 200,000 lbs. of flour was raised at Kaskaskia,* and started from there to Venango, Pa. Ft. Du Quesne (Pittsburgh,) was abandoned, and hence the reinforcement could not go thence by the Ohio river. So he proceeded with his force down to the Mississippi; thence down that river to the mouth of the Ohio; then up the Ohio to the mouth of Wabash; then up the Wabash, to the mouth of Little River; then up that stream to the portage; and then to Ft. Miami, (Ft. Wayne,) where they embarked stores and all on the Maumee; then down the Maumee and along the shore of Lake Erie to Presque'Isle; then across the portage to Le Boeuff; then down French Creek, to Venango, Pa."

From the founding, by the French, of the city of Quebec, in Canada, in 1608, to 1763, for a period of more than one hundred and fifty years, the governments of France and Great Britain, (the latter having begun a settlement at Jamestown, in Virginia, as early as 1607,) were most energetic and resolute rivals in many civil, military, and often sanguinary contests as to territorial limits colonel establishments, and the general trade and commerce of the new world of North America.†

In 1634, the missionaries, Breboeuf and Daniel, joining a party of Hurons, on their return from Quebec, after crossing the Ottowa river, established a mission near a bay of Lake Huron, where they are said daily to have rang a bell, calling the natives of the region to prayer, and who also "performed all those kindly offices which were calculated to secure the confidence and affection of the tribes on the Lake shores."

As early as 1670, Great Britain had established, at different points, between the 32d and 45th degrees of north latitude, as many as nine colonial settlements in America; and it was not until about eighty years later that the English began to make any effort towards a settlement west of the Allegheny mountains.

In 1670, the French colonists in America had persevered in the extension of their settlements to the westward from Quebec, on the shores of the St. Lawrence, and the borders of lakes Ontario and Erie; and their missionaries and traders had succeeded in exploring the bordering regions of the northern lakes, to the west, as far as Lake Superior; and stations, with a view to the Christianization of the Indians, were established at several points, among a number of Indian tribes. To give protection and impetus to the fur trade, then coming to be very extensive in its operations, a number of

*That this point was visited before the establishment of settlements at Kaskaskia and Kahokia, or other points westward, seems to be generally admitted by all the most authenic historical researches that the writer has had occasion to refer to.

†For a more extended summary of these early periods, see Bancroft's History of U. S., Dillon's History of Indiana, Parkman's Conspiracy of Pontiac, Sparks's Life of La Salle, Vol. 1, new series, do. Life of Marquette, &c.

stockade forts and trading posts were also erected at various points best suited for such establishments.

A little minutia as to the efforts, trials, and disappointments of these primitive missionaries and others, in connection with other points, will here be of interest to the reader, and tend to open a more extended view of the relations that surrounded, and, at an early period, evidently influenced, the destiny of the present situation and historic importance of the City of Fort Wayne.

At the period I now refer, Charles II. was King of England, and Louis XIV,—purported to have been a most ambitious man,—was monarch of the French. A statesman of considerable ability, of the name of Colbert, was minister of Finances to the latter, who is said to have inspirited the colonists of Canada with an arduous wish to widen their domain, as well as to increase the power of the French monarch. Thus animated and impelled, with the hope of enjoying the advantages and means of Christian civilization thought necessary to be exerted over the various Indian tribes of the west, at that early period, the civil and religious authorities of Canada were constrained "to engage earnestly in the support of the policy of increasing the number and strength of the forts, trading-posts and missionary stations in the vast regions lying on the borders of the rivers and lakes between Quebec and the head of Lake Superior."

At this early period, the French civil and ecclesiastical authorities of Canada, having given considerable life to renewed action among the missionaries, "in the course of the years 1670, 1671 and 1672," says Dillon, in his researches, "the missionaries, Claude Allouez and Claude Dablon, explored the easternpart of Wisconsin, the north-eastern portion of Illinois, and, probably visited that part of Indiana which lies north of the river Kankakee. In the following year, M. Joliet, an agent of the French colonial Government, and James Marquette, a good and simple-hearted missionary, who had his station at Mackinaw, explored the country lying about the shores of Green Bay, and on the borders of Fox River, and the river Wisconsin, as far westward as the river Mississippi, the banks of which they reached on the 17th day June 1672." In the following month, on the 17th, many obstacles presenting themselves, they set out on their return to Canada, by way of the Illinois river, and arrived at Green Bay, an outlet of Lake Michigan, in the latter part of the month of September, a distance of some 2.500 miles.—At a village of the Illinois Indians; it is related, they were feasted in a most friendly and hospitable manner, upon the choicest food of the tribe, consisting of roast buffalo, fish, hominy and dog meat.

But the curiosity and desires of the French colonists in Canada did not cease with the return of the missionaries. In the early part of 1682, Robert Cavalier de La Salle, with a small exploring party, made his way to the Illinois, and passed down that stream to the Mississippi, thence continuing his voyage,—with short stoppages here and there at the presentation of the friendly calumet or attack from the shore by unfriendly Indians, etc.,—to the Gulf of Mexico, where, on the 9th of April, 1682, they erected a column and cross, attaching thereto the arms of France, with the following inscription: "*Louis the Great, King of France, and Navarre, reigns—the 9th of April*, 1682." All being under arms, after chanting the *Te Deum*, they fired their muskets in honor of the event, and made the air to reverberate with the shouts of "Long live the King!" at once taking formal possession of the entire country, to which they gave the name of *Louisiane*, in honor of their King.

Soon after this event, La Salle and his party returned to Canada, whither he soon after went to France, where he was received with much favor by the King, and the account of his and those of Joliet and Marquette's discoveries were made known. And thus it was that Louis the 14th of France at once laid claim to the whole of the soil lying between Canada and New Mexico,* disregarding all prior or subsequent claims set up by Spain, by reason of the discoveries of Juan Ponce de Leon, in 1512, and Hernando de Soto, during the years 1538 and 1542.

Not long subsequent to the discovery of the mouth of the Mississippi, the French government began to encourage the establishment of a line of trading posts and missionary stations in the country west of the Allegheny mountains, from Canada to the Gulf of Mexico, which policy they seem to have sustained with moderate success during a period of some seventy-five years. The greater part of this long period of time, a few missionaries pursued their labors, but with no lasting or general beneficial results, in so far, at least, as their efforts related to the Indians of the west.

In 1679, the same day that La Salle completed the erection of a fort at its mouth, the river St. Joseph, of Lake Michigan, received the name of "the River Miamies," from the Indians of that name; and it was on the banks of this river that the principal station for the instruction of the Miamies was founded, about that period; after which it was called "the St. Joseph, of Lake Michigan."

Hennepin thus gave the account of the erection of the first French post within the territory† of the Miamies‡ in 1679:

*Afterwards, for many years, called NEW FRANCE.

†Little Turtle, the distinguished chief of the Miamies, who lived here for many years with his tribe, and died here in 1812, at the famous treaty of Greenville, (O.), 1795, thus, in part, addressed General Wayne regarding the territory of his people: "You have pointed out to us the boundary line between the Indians and the United States; but I now take the liberty to inform you that that line cuts off from the Indians a large portion of country which has been enjoyed by my forefathers from time immemorial, without molestation or dispute. The print of my ancestors' houses are everywhere to be seen in this portion. * * * * It is well known by all my brothers present, that my forefather kindled the first fire at Detroit; from thence he extended his lines to the headwaters of Scioto; from thence to its mouth; from thence to Chicago, on Lake Michigan." From the earliest period we have of them, the Miamies have been a leading and most powerful tribe.

‡"When the Miamis were first invited by the French authorities at Chicago, in 1670," says Mr. Chas. B. Lasselle, in one of his interesting sketches, relating to the early history of Fort Wayne, "they were a very powerful Indian nation. A body of them assembled near that place for war against the powerful Iroquis, (Five Nations), of the Hudson, and the still more powerful Sioux, of the Upper Mississippi, consisted of at

"Just at the mouth of the river Miamis there was an eminence with a kind of platform naturally fortified. It was pretty high and steep, of a triangular form—defended on two sides by the river, and on the other by a deep ditch, which the fall of the water had made. We felled the trees that were on the top of the hill, and having cleared the same from bushes for about two musket shot, we began to build a redoubt of eighty feet long, and forty feet broad, with great square pieces of timber, laid one upon another; and prepared a great number of stakes, of about twenty-five feet long, to drive into the ground to make our fort the more inaccessible on the river side. We employed the whole month of November (1769) about that work, which was very hard, though we had no other food but the bear's flesh our savage killed. These beasts are very common in that place, because of the great quantity of grapes that abound there; but their flesh being too fat and luscious, our men began to be weary of it, and desired leave to go a hunting and kill some wild goats. M. La Salle denied them that liberty, which caused some murmurs among them; and it was but unwillingly that they continued the work. This, together with the approach of the winter, and the apprehension that M. La Salle had that his vessel (the Griffin) was lost, made him very melancholy, though he concealed it as much as he could. We made a cabin wherein we performed divine service every Sunday; and father Gabriel and I, who preached alternately, took care to take such texts as were suitable to our present circumstances, and fit to inspire us with courage, concord and brotherly love. * * * * This fort was at last perfected, and called Fort Miamis."

This same missionary, Hennepin, in 1680, visiting some of the Indian villages on the Illinois river, speaks thus of the peculiar ideas and manners of the savages he met there at that early period; which must give the reader to infer that, though the natives of the forest, in their *untutored* state, had but a poor sense of the Christianity taught by the missionaries of the time, they yet possessed a singular intelligence regarding life and the religious nature of man; and were, withal, strangely liberal in their views and actions toward

least three thousand, and were under the head of a chieftain who never sallied forth but with a body-guard of forty warriors. He could at any time lead into the field an army of five thousand men." Of all their villages," says he, "Ke-ki-ong-a was considered by the Miamis the most important, as it was the largest and most central of all their possessions—being situated near the head waters of the Wabash, the Miami, (Maumee), and the St. Joseph of Lake Michigan." Says Bancroft: "The Miamis was the most powerful confederacy of the west, excelling the Six Nations, (Iroquois.) * * * Their influence reached to the Mississippi, and they received frequent visits from tribes beyond that river." As the messenger of St. Clair, Antoine Gamelin, in the spring of 1790, proceeded from Vincennes toward this point with a view to friendly relations with the Indians, he was told at the different villages on his route to go to Ke-ki-ong-a. "You know," said they, "that we can terminate nothing without the consent of our brothers, the Miamies." "The impress of its name," says Mr. Williams, of our city, "upon so many western rivers, shows the predominance of the tribe. The two Miamies of the Ohio will ever perpetuate it. The Miami of Lake Erie (now Maumee) was likewise named for the tribe. * * * * Our own St. Mary's was marked 'Miamies' river,' on the rude skeleton map, made to represent the western country at the time of Colonel Bouquet's expedition in 1763."

those differing from them. But the Indian was a rude child of nature—born in the woods, with the great spirit of the forest deeply impressed upon his soul. He had ever seen the Great Father

"In clouds, and heard him in the winds."

Says Hennepin:—"There were many obstacles that hindered the conversion of the savages, but in general the difficulty proceeds from the indifference they have to every thing. When one speaks to them of the creation of the world, and of the mysteries of the Christian religion, they say we have reason; and they applaud, in general, all that we say on the great affair of our salvation. They would think themselves guilty of a great incivility, if they should show the least suspicion of incredulity, in respect to what is proposed. But, after having approved all the discourses upon these matters, they pretend, likewise, on their side, that we ought to pay all possible defference to the relations and reasonings that they may make on their part. And when we make answer that what they tell us is false, they reply that they have acquiesced to all that we said; and that it is a want of judgement to interrupt a man that speaks, and to tell him that he advances a false proposition. * * * The second obstacle which hinders their conversion, proceeds from their great superstition. * * * The third obstacle consists in this,—that they are not fixed to a place. * * * The traders who deal commonly with the savages, with a design to gain by their traffic, are likewise another obstacle. * * * They think of nothing but cheating and lying to become rich in a short time. They use all manner of stratagems to get the furs of the savages cheap. They make use of lies and cheats to gain double, if they can. This, without doubt, causes an aversion against a religion which they see accompanied, by the professors of it, with so many artifices and cheats." Continues the same missionary, "the Illinois (Indians) will readily suffer us to baptise their children, and would not refuse it themselves; but they are incapable of any previous instruction concerning the truth of the Gospel, and the efficacy of the sacraments. Would I follow the example of some other missionaries, I could have boasted of many conversions; for I might easily have baptised all those nations, and then say, (as I am afraid they do, without any ground,) that I had converted them. * * * Our ancient missionary recollects of Canada, and those that succeeded them in that work, have always given it for their opinion, as I now own it as mine, that the way to succeed in converting the barbarians, is to endeavor to make them men, before we go about to make them Christians. * * * America is no place to go to out of a desire to suffer martyrdom, taking the word in a theological sense. The savages never put any Christian to death on the score of his religion. They leave everybody at liberty in belief; they like the outward ceremonies of our church, but no more. * * * They do not kill people but in particular quarrels, or when they are brutish or drunk, or in revenge, or infatuated with a dream, or some extravagant vision. They are incapable of taking away any person's life out of hatred to his religion."

The best accounts agree that it was through the agency and persevering exertions of missionaries, combined with the active and enterprising movements of traders, that amicable relations and a moderate trade were brought about between the colonists of Canada and the Miami Indians—which occurred before the end of the 17th century.

M. de la Barre, governor-general of Canada, in 1684, in a remonstrance to the English authorities, at Albany, complained that the Iroquois, or Five Nations, (a league of friendship between whom and the English, it was understood, then existed,) had been intermeddling with the rights and property of French traders among the western tribes. To which the Iroquois, upon learning of this remonstrance, said their enemies were furnished with arms and ammunition by the French traders; and, at a subsequent council, held by M. de la Barre with the Five Nations, he accused the Iroquois, Senecas, Cayugas, Onondagas, Oneidas, and Mohawks, with having mistreated and robbed French traders going westward. To which Grangula, chief of the Onondagas, replied that they plundered none of the French, excepting those who took guns, powder, and balls to the Twightwees, (or Miamis) and Chicktaghicks. "These arms," said he, "might have cost us our lives. We have done less wrong," continued he, in a spirit of upbraiding, "than either the English or French, who have taken the lands of so many Indian nations."

In this we have much of the true spirit and trials of those times, which will be found more in detail in many of the prominent histories relating to colonial and subsequent periods. But the intimations of the chief Grangula would seem to have been a forerunner of further and still more extended troubles between the French and the Five Nations; * for, from 1689 to the treaty of Ryswick, in 1697, wars and conflicts, of an almost interminable nature, occurred between the French colonists and the Five Nations, which, it is presumed, tended, in a large degree, to check the ambitious and grasping policy of Louis XIV, and also to prevent and retard the settlement of the French colonists in the Mississippi valley.

Some time during the years 1680 and 1700, a number of missionaries, in succession, used strong endeavors to Christianize and otherwise instruct the Illinois tribes; and historical records state that a church, consisting of a small number of French, with a few Indians, was established on the banks of the Illinois river, at or near the site of a fort called St. Louis, and founded by La Salle at an earlier period.

The traders began early to form matrimonial alliances with the Indian women, and are said to have lived quite amicably with them.

Attracted by a sense of beauty, and with a view to enterprise in

* A century before the signal defeats of Harmar and St. Clair, near this place, Chas. B. Laselle, Esq., in his researches of the early history of Ft. Wayne, says: "In a contest which they, (the Miami Indians) with their kindred, the Illinois, waged for three or four years against the invincible Iroquois, of New York, these 'Romans of America' (Iroquois) were worsted."

the accumulation of furs, a small body of French adventurers, from the Illinois, near the close of the 17th century, moved toward and settled upon the borders of the Kaskaskia, a small river emptying into the Mississippi, about one hundred miles above the mouth of the Ohio, where they founded the little village of Kaskaskia.

Among the first movements of the French in an effort to extend dominion over their western dependencies, from Canada, during the seventeenth century, were the establishment of small settlements at Detroit and Michilimackinac, while many are said to have given themselves up wholly to a life of adventure, rambling here and there, as their inclinations and necessities impelled them, among the different tribes "north-west of the river Ohio."

Among these adventurous spirits, were to be found several quite intelligent, as well as enterprising and ambitious men, who lived in daily hopes of realizing immense "profits and advantages from the prosecution of the fur trade." "This trade," says Dillon, in his interesting researches, "was carried on by means of men * who were hired to manage small vessels on the lakes, and canoes along the shores of the lakes, and on the rivers, and to carry burdens of merchandise from the different trading posts to the principle villages of the Indians who were at peace with the French. At those places the traders exchanged their wares for valuable furs, with which they returned to the places of deposit. The articles of merchandise used by the French traders in carrying on the fur trade, were, chiefly, coarse blue and red cloths, fine scarlet, guns, powder, balls, knives, hatchets, traps, kettles, hoes, blankets, coarse cottons, ribbons, beads, vermillion, tobacco, spirituous liquors, etc. The poorest class of fur traders sometimes carried their packs of merchandise, by means of leather straps suspended from their shoulders, or with the straps resting against their foreheads. It is probable that some of the Indian villages on the borders of the Wabash were visited by a few of this class of traders before the French founded a settlement at Kaskaskia. It has been intimated, conjecturally, by a learned writer, (Bishop Brute), that missionaries and traders, before the close of the seventeenth century, passed down from the river St. Joseph, 'left the Kankakee to the west, and visited the Tippecanoe, the Eel river, and the upper parts of the Wabash.'"

"The Miami villages," continues the same researches, "which stood at the head of the river Maumee, the Wea villages, which were situated about Ouiatenon, on the Wabash river, and the Piankeshaw villages which stood on and about the site of Vincennes, were, it seems, regarded by the early French fur traders as suitable places for the establishing of trading-posts. It is probable, that, before the close of the year 1719, temporary trading-posts were erected at the sites of Ft. Wayne, Ouiatenon, and Vincennes. These points had, it is believed, been often visited by traders before the year 1700."

During the year 1733, an affray having occurred "between some

* Called by the French *voyageurs*, *engagees*, and *coureurs des bois*.

drunken young Ouiatenons and two or three French voyageurs, in an affair of trade," M. de Armand, with a small body of militia, was ordered to make an attack upon the Ouiatenons; but, soon after his arrival at the Miami village here, was persuaded to forego his intentions upon that tribe, and a friendly intercourse was soon re-established between the French and the Ouiatenons, whose villages were near the present site of Lafayette, in this State.

The late Judge Hanna, our esteemed fellow-citizens, Hon. J. W. Borden and J. L. Williams, Esq., in their interesting sketches of Fort Wayne, all make mention of a small French fort that was early erected on the south bank of the St. Mary, not far from the canal acqueduct, and near the residence of Judge McCulloch. The historical account of this fort is, that, as early as 1734, the famous Captain D. M. D'Vincennes, founder of Vincennes, Ind., visited this point in a military capacity, and erected the fort in question; and Vincennes is said then to have referred to this locality as "the key of the west." * How long this fort remained or was garrisoned by the French, it is now unknown.

Two years later, in 1736, by order of his superior officer at New Orleans, Monsieur d'Artaguette, "commandant for the King in Illinois," Captain Vincennes (or, as originally spelt, Vinsenne,) left his post at Vincennes with an expedition against the Chickasaws. In a charge against this tribe of Indians, with a small body of French, aided by about 1000 friendly Indians, Vincennes received a severe wound, and fell soon after, and because of which, his Indian allies became disheartened and fled, leaving Vincennes, D'Artaguette, and the Jesuit, Senat, at the mercy of the savage foe; and on the 31st of May, 1736, the three prisoners were lashed to the stake and burned by their wily captors.

Vincennes had visited the Miamies at this point as early as 1705. M. de Vaudreuille, at that period Governor-general of Canada, in a

* NOTE.—It will readily be seen by the reader, that, at this early period of the history of our country, the west, beginning, as we may say, with the Alleghanies, and beyond, and extending to the borders of Mexico, was an interminable forest, broken only by lakes, water-courses, and prairie regions; and every point, in a general sense, was alike a point of relationship and interest to the other; while this, more especially, both to the Indians and to the whites, was, beyond doubt, very early the key to the north-west. As will be seen, in subsequent pages, there was no point looked upon with greater interest, or which was more beloved or more resolutely and jealously defended by the red man, against any encroachment of a war-like nature, from the first efforts of the formidable Iroquois, or Five Nations, of the east, in the latter part of the 17th century, to the strenuous efforts of Harmar, St. Clair, Wayne, and Harrison; or which was more eagerly sought to be reached and held by the whites, than the ancient site of the present populous city of Fort Wayne. In considering its history, therefore, from the earliest known period, up to the struggles of 1812-14, it is found at once connected, in some way, with every important movement made in the north-west; and instead of forming an extensive Appendix, the connecting links are preserved in future chapters by the interweaving of the general events of the north-west with those more directly transpiring at this point, from the early efforts of LaSalle to discover the Mississippi, to the latest period of warfare, etc., with the Indians of the west. And in thus blending the early and general events of the country, for a long period of years, at once so intimately connected with the history of Fort Wayne,—preserving valuable data, as well as, in many instances, presenting the most important outlines of sieges, marches, etc., the volume readily assumes a more interesting and valuable character.

letter dated "Quebec, 19th October, 1705," said he had "sent Sieur de Vinseine to the Miamis." Another letter, written by M. de Pontchartrain, to M. de Vaudreuille, bearing date "Versailes, 9th June, 1706," said: "His Majesty approves your sending Sieur Jonqueres to the Iroquois, because he is esteemed by them, and has not the reputation of a trader; but you ought not to have sent Sieur de Vincennes to the Miamis, nor Sieur de Louvigny to the Missilimaquina, as they are all accused of carrying on contraband trade. You are aware that the said Sieur de Louvigny has been punished for that; and his Majesty desires that you cause Sieur de Vincennes to be severely punished—he having carried on an open and undisguised trade." In a letter from M. de Vaudreuille to M. de Pontchartrain, dated Nov. 6, 1712, the former says he, "had again sent Sieur de Vincennes to the Miamis." In 1719, M. de Vincennes was reported to M. de Vaudreuille as having died at the Miami village here; but this was a mistake, or it was another officer of that name. It was about this period that the French made some unsuccessful efforts to induce the Miamis to remove from their old homes here towards Lake Michigan, or "to the river St. Joseph of Lake Michigan."

The fort that stood on the east side of the St. Joseph, was early known as the English Fort, which was occupied by a small garrison of English troops subsequent to the overthrow of French rule in Canada, in 1760,—perhaps as early as 1762; though the writer has been unable to gather any positive evidence that this stockade was built *by* the English. All the accounts I have of its early occupation lead to the conclusion that it was "taken possession of by the English" soon after the close of the struggles in Canada in 1760. Gen. Wayne traced both of these forts while here, in 1794; and Col. John Johnston, a sterling patriot of the west, traced "the dim outlines" of the French fort in the vicinity of the canal acqueduct as late as 1800.

Having thus, with other interesting facts and data, followed the missionary, trader, and explorer, in their devious windings and ambitious zeal for the redemption of savage souls on the one hand, and to become suddenly wealthy and famous by the accumulation of large quantities of fur, and the discovery of new regions of territory and tributary streams, to the end that they might be greatly favored by the King, on the other hand, we are readily enabled to see, with other essential reasons, how, at an early period, these zealous and ambitious adventurers found their way to this point, and established here their mission and trading posts; and why, at a later day, the French soldiers erected here a stockade, and long stood guard in view of the confluence of these beautiful rivers.

CHAPTER II.

"The Past bears in her arms the Present and the Future."

Primitive accounts of the New World—Ferocious animals—The Mastodon—Exhumation of bones near Huntertown—The different tribes of Indians—Their names—The Algonquin stock—The Indians and early settlers—Civilization ever disliked by the Indian—The law of change—Derivation of Indian names—The force of barbaric and civilized influences—Indian love of his nativity—Amalgamation—The Miamies in 1718—The Indian race track—Agriculture among the Indians—The old corn field—The old Apple-tree—Indian habits—Ideas of freedom—Ke-ki-ong-a—Labors of the men—The Indian women—Indian eloquence—The Indian mother—An incident—Offspring—Family government—Love of war—Formidable character of the Indians in the latter part of the past century.

THE MOST primitive works relating to the New World, were noted for the great credulity of their authors and highly exagerated accouuts of the inhabitants—both man and beast. The country was considered a marvelous embodiment of the wildest conditions of life, and possessed of a wealth as unfathomable as the land was broad, picturesque, and wild.

Here, in the newly-discovered regions of North America, there were to be met, it was declared, a species of Lilliputians and men of gigantic proportions—men not exactly without heads, wrote Lafitau, but whose heads did not extend above the shoulders—a people subsisting, much as the camelion, upon the air—the black man living a life of concealment in the tropical forests—and that there were also tribes in the more northern boundaries of the New World, who, not unlike the ermine, were quite white; and it was such marvelous tales and exagerated accounts, in part, at least, that awakened the curiosity of the inhabitants of the Old World, and at length peopled the new continent of North America with, to it, a new order of human beings, destined to pave the way for a new and more glorious sense of civilization in all that pertains, let us trust, to the mental and physical welfare of man.

That there were gigantic animals roaming over the land, is a well authenticated fact—the lion, the panther, the bear, the tiger, and, indeed, most of the wild, ferocious animals known to natural history, were, at the period referred to, and to a much later day, doubtless inhabitants of many parts of the New World. The elk, which did not disappear till about 1825, was also common. The

Indians gave accounts* to earlytraders here and at other points of a huge animal they called the *King of Beasts;* and when asked concerning its appearance, their answer was, that "it looked like the white man's hay-stack—*very big*"—and said that it traversed the regions lying between this section of the present State of Indiana and Toledo, Ohio; and seemed to regret, when speaking of it, that it was no longer to be seen here—that the white man had driven it away. From former and recent exhumations of bones† not far from Fort Wayne, it is evident that the accounts given to early traders and others, by the Indians, were not far from correct, at least in so far as the great size of the animals were concerned. In what sense they bore a resemblance, in organization and general structure, to "the white man's hay-stack," is left for the reader to conjecture.

*C. Peltier.

†The Fort Wayne Gazette, of April 22 and September 17, 1867, gave the following account of the exhumation of bones in Noble county, near the Allen county line, and not far from Huntertown, in this county, (Allen) which are evidently remains of the great animals referred to years ago by the Indians here:

"INTERESTING DISCOVERY.—Dr. J. S. Fuller, of Perry, Allen Co., Ind., under date of April 20, 1867, writes us that the skeleton of an elephant was found a few days ago, on the farm of Wm Thrush, of Noble co., near the Allen county line, by some men who were digging a ditch. The discovery was made about four feet below the surface of the marsh. The skeleton is very large, and was found standing upright, which indicates that the animal had mired in the marsh, and died in this position. The doctor has examined the head, under-jaw, hip bones, tusks, and other pieces of the skeleton, and is convinced that they are the remains of an elephant, buried there at least one hundred years ago. The bones are at the residence of Mr. Jas. Potter.

"If the above story is true, (and we have no reason to doubt it, as the doctor is a reliable man) the discovery is one of great interest. There was a tradition among the Indians who inhabited this region that Northern Indiana was once the home of elephants or some animal of a similar size and appearance. We commend the case to the attention of our scientific men."—Ft. Wayne GAZETTE, April 22, 1867.

"The mastodon remains found near Huntertown prove to be more extensive and more interesting than at first anticipated. Part of three skeletons were brought to town yesterday, a male, female, and calf. No one skeleton is complete, but enough of each has been found to determine the sex and age as above mentioned. The lower jaw of the calf was exhumed entire. The teeth, small, and little worn, are the unmistakable signs of 'veal.' A quantity of older and larger teeth, and part of a larger jaw were found. Also five of the upper bones of the fore leg, two upper bones of the hind leg, two thigh bones, shoulder-blade, fragments of tusks, part of a skull, a quantity of ribs, and many other smaller bones.

"The mastodon was an animal similar in size and appearance to the elephant, but larger and more massive in form. It belonged to the geological period immediately preceeding the present, and is supposed to have been the last large animal which became extinct before the creation of man. Its average size, as determined from examination of remains found in various parts of the world, was about seventeen feet in length, and eleven feet in height. Many skeletons have been found in this country, particularly in New York and New Jersey, where the search for them has been more thorough than in other States.

"The skeletons above alluded to were found in a corn field on the farm of a Mr. Thrush, about four miles from Huntertown, in what was once a deep marsh. Twenty or thirty years ago, the proprietor says, it would not have been safe for man or beast to enter it. The bones were found in an area of about forty feet in diameter, from three to four feet below the surface, in a stratum of light clay covering a layer of blue clay. The top soil is a black muck, even now fit for cultivation only in dry seasons.

"As to how they got into the mire, various theories can be framed. A friend who has given the subject some profound thought, suggests that the calf was 'teething,' and crawled into the marsh for something to cool its gums, and sticking fast, the old couple followed to rescue it, and met with a like fate. The last half of this theory, we guess, will pass muster.

"The remains, we understand, will be taken to Chicago, for more careful examination

The uniformity of the aboriginal tribes of North America, in their primitive state,—taking Charlevoix' as among the earliest and best accounts of them—seem at once evident and conclusive; and their habits and customs—institutions and primitive organic relations—seem to have possessed a common identity and bearing.

In an early comparison of the great number of dialects among the various tribes on the continent, it was discovered that not more than eight radically distinct tongues were to be found in the whole territory lying east of the Mississippi river; and but five of these continue to constitute the languages of nations yet remaining; while, of late years, it is discoverable that but three only of these serve to remind the reader that the tribes speaking them have well-nigh become extinct.*

The Algonquin,† or primitive Indian tongue, was not only considered the most extended, but the most exhuberant in dialect. It was the Algonquin which welcomed the early settlers of Plymouth and Roanoake; and was heard, says Bancroft, "from the Bay of Gaspe to the Valley of the Des Moines; from Cape Fear, and, it may be, from the Savannah, to the land of the Esquimaux; from the Cumberland river of Kentucky, to the southern banks of the Mississippi; and "was spoken," continues the same writer, "though not exclusively, in a territory that extended through sixty degrees of longitude, and more than twenty degrees of latitude."

From the earliest accounts known, the Indian was ever disposed to shun the settlements of the white man. He loved his native haunts, the woods, the hills, and the vales of America. He was indigenous to the soil—he knew no other land. From the first troubles with the settlements at Jamestown and Plymouth, to those of a later period, springing up at other points, both east and west, the tribes seemed ever imbued with the belief that the white man would eventually overrun thier hunting-grounds, and at length push the red man far towards the setting sun. How truly thought and said the Indian, from one period to another, may now be most clearly seen. Such is the force of civilization—such the destiny of the unadvancing, unprogressive, uncivilized of the earth, e'en to the lowest kingdom of animal life.

Seeking to find new hunting-grounds, new regions of soil wherein to plant their maize and cultivate the other products common to Indian life, unobtruded by the white man, at an early period, the tribes of the east began gradually to move westward and southward; while many clans very early abandoned their old hunting-grounds, east and northward, to follow a roving life in the deep forests of the south and west—fleeing from the march of civilization, which, a few years later, followed them to their distant and exclusive abode. But a few years ago,—and the same is probably true of

They are at present in charge of Dr. W. H. Meyers and Mr. Simpson, of the Chicago Academy of Natural Sciences."—Fort Wayne GAZETTE, Sept. 17, 1867.

* Albert Gallatin's synopsis. † From the French.

the present time,—"among the tribes of Texas, there were warriors who are said to trace their lineage to Algonquins on the Atlantic; and descendants from the New England Indians," as late as 1852, "roamed over western prairies." *

The eight primitive tribes, exhibiting a radical distinction in language, were:

1. ALGONQUIN,	5. CHEROKEE,
2. DAHCOTA,	6. UCHEE,
3. HURON-IROQUOIS,	7. NATCHEZ,
4. CATAWBA.	8. MOBILIAN.

From these sprang many branches, which, some years subsequent to the earliest settlements in America, had spread over a great part of the country, many of them often becoming greatly reduced by warfare, or, fusing one tribe with another, by amalgamation, gradually very materially changed the primitive tongue. In this way, if not lost through the extinction of clans,† a great number of dialects were developed and diffused over the continent.

The names of the various tribes and clans of late years composing the Algonquin family, many of whom, by permission of the Miamies, had early found their way into, and settled upon, the extensive territory of this tribe, were the

Miamies, (*Twightwees*),	*Sacs*,	*Ottawas*,
Chippewas,	*Corees*,	*Illinois*,
Piankeshaws,	*Foxes*,	*Shawanoes*,
Menomenees,	*Powhatans*,	*Kickapoos*,
Lenni-Lenapes, (*Delawares*,)	*Mohegans*,	*Knisteneaux*,
The New England Indians,	*Abenakes*,	*Monocans*,
Suspuehannocks,	*Mannahoacks*,	*Nanticokes*,
Pottawattamies,	*Winnebagoes*,	*Mascoutens*, ‡

with some other smaller independent clans, many of which were divided into cantons and bodies, it was said, "sometimes so small as to afford only a war party."

Thus we see, more distinctly, the relationship, position, and character of the Miamies. Of the entire Algonquin family, there were perhaps none more stable, heroic and resolute than this tribe.

* Bancroft---Duponceau.

† Nature is everywhere alike as to the principle of CHANGE--mind,—matter of the most gross or most attenuated character,—even to sounds, music, words, dialects, language, of the finest order of developement,--are all subject to the law of change, transmission, growth of the highest grade of unfoldment, or the opposite, to a greater or less degree, to extinction itself.

‡ Each of which had some special meaning in the Indian tongue—as, Ottawa, signified *a trader*; Mascoutens, *dwellers in the prairie*; Menomenies, *we are men*; original men—an expression of dignity, or greatness often used by the braves—such as, "I am a man!" (a Menomenie!); Fox, *red earth*; Sac, or Sauk, *yellow earth*—and so on. And there were probably but few of these tribes or clans that did not, at one period or other, visit this point, or send hither their envoys to sit at the Council Fires of the "Glorious Gate" of the different tribes, which the Miamies "had the happiness to own;" and there were doubtless many seasons of harmony among the tribes gathered here, as there were also periods of bitter feuds and warfare between various nations of the continent.

The limits of their territory has already been quoted in the previous chapter. This extensive domain had been held by their ancestors, said the famous Little Turtle, to General Wayne, "from time immemorial, without molestation or dispute." And had they been a progressive people—readily adapting themselves to the active civilization springing up everywhere about them a few years after the struggles of 1812–14, very many of them might still have been dwelling in this region upon their old familiar hunting-grounds. But, as a mass, they had, with a few exceptions, lived too long in an opposite condition of life to readily enter into the more advanced habits of thought, growth, and culture of the whites, then rapidly settling upon their ancient domain. That the red man could long have lived in the centre of a moderate civilization without feeling its power and influence, any more than the white man, dwelling among savage tribes, in the forest, would be unable to resist, to a greater or less degree, the influences surrounding him, is a matter needing but little consideration in point of fact.

Man ever assimilates, has ever assimilated, to a greater or less extent, in all ages, with that which has surrounded him. If his surroundings are crude, wild, and inflexible, he has readily partaken of them. And in just so far as he has become familiar with the art of subduing and cultivating the soil—clearing the woodlands, and making the untamed conditions of nature to bend to his necessities—producing new vegetative life in the form of fruits, cereals, plants, and flowers, has he improved in organization and the general refinement of blood, brain, and nerve. And it has ever been through the possession, excercise and application of this power and intelligence, however meager and incomplete, at first, the means and implements of cultivation, if steadily pursued, that has laid the ground-work of sure and gradual transition from barbarism to civilization.

The great realm of nature is everywhere progressive—ever looks upward and aspires to a higher sense of beauty and refinement. The flowers of a hundred years ago were less refined in point of essence, and in many instances beauty also, than those of to-day. So also with the fruits and every other species of vegetative life, where a proper degree of care in cultivation is observed. This principle is equally true of man. Give him but the necessary advantages and encouragement in the art of cultivating the soil or improving his mental powers, and he readily begins to refine. Under these auspices the red man, in many instances, from the days of the Jesuit missionaries to the present time, has verified, most clearly and substantially, the truthfulness of this principle of growth and culture in the natural order of existence. And although never becoming truly Anglo-Saxon, in so far as the inventive and higher sense of civilization is manifest—although never losing his tawny skin, save in a sense of amalgamation, nor ceased entirely, perhaps, to entertain an affection for the forest and its wildest haunts—the streams, and a love for the canoe, the spear, the bow and arrow, or trusty rifle—he yet was ever a living evidence of the power and influence of civilization, as brought to bear upon him at various times and in many ways. A rude, uncultivated child of the forest—of nature and the primitive wilds—he was readily and naturally imitative, and soon received from the white man a knowledge of agriculture and the use of various implements, with which to cultivate the soil, cook, fish, hunt, fell the trees, &c.

Beyond these evidences and facts, it had been observed that it was far easier for the white man to become, in manners and custom, an Indian, than for the Indian to become a white man in point of civilization and the progressive march and appliances of life, in art and general culture; *and this is strangely true of no other people with whom the white man has ever associated or come in contact.*

The Indian, though naturally hospitable, by nature and custom, was often a rude example of indifference; knowing and practicing but little of the common sympathetic feeling of the white race. They were accustomed to bewail the loss of friends and their great chiefs and sachems; and the women, on such occasions, in the wildest and most dishevelled appearance, with garments tattered and dirty, their faces blackened, and hair streaming about their shoulders, often wept bitterly, it is true, visiting the graves of the departed for many consecutive days; but, in the ordinary concerns of life, to weep or lament were usages most uncommon to the red man. Even in the midst of the most terrible torture or suffering, he was seldom if ever known to shed a tear or utter complaint. Such was his idea of bravery; yet, if there was one thing more than another that would have had a tendency to awaken the tears and sympathy of the Indian, or cause him to sadly bewail his lot, was to remove him, by force or otherwise, from the scenes of his hunting-ground and early associations—so ardent was his attachment to his native hills and plains—his early home and the many relations that clustered about it; and in this he was much like the rest of mankind.

Our surroundings as naturally become a part of us, as the air we inhale is necessary to our health and vigor of action. The soil we tread upon, bringing forth and nourishing the food we eat, possesses within itself the elements of mutuality and reciprocation; and every organic being as surely gravitates toward the natural, and as readily commingles, in some way, therewith, as the law of gravitation brings a falling body to the earth, or the diurnal action of the globe brings us the constant "shadow of the night" and "the light of day." And the law of sympathy is ever active and earnest within us.

The bleak Esquimaux, the plodding Highlander, and peasant of Northern Russia, no less than the most favored of the English nobility, or the wealthiest and most prosperous merchant or farmer in America, are allied and attached to their native homes, and would as readily take up the cudgel or draw the sword,—load the cannon or shoulder the rifle in defence of their native plains and hills as would we of America, England, France or Germany, were we or they to be suddenly, or otherwise invaded. Nature never fails to express herself—never fails to make a reply when interrogated, no matter how strong the sympathy, or whither the alliance. And the red man, in his primitive fastnesses, native vales and woodlands of America—wandering upon the banks of her many beautiful rivers, chasing the wild animals of the forest, or spearing the fish in her streams,—was no exception to the rule; and when he saw and felt the first act of encroachment upon his native soil, he arose in all the dignity of offended greatness, seized the tomahawk, the war-club, the bow and arrow; assembled the braves; strode vigorously through the war-dance; blackened and painted their faces; and, after the mode of Indian warfare, at once lay in wait to strike the first blow, in hopes to destroy the enemy, or repel him from their boundaries.

And herein is evinced a sad want of wisdom and knowledge on the part of both the Indian and the white man—the one to pass through the ordeal of an almost gradual extermination, while upon the other fell all the trials and dangers of an intestine and savage warfare, amid forest and jungle, united with the vast hardships and vicissitude of the pioneer.

As has already been shown, the uniformity of the Indian dialect, was, in primitive times, or about the period of the discovery of America, strongly related and identical. And the same was mainly true of the general habits and customs of the various tribes of the continent.

At an early period, as the French and English sucessively made inroads upon the territories of the Miamies—or, as they were early called by the English and the Iriquois, *the Twightwees*,—in the establishment of stockades and trading-posts, the spirit of intermarriage soon became rife between the Indian women, fur-traders, adventurers, and soldiers, which, up to the departure of a large body of this tribe for Kansas, several years since, had well-nigh changed the whole number remaining to "half-breeds." At that period, as is well understood, but few full-blooded Indians were to be found throughout the entire extent of their ancient territory. And hence, of late years, looking back upon them, we see the light complexion of the white man clearly visible in their every feature, rather than the brownish-red of the unmixed aboriginal. Many of them, indeed, were quite white, with blue eyes,—though still retaining, in a large degree, the Indian features,—thick lips, large mouth, high cheek bones, and prominent nose; and were, for the most part, still *Indian*—cherishing, to a late day, the ancient customs of their fathers, in hunting, fishing, cultivating the maize, &c.

The following interesting account of the Miamies was written as early as 1718. The writer had made a short stay at the village here, and passed on to their brethren of the Wea and other towns along the Wabash. Says the writer:

"The Miamies are situated sixty leagues from Lake Erie, and number four hundred, all well formed men, and well tattooed; *the women are numerous.* They are hard working, and raise a species of maize unlike that of our Indians at Detroit. It is white, of the same size as the other, the skin much finer, and the meal much whiter. This nation is clad in deer skin.* They love plays and dances; wherefore they have more occupation. The women are well clothed, but the men use scarcely any covering, and are tattooed all over the body. From this Miami village, there is a portage of three leagues to a little and very narrow stream that falls, after a course of twenty leagues,† into the Ohio or the Beautiful River, which discharges into the Oaubache—a fine river that falls into the Missisgippi, forty leagues from Cascachias. Into the Ouabache falls also the Casquinampo, which communicates with Carolina; but this is very far off, and always up stream.

"This river Ouabache is the one on wnich the Ougatenons‡ are settled. They consist of five villages, which are contiguous the one to the other. One is called Oujatanon; the other Peanquinchias; and another Petitscatias; and the fourth Lesgros. The name of the last I do not recollect; but they are all Oujatanons, having the same language as the Miamies—whose brothers they are, and properly all Miamies, having all the same customs and dress. The men are very numerous—fully a thousand or twelve hundred. They have a custom different from all other nations; which is, to keep their fort extremely clean, not allowing a blade of grass to remain in it. The whole of the fort is sanded like the Tuilleries. * * * Their village is situated on a high hill; and they have over two leagues of improvement, where they raise their Indian corn, pumpkins, and melons. From the summit of this elevation, nothing is visible to the eye but prairies full of buffalo."

In stature, for the most part, the Miamies were of medium height, well built, heads rather round than oblong—countenances agreeable, rather than sedate or morose—swift on foot, and excessively fond of racing—both on foot and horse.|| There were, occasionally to be seen among them some men quite tall, yet with well-proportioned bodies. As is intimated in the foregoing, the Twightwees or Miamies, unlike most other tribes, were rather cleanly in their habits; for which they were mostly noted up to a very late period; and were disposed to cultivate the soil—raising the maize, beans, squashes, cucumbers, melons, &c. Around and within view

*From Colonial History of New York, (a Paris document,) vol. ix, p. 891.

†League, (from the French,) three miles. ‡Pronounced as if spelt Weatenons.

|| The Indian race-track, for many years, extended from the south side of the west-end free school building, westward about half a mile. For some years before the departure of the Miamies for the west, while the racing was kept up over this track, men from Ohio, and other parts of the country, were accustomed to bring many fast horses here, and often sold them to the Indians at very extravagant prices.

of the present site of Ft. Wayne, at different points, were several small patches of cleared land, which the Indian women and children regularly cultivated each year, and brought forth considerable quantities of corn and other products; which, together with the game and fish brought in by the men of the tribe, supplied them with food during the winter. It is a well authenticated fact, however, that, at periods, perhaps in seasons of severe drought, or more especially when the products of their fields were destroyed or overrun, and their villages burned by invading armies, or through conflicts with formidable tribes at more remote periods, and often from neglect to prepare for the winter months, the Indians, not unfrequently, found themselves with but scanty supplies for the severe months of winter; and, huddling themselves about their dingy wigwams, with a few smoking embers in the center, scarcely sufficient to keep them warm, have been known to fast for many consecutive days because of their inability to obtain food.

The extensive field* and open point, just east of, and adjacent to, the confluence of the rivers St. Mary and St. Joseph, in which stands the historic Apple Tree,† near and about which were scattered many of the huts and wigwams of the Miamies to a late period in the present century, had been annually cultivated by this ancient tribe for a period of perhaps one hundred and fifty years or more before the erection of the fort at this point under the direction of General Wayne, in 1794. That their women had long been accustomed to

*As early as 1814, the Indians then here informed John P. Hedges, Esq.,—who has now been a resident of Fort Wayne for fifty-five years—coming here with the army in 1812,—that this field had been cultivated by others long before them; and, to quote their own language,—*mingeb-a-westook*,—they had planted and raised corn, beans, &c., in this field for *many* years—a *long*, *long* time.

†Chief Richardville often told the old settlers here that this old apple tree was there when he was a little boy; and that it was then a "bearing tree;" that the hut in which he was born stood very near to it. The chief attained an age of near eighty years, and died in 1841. With these facts it is presumed that, at the present time (September, 1867), the tree is about one hundred and thirty odd years old. From the fact of his early associations, his birth, &c., being so intimately related to this old tree and its adjacent localities, Richardville ever looked upon it with the warmest veneration and regard. The tree is thought to have sprung from a seed accidently dropped or purposely planted by some of the early French traders or missionaries visiting this point. In the spring of 1866, a heavy storm swept away its main trunk, leaving it as now seen in the opposite engraving. The circumference, as measured by the writer and a friend, in the month of June, (1867) was 12 feet. The fruit is small, and usually ripens in the month of October. By the taste of the leaf of the tree, there would seem to be sufficient strength and vitality in it, if not otherwise molested, to survive at least a half century or more to come. Says Mr. J. L. Williams: "We need not question its identity. There are specimens of the hardier varieties in this country now bearing fruit at the age of 150 to 200 years." Let its memory be perpetuated by a careful preservation of it in future years. Its historic renown well entitles it to the careful attention of the present owners of the ancient field of the Miamies, in which it has so long lived, blossomed, and borne its fruit. Let a neat railing be placed about it as a means to its better protection and care. It was out of this tree that an Indian, during the seige of 1812, was shot by one of the soldiers from the fort, a distance of many hundred yards. In an exulting spirit, one of the beseigers was in the habit of climbing the tree each day for several days, and, hrowing his arms, much like the rooster his wings, when crowing, would utter a noise ery like this fowl, which was finally answered by the crack of a rifle from the rt, and the Indian was seen to fall.

THE „OLD APPLE TREE".

extensive agricultural pursuits is most fully confirmed by all the early visitants of this locality, and the regions adjacent.

In a letter to the Secretary of war, General Knox, bearing date August 14, 1794, General Wayne said: "The margin of those beautiful rivers, the Miamis of the lake (or Maumee) and Auglaize, appear like one continued village for a number of miles, both above and below this place (confluence of the Auglaize and Maumee); nor have I ever beheld such immense fields of corn, in any part of America, from Canada to Florida."

The accounts of 1812, are of a similar character. Several villages were then located at different points, here and within a range of some ten miles of Ft. Wayne; the most considerable village then being about ten miles below this point, on the Maumee. A large amount of corn and wheat were then destroyed, much of it purported to have been of a very excellent quality; showing, that, by a long contact with the English and French, from whom had sprung many of the half-breeds, then so numerous among the Miamies and other tribes living near and about them, these Indians had attained many advantages in civilized relations, in the way of agriculture, &c.; and many of the villagers were then living in very good log-cabins, raising annually excellent crops of both corn and wheat. Ox-teams, brought from Canada, were also employed among them, at that period, to very good advantage.*

The Indian loved the wild fruits, and here, in the region of Fort Wayne, there were, at an early period, an abundance of wild plums, haws, berries, &c. The Indians were accustomed to cherish the belief that for them the Great Spirit had especially caused these to come forth and ripen with each season; and every species of food, from the roots, vegetables, and fruits, to the animals themselves, were alike considered as imbued with some peculiar principle in which the Great Spirit had infused some special element of excellence, intended to impart to the red man both health and strength. Here, more especially, the blackberry was most abundant, and from this fact, this point was long known to the Indians as Ke-ki-ong-a,†

*Recollections of Mr. George Taylor, a resident of Plymouth, Ind., who was here in 1812, and, by command of his superior officers of the army, helped to destroy many of the Indian settlements of this region.

†Says Mr. Chas. B. Lasselle, in referring to this point: "The Miami name of this village was Ke-ki-ong-a, which, by an inflection of the last syllable, was pronounced as if writtten Ke-ki-ong'a. The name in English, signifies blackberry patch, which, in its turn, passed among the Miamies as a symbol of antiquity. But whether this name was given it on account of the spot being covered with the blackberry, or was meant to represent it as the most ancient village of their race in this country, is not known, though tradition, their unusual regard for it, (the place) and the tenacity with which they so long defended it, would imply, the latter supposition. The old colonist writers speak of it as the 'Twightwee' village. The French traders called it 'AUME.' The Americans called it 'OMEE,' and sometimes 'THE Miami village.' It extended, principally, along the banks of the St. Joseph river, but was also over the opposite side, and reached to within three or four hundred yards of the confluence of that river with the St. Mary. The inhabitants of this village anciently belonged to that tribe of Miamies called the Twat-t-wahs, (which the early colonists spelt 'Twightwees,') the nation having consisted of the several tribes of Weahs (at We-ah-ta-nong, on the Wabash,) Eel

which, interpreted, signified a blackberry patch. And the reader can well imagine, in the ripening season, a bevy of women and children, with bark baskets, gathering the rich berries of their *ke-ki-ong-a*.

With the red man, to be idle, was to be happy, great, and *free*; and, as we have seen in a former page, the Miamies "loved plays and dances," and thus, with gaming, chanting some familiar refrain, perhaps learned from the medicine men—wrestling, racing, lying, or sitting beneath the shade of some wide-spreading tree, in summer, they whiled away their time during the greater part of the spring, summer, and fall, seldom if ever disturbing the game of the forest, more especially that species (the beaver, the raccoon, the bear, the deer, the buffalo,* &c.,) which afforded them valuable furs and skins, until the hunting season began, which was usually about the first of November of each year. This was life among the Miamies, and, in fact, among every tribe of the northwest.

In games of chance, moccasin, &c., in which they indulged a great deal, at a late period, more especially, they would participate, unless intoxicated, with the greatest good humor, often betting and losing every article they possessed, even to their guns, hatchets, &c., and never thought it amiss to cheat, whenever an opportunity presented. In foot and horse-racing, they as often went to as great extremes in betting as when at a game of moccasin.

The greatest labors of the men, in earlier periods, were those of completing palisades; constructing boats; to aid in the building and repair of their cabins; to prepare the instruments of warfare and the chase; to paint, tattoo, and otherwise adorn their bodies. The women of the red men were ever the toilers; to them fell the burdens of cultivating the fields and patches that brought forth the vegetation of spring and summer that went to nourish them, in part, the remainder of the year; and before the visit of the trader—who supplied them, in exchange for furs, with hoes, and other implements of use,—how meager and indifferent must have been their means and advantages of cultivating the soil. Some wooden implement, perhaps—some sharp bone of an animal, or tortoise shell, doubtless served for a hoe or mattock. And thus toiled the Indian

Rivers (at At-ke-no-pe-kong, on Eel river), Twat-wahs, and perhaps some others, whose names and existence, as separate tribes, have long since ceased, and been merged into those of the nation." Now, the fact of the word Ke-ki-ong-a signifying a blackberry patch warrants a strong supposition, at least, that, in view of the fact of there being very early a large patch of that nature at this point, the name Ke-ki-ong-a must primitively have been derived therefrom.

*November, 9th, 1712, Father Gabriel Marest, a French missionary, writing from some point perhaps along the Wabash, or, as then called, the *Ouabache*, after giving a somewhat full and graphic account of the regions bordering on that stream, said it was "rich in minerals, especially lead and tin, and that if experienced miners were to come out from France and work the mines, he had no doubt that gold and silver would be found in abundance. That the quantity of *buffalo* and bear which was to be found on the banks of the Wabash (*Ouabache*), was incredible;" and further remarked that "the meat of the bear was very delicious, "for," said he, "I have tried it."—Judge Law's Address, page 11.

women in the field, mellowed the soil, beat down the weeds about the corn, cultivated the bean, the squash, the Indian cucumber, the pumpkin and the melon; and she it was that routed the birds from the patches, gathered the maize and other products of her labor; jerked and dried the deer, bear, and buffalo meat; prepared the Indian meal; dried the winter's fruit; gathered the wood for the fires, and cooked the meals. And when a bark canoe was built, it was the Indian woman's work to sew the bark with some stringy substance, berhaps peeled from the elm or root of some small tree, and filling the seams with some adhesive substance, to prevent leakage. When removing from one point to another, or retiring to their hunting-grounds for the winter, to carry the luggage, and material of the wigwam, if taken with them, it was the mission of the Indian women to pack such upon their backs. Did the red man go in pursuit of game, it was the ancient custom of the faithful Indian woman to follow and carry upon her shoulder the fruits of the chase.*

The Indian women were indeed heroes. And when we come to contemplate the toilsome lives they led—their unflinching efforts in all kinds of weather,—in every season of the year—it is not surprising that the early sons of the forest were hardy and active—fleet on foot and wily in the fight. Amid toil and drudgery—trial and vicissitude—the Indian woman often brought forth the offspring of their masters; (for they were evidently nearly all, if not quite, in a large degree, at least, veritable slaves to their husbands.) So hardy were they, from constant physical labor and exposure to the open air, it was said of them, that, "in one quarter of an hour a woman would be merry in the house, and delivered, and merry again; and within two days, abroad; and after four or five days, at work." The powerful will of the Indian women, together with their long accustomed aversion and heroic indifference to pain, ever rose superior to the momentary pangs accompanying the birth of their offspring. In this they possessed a strong native intuition; and thus far, at least, are worthy of emulation by all the mothers of our present heroic conditions of civilization and intellectual advancement. What a world of health and goodness—what an ocean of intellectual excellence and physical beauty might have been germinated through the organism of the Indian mother, had she possess-

*"When the Indians arrived and departed," says Mrs. Kenzie, referring to very early times, in the present century, about Green Bay, "my sense of 'woman's rights' was often outraged. The master of the family, as a general thing, came leisurely bearing a gun and perhaps a lance in his hand. The woman, with the mats and poles of her lodge upon her shoulders, her papoose, if she had one, the kettles, sacks of corn, and wild rice, and not unfrequently, the household dog, perched on the top of all. If there is a horse or pony in the list of family possessions, the man rides, the squaw trudges after. This unequal division of labor is the result of no want of kind, affectionate feeling on the part of the husband. It is rather the instinct of the sex to assert their superiority of position and importance, when a proper occasion offers. When out of the reach of observation, and in no danger of compromising his own dignity, the husband is willing enough to relieve his spouse from the burden that custom imposes on her, by sharing her labors and hardships."—"Early Day in the Northwest," pages 359 and 360.

ed the proper expansion of mind. Even as it was, how many rare and singular examples of oratory came from her. Listen to the stirring appeal of Little Turtle, (Me-che-cannah-quah) addressing Gen. Wayne, and others, at the famous treaty of Greenville, July 15th, 1795:

"Elder brother, and all present! I am going to say a few words," said the orator, "in the name of the Pottawattamies, Weas, and Kickapoos. It is well known to you all, that people are appointed on these occasions, to speak the sentiments of others; therefore am I appointed for those three nations. Elder brother: you told your younger brothers, when we first assembled, that peace was your object; you swore your interpreters before us to the faithful discharge of their duty, and told them the Great Spirit would punish them, did they not perform it. You told us that it was not you, but the President of the fifteen fires of the United States who spoke to us; that whatever he should say should be firm and lasting; that it was impossible he should say what was not true. Rest assured that your younger brothers, the Miamies, Chippewas, Ottawas, Pottawattamies, Shawanees, Weas, Kickapoos, Piankeshaws, and Kaskaskias, are well pleased with your words, and are persuaded of your sincerity. You have told us to consider the boundaries you showed us; your younger brothers have done so, and now proceed to give you their answer.*

"Elder brother: Your younger brothers do not wish to hide their sentiments from you. I wish them to be the same with those of the Wyandots and Delawares. You have told us, that most of the reservations you proposed to us, belonged to our fathers, the French and the British. Permit your younger brothers to make a few observations on this subject. Elder brother: We wish you to listen with attention to our words. You have told your younger brothers that the British imposed falsehoods on us, when they said the United States wished to take our lands from us, and that the United States had no such design: You pointed out to us the boundary line, which crossed a little below Loramie's store, and struck Fort Recovery, and run from thence to Ohio, opposite the mouth of Kentucky river. Elder brother: You have told us to speak our minds freely, and we now do it. This line takes in the greater and best part of your brother's hunting ground; therefore your younger brothers are of opinion you take too much of their lands away, and confine the hunting of our young men within limits too contracted. Your brothers, the Miamis, the proprietors of those lands, and all your younger brothers present, wish you to run the line as you mentioned, to Fort Recovery, and continue it along the road, from thence to Fort Hamilton, on the Great Miami river. This is what your brothers request you to do, and you may rest assured of the free

*This speech not only largely displays the power of Indian oratory,—the native intelligence and goodness of heart of this distinguished Chief, but also carries with it many important historical facts relating to the early history of Fort Wayne.

navigation of that river, from thence to its mouth, forever. Brother: Here is the road we wish to be the boundary between us. What lies to the east we wish to be yours; that to the west, we would desire to be ours. [Presenting a road belt.]

"Elder brother: In speaking of the reservations, you say they are designed for the same purposes as those for which our fathers, the French and English, occupied them. Your younger brothers now wish to make some observations on them. Elder brother: Listen with attention. You told us you discovered on the Great Miami, traces of an old fort. Brother: it was a fort built by me. You perceived another at Loramie's: 'tis true a Frenchman once lived there for a year or two. The Miami villages were occupied as you remarked;* but, it was unknown to your younger brothers, until you told them, that we had sold land there to the French or English. I was surprised to hear you say it was my forefathers had set the example to the other Indians, in selling their lands. I will inform you in what manner the French and English occupied those places. Elder brother: These people were seen by our forefathers first at Detroit: afterwards we saw them at the Miami village—that glorious gate, which your younger brothers had the happiness to own, and through which all the good words of our chiefs had to pass, from the north to the south, and from the east to the west. Brothers, these people never told us they wished to purchase our lands from us.

"Elder brother: I now give you the true sentiments of your younger brothers, the Miamis, with respect to the reservation at the Miami villages. We thank you for kindly contracting the limits you at first proposed. We wish you to take this six miles square on the side of the river where your fort now stands, as your younger brothers wish to inhabit that beloved spot again. You shall cut hay for your cattle wherever you please, and you shall never require in vain the assistance of your younger brothers at that place. Elder brother: The next place you pointed to was the Little River, and said you wanted two miles square at that place.

*The point here referred to, was the following, from General Wayne's speech, made five days previous to the delivery of Little Turtle's speech, and addressed to the Miamies. Said he,

"I will point out to you where I discover strong traces of these establishments; (forts) and, first of all, I find at Detroit a very strong print, where the first fire was kindled by your forefathers: west, at Vincennes, on the Wabash; again at Musquiton, on the same river; a little higher up that stream, they are to be seen at Ouitenon. I discover another strong trace at Chicago; another on the St. Joseph's of Lake Michigan. I have seen distinctly the prints of a French and British post at the Miami villages, and of a British post at the foot of the rapids, now in their possession; prints, very conspicuous, are on the Great Miami, which were possessed by the French forty-five years ago; and another trace is very distinctly to be seen at Sandusky. It appears to me," he continued, "that if the Great Spirit, as you say, charged your forefathers to preserve their lands entire for their posterity, they have paid very little regard to the sacred injunction: for I see they have parted with those lands to your fathers, the French, and the English are now, or have been, in possession of them all; therefore, I think the charge urged against the Ottawas, the Chippewas, and other Indians comes with a bad grace, indeed from the very people perhaps that set them the example. The English and French both wore hats; and yet, your forefathers sold them, at various times, portions of your lands."

This is a request that our fathers, the French and British, never made us; it was always ours. This carrying place has heretofore proved, in a great degree, the subsistence of your younger brothers. That place has brought to us, in the course of one day, the amount of one hundred dollars. Let us both own this place, and enjoy in common the advantages it affords. You told us, at Chicago, the French possessed a fort: we have never heard of it. We thank you for the trade you promised to open in our country; and permit us to remark, that we hope our former traders may be continued, and mixed with yours. Elder brother: On the subject of hostages, I have only to observe, that I trust all my brothers are of my opinion with regard to peace and our future happiness. I expect to be with you every day when you settle on your reservations; and it will be impossible for me or my people to withhold from you a single prisoner; therefore we don't know why any of us should remain here. These are the sentiments of your younger brothers present, on these particulars."

And again, at a council, in the valley of the Muskingum, in 1764, hear the eloquent words of a Shawanoe chief, as he addresses the English commander, Col. Bouquet, then marching against the western tribes:

"Brother," said the chief, "with this belt of wampum, I dispel the black cloud that has so long hung over our heads, that the sunshine of peace may once more descend to warm and gladden us. I wipe the tears from your eyes, and condole with you on the loss of your brethren who have perished in this war. I gather their bones together, and cover them deep in the earth, that the sight of them may no longer bring sorrow to your heart; and I scatter dry leaves over the spot, that it may depart forever from memory.

"The path of peace, which once ran between your dwellings and mine, has of late been choked with thorns, and briars, so that no one could pass that way; and we have both almost forgotten that such a path had ever been. I now clear away all these obstructions, and make a broad, smooth road, so that you and I may freely visit each other, as our fathers used to do. I kindle a great council-fire whose smoke shall rise to heaven, in view of all the nations, while you and I shall sit together and smoke the peace-pipe at its blaze."*

*An Indian council, on solemn occasions, was always opened with preliminary forms, sufficiently wearisome and tedious, but made indispensible by immemorial custom; for this people are as much bound by their conventional usages as the most artificial children of civilization. The forms were varied, to some extent, according to the imagination of the speaker; but in all essential respects they were closely similar, throughout the tribes of the Algonquin and Iroquois lineage. They run somewhat as follows, each sentence being pronounced with great solemnity, and confirmed by the delivery of a wampum belt Brothers, with this belt I open your ears that you may hear—I remove grief and sorrow from your hearts—I draw from your feet the thorns that pierced them as you journeyed thither—I clean the seats of the council-house, that you may sit at ease—I wash your head and body, that your spirits may be refreshed—I condole with you on the loss of the friends who have died since we last met—I wipe out any blood which

Again, in 1762, at the famous council of Lancaster, Pa., a distinguished chief of the Oneidas, with singular emphasis, said:

"In the country of the Oneidas there is a great pine-tree, so huge and old that half its branches are dead with time. I tear it up by the roots, and, looking down into the hole, I see a dark stream of water, flowing with a strong current, deep under ground. Into this stream I fling the hatchet, and the current sweeps it away, no man knows whither. Then I plant the tree again where it stood before; and thus this war will be ended forever."

The love of the Indian mother for her child was most intense. Though seldom expressed by fond caresses, yet it was ever ardent, free, and unextinguishable; and to have entrusted her babe to the care of another to perform the part of mother or nurse, except in cases of death, would indeed, to her, have been a wild, barbarous act. The cradle of the Indian child was usually constructed of bark and small sticks of wood; and was commonly adorned with gaudy feathers, beads, and other attractive objects, of a similar nature. A buffalo or other warm furry skin usually served as a bed and covering for the little nursling.*

When journeying, the Indian mother would wrap her child in furs, or in a blanket, and, placing its back to her own, would travel steadily on to her journey's end, regardless, often, of the wailings of her infant, on the way. When at work in the field or patch, she would often hang her tawny bud, "as spring does its blossoms, on the boughs of a tree, that it might be rocked by the breezes from the land of souls, and soothed to sleep by the lullaby of the birds." And it often occurred, through a peculiar sense of compassion among the aboriginal tribes, that when the mother died, her infant, if very young and feeble, shared the grave with her.

may have been spilt between us. This ceremony, which, by the delivery of so many belts of wampum, entailed no small expense, was never used except on the most important occasions; and at the councils with Col. Bouquet, the angry warriors seem wholly to have dispensed with it.

An Indian orator was provided with a stock of metaphors, which he always made use of for the expression of certain ideas. Thus, to make war was to raise the hatchet; to make peace was to take hold of the chain of friendship; to deliberate was to kindle the council-fire; to cover the bones of the dead was to make reparation and gain forgiveness for the act of killing them. A state of war and disaster was typified by a black cloud; a state of peace by bright sunshine, or by an open path between the two nations.

The orator seldom spoke without careful premeditation of what he was about to say; and his memory was refreshed by belts of wampum, which he delivered after every clause in his harangue, as a pledge of the sincerity and truth of his words. These belts were carefully preserved by the hearers, as a substitute for written records; a use for which they were the better adapted, as they were often worked in hieroglyphics expressing the meaning they were designed to preserve. Thus, at a treaty of peace, the principal belt often bore the figure of an Indian and a white man holding a chain between them. —[Parkman.

*Recollections of Mrs. Griswold (formerly Mrs. Peltier) who, with her grandfather and grandmother, Batis Maloch and wife, (deceased) came from Detroit to Fort Wayne as early as 1807. Mr. James Peltier, her husband, who had, for some years previous, and so continued for some years after, been a trader at this point, and early becoming warmly attached to the American cause, and being much liked by the Indians, was long most useful to the government as an interpreter and messenger, carrying messages often at great risk of life, but always with success.

Many years ago, one of the early mothers of Fort Wayne, with her husband, took up their residence in a little hut at the base of the hill, just west of the bend of the Maumee, nearly under the guns of the old fort. Near their dwelling was another hut, used by her husband for purposes of trade with the Indians. Both, because of their many acts of attention and kindness, had early won the savage heart, and being able to speak freely with the Indians in their native tongue, were often visited and protected by the red children of the region. They seemed indeed to have regarded her as a kind of goddess, and often looked up to her as a spiritual helper. Often, she says, has she joined with them in the wild dance and merry Indian jubilee—all regarding her with special favor on such occasions. A little incident will strikingly illustrate her relationship to them, and serve to exhibit the tender regard of the Indian mother for her offspring. It was a pleasant period of the year, when an Indian woman, approaching the edge of the river, not far from the little huts in question, with a child in her arms, seemingly in great distress, suddenly observing our pioneer mother, then but a girl of some sixteen or seventeen summers, cried most piteously to Mrs. P.* to come to her aid. Anxious to know the cause of the woman's distress, and feeling, as well, a desire to render her what aid she could, Mrs. P. soon stood by the side of the anxious woman in the water. The Indian woman's story was quickly told. She had, but a little while before, observed that her child was dying, and had at once hastened to the river to afford it baptism before its little spirit should take its flight. "If the little papposa die," said she, with much anxiety, "before it is put in the water, it can only see the spirits about it—it can't go up where the *Great* Spirit is." Readily affording the woman the desired aid, the child was speedily baptised, and the mother's heart set at ease. A few moments more, and the spirit of the little pappoose was gone. The great Manito of the red man would now afford it a place in his joyful household.

One of the prime objects of the Indian mother, as, the child advanced, was to enure it to the weather, that it might be strong and active. With this view, soon after being taken from the cradle, with but little covering upon their bodies, the children were permitted to rollick and amuse themselves about the cabin, that they might acquire, as well, a knowledge of the use of their limbs. Freedom of will being the highest idea of governmental excellence with the Indian, there were no special restraints of family government among the Miamies. The children were permitted to do just as they wished, seldom if ever being reproved or chastised; and yet, were unaccustomed, as a general rule, to acts of special incivility

*Mrs. Peltier, (now Griswold), who informed the writer that, in those early times' now some fifty-eight years ago, she was often called upon to aid the Indians in this way. It is most probable that this religious rite came originally from the early missionaries visiting and sojourning here; for the primitive Indian mother seems ever to have entertained the belief that the Great Spirit had placed near her child a guardian angel or spirit that could enable it to surmount all obstacles, here and hereafter.

toward any of the older members of the tribe, or the stranger when visiting them in times of peace.* All were alike attached to their young, and could not, under any circumstances, permit a separation, long at a time, while living. Their own native aspirations led the young Indian early to acquire a knowledge of the bow and arrow, the tomahawk, and the gun, and to use their limbs with dexterity in running and swimming. From oft-repeated stories of the prowess and daring of their ancestors, related to them by the older members of the tribes, as they sat about the fire of the wigwam, the young Indian early became imbued with heroic feelings, and longed to become famous by some special act of bravery and valorous exploit.† As with "the birth of an offspring, or the appearance of a first tooth," there was merry-making in the Indian cabin, so also the wigwam was made a scene of festivity upon the achievement of a first success in hunting. Being thus early schooled, dwelling in, and subsisting upon the wilds of nature, it was not surprising that the young Indian soon became a "brave," longing for war, and to adorn his person, by the most wily means and acts of ferocity, if need be, with the scalps of his red foeman and the pale face. Nothing was so joyous to his soul—nothing made him more eager for the charge, and filled his heart with greater determination to excel as a warrior, or to defeat and put to rout and to death the enemy he was to meet at a special time and place, than to chant beforehand the wild war song, and dance the war-dance around the midnight camp-fires or through the streets of his villages. Painted and blackened; with the feathers of the eagle, hawk, or other bird, as a crown about their heads, or, long, black, coarse hair streaming wildly back over their shoulders, or cut close to their skulls, leaving only a top-lock, standing forth in all their native ardor and self-excellence—brave, resolute, determined — knowing all the country around—every point of possible retreat for an army—every hollow, or special ravine—every deep thicket and clump of trees—every fording-place along the rivers,—the swamps of the woods—every point where the fallen timber was most abundant, or lay the open spaces and prairies—it was not to be wondered the Miamies were often so successful in their efforts against the early pioneers and the armies of Harmar, St. Clair, and others, in the latter part of the past century. Still powerful at that period, commanding at any moment, a numerous alli, with the memory and prowess of their ancestors, and many marks of success to inspire and urge them on, they were not easily to be subdued or driven from the home of their fathers.

*Recollections of J. P. Hedges, Esq., who speaks the Miami tongue quite fluently.

†It was always a common complaint with the chiefs and head men of the different tribes throughout the country,from an early period, that "they could not restrain their young men," and when their early teachings are taken into view, it was not surprising that the young men of the tribes were so often unrestrainable.

CHAPTER III.

"Through the woodland, through the meadow,
As in silence oft I walk,
Softly whispering on the breezes,
Seems to come the red man's talk."—Benj. S. Parker.

Indian mode of reckoning time—Hospitality and Etiquette—The Stranger—The "Green corn dance," as witnessed in 1833—Curative powers of the Indian—Dress of the warrior—Pride of adornment—Restraint—Revenge—Emblems served for names—An incident—The Miamies and Pottawattamies—French settlements among the Miamies—Suggestions of Dr. Franklin—Chiefs and Sachems—Their power—Records of treaties—Force of eloquence—Indian Democracy—The Natchez Indians—The Peace-pipe—Assemblies—Messengers of peace—Councils at the Miami villages—An incident—Indian disregard of death—Declarations of war—Dances—Religious nature of the Indian—The medicine men—Life in the north-west 150 years ago—Civilization here 150 years hence.

THE MIAMIES, like all other tribes of the primitive wilds of America, knew nothing of days, as called after the Saxon gods—took no note of time, save as presented by "the return of snow or the springing of the flowers." The flight of the birds told them of the passage of summer, and the approach of the hunting season. The active instinct of the animal world about them, the appearance of the sky, &c., ever served, by some peculiar expression, to remind them of the approach of storms; and the time of the day was traced by the shadows of the trees, and other objects, as reflected by the sun.

In times of peace, ever hospitable, the stranger,—and, especially those to whom they were attached,—were always welcome, and feasted with the best his cabin afforded. The Indian has often, indeed, been known to go without food himself to appease the hunger of the traveler or those sojourning with them. And when he visited the white man, or was invited by him to a seat at his table, the red man carried with him his own peculiar custom, and ate heartily of all that was set before him. He was most sensitive, too, at such times; and, for any member of the family with whom he was a guest, to have begun to sweep the floor before the departure of his Indian visitor, would have been to lead the red man to infer that you wished to sweep him out also.*

*A fact well known to many of the old citizens of Fort Wayne.

At a late period in the history of the Indians of this region, it was an ordinary thing for the white man to enter the cabin of the red man uninvited. And the same was true of the savage. Nor was it a custom of the Indian to question those who came to see him as to their business there, or how long they intended to remain. Fond of dancing, their festivals were many; at which it was a custom to eat heartily of everything prepared for such occasions. And it was at such times that they were most prodigal, and often greatly exhausted their supplies for the winter.

To show how closely allied to ancient customs were the modern habits and festivities of the Miamies, the reader can now look in upon a gay crowd of dancers at one of their "Green-Corn" dances, at a payment of the Miamies in 1833, at the junction of the Wabash and Little River. "There, upon our arrival," runs the account,* "at a little after dark, we found a party of Indians—consisting of between two and three hundred—assembled for the purpose of participating in or witnessing the dance. A ring was formed, surrounded by a large number of Indian spectators, and about fifty whites—in which were placed the male portion of the dancers, headed by the leaders. At a signal from the music, which consisted of a tap on the drum, of a dull, heavy tone, by one Indian, and a clatter of a set of deer hoofs by another, the leaders broke forth in a wild song of a few ejaculatory notes responded to by the party, and the dancing and singing commenced. The women then fell in one by one; and, selecting their partners as they danced along, the party was completed. The dancers all appeared in their very 'best,' and had attached to their ankles a profusion of small tinkling bells. The music consisted simply of the repeated single taps of the said drum, accompanied with the continuous clatter of the deer-hoofs; while the 'figure' was composed only of three short, rapid leaps upon the balls of the feet, scarcely raising them from the ground, and slightly advancing at the same time. Occasionally, however, an 'extra touch' would be given by the dancers, in some antic or other, which it would be impossible to describe. In this way the dancing, singing, tapping of the drum, clattering of deer-hoofs, tinkling of bells, and an occasional yell, forming a wild and singular medley, which continued for about half an hour, when the party, having danced around the circle some half dozen times, and having gone through the first 'set,' the leader stopped and raised the yell—the men of the party responded in the same way; and the outsiders raised a most furious din of yells, as congratulatory to the performance of the dancers. Here a 'recess' of about a quarter of an hour took place; and a confused scene of congratulations, talking, laughing and yelling, ensued. It may be that, during the interval, many gallant things were said by the grotesque and gaudy beaux, or many witticisms and tender sentiments expressed by the fair Miami damsels; but of this we were not apprised. It is cer-

* As witnessed and described by Chas. B. Laselle, Esq.

tain, however, that the men behaved with a great deal of gallantry; and that no drinking or rowdying whatever occurred upon the occasion. After the conclusion of the recess, the parties resumed their positions, and re-commenced the dance. The same music, dancing, singing, tinkling of bells, and yelling was repeated, as in the first instance; and thus continuing till about 12 o'clock at night, the party then breaking up in one long and loud round of yells."

With the red man, disease was the result of some natural derangement, and the Medicine Man, often strangely skilled in an understanding of the kind, quality, and quantity of some peculiar natural remedial, by the aid of his manipulative powers, at once set about a cure on natural principles; and was seldom—in part because of the great faith of his patient—baffled in his efforts of relief. Among these, the Miamies, at different periods, as known to many early settlers, had several Medicine Men of remarkable ability.

The apparel and address of the warrior ever stood as a history of his achievements in war—his body variously tattooed—often with objects representing different animals, &c., and frequently with the most brilliant dyes. It was a custom in their ordinary adornments to paint the end of the nose, and around the eyes, and the eye brows, with black or some bright colors, and the other portions of the face with vermilion, with perhaps stripes running from one point of the face to the other. Especially—not altogether unlike many of the present civilization,—when visiting, or assembling in council, they resorted to great pains in the arrangement of their dress, decoration and painting of their persons; and, what Marest wrote, years ago, of the Illinois* Indians, was equally true of the Miamies—they were "absolute masters of themselves, subject to no law." Each seemed to have been in a great degree, at least, his own protector—and as often their own avengers. With the Indian, when violence had resulted in the death of a kindred, at the hands of another and different race or tribe, it was a steadfast belief that the spirit of the deceased could not rest in peace or feel appeased until a retaliation was consummated.† To accomplish this, it is a noted fact that an Indian would go a thousand miles for the purpose of revenge, over hills and mountains; through swamps and briars; over broad lakes, rapid rivers, and deep creeks; and all the way endangered by poisonous snakes, exposed to the extremeties of heat and cold, to hunger and thirst. In the carrying out of this spirit, nations‡ and families carried their feuds often to great lengths,

* The Miamies called the Illinois their cousins.

† It is well known here to many old settlers that an Indian, many years ago, followed a white man, who had killed his brother, from point to point, for two years, before he succeeded in avenging the death of his relative, by killing the man he had so long and so assiduously followed and watched.

‡ There had long existed a spirit of animosity between the Miamies and the Pottawattamies; and the latter were very sure to quit the neighborhood of the former if in liquor. This may have arisen in part from the fact that, in the "early part of the 18th century, the Pottawattamies had crowded the Miamies from their dwellings at Chicago."—Schoolcraft.

from which a reconciliation was only attainable through gifts of sufficient quantity "to cover up the graves of the dead." The presents once accepted served both to pacify the living and the dead.* In the relationship of families, emblems served for names. The figure of a crow, the hawk, the turtle, &c., &c., would serve as a distinction or name—as, among the civilized, one is known as the Brown, another the Smith family, and so on; which, to the Indian, was as rational and comprehensive, as to us of to-day is our style of distinction in this relation; and in many instances, in so far, at least, as real beauty, simplicity, and convenience was wont to be manifest, was quite as intelligible and serviceable as the present system of civilization in this particular.

"The rose by any other name would smell as sweet."

At a late period in their history, however, the Miamies, through their intercourse with the French and others, often adopted other names—as, in the case of their chiefs, Le Gris, Richardville, La Fontaine, Godfri, George Hunt, &c.,—the first four being related to families then of distinction in France. †

The quiet, persevering, determined nature of the Miamies was ever a matter of singular interest. If the death of a brother was to be revenged, they proceeded quietly, about the work. Patience, at such a time, was called actively into play; and, if need be, months might roll away before a blow was struck. As illustrative of this fact, a few years prior to the war of 1812, a man of rather reckless character, and who hated the Indian with a rancor only equalled by his unyielding persistence in what he believed or surmised to be false or true, regardless of contradiction or premonition by those best able to give them, moved to this point, and built himself a hut a few miles from Fort Wayne, near Cedar Creek.‡ From the first, he is said never to have lost an opportunity to speak his mind as to the "rascally red skins;" and often used very severe language to

* Parkman.

† In 1754 Gov. Morris, addressing the Pennsylvania Assembly, said the French were "making a settlement of three hundred families in the country of the Twightwees," (Miamies.) It was also in this year, that Benjamin Franklin proposed the establishment of strong English colonies in the territory north-west of the Ohio, as a means of preventing "the dreaded junction of the French settlements in Canada with those of Louisana,"—the Doctor proposing to plant one colony in the valley of the Scioto; to establish small garrisons at Buffalo Creek, on the Ohio; at the mouth of Tioga, south side of Lake Erie; at Hockhocking; and at or near the mouth of the Wabash. He presented also the expediency of capturing "Sandusky, a French fort near Lake Erie," and also suggested that "all the little French forts south and west of the lakes, quite to the Mississippi, be removed or taken and garrisoned by the English." "Every fort," said he, "should have a small settlement around it; as the fort would protect the settlers, and the settlers defend the fort, and supply it with provisions." The propositions thus presented by Dr. Franklin were but foreshadowings, in part, at least, of the results that followed but a few years later, when the English became the temporary masters of about "all the little French forts south and west of the lakes." Providence had not then enabled the Doctor to see the great future that was before him, when the illuminations of '76 were to begin a new era in fortifications and free institutions.

‡ As related by the elder Peltier, and told the writer by Mr. Louis Peltier, son of the former.

express his antipathy towards them. Some time subsequent to his settlement, as mentioned, his horse strayed away, and, after a fruitless search, made bold to accuse the Miamies of having stolen the animal, and declared that he would kill some one of the Indians for it. Talking thus loudly on one occasion, in the hearing of the elder Peltier, long a trader among the Indians, in this and adjacent regions, and who knew the Indian character well, Mr. P. very readily told him that he did not believe the Indians had taken his horse, and that he would advise him not to interfere with them—that he would suffer for it if he did. But the man was resolute in his belief and determination, and paid but little attention to the advice of Peltier, and went away. Not long after this, walking along near the St. Joseph, a short distance above the confluence of the St. Joseph and the St. Mary, with his gun on his shoulder, the stranger suddenly observed an Indian a short distance in advance of him, near the edge of the river, fishing. The season of verdure and sweet-scented flowers had come again—it was spring-time, "ever merry May"—and the birds were again singing their sweet and joyful notes. The lost horse had not yet been found, and now was a good opportunity to "kill an Injun," thought the man. Looking carefully about him, in every direction, and seeing no one, he took deliberate aim and fired. The shot proved effectual—the Indian rolled from his position, and expired. Again looking carefully about him, to ascertain, if possible, if any one had witnessed the act, and observing no one, he at once approached the body, placed some stones in the red man's blanket, in order to sink the carcass, then wrapping the blanket about the murdered Indian, hurled the body into the stream, from whence he carefully strode away, gloating within himself at his seeming seccess.

But, lo! on the opposite side of the stream, concealed by a thick underbrush, lay, unobserved, with eyes glaring upon the entire action of the new-comer, a faithful squaw of the murdered Indian, who, though giving no warning of the danger that stood so near her companion, fearing lest she too might fall a victim to his work of death, yet bore testimony to the whole scene, and soon gave warning to her Indian friends as to what had occurred. All was quiet—a resolution was quickly formed. "White man must die," they whispered among themselves. The shade of their murdered brother called for revenge.

The conduct of the stranger quickly reached the ears of Mr. P., who readily surmised the result, and watched the course of events. Time wore away—months passed—the new-comer had found his horse—and all seemed to have been forgotten; when lo! one bright morning, in the month of October, the sun's march, the falling leaves of Autumn, and the chill winds, all giving token of the approach of winter—the little log-cabin of the stranger was seen to be in ruins, and the inmates gone, no one knew whither, save the friends of the murdered Indian and the Great Spirit of the red man. The revenge was complete, and the departed spirit of their murdered brother could now rest in peace.

How many similar tragedies may have been enacted in the regions of Ke-ki-ong-a during the period of Indian life here, we know not; but doubtless many a tragic event of this kind took place at this point, now known only in the unwritten pages of the Past.

As the head of each family was its chief, so each village had its head chief or sachem; and though the villagers were by no means restricted in their individual relations, each family being privileged to exercise its own peculiar ideas of domestic life, &c., independent of the other, if desiring, in every village,—yet, in a general sense, the habits and customs of each village and family were much the same among, not only the Miamies, but most tribes of the northwest.

The rule and power of control of a chief, sachem, medicine man, prophet, or indeed any member of a tribe, much as with the present state of civilization in America and other parts of the globe, depended largely upon the amount of eloquence the speaker could bring to bear upon his people—a distinction for bravery, or the strongest will, as often gave the Indian prominence among the tribes as those acquiring and exercising power by hereditary descent; and while, in many respects, the government of the Indian seemed to partake of the Monarchical, it was yet of the Democratic order; for no question of grave importance ever presented itself for consideration, but there was sure to follow an assemblage of the braves in council, where no action would be concluded wherein "the people were averse." And it was at such times that the eloquent and stern-willed often held sway.*

To preserve a record of treaties, was to carefully lay by their wampum belts. In cases of important councils between nations, exchange of gifts and belts was mutual, by which each speaker was also greatly aided in memory. The holding of a bundle of small sticks, of a certain number, by the speaker, on such occasions was also common, for each of which, the envoy from one nation to another would recite a message;† and messengers were always selected with

*"It is of the Natchez Indians that the most wonderful tales of despotism and aristocratic distinctions have been promulgated. Their chiefs, like those of the Hurons, were esteemed descendants of the sun, had greater power than could have been established in the colder regions of the north, where the severities of nature compel the savage to rely on himself and be free; yet, as the Natchez, in exterior, resembled the tribes by which they were surrounded, so their customs and institutions were but more marked developements of the same characteristics. Everywhere at the north, there was the same distribution into families, and the same order in each separate town. The affairs relating to the whole nation, were transacted in general council, and with such equality, and such zeal for the common good, that, while any one might have dissented with impunity, the voice of the tribe would yet be unanimous in its decision."—Bancroft's His. U. S., vol. 3, pages 278 and 279.

†Referring to the Indians of the north, Bancroft says: "Their delight was in assembling together, and listening to messengers from abroad. Seated in a semicircle on the ground, in double or triple rows, with the knees almost meeting the face,—the painted and tattooed chiefs adorned with skins and plumes, with the beaks of the red-bird, or the claws of the bear,—each listener perhaps with a pipe in his mouth, and preserving

a view as well to ability as to the knowledge of the task to be performed. And it is said that "often an orator, without the aid of rank as a chief, by the brilliancy of his eloquence, swayed the minds of a confederacy."

Another interesting feature in Indian usage, was the Peace-Pipe, or Friendly Calumet. The writings concerning the early missionaries, traders, explorers, and military officers, make repeated mention of it; and the beauty and simplicity of the custom must be readily seen and admitted. The calumet, to the red man, was always esteemed and reverenced as the most sacred of all their emblematic relations and devices; and no village, in earlier times, when the red man held sway over the western wilds, was without its specially ornamented calumet,—which was often adorned with the feathers of the bird of liberty, the eagle, or other plumage or ornamental device, and always "consecrated in the general assembly of the nation." The messenger, traversing the wildest regions, on an errand of friendship, felt always secure, by a presentation of the peace-pipe, from all attack from ferocious or unfriendly tribes. The primitive custom of the messengers of Peace, bearing the calumet, was for the envoys to approach within a given distance of the village, first making a loud noise, then seating themselves upon the ground. Then the villagers, headed by their principal chief, or sachem, bearing the peace-pipe in his hand, all singing the Indian song of peace, went forth to meet them. Approaching the envoys, the latter rose to greet them, they, too, chanting a hymn, "to put away all wars, and to bury all revenge." At once exchanging pipes, and smoking freely, peace was terminated, and the messengers were escorted to the villages where it was made known, in loud declamation, that the strangers were friends; and a great feast of hominy, dog, and bear's meat, was spread out and partaken of in honor of the messengers.

As the ancient Twightwee (Miami) villages, located within and about the present site of Fort Wayne, in the words of their famous chief, Little Turtle, formed "that glorious gate which the Miamis had the happiness to own, and through which all the good words of their chiefs had to pass from the north to the south, and from the east to the west," how many such solemn and interesting occasions as that of exchanging the friendly calumet and entertaining the embassy of a distant tribe with a great feast, may have made the woods and surrounding vales of this locality reverberate with the glad strains of the Indian peace song and jubilant dance of the villagers, none can now tell; yet the strong supposition is that there were many such occasions here.

deep silence,—they would give solemn attention to the speaker, who, with great action and energy of language, delivered his message; and, if his eloquence pleased, they esteemed him as a god. Decorum was never broken; there were never two speakers struggling to anticipate each other; they did not express their spleen by blows; they restrained passionate invective; the debate was never disturbed by an uproar; questions of order were unknown."- His. U. S. vol. 3, page 279.

The Indian, though holding life as dear, perhaps, as most mortals, had, yet, withal, a singular disregard for death—a stoical indifference and fortitude that rendered him seemingly unsusceptible of pain; and, as all history relating to the Indians most fully attests, at times, could kill and scalp a savage or civilized foe with as much ease and zest as if partaking of a pot of hominy, or feasting upon a portion of roast bear.

Some fifty years ago, a party of Indians, as was often their habit at that period, had congregated about the little trading hut of J. Peltier,—then conspicuous at the foot of the hill, just below the old fort,—and becoming somewhat intoxicated, two of the party, of different tribes, became excited about some trivial matter, and one of them drew a knife from his belt, and cut the other across the abdomen so severely as to let his intestines partially out.* Seating himself upon the ground, the wounded Indian soon deliberately drew his own knife, cut a piece of flesh from the outer part of the stomach, and began to eat it.

The Indian cutting him, suddenly seeing this, proudly ejaculated *Del-au-aweah!* (that's a brave man, or he is a brave man!) And to show his compassion for the wounded brave, he at once approached him, and, with a blow from his tomahawk, ended the further suffering of the wounded Indian†

In the ancient songs of the red men there was always a vein of disregard or contempt for death; and it was no uncommon thing for the chiefs to declare that "the spirits on high would repeat their names." Where they wished to exhibit a spirit of defiance towards an antagonist, it was no unusual thing for the Indian to prepare a red-colored belt, a small bundle of "blo ody sticks," and dispatch them to the enemy. In early times, the Indians were most feared when they prowled about in small parties, laying in wait, here and there—suddenly bounding upon a small settlement, or waylaying the emigrant. Concealment and surprise constituted their highest sense of warfare. When least anticipated, they were upon and scalping the early settler. And sad was the havoc many times during the pioneer days of the western frontiersmen. On more than one occasion, as subsequent pages will attest, has the tragedy of an Indian massacre been enacted within the boundaries of the territory of the Miamies.

*Capt. Wells, who resided at this point for many years with the Miamies, while in Philadelphia with Little Turtle, in 1797, in a conversation with the distinguished French philosopher and traveler, Count Volney, referring to one of the chiefs of the Miamies, at old Fort Miamis, here, known as Blue Jocky, said: "This man, (on one occasion) when drunk, met an old enemy, to whom he had borne a grudge of twenty-two years standing. Blue Jocky seized the opportunity and killed him. Next day all the family were in arms to revenge the murder. He came to the fort, and said to the commanding officer, who repeated the tale to me, 'Let them kill me. It is but right. My heart betrayed me, and the liquor robbed me of my wits. But they threatened to kill my son, and that was not just. Father, try to make it up for me. I will give them all I have; my two horses, my trinkets, my weapons, except one set, and, if that will not content them, I will meet them at any time and place, and they may kill me.'"

For some years after the war of 1812, it was no uncommon thing for them to kill each other here in their drunken sprees.

†Recollections of Mrs. Griswold.

Every people, however barbarous or civilized, ever had their seasons of relaxation and merry-making. Among the most favorite pastimes of the Miamies, were their dances.

In the spring time, as a matter of reverence to the Great Spirit (Much-a-te-Auceke), "the man with the black robe; the good man or preacher,"—asking him to aid in the production or growth of a bountiful crop, they had the corn-planting dance. A great deal of importance was attached to this dance, which was conducted with an air of marked solemnity and earnestness,—all the villagers partaking in it.*

It was a time-honored custom with the Miamies and most tribes of the West, that when a member of a family died, a meeting of the family and immediate villagers would take place at a certain time, subsequent to the death of the person, with a view to replacing the deceased, which was done by means of a game of chance, there being often a number of candidates for the place. The lucky one at once fell heir to all the effects of the deceased. After which they all joined in a merry dance, called the *Replacement Dance.*

The Beggar Dance was also frequent here; but was seldom if ever indulged in by the Miamies. The Pottawattamies,† who were frequently here, with perhaps a few others of the Shawanoe, Wyandot, or Kickapoo nations, were the only ones who commonly indulged in this dance.

The object of the beggar dance was to obtain presents, or indeed anything the stranger, trader, or settler might feel disposed to give them; and, with no covering on their bodies, but a part of a deer or other skin about their waists, the rest of the body and face painted with some bright colors, with perhaps some gay ornament or feathers, about their heads, often several in number, would pass from agency to agency, in front of whose doors they would go through the liveliest movements of dancing, singing, &c., which, to the spectators, was often very amusing, and who seldom failed to give the rude dancers some tobacco, a loaf or two of bread, some whiskey, or other article that would be pleasing to them.

The Indians of the Northwest had many social pastimes, and their *complimentary dances* were probably frequent. The "medicine-dance" was one of some rarity, which usually took place only out of respect or courtesy to the medicine-men. In the complimentary dance, it was a custom to obtain permission of the party to "be complimented to dance for him." This granted, preparations were made by painting the face elaborately, and marking the body, which was usually bare about the chest and shoulders. In addition to this, a profusion of ornaments, in the form of feathers, &c., were added to the hair; and most "happy was he, who, in virtue of having taken one or more scalps, was entitled to proclaim it by a corresponding number of eagle's feathers. The less fortunate made a substitute of the feathers of the wild turkey," or other game. For which purpose too, the fowls of the pioneers were often closely "plucked."

* John P. Hedges. †The Pottawattamies lived a few miles north of Ft. Wayne.

The preparations for the complimentary dance being ready, the dancers congregated at some point selected, "and then marched to the spot in view for the dance, attended by the dull, coarse sound of the Indian drum and shee-shee-qua, or rattle. Arranging themselves in a circle, they would dance with violent contortions and jesticulations, some of them graceful, others only energetical, the squaws, who usually stood a little apart, and mingled their discordant voices with the music of the instruments, rarely participating in the dance. Occasionally, however, when excited by the general gaiety, a few of them would form a circle outside and perform a sort of ungraceful up-and-down movement, which possessed no merit, save the perfect time which was kept, and for which the Indians seemed, without exception, to have possessed a natural ear. The dance finished, which was often only when the strength of the dancers was quite exhausted, a quantity of presents were brought and placed in the middle of the circle, by request of the party complimented. An equitable distribution of the gifts having taken place, and the object of the gathering terminated, all withdrew."*

The medicine-dance was mainly to celebrate the power and skill of the Medicine Man in the cure of disease, and as a means of respect to him as a supposed interpreter of the will and desires of the Great Spirit, as related to the direction of his people.

Says Mrs. J. H. Kinzie, in her interesting narration of experiences and observations among the Indians of the North-West, during the early part of the present century, "a person was selected to join the fraternity of the 'Medicine Man' by those initiated, chiefly on account of some skill or sagacity that had been observed in him. Sometimes it happened that a person who had had a severe illness which had yielded to the prescriptions of one of the members, was considered a proper object of choice from a sort of claim thus established. When he was about to be initiated, a great feast was made, of course at the expense of the candidate, for in the most simple, as in the most civilized life, the same principle of politics held good, and 'honors were to be paid for.' An animal was killed and dressed, of which the people at large partook—there were dances and songs and speeches in abundance. Then the chief Medicine Man took the candidate and privately began to instruct him in all the ceremonies and knowledge necessary to make him an accomplished member of the fraternity. Sometimes the new member selected was yet a child. In that case, he was taken by the Medicine Man so soon as he reached the proper age, and qualified by instruction and example to become a creditable member of the fraternity.

"Each Medicine Man usually had a bag or some receptacle in

*The medicine, man "occasionally made offerings and sacrifices which were regarded as propitiatory. * * * He was also a 'prophet,' in so far as he was, in a limited degree, an instructor, but did not claim to possess the power of foretelling future events."—"Wau-Bun, the 'Early Day' in the North-West,"—pages 360, 361, and 362.

which was supposed to be enclosed some animal to whom in the course of their *pow-wows*, he addressed himself, crying to him in the note common to his imagined species, and the people seem all to have been persuaded that the answers which were announced were really communications in this form, from the Great Spirit.

"The Indians appear," continues Mrs. Kenzie, "to have no idea of a retribution beyond this life. They have a strong appreciation of the great fundamental virtues of natural religion—the worship of the Great Spirit, brotherly love, parental affection, honesty, temperance, and chastity. Any infringement of the laws of the Great Spirit, by a departure from these virtues, they believe will excite his anger, and draw down punishment. These are their principles. That their practice evinces more and more," says she, "a departure from them, under the debasing influences of a proximity to the whites, is a melancholy truth, which no one will admit with so much sorrow as those who lived among them, and esteemed them a quarter of a century ago, before this signal change had taken place."

There were many dances, however, among the Miamies, as well as many periods of the year in which they indulged in such festivities, throughout their villages. Evening, and often through the greater part of the night, during the milder seasons, was the usual time for such enjoyment. Their music consisted, usually, of a deer skin entirely free of hair, which they stretched in some way, similar to our common drum-head, and upon which their "music man" would keep time and hum an air adapted to the Indian's style of dancing. It was very common on such occasions to have a large pot of hominy cooking over a moderate fire, to which the dancers would occasionally repair and partake, all from the same spoon or wooden ladel.

But the red man was never entirely fixed or permanent in his location. Hunting and fishing occupied a very large share of his time. The summer months especially, were much devoted to fishing. The furry animals and the deer, from which he expected each season to realize a moderate income, with which to procure ammunition, blankets, &c., for another season, were never disturbed by the Indian until the period arrived for their furs and hides to be fully matured for the market. Then the Indians and their familes (excepting there were some who, from age or infirmity, were unable to go,) left their villages, and sought new homes in the woods, or near some large prairie, where the deer, the ottar, the raccoon, &c., were most abundant. And their return, to renew their old homes, was only hailed by the springing of the early grass, or the joyful song of some sweet bird of passage that had again, at the first tokens of Spring, ventured a return to the Northwest. And this was life among the Miamies here, to a late period of their history. This was life in the primitive wilds of the great Northwest a hundred and fifty years or more ago. What a civilization may be ours one hundred and fifty years hence!

CHAPTER IV.

"The junction of these rivers (the St. Mary and the St. Joseph), may even claim a page in the annals of that momentous contest between French and English civilization—between Romanism and Protestantism—which was waged with alternating success, and with short intervals of repose, for more than a hundred years, terminating, soon after the fall of Quebec, in the establishment of Anglo-Saxon supremacy by the treaty of 1763."—Extract from a lecture of J. L. Williams, Esq., delivered in Fort Wayne, March 7, 1860.

Death of La Salle—A line of stockade forts contemplated and established by the French—Progress of events following this movement of the French—Movements of the English—The French become aroused—Feuds of the Old World rekindled in the New—The French and the Indians—Washington sent as a Messenger—War—Braddock's Defeat—Activity of the Contending Armies—Wolfe's Advance upon Quebec—Final triumph of the English Army on the Plains of Abraham—A new Era dawned upon the New World.

SIXTEEN hundred and eighty-two had passed. The shouts of "vive le roi," by La Salle and his *voyageurs*, near the mouth of the great Father of Waters had long since died away on the still air, and La Salle himself fallen a victim, on the shores of Texas, to the treachery of his followers. 1699 came. Lemoine d'Iberville had planted a little colony on the newly-possessed territory of *Louisiane*. And again years sped away. The little settlement upon the newly acquired dominion of the South grew and prospered amid the spontaneous growths of nature everywhere about it; and the French Government had begun seriously to contemplate the union of her Northern and Southern extremities by the arrangement and establishment of a continuous line of stockade forts and settlements through the interminable forests and prairies, along the shores of beautiful rivers, by the margin of dreary lakes, lowly vales, and towering cliffs—from the river St. Lawrence to the dark blue waters of the Gulf of Mexico. The middle of the 18th century came, and the great enterprise was rapidly hastening toward a complete consummation. A fort on the strait of Niagara stood in full view of, and guarded the entrance to, the vast interior extending towards the great Southwest. A second sprang up at Detroit, overlooking and controlling the route from Lake Erie to the North. A third soon stood defiantly forth at St.

Mary's, guarding with jealous eye all access to Lake Superior. A fourth was completed at Michillimackinac, which stood guard to the mouth of Lake Michigan. Soon a fifth appeared at Green Bay, and a sixth at St. Joseph, guarding the routes to the great Father of Waters, via the Wisconsin and Illinois rivers; and two more,—making eight—one, Fort Miamies, near the confluence of the St. Joseph and St. Mary's rivers, (in view of the present site of Fort Wayne,) the other, Fort Ouiatenon, on the Wabash, below Lafayette. Small settlements of French soon sprang up at Kaskaskia, Cahokia, and at other points, some in the territory of the Illinois Indians, along the Illinois river, while, here and there along the banks of the Mississippi, were to be seen, amid the thick jungle, long peculiar to this broad and beautiful river, an occasional stockade fort; while, upon reaching the present site of the city of Natchez, on the Mississippi, they were met by their kinsmen of Louisiana, extending their settlements to meet the *voyageurs* from the shores of Canada.

France was now a power in the great Northwest. Her military strength was seemingly complete. The great forest was hers. She amalgamated with the wild tribes of the land wherever she went, and thus became a part of the great family of natives at every point. This alliance grew into a warm attachment, and the Indians knew the king of the French as their Great Father, and long looked up to him, through his subjects on this side of the great waters, as a protector and aid in time of need. From the French they early obtained guns, powder, and balls, and from them soon learned their use in hunting, whereby the French obtained vast quantities of valuable furs at such prices as they were pleased to dictate. The missionaries pursued their labors, and at every post were to be met with their crosses and symbols; many of them, in accordance with their peculiar school and ideas of religious zeal, were ready to suffer martyrdom, if need be, even at the hand of the savage.

Time wore on. The French settlements and forts had succeeded but poorly. They had sadly neglected agricultural pursuits. Speculation had warped and twisted their better natures, and their former sense of civilization had now become so strongly interwoven with those of the habits and customs of the red man, that they had well-nigh lost that higher feeling of mental and physical growth upon which the white race had so long prided itself and sought to attain.

And as they were often wanting in sobriety and civic continuity, so the French Government at that period, because of its ambitious tendency and ardent desire for dominion and conquest, with other causes of a no less deleterious character about the French court, was but feebly prepared to render the necessary aid or give that impetus to her colonial settlements in America that would have secured at least a moderate expression of prolonged and energetic civil culture.

1748 at length came, and France was still secure in her posses-

*See Smith's History of Canada, I. 208.

sions in the New World. Her line of stockade forts were still maintained. A new scheme had arisen in the mind of the somewhat acute Count Galissonniere* of bringing over to the New World ten thousand French peasants to be settled upon the regions bordering the Ohio, which, at that time, the French government was proposing to embrace within her already extensive domain. Many of these peasants were also to inhabit the lake borders. While thus passing their time in the castle of St. Louis, at Quebec,—civilians, soldiers, and men of State,—the English lion had been quietly looking about in search of prey, and now began to move cautiously along the beautiful valley of the Mohawk, and, soon issuing from the lowlands, he was heard to roar along the eastern slopes of the Alleghany Mountains. His march was still westward, and gradually onward he moved, until at length, he saw beyond, in the distance, where here and there an open spot was visible, small moving objects, and the smoke of the Canadian hut continued for a time to curl peacefully away amid the surrounding forest and over the broad blue face of the great lakes of their dominion. Forests fell before the westward march of the English settlements; "and while, on one side of the Alleghanies, Celeron de Bienville was burying plates of lead, engraved with the arms of France," says Parkman, "the ploughs and axes of Virginia woodsmen were enforcing a surer title on the other." The right of possession was soon to be tested. The two powers of the day were destined, ere many moons, to measure swords and struggle for supremacy on the new Continent.

The peculiar intimacy of the French with the Indians had long given them a strength of no mean consideration. The opposite was true of the English; and often, instead of drawing the Indians about them in a spirit of amity and friendship, by making them many little presents of trinkets, &c., as did the French then and long before, the phlegmatic nature of the Englishman drove him sullenly away. The Jesuit missionaries, too, still exerted a wide influence, in their peculiar way, over the western tribes. The English had no missionaries. They were simply agriculturalists—desired to till the soil and pursue a moderate, though sure system of commerce. The French were principally fur traders, and their government had long been actuated by, and inflated with, a spirit of conquest and dominion. The one was heretic to the other—had long been so; and the bitter feuds of the Old World were now about to take form and action upon the soil of the New. England was stern and resolute. The "Church of England" was the Englishman's church, and his God was not the God of his rival. The "Church of Rome" was the church of the Frenchman of the day; and his God was not the God of the Englishman. The contest was destined to be a bitter one, and the vantage ground seemed all on the side of the French. Time wore heavily on. 1749 came. The English had begun to make some inroads upon the French domin-

*See History of Canada, I, 214.

ions as traders; and it was in this year that La Jonquiere, then governor of Canada, made the discovery that a number of English traders had come to Sandusky,* and "were exerting a bad influence upon the Indians of that quarter." The Canadian Governor, says the account, "caused four of the intruders to be seized near the Ohio and sent prisoners to Canada." Events were now surely and successively "casting their shadows." The English, at that period being much disaffected and broken in their governmental relations, to awaken at New York, Philadelphia, Virginia, and other points, a policy that would attract the attention of, and draw the Indians to them, seemed most difficult indeed. Even the powerful Iroquois or Five Nations, then dwelling, for the most part, in the Province of New York, and who, from an ill-will unthoughtedly engendered by Champlain, in May 1609, in uniting, at Quebec, with a party of Algonquin Indians against them, causing their defeat and utter rout near the rocky promontory of Ticonderoga, and who, therefore, during many years subsequent, were a great source of trouble to the French settlements in Canada, well-nigh, at times, desolating the homes and fields of her interior provinces—even this formidable tribe, the English failed to win over, to their cause. And "the cold and haughty bearing of the English officials," together with often depriving them, by unfair means, of their annual presents from England; the habit of arranging negotiations with them through a class of rum dealers, persons looked upon with but little regard by this powerful tribe; with other causes of complaint arising from neglect,† &c., are said to have quite disgusted "the proud chiefs" of the Iroquois.‡

It is true, these causes and disquietudes did not wholly apply to all parts of the English Provinces. The Friends, and some other souls, were exceptions, mainly in a philanthropic sense; but these bodies were usually small in numbers, and often ineffectual in their efforts. No such condition of affairs was anywhere visible among

*His. of Canada, I, 214. †Massachusetts Historical Collection, 1st series, VII, 67.

‡Among the MSS. papers of the famous Sir Wm. Johnson, to the Board of Trade, London, dated May 24, and Nov. 13, 1763, was the following: "We find the Indians, as far back as the very confused manuscript records in my possession, repeatedly upbraiding their province for their negligence, their avarice, and their want of assisting them at a time when it was certainly in their power to destroy the infant colony of Canada, although supported by many nations; and this is likewise confessed by the writings of the managers of these times."

"I apprehend that it will clearly appear to you, that the colonies had, all along, neglected to cultivate a proper understanding with the Indians, and from a mistaken notion have greatly despised them, without considering that it is in their power to lay waste and destroy the frontiers. This opinion arose from our confidence in our scattered numbers, and the parsimony of our people, who, from an error in politics, would not expend five pounds to save twenty." Sir William was a wise manager of Indian affairs, and from a long and close intimacy with many of the tribes of the North-East, at an early period, became remarkable for his knowledge of Indian character and the strong influence he exerted over them. His headquarters, known as Johnson's Hall, were long at Oswego, N. Y., where great numbers of Indians were more or less always about him, and whither various tribes, through their chiefs and sachems, often repaired to hold their council fires and treaties. And the Indians ever knew him as their great father. Through his agency the Iroquois, in after years, became firm friends of the English.

the French of the time. Their relations and developements were widely different. So diligent and careful were they in their attentions to the chiefs and others of the different tribes, that often on the approach of such to their forts, the loud roll of the drum or booming of cannon would announce their coming; and this attention was most pleasing to the red man, and made him to feel that he was not only a power in the land, but welcome. At the tables of the French officers "they were regaled" and often bribed with medals and decorations,—scarlet uniforms, and French flags. Far wiser than their rivals, the French never ruffled the self-complacent dignity of their guests; never insulted their religious notions; nor ridiculed their ancient customs. They met the savage half way, and showed an abundant readiness to "mould their own features after his likeness."* And it is noted that "Count Frontenac himself, plumed and painted like an Indian chief, danced the war-dance, and yelled the war-song at the camp-fires of his delighted allies." Such were the peculiarities of the French—such their wisdom and sense of harmony in so far as related to the wild aborigines of the new continent at that early period.

As little by little, the delicious fruit ripens, the flowers bud and blossom, or the tiny acorn expands into the mighty oak of the forest, so event followed event; as the leaves of Autumn whirl upon the passing breeze, and at length disrobe the thick forest.

The movements and apprehensions of the French steadily became more and more apparent to the English. Soon a French Priest, of the name of Piquet, made bold, in the midst of his opposers, to open a mission at the site of Ogdensburg, on the St. Lawrence,† mainly with a view to win the friendship of the Iroquois, in which he was highly successful, having at one time gained the heart and attention of a very large body of that famous confederacy, which gave the English great uneasiness. But Sir William Johnson soon began to exert a remarkable influence over the various tribes, and at length succeeded in gaining the attention of the Iroquois; and not only did this tribe become friendly, to a considerable degree, towards the English, but the Delawares, and the Miamies, dwelling along the Ohio, come to regard them with much favor; while the mass of the other tribes lying to the North, West, and South, stood ready at the bidding of their French father.

Matters now began to assume a formidable attitude. The enmity of the rival colonies grew intense. Their hatred had assumed a double aspect of religious and national antipathy. Formerly the Indians had been the instruments of French aggressions upon the English settlements; and "with them," says Parkman, "the very name of Canada called up horrible recollections and ghastly images; the midnight massacre of Schenectady, and the desolation of many

*Accounts of Adair, Post's Journals, Croghan's Journal, and MSS. of Sir Wm. Johnson, and others.

†History of New York, L., 423.

a New England Hamlet." A French fort had been erected at Crown Point, upon English territory. The treaty of Utretcht and confirmation of same at Aix la Chapelle, had made English ground of Acadia; but a doubt as to the limits of the province soon sprang up, and appointed commissioners, from both sides, failing to agree, belligerant attitudes between the soldiery of the two nations, soon became manifest on Acadian soil. Gist, surveyor, of the "Ohio Company," which had been organized in 1748, with a view to the formation of settlements west of the Alleghanies, had made his way to the falls of the Ohio. The Indians were startled. The French soon snuffed the discontented air of the red man, and before the surveyor and his party had scarcely begun their operations, the French confronted them, and the work ceased.

1753 came. The season of verdure had approached. The birds of the forest were already warbling their sweet notes of welcome to the spring. The French had made their way across Lake Erie, and Presque 'Isle had already become a fortification. From Presque 'Isle they strode rapidly towards the Ohio. The news soon found its way among the middle provinces, and Governor Dinwiddie, of Virginia, began at once to look calmly about him to select an efficient envoy to bear a message to the invaders, ordering their immediate evacuation of the soil. GEORGE WASHINGTON, then in his twenty-first year, was the one selected. Months had gone by. Spring had passed. Another summer had ended—Autumn had left bear the trees, and the cold bleak of winter had come again. The winds moaned through the forest; and the fourth of December, 1753, saw Washington journeying along the banks of the Alleghany. Soon he reached the Indian village of Venango, at the mouth of French Creek. The advanced post of the French was there. The English trader, formerly at that point had departed, and the French flag was flying over his cabin. The French gave the young messenger a fair reception and hearing, and bade him see the commanding officer at Le Bœuf, still above Venango, on French Creek, whither Washington started and soon arrived. Upon communicating with Legardeur de St. Pierre, the commanding officer, he was told by the latter that he would send the message to the Governor-General of Canada; that his orders were to hold possession of the country; and that he would do it "to the best of his ability." Washington returned. The ultimatum had been revealed, and, at the opening of another spring, a large body of the backwoodsmen of Virginia had formed themselves into a company under Trent, as Captain. Soon crossing the Alleghanies, and descending to the point where now flourishes the city of Pittsburg, Pa., they began the erection of a fort. Le Bœuf and Venango soon got scent of it, and, sweeping down with a large body of French and Indians, the fort of the backwoodsmen was soon evacuated. Then followed young Washington at the head of a second party. Reaching the Monongahela, he threw up a temporary fortification, and one dark, stormy night, M. Jumonville, with a French scouting party, was suddenly surprised and all taken prisoners by Washington and his backwoodsmen. Soon evacuating this point, he made another halt at the Great Meadows, where, behind some former entrenchments, he was soon assailed by nearly a thousand French and Indians, whom they fought most valiantly, until the French beat a truce-parley, and presented terms of capitulation; and Washington and his men being free to move, soon began to recross the mountains. The Indians now began to wonder at these movements upon their soil—two foreign parties struggling for a territory that belonged to neither, had aroused their attention, and the red men soon began to see that, as one of their sagacious chiefs suggested, a few years later, the French and English were very much "like the two edges of a pair of shears," and that they, (the Indians) were "the cloth which was being cut to pieces between them."

The war dog now began to howl fiercer than ever. 1755 found the courts of London and Versailes still maintaining diplomatic relations, and while yet persisting in a desire for a peaceful adjustment of affairs, they were both arranging for a conflict of arms in the New World. Braddock, with a considerable English fleet, soon sailed from the harbor of Cork, in Ireland; and, a little later, a French fleet put to sea from Brest, under command of Baron Dieskau. While the English fleet came safely over, and landed her troops as designed, the French were less fortunate, and lost two of their vessels by drifting, in a fog, too near the guns of a strong British fort, near the banks of Newfoundland, who took the vessels, after a short contest, and made prisoners of the crew. The British now ordered a general attack upon the French marine, and before the end of this year, had captured three hundred French vessels and some eight thousand of her sailors.

The French were discomfited, but not beaten. Braddock became commander-in-chief of the English forces in America. Negotiations were soon broken off between the two great powers, before which, however, the English ministry had hit upon a plan by which they proposed to strike a simultaneous and general blow against the French on the new continent, and thus, if possible, to sweep them from the land at once, as it were. The plan of attack was to move upon Acadia, Crown Point, Niagara, and Fort Du Quesne, (Pittsburg)—Braddock, with his troops from the Old World, aided by two regiments of provincials, to secure the latter point. But he was a new-comer in the land, and knew but little of the perils and difficulties to be encountered. He was not "the right man in the right place" for such a field of action at such a time, in so far, at least, as ultimate success was concerned. Having explained, however, to the several governors of the Provinces his intentions, he began, in a stern, austere, and rigid manner, the adjustment of his plans; which being consummated, he took up his line of march toward the borders of Virginia, and soon encamped at Fort Cumberland. Weeks passed away in preparation. The backwoodsmen knew how to sling an axe, but were little acquainted with the close drilling and sterner discipline of the Braddock school. He was often out of humor with them—abused his contractors, for obtaining bad horses, and said hard things of the country and its people generally. But the hour of march at length came. June, 1755, saw the army of Braddock on the move, with an immense baggage, for Fort Du Quesne,—the axemen felling the trees, and opening the way for the advancing forces. "Large bodies move slowly." The opening was rough, and all was tedious. Nearly a month had passed, and on the eighth of July, an advance body of some twelve hundred men, with the less cumbersome baggage and artillery, stood upon the bank of the Monongahela, about fifteen miles from Fort Du Quesne. A rocky barrier, and somewhat uneven ground, prevented a direct passage to the fort, and an order from the general to cross the river with a view to finding a better path, and then to recross it again a few miles still lower down, was readily entered upon, and the army soon made the first crossing, and rapidly filed along the shore, all aglow with joy at the prospect of a speedy arrival at the fort.

Du Quesne was already in the hands of the French. Bands of Indians and French scouts had spied the approach of Braddock. The fort was all alive with preparation. Retreat was the first thought of Contrecœur, its commander. But Beaujeu, his captain, said *fight*. His suggestion was listened to and accepted; he at once proposed to lead a band of Indians and French to waylay and intercept the further march of Braddock. The camps of the fierce Caughnawages, Ottawas, Abenakis, Ojibwas, and Hurons, were near and soon reached by Beaujeu, who assembled the warriors, and at once threw the hatchet on the ground before them.* All was hesitancy. Again he appealed to them, and still they were silent. At length he approached them with a stern resolution. "I am determined to go," he shouted. "What," continued Beaujeu, "will you suffer your father to go alone? I am sure we shall conquer." He succeeded, and, on the morning of the ninth of July, word having reached them that the English were near, the chiefs collected their braves; all painted their faces, greased themselves, whooped, danced, and "hung feathers in their scalp-locks." All was heroism and determination with them. Great quantities of gun-powder and bullets were given them, and, with some two hundred and fifty French soldiers, to bring up the rear, the savages, band after band, glided wildly away to the forest. A few miles brought them to a thick clump of woods, near a path leading to the river, which was close by, and where two ravines formed a most remarkable ambuscade, sufficient in extent to contain and conceal "at least *ten thousand men*;" and the savages, with Beaujeu and his men, were here soon concealed, with guns all ready for action. The drums of the advancing army were beating. It was midsummer. All was bright and beautiful. The sun

*Which, if taken up by the Indians, meant that they would join in the fight.

shone forth in all his splendor, and the wild flowers spangled the forest at every side, freighting the undulating currents with delicious odor. On came the army of Braddock. The fated spot was at hand. The army filed along the little road leading to the river, and began to re-cross. All over, they indifferently continued their march, with no scouts in front or at the side to give token of danger. Soon the ravine was neared. Upon every side there seemed a barrier of some kind—thick trees, close underbrush, high grass, and heavy fallen timber—and their progress was slow, while a rapid retreat, with such an army, would have been utterly impossible. Lo! a sudden whoop from the savages, a volley of musketry from behind the ambuscade of the enemy, soon told the sad story. No one had seen the peril. The English grenadiers were confounded, and many fell. The survivors returned the charge. The resolute Beaujeu was killed, and the Indians wavered, but his second, Dumas, rallied them to the charge, and in the front the Canadians and French poured a heavy volley, while the Indians did a similar execution on the right and left. The whole body of the army soon felt the charge; dismay and disorder took possession of the soldiery. The advancing columns fell back upon the main body. The enemy was everywhere wholly or partially concealed. Few were to be seen. Yell upon yell resounded at every side. Every tree—every log—served as a place of concealment, and every shot told its own sad tale. The grenadiers had never seen or heard the like before. Huddling together in crowds, each seemed struggling to form a shield and barrier of the other. Their muskets were as often fired in the air as towards the enemy; and many fell at the hands of their own comrades. The officers were generally brave and active. Braddock, though seemingly fearful in the onset, had five horses shot under him. The Virginians, like the Indians, at length took to the trees. Braddock rallied them into the ranks again, and the enemy mowed them down with terrible effect; and soon Braddock himself fell, and was borne from the field. Washington was there, as if taking his first great lesson in warfare. He rode heroically through the ranks. Two horses were killed under him, and four bullets pierced his clothes, says the account;* but he came off unhurt. Gates and Gage were there. The former was shot through the body—the latter, badly wounded. Out of eighty-six officers, but twenty-three escaped injury. Of the twelve hundred who crossed the Monongahela, seven hundred were cut down and wounded. The Virginians suffered much. Their bravery was great. The grenadiers quailed. The open fields of the Old World were not there. The work of death continued three hours. There was no relief but retreat, and the remaining body precipitately turned back and crossed the Monongahela. The enemy pursued only to the river. The rout was complete, and the field left to the enemy to plunder and scalp.

*See Spark's life of Washington, I. 67.

Braddock's defeat, and the fording-place became memorable. The rout continued to Philadelphia. Meeting the rear division of Dunbar, the panic communicated to the balance of the division; and cannon, baggage, wagons, &c., were destroyed, and left behind. The frontier settlements were passed and left to the ravages of the savage men, who, soon after, waged a destructive war upon them.

The expedition against Acadia resulted in the speedy reduction of that point; but three thousand inhabitants thereof, stoutly refusing to subscribe to the English oath of allegiance, were speedily placed upon vessels and shipped to British dominions.

The movement against Niagara failed entirely—the forces being unable even to reach the falls. The one against Crown Point, in part, at first, much like Braddock, were surprised by the enemy,—French and Indians,—in a thick, woody ambuscade, and badly cut up; but afterwards rallied with superior force, and the victory on the beautiful borders of Lake George, under Sir William Johnson, was considered tolerably complete and decisive.

Five wearisome years thus passed away—Indians, English, and French waging a ceaseless warfare upon and destroying each other, in surprising, cannonading, and also attacks upon defenseless settlements by the savages. Great suffering necessarily awakened strong efforts and energy on the part of both the French and the English.

In 1758, from Cape Breton and Nova Scotia, extending to the Ohio river, and along the bordering regions of Lake George, the war between the rival claimants became rife again. Lord Abercrombie was in command of the English forces of America, with some fifty thousand men under him; and with Montcalm, who had, about two years before, with a superior force of French and Indians, achieved many important victories in the capture and destruction of Oswego, the reduction and capture of Fort William Henry—the aspect of affairs began to assume another and different shape. The English now began to regain lost ground and to capture other important points. The formidable fortress of Louisburg was taken; Fort DuQuesne, (Pittsburg—lost by Braddock)—soon fell into English hands. Bradstreet soon struck a favorable blow, and captured Fort Frontenac. Lord Abercrombie, with a force of some sixty thousand men, advanced upon Ticonderoga, and though the many brave Highlanders under him were badly cut up—though a retreat became necessary, from the great disadvantage of the attack,—yet the English never lost heart, but pushed forward with renewed vigor. Canada was to be reduced and taken. A new plan of assailing the province, from three sides, found a lodgement in the British mind—General Prideaux was to move upon Niagara from the west; Ticonderoga and Crown Point were to be reduced or captured from the south by General Amherst; while the brave Wolfe, from the east, was to move upon Quebec. General Prideaux, of the first, having been killed by the bursting of a cohorn, the command and capture of Niagara fell upon Sir Willam Johnson. The loss of Niagara was equal to the loss of the Province, and the French began to exhibit strenuous efforts to save the fort and beat back the enemy. The French and Indian forces then holding Detroit, Presque'Isle, Venango and Le Bœuf, were speedily ordered to the rescue of Niagara. Sir William advanced upon the enemy. They soon fled, and for five miles Sir William pursued the retreating forces. The success of Niagara was complete. Amherst's advancement upon Ticonderoga was the signal for its destruction, and the French blew it up, passing down Lake Champlain to Crown Point, whither they soon retreated, and concentrated their forces upon Isle Aux Noix. Preparing formidable breast-works here, they determined to brave the worst, and put a stop, if possible, to the further invasion of the enemy. But winter came, and the armies ceased hostilities for a season.

The rigid winter months soon passed—May had glided into June, and Wolfe, with an army of eight thousand men, was sailing up the St. Lawrence. Soon forming an encampment upon the Island of Orleans, Quebec, with her "churches and convents of stone; its ramparts, bastions, and batteries"—high cliffs, and the noted castle of St. Louis, all in full view,—he began to survey the field of operations. Still beyond the rocky promontory which formed the base-work of the boasted city, presenting a continuous line of intrenchments and batteries for some distance along the St. Lawrence, his right resting on Quebec and the river St. Charles, lay the army of Montcalm, fourteen thousand strong. Every aspect of nature seemed to have conspired against the operations of Wolfe. A thick forest shielded Montcalm in the rear; opposite stood the towering promontory of Point Levi, and to his left appeared the cascade and gulf of Montmorenci. The task before Wolfe was herculean. "I have this day (Dec. 1, 1758,) signified to Mr. Pitt," wrote Wolfe to Wm. Rickson, "that he may dispose of my slight carcass as he pleases, and that I am ready for any undertaking within the reach and compass of my skill and cunning. I am in a very bad condition, both with gravel and rheumatism: but I had much rather die than decline any kind of service that offers; if I followed my own taste, it would lead me into Germany; and if my poor talent was consulted, they should place me to the cavalry, because nature has given me good eyes, and a warmth of temper to follow the first impressions. However, it is not our part to choose, but to obey." The meridian of the 31st of July, 1759, had passed. Wolfe had determined to move upon Montcalm's front, and was soon embarked with a strong force. Heavy cannonading from his vessels, soon enabled him to gain a landing "just above the mouth of the Montmorenci." The ambition of the grenadiers and Royal Americans "o'er leaped itself." Eager for the victory, they sprang upon the shore. Illy directed and without orders, with loud shouts, they rushed over the plain and began, in the face of a terrible fire of the enemy, to clamber up the ramparts of the French. Hundreds of their slain soon covered the slopes. A moment of comparative stillness soon elapsed. The great volleys of smoke arising from the heavy cannonading had been effectual in attracting thick clouds over the scene of action, and a pelting rain put a stop to the bloody contest. Night set in. A retreat was ordered. The surviving forces regained their vessels, and, as they moved away, the loud *vive le roi* from the ramparts, and the wild whoops of the Indians, as they descended the heights to tomahawk and scalp the wounded, and plunder the the dead, all told how complete they esteemed the victory.

Wolfe was sad. "More than four hundred of the flower of his army had fallen a useless sacrifice." The vital powers of his rather slender frame had been greatly overcome, and a burning and protracted fever confined him for a period of several days to his bed; and here it was, while suffering under the weight of a painful fever, that his soul seemed to rise above the surrounding obstacles of success, and enabled him to conceive the plan of future triumph. The scheme thus evolved was deep and daring. The army was to be divided into two divisions,—one, by seeming attacks, to engage the attention of Montcalm before Quebec—the other to move, at night, above the place, on the north side, and scale the rugged heights of Abraham. September came, and all was readiness. All worked well. The plan developed was pushed forward, and on the night of the 12th of September, clear and beautiful—the stars looking down with a glorious harmony upon the scene—noiselessly, the vessels of Wolfe floated down the stream to the point of embarkation. "*Qui vive?*" cried a sentinel of the French, as he caught a glimpse of the moving objects.

"*La France!*" was the word echoed back by one of the captains of the fleet.

"*A quel regiment?*" enquired the French guard. "*De la Reine?*"* was the ready response of the captain.

The sentinel, thinking no ill, and as a vessel was hourly looked for from Bougainville, all suspicions were hidden in the darkness of the hour, and the English fleet passed on. Soon another summons from a sentinel brought forth similar responses from the captain of the English vessel, and all was well. The designated point, at the base of the heights, was reached,—ever after memorable as "Wolfe's cove." The ascent was very great. Wolfe felt doubtful. Said he, to one of his officers, "you can try it, but I don't think you'll get up."

Soon one Donald McDonald, the same, doubtless, who had just before so readily responded to the French sentinel, began to scale the heights. Again came a challenge from a guard above. The

*This was the name of a corps under the French commander, Bougainville, a fact known to the captain referred to.

reply was prompt and satisfactory. He had come, said he in French, to relieve him, (the French sentinel) and the guard was silenced. Close upon the ascent of McDonald, came a number of Highlanders, scrambling up by every available means—and still they came, until the height above swarmed with the English soldiery. A fierce resistance ensued between the guards and the English. The guards were compelled to give way. Wolfe's idea and the stratagem of the Highlander had done the work. Morning came, and with it the clear sunlight. The Plains of Abraham presented to the opposite ramparts of Quebec a scene of terror and dismay. The shining bayonets of the enemy, "and the dark-red lines of the English forming in array of battle," readily told the French what was coming. The long siege had already greatly exhausted the French supplies—their militia had withdrawn for want of food. Their alarm drums were beaten; and all was excitement. "They have gotten to the weak side of us at last, and we must crush them with our numbers," said Montcalm; and the French soldiers began to move to the front of the English. Firing began, and nine o'clock saw the two armies confronting each other. Montcalm soon began to advance. Coming yet nearer, his troops opened a heavy fire upon the English. All was still in the English ranks. No one ventured to pull a trigger, until the army of Montcalm had advanced within some forty yards of the regulars. "At once," runs the account, "from end to end of the British line, the muskets rose to the level, as if with the sway of some great machine, and the whole blazed forth at once in one crashing explosion." The smoke became intense, and for a time enveloped the soldiery in darkness. The execution of the English had been great; and now, that the smoke had cleared away, they began to redouble their efforts—"hewing down the Frenchmen with their broadswords, and slaying many in the very ditch of the fortifications." The action was short and rapid. The French loss was estimated at "fifteen hundred men, killed, wounded, and taken." The French now fled precipitately. Wolfe had fallen, mortally wounded, and been conveyed to the rear, before the flight of the French began. "See how they run," cried an English officer standing near to Wolfe, as he lay upon the soft turf. "Who run?" anxiously enquired Wolfe, "opening his eyes," says the account, "like a man aroused from sleep." "The enemy, sir," replied the officer; "they give way everywhere." "Then," returned the dying Wolfe, "tell Colonel Burton to march Webb's regiment down to Charles river, to cut off their retreat from the bridge. Now, God be praised," he softly murmured, turning on his side, "I will die in peace;" and his heroic spirit passed away. Montcalm had also received a mortal wound, and was dying. "I am happy," said he, "that I shall not live to see the surrender of Quebec." Being interrogated as to instructions, his reply was, "I will give no more orders; I have much business that must be attended to, of greater moment than your ruined garrison and this wretched country;" and Montcalm, too, soon went out. The white flag was run up on the ramparts of Quebec, and on the 18th of September, 1759, that point was forever wrested from the power of the French. A year later, September 8, 1760, and the whole dominion was swept from their grasp, and England ever after swayed the province. A new rule began at once to extend itself over the north-western territory.

A new era had dawned upon the New World. The sun-light of a new governmental superstructure—a broad Democratic-Republican basis,—wherein the great principles of "life, liberty, and the pursuit of HAPPINESS," were to form the pillars of a beautiful edifice,—had already risen above the hill-tops of the Future, soon to penetrate the thick forests and glimmer along the valleys and hill-sides of the far west.

CHAPTER VI.

* * * * *

"O'er a pulse from chaos beating,
With its mystic flow of pride,
We are drifting—ever drifting,
And are floating down the tide."—WM. H. BUSHNELL.

Numbers and condition of the tribes of the northwest at the close of the French and Indian war—The western route—The Shawanoes and Miamies—Indian attachment to the French—Their hatred of the English—The Delaware Prophet—British occupancy of forts Miami and Ouiatenon—Treaty of 1763—The Indian domain—The conspiracy of Pontiac—His designs first discovered at this point—Discovery of the "bloody belt"—Council called—Holmes' letter—Office of the chiefs—The great council at the river Ecorces—Great speech of Pontiac—The Ojibwa girl's warning—Pontiac's visit to the fort—His failure—Further efforts—Gladwyn's letter—Further efforts of Pontiac—Visit and retention of Campbell and McDougal at the camp of Pontiac—Capture of the forts—The conspiracy at this point—Betrayal and death of Holmes—surrender of the fort—One hundred and four years have passed—"Progress! Civilization! Onward!

AT the close of the French struggle, so great had been the havoc among the various tribes of the north-west, that, from the estimates of Sir William Johnson, it was presumed there were not more than ten thousand fighting men to be found in the whole territory lying "between the Mississippi on the west, and the ocean on the east; between the Ohio on the south, and Lake Superior on the north;" which, according to a further estimate by Sir William, in 1763, placed the Iroquois at 1950; the Delawares at about 600; the Shawanoes at about 300; the Wyandotts at about 450; the Miamies, with their neighbors, the Kickapoos, at about 800; while the Ottawas, Ojibwas, and a few wandering tribes, northward, were left without any enumeration at all. At that period, so thin and scattered was the population," say the best accounts,* "that, even in those parts which were thought well populated, one might sometimes journey for days together through the twilight forest, and meet no human form. Broad tracts were left in solitude. All Kentucky was a vacant waste, a mere skirmishing ground for hostile war-parties of the north and south. A great part of Upper Canada, of Michigan, and of Illinois, besides other portions of the west, were tenanted by wild beasts alone."

*See Parkman's History of Conspiracy of Pontiac, p 132.

The most favored route westward from the central colonial districts, at that period, "was from Philadelphia across the Alleghanies, to the valley of the Ohio," by way of Fort du Quesne, (after the war, being rebuilt by the English, called "Fort Pitt,") where Pittsburg now stands. It was this route that most of the traders westward took, whither, from that point, they penetrated the interior with their goods, upon pack-horses, to traffic with the Indians. An Englishman, for sometime subsequent to the war, became a ready subject for the scalping-knife, and, consequently, was compelled to move with great precaution.

At this period, says Parkman, in his interesting researches, "the Shawanoes had fixed their abode upon the Scioto and its branches. Farther towards the west, on the waters of the Wabash and the Maumee, dwelt the Miamies, who, less exposed, from their position, to the poison of the whiskey keg, and the example of debauched traders, retained their ancient character and custom in greater purity than their eastern neighbors," "From Vincennes," says the same writer, "one might paddle his canoe northward up the Wabash, until he reached the little wooden fort of Ouiatenon. Thence a path through the woods led to the banks of the Maumee. Two or three Canadians, or half breeds, of whom there were numbers about the fort, would carry the canoe on their shoulders, or, for a bottle of whisky, a few Miami Indians might be bribed to undertake the task. On the Maumee, at the end of the path, stood Fort Miami, near the spot where Fort Wayne was afterwards built. From this point," continues he, "one might descend the Maumee to Lake Erie, and visit the neighboring Fort of Sandusky; or, if he chose, steer through the strait of Detroit, and explore the watery wastes of the northern lakes, finding occasional harborage at the little military posts which commanded their important points. Most of these western posts were transferred to the English during the autumn of 1760; but the settlements of the Illinois (Kaskaskia, Cahokia, &c.,) remained," says Parkman, "several years longer under French control."

The Indians of the northwest had lost their French Father, and with him, for a time, their trinkets, and much besides, in the form of powder, balls, &c., that they had long annually been accustomed to receive from that quarter. They could hardly realize, notwithstanding the many whisperings to that effect, that their French Father was forever divested of his power in America, and that his rule this side of the great waters had ceased. They believed the oft repeated stories of the many *habitans*, *coureurs des bois*, &c., of the various villages, and wandering from point to point among the tribes of the northwest, which were also greatly strengthened by similar assurances from those of the French still holding possession of the territory along the Illinois and Mississippi rivers, and at other points, that their French Father "had of late years fallen asleep," and that his numerous vessels and soldiers would soon be moving up the Mississippi and St. Lawrence, to drive the English from their dominions, leaving them again in quiet possession of their former hunting grounds. Every means was now resorted to by the French thus scattered about the wilderness to arouse the savages, and their efforts were not in vain. The rancor of the Indians was greatly increased from time to time, until at length, after a laspe of two years, a great scheme was developed and put on foot for the overthrow and destruction of the English and the various posts so recently occupied by them. As had been frequent at other periods among the aborignies in the wilds of the New World, a great Prophet suddenly began to exert a powerful influence among the tribes of the northwest. He held his mission under the Great Spirit, and earnestly enjoined upon the tribes to return again to their primitive habits—to throw away the weapons, apparel, &c., obtained from the pale faces. Here, said he, is the starting point of success. The force of the new prophet's teachings were truly great, and the tribes came from long distances to hear him. For the most part his suggestions were much regarded by the tribes; but the weapons of the white man could not be dispensed with. These they retained. The prophet was a Delaware, and the great leader of the movement, was an Ottawa chieftain, whose Indian name was PONTIAC. Detroit was surrendered to the English on the 29th of November, 1760; and while many prisoners were removed down the lake, "the Canadian inhabitants were allowed to retain their farms and houses, on condition of swearing allegiance to the British crown." An officer being speedily dispatched to the southwest, Fort Miami, at the confluence of the rivers St. Mary and St. Joseph, and Ouiatenon, below the present site of Lafayette, so long standing guard between the Ohio river and Lake Erie, were soon possessed by the English, and a new rule begun.

For over two years, forts Miami and Ouiatenon remained in comparative security. No hostile movement on the part of the French or savages had thus far conspired to greatly ruffle the complacency of their guardianship.

The tenth of February, 1763, at length arriving, a treaty of Peace was convened at Paris, France, between the two great Powers of France and England—the former surrendering to the latter all claims to the vast region lying east of the Mississippi, making the great Father of Waters the boundary line of the British possessions in America.

A few months later, on the 7th of October, the English government, "proportioning out her new acquisitions into separate governments," set apart "the valley of the Ohio and adjacent regions as an Indian domain," and, by proclamation, strictly forbade "the intrusion of settlers" thereon. Each came at an unpropitious period. The seeds of future trouble had long since been sown, and the little forts in the wilderness, here (Fort Miami) and at

Ouiatenon, were destined ere long to feel the shock of "coming events." The great plot of Pontiac and the efforts of the Delaware prophet for the destruction of the English and the recapture of the posts so recently lost to the French, were rapidly though silently maturing. Intimations and surmises were all that could be gained, so still and cautious were the movements of the savages; and the first really positive assurance (as it afterwards proved) of the efforts and designs of the Ottawa chieftain and his followers, was disclosed at Fort Miami, opposite the present site of Fort Wayne.

With the utmost vigilance, on the one hand, and the greatest possible activity on the other, Pontiac was now pushing forward his scheme of destruction against the English. War belts were dispatched to various tribes at a distance, inviting them to join in the overthrow of the invaders and capture of the forts; and soon the entire Algonquin race, combined with the Senecas (of the Six Nations) the Wyandotts, and many tribes from the valley of the Lower Mississippi, were allied to the great scheme of destruction. An English officer, by the name of Holmes, was in command, with a small body of men, at this point, Fort Miami; and it was through Holmes that the first most positive intimations were received of the premeditated plot of the Indians.

One day, early in the month of March, 1763, Holmes was startled by a friendly admonition. A neighboring Indian, who, through some acts of kindness, perhaps, on the part of Holmes, had formed a strong friendship for the ensign. The Indian told him that the warriors of one of the villages near by had recently received a *bloody belt*,* with a "speech," pressing them to kill him (Holmes) and demolish the fort here, and which, whispered the friendly Indian, the warriors were then making preparations to do. The peril was iminent, and Holmes began at once to look about him. Soon summoning the neighboring Indians to a council, he made bold to charge them with the design, which they readily acknowledged, with seeming contriteness and regret, charging the whole affair upon a tribe at another locality in the region. Holmes obtained the belt, and, from a speech of one of the chiefs of the Miamies, was at least partially induced to entertain the belief that all would now be tranquil.

A few days later, and the following letter, from Ensign Holmes, at this point, was on its way to Major Gladwyn, commanding at Detroit:

"FORT MIAMIS, MARCH 30TH, 1763.

"Since my Last Letter to You, wherein I Acquainted You of the Bloody Belt being in this village,† I have made all the search

*It was a custom with many tribes in those days to send belts of wampum and somtimes tobacco when aid was desired, or peace was to be made. The white belt denoted peace; the black or red belt were emblamatic of war.

†The old Twightwee or Miami village, on the west side of the St. Joseph, and scattered in the neighborhood of the "Old Apple Tree," nearly opposite the site of old fort Wayne.

I could about it, and have found it out to be True; Whereon I Assembled all the Chiefs of this Nation,* & and after a long and troublesome Spell with them, I Obtained the Belt, with a Speech; as you will Receive Enclosed; This Affair is very timely Stopt, and I hope the News of a Peace will put a Stop to any further Troubles with these Indians, who are the Principle Ones of Setting Mischief on Foot. I send You the Belt with this Packet, which I hope You will Forward to the General."

The peculiar organization of the Indian—his habits; the wild roaving life of many of the tribes—their want of military order; the lack of proper central governmental relations to unite and hold the tribes together; their inability and want of judgment in furnishing supplies for a large body of men in time of war; their custom of rapid blows to secure speedy victory; their native idea of individual and collective freedom;† small producers and large consumers—subsisting mainly upon the wild animals of the forest, and the fish of the streams—"loose and disjointed as a whole;" scattered, for the most part, in small bodies over large regions of territory—all combined, at the period in question, to render it impossible for the tribes of America long successfully to conduct a seige or sustain themselves,—however cunning, intelligent, resolute, and brave their chief or chiefs,—in a contest with the active civilization and formidable means of warfare of the English. It is true, that soon after the French war, the strength of the British became greatly diminished—the army which had been brought to bear upon Canada with such salutary effect, having soon after been dissolved, and the main body of the regulars recrossed the ocean to join their friends again in the Old World. Yet, with small garrisons, they were, to a considerable extent, still formidable, as compared with the advantages possessed by the savages, unaided by the French.

Signs of coming trouble with the Indians at length became more apparent. They had now begun to hang about the forts, "with calm, impenetrable faces," asking "for tobacco, gunpowder, and whisky. Now and then some slight intimation of danger would startle the garrison from security, and an English trader, coming in from the Indian villages, would report that, from their manners and behavior, he suspected them of mischievous designs." Occa-

*The Miamies.

†It was the office of the chiefs, says Parkman, "to declare war and make peace; but when war was declared, they had no power to carry the declaration into effect. The warriors fought if they chose to do so; but if, on the contrary, they preferred to remain quiet, no man could force them to lift the hatchet. The war-chief, whose part it was to lead them to battle, was a mere partizan, whom his bravery and exploits had led to distinction. If he thought proper, he sang his war-song, and danced his war-dance, and as many of the young men as were disposed to follow him gathered around and enlisted themselves under him. Over these volunteers he had no legal authority, and they could desert him at any moment with no other penalty than disgrace. * * * Many an Indian army, before reaching the enemy's country, has been known to dwindle away until it was reduced to a mere scalping party."

sionally some "half-breed would be heard boasting in his cups that before the next summer he would have English hair to fringe his hunting-frock."*

By the 27th of April, 1763, Pontiac having largely matured his plans—great numbers of the villages and camps of the western tribes, including all grades and ages, women and children, of the tribes, having celebrated the savage rites of war; magicians "consulted their oracles, and prepared charms to insure success;" many warriors, as was long the Indian custom, before great events in war, withdrawing to the deep recesses of the forest, or hiding in caves to fast and pray, that the Great Spirit might give them victory,—of the tribes already mentioned a grand council was convened at the river Ecorces, where Pontiac delivered to the vast throng a speech rife with both eloquence and art.

On the morning of the great council, "several old men, heralds of the camp, passed to and fro among the lodges, calling the warriors, in a loud voice, to attend the meeting. In accordance with the summons, they came issuing from their cabins—the tall, naked figures of the wild Ojibwas, with quivers slung at their backs, and light war-clubs resting in the hollow of their arms; Ottawas, wrapped close in their gaudy blankets; Wyandotts, fluttering in painted shirts, their heads adorned with feathers, and their leggins garnished with bells. All were soon seated in a wide circle upon the grass, row within row,—a grave and silent assembly. Each savage countenance seemed carved in wood, and none could have detected the deep and firey passions hidden beneath that unmovable exterior. Pipes, with ornamented stems, were lighted and passed from hand to hand."†

Soon placing himself in the centre of the wild, though silent multitude, with long black hair flowing about his shoulders; stern, resolute, with an imperious, preemptory bearing, "like that of a man accustomed to sweep away all opposition by force of his impetuous will," plumed and painted, with a girt about his loins, Pontiac began at once to arouse his auditors by a recital of the injustice of the English, and by drawing a contrast between the conduct of the French and the British towards the tribes assembled; presenting to them the terrible consequences of English supremacy—persisting that it was the aim of the British to destroy and drive them from the land of their fathers. They have driven away the French, he recounted, and now they seek an opportunity to remove us also. He told them that their French Father had long been asleep, but that then he was awake again, and would soon return in his many canoes to regain his old possessions in Canada.

Every sentence was rounded with a fierce ejaculation; and as the impetuous orator proceeded, his auditory grew restless to spring at once into the bloody arena of battle and bury the scalping knife and tomahawk in the body of the enemy. Turning to the

*Hist. Consp. Pontiac, p 167. †Parkman.

opposite side of savage nature, appealing to their sense of the mysterious, in a somewhat mellowed tone, though still as earnest in demeanor, he said:

"A Delaware Indian conceived an eager desire to learn wisdom from the Master of Life; but, being ignorant where to find him, he had recourse to fasting, dreaming, and magical incantations. By these means it was revealed to him, that, by moving forward in a straight, undeviating course, he would reach the abode of the Great Spirit. He told his purpose to no one, and having provided the equipments of a hunter,—gun, powder-horn, ammunition, and a kettle for preparing his food,—he set forth on his errand. For some time he journied on in high hope and confidence. On the evening of the eighth day, he stopped by the side of a brook, at the edge of a small prairie, where he began to make ready his evening meal, when, looking up, he saw three large openings in the woods, on the opposite side of the meadow, and three well-beaten paths which entered them. He was much surprised; but his wonder increased, when, after it had grown dark, the three paths were more clearly visible than ever. Remembering the important object of his journey, he could neither rest nor sleep; and leaving his fire, he crossed the meadow, and entered the largest of the three openings. He had advanced but a short distance into the forest, when a bright flame sprang out of the ground before him, and arrested his steps. In great amazement, he turned back, and entered the second path, where the same wonderful phenomenon again encountered him; and now, in terror and bewilderment, yet still resolved to persevere, he pursued the last of the three paths. On this he journied a whole day without interruption, when, at length, emerging from the forest, he saw before him a vast mountain, of dazzling whiteness. So precipitous was the ascent, that the Indian thought it hopeless to go farther, and looked around him in despair; at that moment, he saw, seated at some distance above, the figure of a beautiful woman arrayed in white, who arose as he looked upon her, and thus accosted him: 'How can you hope, encumbered as you are, to succeed in your design? Go down to the foot of the mountain, throw away your gun, your ammunition, your provisions, and your clothing; wash yourself in the stream which flows there, and then you will be prepared to stand before the Master of Life! The Indian obeyed, and then began to ascend among the rocks, while the woman, seeing him still discouraged, laughed at his faintness of heart, and told him that, if he wished for success, he must climb by the aid of one hand and one foot only. After great toil and suffering, he at length found himself at the summit. The woman had disappeared, and he was left alone. A rich and beautiful plain lay before him, and at a little distance he saw three great villages, far superior to the squallid dwellings of the Delawares. As he approached the largest, and stood hesitating, whether he should enter, a man gorgeously attired, stepped forth, and, taking him by the hand, welcomed him to the celestial abode. He then conducted him into the presence of the Great Spirit, where the Indian stood confounded at the unspeakable splendor which surrounded him. The Great Spirit bade him be seated, and thus addressed him:

"'I am the maker of heaven and earth, the trees, lakes, rivers, and all things else. I am the maker of mankind; and because I love you, you must do my will. The land on which you live, I made for you, and not for others. Why do you suffer the white man to dwell among you? My children, you have forgotten the customs and traditions of your fathers. Why do you not clothe yourselves in skins as they did, and use the bows and arrows, and stone-pointed lances, which they used? You have bought guns, knives, kettles, and blankets of the white man, until you can no longer do without them; and what is worse, you have drunk the poison fire-water, which turns you into fools. Fling all these away; live as your wise fore-fathers lived before you. And, as for these English,—these dogs dressed in red, who have come to rob you of your hunting-grounds, and drive away the game,—you must lift the hatchet against them, wipe them from the face of the earth, and then you will win my favor back again, and once more be happy and prosperous. The children of your great father, the King of France, are not like the English. Never forget that they are your brethren. They are very dear to me, for they love the red men, and understand the true mode of worshiping me!"

With some further admonition from the Great Spirit, of a moral and religious nature, says the account,* the Indian took leave of the Master of Life, and returned again to terra firma, where, among his people, he told all he had seen and heard in the wonderful land of the Great Spirit.

All was now ripe for action. Pontiac's words and the glowing allegory he had presented, had spread a magnetic fire among the great throng of listeners that nothing short of a desperate encounter or defeat would smother. The first great move was destined to culminate upon Detroit.

A beautiful Ojibwa girl, whose love for the commander, Gladwyn, seems to have been only equalled by her precaution and care, was in the secret. Had probably attended the council, and heard the plan of Pontiac's movement to surprise and capture the fort; and true to her sense of regard for her kind friend, Major Gladwyn, on the afternoon of the 6th of May, she found occasion, (having made a handsome pair of moccasins for the commander,) to visit the fort, whither she quietly strode, with anxious heart, in hopes to reveal to her lover his perilous situation, and unfold to

*From the Pontiac MSS., originally in the hand of one McDougal, who, says Parkman, "states that he derived his information from the Indians." And further says that "the author of the Pontiac MSS. probably writes on the authority of Canadians, some of whom were present at the council." See History Conspiracy of Pontiac, pp. 180, 181, 182, 183.

him the movement about to be made upon the fort by Pontiac and his warriors—his plan of surprise, &c. As she entered, Gladwyn observed that she wore a different air than on other occasions. Her countenance assumed the expression of one in distress. Fear and depression both seemed to sway her, and she could say but little. Remaining but a short time, she stepped forth again into the open air, to look about, perhaps, to see who might chanced to have seen her enter the fort. Sorrow still weighed heavily upon her. She could not depart from the scene of her friend without acquainting him with the work that was fast maturing for his death, and the destruction of all within the garrison. With this feeling, she lingered about the fort until quite late, which not only attracted the attention of the sentinel, but Gladwyn himself, who, noticing her strange conduct, called her to him, and asked her what was giving her trouble. Her heart beat heavily. She could not speak. Still her friend pressed her for a response, assuring her that he would not, under any consideration, betray her—that, with him, whatever she told would be safe—that no harm should befall her. Her fear was suddenly overcome, and her admiration for her friend, united with an irresistible determination to save him, even in the midst of danger, as the beautiful Pocahontas had saved the life of Captain Smith, she confidingly told him all.

Said she, very sadly, "to-morrow Pontiac with sixty of his warriors will come to the fort. All will have short guns hidden under their blankets—blankets close about their necks, so as to hide guns. Pontiac will want to hold peace-council, will make a great speech; then offer you peace-wampum. With hands on short guns, warriors all to make a quick jump and fire, killing all English officers. Then come all Indians outside, and kill all but French—leave no English alive."

The soul of Gladwyn suddenly loomed above the perilous hour that awaited him on the morrow. His naturally courageous heart began to beat with renewed activity and determination. Bidding the faithful squaw* be faithful still and fear not; to acquaint him, if possible, with any further movements that might transpire, with a lighter heart, and a freer air, the Ojibwa beauty strode quietly out and was soon lost to the view of her lover and the perilous garrison.

If the Great Spirit had inspired an Indian to destroy, he had also superinduced one of his red children to save; and thus moved, the Ojibwa girl had already won the victory. Acting at once upon the admonition of the Indian girl, Gladwyn soon acquainted his

*One M. Peltier, who lived at Detroit during most of the period of the siege, and who, though but 17 years old at the time, remembered much that then occurred, in 1824, in a statement made to Gen. Cass, said that "he remembered that soon after the failure of Pontiac's attempt to surprise the garrison, he punished, by severe flogging, a woman named Catherine, accused of having betrayed the plot." He also remembered "the several attacks on the armed vessels, by the Indians, and the attempts to set them on fire by means of blazing rafts."

officers of the event to be looked for on the morrow, and all was preparation and readiness. From mist and rain, the sky cleared away, and the sun disappeared in a glow of brightness. Night came gradually on; and while all was stillness and anxiety within the garrison, no hostile movement intruded from without. All night the English soldiers, without knowing why, (for the secret of the Ojibwa girl had not been told the privates, for prudential reasons,) kept watch and paraded the ramparts with anxious and sleepless vigil. Nothing, however, served to ruffle the air, save the distant bum-bum of the Indian drum, and the fierce whoop of the warriors as they mingled their hoarse voices in the wily dance and pushed forward their arrangements for the strategetic effort that was to begin with the dawning of another day.

The night at length passed, and with its passing soon came the evidence of Pontiac's design, as told by the Ojibwa girl. Soon, in the distance, many canoes could be seen, from the palisades of the fort, slowly moving across the river, as was subsequently learned, laden with Indians lying compactly in the bottom of each canoe, well concealed, that a knowledge of their strength might be kept from the garrison.

The open ground without the fort began gradually to fill up. Warriors, fancifully decorated, with here and there many women and children, gathered upon the ground. To allay suspicion, with marked activity and restless anxiety, preparations were soon making in front of the garrison for a great game of baggattaway. "At ten o'clock," says Parkman, "the great war-chief, with his treacherous followers, reached the fort, and the gate-way was thronged with their savage faces. All were wrapped to the throats in colored blankets. Some were crested with hawk, eagle, or raven plumes; others had shaved their heads, leaving only the fluttering scalp-lock on the crown; while others, again, wore their long, black hair, flowing loosely at their backs, or wildly hanging about their brows like a lion's mane."

The account runs, that, as Pontiac, followed by his warriors, stepped within the enclosure, (the entire garrison being on duty, with sabers and bayonets glistening, ready for action at every point, by special order of the commander,) "a deep ejaculation half escaped from his broad chest." The very air about him seemed to whisper: "Pontiac, your plot is known." But he moved on, and soon passed into the doorway of the council-house, followed by his fierce coadjutors. The commandant, Gladwyn, and his officers, with swords at their sides, and a brace of pistols in their belts, all seated, in readiness for the reception of the wily chief and his followers. The Indian, as a general rule, always sat upon the ground or upon a coarse mat. Before taking their seats, Pontiac's perturbed spirit led him to enquire as to the cause of so many of his "father's young men standing in the street with their guns?" To which the commandant replied, through his interpreter, that "he had ordered the soldiers under arms for the sake of exercise and discipline." Seating themselves at once upon the matts arranged for them upon the floor, with much discomfiture and evident mistrust, in each countenance, Pontiac arose holding in one hand the peace-belt, referred to by the Ojibwa girl, and at once began to express to Gladwyn his strong admiration and love for the English—said that "he had come to smoke the pipe of peace and brighten the chain of friendship with his English brothers." And it is said, that though evidently conscious of his detection, "he raised the belt and was about to give the fatal signal," when, instantly, "Gladwyn waved his hand"—and, as if by magic—so well matured were the plans of the commandant,—the garrison drum beat a most stunning roll, filling the air with its reverberations, and startling the warriors, both within and without the fort, into sudden dismay; while the guards in the passage to the council-house suddenly made their arms to clash and rattle as they brought them into a position for action; and the officers, with Gladwyn, looking stearnly upon the figures of the "tall, strong men" before them, had simultaneously clasped their swords, in anticipation of, and with a view to meet, if need be, the premeditated on-slaught of Pontiac and his warriors. The moment was one of heroic determination on the part of the little garrison of Detroit, and of the utmost discomfiture and chagrin with the savages. The plans of the great Ottawa chieftain were foiled, and he stood before the commandant and his officers like one suddenly overcome by a terrible shock.

Says Gladwyn, in a letter dated May 14th, 1763, "they were so much surprised to see our disposition, that they would scarcely sit down to council: However, in about half an hour, after they saw their designs were discovered, they sat down, and Pontiac made a speech, which I answered calmly, without intimating my suspicions of their intentions, and after receiving some trifling presents, they went away to their camp."

Accompanied by three of his chiefs, he returned to the fort the next morning, with a calumet or peace-pipe, neatly ornamented with different colored plumage, which he offered to the commandant, with the following speech: "My fathers, evil birds have sung lies in your ears. We that stand before you are friends of the English. We love them as our brothers, and, to prove our love, we have come this day to smoke the pipe of peace." Presenting the pipe to Major Campbell, second in command, as a pledge of friendship, the chiefs again took their departure.

A great game of ball was played that afternoon, and Pontiac strode among the villagers arousing them to action. On the next day, surrounded by an immense throng upon the grounds near the fort, Pontiac stepped forth, and again approached the entrance to the fort, but could not now gain an admission—all was barred against him. Enquiring as to the cause of this, the commandant replied that the Great Chief could enter, but none others. To which Pontiac replied that "he wanted all his warriors to enjoy the fragrance of the friendly calumet." But all was of no avail. None could enter but the chief. Pontiac is here said to have thrown off the mask of friendship, and exhibited, in unmistakable action, a determination for vengeance against the English. His followers now repaired to the dwellings of two English residents near, murdered and scalped them. Pontiac repaired to the Ottawa village, aroused his warriors, and danced the war-dance. Two English officers had been waylayed and killed by the savages near Lake St. Clair; and on the morning of the 10th of May (1763), all the tribes combined under Pontiac, aided by a few French *engagees*, by shouts, at least, approached the fort, and began an attack, which lasted some six hours. Efforts now being made for a reconciliation, La Butte, the interpreter, accompanied by two old Canadians, was sent to the camp of Pontiac to ascertain the cause of his action, and to assure him that any grievance he had to complain of, would be speedily redressed. Pontiac listened attentively, and seemed to assent to all proposed, and La Butte soon hastened back to the fort to report progress; but shortly after, returning to the camp of Pontiac, learned that he had been deceived. Pontiac, with his chiefs, now wished to hold an interview with their English fathers themselves, that the peace might be the more complete and binding. Major Campbell was much liked by many of the savages, and with him they wished to speak. Upon hearing of this desire from La Butte and the two Canadians, Campbell unsuspectingly expressed a wish to visit the camp of the savages. Gladwyn was fearful. He suspected the intentions of Pontiac. But Campbell went, accompanied by Lieutenant McDougal, a junior officer of the garrison, "La Butte, and several other Canadians." One Mr. Gouin, who had just made himself sufficiently well acquainted with the designs of the Indians in getting Campbell and McDougal into their camp, hastened to warn them of their danger; but all was of no avail. They went, and were taken prisoners. After a few hours parley, feeling that his fate was already sealed, to test his position more fully, it is stated that Campbell once arose to depart for the fort again, after finding all efforts for reconciliation unavailing, when Pontiac bade him be seated, saying "My fathers will sleep to-night in the lodges of his red children." Their lives were at once eagerly sought by the savages, but Pontiac would not then permit them to be injured, though Campbell was subsequently destroyed by the Indians, while McDougal is said to have made his escape.

On the 13th of May the attack was renewed, with an increased force and great vigor. The condition of the fort seemed most perilous, and the officers had a consultation as to what was best to do, in view of their garrison being but weak at best, and a powerful enemy to contend with. (From 600 to 2,000 Indians was the estimate against which the fort at that time had to contend.) But there was now no means of escape. To fight and defend were the only alternatives; and for several weeks the siege continued; during which time, it was told by an officer at Detroit, "no man lay down to sleep, except in his clothes, and with his weapons by his side." Pontiac strove in vain to gain the Canadians as allies. The provisions of the garrison became reduced; and but for the timely aid they received from the Canadians, they would have been compelled to suffer defeat. But the tables, in this respect, were soon turned, and the Indians began to want for the necessaries of life. Not being able to demolish or capture the fort as easily as they had anticipated,—the Indian never accustomed to lay in stores for such occasions—their food became exhausted, and they too called upon and received from the Canadians like aid. It was about this period that several attempts, from other points, were made to relieve the garrison, by additional troops and provisions; but without success. The action of the Indians at other points, embraced in the great conspiracy of Pontiac, were now also becoming important. Nine Posts, held by the English, had been included in the great conspiracy and sought to be captured, viz: Detroit, Presque' Isle, Michillimackinac, Miami, (at this point,) Ouiatenon, (below Lafayette, Ind.) Le Bœuf, Venango, Fort Pitt, (Pittsburg) and Fort Sandusky. The plan of capture seems to have embodied the cunning and resolution of Pontiac at every point; and the pretensions somewhat similar to those at first presented by the great head of the conspiracy at Detroit, were mostly manifested at every post essayed to be taken; and one after another, excepting Detroit alone, rapidly fell into the hands of the Indians. Many were the bloody scenes enacted.

On the 16th of May, Sandusky fell; on the 1st of June, Ouiatenon was captured; Michillimackinac on the 12th, and Presque'Isle, on the 15th of June, also fell into the hands of the wild conspirators.

After Presque'Isle was taken, runs the narration of Parkman, the neighboring little posts of Le Bœuf and Venango shared its fate, while, farther southward, at the forks of the Ohio, a host of Delaware and Shawnoe warriors were gathering around Fort Pitt, and blood and havoc reigned along the whole frontier.

Father Jonois, a Jesuit missionary, had reached Detroit and conveyed to the garrison a letter from Captain Etherington, at Michillimackinac, giving an account of the capture of that post. Soon after, a letter from Lieut. Jenkins, at Ouiatenon, telling of the capture of that post, was also received by Major Gladwyn. "Close upon these tidings," says the account, as given by Parkman, "came the news that Fort Miami (at this point, Fort Wayne) was taken. This Post, " continues the narration, * * * * "was commanded by Ensign Holmes; and here I cannot but remark," says the same writer, "on the forlorn situation of these officers, isolated in the wilderness, hundreds of miles, in some instances, from any congenial associates, separated from every human being except the rude soldiers under their command, and the white or red savages who ranged the surrounding woods."

The Miamies at this point, had been deeply embroiled in the great conspiracy, and the region of "Ke-ki-ong-a" resounded with many a savage yell of hatred towards the English.

Stratagem ever formed a part of Indian warfare and savage character. By its skillful employment, the red man as readily looked for success in war, as, with his rifle or bow and arrow, by deliberate and steady aim, he sought to bring down the wild game of the forest.

Holmes had long suspected the designs of the Indians, and, for that reason, had, for some months, been somewhat vigilant in his observations of their conduct, more especially after the discovery in the neighborhood of the bloody belt, already referred to. But savage ingenuity and deception were striving hard, and Holmes, seemed destined to fall a victim to the perfidy of the conspirators, white and red, prowling about the village and neighborhood.

The 27th of May had come. All nature was radiant again with the beauties of spring. The great, expanding foliage of the forest waved gracefully over and mainly shut out from the broad blaze of a vivifying sunlight, the beautiful blosoms and sweet-scented wild flowers that grew profusely beneath the tall majestic oaks, maple, and sycamores, and countless other and smaller trees, that lined the margins of our beautiful rivers, and mainly covered the vast regions of soil, where now, under a new reign of civilization and human progress, the same great sun daily reveals to the civilized eye, innumerable fields and meadows; beautiful towns and cities; fine orchards; and, each season, vast numbers of blooming and fruitful gardens.

An Indian girl,* with whom Holmes had for some time been intimate, and in whom he placed much confidence, by compulsion on the part of the conspirators, came into the fort and told Holmes that there was a sick squaw lying in a wigwam not far from the fort, and expressed a desire that he should go and see her. The fatal hour had come. Unsuspectingly, and with a view to serve and perhaps relieve the supposed sick squaw, (knowing perhaps something of medicine; for it would seem, had there been a sur-

*Mrs. Suttenfield, one of the early mothers of Fort Wayne, living here since 1814, informed the writer that she became acquainted with this woman in 1815; that she and her family lived neighbors to her for several years. At the period of Mrs. S.'s acquaintance with the woman, she had a son, a man of some years. On one occasion, being at the hut of the woman, the man, her son, came in intoxicated, and somewhat noisy, and the woman, by way of an apology to Mrs. S., remarked that he was a little SQUABBY, or drunk; and concluded with the remark that he was a SAGINASH, (English); and from the age of the man, the inference is drawn that he was a son of Holmes. After leaving here, the women took up her residence at Raccoon Village. She lived to a very old age, and was known to many of the early settlers of Ft. Wayne. Mrs. Suttenfield's recollections of the account she received are, that the Indians at the time of the conspiracy, (probably induced by Godefroi and his associates) forced her to act as she did towards Holmes, which is quite probable.

geon in the fort, he would have been more likely to have at least been called on by the Ensign than for Holmes to have gone himself,) preceded by the Indian girl, he was soon without the enclosure of the garrison, and advancing with cautious steps in the direction of the hut wherein lay the object of his philanthropic mission. Nearing a cluster of huts, which are described* to have been situated at the edge of an open space, "hidden from view by an intervening spur of the woodland," the squaw directed him to the hut wherein lay the supposed invalid. Another instant,—a few more paces,—and the sudden crack of two rifles from behind the wigwam in view, felled Holmes to the earth, and echoed over the little garrison, startling the guards and inmates into momentary surprise and wonder. Amid the confusion, the sergeant unthoughtedly passed without the fort to ascertain the cause of the rifle shots. But a few paces were gained, when, with loud, triumphant shouts, he was sprung upon by the savages and made a captive; which, in turn, brought the soldiers within, about nine in all, to the palisades of the garrison, who clambered up to see the movement without, when a Canadian, of the name of Godfroi, (or Godfri) accompanied by "two other white men," stepped defiantly forth, and demanded a surrender of the fort, with the assurance to the soldiers that, if at once complied with, their lives would be spared; but, refusing, they should "all be killed without mercy."†

The aspect before them was now sadly embarrassing. Without a commander—without hope, and full of fear, to hesitate, seemed only to make death the more certain, and the garrison gate soon swung back upon its hinges; the surrender was complete, and English rule, at this point, and for a time, at least, had ceased to exercise its power.

More than a hundred and four years have now rolled away since this eventful hour; and the placid and beautiful St. Joseph, (near which the fort stood), with its high embankments and overhanging boughs, sweeps as noiselessly and unpretendingly by the scene, as when the fort, with its bastions and palisades, overlooked its waters, and the Indian huts, with their dusky inmates, dotted the adjacent localities; while, in the distance, appears a beautiful city, with numerous tall spires and handsome edifices, covering more than two thousand acres of ground, and containing nearly thirty thousand inhabitants, whose busy tread, mechanical industry, active pursuits, and habits of thought, tell of a glorious, free, and happy Future. In silent awe, indifferent alike of the Past, the Present, and the Coming Time, the long line of buildings, gazing complacently, as it were, upon the scene of the ancient garrison, and the site of the Indian village, seem to say: "Whither and why have

*In the MSS. of the "Loss of the Posts." See His. of Consp. Pontiac, pages 244 and 245.

†One statement is, that they were all killed; but I have been unable to find its verification in any of the printed accounts I have examined.

you vanished? Where are the years that have gone by? And why are WE here?" And the great clock, near the center, (the Court-house) looking from all sides, momentarily responds:

"PROGRESS!—CIVILIZATION!—ONWARD!"

CHAPTER VII.

"These forest-isles are full of story :—
Here many a one of old renown
First sought the meteor-light of glory,
And 'mid its transient flash went down.
*   *   *   *   *
And all the bright and teeming Present
Thrills with the great and *evenescent* Past."
W. D. GALLAGHER.

A return to the beleagured garrison at Detroit—Aid hourly expected—Anxiety of the inmates—Pontiac solicits aid from the Canadians—Relief approaches the fort—"Broadside" from a schooner—Pottawattamies and Wyandotts sue for peace—A calm comes over the troubled waters—Fight at "bloody bridge"—New recruits to the army of Pontiac—Indians board the schooner "Gladwyn"—A panic—Escape of the vessel—The siege abandoned by the main body of the tribes—Pontiac and his tribe left alone to carry on the siege—Pontiac abandons the siege—Starts for the Maumee—A hard winter—Much suffering—Great council at Niagara—A new campaign against the western tribes—Bradstreet relieves the besieged fort—Makes a treaty—Speech of Wasson—Captain Morris—He arrives at the camp of Pontiac—Rough treatment—Escapes—Reaches this point—Miamies want to kill him—Is lodged in old fort Miami—Taken across the St. Joseph—His final release and return to Detroit—Bradstreet's movements—Bouquet penetrates the Indian country—The captives—Indians subdued—Croghan's visit to the west—His capture—Meets Pontiac—Council at Ouiatenon—Croghan's return—Visit to this point—His journal—His arrival at Detroit—Holds a council there—The great council at Oswego—Pontiac attends—English rule again in the west—Pontiac visits St. Louis—His death.

RETURNING again to Detroit, we find the Indians still active in their efforts to capture the garrison, and all within the palisades of the fort anxiously expecting the arrival of vessels with men and provisions. Pontiac had called a council with the Canadians, and made a strong speech, and again importuned them to join him in the overthrow of the English. The Canadians had refused, on the ground, that the French King and the English had signed a paper stipulating certain bounds, that then belonged to the English; and being under English rule, the French King having told them to remain still for a time, until he could come to their relief, to join the Indians would be to bring the wrath of the King upon both the Canadians and the Indians, "But, my brothers," said the Canadian speaker, at the council with Pontice, "you must first untie the knot with which our father, the King, has bound us;" and, though a few reckless characters among the Canadians are said to have joined the Indians at the time, in compliance with Pontiac's desire, yet the effort was nevertheless a failure. Pontiac was defeated in his designs, and was destined soon to meet with utter failure in his effort to capture the garrison. On the 19th of June, Gladwyn had received news to the effect that a "vessel had been seen near Turkey Island, not far distant from Detroit; and the anxiety for her arrival became very great. On the 23d the vessel began to near the point of landing, opposite the fort, and the Indians could be seen in the distance preparing to make an attack upon her; which induced Gladwyn to fire two cannon shots, as well to put the Indians to flight as to let the vessel know all was yet safe within the fort. Having encountered some resistence on the part of the Indians, and desiring to move with care, several days now elapsed before the vessel succeeded in reaching the place of landing, beside another schooner that had for some time previously been lying at anchor there. Bringing a supply of provision and a number of fresh recruits, the new schooners had readily become objects of no little aversion to the wild assailants. On one occasion, shortly after the arrival of the last vessel, thinking to assail the Indians with a few broadsides from some point in the stream, "Gladwyn himself, with several of his officers, had embarked on board the smaller vessel, while a fresh breeze was blowing from the northwest. The Indians on the bank stood watching her as she tacked from shore to shore, and pressed their hands against their mouths, in amazement, thinking that magic power alone could enable her thus to make her way against wind and current. Making a long reach from the opposite shore, she came on directly towards the camp of Pontiac, her sails swelling, her masts leaning over till the black muzzles of her guns almost touched the river. The Indians watched her in astonishment. On she came, till their fierce hearts exulted in the idea that she would run ashore within their clutches, when, suddenly a shout of command was heard on board; her progress was arrested; she rose upright, and her sails flapped and fluttered as if tearing loose from their fastenings. Steadily she came round, broadside to the shore; then, leaning once more to the wind, bore away gallantly on the other tack. She did not go far. The wondering spectators, quite at a loss to understand her movements, soon heard the coarse rattling of her cables as the anchor dragged it out, and saw her furling her vast white wings. As they looked unsuspectingly on, a puff of smoke was emitted from her side; a long report followed; then another, and another; and the balls, rushing over their heads, flew through the midst of their camp, and tore wildly among the thick forest trees beyond. All was terror and consternation. The startled warriors bounded away on all sides; the squaws snatched up their children, and fled screaming; and, with a general chorus of yells, the whole encampment scattered in such haste, that little damage was done, except knocking to pieces their frail cabins of bark."*

This procedure being followed by similar efforts, the Indians now sought to destroy their new opposers by means of floating rafts of fire; but all to no great purpose, as the vessels always managed to escape their contact. And thus the besiegers, with occasional new recruits, continued, in various ways, until the middle of July, when some Pottawattamies and Wyandotts sued for peace, which, under certain considerations, being granted, but little of interest is said to have occurred until the end of July, when the garrison was again reinforced by the arrival, after a sharp encounter with the Indians, (those who had recently made peace), of twenty-two barges, with about two hundred and eighty men, including "several small cannon, and a fresh supply of provisions and ammunition."

The new body of troops, under command of Captain Dalzell, a brave officer, who was killed soon after his arrival, were not long idle. On the 31st of July they moved out with a view of silently attacking the Indians at a certain point, afterwards known as the "bloody bridge." The Indians heard of the movement, and lay in ambush. The fight was a short but bloody one for the English, loosing, as they did, about fifty-nine men, killed and wounded, their captain among the number; and the Indians some fifteen or twenty, which greatly elated the latter, who sent the news to the tribes in every direction; and "fresh warriors," wrote Gladwyn, soon began to "arrive almost every day;" until "upwards of a thousand" were thought by him to be engaged in the attack under Pontiac. With a few skirmishes, now and then, nothing of special interest occurred until the night of September the 4th, when the schooner "Gladwyn", returning to Niagara, was attacked by the Indians, not far from the fort, as she lay anchored in the stream, having been detained for the want of sufficient wind. The Indians, some three hundred in number, the night being densely dark, dropped silently down with the current, and were unobserved until near the vessel, when a broadside, with musketry, was opened upon them, of whom many were killed; but they soon began to board the vessel. "The master of the vessel was killed; several of the crew were disabled; and the assailants were leaping over the bulwarks, when Jacobs, the mate, called out to blow up the schooner," which "saved her and her crew"—some of the Wyandotts, having comprehended "the

*Parkman.

meaning of his words," giving "the alarm to their companions, instantly causing every Indian to leap overboard in a panic, and the whole were seen diving and swimming off in all directions to escape the threatened explosion."* The schooner being thus freed, and the Indians fearing to make further effort, "on the following morning she sailed for the fort," and reached Niagara in safety.

At length, towards the close of September, hearing that a large force was coming to relieve the garrison, and being weary of their labors, the Indians, with the exception of Pontiac and his tribe, the Ottawas, began to sue for peace, and a truce being granted them, they soon departed from the scene of the besieged fort, and took to the forest to provide food for their families and obtain the furs and hides of the animals so long left unmolested.

The Ottawas, with Pontiac, being now left alone to carry on the siege, kept up the attack till the last of October, when, learning from the French that a lasting peace had been made between the French and the English, and that aid from their French father, the King, was now no longer to be hoped for, "in rage and mortification," he left Detroit, and, with a number of his chiefs, "repaired to the River Maumee, with the design of stirring up the Indians in that quarter, and renewing hostilities in the spring."†

The winter proved a hard one; and the Indians suffered much from cold and hunger. The siege had exhausted their ammunition; the fur-trade having been interfered with, left them without many articles they had previously been in the habit of enjoying. But before the cold had spent itself, Sir William Johnson had dispatched messengers to many tribes, inviting them to a great peace-council, at Niagara, which was readily responded to; and some two thousand warriors, were soon gathered about Niagara to meet and talk with Sir William.

There were yet, however, many who were still much embittered in their feelings towards the English, and would not attend the council.

The "Menomenies, Ottawas, Ojibwas, Mississaugas, from the north, Caughnawas, from Canada, even Wyandotts, from Detroit, with a host of Iroquois;" while "the Sacs, Foxes, and the Winnebagoes had sent their deputies; and also the Osages, a tribe beyond the Mississippi, had their representatives in the general meeting."

The attitude of many of the tribes of the northwest, had early superinduced a vigorous movement on the part of the English government for their chastisement.

The plan of this campaign embraced two armies,—one to be led by Colonel Bouquet, and the other by Colonel Bradstreet, the former to move towards Fort Pitt, and to the country of the hostile Shawanoes and Delawares, along the Scioto and Muskingum rivers; while Bradstreet was to push forward to Detroit.

*Parkman. †Ibid.

Bradstreet had preceeded Bouquet, and being of a most ambitious turn of mind, or at least quite anxious to do as much of the work as possible, met some of the hostile tribes, on his march who, to delay the action of the army, sought for peace, and he concluded treaties with them, on certain stipulated grounds, a matter that belonged entirely to Sir William Johnson. Supposing that he had done about all the work, (though the Indians were then menacing the frontier settlements,) sent word to Bouquet to that effect; and "while Bradstreet's troops were advancing upon the lakes, or lying idle in their camps at Sandusky, another expedition (Bouquet's) was in progress southward, with abler conduct and a more auspicious result."*

On the 26th of August, Bradstreet reached the long-besieged fort of Detroit, which was a most happy moment to Gladwyn and his little corps of soldiers within the garrison, who had been more or less beset by the beseigers up to that time,—the Indians, having resumed hostilities, in the spring, as proposed by Pontiac—a period of upwards of fifteen months.

Before quiting Sandusky, Bradstreet had commissioned and sent one Captain Morris, an Englishman, accompanied by a number of Canadians and friendly Indians, as attendants, towards the country of the Illinois to treat with and bring the Indians of that portion of the west to friendly terms.

Pontiac and his followers, sullen and intractable, had left Detroit, and again taken up his abode, for the time, on the Maumee, a few miles below the present site of Fort Wayne, whence he is said to have "sent a haughty defiance to the English commander" at Detroit; and many of the Indians about Detroit had gone with Pontiac, leaving there but a few remnant tribes, who, for the most part, exhibiting a desire for peace, Bradstreet soon gave them an opportunity to express their sense of feeling in this relation, and a council was held with this view, at that point, on the 7th of September.

Upon the condition,—which they are said to have happily not understood at all, and which, not understanding, they readily accepted,—"that they become subjects of the King of England,"—a treaty of peace was concluded with them.

At this council were present portions of the Miamies, Pottawattamies, Ottawas, Ojibwas, Sacs, and Wyandotts. Said Wasson, an Ojibwa chief, to the English commander, on this occasion:

"My Brother, last year God forsook us. God has now opened our eyes, and we desire to be heard. It was God's will you had such fine weather to come to us. It is God's will also that there should be peace and tranquility over the face of the earth and of the waters"—openly acknowledging that "the tribes he repre-

*Parkman.

sented were justly chargeable with the war, and deeply regreted their absence."

But let us look after Morris and his companions, who are now rowing, as rapidly as their strength and the current will admit, up the beautiful Maumee.

Ascending this stream in a canoe, runs the narration,* he soon approached the camp of Pontiac, who, as we have seen, had withdrawn to the banks of this river, with his chosen warriors. While yet at some distance, Morris and his party were met by about two hundred Indians, who treated him with great violence, while they offered a friendly welcome to the Iroquois and Canadian attendants. Accompanied by this clamorous escort, all moved together towards the camp. At its outskirts stood Pontiac himself. He met the ambassador with a scowling brow, and refused to offer his hand. "The English are liars," was his first fierce salutation. He then displayed a letter addressed to himself, and purporting to have been written by the King of France, containing, as Morris declared, "the grossest calumnies which the most ingenious malice could devise, to incense the Indians against the English." The old story had not been forgotten. "Your French Father," said the writer, "is neither dead nor asleep; he is already on his way, with sixty great ships, to revenge himself on the English, and drive them out of America." It is evident, concluded the account, "that the letter had emenated from a French officer, or more probably a French fur-trader, who, for his own aggrandizment, sought to arouse the antipathy of the natives to the detriment and further encroachment of the English; and Bradstreet, for not having brought the Indians to a state of subjection before his departure from Sandusky, is in no little degree censured for the result of Morris' subsequent efforts and harsh treatment in meeting with Pontiac; for the fact of so many of the Indians being held as prisoners by the English, at Detroit, even acted as a powerful check to the Ottawas in their action towards Morris.

"The Indians led me," says Morris,† "up to a person, who stood advanced before two slaves, (prisoners of the Panis nation, taken in war and kept in slavery,) who had arms, himself holding a fusee, with the butt on the ground. By his dress and the air he assumed, he appeared to be a French officer: I afterwards found he was a native of old France, had been long in the regular troops as a drummer, and that his war-name was St. Vincent. This fine-dressed, half-French, half-Indian figure desired me to dismount; a bear-skin was spread on the ground, and St. Vincent and I sat upon

*As compiled from Morris' own statement and the testimony of the Canadian and Indian guides. See History of the Consp. of Pontiac, pages 469 to 474, and in Appendix F.

†Says Parkman: "Morris appears to have been a person of strong literary tastes. His portrait, prefixed to the little volume, (containing this narration) exhibits a round English face and features more indicative of placid good humor than of the resolution which must have characterized him." The volume referred to, was published in London, in 1791, in connection with other matter of a miscellaneous character.

it, the whole Indian army, circle within circle, standing round us. Godefroi sat at a little distance from us; and presently came Pondiac,* and squatted himself, after his fashion, opposite to me. This Indian," continues he, "has a more extensive power than ever was known among that people; for every chief used to command his own tribe: but eighteen nations, by French intrigue, had been brought to unite, and chuse this man for their commander, after the English had conquered Canada; having been taught to believe, that, aided by France, they might make a vigorous push and drive us out of North America." * * * * * "Pondiac said to my chief: 'If you have made peace with the English, we have no business to make war on them. The war-belt came from you.' He afterwards said to Godefroi: 'I will lead the nations to war no more; let 'em be at peace, if they chuse it; but I myself will never be a friend to the English. I shall now become a wanderer in the woods; and if they come to seek me there, while I have an arrow left I will shoot at them.'

"He made a speech to the chiefs," continues Morris, "who wanted to put me to death, which does him honor; and shows that he was acquainted with the law of nations; 'We must not,' said he, 'kill ambassadors; do we not send them to the Flat-heads, our greatest enemies, and they to us? Yet these are always treated with hospitality.'"

After relieving the party of all but their canoe, clothing, and arms, they were permitted to resume their course without further molestation.

Quitting the inhospitable camp of Pontiac, with poles and paddles, against a strong current, they continued their course up the beautiful Maumee, and, in seven days from their first out-set, in the morning, they arrived and made a landing, within sight of Fort Miami, (at this point) which, from the time of its capture, after the death of Holmes, the previous year, had been without a garrison, its only occupants being a few Canadians who had erected some huts within its enclosure, together with a small number of Indians who made it their place of shelter for a time. The open points in the locality of the fort, at that time, were principally covered with the wigwams of the Kickapoos, quite a large body of whom having but lately reached here. On the opposite side,† covered by an intervening strip of forest, quite hiden from view, stood the Miami villages.

Having brought the canoe to a place of landing, a short distance below the fort, and began the adjustment of some necessary affairs,

*The former style of spelling the name, or at least as usually spelt by the English at that time.

†At the period of Morris' arrival at this point, and for many years after, the reader must infer that the huts of the Miamies extended on both sides of the St. Joseph, dotting much of the field adjacent to the "Mad Anthony Park" or orchard, including, perhaps, much of the present site of the orchard itself, and on the opposite side, running as far west, as the Agricultural Works and thereabout.

his attendants strode off through the strip of woods* towards the village; and it is stated as most fortunate that he thus remained behind, for, scarcely had his attendants reached the open space beyond the woods, when they were met by a band of savages, armed with spears, hatchets, and bows and arrows, resolutely determining to destroy the Englishman, Morris.† Not yet perceiving him, the chiefs accompanying Morris, began at once to address them, and to endeavor to dissuade them from their purpose, which had the desired effect, at least, in so far as taking his life was concerned. Coming up, in a few moments, to the point where Morris stood, they at once began to threaten him and treat him very roughly, and took him to the fort, where he was commanded to remain, forbidding the Canadians there to permit him to enter their huts. A deputation of Shawanoe and Delaware chiefs, which tribes, the reader will remember, were at that time making great preparations to move against the English, though pretending to be friendly, had recently come to the Miami village here, with fourteen war-belts, and with a view of arousing the Miamies again to arms against the English; and it was to these that was mainly ascribed the cause of Morris' treatment on his arrival here. From this point they had proceeded westward, arousing a similar spirit among all the tribes from the Mississippi to the Ohio, avowing that they would never make friends with the English—that they would fight them as long as the sun shone; and earnestly pressed the Illinois tribes to join them in their terrible determination.

But Morris had not long remained at the fort, before two Miami warriors came to him, and, with raised tomahawks, grasped him by the arms, forced him without the garrison, and led him to the river. Walking forward into the water with him, Morris' first thought was that the Indians sought to drown him, and then take his scalp; but, instead, they led him across the stream, then quite low, and moved towards the center of the Miami village, on the west side of the St. Joseph. Nearing the wigwams, the Indians ceased to go further, and at once sought to undress him; but finding the task rather difficult, they became quite angry thereat; and Morris himself, "in rage and despair," "tore off his uniform." Then tying his arms behind him with his own sash, the Indians drove him forward into the village. Speedily issuing from all the wigwams to see and receive the prisoner, in great numbers, the Indians gathered about him, "like a swarm of angry bees," giving vent to terrific yells—"sounds compared to which, the nocturnal howlings of starved wolves are gentle and melodious."‡ The largest portion of the villagers were for killing him; but a division arising between them, as to what was best to do with him, readily

*This point must have been near or just below the confluence of the St. Mary and St. Joseph. A visit to and little survey of all these points, would render them the more interesting and familiar to the thoughtful and curious.

†His. Consp. Pontiac, p 471.

‡Parkman.

developed a vociferous debate; when two of the Canadians, of the names of Godefroi and St. Vincent, who had accompanied him to this point, and who had now followed him to the village, came forward and began to intercede with the chiefs in behalf of their prisoner. A nephew of Pontiac was among the chiefs,—who is represented as a young man, possessing much of the bold spirit of his uncle, and who heroically spoke against the propriety of killing the prisoner; and Godefroi desisted, saying "that he would not see one of the Englishmen put to death, when so many of the Indians were in the hands of the army at Detroit." A Miami chief, called the Swan, is also represented as having protected the prisoner, and cut the sash binding his arms. Morris, beginning now to speak in his own defense, was again seized by a chief called the White Cat, and bound to a post by the neck; at which another chief, called the Pacanne, rode up on horseback, cut the band with his hatchet, at once giving Morris his freedom again, exclaiming, as he did so, "I give this Englishman his life. If you want English meat, go to Detroit or to the lake, and you will find enough of it. What business have you with this man, who has come to speak with us?"

The determined will and bold words of Pacanne had the desired effect. A change of feeling now readily began to show itself; and the prisoner, without further words or beating from any of the crowd, was soon violently driven out of the village, whither he soon made his way to the fort. On his way, however, it is stated, an Indian met him, and, with a stick, beat his exposed body.

His position was now most critical; and while the Canadians in the fort were disposed to protect him, they were yet loth to lay themselves liable to distrust or danger; and the same warriors who had taken him to the village, were now lurking about, ready to embrace the first opportunity to kill him; while the Kickapoos, near by, had sent him word that, if the Miamies did not kill him, they would whenever he passed their camp. Again, on the eve of setting out on his journey to the Illinois, notwithstanding the dangers now thickening about him, and the great distance yet before him, his Canadian and Indian attendants strongly urged him not to proceed farther; and, on the evening of this day, they held a council with the Miami chiefs, wherein it became the more evident that his situation was most perilous, and that any attempt to continue his journey would be most disastrous; and while many messages were continually reaching him, threatening to put an end to his life, should he attempt to fulfill his mission, report was also conveyed to him that several of the Shawanoe deputies were then returning to the garrison expressly to kill him. Under these circumstances, readily abandoning his determination to proceed farther, he soon began to row his bark towards Detroit, whither he arrived on the 17th of September. Not finding Bradstreet there, as he had anticipated, he having returned to Sandusky, and Morris, now quite weary and fatigued, unable to proceed farther, from the hardships he had undergone, soon sent the former an account of his efforts, in which, together with the facts already presented, was the following, bearing date September 18:

"The villains have nipped our fairest hopes in the bud. I tremble for you at Sandusky; though I was pleased to find you have one of the vessels with you, and artillery. I wish the chiefs were assembled on board the vessel, and that she had a hole in her bottom. Treachery should be paid with treachery; and it is more than ordinary pleasure to deceive those who would deceive us."

Bradstreet's main object in returning to Sandusky, was to fulfill his promise with the Delaware and Shawanoe ambassadors to meet them at that point,—about the period of Morris' return,—to receive the prisoners held by them, and conclude a treaty of peace. The deputation not coming to time, left him much disappointed for several days, when a number of warriors of these tribes came to Bradstreet's camp with the plea, that, if he would not attack them, they would bring the prisoners the next week, which Bradstreet readily accepted, and, removing his camp to the carrying-place of Sandusky, lay in waiting for the Indians and the prisoners. Soon receiving a letter from General Gage, condemnatory of his course,—insisting that his mode of treatment with the Indians was inadequate to effect any good results with them, and ordering him to break engagements with them, and move upon the enemy at once,—close upon the receipt of which also came the journal of Captain Morris, enabling him readily to see "how signally he had been duped;" though subsequent facts proved that some good did result from Bradstreet's course with the Indians at Detroit, as many of them had become more reasonable and tranquil in their actions. Becoming dispirited and not seeing fit to comply with Gage's commands, he broke up his camp at Sandusky, and wended his way towards Niagara, meeting with many disasters on his voyage thither.

The expedition under Bouquet, to the southward, had now done the work. Having penetrated to the center of the Delaware towns, and into the most extensive settlements of the Shawanœs, about 150 miles from Fort Pitt, to the northwest, with a large body of regular and provincial troops, he soon humbled these wily and unrelenting tribes, and speedily compelled them to deliver all the prisoners in their possession.

During the frontier struggles, for some years prior to Bouquet's campaign, hundreds of families along the borders had been massacred and many carried away to the forest by the Indians; and when Bouquet started on his expedition against the Shawanœs and Delawares, in the interior, leaving the border settlements, he was eagerly joined by many who, years before, had lost their friends. Among the many prisoners brought into the camp of Bouquet, (over two hundred, in all,) while in the settlements of these tribes, husbands found their wives, and parents their children, from whom they had been separated for years. Women, frantic between hope and fear, were running hither and thither, looking piercingly into the face of every child, to find their own, which, perhaps, had died—and then such shrieks of agony! Some of the little captives shrank from their own forgotten mothers, and hid in terror in the blankets of the squaws that had adopted them. Some that had been taken away young, had grown up and married Indian husbands or Indian wives, now stood utterly bewildered with conflicting emotions. A young Virginian had found his wife; but his little boy, not two years old when captured, had been torn from her, and had been carried off no one knew whither. One day, a warrior came in leading a child. No one seemed to own it. But soon the mother knew her offspring, and screaming with joy, folded her son to her bosom. An old woman had lost her granddaughter in the French war, nine years before. All her other relatives had died under the knife. Searching, with trembling eagerness, in each face, she at last recognized the altered features of her child. But the girl had forgotten her native tongue, and returned no answer, and made no sign. The old woman groaned, and complained bitterly, that the daughter she had so often sung to sleep on her knees, had forgotten her in her old age. Soldiers and officers were alike overcome. "Sing," said Bouquet to the old lady, "sing the song you used to sing." As the low trembling tones began to ascend, the wild girl gave one sudden start, then listening for a moment longer, her frame shaking like an ague, she burst into a passionate flood of tears. She was indeed the lost child. All else had been effaced from her memory, save the recollection of that sweet song of her infancy. She had heard it in her dreams.* The tender sensibilities and affectionate throbbings so often manifested by the civilized soul under heavy affliction, were feelings foreign, as a general rule, to the Indian heart. His temperament was iron; he had ever been nurtured in an opposite condition of growth; and, consequently, he is said to have held such expressions of the heart in contempt; but when the song of the old lady was seen by them to touch the captive's heart and bring her again to a mother's arms, they were overcome with emotion, and the heart of the Indian beat heavily under the weight of feeling that suddenly convulsed him as he gazed upon the strange scene then enacted.

Many captive women who returned to the settlements with their friends soon after made their escape, and wandered back to their Indian husbands again, so great was the change that had taken place in their natures. Such was the magnetic power of the Indian and the wilds of the forest over the civilized soul.

The English having now subdued the tribes of the northwest, and completed definite treaties with them at Niagara, began to contemplate a further move to the west and north, with a view to securing the country and posts along the Illinois and Mississippi;

* "States and Territories of the Great West," pages 136, 137.

of which Pontiac soon became aware, and, leaving his place of seclusion on the Maumee, where Morris had met him and received such harsh treatment at the hands of his warriors, with four hundred of his chiefs, about the close of autumn, passed up to this point, (Fort Wayne) and, after a short stay, on to the Wabash, and thence to the Mississippi, arousing the tribes at every point to prepare to meet and destroy the English; and, having gained the French settlements and other places where the French traders and *habitans* were to be met, and where the flag of France was still displayed, (for the French held the country about the Illinois, Mississippi, and to the southward, as far as New Orleans, for some time after the loss of Canada and the upper posts,) the French fur-traders and *engagees*, who dreaded the rivalry of the English in the fur-trade, readily gave encouragement to Pontiac and his followers, still insisting that the King of France was again awake, and his great armies were coming; "that the bayonets of the white-coated warriors would soon glitter amid the forests of the Mississippi." But Pontiac seemed doomed to disappointment and failure; and, after repeated efforts, having visited New Orleans, to gain the aid of the French governor of Louisiana, he returned again to the west.

Determining to try the virtues of peace proposals in advance of the army to the westward and southward, Sir William Johnson sent forward two messengers, Lieut. Fraser and George Croghan, to treat with the Indians on the Mississippi and Illinois. After many hardships, and the loss of their stores, through the severity of the winter, &c., they reached Fort Pitt, where, after some delay and the severe cold had subsided, with a few attendants, Fraser made his way safely down the Ohio for a thousand miles, where, coming to a halt, he met with very rough treatment from the Indians. A short time after, in the month of May, Croghan, with some Shawnoe and Delaware attendants, also moved down the Ohio, as far as the mouth of the Wabash, where, being fired upon by a party of Kickapoos, and several of the attendants killed, Croghan and the remainder were taken prisoners, whither they proceeded to Vincennes, where, finding many friendly Indians, he was well received, and the Kickapoos strongly censured for their work. From this point they went to Ouiatenon, arriving there on the 23d, where also Croghan met a great many friendly Indians. Here he began to make preparations for a council, and was met by a large number of Indians, who smoked the pipe of peace with him. Soon receiving an invitation, from St. Ange, to visit Fort Chartres, lower down, Croghan, accompanied by a large number of Indians, left Ouiatenon for that point, and had not journeyed far when they met Pontiac and a large body of chiefs and warriors. Pontiac shook the hand of Croghan, who at once returned with the party to Ouiatenon, where a great concourse of chiefs and warriors were gathered.

Pontiac complained that the French had deceived him, and offered the calumet and peace-belt, professing strong concurrence with the Ouiatenon chiefs in their expressions of friendship for the English.

At the conclusion of this meeting, collecting the tribes here he had desired to meet, he soon took up his line of march, followed by Pontiac and a large number of chiefs, and set out towards Detroit, crossing over to this point, Fort Miami, and the village adjacent.

Having kept a regular journal of his mission, filling it up at every point on the route,—from which the foregoing is principally drawn,—while here, he wrote,

"*August* 1*st*, (1765). The Twigtwee (Twightwee) village is situated on both sides of a river, called St. Joseph. This river where it falls into the Miami (Maumee) river, about a quarter of a mile from this place, is one hundred yards wide, on the east side of which stands a stockade fort, somewhat ruinous.*

"The Indian village consists of about forty or fifty cabins, besides nine or ten French houses, a runaway colony from Detroit, during the late Indian war; they were concerned in it, and being afraid of punishment, came to this point, where ever since they have spirited up the Indians against the English. * * * * * The country is pleasant, the soil is rich and well watered. After several conferences with these Indians, and their delivering me up all the English prisoners they had, on the 6th of August we set out for Detroit, down the Miamis river in a canoe.

"*August* 17*th*.—In the morning we arrived at the fort, (Detroit) which is a large stockade, inclosing about eighty houses; It stands close on the north side of the river, on a high bank, commands a very pleasant prospect for nine miles above, and nine miles below the fort; the country is thickly settled with French, their plantations are generally laid about three or four acres in breadth on the river, and eighty acres in depth; the soil is good, producing plenty of grain."† Says the Canadians were both poor and idle,—some 300 or 400 families, depending mainly upon the Indians for subsistence; had adopted the Indian manners and customs, raising but little grain, and all, men, women, and children, speaking the Indian language perfectly well, etc.

Many Ottawas, Pottawattamies, and Ojibwas were now assembled, and, in the same old council hall where Pontiac, some months before, by stratagem, had essayed to overthrow the English, great throngs of relenting warriors readily convened in obedience to the call of the English ambassador. The expressions among the tribes and deputies of tribes present, was one of mingled repentence and regret; and on the twenty-seventh of August, Croghan addressed them, after their own figurative style, as follows:

"Children, we are very glad to see so many of you here present

*Any one, from this account, can at any time easily ascertain the site of the old English fort, Miami, of which the reader is already quite familiar.

†"Western Annals," pages 184 and 185.

at your ancient council-fire, which has been neglected for some time past; since then, high winds have blown, and raised heavy clouds over your country. I now, by this belt, rekindle your ancient fire, and throw dry wood upon it, that the blaze may ascend to heaven, so that all nations may see it, and know that you live in peace and tranquility with your fathers the English.

"By this belt I disperse all the black clouds from over your heads, that the sun may shine clear on your women and children, that those unborn may enjoy the blessings of this general peace, now so happily settled between your fathers the English and you, and all your younger brethren to the sun-setting.

"Children, by this belt I gather up all the bones of your deceased friends, and bury them deep in the ground, that the buds and sweet flowers of the earth may grow over them, that we may not see them any more.

"Children, with this belt I take the hatchet out of your hands, and pluck up a large tree, and bury it deep, so that it may never be found any more; and I plant the tree of peace, which all our children may sit under, and smoke in peace with their fathers.

"Children, we have made a road from the sunrising to the sun-setting. I desire that you will preserve that road good and pleasant to travel upon, that we may all share the blessing of this happy union."

Closing this great peace-gathering about the last of September, 1765, and after exacting a promise from Pontiac that he would visit Oswego in the spring, and, in behalf of all the tribes he had so recently led against the English, conclude a treaty of peace and amity with Sir William Johnson, Croghan left the scene of his successful labors, and wended his way towards Niagara.

About the period of the first snow, the 42d regiment of Highlanders, a hundred strong, having moved down the Ohio, from Fort Pitt, commanded by Capt. Sterling, arrived at Fort Chartres. The *fleur de lis* of France was soon lowered; and, in its stead, the English planted their standard and forever destroyed the French power in America—holding, as the English then did, and for many years subsequent, all the western posts, from Canada to the Illinois—which left the Indians also with but little to hope for.

When spring came, Pontiac, true to his word, with his canoe, left his old home on the Maumee, for Oswego, whither he soon arrived, and where he made a great speech, and "sealed his submission to the English" forever.

His canoe laden with the presents he had received at the great council of Oswego, he rowed rapidly toward the Maumee again, where he is said to have spent the following winter, living "in the forest with his wives and children, and hunting like an ordinary warrior." In the spring of 1767, considerable discontent began again to manifest itself among the tribes "from the lakes to the Potomac," and from which eventually came the spilling of much blood, as at former periods, along the frontier. The Indians had been disturbed in the possession of their lands, and had begun another terrible resentment. Pontiac had now long strangely kept out of the way. Whether he had been party to the agitation along the border or not, was not known; but many had their suspicions. For two years subsequent to this period, Pontiac seems to have kept so close, some where, that few, if any, but his own immediate friends, perhaps, knew or heard of his whereabouts. In the month of April,* 1769, however, he seems again to have visited the Illinois, and though not knowing that he had anything special in view, yet the English in that region were excited by his movements. From this point, he soon after started for the (then) French settlement of St. Louis, (Mo.), where he was soon after murdered.

The account of his death, as derived from the most reliable sources, is, that he was killed by an Illinois Indian, of the Kaskaskia tribe; that he had been to a feast with some of the French Creoles of Cahokia, opposite the present site of the city of St. Louis, and became drunk. Leaving the place of carousal, and entering an adjacent forest, the murderer stole quickly upon him and dispatched him with his tomahawk, striking him on the head; that the assassin had been instigated to the act by an Englishman of the name of Williamson, who had agreed to give him a barrel of whisky, with a promise of something besides, if he would kill the Ottawa chieftain, which he readily accepted. Says Gouin's account:

"From Miami (here) Pontiac went to Fort Chartres, on the Illinois. In a few years, the English, who had possession of the fort, procured an Indian of the Peoria nation to kill him. The news spread like lightning through the country. The Indians assembled in great numbers, attacked and destroyed all the Peorias, except about thirty families, which were received into the fort." And the death of Pontiac was revenged. His spirit could rest in peace. Such was Indian usage. And thus closed the career of one of Nature's most singular and resolute types of aboriginal character; of whom Croghan wrote in his journal and sent to Gen. Gage in 1765: "Pontiac is a shrewd, sensible Indian, of few words, and commands more respect among his own nation than any Indian I ever saw could do among his own tribe."

*It was in this year that a definitive cession of the province of Louisiana,—which had formerly extended over the entire territory now known as the State of Indiana,—was terminated (because of the great losses sustained at various times in its maintenance by the French government) between France and Spain, the latter becoming,—by secret treaty, made some years prior, (1764) between Louis 14th, and the King of Spain,—sole possessor of the province. And the surrender of St. Louis, by St. Ange, with the English already in possession of all Louisiana east of the Mississippi, closed forever the dominion of the French in the New World.

CHAPTER VIII.

" A sound like a sound of thunder rolled,
And the heart of a nation stirred—
For the bell of Freedom at midnight tolled,
Through a mighty land was heard,
* * * * * * * *
It was heard by the fettered and the brave—
It was heard in the cottage, and in the hall—
And its chime gave a glorious summons to all."

WM. ROSS WALLACE.

The struggle for Independence—Causes that led to the Revolution—The men of '76—Triumph over old conditions—Final treaty of peace—Foreshadowings of former ages realized in the founding of the New Republic.

AS the great earth upon which we live swings with a lighter air in its orbit as the many inharmonious conditions and the great forests upon its surface are cleared away and reduced to ashes by the necessities of improvement, so the advancing tide of human civilization brings to the circumambient air of human relations a less rarefied and more brilliant atmosphere of intellectual strength and love of Freedom.

But the great soul of nature is never still—never ceases to act, to push forward, as with some imponderable impulse, to work out and develop a great and beautiful Future; and scarcely had the French and Indian war of 1759 and 1760 ceased its action, when the colonial settlements of the New World began to exhibit a spirit of dissatisfaction, produced by the acts of the English parliament, and King, that foreshadowed in the (then) not far distant future a momentous and long-protracted struggle; and the heroic James Otis, then advocate-general of the province of Massachusetts, replying to Gridley, advocate for the crown, readily gave new strength and vigor to the foreshadowing. Said he, with great emphasis, on the occasion in question: "To my dying day, I will oppose, with all the power and faculties God has given me, all such instruments (*Writs of Assistance* for the collection of revenue from the colonists) of slavery on one hand, and villainy on the other."

The same formidable power, with colonial aid, that had crushed and despoiled the French in Canada, and, for a time, mainly subdued the Indians of the northwest, had now (1761) begun to present a rigorous front towards the colonists; and though this point, a few years subsequent to the formidable effort of Pontiac, against the English, had remained in comparative quiet, in so far, at least, as the historic accounts run, yet, as step by step the struggle for Independence continued, and at length the strengthened voice of civilization on the new continent, echoing along the ridges of the Alleghanies and through the massive gloom of forest towards the setting sun, startling the little English garrisons at Detroit and other points into momentary activity, and awakening again the aboriginal tribes to a new consideration of their future, this again readily became a point of the greatest importance in both a civil and military point of view; and dearly was it bought by the efforts of the American army, as will be seen in subsequent pages.

The first struggle on the new continent had readily scattered the seed that was to bring forth a second, a third, and a fourth revolution. And, as the accelerated action of the globe becomes less commotionate and easier in its rotative movement, as the refining process of its surface advances, and its internal heat and compressed air are reduced and evolved through volcanic eruptions, earthquakes, and fissury expansion, so the new colonial settlements were destined only to enjoy a wider range of social and governmental Freedom in proportion as they removed the barriers of the forest, and became earnest, efficient, and resolute in action against the further aggression and power of the British Crown on the new continent; and, as this germ of glorious determination and advancement in the establishment of free institutions seemed only destined to expand to a fair expression of vital force and activity through the aggressive movements of the English Government; so the latter began to exercise an undue control over the colonies of the New World, by a gradual disturbance, in various ways, of their colonial relations—at one time interfering with the charter of Connecticut; at another, levying heavy duties upon certain articles of importation into America; and the adoption, soon after, of strenuous measures for the collection thereof—insisting that the colonists should defray the expenses of the French andIndian war, upon the ground that it had been waged in defence of the colonies.

Intense discord and excitement rapidly arose among the colonists. The people gathered at different points. Declamation met declamation. Protest followed protest; and the agitation was still increased by the passage of the famous "Stamp Act," by the English Parliament of 1765, which imposed heavy stamp duties upon all newspapers, almanacs, bonds, notes, etc., issued in America. And again determination followed determination. Resistance became universal and uncontrollable. The spirit of Freedom had found a place in every true colonial heart; and resistence, even to the sword and bayonet, if need be, became at length a fixed and unalterable determination throughout the colonies. Patrick Henry, amid the cries of "Treason!" "Treason!" in the House of Burgesses, in Virginia, thrilled the masses with a magnetic fire of determination that gave new impetus to colonial resentment. And "treason!" "treason!" as the yellow leaf of autumn, fluttering for a moment upon the passing breeze, falls gently to the earth, was as soon drowned by the eloquent voice of Henry; and "give me liberty, or give me death!" rapidly arose upon the tumultuous air of the colonial settlements.

English soldiers soon making their appearance in Boston, (Sept. 27, 1768,) harsh treatment and imperious demands soon awakened resentment. A collision between the citizens and soldiers, in which three Americans were killed, was the result. Determining neither to use, nor to pay tax upon tea, three ships laden with this article, arriving in Boston harbor, were boarded at night by a party of disguised Bostonians, and the tea was hurled into the water.

Parliament still sternly demanding to be regarded in her claims, and finding it out of the question either to bribe or buy the patriotic colonists, soon began more strenuous measures of control. The colonists rapidly formed into bodies of militia. "Minute men," ready for action at a moment's notice, sprang up at every hand. The English Parliament had declared Massachusetts to be in a state of rebellion, and more troops came over. "Boston Neck" was fortified by the English, and the Patriots, concealing their cannons in loads of manure, and their ammunition and cartridges in market baskets and candle-boxes, gradually passed the guards to a point beyond Boston, unmolested. Concord, N. H., became a prominent point, whither the patriots gathered their stores and ammunition, etc. General Gage, then commanding the English forces, thought to route the colonists from this point, and one night secretly dispatched an army of eight hundred men towards Concord for the purpose. The Patriots heard of their coming. The bells of the place were rung; guns were fired, and the minute men were in arms. "Disperse, ye rebels," cried Gage, confronting the colonists and discharging his horse-pistols. The English soldiery followed with a discharge of musketry. A number fell on the colonial side, and, giving way, the British passed on to Concord. A few hours later, the English, starting on their return to Boston, the colonists having gathered in large numbers from different points, and posted themselves behind barns, trees, houses, and fences, opened a terrible fire upon them from every side, and before reaching Boston, the former were well-nigh destroyed.

The first blood was now spilled, and the account of the battle of Lexington aroused, at every point, the whole colonial population of America. "The farmer left his plow, and the mechanic his work-shop. Even old men and boys," says the records, "hastened to arm themselves"—the wife girding "the sword about her husband;" the mother blessing her son, and bidding him "go strike a blow for his country." The colonists were ripe for the struggle. A new era was to dawn upon the world; and Freedom was destined to triumph.

As demand calls for supply; as necessities superinduce and develope the requisites of any great movement, so there soon appeared upon the colonial stage a Franklin, a Washington, a Jay, a Jefferson, a Hancock, an Adams, a Monroe, a Randolph, a Thompson, a Lee, an Otis, a Wayne, a Henry, a Hamilton, a Knox, a Clinton, a Mifflin, a Pickens, a Morgan, a Green, a Morris, a Lincoln, a Marion, a Sumpter, a Tarleton, a Sullivan, a Jones, a Hopkins, a Rutledge, a Gates, a Putnam, a Trumbull, a Wm. Washington, a Bainbridge, a Schuyler, a Warren, etc.

Ticonderoga, had now, (May 10th, 1765,) fallen into the hands of the Americans; the Continential Congress, for the second time, was in session at Philadelphia; GEORGE WASHINGTON became commander-in-chief of the colonial army; great quantities of paper currency were issued; the great battle of Bunker Hill was soon fought; and the war for American Independence had begun with an earnestness and determination only equalled by the glorious spirit that gave birth and impetus to the struggle.

At length the 4th of July, 1776, came. The Continental Congress had received, considered, and, on this hallowed and ever-memorable day, adopted a DECLARATION OF INDEPENDENCE. The great old bell of Independence Hall soon rang out upon the still air the glorious consummation; and every where the heart of the colonist thrilled with joy. In the midst of discord, and under heavy travail, the new continent had given birth to a rare and beautiful child of Freedom and Progress, destined to live and become more glorious, happy, free, and beautiful as time rolled on.

As before this eventful and happy hour,—with now a victory; now retreat and momentary defeat; now suffering with cold and hunger; annon encountering the savages of the forest, pushed on by British influence, for seven years the war continued; during which period, the American forces had been joined by many brave and patriotic men from the Old World, whose souls had caught the spirit of the hour, and whose great love of Freedom brought them to the rescue of the struggling cause on the new continent; amoug whom were Lafayette, Kosciusko, De Kalb, Pulaski, Baron Steuben, and France herself, but a few years before defeated by the British in Canada, and at other points, also became an ally of the Americans, and rendered valuable aid in the cause of Freedom.

Effecting a final treaty of peace with the British September 3, 1783; and from that time forward rapidly gaining strength and recovering from the great pressure so long hanging over them, on the 4th of March the old Continental Congress ceased to be, and the main elements of the present FEDERAL CONSTITUTION, under which our Republic has for so many years existed, and, under every adversity, maintained its primitive spirit of independence, became the organic basis of the new governmental superstructure of America. A glorious era in the World's History had now begun.

A month and two days later, (April 6th, 1789,) by the unanimous voice of the electors, the surveyor, the hero, and the soldier; the statesman and the philanthropist; the lover of Truth and Goodness; the successful leader of the colonial army, and the man of Progress in Governmental Freedom "and the pursuit of HAPPINESS"—GEORGE WASHINGTON, of Virginia, became first President, and the good and patriotic JOHN ADAMS, of Massachusetts, first Vice-President of the United States.

The beautiful germ of the Ideal Republic of Plato, cast upon the soil of the World's necessities more than two thousand years before; the great principles of civil and religious liberty, involving at once "the inalienable rights of man" and the fundamental truths and necessities of continued progression in all that pertained to his welfare in mental and physical growth, as the only safe and sure road to ultimate happiness and good government, seen, acknowledged, and declared years prior to the departure of Columbus on his great voyage of discovery; and which "had shaken thrones and overturned dynasties" long before the regicidal fate of Charles the First, had now, within the wild domain of the New World, begun to bear their first fruits, and to give promise of a continued and still more glorious fruitage in the years to come.

CHAPTER IX.

"Where are the hardy yeomen
Who battled for this land,
And trode these hoar old forests,
A brave and gallant band?
* * * * * *
They knew no dread of danger,
When rose the Indian's yell;
Right gallantly they struggled,
Right gallantly they fell."—CHARLES A. JONES.

—o—

Peaceful attitude of affairs at the close of the great council at Oswego—A desire for more room—Movements of small parties westward—How they lived—Their dislike of extensive settlements—The English colonists—Habits and vicissitudes of the early pioneers—Their appearance, houses, furniture, etc.—"Tomahawk rights"—The cabins often too "cluss"—Dangers and hardships—Efforts of Patrick Henry—Appointment of George Rogers Clark—His movement down the Ohio—Reaches Louisville, Ky.—Starts for Kaskaskia—Takes the place by storm—The "Long Knives"—The stratagem—Fright of the villagers—Father Gibault and others visit Clark—The inhabitants permitted to attend church—Expect to be separated—Revisit of Father Gibault and party—Clark's response—Joy of the villagers—An expedition against Cahokia—Capture of that place and Vincennes—Appointments by Clark—"Big Door"—A "talk"—Big Door declares for the Long Knives—Clark organizes a company of French—Moves against the Indians—Brings them to terms—His movements reach the English at Detroit—Hamilton, the English Governor, moves against Vincennes, with a view to re-capture the lost posts—Vincennes retaken by the British—Clark hears of the event, and soon captures the fort again—Hamilton and others sent to Virginia—No further troubles from the English—La Balme's expedition to this point—Flight of the Indians—La Balme withdraws—Pursued by the Indians, under Little Turtle, and the whole party destroyed.

—o—

AT THE CLOSE of the great treaty of Sir William Johnson with the different tribes of the north-west, at Oswego, in the spring of 1766, at which Pontiac himself appeared and concluded a final reconciliation in behalf of all the tribes formerly banded under his leadership, it was generally thought by the colonists and those settlements along the Alleghenies and at other points westward, that further danger from the tribes was at an end. The English flag was now waving over all the posts from Niagara to the Mississippi; and while the settlements along the borders* and beyond were yet sparse and scattering, there arose a strong

*Which, at that period, extended but little westward of the Alleghany mountains.

desire for more room among the settlers, and hundreds of resolute men were soon on the march seeking new homes in the wilderness of the west. After so much warfare, the peaceful quietudes of the border and more easterly settlements were more than they could abide, and the wild scenes of the distant forest afforded a fair interchange for the former excitement and vicissitudes of war.

Starting out in small parties, the adventurous settlers would move westward far interiorward, then separating, they would traverse large extents of country, and at length, each selecting a site for himself, would settle down in the primeval forest, far from any scenes of civilization or civilized associates, and living much like the Indians, they soon became as reckless and indifferent as the most savage of the red men around them. It is related of those early times that one of those pioneer settlers left his clearing and started for the forests of the west, for the reason that another had settled so near to him that he could hear the report of his rifle; while yet another, seeing from the valley of his location, smoke curling in the distance, is said to have gone fifteen miles to discover its emanation, and finding new-comers there, "quit the country in disgust." More "elbow-room" was wanted. Such were at least some of the extreme expressions of the time.

The English colonists were hardy, daring, self-reliant men. Unlike former periods in the old world, when one nation was often suddenly overrun by another, both in their military and migratory movements, they pushed gradually forward; and while many were destroyed, they yet, on the one hand, succeeded in reducing the Indians to a state of submission, through fear of extermination, while, on the other, the pioneer, relying entirely on his own bravery and prowess, with what aid each could render the other, in times of attack upon the settlements, &c., long held possession of a large region of country, and thus aided in laying the basic structure of future greatness. Long accustomed to the exposure and the vicissitudes of a life on the frontier and in the wilderness, it is not surprising that these hardy men became daring and implacable, often restless for the achievement of some momentary victory or revenge.

Adventurous men now soon began to crowd upon the Indians; their lands were being overrun by the colonists; and while the Indians were disposed to present, for the most part, a friendly front towards the British, they yet cut down the settlers, and, through the English, readily made war upon the colonial settlements during the Revolution. Born and bred amid scenes of hardship, these early pioneers were naturally hardy and active, often caring but little for the common comforts of life or the roughest weather. "Wild as untamed nature, they could scream with the panther, howl with the wolf, whoop with the Indian, and fight all creation." It is related of one of these strangely rough adventurers in the history of the west, that, having "been tomahawked, and his scalp started, he might yet be killed sometime, as the lightning had tried him on once, and would have done the business up for him, if he hadn't dodged." Constantly associating with the Indians, many of them not only became demi-savage in appearance, but "frequently assumed the whole savage character."

A little description of their appearance, ordinary costumes, habits of life, houses, etc., will be of interest to the present generation. A coonskin cap, with the tail dangling at the back of the neck, and the snout drooping upon the forehead; long buckskin leggins, sewed with a wide, fringed welt, down the outside of the legs; a long, narrow strip of coarse cloth, passing around the hips and between the thighs, was brought up before and behind under the belt, and hung down flapping as they walked; a loose deerskin frock, open in front, and lapping once and a half round the body, was belted at the middle, forming convenient wallets on each side for chunks of hoecake, tow, jerked venison, screw-driver, and other fixings; and a pair of Indian moccasins completed the primitive hunter's most unique apparel. Over the whole was slung a bullet-pouch and powder-horn. From behind the left hip dangled a scalping-knife; from the right protruded the handle of a hatchet; both weapons stuck in leathern cases. Every hunter carried an awl, a roll ot buckshin, and strings of hide, called "whangs," for thread. In the winter loose deer-hair was stuffed into the moccasins to keep the feet warm. The pioneers lived in rude log-houses, covered, generally, with pieces of timber, about three feet in length and six inches in width, called "shakes," and laid over the roof instead of shingles. They had neither nails, glass, saws, nor brick. The houses had huge slab doors, pinned together with wooden pins. The light came down the chimney, or through a hole in the logs, covered with a greased cloth. A scraggy hemlock sapling, the knots left a foot long, served for a stairway to the upper story. Their furniture consisted of tamarack bedsteads, framed into the walls, and a few shelves supported on long wooden pins; sometimes a chair or two, but more often, a piece split off a tree, and so trimmed, that the branches served for legs. Their utensils were very simple; generally nothing but a skillet, which served for baking, boiling, roasting, washing dishes, making mush, scalding turkeys, cooking sassafras tea, and making soap. A Johnycake board, instead of a dripping-pan, hung on a peg in every house. The corn was cracked into s coarse meal, by pounding it in a wooden mortar. As soon as swine could be kept away from the bears, or, rather, the bears away from them, the pioneers indulged in a dish of pork and corn, boiled together, and known among them as "hog and hominy." Fried pork they called "Old Ned."*

Quite the opposite of the early French settlers, who formed themselves into small communities, and tended their fields in com-

*"States and Territories of the Great West," pages 142, 143, 144, 145.

mon, the yankee pioneer "went the whole length for individual property," each settler claiming for himself three hundred acres of land, and the privilege of taking a thousand more, contiguous to his clearing; each running out his own lines for himself, chipping the bark off the trees, and cutting his name in the wood; which claims, thus loosely asserted, were then called "tomahawk rights," and were readily regarded by each emigrant. The first work that claimed the attention of the settler was that of felling the trees about him in order to make an opening and to prepare his house-logs, for the erection of a cabin, "sleeping, meanwhile, under a bark cover, raised on crotches, or under a tree." A story is related of one of these pioneers, that, after the completion of his cabin, "he could hardly stomach it." The logs were unchinked, the doorway open, the chimney gaping widely above him, but he complained that the air was yet too "cluss," and that he was compelled to sleep outside for a night or so in order "to get used to it."

Such, runs the record, "were the people, and such their modes of living, that began to spread themselves throughout the west, between the close of Pontiac's war and the commencement of the Revolution. Then, when that struggle came on, new difficulties gathered thickly around the scattered settlements. The reduction of the wilderness was a huge task of itself, even with every encouragement, and without opposition of any sort. But the Anglo Saxon seemed to have had everything arrayed against him. Not only the forest, and the wild beasts, and untold privations, stood in the way of his progress, but the French first tried to crowd him out; then the Indians sought to kill him; and, lastly, the British turned against their own flesh and blood, and bribed the savages to take his life. While the armies of England were roving over and wasting the whole Atlantic coast, from Massachusetts to Georgia, the British Governor at Detroit, and his agents at the forts on the Wabash, and Maumee rivers, (including the fort at this point,) and at Kaskaskia, were busily engaged in inciting the Indians to deeds of rapine and murder on the western frontier. The terrible scenes of the old French war, and of Pontiac's war, were often re-enacted. The pioneers, however, were a different class of men from those who had previously suffered in Virginia and Pennsylvania, and who frequently precipitately fled from their burning dwellings. There was an iron will and temper in these later settlers that presented a front far different from those who, some years before, had fled before the combined forces of the savages and French. Not waiting to be smoked or burnt out, or have their skulls opened with the tomahawk; their throats cut or scalps taken, the yankee pioneers met their assailants and took a ready hand in the game of fight; and no sooner was it understood that the British were engaged in inciting the Indians against the American settlers, than it was resolved to push the war into the very forest itself—to the very threshold of the enemy. Patrick Henry, then Governor of Virginia, soon snuffed the air of the pioneer settlements. He saw the situation. His soul arose equal to the emergency, and was among the first to propose a plan of relief for these sufferers of the forest. On the 2d of January, 1778, he issued instructions to the farmers, and directed the heroic Lt.-Col. Geo. Rogers Clark, of Albermarle county, Virginia, to "proceed with all convenient speed to raise seven companies of soldiers, to consist of fifty men each, officered in the usual manner, and armed most properly for the enterprise, and with that force to attack the British fort at Kaskaskia;" charging him, most explicitly, as follows: "During the whole transaction, you are to take especial care to keep the true destination of your force secret;—its success depends on this." The sagacious foresight of Henry knew the man for the work.

Clark set about the task with a will. He was born a hero, and was said to be one of the finest looking men of his day, and would readily "have attracted attention among a thousand." Conscious dignity is said to have sat gracefully upon him. Agreeable in temper; manly in deportment; intelligent in conversation; largely competent as an officer; vivacious and bold of spirit, Col. Clarke was the man for the occasion.

His captains having reached Fort Pitt in the month of June,* with less than six lines, in companies, with boats in readiness, Clark and his little army were soon aboard, and floating down the Ohio, whither they descended to the falls, in view of the present site of Louisville, Ky., where they encamped, hoping to obtain additional force from Kentucky stations; but, after some consideration touching these posts, deeming it unwise to reduce their strengh, with one hundred and fifty-three men, Col. Clark, armed after the Indian style, continued his course to the mouth of the Tennessee river. Obtaining important information at this point relative to the British posts on the Upper Mississippi, and sinking his boats to prevent discovery, he started overland to surprise and capture Kaskaskia. Each man carrying his own baggage and rations, through marshes and forests, for a distance of one hundred and twenty miles, often knee-deep in water, with their apparel dirty and ragged, beards unshaven for three weeks, presenting altogether a wild, frightful aspect, on the evening of the Fourth of July, 1778, Clark and his men approached Kaskaskia, and concealed themselves about the hills east of the Kaskaskia river. Sending out spies to watch the inhabitants, soon after night-fall, he was again in motion, and took possession of a house, in which a family resided, about three-quarters of a mile from the town, which contained about two hundred and fifty dwellings. Finding boats and canoes at this point, Clark divided his troops into three par-

*The general inconveniences of the day—the thick forests, etc., all combined to render everything in the way of military and pioneer movements exceedingly slow, and often precarious.

ties—two to cross the river, while the other, with Clark himself, moved forward and took command of the fort.

The Indians and French had long known the New Englanders by the appellation of "Bostonias," and the Virginians by that of "Long-Knives." Many strange and fearful stories had long gone forth among the French of these posts concerning the Long-Knives. English officers visiting the Kaskaskians, had told them that the Long-Knives would not only take their property, but were so brutal and ferocious that they "would butcher, in the most horrible manner, men, women, and children!"—a fact that had previously reached the ear of Clark, and in pretension, at least, as the most salutary means of effecting his purpose, he determined to carry out the idea and take the inhabitants by storm; and, accordingly, persons who could speak the French language, were directed to pass through the streets of the town and warn the inhabitants to keep within their dwellings, "under penalty of being shot down in the streets."

Crossing the river, the two parties strode into the yet "quiet and unsuspecting village at both extremes, yelling in the most furious manner, while those who made the proclamation in French, ordered the people into their houses on pain of instant death."* The word was out. The little village of Kaskaskia was in an uproar. All was consternation, fear, and trembling. Men, women, and children ran for dear life, and "*Les long couteaux!—les long couteaux!*"—the Long-Knives!—the Long-Knives! rapidly arose upon the theretofore quiet air of Kaskaskia, and the inhabitants precipitately betook themselves to their dwellings to escape the vengeance of the intruders. The victory was short and decisive. No blood had been shed; and two hours later, the inhabitants of the village had all surrendered and delivered up their firearms. All consummated after the best style of a commander well adapted to the occasion, and who knew just how to carry out the plan of action to the best advantage,—a movement termed by the French *rouse de guerre*,—the policy of war; and to render the movement the more earnest and effectual in its character, the French Governor, M. Rocheblave, was taken prisoner in his own chamber, and the night was passed by the Virginia soldiers in patroling the streets with whoops and yells after the manner of the Indians, which gave the inhabitants great uneasiness, but was all turned to the best account by Col. Clark. The inhabitants were now fully pursuaded that all they had previously heard concerning the Long-Knives was too true. Clark had even carried his plan so far as to prohibit intercourse with each other or his men; and for five days they were thus held in suspense within their cottages. His troops now, (the fifth day) being removed to the outskirts of the village, the inhaditants were privileged again to walk the streets; but soon observing them conversing with each other, without giving any cause therefor, or permitting a word to be said in self-defence,

*"Western Annals," pages 268, 269.

Clark ordered several of the officers of the place to be put in irons. Not that he wished to be cruel or despotic, but that his strategetic plan might prove more effectual and certain in its operations; and the wild, reckless, indifferent, dirty, ragged appearance and manner of Clark and his men, gave the greater awe and force to his plan of action.

At length, M. Gibault, the parish priest, accompanied by "five or six elderly gentlemen," by permission, called upon Col. Clark. All looking alike dirty, and but little different in their general appearance, the deputation were greatly at a loss to know with whom to confer as commandant, and thus some moments elapsed before they were able to speak. But, very submissively, the priest, after a short interval, began to make known their mission. He said "the inhabitants expected to be separated, perhaps never to meet again, and they begged through him, as a great favor from their conqueror, to be permitted to assemble in the church, offer up their prayers to God for their souls, and take leave of each other."

To this Clark, with an air of seeming carelessness, replied that "the Americans did not trouble themselves about the religion of others, but left every man to worship God as he pleased;" and readily granted the privilege desired, but charged them on no account to attempt to leave the place; and no further conversation was permitted with the deputation.

The little church was soon open, and the people rapidly crowded into it. As though the last opportunity they would have thus to assemble, all mournfully chanted their prayers, and bid each other *adieu*, little presuming that they would ever meet again in this life; and so great did they esteem the privilege granted them, that, at the close of the exercises, the priest and deputation repaired again to the quarters of Clark, and, on behalf of the people of the village, graciously thanked him for the indulgence granted them. Begging leave to say a word regarding their separation and their lives, they asserted that they knew nothing of the troubles between Great Britain and the colonists; that all that they had done was in subjection to the English commandants; and that while they were willing to abide by the fate of war in the loss of their property, they prayed that they might not be separated from their families; and that "clothes and provisions might be allowed them, barely sufficient for their present necessities."

The stratagem was now complete. Fear had lapsed into resignation; and the spirit of hope in the Kaskaskians had fallen below the common ebb of even partial security. The achievement of Clark's plan was complete, and, with an air of surprise, he abruptly responded: "Do you mistake us for savages? I am almost certain that you do from your language! Do you think that Americans intend to strip women and children, or take the bread out of their mouths?" "My countrymen," continued he, "disdain to make war upon helpless innocence. It was to prevent the horrors of Indian butchery upon our own wives and children that we have taken arms and penetrated into this remote stronghold of British and Indian barbarity, and not the despicable prospect of plunder. That now the King of France had united his powerful arms with that of America, the war would not, in all probability, continue long; but the inhabitants of Kaskaskia were at liberty to take which side they pleased, without the least danger to either their property or families. Nor would their religion be any source of disagreement, as all religions were regarded with equal respect in the eye of the American law, and that any insult offered it would be immediately punished. And now, to prove my sincerity, you will please inform your fellow-citizens that they are quite at liberty to conduct themselves as usual, without the least apprehension. I am now convinced, from what I have learned since my arrival among you, that you have been misinformed and prejudiced against us by British officers; and your friends who are in confinement shall immediately be released."

The utterances of Clark were soon conveyed to the people; and from fear and apprehension all was changed to joy and praise. The bells rang, and *te deums* were sung. All the night long the villagers made merry. All the privileges they could have desired were granted them, and Col. Clark was readily acknowledged "the commandant of the country."

Soon planning an expedition against Cahokia, in which the Kaskaskians themselves took part, that place was taken with but little trouble and no bloodshed. Close upon the achievement of this success, through the aid and friendship of M. Gibault, the priest of Kaskaskia, Vincennes was also soon captured, with but little effort, and the American flag displayed from the garrison. Capt. Williams was now appointed commandant at Kaskaskia; Capt. Bowman at Cahokia, and Capt. Helm at Vincennes.* The French at these points were now all fast friends of the Americans, and rejoiced at the change that had been made from British to American rule; and Clark proceeded to re-organize the civil government among them, appointing influential and prominent French residents to fill the offices.

At this period a Piankeshaw chief, of great influence among his tribe, known as the "Big Gate," or "Big Door," and called by the Indians "The Grand Door to the Wabash," from the fact that, much as with the famous Pontiac and the Delaware Prophet, farther to the eastward, with whom the reader is already familiar, nothing could be accomplished by the Indian confederation on the Wabash at that period, without his approbation. Receiving "a spirited compliment" from father Gibault, (who was much liked by the Indians,) through his father, known as "Old Tobac," Big Door returned it, which was soon followed with a "great talk" and a belt of wampum. These Indians, under British influence, had previ-

*The fort at Vincennes was called Fort Patrick Henry, after its capture by Clark.

ously done much "mischief to the frontier settlements." Capt. Helm now soon sent a "talk" and wampum to the "Big Door." The chief was very much elated, and sent a message to Helm, stating that he was glad to see one of the Big Knife chiefs in town; that here he joined the English against the Big Knives, but he long thought they "looked a little gloomy;" that he must consult his counselors; take time to deliberate, as was the Indian custom; and hoped the Captain of the Big Knives would be patient. After several days, Old Tobac invited Captain Helm to a council; and it is said Tobac played quite a subordinate to his son (Big Door) in the proceedings thereof.*

After some display of eloquence in reference to the sky having been dark, and the clouds now having been brushed away, the Grand Door announced "that his ideas were much changed; and that "the Big Knives was in the right;" "that he would tell all the red people on the Wabash to bloody the hand no more for the English;" and jumping up, striking his breast, said he was "a man and a warrior;" "that he was now a Big Knife," and shook the hand of Capt. Helm, his example being followed by all present; and soon all the tribes along the Wabash, as high as Ouiatenon, came flocking to Vincennes to welcome the Big Knives. The interests of the British are now said to have lost ground in all the villages south of Lake Michigan.

A few months later, and the jurisdiction of Virginia was extended over the settlements of the Wabash and the Upper Mississippi, through the organization of the "County of Illinois," over which Col. John Todd had been made civil commander.

On the first of September, the time of enlistment of the troops under Clark having expired, and seventy of his men already returned home, to take their places, Clark at once organized a company of the inhabitants of Kaskaskia and Cahokia, commanded by their own officers, and soon started a formidable and rapid movement against the Indians, with whom he made no treaties or gave any quarters. His idea and spirit was to reduce them to terms, without any parley; and soon the name of Clark became a terror among the tribes of the northwest. Before the close of December, (1778) these hostilities had nearly ceased, and everything wore a friendly air among the French settlers.

The news of Clark's success having at length reached Detroit, by way of this point, Hamilton,† the British Governor, at once determined to recapture the posts again, and accordingly with eighty reg-

*"Western Annals," pages 173, 174.

†The following passport, issued by Governor Hamilton, at Detroit, will convey a lively sense of the condition of affairs, and spirit of the northwest at this early period; "By Henry Hamilton, Esq., Lieut. Governor and Superintendent of Detroit and Dependencies, &c., &c. "Detroit St., No. 254. It is permitted to John Bte. Dubois and Amable Delisle, employed by Mr. Macleod, to depart from this post and go to St. Vincennes;—they having been posted, taken the usual oath, and that of fidelity, and given bond in the penalty of Two hundred and Fifty Pounds, New York currency, by which they bind themselves that they will not sell rum, wine, cider, or other strong

ulars, a large number of Canadian militia, and six hundred Indians, he ascended the Maumee, to this point, crossed over to the Wabash, and made a rapid movement upon Vincennes, thinking to take the fort by storm, and destroy all within the garrison. Thus they moved forward. Helm was not to be dismayed. Full of confidence, and with an air that served to signify that the fort was full of soldiers, he leaped upon the bastion, near a cannon, and, swinging his lighted match, shouted with great force, as the advancing column approached, "Halt! or I will blow you to atoms!" At which the Indians precipitately took to the woods, and the Canadians fell back out of range of the cannon. Fearing that the fort was well manned, and that a desperate encounter would ensue, Hamilton thought best to offer a parley. Capt. Helm declaring that he would fight as long as a man was left to bear arms, unless permitted to march out with the full honors of war, which were at length agreed upon, and the garrison thrown open, Helm and *five men*, all told, marching out, to the utmost astonishment of the British commander. But Helm was afterwards detained in the fort as a prisoner.

The season now being late and unfavorable, Hamilton determined to take no further steps toward a capture of the other posts till spring. But in the meantime Clark, towards the last of January, 1779, received word as to the loss of Vincennes, and on the seventh of February, with one hundred and thirty men, he took up his line of march through the forest for Vincennes, a distance of one hundred and fifty miles, ordering Captain Rogers, with forty men, on board a large keel-boat, with two four-pounders and four swivels, to ascend the Wabash within a few miles of the mouth of White River—there to await further orders.* The march through the wilderness was one of peril and hardship—the river bottoms were inundated; and, as they moved through these lowlands, the soldiers were often, while having to feel for the trail with their feet, compelled to hold their guns and amunition above their heads. Their food on the march was parched corn and jerked beef. At

liquors to the Indians, directly or indirectly, nor allow the same to be done by any one in their employ; that they will demean themselves as good and faithful subjects; that they will exhibit their passport, on arriving at the Miamis (this point) and at the Weas, (Ouiatenon, below Lafayette) to those who are invested with authority; and they bind themselves, under the pains of severe punishment, not to aid, assist, or correspond with the enemies of his Majesty; and also that they will give information, as soon as possible, to the governors or officers commanding the nearest forts or posts, of those who violate any of the provisions above mentioned. And if any one should escape from any of the posts dependent to this Government, they shall immediately give notice thereof to the Lieut. Governor.

Given at Detroit, under my hand and seal, House of the King, the 17th of June, 1778. HENRY HAMILTON, L. S. By order of the Lieut. Governor, P. DEJEAN."

*Col. Clark seems to have had his attention long fixed upon this point, but was doubtless governed by a fair sense of wisdom in all his movements. In a letter to one Major Boseron, of Vincennes, bearing date, "Louisville, Feb. 28, 1780," Clark said: "I learn that there is a report of a number of savages collected at Omi (the Miami village at this point) with an intention to disturb the settlement of St. Vincents. I hope it is groundless; if not, I could only wish that they would keep off for a few weeks, and I think they would be more sensible of their interest."

length, after some delay,' on the evening of the 23d of February, arriving upon an eminence within sight of the fort, Clark ordered his men on parade, near the summit of the hill, overlooking the fort, keeping them marching for some time, in a manner that seemed to the English commander as if there was a large army approaching—at least a thousand men, he thought, with colors plainly visible. During the night a deep ditch was dug to within rifle-shot of the fort, and before day-break, a number of men were stationed therein "to pick off the garrison." It was a success; every gunner attempting to show his head along the cannon of the fort, or peer through a loop-hole was shot; and on the 25th of February the fort was surrendered, and Hamilton, Major Hay, and a few others, as instigators in the incitement of Indian murders on the frontiers, accompanied by a strong guard, were sent to Virginia to answer for the crimes charged upon them, and where they were put in irons and held for a time in close confinement in retaliation for the massacres that had occurred; but were finally released at the suggestion of General Washington.

This achievement on the part of Clark and his brave comrades, left them,—with no further attempts of the English to regain the lost forts, on the Wabash and Upper Mississippi,—in possession of all the lower portion of the West until the close of the Revolution, when, at the treaty of peace with the English in 1783, on the basis of its having been conquered and held by Col. Clark, Great Britain conceded that all of this extended region of territory belonged to the United States.

In the fall of the year (1780) following this signal success of Clark at Vincennes, a Frenchman, by the name of La Balme* formed a plan at Kaskaskia for the capture of Ke-ki-ong-a, (this point) then held by the British.

"This village," says the account,† "was situated on the banks of the St. Joseph river, commencing about a quarter of a mile above its confluence with the St. Mary, which forms the Miami, (Maumee) and was near the present city of Fort Wayne. It had been a principal town of the Miami Indians for at least sixty years before the Revolution, and had been occupied by the French before the fall of Canada, who had erected a fort at the confluence of the rivers, on the eastern side of the St. Joseph. At the period of the Revolution," continues the account, "it had become a place of much importance, in a trading and military point of view, and as such, ranked, in the north-west, next to Detroit and Vincennes. It was, accordingly, occupied as a post or seat of an official for Indian affairs, by the British in the beginning of the war. Col. Clark, on the capture of Vincennes, had meditated an expedition against this place, as well as against Detroit; and though he seems never

*Pronounced by the French settlers of the time *La Bal.*

†By Charles B. Lasselle, Esq., formerly a resident of Fort Wayne, but now residing at Logansport, Ind., first published in the "Democratic Pharos," of Logansport, 1857

to have abandoned the idea, yet he could not succeed in his arrangements to attempt its execution. But while the subject was still fresh in the mind of Clark and the inhabitants of the Lower Wabash, another individual made his appearance to undertake what even the daring Clark, with greater resources, did not deem *prudent* to venture upon. This was LA BALME. But of him and his expedition, it may be here stated, very little information of an entirely authentic shape, is within our reach. Excepting about a dozen lines in Mr. Dillon's Historical Notes, no published account whatever of this expedition has ever appeared. Whatever may be given in this brief sketch, has been obtained mostly from some of those who were in part eye-witnesses to the events, and from tradition as handed down by the old inhabitants. La Balme was a native of France, and had come to this country as some kind of an officer, with the French troops, under LaFayette, in 1779. We are not apprised whether he came to the west on his own responsibility, or whether he was directed by some authority; but we find him, in the summer of 1780, in Kaskaskia, raising volunteers to form an expedition against the post of Ke-ki-ong-a, with the ulterior view, in case of success, of extending his operations against the fort and towns of Detroit. At Kaskaskia he succeeded in obtaining only between twenty and thirty men. With these he proceeded to Vincennes, where he opened a recruiting establishment for the purpose of raising the number necessary for his object.* But he does not seem to have met here with the favor and encouragement of the principal inhabitants, or to have had much success in his enlistment. His expedition was looked upon as one of doubtful propriety, both as to its means and objects, and it met with the encouragement, generally, of only the less considerate. Indeed, from the fragment of an old song,† as sung at the time by the maidens of Vincennes on the subject of La Balme and his expedition, preserved by the writer, it would seem that plunder and fame were as much its objects, as that of conquest for the general good. Injustice may have been done him, in this respect; but it is quite certain, from all accounts, that though a generous and gallant man, well calculated to be of service in his proper sphere, yet he was too reckless and inconsiderate to lead such an expedition. How long he remained at Vincennes, we have not now, perhaps, any means of knowing. But sometime in the fall of that year—1780—with, as is supposed, between fifty and sixty men, he proceeded up the Wabash on his adventure.

"He conducted his march with such caution and celerity, that

*This establishment, says Mr. Lasselle, in a note, was situate on lot No. 106, near the corner of Market and Third streets, in what had been called the "Old Yellow Tavern."

†The following is the beginning of the song referred to, as "sung by the inhabitants of Vincennes, July, 1778," in the language of Mr. Lasselle, "when the priest, M. Gibault, won them to the American side:"

"Notre bon cure, plus brave que Devaux,
A pris Notre village sans tambour drapeau."

he appeared at the village (here) before even the watchful inhabitants had apprehended his approach. The sudden appearance of a foe, unknown as to character, numbers, and designs, threw them into the greatest alarm, and they fled on all sides. La Balme took possession of the place without resistence. It was, probably, his intention, in imitation of Clark's capture of Kaskaskia, to take the village and its inhabitants by surprise, and then by acts and professions of kindness and friendship, to win them over to the American cause; but the inhabitants, including some six or eight French traders, totally eluded his grasp. His occupation of the village was not of long duration. After remaining a short time, and making plunder of the goods of some of the French traders and Indians, he retired to near the Aboite Creek* and encamped. The Indians having soon ascertained the number and character of La Balme's forces, and learning that they were Frenchmen, were not disposed at first to avenge the attack. But of the traders living there, (here), there were two, named Beaubien† and La Fontaine,‡ who, nettled and injured by the invasion and plunder of the place, were not disposed to let the invaders off without a blow. These men having incited the Indians to follow and attack La Balme, they soon rallied their warriors of the village and vicinity under the lead of their war chief, the Little Turtle, and falling upon them in the night time, massacred the entire party. Not one is said to have survived to relate the sad story of the expedition.

"Such," says Mr. Lasselle, "is a brief and imperfect account of La Balme's expedition, of which so little is known. It may," continues he, "not have been impelled by the most patriotic motives, nor guided by wise counsels, nor attended with results especially beneficial to the country; yet, as an interesting event, connected with the early history of the country, it should be rescued from the oblivion which rests upon it."||

*About the point where the Wabash and Erie Canal crosses this stream.

†Says a note to this account: "Beaubien married the chiefess, widow of Joseph Drouet de Richardville, and mother of the late chief of the nation, John B. Richardville."

‡Father of the late Miami chief, La Fontaine.

||A short account of La Balme's expedition may also be found in "Annals of the West," pages 318, 319.

CHAPTER X.

"Like the dim traditions, hoary,
Of our loved and native clime;
Like some half-forgotten story,
Read or heard in olden time."—Lewis J. Cist.

—o—

Emigration westward—Organization of a territorial government—Settlements at Cincinnati (Losantiville) and North Bend—Emigrant boats—Movements from Fort Washington to this point—Spanish and Indians—Dissolution—Suggestions of General Washington—His letter to Richard Henry Lee—The importance of the Miami village—Treaties and cessions—Congress and Indian lands—Indian basis of complaint—Council of 1793—Indian speech—Further troubles—What the Indians thought would be the result—Miamies, under Little Turtle, lead a confederacy—Depredations—Report of Gen. Knox—The Wabash Indians—Letter of Gov. St. Clair—The President of the U. S. empowered to call forth the militia of the States—Washington's instructions to Gov. St. Clair—Gov. St. Clair proceeds to the Illinois—Losantiville changed to Cincinnati—Speeches to the Wabash Indians—Antoine Gamelin delivers the messages—Reaches this point—Gamelin's journal—The man-eating society at this point—Gen. Cass' address, &c.—St. Clair's return—Movement against the Indians—British commandant at Detroit notified—British aid to the Indians—Militia arrive at Cincinnati—Organization of the army under Gen Harmar, and movement upon the Miami village here—The army reach the village and find it deserted—Disorder of the troops—A detachment—Return of the scouts—An order—Another scout—Fires of the Indians discovered—Indians discovered—Detachment moves forward—Indians concealed—An attack—Detachment put to flight—Village destroyed—Harmar moves down the Maumee—Issues more orders—Starts for Fort Washington—Encampment—Col Hardin desires to return to the village—His desire granted—Indians discovered—Some disorder—An attack—An account of one of the wounded Indians again victorious—Retreat—Army starts again for Fort Washington, where it arrives in safety—Names of the killed—Expedition of Major Hamtramck—Another dreary winter.

—o—

BUT A FEW YEARS had elapsed, after the struggle for Independence, when a tide of emigration began to set in to the westward again, and a territorial government, with a small settlement, was established at Campus Martius, now Marietta, Ohio, in July, 1788. The officers of the government were General Arthur St. Clair, Governor; Winthrop Sargent, Secretary; and three judges for the executive council. Campus Martius was of square form, one hundred and eighty feet each way. Small steeples extended from the top of each block house, which were bullet-proof, and served as sentry-boxes; while the square was encompassed by a strong palisade, some ten feet in height, and the buildings, all within the enclosure, were constructed of whip-sawed timber, about four inches thick, dove-tailed at the corners, and covered with shingle roofs, each room of which had fire-places and brick chimneys. The towers and bastions were bright with whitewash.

For the most part, the settlers of the Northwestern Territory were men who had spent a large part of their lives, as well as fortunes, in the Revolutionary War. Such was the character of a party of emigrants, under the leadership of General Rufus Putnam, who left New England in 1787, and, descending the Ohio, to a point below Marietta, began the settlement of Belpre, bringing thither with them, and establishing there, many of the primitive habits and customs of their ancestors. First erecting substantial buildings for their families, they set about the erection and organization of a church and school, toward which all are said to have contributed "with a right good will;" and these were the first institutions of the kind established in the Northwestern Territory.

Two years later, in 1789, the first settlement was formed at or near the present site of Cincinnati, Ohio, by some twenty persons, under the lead of Israel Ludlow and Robert Patterson, and then called Losantiville. The original appearance of the present Cincinnati, as at the time of its first settlement, is described as "a beautiful woodland bottom, on the bank of the river, sixty feet above low-water mark, and extending back three hundred yards to the base of a second bank, which rose forty feet higher, and then sloped gently more than a half mile to the foot of the bluff; the bottom being covered with a heavy growth of sycamore, maple, and black-walnut; the second with beech, oak, and hickory timber." In January of this year, another party moved down the Ohio, and began a settlement at North Bend. The craft or boats in which these early settlers descended the river, to the present generation, would indeed seem novel. They usually consisted of a frame-work of logs, covered with green oak planks, and caulked with rags. Snugly ensconsed in these, men, women, and children floated down the rivers to their destination, unexposed to the attacks of the Indians, who often fired upon them from the river banks.

For some years, a spirit of rivalry existed between the settlements of Cincinnati (Losantiville) and North Bend as to the best point for the establishment of a military post, and for a time North Bend, from its natural security against the attacks of the Indians, seemed destined to become the most advantageous and permanent point, and many emigrants came flocking thitherward. But at length, the commanding officer becoming enamored with a beautiful woman at the Bend, the wife of one of the settlers, the husband became alarmed or jealous, and removed to Losantiville,* so runs

*A school-teacher, by the name of Filson, being called on to name the settlement

the record; and North Bend at once began to decline in the appreciation of the commanding officer, as the most available military point for the protection of the northwest territory, and the troops were soon removed to Losantiville, which post was called Fort Washington. It was from this point that the first movement, under Gen. Harmar, who was then commandant at Fort Washington, was made against the Indians at the present site of Fort Wayne, under the administration of Gen. Washington, in October, 1790. It was also from these points, which, at an early period here, were known as "the settlements," that came most of the earlier sojourners and settlers of Fort Wayne; then still known as the Miami village or Omi;* not only Harmar's, but the subsequent expeditions of Gens. St. Clair and Wayne, started from Fort Washington for this point.

During 1780, 1781, to 1785-6, difficulties had arisen between the colonial government and the Spanish on the Lower Mississippi, as to the navigation of that river, and the possession of a large part of the western territory, together with much trouble with the Indians of the west, more especially along the Ohio, which continued to give the settlements great trouble for some time subsequent, and also greatly to disturb the internal relations of the country generally. In addition to, and effects arising mainly from, these causes, Kentucky, at an early day during the foregoing period, began and continued for some years to manifest, with other parts of the southwest, considerable dissatisfaction. The government had permitted the Spaniards of the south to control the navigation of the Mississippi; many privations had come upon the people of the west in consequence, and a spirit of distrust had gradually given rise to a spirit of dissolution,† especially in Kentucky, which, at that period, and for some years later, yet formed a part of Virginia. Washing-

here begun, called it "Losantiville," the interpretation of which ran as follows: *Ville*, the town; *anti*, opposite to; *os*, the mouth; *L*, of Licking river; which, at the time, was considered, we believe, a pretty fine effort on the part of Mr. Filson.

*" A corrupt orthography and abridgement of the French term Au, or Aux Miamis; as Au Cas is a corruption of Au Kaskaskias, to Kaskaskia."---History of Kentucky.

†A person, thought to have been a man by the name of Green, of Louisville, Kentucky, writing to some person in New England, under date of December 4, 1786, said: "Our situation is as bad as it possibly can be, therefore every exertion to retrieve our circumstances must be manly, eligible and just. We can raise twenty thousand troops this side of the Allegheny and Apalachian Mountains, and the annual increase of them by emigration from other parts, is from two to four thousand.

"We have taken all the goods belonging to the Spanish merchants of Post Vincennes and the Illinois, and are determined they shall not trade up the river, provided they will not let us trade down it. Preparations are now being made here (if necessary) to drive the Spaniards from their settlements, at the mouth of the Mississippi. In case we are not countenanced and succored by the United States, (if we need it) our allegiance will be thrown off, and some other power applied to.

"Great Britain stands ready with open arms to receive and support us. They have already offered to open their resources for our supplies. When once re-united to them, 'farewell, a long farewell to all your boasted greatness.' The province of Canada and the inhabitants of these waters, of themselves, in time, will be able to conquer you. You are as ignorant of this country as Great Britain was of America. These are hints, which, if rightly improved, may be of service; if not, blame yourselves for the neglect."

ton had felt the pressure, and soon presented important suggestions, as he had done before the revolution, relative to the organization of commercial and navigation companies, as the best means of protecting and cementing the interests of the East and West.

In a letter to Governor Harrison in this year, (1784) he strenuously urged the importance of binding together all parts of the Union, and especially the West and East, with the indissoluble bonds of interest, with a view to prevent the formation of commercial, and, in consequence, political connections with either the *Spaniards on the South, or the English on the North*; and recommended the speedy survey of the Potomac and James rivers; of the portage to the waters of the Ohio; of the Muskingum; and the portage from that river to the Cuyahoga; for the purpose of opening a water communication for the commerce of the Ohio and the lakes, to the seaboard, and denominated it as an object of great political and commercial importance.

To Richard Henry Lee, in the same year, Washington wrote: "Would it not be worthy of the wisdom and attention of Congress to have the western waters well explored, the navigation of them fully ascertained and accurately laid down, and a complete and perfect map made of the country, at least as far westerly as the Miamis, running into the Ohio, and Lake Erie, and to see how the waters of these communicate with the river St. Joseph, which empties into Lake Michigan, and with the Wabash? *for I cannot forbear observing that the Miami village* points to a very important post for the Union.*"

The Indian, though usually called a savage, and doubtless, as a general rule in earlier days, properly so, yet possessed, with all, a singular intelligence. From the first dealings of the colonists of Virginia with the famous Powhattans; the Pilgrims, at Plymouth; with Massasoit and his son Metacomet, (King Phillip) of the Wampanoags, about Mount Hope, to the later settlements of the West and the various tribes of the southwest, they ever exhibited a peculiar knowledge of etiquette, and seldom forgot this sense of regard even for their enemies or the most presumptive intruders, where the chiefs and sachems could exercise a voice.

It was not a custom with the French, at any time at any of the points of their settlements in the West, to make large purchases of lands from the Indians; small tracts about their settlements invariably served to supply their wants; and at the treaty of Paris, in 1763, these small grants, about the forts of Detroit, Vincennes, Kaskaskia, Cahokia, &c., were all that they ceded to the English.

*At this point. I have italicised this part of Washington's letter to call attention to the importance then attached to the present site of Fort Wayne. Had dissolution been attempted at any time during the above period, and the British called to the aid of the West, this would have been an admirable base for the operations of the colonial army, once having fortified themselves and prepared for a siege—a fact which Washington seems most fully to have been aware of.

Following close upon this treaty came the war and the defeat of Pontiac; and in 1768, a grant by the Iroquois or Six Nations, at Fort Stanwix, or the land *south* of the Ohio, which grant was not respected by those hunting on the grounds thus conveyed. Dunmore's War, of 1774, was concluded without any transfer of lands to the whites; and, at the close of the revolution, in 1783, when Great Britain transferred her western claims to the United States, she conveyed nothing but what she had previously received from France, excepting the guarantee of the Six Nations and the southern tribes to a part of the land *south* of the Ohio; while none of the territory claimed by the Miamies, western Delawares, Shawanoes, Wyandotts or Hurons, and some other tribes still to the west and north, was ceded to the United States by this treaty.

But a different view was taken of the matter by Congress at this period; and concluding that the treaty guaranteed to the United States the full right to all territory then transferred, and, at the same time, considering the right of the Indians to the territory as forfeited by acts of warfare against the colonial government during the struggle for Independence, made no movement towards a purchase of the lands from the Indians, but began to form treaties of peace with them, and to suggest its own boundary lines.

It was in this way, in October, 1784, at the second treaty of Stanwix, that the United States obtained the right possessed by the Iroquois to the western territory, north and south of the Ohio; and though publicly and honorably concluded, its legality was yet questioned by many of the Iroquois, the basis of their opposition resting upon the fact that that treaty was with only a part of the Indian tribes; and that it was the desire of the tribes that the United States Government should treat with them as a body, including all the Indians bordering upon the lakes of the north.

The provisions of October, 1783, had arranged for one great council of all the tribes; but in the month of March following, 1784, this provision was changed to that of holding councils with each separate tribe or nation; and the commissioners appointed by the Government to superintend these affairs, refusing to pay further attention to the subject of a general council with the northern tribes, in October, 1784, as against the wishes of Red Jacket, Brant, and other chiefs, of the Iroquois, terminated the treaty of Fort Stanwix.

After which, in January, of the following year, (1785), a treaty was concluded with the Wyandotts, Delawares, Chipewas, and Ottawas; but the legality of the former treaty seems not then to have been questioned, by the Wyandotts and Delawares, at least; and yet it was asserted at a general council of some sixteen tribes of northwestern Indians, in 1793, that the treaties of Forts Stanwix, McIntosh, and Finney, (the latter at the mouth of the Great Miami,) were the result of intimidation, and held only with single tribes, at which, they asserted that the Indians had been invited to form treaties of peace, but, instead, forced to make cessions of land.

In January, 1786, a third treaty was held by the United States, at Fort Finney, with the Shawanoes; and the Wabash tribes being invited to be present, would not go. In 1789, confirmatory of preceding treaties, the fourth and fifth treaties were held at Fort Harmar, one with the Six Nations; the other with the Wyandotts, Delawares, Ottawas, Chippewas, Pottawattamies, and Sacs; and it seems, from speeches made at a subsequent council of the confederated tribes, more particularly of the lake, (1793) that they would not accept those treaties as at all binding upon them. Said one of the chiefs at this latter council:

"Brothers: We are in possession of the speeches and letters which passed on that occasion, (council convened by Governor Arthur St. Clair, in 1788,) between those deputied by the confederate Indians, and Gov. St. Clair, the commissioner of the United States. These papers prove that your said commissioner, in the beginning of the year 1789, after having been informed by the general council of the preceding fall that no bargain or sale of any part of these lands would be considered as valid or binding, unless agreed to by a general council, nevertheless persisted in collecting together a few chiefs of two or three nations only, and with them held a treaty for the cession of an immense country, in which they were no more interested, than as a branch of the general confederacy, and who were in no manner authorized to make any grant or cession whatever.

"Brothers: How then was it possible for you to expect to enjoy peace, and quietly to hold these lands, when your commissioner was informed, long before he held the treaty of Fort Harmar, that the consent of a general council was absolutely necessary for the sale of any part of these lands to the United States."*

From these facts, in part, at least, it will be seen why the expeditions of 1790–'91, and 1793–'4, with the efforts of 1811–'12 and '13, met with such stubborn and relentless resistence from the Miamies and other tribes, as detailed in subsequent pages. The impression that they would, without remuneration or mercy be despoiled of their lands and at length driven away, seems to have gained possession of the tribes generally of the northwest before and during the early campaigns of Harmar, St. Clair, and Wayne; and the Miamies,—though, as it would seem from Gamelin's journal, a strong spirit of unity did not prevail among the different tribes, before and during 1780,—led the way under the lead of Little Turtle, with formidable effect.

With a feeling of bitterness and revenge towards the United States, small bands of Indians had begun, in the spring of 1789 to attack the settlements along the western borders of Virginia and Kentucky.

*"Western Annals," pages 522, 523, 524.

The Secretary of War of the period, General Knox, in a report to the President, 15th of June, 1789, presented this subject as follows:

"By information from Brigd'r-General Harmar, the commanding officer of the troops on the frontier, it appears that several murders have been lately committed on the inhabitants, by small parties of Indians, probably from the Wabash country. Some of the said murders having been perpetrated on the south side of the Ohio, the inhabitants on the waters of that river are exceedingly alarmed, for the extent of six or seven hundred miles along the same. It is to be observed that the United States have not formed any treaties with the Wabash Indians; on the contrary, since the conclusion of the war with Great Britain, hostilities have almost constantly existed between the people of Kentucky and the said Indians. The injuries and murders have been so reciprocal that it would be a point of critical investigation to know on which side they have been the greatest. Some of the inhabitants of Kentucky during the past year, roused by recent injuries, made an incursion into the Wabash country, and possessing an equal aversion to all bearing the the name of Indians, they destroyed a number of peaceable Piankeshaws* who prided themselves in their attachment to the United States. Things being thus circumstanced, it is greatly to be apprehended that hostilities may be so far extended as to involve the Indian tribes with whom the United States have recently made treaties. It is well known how strong the passion for war exists in the mind of a young savage, and how easily it may be inflamed, so as to disregard every precept of the older and wiser part of the tribes who may have a more just opinion of the force of a treaty. Hence, it results that unless some decisive measures are immediately adopted to terminate those mutual hostilities, they will probably become general among all the Indians northwest of the Ohio.

"In examining the question how the disturbances on the frontiers are to be quieted, two modes present themselves by which the object might perhaps be effected—the first of which is by raising an army and extirpating the refractory tribes entirely; or, secondly, by forming treaties of peace with them in which their rights and limits should be explicitly defined, and the treaties observed on the part of the United States with the most rigid justice, by punishing the whites who should violate the same.

"In considering the first mode, an inquiry would arise, *whether, under the existing circumstances of affairs, the United States have a clear right, consistently with the principles of justice and the laws of nature, to proceed to the destruction or expulsion of the savages on the Wabash, supposing the force for that object easily attainable.* It is presumable that a nation solicitous of establishing its character on the broad basis of justice, would not only hesi-

*The same, doubtless, under the lead of the "Grand Door," who gave so hearty a welcome to Capt. Helm, at Vincennes, after the capture of that post by Col. Clark.

tate at but reject every proposition to benefit itself by the injury of any neighboring community, however contemptible and weak it may be, either with respect to its manners or power. When it shall be considered that the Indians derive their subsistence chiefly by hunting, and that, according to fixed principles, their population is in proportion to the facility with which they procure their food, it would most probably be found that the expulsion or destruction of the Indian tribes have nearly the same effect; for if they are removed from their usual hunting-grounds, they must necessarily encroach on the hunting-grounds of another tribe, who will not suffer the encroachment with impunity—hence they destroy each other. The Indians, being the prior occupants, possess the right of the soil. It can not be taken from them unless by their free consent, or by the right of conquest in case of a just war. To dispossess them on any other principle, would be a gross violation of the fundamental laws of nature, and of that distributive justice which is the glory of a nation. But if it should be decided, on an abstract view of the question, to be just to remove by force the Wabash Indians from the territory they occupy, the finances of the United States would not at present admit of the operation.

"By the best and latest information, it appears that on the Wabash and its communications, there are from fifteen hundred to two thousand warriors. An expedition against them, with a view of extirpating them, or destroying their towns, could not be undertaken, with a probability of success, with less than an army of two thousand five hundred men. The regular troops of the United States on the frontiers are less than six hundred:* of that number not more than four hundred could be collected from the posts for the purpose of the expedition. To raise, pay, feed, arm, and equip one thousand nine hundred additional men, with the necessary officers, for six months, and to provide every thing in the hospital and quartermaster's line, would require the sum of two hundred thousand dollars, a sum far exceeding the ability of the United States to advance, consistently with a due regard to other indispensable objects."

On the 26th of August, 1789, about two hundred mounted volunteers, under the command of Colonel John Hardin, marched from the Falls of the Ohio to attack some of the Indian towns on the Wabash. This expedition returned to the Falls on the 28th of September, without the loss of a man—having killed six Indians, plundered and burnt one deserted village, and destroyed a considerable quantity of corn.†

In a letter, addressed to President Washington, bearing date "September, 14, 1789," Governor St. Clair said:

"The constant hostilities between the Indians who live upon the river Wabash and the people of Kentucky, must necessarily be attended with such embarrassing circumstances to the government

*Detachments of regular troops were stationed at Fort Pitt, Fort Harmar, Fort Washington, Fort Steuben, (at the Falls of the Ohio,) and at Post Vincennes.—His. Ind.

†Dillon.

of the northwestern territory, that I am induced to request you will be pleased to take the matter into consideration, and give me the orders you may think proper. It is not to be expected, sir, that the Kentucky people will or can submit patiently to the cruelties and depredations of those savages. They are in the habit of retaliation, perhaps without attending precisely to the nations from which the injuries are received. They will continue to retaliate, or they will apply to the governor of the northwestern territory (through which the Indians must pass to attack them) for redress. If he can not redress them, (and in the present circumstances he cannot,) they also will march through that country to redress themselves, and the government will be laid prostrate. The United State, on the other hand, are at peace with several of the nations, and should the resentment of these people [the Kentuckians] fall upon any of them, which it is likely enough to happen, very bad consequences may follow. For it must appear to them [the Indians] that the United States either pay no regard to their treaties, or that they are unable or unwilling to carry their engagement into effect. * * * They will unite with the hostile nations, prudently preferring open war to a delusive and uncertain peace."

Being empowered, by an act of Congress of the 29th of September, 1789, to call out the militia of the several States for the protection of the frontier settlements, President Washington, on the 6th of Oct., 1789, addressed Governor St. Clair officially as follows:

"It is highly necessary that I should, as soon as possible, possess full information whether the Wabash and Illinois Indians are most inclined for war or peace. If for the former, it is proper that I should be informed of the means which will most probably induce them to peace. If a peace can be established with the said Indians on reasonable terms, the interests of the United States dictate that it should be effected as soon as possible. You will, therefore, inform the said Indians of the disposition of the general government on this subject, and of their reasonable desire that there should be a cessation of hostilities as a prelude to a treaty.

"If, however, notwithstanding your intimations to them, they should continue their hostilities, or meditate any incursion against the frontiers of Virginia and Pennsylvania, or against any of the troops or posts of the United States, and it should appear to you that the time of execution would be so near as to forbid your transmitting the information to me, and receiving my orders thereon, then you are hereby authorized and empowered, in my name, to call on the lieutenants of the nearest counties of Virginia and Pennsylvania for such detachments of militia as you may judge proper, not exceeding, however, one thousand from Virginia and five hundred from Pennsylvania. * * * The said militia to act in conjunction with the Federal troops in such operations, offensive or defensive, as you and the commanding officer of the troops, conjointly, shall judge necessary for the public service, and the protection of the inhabitants and the posts. The said militia, while in actual service, to be on the continental establishment of pay and rations; they are to arm and equip themselves, but to be furnished with public ammunition if necessary; and no charge for the pay of said militia will be valid unless supported by regular musters made by a field or other officer of the Federal troops.

"I would have it observed, forcibly, that a war with the Wabash Indians ought to be avoided by all means consistently with the security of the troops and the national dignity. In the exercise of the present indiscriminate hostilities, it is extremely difficult, if not impossible, to say that a war without further measures would be just on the part of the United States. But if, after manifesting clearly to the Indians the disposition of the general government for the preservation of peace and the extension of a just protection to the said Indians, they should continue their incursions, the United States will be constrained to punish them with severity.

"You will also proceed, as soon as you can, with safety, to execute the orders of the late Congress, respecting the inhabitants at Post Vincennes, and at the Kaskaskias, and the other villages on the Mississippi. It is a circumstance of some importance, that the said inhabitants should, as soon as possible, possess the lands to which they are entitled, by some known and fixed principles."

The last paragraph of the foregoing instructions was based upon the resolutions of Congress, of the 20th June and 29th August, 1788.* By these resolutions, provisions were made for confirming in their possessions and titles the French and Canadian inhabitants, and other settlers, about Kaskaskia and post Vincennes, who, on or before the year 1783, had professed themselves citizens of the United States, or any of them. By the same resolutions, a tract of four hundred acres of land was donated to each head of a family of this description of settlers.†

About the 1st of January, 1790, Governor St. Clair, with the judges of the supreme court of the territory, descended the river Ohio, from Marietta to Fort Washington, at Losantiville. At this place the governor laid out the county of Hamilton, appointed magistrates and other civil officers for the administration of justice in that county, and induced the proprietors of the little village to change its name from Losantiville to Cincinnati. On the 8th of January, 1790, St. Clair and Winthrop Sargent, secretary of the territory, arrived at Clarksville, whence they proceeded to the Illinois country, to organize the government in that quarter, and to carry into effect the resolutions of Congress relative to the lands and settlers about Kaskaskia and Post Vincennes. Before the governor left Clarksville, however, he sent to Major Hamtramck, the commanding officer at Post Vincennes, dispatches containing speeches which were addressed to the Indian tribes on the Wabash.‡

*Old Journals, vol. iv, 823, 858. †Dillon. ‡Ibid.

Having received the instructions of Gov. St. Clair, after the necessary preparations, Major Hamtramck, then commanding at Post Vincennes, on the 15th of April, despatched Antoine Gamelin from that point with the speeches of St. Clair to the tribes of the Wabash. Reaching the Indian settlements, Mr. Gamelin delivered the speeches at all the villages bordering this stream, and came as far eastward as the Miami village, opposite the present site of Fort Wayne. The following is the journal of Gamelin, much of which relates to his conference at the Miami village here; and will give the imaginative reader quite a fair view of the spirit of the Miamies at this point at that period. Says the journal of Gamelin:

"The first village I arrived to, is called Kikapouguoi. The name of the chief of this village is called Les Jambes Croches. Him and his tribe have a good heart, and accepted the speech. The second village is at the river du Vermillion, called Piankeshaws. The first chief and all his warriors, were well pleased with the speeches concerning the peace: but they said they could not give presently a proper answer, before they consult the Miami nation, their eldest brethren. They desired me to proceed to the Miami town, (Ke-ki-ong-gay,) and, by coming back, to let them know what reception I got from them. The said head chief told me that he thought the nations of the lake had a bad heart, and were ill disposed for the Americans: that the speeches would not be received, particularly by the Shawnees at Miamitown. * * The 11th of April, I reached a tribe of Kickapoos. The head chief and all the warriors being assembled, I gave them two branches of white wampum, with the speeches of his excellency Arthur St. Clair, and those of Major Hamtramck. It must be observed that the speeches have been in another hand before me. The messenger could not proceed further than the Vermillion, on account of some private wrangling between the interpreter and some chief men of the tribe. Moreover, something in the speech displeased them very much, which is included in the third article, which says, '*I do now make you the offer of peace: accept it, or reject it, as you please.*' These words appeared to displease all the tribes to whom the first messenger was sent. They told me they were menacing; and finding that it might have a bad effect, I took upon myself to exclude them; and, after making some apology, they answered that he and his tribe were pleased with my speech, and that I could go up without danger, but they could not presently give me an answer, having some warriors absent, and without consulting the Ouiatenons, being the owners of their lands. They desired me to stop at Quitepiconnæ, [Tippecanoe,] that they would have the chiefs and warriors of Ouiatenons and those of their nation assembled there, and would receive a proper answer. They said that they expected by me a draught of milk from the great chief, and the commanding officer of the post, for to put the old people in good humor; also some powder and ball for the young men for hunting, and to get some good broth for their women and children: that I should know a bearer of speeches should never be with empty hands. They promised me to keep their young men from stealing, and to send speeches to their nations in the prairies for to do the same.

"The 14th April the Ouiatenons and the Kickapoos were assembled. After my speech, one of the head chiefs got up and told me 'You, Gamelin, my friend and son-in-law, we are pleased to see in our village, and to hear by your mouth, the good words of the great chief. We thought to receive a few words from the French people; but I see the contrary. None but the Big Knife is sending speeches to us. You know that we can terminate nothing without the consent of our brethren the Miamis. I invite you to proceed to their village, and to speak to them. There is one thing in your speech I do not like: I will not tell of it: even was I drunk, I would perceive it: but our elder brethren will certainly take notice of it in your speech. You invite us to stop our young men. It is impossible to do it, being constantly encouraged by the British.' Another chief got up and said—'The Americans are very flattering in their speeches; many times our nation went to their rendezvous. I was once myself. Some of our chiefs died on the route; and we always came back all naked: and you, Gamelin, you come with speech, with empty hands.' Another chief got up and said to his young men, 'If we are poor, and dressed in deer skins, it is our own fault. Our French traders are leaving us and our villages, because you plunder them every day; and it is time for us to have another conduct.' Another chief got up and said—'Know ye that the village of Ouiatenon is the sepulcher of all our ancestors. The chief of America invites us to go to him if we are for peace. He has not his leg broke, having been able to go as far as the Illinois. He might come here himself; and we should be glad to see him at our village. We confess that we accepted the ax, but it is by the reproach we continually receive from the English and other nations, which received the ax first, calling us women: at the present time they invite our young men to war. As to the old people, they are wishing for peace.' They could not give me an answer before they receive advice from the Miamis, their elder brethren.

"The 18th April I arrived at the river a l'Anguille, [Eel river.] The chief of the village,* and those of war were not present. I explained the speeches to some of the tribe. They said they were well pleased; but they could not give me an answer, their chief men being absent. They desired me to stop at their village coming back; and they sent with me one of their men for to hear the answer of their eldest brethren.

"The 23d April I arrived at the Miami town.† The next day I

*The site of this village is on the north side of Eel river, six miles above the point of the junction of this stream with the Wabash.

†At this point.

got the Miami nation, the Shawanees, and Delawares all assembled. I gave to each nation two branches of wampum, and began the speeches, before the French and English traders, being invited by the chiefs to be present, having told them myself I would be glad to have them present, having nothing to say against any body. After the speech, I showed them the treaty concluded at Muskingum, [Fort Harmar,] between his excellency, Governor St. Clair, and sundry nations, which displeased them. I told them that the purpose of this present time was not to submit them to any condition, but to offer them the peace, which made disappear their displeasure. The great chief told me that he was pleased with the speech; that he would soon give me an answer. In a private discourse with the great chief, he told me not to mind what the Shawanees would tell me, having a bad heart, and being the pertubators of all the nations. He said the Miamis had a bad name, on account of the mischief done on the river Ohio; but he told me, it was not occasioned by his young men, but by the Shawanees; his young men going out only for to hunt.

"The 25th of April, Blue Jacket, chief warrior of the Shawanees, invited me to go to his house, and told me—'My friend, by the name and consent of the Shawanees and Delawares, I will speak to you. We are all sensible of your speech, and pleased with it: but, after consultation, we can not give an answer without hearing from our father at Detroit; and we are determined to give you back the two branches of wampum, and to send you to Detroit to see and hear the chief, or to stay here twenty nights for to receive his answer. From all quarters we receive speeches from the Americans, and not one is alike. We suppose that they intend to deceive us. Then take back your branches of wampum.'

"The 26th, five Pottawattamies arrived here with two negro men, which they sold to English traders. The next day I went to the great chief of the Miamis, called Le Gris. His chief warrior was present. I told him how I had been served by the Shawanees. He answered me that he had heard of it: that the said nations behaved contrary to his intentions. He desired me not to mind those strangers, and that he would soon give me a positive answer.

"The 28th of April, the great chief desired me to call at the French trader's and receive his answer. 'Don't take bad,' said he, 'of what I am to tell you. You may go back when you please. We can not give you a positive answer. We must send your speeches to all our neighbors, and to the lake nations. We can not give a definitive answer without consulting the commandant at Detroit.' And he desired me to render him the two branches of wampum refused by the Shawanees; also a copy of speeches in writing. He promised me that, in thirty nights, he would send an answer to Post Vincennes by a young man of each nation. He was well pleased with the speeches, and said to be worthy of attention, and should be communicated to all their confederates, *having resolved among them not do anything without a unanimous consent.* I agreed to his requisitions, and rendered him the two branches of wampum and a copy of the speech. Afterward he told me that the Five Nations, so called, or Iroquois, were training something; that five of them, and three Wyandotts, were in this village with branches of wampum. He could not tell me presently their purpose, but he said I would know of it very soon.

"The same day Blue Jacket, chief of the Shawanees, invited me to his house for supper; and, before the other chiefs, told me that, after another deliberation, they thought necessary that I should go myself to Detroit for to see the commandant, who would get all his children assembled to hear my speech. I told them I would not answer them in the night; that I was not ashamed to speak before the sun.

"The 29th of April I got them all assembled. I told them that I was not to go to Detroit; that the speeches were directed to the nations of the river Wabash and the Miami; and that, for to prove the sincerity of the speech, and the heart of Governor St. Clair, I have willingly given a copy of the speeches to be shown to the commandant of Detroit; and, according to a letter wrote by the commandant of Detroit to the Miamis, Shawanees, and Delawares, mentioning to you to be peaceable with the Americans, I would go to him very willingly, if it was in my directions, being sensible of his sentiments. I told them I had nothing to say to the commandant; neither him to me. You must immediately resolve, if you intend to take me to Detroit, or else I am to go back as soon as possible. Blue Jacket got up and told me, 'My friend, we are well pleased with what you say. Our intention is not to force you to go to Detroit. It is only a proposal, thinking it for the best. Our answer is the same as the Miamis. We will send, in thirty nights, a full and positive answer by a young man of each nation by writing to Post Vincennes.' In the evening, Blue Jacket, chief of the Shawanees, having taken me to supper with him, told me, in a private manner, that the Shawanee nation was in doubt of the sincerity of the Big Knives, so called, having been already deceived by them. That they had first destroyed their lands, put out their fire, and sent away their young men, being a hunting, without a mouthful of meat; also had taken away their women—wherefore, many of them would, with a great deal of pain, forget these affronts. Moreever, that some other nations were apprehending that offers of peace would, may be, tend to take away, by degrees, their lands, and would serve them as they did before: a certain proof that they intend to encroach on our lands, is their new settlement on the Ohio. If they don't keep this side [of the Ohio] clear, it will never be a proper reconcilement with the nations Shawanees, Iroquois, Wyandotts, and perhaps many others. Le Gris, chief of the Miamis, asked me, in a private discourse, what chiefs had made a treaty with the Americans at Muskingdum [Fort Harmar]? I answered him that their names were mentioned in the treaty. He told me he had heard of it some time ago; but they are not chiefs, neither delegates, who made that treaty—they are only young men who, without authority and instructions from their chiefs, have concluded that treaty, which will not be approved. They went to the treaty clandestinely, and they intend to make mention of it in the next council to be held.

"The 2d of May I came back to the river a l'Anguille. One of the chief men of the tribe being witness of the council at Miami town, repeated the whole to them; and whereas, the first chief was absent, they said they could not for the present time give answer, but they were willing to join their speech to those of their eldest brethren. 'To give you proof of an open heart, we let you know that one of our chiefs is gone to war on the Americans; but it was before we heard of you, for certain they would not have been gone thither.' They also told me that a few days after I passed their village seventy warriors, Chippewas and Ottawas, from Michilimacinac, arrived there. Some of them were Pottawattamies, who, meeting in their route, the Chippewas and Ottawas, joined them. 'We told them what we heard by you; that your speech is fair and true. We could not stop them from going to war. The Pottawattamies told us that, as the Chippewas and Ottawas were more numerous than them, they were forced to follow them.'

"The 3d of May I got to the Weas. They told me that they were waiting for an answer from their eldest brethren. 'We approve very much our brethren for not to give a definitive answer, without informing of it all the lake Nations; that Detroit was the place where the fire was lighted; then it ought first to be put out there; that the English commandant is their father, since he threw down our French father. They could do nothing without his approbation.'

"The 4th of May I arrived at the village of the Kickapoos. The chief, presenting me two branches of wampum, black and white, said: 'My son, we can not stop our young men from going to war. Every day some set off clandestinely for that purpose. After such behavior from our young men, we are ashamed to say to the great chief at the Illinois and of the Post Vincennnes, that we are busy about some good affairs for the reconcilement; but be persuaded that we will speak to them continually concerning the peace; and that, when our eldest brethren will have sent their answer, we will join ours to it.'

"The 5th of May I arrived at Vermillion. I found nobody but two chiefs; all the rest were gone a hunting. They told me they had nothing else to say but what I was told going up."

Gov. St. Clair being at Kaskaskia, in the fore part of the month of June of this year, (1790) received from Major Hamtramck the following, bearing date, "Post Vincennes, May 22d, 1790:" "I now inclose the proceedings of Mr. Gamelin, by which your excellency can have no great hopes of bringing the Indians to a peace with the United States. The 8th of May, Gamelin arrived, and on the 11th some merchants arrived and informed me that, as soon as Gamelin had passed their villages on his return, all the Indians had gone to war; that a large party of Indians from Michilemacinac, and some Pottawattamies, had gone to Kentucky; and that three days after Gamelin had left the Miami (village—here) an American was brought there and burnt."*

* According to the statement of chief Richardville, Mr. Peltier, and others, says Mr. J. L. Williams, in his researches, page 11, "Historical Sketch of the First Presbyterian Church of Fort Wayne," "the extreme point of land just below the mouth of the St. Joseph, now so attractive in rural peaceful beauty, is said to have been the accustomed place for burning prisoners." Some years ago, chief Richardville also pointed out a spot, to an old citizen of Fort Wayne, lying near Mr. J. S. Mason's line, a few rods from a grave-yard on the west side of the Bluffton Plank Road, where he said a Kentuckian had been burned by the Indians sometime during 1812. This, as the reader is already aware, being long a familiar and beloved spot, not only with the Miamies, but many other friendly tribes, to hold and maintain it, they seem to have early devised many plans and means of security, both against their enemies of other savage tribes and the whites, at different periods. At a very early time, the Miamies were called and familiarly known among the tribes of the country as "LINNEWAYS," or "MINNEWAYS," which, as with the name MENOMENIES, signified MEN. As a means of terror to their enemies, the Minneways or Miamies had early formed here what was commonly known as a "man-eating society," which, to make it the more fearful to their opponents, was firmly established on a hereditary basis, confined to one family alone, whose descendants continued to exercise, by right of descent, the savage rites and duties of the man-eating family. One Major Thomas Forsyth, who lived for a period of more than twenty years among the Sauks and Fox Indians, in a written narration of these two tribes, first published in Drake's "Life of Black Hawk," as early as 1838, said: "More than a century ago, all the country, commencing above Rock river, and running down the Mississippi to the mouth of the Ohio, up that river to the mouth of the Wabash, thence up that river to Fort Wayne, thence down the Miami of the Lake some distance, thence north to the St. Joseph's and Chicago; also the country lying south of the Des Moines, down perhaps, to the Mississippi, was inhabited by a numerous nation of Indians, who called themselves Linneway, and were called by others, Minneway, signifying "men." This great nation was divided into several bands, and inhabited different parts of this extensive region, as follows: The Michigamies, the country south of the Des Moines; the Cahokias that east of the present village of Cahokia in Illinois; the Kaskaskias that east of the town of that name; the Tamarois had their village nearly central between Cahokia and Kaskaskia; the Piankeshaws near Vincennes; the Weas up the Wabash; the Miamies on the head waters of the Miami of the Lakes, on St. Joseph's river and at Chicago. The Piankeshaws, Weas and Miamies, must at this time have hunted south towards and on the Ohio. The Peorias, another band of the same nation, lived and hunted on the Illinois river: The Mascos or Mascontins, called by the French GENS DES PRARIES, lived and hunted on the great prairies, between the Wabash and Illinois rivers. All these different bands of the Minneway nation, spoke the language of the present Miamies, and the whole considered themselves as one and the same people; yet from their local situation, and having no standard to go by, their language became broken up into different dialects. These Indians, the Minneways, were attacked by a general confederacy of other nations, such as the Sauks and Foxes, resident at Green Bay and on the Ouisconsin; the Sioux, whose frontiers extended south to the river des Moines: the Chippeways, Ottoways, and Potawatimies from the lakes, and also the Cherokees and Choctaws from the south. The war continued for a great many years and until that great nation the Minneways were destroyed, except a few Miamies and Weas on the Wabash, and a few who are scattered among strangers. Of the Kaskaskias, owing to their wars and their fondness for spirituous liquors, there now (1826) remain but thirty or forty souls:—of the Peorias near St. Genevieve ten or fifteen; of the Piankeshaws forty or fifty. The Miamies are the most numerous; a few years ago they consisted of about four hundred souls. There do not exist at the present day (1826) more than five hundred souls of the once great and powerful Minneway or Illini nation. These Indians, the Minneways, are said to have been very cruel to their prisoners, not unfrequently burning them. I have

Being readily induced to believe, from the dispatches received from Hamtramck, that there was no possibility of forming a treaty of peace with the Miamie Indians and other tribes banded with them, Governor St. Clair determined to return to Fort Washington (Cincinnati,) with a view of consulting with General Harmar as to the expediency of an expedition against the hostile tribes; and, accordingly, on the 11th of June, he quit Kaskaskia, and by water, reached Fort Washington on the 13th of July.

Having consulted with General Harmar, and concluding to send a formidable force against the Indians about the head waters of the Wabash, by authority of President Washington, on the 15th of July (1790,) he addressed circular letters to a number of Lieutenants of the western counties (of Virginia, of which Kentucky was then a part) and Pennsylvania, for the purpose of raising one thousand militia in the former, and five hundred in the latter. The regular troops then in service in the west General Harmar estimated at about four hundred efficient men, with whom the militia were to operate as follows: Of the Virginia militia, 300 were to rendezvous at Fort Steuben, and, with a garrison at that post, to proceed to Vincennes, to join Major Hamtramck, who had orders to call to his aid the militia of that place. From thence to move up the Wabash, with a view of attacking such points among the Indian villages along that river as his force might seem adequate. The twelve hundred militia remaining were to join the regular troops, under General Harmar, at Fort Washington. That the British commandant at Detroit might know the true cause and course of the movement, on the 19th of September, Gov. St. Clair addressed a letter to him, which he sent by a private conveyance, assuring the said com-

heard of a certain family among the Miamies who were called man-eaters, as they were accustomed to make a feast of human flesh when a prisoner was killed. For these enormities, the Sauks and Foxes, when they took any of the Minneways prisoners, gave them up to their women to be buffeted to death. They speak also of the Mascontins with abhorrence, on account of their cruelties. The Sauks and Foxes have a historical legned of a severe battle having been fought opposite the mouth of the Iowa river, about fifty or sixty miles above the mouth of Rock riverr The Sauks and Foxes descended the Mississippi in canoes, and landing at the place above described, started east, towards the enemy: they had not gone far before they were attacked by a party of the Mascontins. The battle continued nearly all day; the Sauks and Foxes, for want of ammunition, finally gave way and fled to their canoes: the Mascontins pursued them and fought desperately, and left but few of the Sauks and Foxes to carry home the story of their defeat. Some forty or fifty years ago, the Sauks and Foxes attacked a small village of Peorias, about a mile below St. Louis and were there defeated. At a place on the Illinois river, called Little Rock, there were formerly killed by the Chippeways and Ottowas, a number of men, women and children of the Minneway nation. In 1800 the Kickapoos made a great slaughter of the Kaskaskia Indians. The Main-Pogue, or Potawatimie juggler, in 1801, killed a great many of the Piankeshaws on the Wabash."

In proof of the foregoing, relative to the society of man-eaters among the Indians at this point, General Lewis Cass, in a speech here, delivered at the canal celebration of July 4th 1843, in "Swinney's Grove," near the site of the presant Catholic cemetery, said:

"For many years during the frontier history of this place and region, the line of your canal was a bloody war-path, which has seen many a deed of horror. And this peaceful town has had its Moloch, and the records of human depravity furnish no more terrible examples of cruelty than were offered at his shrine. The Miami Indians, our predecessors in the occupation of this district, had a terrible institution whose origin and mandant that the purposes of the United States were pacific in so far as their relations to Great Britain were concerned; that the expedition was to quell the vindictive and intolerable spirit of the Indians towards the settlements, whither and against whom they had so long, so inhumanly, and destructively carried their savage warfare.

That the English, towards Lake Erie, notwithstanding this spirit of candor and courtesy on the part of St. Clair, gave aid to the Indians in their efforts against the United States during 1790–'91, the evidence is clear enough; but to what extent, was not fully known. The following paragraphs from a certificate of one Thomas Rhea, taken in the early part of 1790, will give some clue, at least, as to the aid then and subsequently rendered the Indians by the British:

"At this place, the *Miami*," said Rhea, in his account, "were Colonels Brant* and McKee, with his son Thomas; and Captains Bunbury and Silvie, of the British troops. These officers, &c., were all encamped on the south side of the Miami or Ottawa river, at the rapids above Lake Erie, about eighteen miles; they had clever houses, built chiefly by the Po'tawattamies and other Indians; in these they had stores of goods, with arms, ammunition and provision, which they issued to the Indians in great abundance, viz: corn, pork, peas, &c.

* Brant was a Mohawk chieftain, of considerable intelligence, educated at Philadelphia; a favorite of Sir William Johnson, and ever greatly attached to the British.—After the struggles of these periods, he took up his residence in Canada, where he died in 1807.

object have been lost in the darkness of aboriginal history, but which was continued to a late period, and whose orgies were held upon the very spot where we now are. It was called the man-eating society, and it was the duty of its associates to eat such prisoners as were preserved and delivered to them for that purpose. The members of this society belonged to a particular family, and the dreadful inheritance descended to all the children, male and female. The duties it imposed could not be avoided, and the sanctions of religion were added to the obligations of immemorial usage. The feast was a solemn ceremony, at which the whole tribe was collected as actors or spectators. The miserable victim was bound to a stake, and burned at a slow fire, with all the refinements of cruelty, which savage ingenuity could invent. There was a traditionary ritual, which regulated with revolting precision, the whole course of procedure at these ceremonies Latterly the authority and obligations of the institution had declined, and I presume it has now wholly disappeared. But I have seen and conversed with the head of the family, the chief of the society, whose name was White Skin—with what feeling of disgust, I need not attempt to describe. I well knew an intelligent Canadian, who was present at one of the last sacrifices made at this horrible institution. The victim was a young American captured in Kentucky, towards the close of our Revolutionary War. Here where we are now assembled, in peace and security, celebrating the triumph of art and industry, within the memory of the present generation, our countrymen have been thus tortured, and murdered, and devoured. But, thank God, that council-fire is extinguished. The impious feast is over; the war-dance is ended; the war-song is sung: the war-drum is silent, and the Indian has departed to find, I hope, in the distant West, a comfortable residence, and I hope also to find, under the protection, and, if need be, under the power of the United States, a radical change in the institutions and general improvement in his morals and condition. A feeble remnant of the once powerful tribe, which formerly won their way to the dominion of this region, by blood, and by blood maintained it, have to-day appeared among us like passing shadows, flitting round the places that know them no more. Their resurrection, if I may so speak, is not the least impressive spectacle, which marks the progress of this imposing ceremony. They are the broken column which connect us with

"The Indians came to this place in parties of one, two, three, four and five hundred at a time, from different quarters, and received from Mr. McKee and the Indian officers, clothing, arms, ammunition, provisions, &c., and set out immediately for the upper Miami towns, where they understood the forces of the United States were bending their course, and in order to supply the Indians from other quarters collected there, pirogues, loaded with the above-mentioned articles, were sent up the Miami (Maumee) river, wrought by French Canadians."

About the middle of September, the Virginia militia began to gather about the mouth of Licking river, opposite Cincinnati, all of whom were, for the most part, badly armed and lacked for camp-kettles and axes; but were readily organized by General Harmar, and soon formed into three battalions, under Majors Hall, McMullen, and Ray, with Trotter, as Lieutenant-Colonel to lead them. About the 24th of September, came the militia of Pennsylvania to Fort Washington, who were also badly equipped, and many of whom were substitutes—"old, infirm men, and young boys." These were formed into one battalion, under Lieut.-Colonel Truby and Major Paul; while four battalions of militia, subject to General Harmar's command, were commanded by Col. John Hardin. Majors John Plasgrave Wylles, and John Doughty commanded the regular troops, in two small battalions. The artilery corps, with but three pieces of ordinance, was under the command of Captain William Ferguson; while under James Fontaine was placed a small battalion of light troops or mounted militia—amounting in all to about 1,453 regular and raw militia troops.

The militia under Col. Hardin, on the 26th of September, advanced from Fort Washington into the country, for the double purpose of opening a road for the artillery and to obtain feed for their cattle. On the 30th of September, the regular troops marched, commanded by General Harmar; and on the 3d day of October joined the militia.

A journal of the daily movements of the army was regularly kept by Captain John Armstrong, of the regulars, up to its arrival at the Miami village, at this point.

After an uninterrupted march of sixteen days, on the afternoon of the 15th of October, Colonel Hardin, with an advanced detachment, reached this point, and stole in upon the Miami village, only

the past. The edifice is in ruins, and the giant vegetation, which covered and protected it, lies as low as the once mighty structure, which was shelved in its recesses. They have come to witness the first great act of peace in our frontier history, as their presence here is the last in their own. The ceremonies upon which you heretofore gazed with interest, will never again be seen by the white man, in this seat of their former power. But thanks to our ascendancy, these representations are but a pageant; but a theatrical exhibition which, with barbarous motions, and sounds and contortions, shew how their ancestors conquered their enemies, and how they glutted their revenge in blood. To-day, this last of the race is here—to-morrow they will commence their journey towards the setting sun, where their fathers, agreeable to their rude faith, have preceded them, and where the red man will find rest and safety."

to find it deserted by men, women and children. A few cows, some vegetables, and about twenty thousand bushels of corn in the ear, save the wigwams, huts, and surrounding scenery, were all that greeted them; and the militia, in much disorder, soon began to move about in search of plunder.

On the 17th, about one o'clock, the main body of the army came up and crossed the Maumee to the village.

Major McMullen, of Col. Hardin's command, having discovered the tracks of women and children leading in a north-westerly direction, and so reported to General Harmar on his arrival, the latter determined at once upon an effort to discover their place of rendezvous; and, to that end, on the morning of the 18th, detailed Col. Trotter, Major Hall, Major Ray, and Major McMullen, with three hundred men, among whom were thirty regulars, forty light-horse, and two hundred and thirty active riflemen. Furnished with three days' provision, they were ordered to reconnoiter the country around the village. About one mile from the encampment, an Indian on horseback was discovered, pursued, and killed, by a part of the detachment, under Trotter; and before returning to the main body of the party, another Indian was seen, "when the four field officers left their commands, and pursued him, leaving the troops for the space of about half an hour without any direction whatever." Being intercepted by the light-horsemen, one of which party he had wounded, the Indian was at length killed. Changing the route of his detatchment, and moving in different directions, till night, Col. Trotter again, unexpectedly to, and without the approbation of General Harmar, returned to the Miami village.

In consequence of the disorderly course of the militia on their arrival at the village, in their desire for plunder, General Harmar ordered cannon to be fired for the purpose of calling them to their ranks, and also harangued the officers on the bad results liable to follow such indifference. On the 18th he issued the following general order:

"CAMP AT THE MIAMI VILLAGE, Oct. 18, 1790.

"The general is much mortified at the unsoldier-like behavior of many of the men in the army, who make it a practice to straggle from the camp in search of plunder. He, in the most positive terms, forbids this practice in future, and the guards will be answerable to prevent it. No party is to go beyond the line of sentinels without a commissioned officer, who, if of the militia, will apply to Colonel Hardin for his orders. The regular troops will apply to the general. All the plunder that may be hereafter collected, will be equally distributed among the army. The kettles, and every other article already taken, are to be collected by the commanding officers of batalions, and to be delivered to-morrow morning to Mr. Belli, the quartermaster, that a fair distribution may take place. The rolls are to be called at troop and retreat beating, and every man absent is to be reported. The general expects that these orders will be pointedly attended to: they are to be read to the troops this evening. The army is to march to-morrow morning early for their new encampment at Chillicothe,* about two miles from hence.

"JOSIAH HARMAR, BRIGADIER-GENERAL."

Col. Hardin, having asked for the command of the troops returned to camp under Trotter, for the remaining two days, Gen. Harmar readily complied; and on the next day, (19th) Col. Hardin led the detachment along an Indian trail to the northwest, in the direction of the Kickapoo villages. Coming to a point, near a morass, some five miles distant from the confluence of the St. Mary and St. Joseph rivers, where, on the preceding day, there had been an Indian encampment, the detachment came to a halt, and were soon stationed at different points, in readiness for an attack, should the enemy still be near. A half hour passed, and no sign of the enemy. The order now being given to the companies in the front to advance, the company under Faulkner, not having received the order of march, a neglect on the part of Col. Hardin, was left behind. Having advanced some three miles, two Indians afoot, with packs, were discovered; but, the brush being thick, and suddenly throwing aside their burdens at the sight of the detachment, were soon lost sight of and escaped. The absence of Faulkner at this time becoming apparent, Major Fontaine, with a portion of the cavalry, was at once sent in pursuit of him, with the supposition that he was lost.

The report of a gun, in front of the detachment, soon fell upon the attentive ear of Captain Armstrong, in command of the regulars—an alarm gun, perhaps, suggested he. He had discovered the "tracks of a horse that had come down the road and returned." These facts were readily conveyed to the ear of Colonel Hardin. Captain Armstrong now observed the fires of the Indians—they were only discernible in the distance. Caution was large in the soul of Armstrong. Hardin thought the Indians would not fight, and moved forward, in the direction of the fires, neither giving orders or preparing for an attack. The little army of three hundred were now strangely separated—they were in the forest, several miles from camp. The enemy were in ambush—were numerous† —and Me-che-cannah-quah,—Little Turtle—was their leader. Hardin continued to advance, and the columns moved forward in obedience to orders. Behind the fires lay the red men, hidden from view, with guns leveled. Steadily the broken detachment moved forward, under the intrepid control of their commander; and no sooner had they approached the fires than a terrible volley was opened upon them from behind the smoking entrenchments. The shock was sudden—the columns were unprepared for it. The mi-

*A Shawanoe village.

†Thought by some to have been as many as seven hundred—by others only about one hundred. The locality of this engagement was near Eel River, about the point where the Goshen State Road crosses this stream, now known as "Heller's Corners."

litia were panic stricken, and all but nine broke the ranks and began a precipitate flight for the camp of Gen. Harmar. Hardin had retreated with them, and in vain strove to rally them. The resolute regulars bravely faced the enemy, and returned the fire. The nine remaining militia were pierced by the balls of the enemy, and twenty-two of the regulars fell, while Captain Armstrong, Ensign Hartshorn, and some five or six privates, alone made their escape, and reached the camp again at the village. The victory was with the Indians, and the retreating columns all reached the camp of Harmer without further loss.

Having, after the departure of Hardin and the detachment in the morning, destroyed the Miami village, Harmar, in the meantime, had moved about two miles down the Maumee, to the Shawanoe village, known as Chillicothe, and on the 20th issued the following orders:

"CAMP AT CHILLICOTHE, *one of the Shawanese towns, on the Omee* [*Maumee*] *river*, Oct. 20th, 1790.

"The party under command of Captain Strong is ordered to burn and destroy every house and wigwam in this village, together with all the corn, etc., which he can collect. A party of one hundred men (militia), properly officered, under the command of Col. Hardin, is to burn and destroy effectually, this afternoon, the Pickaway town,* with all the corn, etc., which he can find in it and its vicinity.

"The cause of the detatchment being worsted yesterday, was entirely owing to the shameful, cowardly conduct of the militia, who ran away, and threw down their arms, without firing scarcely a single gun. In returning to Fort Washington, if any officer or men presume to quit the ranks, or not to march in the form that they are ordered, the general will most assuredly order the artillery to fire on them. He hopes the check they received yesterday will make them in future obedient to orders."

"JOSIAH HARMAR, BRIGADIER-GENERAL."

From the scene of the yet smoking and charred remains of the Indian village of Chillicothe,† at ten o'clock on the morning of the 21st, the army under Harmar took up its line of march towards Fort Washington, and proceeded about seven miles, when a halt was made, and the army encamped for the night.

The evening was clear and beautiful—one of those glorious nights in the month of October, when the stars, all in harmony, with no clouds intervening between the earth and the etherial blue to

*A Shawanoe village.

†The scene of this village, some two miles below Fort Wayne, on the Maumee, was about the site of the residence of Mrs. Phelps. Says Mr. J. W. Dawson, in his researches, concerning the history of Fort Wayne, "from Judge Colman, who settled on the farm now owned by Mrs. Phelps, in 1827, we learn that every evidence of former cultivation of the ground there, was seen; there being no timber growing, evidences of ancient building, of gardening, such as asparagus, &c.; and also there found many bayonets, gun-barrels, knives, pack-saddle frames, &c."

shut out their joyous example, seem to twinkle a heavenly anthem to the sombre hues and waneing aspects of Autumn. No stealthy tread was heard—no savage form was to be seen—the whoo-whoo, wh-o-o of the night-owl; the careful movement of the sentinel; the mingled voices of the soldiery, and the falling leaves, rustling through the branches to the earth, were all the sounds that fell upon the attentive ears of Harmar and his army.

Looking thus out upon the stillness and beauty of the night, a thought had stolen upon the mind of Colonel Hardin. His ambition—his desire for the chastisement of the Indian—was by no means appeased. The Miamies had perhaps returned to the village immediately after the departure of the army, thought he; and a most propitious opportunity was presented to return and "steal a march upon them." Thus imbued, he readily imparted his feelings to General Harmar—urging "that, as he had been unfortunate the other day, he wished to have it in his power to pick the militia and try it again." He sought to explain the cause of the militia not meeting the Indians on the 19th; and insisted that he then wished to retrieve their course. The earnest demeanor of Hardin prevailed. Harmer gave his consent. The commanding general was anxious that the Indians should be as well subdued as possible, that they might not give the army trouble on its return march to Fort Washington; and, as the night advanced, amid the stillness of the scene about them, with a body of three hundred and forty militia, and sixty regulars under Major Wyllys, with a view of advancing upon the Miami village before daylight, and thus be enabled the more effectually to surprise the Indians, the force took up its line of march in three columns, the regulars in the centre, and the militia to the right and left. Captain Joseph Ashton moved at the head of the regulars, while Major Wyllys and Colonel Hardin were in his front. Contrary to expectations, some delay having occurred by the halting of the militia, the banks of the Maumee were not gained till after sunrise. Indians were now soon discovered by the spies, at the announcement of which, Major Wyllys called the regulars to a halt, and ordered the militia on to a point in front, and presented his plan of attack to the commanding officers of the detachment. Major Wyllys reserving to himself the command of the regulars, Major Hall was directed, with his battalion, to move circuitously round the bend of the Maumee, crossing the St. Mary's and, in the rear of the Indians, to halt until an attack should be made "by Major McMullen's battalion, Major Fontaine's cavalry, and the regular troops under Major Wyllys, who were all ordered to cross the Maumee at and near the common fording place, which was about opposite the residence of Mr. J. J. Comparet.* Hardin

*Among the wounded in this engagement, there was a man by the name of John Smith, who, during the engagement, with several others fell in the river. He had received a severe wound, and, as a means of safety, had remained quiet until all had left, when he crawled to the bank of the river and concealed himself until some time during the night. When all seemed still, he cautiously left his hidding place, moved

and Wyllys had aimed to surround the Indians in their encampment; but Major Hall, having reached his position unobserved, disregarded the orders given by firing upon a single Indian that appeared in sight before the general attack was made. The report from the point of Hall's battalion had startled the Indians, and small squads of them were seen hurrying away in many directions, rapidly pursued, contrary to orders, by the militia under McMullen, and the cavalry under Fontaine, leaving Wyllys, at the head of the regulars, without support, and who, crossing the Maumee, were attacked by a superior body of Indians, under the lead of Little Turtle, and at length, after the fall of Wyllys and the largest portion of the regular troops, were forced to retreat. Major Fontaine, at the head of the mounted militia, in a charge upon a small body of Indians, with a number of his men were killed,* while the remainder sought safety in retreat. In the meantime, while the regulars were engaged with the party under Little Turtle, the militia under Hall and McMullen, at the confluence of the St. Mary and St. Joseph, were briskly engaged in combating small parties of Indians; but soon retreated after the defeat of the regulars, having killed and wounded many of the red men, who made no attempt to follow them, in their rapid march towards the main body under Harmar. A single horseman having reached the camp of the main army, about 11 o'clock, a. m., Harmar at once, upon learning the news of the defeat of the detachment, ordered Major Ray, with his battalion, to advance to the aid of the retreating forces. But the effect of the panic on the militia was too great—but thirty men could be prevailed on to advance to the rescue under Major Ray, who had advanced but a short distance, when they were met by Hardin and the retreating forces under him. Gaining the encampment, Colonel Hardin, flushed with excitement, and still entertaining a strong desire to carry his point against the Indians, urged Harmar to set out at once, with the entire force, for the Mi-

*The remains of Majors Wyllys and Fontaine, with some eight other officers and valiant men who fell on the occasion, were buried in some trenches, near the banks of the Maumee, some twenty rods below the residence of J. J. Comparet, Esq. The indentations on either side of the Maumee, just below Mr. Comparet's dwelling, still exhibits to the stranger the fatal ford where so many brave men fell, and whose blood reddened the stream.

down the Maumee a short distance, and made his escape, reaching Fort Washington in safety, and recovered from his wounds. When Wayne's army came here, this man Smith came with it, and ever after lived, and, some years ago, died here. Mrs. Suttenfield, whose name is already familiar to the reader, informed the writer that Smith lived for two years in her family, and many times heard him relate his adventures and narrow escape from the Indians on the occasion in question. The Indians being in ambush, along the banks of the Maumee, both above and below, at the time Harmar's men began to move over the river, a cross fire was opened upon them by the Indians, and a large number fell in the river, rendering the water, which was not then deep enough to cover the bodies, quite bloody, so much so, that Smith, though very dry, would not drink it. When it grew dark, the Indians, none of whom had pursued the retreating forces, came to the river, and began to strip the bodies, exulting greatly over their victory. In describing the noise they made while thus engaged, Smith who was still concealed, said their voices "sounded like the chattering of a parcel of black birds."

ami village again. But Harmar would not venture a return. Said he: "You see the situation of the army: we are now scarcely able to move our baggage: it will take up three days to go and return to this place: we have no more forage for our horses: the Indians have got a very good scourging; and I will keep the army in perfect readiness to receive them, should they think proper to follow."*

The militia had now become little better than wooden men in the eyes of General Harmar. He had lost all faith in them, and began at once to narrow the bounds of the camp. A second defeat and retreat were complete; and without further attempt to move upon the Indians, on the morning of the 23d of October, after a loss of one hundred and eighty-three killed, and thirty-one wounded, the army again took up its line of march for Fort Washington, whither it arrived on the 4th of November, having met with no further attack or trouble with the Indians after the movement of the 22d, about and near the ruins of the Miami village.

Among the names of the killed during the efforts of the army in this campaign, were Major Wyllys and Lieutenant Ebenezer Frothingham, of the regulars; Major Fontaine, Captains Thorp, McMurtrey, and Scott, Lieutenants Clark and Rogers, and Ensigns Bridges, Sweet, Higgins, and Thielkeld, of the militia. The loss on the part of the Indians was thought to be about equal that of the forces under Harmar.

Turning our attention to the expedition of Major Hamtramck, who, as the reader will remember, had moved from Vincennes up the Wabash, we find that while Harmar was moving upon the Miami village at this point, and destroying the villages, corn, etc., of the Indians in the region, the former had proceeded with his command to the mouth of Vermillion river, and laid waste several deserted villages, returning again to Vincennes, uninterrupted in his efforts.

The campaigns of 1790, against the Indians of the Northwest, were now closed, and the chilling blasts of another long, dreary winter, with its anxieties, its hardships, and its perils, had begun to set in about the sparse and lonely settlements of the west.

*Deposition of Hardin, Sept. 14, 1791.

CHAPTER XI.

"Those western Pioneers an impulse felt,
Which their less hardy sons scarce comprehend;
Alone, in Nature's wildest scenes they dwelt;
* * * * * *
And fought with deadly strife for every inch of ground."
F. W. THOMAS.

Effect of the movement of Gen. Harmar—Hostilities renewed by the Indians—Opposition to the Militia—Petition of the settlers—Increase of the regular army—Appointment of Gen. St. Clair—Preparations for another movement against the Miami village here—Instructions of the Secretary of War—Expedition of Gen. Scott—A second expedition from Kentucky—Gen. Wilkinson's account of the same—Effect of these expeditions—What the Indians believed—Organization of an Indian confederacy—British influence—Simon Girty—Mrs. Suttenfield's recollections—Treaty of 1783—British disregard of it—Army under St. Clair move for this point—Unfavorable weather, &c.—The army reach the site of the present town of Fort Recovery—Approach of winter—The army encamp for the night—Indians on the alert—Preparations for an early move next morning—Sudden and furious attack by the Indians—Militia give way—Great consternation—St. Clair's account—Great slaughter—Officers nearly all killed—Artillery silenced—Retreat the only hope, which is effected—Horses nearly all killed—Cannon left behind—Main road gained—Guns, knapsacks, &c., strewn for miles along the road—Rout continued for 29 miles—Statement of the killed, wounded, &c—Many women had followed the expedition—terrible Treatment by the Indians—B. Van Cleve's account—A new order of things the only hope of the west.

———o———

THE INDIANS, though much effected by the campaign of Harmar, both in the destruction of their villages and the loss of considerable numbers of their braves in the skirmishes with the troops at this point and near Eel river, were yet much "elated at the departure of Harmar, and so much did they esteem it a success on their part, that they renewed their attacks on the frontier with increased force and ferocity. Meetings were called to devise means for defending the settlements. The policy of employing regular officers to command militia was denounced, and petitions were extensively circulated, praying the President to employ militia only in defence of the frontier, and offering to raise a sufficient force to carry the war immediately into the Indian country."*

The prayer of the petitioners, however, was not granted, but the

*"American Pioneer," p. 205.

President readily favored the increase of the regular army on the frontier, and appointed General St. Clair to the command. Energetic measures were adopted to furnish him with arms, stores, &c., for an early campaign; but the difficulties and delays incident to furnishing an army, so far removed from military depots, with cannon, ammunition, provisions, and the means of transportation, were so great, that much time was lost before General St. Clair was able to move his army from Fort Washington; and then it was said to be in obedience to express orders, and against his own judgment, as he was neither provided with sufficient force, nor the means of transportation.

It was on the 3d of March, 1791, that Congress passed the "act for raising and adding another regiment to the militia establishment of the United States, and for making further provision for the protection of the frontier." An army of some three thousand troops was proposed to be placed under the command of General Arthur St. Clair. On the 21st of March, ('91), the following instructions were addressed, by the Secretary of War, Gen. Henry Knox, to General St. Clair; which shows with what importance the possession of this point was still held, and in which President Washington, doubtless, wielded a large share of influence. Said the Secretary; "While you are making use of such desultory operations as in your judgment the occasion may require, you will proceed vigorously, in every preparation in your power, for the purpose of the main expedition; and having assembled your force, and all things being in readiness, if no decisive indications of peace should have been produced, either by the messengers or by the desultory operations, you will commence your march for the Miami village, in order to establish a strong and permanent military post at that place. In your advance you will establish such posts of communication with Fort Washington, on the Ohio, as you may judge proper. The post at the Miami village is intended for awing and curbing the Indians in that quarter, and as the only preventive of future hostilities. It ought, therefore, to be rendered secure against all attempts and insults of the Indians. The garrison which should be stationed there ought not only to be sufficient for the defense of the place, but always to afford a detachment of five or six hundred men, either to chastise any of the Wabash or other hostile Indians, or to secure any convoy of provisions. The establishment of said post is considered as an important object of the campaign, and is to take place in all events. In case of a previous treaty, the Indians are to be conciliated upon this point if possible; and it is presumed good arguments may be offered to induce their acquiescence. * * * Having commenced your march upon the main expedition, and the Indians continuing hostile, you will use every possible exertion to make them feel the effects of your superiority; and, after having arrived at the Miami village, and put your works in a defensible state, you will seek the enemy with the whole of your remaining force, and endeavor, by all possible means to strike them with great severity. * * * In order to avoid future wars, it might be proper to make the Wabash, and thence over to the Maumee, and down the same to its mouth at lake Erie, the boundary [between the people of the United States and the Indians], excepting so far as the same should relate to the Wyandots and Delawares, on the supposition of their continuing faithful to the treaties. But if they should join in the war against the United States, and your army be victorious, the said tribes ought to be removed without the boundary mentioned."

On the 9th of March, some days before instructions were addressed to General St. Clair, General Knox, had communicated similar instructions to Brigadier-General Scott, of Kentucky, to move, with a sufficient body, against the Wea or Ouiatenon towns* on the Wabash. Accordingly on the 23d of May, following, "with a force of about eight hundred mounted and armed men," Scott "crossed the Ohio, at the mouth of the Kentucky river," and took up his line of march for Ouiatenon, and on the afternoon of the first of June, after a most disagreeable march of over 150 miles, through rain and storm, and the encounter of many obstacles, they succeeded in reaching and surprising the village of Ouiatenon, which, with other towns, the growing corn, &c., in the region, were soon after destroyed, and thirty Indians, mostly warriors, killed, and fifty-eight taken prisoners; from whence, without the loss of a man, and but six wounded, on the 14th of June, they started on their return march for the rapids of the Ohio. On the 4th of the month, while at the Ouiatenon towns, Scott gave the Indians a written speech, in which he assured them of the pacific and humane feelings of the United States government towards them, in view of their becoming peaceable and quiet in their future relations with the government and people of the country.

Scarcely had Gen. Scott and his corps of mounted men returned to Kentucky, when General St. Clair addressed a letter to the board of war of the district of Kentucky, authorizing them to send a second expedition of five hundred men up the Wabash. Readily complying with this request, on the 5th of July, at Danville, Brigadier-General James Wilkinson was appointed to the command of the second expedition, and ordered to be in readiness at Fort Washington by the 20th of July with the number of men specified, "well mounted on horseback, well armed, and provided with thirty days' provisions." Accordingly, on the first of August, with five hundred and twenty-five men, Wilkinson left Fort Washington, moving, by way of feint, in the direction of the Miami village, at this point, and soon brought up at the Indian town of Ke-na-pa-com-a-qua, on the north bank of Eel river, about six miles from the present town of Logansport. After cutting up the corn, then in the milk, and

*Situated on the south side of the river, about eight miles below the present site of Lafayette. The site of the old village of Ouiatenon is now known as "Wea Prairie."

burning the cabins the next morning, set out for the Indian towns beyond. Striking the village of Tippecanoe on the route, it in turn, with the growing corn, was destroyed; and advancing to one of the Kickapoo towns, it too with considerable corn, were burned and cut down. Moving on, the same day, to the town of Ouiatenon, the same destroyed by General Scott in June, and where the corn had been replanted, and which had now gained considerable growth, was cut down again; and from here, striking the trail of Scott, they took up the line of march for the rapids of the Ohio, where they arrived on the 21st of August, after a march of some four hundred and fifty-one miles, "without any material incident."

In his report, General Wilkinson said: "The volunteers of Kentucky have, on this occasion, acquitted themselves with their usual good conduct; but, as no opportunity offered for individual distinction, it would be unjust to give one the plaudits to which they all have an equal title. * * * * But, sir, when you reflect on the causes which checked my career and blasted my designs, I flatter myself you will believe every thing has been done which could be done in my circumstances.* I have destroyed the chief town of the Ouiatenon nation, and made prisoners of the sons and sisters of the King: I have burned a respectable Kickapoo village, and cut down at least four hundred and thirty acres of corn, chiefly in the milk. The Ouiatenons, (Weas) left without houses, home, or provisions, must cease to war, and will find active employ to subsist their squaws and children during the impending winter."

The principal design of the campaigns of Generals Scott and Wilkinson was that of weakening the strength of the Indians of the Wabash country, with a view to giving material aid to General St. Clair in his approaching campaign against the Miamies of Ke-ki-on-ga and the region here; but an opposite effect was the result. From formerly having entertained the belief that the Americans designed to despoil them of their lands, and destroy the whole Indian race, after these and the former efforts of General Harmar, the Indians of the northwest, still instigated by the English, began now most fully to believe that such was truly their design; and instead of slackening their efforts or ceasing to make war upon the Americans, the Miamies and Shawanoes, more espescially, began to call to their aid a numerous body of warriors from the surrounding tribes of the Pottawattamies, Kickapoos, Delawares, Ottawas, Wyandotts, and other tribes of the northwest; "and while Gen. St. Clair was making preparations to establish a military post at the Miami village, the Miami chief, Little Turtle, the Shawanoe chief, Blue Jacket, and the Delaware chief, Buck-ong-a-helas, were actively engaged in an effort to organize a confederacy of tribes sufficiently powerful to drive the white settlers from the territory lying

*The difficult marches through swamps, thickets, &c., had lamed and worn down some two hundred and seventy horses, with other impediments, which made it difficult to take further action.

on the northwestern side of the river Ohio"—receiving aid and counsel "from Simon Girty,* Alexander McKee, Mathew Elliott, (the latter two the sub-agents in the British Indian department), and from a number of British, French, and American traders who generally resided among the Indians, and supplied them with arms and ammunition, in exchange for furs and peltries."

It will here be proper to notice that although, at the definitive treaty of 1783, between the colonial government of America and Great Britain, it was declared in the seventh article of that document that the King of the latter would, "with all convenient speed, and without causing any destruction, or carrying away any negroes or property of the American inhabitants, withdraw all his forces garrisons, and fleets, from the United States, and from every post, place, and harbor, within the same,"† yet, at the time of Harmar's, St. Clair's, and Wayne's campaigns, the British Government still held and garrisoned the posts of Niagara, Detroit, and Michilmacinac; and from these points, under the plea that that part of the treaty‡ of 1783, relating to the collection and payment of all debts‖ theretofore contracted with and due to the King's subjects, had not been faithfully complied with by the Americans, much to the detriment of the former, the English Government persisted in hold-

*This man seems to have been a noted character through most of the early struggles in the north and west, from Dunmore's war, in 1774, till after the war of 1812. He was once adopted by the Senecas, the same year that he joined Lord Dunmore's campaign; but subsequently allied himself to the Wyandotts, and long after led a roving, savage life among the Indians of the northwest, usually leading them to battle, or instigating them to deeds of ferocity against the Americans, under British employ or encouragement. He was of Irish descent, and said to have been the wildest and most reckless of the family. He had three brothers—Thomas, George, and James. Mrs. Suttenfield informed the writer that she learned some time suqsequent to the arrival of herself and husband at the Fort here, in 1814, that Simon and James Girty had lived for some time, prior to the war of 1812, near the bend of the Maumee, about two miles below Fort Wayne. At the capitulation of Detroit, in 1812, Mrs. S. and her husband being there, saw Simon Girty, and described him as a short, heavy set, rough looking character, with grey hair. When he had last visited Detroit, some years prior, he had caused his horse to jump off a considerable embankment into the river, and then swam her over the same. "Here's old Simon Girty again on American soil!" he exclaimed, as he approached a crowd gathered at a prominent point in the place, at the time Mrs. S. and her husband saw him at Detroit. "What did you do with that black mare you jumped into the river when Wayne was after you?" enquired one of the crowd. "O, she's dead, and I buried her with the honors of war," replied Girty.

Notwithstanding his peculiar organization and the many unfortunate traits of character ascribed to him, he is said to have possessed some redeeming points—was strong in his friendship towards those he became attached, and, in many respects, was somewhat honorable. He was often at the Miami village here, and doubtless had much to do, at various times, with exciting the Indians to warfare against the Americans, against whom, with the Indians, he fought at St. Clair's defeat. Generally attired in the Indian costume, it was of course difficult to distinguish him, except when he spoke the English language. He is said to have lived to the age of near a hundred years, and died in Canada, some years subsequent to the war of 1812. Interesting accounts of him will be found in "Annals of the West," beginning on page 281, and in the "American Pioneer," beginning on page 282.

†Laws U. S., i, 205.

‡Article 4, U. S. Laws

‖Some of the States had passed laws, soon after the treaty of 1783, tending to prevent or restrain the collection of debts due from American citizens to the King's subjects.

ing these posts, (more especially to retain the fur trade) and continued, from time to time, to give aid and comfort to the Indians and others in open warfare and attacks upon the U. S. forces and the settlements along the Ohio, and other points in the west.

With the advantages presented by the fur trade, carried on by the English and Canadians, (the latter being then subjects of the King of England) and withal not a little jealous of the United States in her efforts to extend her dominion over the tribes and territory north of the Ohio, to relinquish her hold upon the country and leave the tribes to the control and influence of the Americans, were points not easily to be set aside by the British Government. And accordingly, while Gen. St Clair was preparing to march upon the Miami village, at the junction of the St. Mary and St. Joseph, the English, at Niagara, Detroit, and Michilimacinac were using what means they could to defeat the purposes of the United States Government; and but a small insight as to their movements, at that time, in league with the Indians and others, would doubtless have been sufficient to have convinced St. Clair and his officers of the utter futility of any effort to capture the Miami village, or establish a military post at this point, as then being pushed forward. But the effort seemed destined to be made; and after much delay and many impeding and perplexing circumstances, in the early part of the month of September, 1791, the main body of St. Clair's army, under General Butler, took up its line of march from the vicinity of Fort Washington, and, moving northward some twenty-five miles, on the eastern bank of the Great Miami, erected a post, which they called Fort Hamilton. On the 4th of October, Fort Hamilton being completed, the army began its further march for the Miami village. Having advanced forty-two miles from Fort Hamilton, they erected another garrison, calling it Fort Jefferson, six miles south of Greenville, Ohio. The season was now far advanced; and the 24th of October had arrived before the army was again on its move for the village.

After a march of nine days, during which time a number of the militia deserted; heavy rains fell; provisions became short; a reconnoitering party from the main army, was fired upon, two killed, and one supposed to have been taken prisoner; and St. Clair sick much of the way, on the 3d of November the main army reached the site of the present town of Fort Recovery, Ohio, and encamped, at the head waters of the Wabash, in view of several small creeks, about fifteen miles from the Miami village here.

The chill of winter now begun to be perceptibly felt—snow had already fallen, and the earth was white therewith. Some Indians were here seen, but they fled as soon as observed.

The advance and general movement of St. Clair was sufficiently well known* to the confederated tribes and their allies to inspire

*Ths news of St. Clair's march upon the Miami villages having reached the Indians during the autumn of 1791, the famous Shawanoes chief, Tecumseh, says the life of

them with great courage and determination, and had already begun a resort to strategem to draw the army into their clutches; and had even advanced to within a few miles of the main body of the army, where, under the lead of the famous Little Turtle, Buck-ong-a-helas, Blue Jacket, Simon Girty, and several other white men, lay—in readiness to meet the advancing columns of St. Clair—some twelve hundred warriors.

The army was now some fifteen miles from the Miami village. With a view to a place of safety for the knapsacks of the soldiers, St. Clair, with Major Ferguson, had, on the evening of the arrival of the army at its present encampment, concluded "to throw up a slight work," and then, with the regiment yet back, to move on to attack the enemy. But neither were consummated; and before the sun had sent his rays over the western wilds—between that hour which the adage has accounted the darkest just before day, and the full twilight of the morning—the Indian whoop and wild yell of the enemy startled the army of St. Clair, already under arms, into the wildest commotion, and at once began a furious attack upon the militia, which soon gave way, and pell-mell, came rushing into the midst of the camp, through Major Butler's battalion, creating the wildest disorder on every side, and closely pursued by the Indians. "The fire, however, of the front line checked them; but almost instantly a very heavy attack began upon that line; and in a few minutes it was extended to the second likewise. The great weight of it was directed against the center of each, where the artillery was placed, and from which the men were repeatedly driven with great slaughter."* Soon perceiving but little effect from the fire of the artillery, a bayonet charge was ordered, led by Lieut.-Colonel Darke, which drove the Indians back some distance, but, for the want of sufficient force, they soon moved forward to the attack again, and the troops of Darke were, in turn, compelled to give way; while, at the same time, the enemy had pushed their way into camp by the left flank, and the troops there also were giving way. Repeated and effectual charges were now made by Butler and Clarke's battallions, but with great loss; many officers fell, leaving the raw troops without direction—Major Butler himself being dangerously wounded. In the second regiment every officer had fallen, except three, and one of these had been shot through the body.

The "artillery being now silenced, and all the officers killed, except Captain Ford, who was very badly wounded and more than

*St. Clair's report.

that chief, was soon placed at the head of a small party of spies or scouts, with instructions to watch and report the advancement of St. Clair; and he is said to have done his work most faithfully, for, while concealed near a small tributary of the Great Miami, he and his party saw St. Clair and his army pass on their way to Greenville. Though prevented from taking part in the hostile movements that followed, yet, it is evident that the efforts of Tecumseh and his little band, whose report soon reached the head chiefs in action against St. Clair, had much to do with the subsequent defeat and rout of the army.

half of the army fallen, being cut off from the road, it became necessary to attempt the regaining of it, and to make a retreat, if possible. For this purpose the remains of the army were formed, as well as circumstances would admit, towards the right of the encampment, from which, by the way of the second line, another charge was made upon the enemy, as if with the design to turn their right flank, but in fact to gain the road. This was effected, and as soon as it was open, the militia took along it, followed by the troops; Major Clarke, with his battalion covering the rear."* Everything was now precipitate. The panic had assumed a terrible flight. The camp and artillery were all abandoned—not a horse was left alive to remove the cannon; and the soldiery threw away their arms and accouterments as they ran, strewing the road for miles with them. The retreat began about half-past nine o'clock, and continued a distance of twenty-nine miles, to Fort Jefferson, where they arrived soon after sunset, having lost thirty-nine officers, killed, and five hundred and ninety-three men killed and missing; twenty-two officers, and two hundred and forty-two men wounded; with a loss to the public, in stores and other valuable property, to the amount of some thirty-two thousand eight hundred and ten dollars and seventy-five cents.†

The following were the names of the officers who fell on this memorable occasion: Major-general Richard Butler, Lieutenant-colonel Oldham, of the Kentucky militia; Majors Ferguson, Clarke, and Hart; Captains Bradford, Phelon, Kirkwood, Price, Van Swearingen, Tipton, Smith, Purdy, Piatt, Guthrie, Cribbs, and Newman; Lieutenants Spear, Warren, Boyd, McMath, Bead, Burgess, Kelso, Little, Hopper, and Lickens; Ensigns Balch, Cobb, Chase, Turner, Wilson, Brooks, Beatty, and Purdy; Quartermasters Reynolds and Ward; Adjutant Anderson; and Doctor Grasson. The officers wounded were:—Lieutenant-colonels Gibson, Darke, and Sargent, (adjutant-general;) Major Butler; Captains Doyle, Trueman, Ford, Buchanan, Darke, and Hough; Lieutenants Greaton, Davidson, De Butts, Price, Morgan, McCroa, Lysle, and Thomson; Ensign Bines; Adjutants Whisler and Crawford; and the Viscount Malartie, volunteer aid-de-camp to the commander-in-chief.

Many women‡ had followed the army of St. Clair in its march towards the Miami village, prefering to be with their husbands than to remain behind, most of whom were destroyed; and "after the flight of the remnant of the army, the Indians began to avenge their own real and imaginary wrongs by perpetrating the most horrible acts of cruelty and brutality upon the bodies of the living and dead Americans who fell into their hands. Believing that the whites, for many years, made war merely to acquire land, the Indians

*St. Clair's report. †Report of Secretary of War, Dec. 11, 1792.

‡"History of Ohio," by Atwater, says 250; Dillon, in his His. of Ind., says "more than one hundred."

crammed clay and sand into the eyes and down the throats of the dying and the dead."*

B. Van Cleve, who was in the quartermaster-general's department, of the army of St. Clair, says: †" On the fourth [of November] at daybreak, I began to prepare for returning [to Fort Washington,]‡ and had got about half my luggage on my horse, when the firing commenced. We were encamped just within the lines, on the right. The attack was made on the Kentucky militia. Almost instantaneously, the small remnant of them that escaped broke through the line near us, and this line gave away. Followed by a tremendous fire from the enemy, they passed me. I threw my bridle over a stump, from which a tent pole had been cut, and followed a short distance, when finding the troops had halted, I returned and brought my horse a little further. I was now between the fires, and finding the troops giving away again, was obliged to leave him a second time. As I quitted him he was shot down, and I felt rather glad of it, as I concluded that now I shall be at liberty to share in the engagement. My inexperience prompted me to calculate on our forces being far superior to any that the savages could assemble, and that we should soon have the pleasure of driving them. Not more than five minutes had yet elapsed, when a soldier near me had his arm swinging with a wound. I requested his arms and accoutrements, as he was unable to use them, promising to return them to him, and commenced firing. The smoke was settled down to within about three feet of the ground, but I generally put one knee to the ground and with a rest from behind a tree, waited the appearance of an Indian's head from behind his cover, or for one to run and change his position. Before I was convinced of my mistaken calculations, the battle was half over and I had become familiarised to the scene. Hearing the firing at one time unusually brisk near the rear of the left wing, I crossed the encampment. Two levy officers were just ordering a charge. I had fired away my ammunition and some of the bands of my musket had flown off. I picked up another, and a cartridge box nearly full, and pushed forward with about thirty others. The Indians ran to

*Dillon's His. Ind., p. 283. From a letter to General St. Clair, dated Fort Washington, February 13, 1792, written by Capt. Robert Bunti, who had previously accompanied Gen. James Wilkinson with a small detachment of mounted men to the scene of St. Clair's defeat, the following extract is made: "We left Fort Jefferson about nine o'clock on the 31st (of January), with the volunteers, and arrived within eight miles of the field of battle that evening, and next day we arrived at the ground about ten o'clock. The scene was truly melancholy. In my opinion those unfortunate men who fell into the enemy's hands, with life, were used with the greatest torture—having their limbs torn off; and the women have been treated with the most indecent cruelty, having stakes as thick as a person's arm, drove through their bodies. The first, I observed when burrying the dead; and the latter was discovered by Colonel Sargent and Dr. Brown." Pits being dug, all the bodies found were burried by the detachment under Wilkinson. The Indians seldom if ever buried those they killed in battle, or otherwise.

†As published from the manuscript of Van Cleve in the "American Pioneer," 1843.

‡Says a note to this account; "He was in the quartermaster-general's service; so that he 'fought on his own hook.'"

the right, where there was a small ravine filled with logs. I bent my course after them, and on looking round, found I was with only seven or eight men, the others having kept straight forward and halted about thirty yards off. We halted also, and being so near to where the savages lay concealed, the second fire from them left me standing alone. My cover was a small sugar tree or beach, scarcely large enough to hide me. I fired away all my ammunition; I am uncertain whether with any effect or not. I then looked for the party near me, and saw them retreating and half way back to the lines. I followed them, running my best, and was soon in. By this time our artillery had been taken, I do not know whether the first or second time, and our troops had just retaken it, and were charging the enemy across the creek in front; and some person told me to look at an Indian running with one of our kegs of powder, but I did not see him. There were about thirty of our men and officers lying scalped around the pieces of artillery. It appeared that the Indians had not been in a hurry, for their hair was all skinned off."

"Daniel Bonham, a young man raised by my uncle and brought up with me, and whom I regarded as a brother, had by this time received a shot through his hips, and was unable to walk. I procured a horse and got him on. My uncle had received a ball near his wrist that lodged near his elbow. The ground was literally covered with dead and dying men, and the commander gave orders to take the way—perhaps they had been given more explicitly. Happening to see my uncle, he told me a retreat was ordered, and that I must do the best I could, and take care of myself. Bonham insisted that he had a better chance of escaping than I had, and urged me to look to my own safety alone. I found the troops pressing like a drove of bullocks to the right. I saw an officer, whom I took to be lieut. Morgan, an aid to general Butler, with six or eight men, start on a run a little to the left of where I was. I immediately ran and fell in with them. In a short distance we were so suddenly among the Indians, who were not apprised of our object, that they opened to us, and ran to the right and left without firing. I think about two hundred of our men passed through them before they fired, except a chance shot. When we had proceeded about two miles, most of those mounted had passed me. A boy had been thrown or fell off a horse, and begged my assistance. I ran, pulling him along, about two miles further, until I had become nearly exhausted. Of the last two horses in the rear, one carried two men, and the other three. I made an exertion and threw him on behind the two men. The Indians followed but about half a mile further. The boy was thrown off some time afterwards, but escaped and got in safely. My friend Bonham I did not see on the retreat, but understood he was thrown off about this place, and lay on the left of the trace, where he was found in the winter and was buried. I took the cramp violently in my thighs, and could scarcely walk, until I got within a hundred yards of the rear, where the Indians were tomahawking the old and wounded men; and I stopped here to tie my pocket handkerchief around a man's wounded knee. I saw the Indians close in pursuit at this time, and for a moment my spirits sunk, and I felt in despair for my safety. I considered whether I should leave the road, or whether I was capable of any further exertion. If I left the road, the Indians were in plain sight and could easily overtake me. I threw the shoes off my feet and the coolness of the ground seemed to revive me. I again began a trot, and recollect that, when a bend in the road offered, and I got before half a dozen persons, I thought it would occupy some time for the enemy to massacre them, before my turn would come. By the time I had got to Stillwater, about eleven miles, I had gained the centre of the flying troops, and, like them, came to a walk. I fell in with lieutenant Shaumburg, who, I think, was the only officer of artillery that got away unhurt, with corporal Mott, and a woman who was called red-headed Nance. The latter two were both crying. Mott was lamenting the loss of his wife, and Nance that of an infant child. Shaumburg was nearly exhausted, and hung on Mott's arm. I carried his fusee and accoutrements, and led Nance; and in this sociable way we arrived at Fort Jefferson, a little after sunset.

"The commander-in-chief had ordered Col. Darke to press forward to the convoys of provisions, and hurry them on to the army. Major Truman, captain Sedan and my uncle were setting forward with him. A number of soldiers, and packhorsemen on foot, and myself among them, joined them. We came on a few miles, when all, overcome with fatigue, agreed to a halt. Darius Curtus Orcutt,* a packhorse master, had stolen at Jefferson, one pocket full of flour and the other full of beef. One of the men had a kettle, and one Jacob Fowler and myself groped about in the dark, until we found some water, where a tree had been blown out of root. We made a kettle of soup, of which I got a small portion among the many. It was then concluded, as there was a bend in the road a few miles further on, that the Indians might undertake to intercept us there, and we decamped and traveled about four or five miles further. I had got a rifle and ammunition at Jefferson, from a wounded militiaman, an old acquaintance, to bring in. A sentinel was set, and we laid down and slept, until the governor came up a few hours afterward. I think I never slept so profoundly. I could hardly get awake after I was on my feet. On the day before the defeat, the ground was covered with snow. The flats were now filled with water frozen over, the ice as thick as a knife-blade. I was worn out with fatigue, with my feet knocked to pieces against the roots in the night, and splashing through the ice without shoes. In the

*Orcutt's packhorses were branded D. C. O., and it was a standing joke, when any one asked what the brand meant, to answer that D. C. stood for Darby Carey, and the round O for his wife.—Western Pioneer.

morning we got to a camp of packhorsemen, and amongst them I got a doughboy or water-dumpling, and proceeded. We got within seven miles of Hamilton on this day, and arrived there soon on the morning of the sixth."

The efforts against the Miami village were, for a time, at least, brought to a close. A new order of things now became necessary, if success was to be attained in any further movement towards this point.

CHAPTER XII.

* * * * * *

"Fill up life's little span
With God-like deeds—it is the test—
Test of the high-born soul,
And lofty aim;
The test in History's scroll
Of every honored name!
None but the brave shall win the goal."—HARVEY RICE.

—o—

How Washington was effected by the defeat of St. Clair—Frontier settlements exposed to the ravages of the Indians—Appointment of General Wayne to the command of the western army—Relief of the frontier settlements—Party spirit—Efforts of the government to form treaties with the Indians—General Wayne advances towards this point—Establishes his headquarters at Fort Greenville—Erects a fortification on the site of St. Clair's defeat—Indians begin to be fearful of success—Send General Wayne a speech—Can't accept the terms of Wayne—They still hope for British aid—The Spanish of the Lower Mississippi—Detachment sent to Fort Massac—Fierce attack upon Fort Recovery—The army starts for the Miami village—Erection of Fort Adams—Army reaches mouth of the Anglaize and Maumee—Erection there of Fort Defiance—Wayne's report to the Secretary of War—Distrust of the Indians—Capt. William Wells and Little Turtle—Wells quits the Miamies and joins Wayne—Council of the tribes—Speech of Little Turtle—Movements of the army—Attack by the Indians—The wisdom of Little Turtle—Anthony Shane's account of Tecumseh—Report of General Wayne—Return to Fort Defiance—Destruction of corn-fields and villages—General Wayne and the British commander at the Rapids of the Maumee—Repairs upon Fort Defiance—Army moves again for the village here—Its arrival—Selection of the site for the erection of a fort—Journal of the army—Completion of the fort—Lieut.-Col Hamtramck assumes command, and names it FORT WAYNE—Main body of the army, under Wayne, starts for Fort Greenville—Glorious effect of Wayne's victory throughout the country—Indians invited to hold a treaty of peace—efforts of the British Indian agents—Agreeable adjustment of affairs with Great Britain—Indians dispirited thereby—They begin to visit Wayne at Greenville—Letters of Col. Hamtramck—The treaty of Greenville—effecting address of Wayne—Great rejoicing throughout the country—"Westward, ho!"

—o—

THE NEWS of the defeat of Gen. St. Clair fell heavily upon the mind of Washington. He had long looked upon the capture of this locality and the establishment here of formidable fortifications with the highest degree of interest and concern; and to learn of the defeat of an army like that under St. Clair—a defeat greater than that of Braddock in his movement against Fort Du Quesne, in 1755—was to be most severely felt by him.

He had hoped for speedy relief to the sparse and greatly exposed settlements of the west, and had relied largely upon General St. Clair to carry his designs and those of the government to a successful termination; and while, in the main, Gen. St. Clair was but little if any to blame for the terrible defeat that impeded his march to the Miami village, yet Washington could but feel it most sorely. His feelings are said suddenly to have overcome him; and though most unlike the man of courage, hope, perseverance, and usual calm, self-complacency, when told of St. Clair's ill success, his better feelings suddenly gave way to those of the most intense discomfiture. "It's all over!" he exclaimed; "St. Clair is defeated! routed!" His private secretary, according to the account, was the only one present, and he is said to have been "awed into breathless silence by the appalling tones in which the torrent of invective was poured forth by Washington. But his composure was as soon restored, and new resolution as readily formed in the plastic mind of the President.

The defeat of St. Clair's force was doubly embarrassing. Besides disappointing and perplexing the government, it had "exposed the whole range of the frontier settlements on the Ohio to the fury of the Indians," against which they made the best arrangements in their power for their own defence; while the government took measures for recruiting, as soon as possible, the Western army. Among the military commandants of the time, General Wayne was a great favorite with the people of the west, and he readily received the appointment to the command of the western troops; though "a factious opposition in Congress, at that time, to the military and financial plans of the administration, delayed the equipment of the army for nearly two years;" and thus, "while General Wayne was preparing to penetrate the Indian country in the summer of 1794, the attention of the Indians was drawn to their own defence, and the frontiers were relieved from their attacks."* Party spirit now ran high. The west felt sorely agrieved, and every act of the general government tending towards conciliation with the British, who were charged with inciting the Indians on the frontier, was looked upon in the most disapprobative feeling; and while General Wayne, from 1792 to August, 1793, was gathering his forces for the renewal of efforts against the Indians of this point, the government of the United States used strenuous efforts to establish treaties of peace and good-will among the tribes hostile to the Americans in the nerthwestern territory, by sending out messengers with speeches. On the 7th of April, 1792, Brig.-General Wilkinson dispatched such messengers (Freeman and Gerrard) from Fort Washington to the Indians on the Maumee;† but who were captured, and being taken for spies, were murdered some where near the rapids of this river; and the efforts of the government resulted in but little success, in so far as the direct desire for peace

*"American Pioneer," p. 206. †Dillon's His. Ind. pp. 287, 289,

was concerned. The strong arm of war seemed the only means left to bring the tribes to a true sense of regard for the government and its real purposes towards the Indians of the western country. Thus stood matters from the time of the last efforts of the United States, on the part of its last commissioners to the Indians, (Benjamin Lincoln, Beverley Randolph, and Timothy Pickering) in August, 1793, with some activity on the part of the Indians, and much hope and anxiety on the part of the settlements of Marietta and other points in the west, till Wayne had advanced from his headquarters, at "Hobson's Choice," near Fort Washington, on the 6th of October, 1793, to the southwest branch of the Great Miami, within six miles of Fort Jefferson, and, about a month subsequently, established his headquarters at Fort Greenville,* which was built by him about the period of his arrival at that point. On the 23d of December, of this year, from this fort, he gave orders for the erection of a fort on the site of St. Clair's defeat, in '91, and for that purpose ordered Major Henry Burbeck, with eight companies of infantry, and a detachment of artillery, to proceed to the ground, whither the soldiers arrived, executed the order of General Wayne, and the fortification was appropriately called "Fort Recovery." At this bold procedure, the Indians began to exhibit signs of uneasiness, and soon sent General Wayne a "speech," desiring to present overtures of peace with the United States; but the terms presented by Wayne were not then agreeable to the Indians, who had, about the time of Wayne's proposition, much as in the case of the French, at the time of the Pontiac struggle against the British, been led to hope that early in the coming year ('94), Great Britain would render them sufficient aid to enable them to expel and destroy the American settlers situated on the territory northwest of the Ohio.†

Matters now agitating the general mind, and, to a considerable extent, calling away the attention of the Government, relative to a proposed expedition against the Spaniards of the Lower Mississippi, and to oppose which, General Wayne was ordered by President Washington to send a detachment to Fort Massac, on the Ohio, about eight miles below the Tennessee river, there "to erect a strong redoubt and blockhouse, with some suitable cannon from Fort Washington," the expedition of Wayne remained in comparative quiet at the different posts, (Jefferson, Greenville, Recovery, &c.,) till the morning of the 30th of June, '94 when Major

*Which formerly stood in the vicinity of what is now the town of Greenville, Darke county, Ohio.

†In February, 1794, Lord Dorchester, then Governor-general of Canada, at a council of chiefs at Quebec, told the Indians "that he should not be surprised if Great Britain and the United States were at war in course of the year." Hence their encouragement in part, at least. It was about this period also that France was experiencing much trouble of a revolutionary nature, and that Genet, the French Minister in this country, had sought to raise a body of troops, &c., to move against the Spaniards of Florida and Louisiana. Lord Dorchester, doubtless infering that such a movement, aided by the United States, would soon precipitate the two countries into a war again, was most probably led to encourage the Indians by the remark quoted above. A proclamation was issued by Washington against the movement, March 24, 1794.

McMahon, commanding, with an escort of ninety riflemen and fifty dragoons, was fiercely assailed by a body of some fifteen hundred Indians "under the walls of Fort Recovery." Assisted, as was thought, by a "number of British agents and a few French Canadian volunteers," the Indians, during a period of about twenty-four hours, made several sallies upon this fort, but finding their efforts unavailable, retired. The loss, however, to the garrison was by no means trifling—twenty-two men being killed, and thirty wounded, and three were missing; two hundred and twenty-one horses were also killed, wounded and missing. The Indians having been engaged in carrying away their dead during the night, but eight or ten of their warriors were found dead near the fort. Major McMahon, Captain Hartshorne, Lieutenant Craig, and Cornet Torry, fell on this occasion.

Major-General Scott, with some sixteen hundred mounted volunteers, having arrived at Fort Greenville, on the 26th of July, ('94), and joined the regulars under General Wayne, on the 28th of July, the army began its march upon the Indian villages along the Maumee. On this march, some twenty-four miles to the north of Fort Recovery, Wayne had built and garrisoned a small Post, which he called Fort Adams. From this point, on the 4th of August, the army moved toward the confluence of the Auglaize and Maumee rivers, where they arrived on the 8th of August. At this point, "a strong stockade fort, with four good stockhouses, by way of bastions," was soon concluded, which was called by Gen. Wayne Fort Defiance. On the 14th of August, General Wayne wrote as follows to the Secretary of War: "I have," said he, "the honor to inform you that the army under my command took possession of this very important post on the morning of the 8th instant—the enemy, on the preceding evening, having abandoned all their settlements, towns, and villages, with such apparent marks of surprise and precipitation, as to amount to a positive proof that our approach was not discerned by them until the arrival of a Mr. Newman, of the quartermaster-general's department, who deserted from the army near the St. Mary's. * * * I had made such demonstrations, for a length of time previously to taking up our line of march, as to induce the savages to expect our advance by the route of the Miami villages, to the left, or toward Roche de Bout, by the right—which feints appear to have produced the desired effect, by drawing the attention of the enemy to those points, and gave an opening for the army to approach undiscovered by a devious, *i. e.*, in a central direction. Thus, sir, we have gained possession of the grand emporium of the hostile Indians of the west, without loss of blood. * * * Everything is now prepared for a forward move to-morrow morning toward Roche de Boute, or foot of the rapids. * * * Yet I have thought proper to offer the enemy a last overture of peace; and as they have everything that is dear and interesting now at stake, I have reason to expect that they will listen to the proposition mentioned in the enclosed copy of an address, dispatched yesterday by a special flag (Christopher Miller,) who I sent under circumstances that will insure his safe return, and which may eventually spare the effusion of much human blood. But should war be their choice, that blood be upon their own heads. America shall no longer be insulted with impunity. To an all-powerful and just God I therefore commit myself and gallant army."

In his address to the Indians, as dispatched by Miller "to the Delewares, Shawanees, Miamis, and Wyandots, and to each and every of them; and to all other nations of Indians northwest of the Ohio, whom it may concern," said General Wayne: "Brothers—Be no longer deceived or led astray by the false promises and language of the bad white men at the foot of the rapids: they have neither the power nor inclination to protect you. No longer shut your eyes to your true interest and happiness, nor your ears to this last overture of peace. But, in pity to your innocent women and children, come and prevent the further effusion of your blood. Let them experience the kindness and friendship of the United States of America, and the invaluable blessings of peace and tranquility." He urged them also—"each and every hostile tribe of Indians to appoint deputies" to assemble without delay at the junction of the Auglaize and foot of the rapids, "in order to settle the preliminaries of a lasting peace." The answer brought by Miller on his return, on the 16th, was, "that if he (General Wayne) waited where he was ten days, and then sent Miller for them, they would treat with him; but that if he advanced, they would give him battle."

The slow movement of Wayne towards the Miami village had caused many of the Indians to feel no little distrust as to their ability to defeat the great chief* of the Americans who was creeping so cautiously upon their strongholds.

A man by the name of Wells, already referred to in a previous chapter, who, at the age of twelve years, had been captured in Kentucky and adopted by the Miamies, and who had lived to manhood and raised a family among them, just prior to the advance of the army towards the rapids, began to feel a new awakening in his mind. He had fought by the side of Little Turtle against both Harmar and St. Clair; and it was said of him, that "afterwards, in the times of calm reflection, with dim memories still of his childhood home, of brothers and playmates, he seemed to have been harrowed with the thought that amongst the slain, by his own hand, may have been his kindred." He had resolved to break his attachment to the tribe, even to his wife and children. In this state of mind, with much of the Indian characteristics, inviting the war chief of the Miamies—Little Turtle—to accompany him to a point on the Maumee, about two miles east of Fort Wayne, at what was long known as the "Big Elm," whither they at once repaired. Wells

*From his great vigilence, Wayne was called by the Indians the Black Snake.

readily told the chief his purpose. "I now leave your nation," said he, "for my own people. We have long been friends. We are friends yet, until the sun reaches a certain height, (which was mentioned). From that time we are enemies. Then if you wish to kill me, you may. If I want to kill you, I may." When the time indicated had come, Capt. Wells crossed the river, and was soon lost to the view of his old friend and chieftain, Little Turtle. Moving in an easterly course, with a view to striking the trail of Wayne's forces, he was successful in obtaining an interview with the General, and ever thereafter proved the fast friend of the Americans.* The resolute movement of Wells was a severe blow upon the Miamies. To Turtle's mind it seemed to have been an unmistakable foreboding of sure and speedy defeat to the confederated tribes of the northwest, as already referred to.

In accordance with previous arrangements, on the 15th of August, General Wayne moved with his forces towards the foot of the rapids, and came to a halt a few miles above that point, on the 18th, and the next day began the erection of a temporary garrison, more especially for the reception of stores, baggage, and the better to reconnoitre the enemy's ground, which lay "behind a thick, bushy wood, and the British fort."† This post was called "Fort Deposit."

The Miamies were now undecided as to the policy of attacking General Wayne, notwithstanding the fact that they, with the aid of other tribes, and through the influence of the British, had succeeded in defeating the former expeditions of Harmar and St. Clair. At a general council of the confederated tribes, held on the 19th of August, Little Turtle was most earnest in his endeavors to pursuade a peace with general Wayne. Said he, "we have beaten the enemy twice under different commanders. We cannot expect the same good fortune to attend us always. The Americans are now led by a chief who never sleeps. The nights and the days are alike to him, and during all the time that he has been marching on our villages, notwithstanding the watchfulness of our young men, we have never been able to surprise him. Think well of it. There is something whispers me, it would be prudent to listen to his offers of peace." But his words of wisdom were but little regarded. One of the chiefs of the council even went so far as to charge him with cowardice, which he readily enough spurned, for there were none braver or

*After the arrival here of the army under Wayne, Wells was made captain of the Spies, and settling at the "Old Orchard," a short distance from the confluence of the St. Mary and St. Joseph, on the banks of a little stream there, afterwards called "Spy Run," and which still bears that name, the government subsequently granted him a pre-emption of some three hundred and twenty acres of land thereabout, including his improvement thereon, the old orchard, etc. Wells afterwards, also became, by appointment of the Government, Indian Agent here, in which capacity he served for several years.

†This fort, at the foot of the Rapids, called Fort Miami, was about seven miles from Fort Deposit, and stood on the northwestern bank of the Maumee, near where Maumee City now stands.

more ready to act where victory was to be won or a defense required, than Little Turtle, and so, without further parley, the council broke up, and Turtle, at the head of his braves, took his stand to meet and give battle to the advancing army.

"At eight o'clock," says Wayne, in his report to Secretary Knox, on the 28th of August, 1794, "on the morning of the 20th, the army again advanced in columns, agreeably to the standing order of march; the legion on the right, its flank covered by the Maumee: one brigade of mounted volunteers on the left, under Brigadier-general Todd, and the other in the rear, under Brigadier-general Barbee. A select battallion of mounted volunteers moved in front of the legion, commanded by Major Price, who was directed to keep sufficiently advanced, so as to give timely notice for the troops to form in case of action, it being yet undetermined whether the Indians would decide for peace or war.

"After advancing about five miles," continued the report, "Major Price's corps received so severe a fire from the enemy, who were secreted in the woods and high grass, as to compel them to retreat. The legion was immediately formed in two lines, principally in a close, thick wood, which extended for miles on our left, and for a very considerable distance in front, the ground being covered with old fallen timber, probably occasioned by a tornado, which rendered it impracticable for the cavalry to act with effect, and afforded the enemy the most favorable covert for their mode of warfare. The savages were formed in three lines, within supporting distance of each other, and extending for near two miles, at right angles with the river. I soon discovered, from the weight of the fire and extent of their lines, that the enemy were in full force in front, in possession of their favorite ground, and endeavoring to turn our left flank. I therefore gave orders for the second line to advance and support the first; and directed Major-general Scott to gain and turn the right flank of the savages, with the whole of the mounted volunteers, by a circuitous route; at the same time I ordered the front line to advance and charge with trailed arms, and rouse the Indians from their coverts at the point of the bayonet, and when up, to deliver a close and well-directed fire on their backs, followed by a brisk charge, so as not to give them time to load again.

"I also ordered Captain Mis Campbell, who commanded the legionary cavalry, to turn the left flank of the enemy next the river, and which afforded a favorable field for that corps to act in. All these orders were obeyed with spirit and promptitude; but such was the impetuosity of the charge by the first line of infantry, that the Indians and Canadian militia and volunteers were drove from all their coverts in so short a time, that, although every possible exertion was used by the officers of the second line of the legion, and by Generals Scott, Todd, and Barbee, of the mounted volunteers, to gain their proper positions, but part of each could get up in season to participate in the action; the enemy being drove, in the course of one hour, more than two miles through the thick woods already mentioned by less than one-half their numbers. From every account, the enemy amounted to two thousand combatants. The troops actually engaged against them were short of nine hundred.* This horde of savages, with their allies, abandoned themselves to flight, and dispersed with terror and dismay, leaving our victorious army in full and quiet possession of the field of battle, which terminated under the influence of the guns of the British garrison."

The wisdom, foresight and valor of Little Turtle were now no longer to be questioned. At the Indian council, on the night before the attack, he clearly saw the end of all their efforts against the army of Wayne; and the Indians soon began to feel and realize that their main hold upon the northwest was broken forever.

Though it is not positively known whether Tecumseh was at the council or not, the night before the battle, yet it is authentically recorded, in the life of this chief, in accordance with the following account by Anthony Shane, that he led a party of Shawanoes in the attack upon the army of General Wayne. And it was in this engagement that he first encountered the white chief, Gen. Harrison, then a Lieutenant, with whom, a few years later, he had so much dealing. Says the account of Shane: He occupied an advanced position in the battle, and while attempting to load his rifle, he put in a bullet before the powder, and was thus unable to use his gun. Being at this moment pressed in front by some infantry, he fell back with his party, till they met another detachment of Indians. Tecumseh urged them to stand fast and fight, saying if any one would lend him a gun, he would show them how to use it. A fowling-piece was handed to him, with which he fought for some time, till the Indians were again compelled to give ground. While falling back, he met another party of Shawanoes; and, although the whites were pressing on them, he rallied the Indians, and induced them to make a stand in a thicket. When the infantry pressed close upon them, and had discharged their muskets into the bushes, Tecumseh and his party returned the fire, and then retreated till they had joined the main body of the Indians below the rapids of the Maumee.

As presented in the foregoing report, "the bravery and conduct of every officer belonging to the army, from the generals down to the ensign," merited the "highest approbation. There were, however, some," says Wayne, "whose rank and situation placed their conduct in a very conspicuous point of view, and which I observed with pleasure, and the most lively gratitude. Among whom, I must beg leave to mention Brigadier-general Wilkinson, and Col.

*The exact number of Indians engaged in this action, against Wayne's army has never been ascertained. There were, however, about 450 Delawares, 175 Miamies, 275 Shawanees, 225 Ottawas, 275 Wyandotts, and a small number of Senecas, Pottawattamies, and Chippewas. The number of white men who fought in defense of the Indians in this engagement, was about seventy, including a corps of volunteers from Detroit, under the command of Captain Caldwell.—His. Ind.

Hamtramck, the commandants of the right and left wings of the legion, whose brave example inspired the troops. To those I must add," said he, " the names of my faithful and gallant aids-de-camp, Captain De Butt and T. Lewis; and Lieutenant Harrison, who, with the adjutant-general, Major Mills, rendered the most essential service by communicating my orders in every direction, and by their conduct and bravery exciting the troops to press for victory. Lieutenant Covington, upon whom the command of the cavalry now devolved, cut down two savages with his own hand; and Lieutenant Webb one, in turning the enemy's left flank. The wounds received by Captains Slough and Prior, and Lieutenant Campbell Smith, an extra aid-de-camp to General Wilkinson, of the legionary infantry, and Captain Van Rensselear, of the dragoons, Captain Rawlins, Lieutenant McKenny, and Ensign Duncan, of the mounted volunteers, bear honorable testimony of their bravery and conduct.

" Captains H. Lewis and Brock, with their companies of light infantry, had to sustain an unequal fire for some time, which they supported with fortitude. In fact, every officer and soldier, who had an opportunity to come into action, displayed that true bravery which will always ensure success. And here permit me to declare, that I never discovered more true spirit and anxiety for action, than appeared to pervade the whole of the mounted volunteers; and I am well persuaded that, had the enemy maintained their favorite ground for one-half hour longer, they would have most severely felt the prowess of that corps. But, while I pay this tribute to the living, I must not neglect the gallant dead, among whom we have to lament the early death of those worthy and brave officers, Captain Mis Campbell, of the dragoons, and Lieutenant Towles, of the light infantry, of the legion, who fell in the first charge."

Of the killed and wounded, in this engagement, according to the report of General Wayne, the regular troops, lost twenty-six killed, and eighty-seven wounded. Of the Kentucky volunteers, seven were killed and thirteen were wounded; and nine regulars and two volunteers died of their wounds before the 28th of the month. The loss of the enemy was more than twice that of the army under Wayne; and "the woods were strewn for a considerable distance with the dead bodies of Indians."

Wayne's victory was now complete. It was short and decisive; and after remaining "three days and nights on the banks of the Maumee, in front of the field of battle, during which time all the houses and cornfields (of the enemy) were consumed and destroyed for a considerable distance both above and below Fort Miami, as well as within pistol shot of the garrison, who were compelled to remain tacit spectators to this general devastation and conflagration; among which were the houses, stores, and property of Colonel McKee, the British Indian agent, and principal stimulator of the war now existing between the United States and the savages,"* on the 27th, the army started upon its return march for Fort Defiance, laying waste, as it moved, villages and cornfields for a distance of some fifty miles along the Maumee.

It will be proper here to mention, that while the American forces occupied their position within range of the British fort† at the rapids, from the afternoon of the 20th to the forenoon of the 23d, five letters passed between the British commander (Major Campbell) and General Wayne; the first coming from the British commandant, enquiring the cause of the army of the United States approaching so near his majesty's fort—that he knew "of no war existing between Great Britain and America," etc. To which Gen. Wayne replied: "Without questioning the authority or the propriety, sir, of your interrogatory, I think I may, without breach of decorum, observe to you, that, were you entitled to an answer, the most full and satisfactory one was announced to you from the muzzles of my small arms, yesterday morning, in the action against the horde of savages in the vicinity of your post, which terminated gloriously to the American arms; but, had it continued until the Indians, etc., were driven under the influence of the post and guns you mention, they would not have much impeded the progress of the victorious army under my command, as no such post was established at the commencement of the present war between the Indians and the United States." To which, in turn, the British commandant, having taken the rejoinder of Wayne as an insult to the British flag, threatened to open his batteries upon the American forces, should they continue to approach his post "in the threatening manner" they were then doing, etc. Wayne's reply was this time to the effect that he also knew of no war then existing between Great Britain and America—reminding him of the definitive treaty of 1783—showing him that Great Britain was then and there maintaining a post beyond the limits and stipulations of that treaty; and ordering him to retire peacefully within the limits of the British lines. To which the British commandant replied that he certainly would not abandon the post at the summons of any power whatever, until he received orders to that effect from those he had the honor to serve under, or the fortunes of war should oblige him so to act; and still firmly adhered to his previous proposition, or threat. And thus the controversy ended.

Reaching Fort Defiance again, the army soon began repairs upon the fort, in order to render it the more substantial in its general structure; and here the army remained till the morning of the 14th of September, 1794, when "the legion began their march for the Miami village," (this point) whither they arrived at 5 o'clock, P. M., on the 17th of September, and on the following day, the

*Wayne's report.

†At the period of Wayne's engagement near the rapids, there were about 250 regulars and 210 militia in this fort, with "four nine-pounders, two large howitzers, and six six-pounders mounted in the fort, and two swivels."—American State papers.

troops fortified their camps, while "the commander-in-chief reconnoitered the ground and determined on the spot to build a garrison."*

The history of events, from the time of the arrival of Wayne and his army at the Miami village, on the afternoon of the 17th, to the completion of the fort, will be partially seen, at least, from the following dates at the Miami village, as presented in the daily journal of Wayne's campaign:

Camp Miami Villages, 18th Sep. 1794.—* * * * Four deserters from the British came to us this day; they bring the information that the Indians are encamped 8 miles below the British fort to the number of 1600.

20th *Sep.*—Last night it rained violently and the wind blew from the N. W. harder than I knew heretofore. Gen. Barber with his command arrived in camp about 9 o'clock this morning with 553 kegs of flour, each containing 100 pounds.

23*d Sep.*—Four deserters from the British garrison arrived at our camp; they mention that the Indians are still embodied on the Miami, 9 miles below the British fort; that they are somewhat divided in opinion, some are for peace and others for war.

24*th Sep.*—This day the work commenced on the garrison, which I am apprehensive will take some time to complete it. A keg of whisky containing ten gallons, was purchased this day for eighty dollars, a sheep for ten dollars: three dollars was offered for one pint of salt, but it could not be obtained for less than six.

25*th Sep.*—Lieutenant Blue, of the dragoons, was this day arrested by ensign Johnson, of the 4th S. L., but a number of their friends interfering, the dispute was settled upon lieutenant Blue asking Johnson's pardon.

26*th Sep.*—M'Cleland, one of our spies, with a small party came in this evening from Fort Defiance, who brings information that the enemy are troublesome about the garrison, and that they have killed some of our men under the walls of the fort. Sixteen Indians were seen to-day near this place; a small party went in pursuit of them. I have not heard what discoveries they have made.

30*th Sep.*—Salt and whisky were drawn by the troops this day, and a number of the soldiery became much intoxicated, they having stolen a quantity of liquor from the quartermaster.

4*th Oct.*—This morning we had the hardest frost I ever saw in the middle of December, it was like a small snow; there was ice in our camp kettles ¾ of an inch thick; the fatigues go on with velocity, considering the rations the troops are obliged to live on.

5*th Oct.*—The weather extremely cold, and hard frosts, the wind N. W.; every thing quiet and nothing but harmony and peace throughout the camp, which is something uncommon.

6*th Oct.*—Plenty and quietness the same as yesterday; the volunteers engaged to work on the garrison, for which they are to receive three gills of whisky per man per day; their employment is digging the ditch and filling up the parapet.

8*th Oct.*—The troops drew but half rations of flour this day. The cavalry and other horses die very fast, not less than four or five per day.

9*th Oct.*—The volunteers have agreed to build a block-house in front of the garrison.

11*th Oct.*—A Canadian (Rozelie) with a flag arrived this evening; his business was to deliver up three prisoners in exchange for his brother, who was taken on the 20th August; he brings information that the Indians are in council with Girty and M'Kee near the fort of Detroit, that all the tribes are for peace except the Shawanees, who are determined to prosecute the war.

16*th Oct.*—Nothing new, weather wet, and cold, wind from N. W. The troops healthy in general.

17*th Oct.*—This day Captain Gibson arrived with a large quantity of flour, beef, and sheep.

19*th Oct.*—This day the troops were not ordered for labor, being the first day for four weeks, and accordingly attended divine service.

*Daily journal Wayne's campaign.

20th Oct.—An express arrived this day with dispatches to the commander-in-chief; the contents are kept secret.

A court-martial to sit this day for the trial of Charles Hyde.

21st Oct.—This day were read the proceedings of a general court martial, held on lieutenant Charles Hyde, (yesterday) was found not guilty of the charges exhibited against him, and was therefore acquitted.

On the morning of the 22d of October, 1794, the garrison was in readiness, and Lieutenant-colonel Hamtramck assumed command of the Post, with the following sub-legions: Captain Kingsbury's 1st; Captain Greaton's 2d; Captains Spark's and Reed's 3d; Captain Preston's 4th; and Captain Porter's of artillery; and after firing fifteen rounds of cannon, Colonel Hamtramck gave it the name of FORT WAYNE.

And here was the starting-point of a new era in civilization in the great northwest!

On the 28th of October, having completed his work at the point now bearing his name, General Wayne, with the main body of the regulars, took up his line of march for Fort Greenville, arriving at that point on the 2d of November.

Early in September the news of Wayne's victory had spread over a large part of the country, and operated most favorably for the government. It not only removed the dissatisfaction to which the great delays attending the campaign had given rise, but it was the best possible illustration of the benefits to be derived from the protection of the general government, which had been greatly underrated. As a permanent peace with the Indians was now considered certain, this increased the desire for tranquility at home. And the troubles which, but a short period before, had threatened to involve the government in much trouble, through the desire of Genet and his followers to move upon the Spaniards of the Lower Mississippi, began greatly to dispirit the insurgents; and by the first of October, ('94) tranquility and good order were in a great measure restored throughout the country.*

After the close of the engagement of the 20th of August, Wayne continued to invite the Indians to a friendly meeting, with a view to permanent peace between the tribes and the United States. But the Indians, for some time, seemed to be balancing between a desire still for the overthrow of the Americans and the hope of "effectual support from the British," on the one hand, and the fear of ultimate defeat on the other, let their own strength or aid from the English be as formidable as it might; and while Wayne was inviting them to meet him at Greenville to conclude a treaty with him there, "Lieutenant-general Simcoe, Col. McKee, and other officers of the British Indian department, persuaded Little Turtle, Blue Jacket, Buck-ong-a-helas, and other distinguished chiefs, to agree to hold an Indian council at the mouth of Detroit river."†

The troubles with England, which had, but a few months before, threatened to break out into warfare again, were now, through the

* American Pioneer.

†Dillon's His' Ind.

FORT WAYNE 1795

wisdom of Washington, in a great measure, and the admirable efforts of John Jay, as envoy extraordinary from this country to the court of St. James, amicably adjusted in the conclusion of "a treaty of amity, commerce, and navigation, between the United States and Great Britain." This treaty was concluded on the 19th of November; and one of its main stipulations was that of a withdrawal, "on or before the first day of June, 1796, all (of the Kings) troops and garrisons, from all posts and places within the boundry lines assigned to the United States by the treaty of peace of 1783."

The news of this treaty having reached America, the Indians soon felt their last hope of aid from the English fading away, and began seriously to think of peace; and during the months of December and January, 1794-5, small parties of Miamies, Ottawas, Chippewas, Pottawattamies, Sacs, Delawares, and Shawanoes began to visit General Wayne at his headquarters at Greenville, signing respectively, preliminary articles of peace, and agreeing "to meet Wayne at Greenville on or about the 15th of June, 1795, with all the sachems and war-chiefs of their nations," with a view of arranging a final treaty of peace and amity between the United States and the Indians of the northwestern territory.

During the period that elapsed between the departure (28th of October,) of Wayne for Fort Greenville from the newly completed garrison bearing his name here, until the 17th of May 1796, Col. Hamtramck remained in command at Fort Wayne; and though nothing of a very important nature transpired during that time, yet there is much of interest to be gathered from the many letters* of Col. H., written from the fort here, and addressed to generals Wayne and Wilkinson.

On the 5th December, '94, he wrote to Gen. Wayne:

"It is with a great degree of mortification that I am obliged to inform your excellency of the great propensity many of the soldiers have to larceny. I have flogged them till I am tired. The economic allowance of one hundred lashes, allowed by government, does not appear a sufficient inducement for a rascal to act the part of an honest man. I have now a number in confinement and in irons for having stolen four quarters of beef on the night of the 3rd instant. I could wish them to be tried by a general court-martial, in order to make an example of some of them. I shall keep them confined until the pleasure of your excellency is known."

"*Fort Wayne, December* 29, 1794.

"SIR—Yesterday a number of chiefs of the Chippeways, Ottawas, Sacks, and Pottawattamies arrived here with the two Lassells.† It appears that the Shawanees, Delawares, and Miamies remain still under the influence of McKee; but Lassel‡ thinks they will be compelled to come into the measures of the other Indians. After the chiefs have rested a day or two, I will send them to head-quarters"

"*Fort Wayne, December* 29, 1794.

SIR—Since my last letter to your excellency of the present date, two war-chiefs have arrived from the Miami nation, and inform me that their nation will be here in a few days, from whence they will proceed to Greenville. They also bring intelligence of the remaining tribes of savages acceding to the prevalent wish for peace, and collecting for the purpose the chiefs of their nations, who, it is expected, will make their appearance at this post about the same time the Miamies may come forward."

*Published from the manuscript of Col Hamtramck in the "American Pioneer, 1843.

†Jacques and Antoine Lasselle. ‡Jacques Lasselle

"*December* 13, 1795

"The issues to the Indians would be very inconsiderable this winter, if it was not for about ninety old women and children with some very old men, who live near us and have no other mode of subsisting but by garrison. I have repeatedly tried to get clear of them, but without success.

"*January* 13, 1796.

"About ninety old women and children have been victualled by the garrison. I have, yesterday, given them five days' provision, and told them it was the last they should have until spring. I was obliged to do so because, from calculation, I have no more flour than will last me until spring. But, sir, if other supplies could be got by land, I consider it politic to feed these poor creatures, who will suffer very much for want of subsistence."

[*To General Wilkinson*] "*March* 28, 1796.

"I am out of wampum. I will be very much obliged to you to send me some, for speaking to an Indian without it is like consulting a lawyer without a fee."

[*To General Wilkinson*] ' *April* 5, 1796.

"Little Turtle arrived yesterday, to whom I delivered your message. H's answer was, to present his compliments to you, that he was very glad of the invitation, as he wished very much to see general Wilkinson, but it was impossible for him to go to Greenville at present, as he had ordered all his young men to repair to a rendezvous, in order, when assembled, to chose a place for their permanent residence; that, as soon as that object shall be accomplished, he would go to see you, which, he said, would be by the time he hears form you again."

[*To General Wilkinson.*] "*April* 18, 1796.

"The bearer is captain Blue Jacket, who, at your request, is now going to Greenville. Blue Jacket is used to good company and is always treated with more attention than other Indians. He appears to be very well disposed, and I believe him sincere."

True to their promise, in the early part of June, 1795, deputations from the different tribes of the northwest began to arrive at Greenville with a view to the consummation of the treaty already referred to. This treaty, which was one of much interest throughout, lasted from the 16th of June, to the 10th of August, (1795) many of the principal chiefs making strong speeches, and each nation openly and separately assenting to the articles and stipulations of the treaty. At the conclusion of his speech to deputies on the 10th of August, at the termination of the treaty, General Wayne addressed the assemblage as follows: "I now fervently pray to the Great Spirit, that the peace now established may be permanent, and that it may hold us together in the bonds of friendship, until time shall be no more. I also pray that the Great Spirit above may enlighten your minds, and open your eyes to your true happiness, that your children may learn to cultivate the earth, and enjoy the fruits of peace and industry. As it is probable, my children, that we shall not soon meet again in public council, I take this opportunity of bidding you all an affectionate farewell, and wishing you a safe and happy return to your respective homes and families."

A general feeling of rejoicing soon pervaded the country at the happy termination of this treaty;* and it was as pleasing and accep-

* The boundry lines established at this treaty, between the northwestern Indians and the U. S., secured to the Indians all the territory within the present limits of the State of Indiana, excepting, First:—One tract of land, six miles square, at the confluence of the St. Mary and St. Joseph rivers. Secondly:—One tract of land, two miles square, on the Wabash river, at the end of the portage, from the head of the river Maumee, and about eight miles westward from Fort Wayne. Thirdly:—One tract of land, six miles square, at Ouiatenon, or the old Wea town on the river Wabash.

table to the Government, as it was agreeable to the Indians. With these pacific relations came the cry of "WESTWARD, HO!" and soon a tide of emigration began to set in from the eastern States, many selecting sites along the Ohio, the Sciota, and Muskingum rivers; and others again selected and began settlements along the fertile regions lying between the two Miami rivers, and at other points westward. And thus had begun a new life and a new freedom in the wide domain of the northwest.

Fourthly:—The tract of one hundred and fifty thousand acres, near the falls of the Ohio; which tract was called the "Illinois Grant," or "Clark's Grant." Fifthly:—The town of Vincennes, on the river Wabash, and the adjacent lands to which the Indian title had been extinguished; and all similar lands, at other places, in possession of the French people, or other white settlers among them. And, sixthly:—The strip of land lying east of a line running directly from the site of Fort Recovery, so as to intersect the River Ohio at a point opposite to the mouth of the Kentucky river.

CHAPTER XIII.

"All along the winding river
And adown the shady glen,
On the hill and in the valley,"
The voice of war resounds again.

Emigration westward—The Shawanoes Prophet—Enactments of laws—Treaty between the U S. and Spain—Efforts to dissolve the Union—Col. Hamtramck leaves Fort Wayne—British evacuate Fort Miami—Death of General Wayne—General Wilkinson assumes command of the western forces—Movements of Baron Carondelet—Failure of the Spanish and French scheme—Treaty of peace with France—cession of Louisiana to France—Cession of same to the U. S.—Legislative session at Cincinnati—Wm. Henry Harrison chosen representative in Congress—Division of territory—Harrison appointed Governor—Principal events from 1800 to 1810—Efforts of Governor Harrison to induce the Indians to engage in agricultural pursuits—Extinguishment of Indian claims—Treaty at Fort Wayne in 1803—Peaceable relations between the Indians and the U. S.—Beginning of new troubles—Short account of the Shawanoes—Indians put to death by order of the Prophet—Speech of Gov. Harrison—Capt. Wm. Wells, Indian agent here—Sends a message to Tecumseh by Anthony Shane—Shane's reception—Tecumseh's reply—Wells refuses to comply with Tecumseh's request—Shane again sent to Tecumseh—Second reply of Tecumseh—Indians continue to assemble at Greenville—Many about Fort Wayne—Great alarm of the settlers—Governor of Ohio sends a deputation to Greenville—Address of the commissioners—Speech of Blue Jacket—Tecumseh and others return with the commissioners—Further alarm—A white man killed—Militia called out—Investigation of the murder—Settlers still uneasy—Speech of Gov. Harrison—Protestations of the Prophet—He removes to Tippecanoe—Warlike sports begun—Settlers again alarmed—The Prophet visits Gov. Harrison—His Speech—Harrison tests him—Secret movements of Tecumseh and the Prophet—Many of their followers leave them—Militia organized—Alarm subsides—Treaty of Fort Wayne, 1809—Further movements of Tecumseh and the Prophet—Gov. Harrison prepares for the safety of the frontier.

THE TIDE of emigration westward, that had begun soon after the treaty of Greenville, steadily continued for a number of years, and the peace of the country was not materially interrupted till some time during the year 1810, when the famous Shawanoe Prophet, Ells-kwata-wa, through a singular and somewhat powerful influence, began to exert a wide control over many tribes of the northwest, thus creating much alarm among the western settlements, which, in turn, much impeded the influx of emigrants to the Indiana Territory.

The most important events that transpired from 1795 to 1810, were the meeting of Governor St.Clair,with John Cleves Symmes and George Turner, the latter as judges of the northwestern territory, Cincinnati, May 29th, 1795, wherein they adopted and made thirty-eight laws for the better regulation and government of the territory.

On the 27th of October of this year ('95) a treaty of "friendship, limits, and navigation, between the United States of America and the King of Spain," was concluded, at the court of Spain, between Thos. Pinckney, envoy extraordianary of the United States, and the Duke of Alcudia, which extended from the southern boundry of the U. S. to "the northernmost post of the thirty-first degree of latitude north of the equator," which was to extend "due east to the middle of the river Apalachicola or Catahoucha, thence along the middle thereof, to its junction with the Flint; thence straight to the head of St. Mary's river, and thence down the middle thereof, to the Atlantic Ocean;" and was ratified on the 3d of March, 1796.

In July of 1796, the French Executive Directory, because of this treaty of amity, commerce, and navigation between the United States and Spain, charged the American government with "a breach of friendship and abandonment of neutrality, and a violation of tacit engagements;" and during 1796 and 1797, as in keeping with a similar spirit exhibited in 1795, before the Spanish garrisons on the eastern side of the Mississipppi were surrendered to the United States, strong efforts were made, on the part of French and Spanish agents, to persuade the inhabitants of the western country to withdraw their connection from the American Union, and, with those governments, to form a separate and independent government, extending westward from the Allegheny Mountains. But the inducements were of no avail, and the scheme failed.

Before the end of July, (1796) the English had withdrawn from all "the posts within the boundry of the United States northwest of the Ohio;" and about the 17th of May of this year, Colonel Hamtramck had left Fort Wayne, passing down the Maumee to Fort Deposit, where the famous engagement of Wayne had but a few months before occured, and on the 11th of July the British fort, Miami, at the foot of the rapids, was evacuated, Capt. Moses Porter soon taking command. On the 13th of July, Colonel Hamtramck took possession of the Post at Detroit.

In December of this year, '96, General Wayne died, and General James Wilkinson was put in command of the western army of the United States, and a small detachment still continued at Fort Wayne.

In the month of June 1797, some feeling still existing on the part of Spain as well as France, the two governments being somewhat allied in their motives against the United States, the governor of Louisiana (Baron de Carondelet) sent a request to General Wilkinson to delay the movement of the United States troops that were to occupy the posts on the Mississippi river until such time as the adjustments of certain questions then pending between the American and Spanish governments could be adjusted. But the true object of Carondelet, through his agent (Thomas Power,) seems to have been only to ascertain the true feeling of the western people regarding a dissolution of the Union. Power having passed through the western territory as far as Detroit, in the month of August, '97, he met General Wilkinson, and explained the object of his mission, which the general readily concluded to be "a chimerical project, which it was impossible to execute, that the inhabitants of the western states, having obtained by treaty all they desired, would not wish to form any other political or commercial alliance." Because of these intrigues on the part of Spain, and the conduct of France, in December, 1796,* in refusing to receive Minister Monroe, at Paris, on the ground of complaints already mentioned, relative to the treaty with Spain, and because of the depredation of French vessels against American commerce, the United States government, during 1798, impelled the latter to adopt and enforce strenuous measures of retaliation; the first of which was that of "an act authorizing the President of the U. S. to raise a provisional army." The second, "to suspend the commercial intercourse between the U. S. and France and the dependencies thereof." The third, "to authorize the defense of the merchant vessels of the U. S. against French depredations;" and fourth, "an act concerning alien enemies."

The Spaniads had hoped for aid, by way of Canada, from the English, in 1798. But they were doomed to disappointment, and having reluctantly evacuated the posts on the Mississippi during the summer of 1798, in the fall of that year Gen. Wilkinson moved down that river and took up his headquarters at Loftus' Heights, where he soon erected Fort Adams. In September of this year, France having exhibited a desire for peaceable relations with the United States, subsequent negotiations were had at Paris, and on the 30th of September, 1800, a "treaty of peace and commerce" was consummated between the United States and France.

In October of this year, (1800), by the conclusion of a treaty at St. Ildefonso, Spain retroceded to France the province of Louisiana, embracing the original lines of territory as when before held by France; and under Jefferson's administration, three years later, (30th of April, 1803,) the French government "sold and ceded Louisiana, in its greatest extent, to the United States, for a sum about equal to fifteen millions of dollars."

On the 23d of April, 1798, a legislative session was convened at Cincinnati, which closed on the 7th of May, same year, Winthrop Sargent, acting governor, and John Cleves Symmes. Joseph Gilman, and Return Jonathan Meigs, Jr., territorial judges. On the 29th of October of this year, Gov. St. Clair issued a proclamation,

* It was in September of this year that Washington, then soon to vacate the Presidential chair for John Adams, who, that year, was elected President, and Thomas Jefferson vice President of the United States, issued his fervent and ever memorable FAREWELL ADDRESS.

"directing the qualified voters of the Northwestern Territory to hold elections in their respective counties on the third Monday of December," with a view to electing representatives to a general assembly, to convene at Cincinnati on the 22d of January, 1799. The representatives having met at the appointed place, in compliance with the ordinance of 1787, for the establishment of legislative councils, ten persons were chosen as nominees, and their names forwarded to the President of the United States, who, on the second of March, 1799, selected therefrom, the names of Jacob Burnett, James Findlay, Henry Vanderburgh, Robert Oliver, and David Vance, as suitable persons to form the legislative council of the territory of the United States, lying northwest of the Ohio river, which names were, on the following day, confirmed by the U. S. Senate. This body met at Cincinnati on the 16th day of September, and were fully organized on the 25th of that month, 1799, of which Henry Vanderburgh was elected President, and William C. Schenk, Secretary. The following counties were represented: Hamilton, Ross, Wayne, Adams, Knox, Jefferson, and Washington; sending nineteen members.

On the third of October, of this year, the names of two candidates (Wm. H. Harrison and Arthur St. Clair, Jr.,) to represent the Northwestern Territory in Congress, being presented to that body, Harrison was chosen—the one receiving eleven votes, and the other ten.*

In 1800, a division of the territory northwest of the Ohio river having occurred, on the 13th of May of that year, Wm. Henry Harrison was appointed governor of the Indiana Territory. The seat, of government for the Territory was established at Vincennes, where, with the judge of the same, the governor met on Monday, 12th of January, 1801, with a view of adopting and issuing "such laws as the exegencies of the times" might call for, and likewise for the "performance of other acts conformable to the ordinances and laws of Congress (1787) for the government of the Territory."

From the period of the formation of the new territory to 1810, the principal subjects of attention and interest to the people therein, "were land speculations, the adjustment of land titles, the question of negro slavery, the purchase of Indian lands by treaties, the organization of territorial legislatures, the extension of the right of suffrage, the division of the Indiana Territory, the movements of Aaron Burr, and the hostile views and proceedings of the Shawanoe chief, Tecumseh, and his brother, the Prophet."†

With a view to peace and good-will between the United States and the Indians of the northwest, through certain laws and regulations of the government, Gov. Harrison, at an early period of his administration, made efforts to induce the different tribes to engage in agricultural and other pursuits of a civilized nature, to the end that they might be more agreeably situated and live more in har-

* Dillon's His. Ind., page 392. †Ibid, page 409

mony with the advancing civilization of the time. Being also invested with powers authorizing him to negotiate treaties between the U. S. government and the different tribes of the Indiana Territory, and also to extinguish, by such treaties, the Indian title to lands situate within the said territory. Between the fore part of 1802 and 1805, the governor was most actively employed in the discharge of these duties.

On the 17th day of September, 1802, at a conference held at Vincennes, certain chiefs and head men of the Pottawattamie, Eel River, Piankeshaw, Wea, Kaskaskia, and Kickapoo tribes appointed the Miami chiefs, Little Turtle and Richardville, and also the Pottawattamie chiefs, Wine-mac and To-pin-e-pik to adjust, by treaty, the extinguishment of certain Indian claims to lands on the Wabash, near Vincennes. And on the 7th of June, the year following, (1803,) Gov. Harrison held a treaty at Fort Wayne, with certain chiefs and head men of the Delaware, Shawanoe, Pottawattamie, Eel River, Kickapoo, Piankeshaw, and Kaskaskia tribes, wherein was ceded to the United States about one million six hundred thousand acres of land.*

For a period of sixteen years, subsequent to the treaty of Greenville, (1795 to 1811) agreeable relations were maintained, by the U. S., between the Miamies and some other tribes represented at that famous treaty. During this time the Indians seemed mainly to have betaken themselves to the forest and priaries in pursuit of game; and the result was that a considerable traffic was steadily "carried on with the Indians, by fur-traders of Fort Wayne, and Vincennes, and at different small trading posts which were established on the borders of the Wabash river and its tributaries. The furs and peltries which were obtained from the Indians, were generally transported to Detroit. The skins were dried, compressed, and secured in packs. Each pack weighed about one hundred pounds. A pirogue, or boat, that was sufficiently large to carry forty packs, required the labor of four men to manage it on its voyage. In favorable stages of the Wabash river, such a vessel, under the management of skillful boatmen, was propelled fifteen or twenty miles a day, against the current. After ascending the river Wabash and the Little River to the portage near Fort Wayne, the traders carried their packs over the portage, to the head of the river Maumee, where they were again placed in pirogues, or in keel-boats, to be transportated to Detroit. At this place the furs and skins were exchanged for blankets, guns, knives, powder, bullets,† intoxicating liquors, etc., with which the traders returned to their several posts. According to the records of the customhouse at Quebec, the value of the furs and peltries exported from Canada, in the year 1786, was estimated at the sum of two hundred and twenty-five thousand nine hundred and seventy-seven ponnds sterling."

* Dillon's His. Ind.

†The bullets, which were made to fit the guns in use among the Indians, were valued at four dollars per hundred. Powder, at one dollar per pint.

But the volcanic fire of revolution had already begun its upheavel. The past had witnessed many periodical struggles in the new world, and the hour for another was near at hand. The Indians of the northwest, for the most part, began to grow restive. The game of the forest had now long been hunted and killed for their hides, fur, and meat, while many of the traders had grown wealthy upon the profits yielded therefrom. The life of the hunter seemed too monotinous for the Indian, and he sought, as at other periods, and, in many relations, for good reasons, as he had thought, to change it for one of war; and as the larger fish of the ocean are said to devour the lesser ones, so it would seem that, by continued irritation, brought on through the efforts of both the white and red man, Civilization, with its strange and active impulse, was at length destined to supplant the early and endearing homes and soil of the red children of the northwest with new and more advanced human and physical relations.

As the reader has already seen, the Shawanoes played a conspicuous part at various times during the early efforts of the English and Americans to gain possession of the western frontier. Col. Bouquet's expedition was directed mainly against them, at which time they dwelt principally about the Sciota river, some miles to the southeast of the Miami villages.

Not unlike most Indian tribes, the origin of the Shawanoes is enveloped in much obscurity. Many tribes, it is true, can be traced back for many centuries; but beyond that, all is conjecture or so wrapped in legendary accounts, that it is most difficult indeed to trace them further.

The Lenni-Lenape, or Delawares, have long received the first claim to attention as an active and war-like branch of the Algonquin family; but the Shawanoes are evidently, in so far, at least, as their chiefs and the spirit of war is concerned, entitled to a first consideration, while the Miamies, evidently, were early the superiors, in many essential respects, of most of the Algonquin tribes of the northwest.

The French knew the Shawanoes as the Chaouanous, and were often called the Massawomees. The famous Iroquois called them the Satanas; and the name was often spelt Shawanees, Shawaneus, Sawanos, Shawanos, and Shawanoes. The latter style of spelling the name is the one adopted in these pages.

Mr. Jefferson, in his "Notes on Virginia," speaks of a savage warfare between several tribes, one of which was the Shawanoe, at the period of Capt. John Smiths's advent in America. In 1632, by another historian, the Shawanoes were dwelling upon one of the banks of the Delaware; and it is variously conceded that this tribe participated in the treaty with Wm. Penn, in 1682. Accounts agree that "they were a marauding, adventurous tribe," while "their numerous wanderings and appearances in different parts of the continent, almost place research at defiance." To become embroiled with neighboring tribes, wherever they dwelt, seems to have been their fate; and to save themselves from utter destruction as a tribe, it is told that they had more than once been obliged to fly for other and more secure parts of the country.

Parkman is of opinion that the Five Nations (Iroquois) overcame them about the year 1672, and that a large portion of them sought safety in the Carolinas and Florida; where they soon again became involved in trouble, and the Mobilians sought to exterminate them. Returning northward, with others, they settled in what is now the Ohio valley. Gallatin, who is well versed in the aboriginal tongues, is of opinion that this tribe was of the Lenni-Lenape branch of the Algonquin family, and thinks that their dispersion took place about 1732. The Suwanee river, in the southern part of the United States, takes its name from this tribe, whither they had wandered before settling in the northwest. Says Heckwelder, referring to this tribe before their settlement upon the Ohio, they "sent messengers to their *elder brother*, the Mohicans, requesting them to intercede for them with their grandfather, the Lenni-Lenape, to take them under his protection. This the Mohicans willingly did, and even sent a body of their own people to conduct their younger brother into the country of the Delawares. The Shawanoes, finding themselves safe under the protection of their grandfather, did not choose to proceed to the eastward, but many of them remained on the Ohio, some of whom settled as far up that river as the Long Island, above which the French afterward built Fort Duquesne, on the spot where Pittsburgh now stands. Those who proceeded further, were accompanied by their chief, Gachgawatschiqua, and settled principally at and about the forks of the Delaware, between that and the confluence of the Delaware and Schuylkill rivers; and some, even on the spot where Philadelphia now stands; others were conducted by the Mohicans into their own country, where they intermarried with them and became one people. When those who settled near the Delaware had multiplied, they returned to Wyoming, on the Susquehanna, where they resided for a great number of years."

In 1754, during the French and English war, the Shawanoes took part with the French. The Wyoming branch, through the efforts of the missionary Zingendorf, through this period, remained quiet, taking no part in the struggle. A few years later, however, a trivial dispute having arisen between this tribe and the Delawares as to the possession of a grasshopper, a bloody conflict ensued between them, wherein about one-half of the Shawanoe warriors were destroyed, while the remainder removed to the Ohio, where they dwelt for several years, during all the period of those desolating struggles of the early frontier settlements, referred to in former chapters, during the latter part of the past and the first of the present century. In what is now the State of Ohio, they had many considerable towns. Tecumseh was born at one of these, known as

Piqua, which stands upon Mad River, a few miles below Springfield. This village was destroyed by the Kentuckians, under Clark, in 1780.

After their defeat by Col. Bouquet, in 1764, and the treaty of Sir William Johnson, they soon became embroiled in a difficulty with the Cherokees, maintaining the struggle until 1768, when they were forced to sue for peace. Remaining comparatively quiet for several years, but little is known of them, of a war-like nature, until 1774, soon after the breaking out of the "Dunmore War." But for the results that brought them into this struggle, it is said the Shawanoes were in no wise responsible. A report having gained credence among the whites that the Indians had stolen several of their horses, a couple of Shawanoes were taken and put to death by them, without knowing whether they were the guilty ones or not; and on the same day, the whites fired upon and killed several of the Shawanoes, the latter returning the fire and severely wounding one of the whites. Cresap also killed the famous Logan family about this period. An old Delaware sachem, known as "Bald Eagle," for many years the friend of the whites, was murdered, and the famous chief of the Shawanoes, one much beloved by that tribe, known as "Silver Heels," was fatally wounded, while returning in a canoe from Albany, where he had accompanied some white traders seeking safety. When found by his friends, "Bald Eagle" was floating in his canoe, in an upright position, and scalped. The Indians were now exasperated to a high degree; Logan, at the merciless death of his wife and children,—and a sanguinary war was the result. It was in the month of October of the year in question that occured the famous battle of Point Pleasant, in which Colonel Lewis was killed, with some fifty odd other white men, with about a hundred wounded. The Indians were defeated, but the defeat was dearly bought.

After this, the Shawanoes allied themselves to the English, and became the implacable foe of the colonists in the struggle for Independence; and even after peace was declared, in 1783, they refused to be friendly, and continued to wage war upon the whites, obstinately opposing the advancing army to the west. Several small expeditions were sent against them after the revolution, which they strongly opposed—Clark's, in 1780 and 1782; Logan's in 1786; Edward's in 1787; Todd's in 1788; and the reader is already familiar with their efforts, combined with other tribes, against the expeditions of Harmar, St. Clair, and Wayne.

In the spring of 1803, Captain Thomas Herrod, living a short distance from Chilicothe, was murdered and scalped near his own house. A party of hunters coming upon the body, recognized it, and, from the appearance, were convinced that it had been done by Indians. The treaty of Greenville up to this time had suffered no violation, and the settlers now believed hostilities were about to commence. Who committed this deed has never been ascertained, but there was strong suspicions among the immediate neighbors against a white man who had been a rival candidate with Herrod for a captaincy in the Ohio militia. There being no tangible evidence against the man, he was allowed to remain unmolested, while those who suspected the Indians most cowardly retaliated upon them. The account of the death, as if borne on the wings of the wind, spread with great rapidity all over the Sciota valley, and the excitement and alarm produced among the citizens was most intense. Whole families, from five to fifteen miles apart, flocked together for purposes of self-defense. In some places block-houses were run up, and preparations for war made in every direction. The citizens of Chilicothe, though in the center of population, collected together for the purpose of fortifying the town. The inhabitants living on the north fork of Paint Creek were all collected at Old Town, now Frankfort, and among others was David Wolf, an old hunter, a man of wealth and some influence. He had settled on the north fork, twenty miles above Old Town. After remaining in the town several days, he employed two men, Williams and Ferguson, to go with him to his farm, with the view of examining into the condition of his stock. When they had proceeded about six miles, and were passing across a prairie, they saw an Indian approaching them in the distance, and walking in the same path over which they were traveling. On a nearer approach, it was found to be the Shawanoe chief, Waw-wil-a-way, the old and faithful hunter of General Massie during his surveying tours, and an unwavering friend of the white men. He was a sober, brave, intelligent man, well known to most of the settlers in the country, and beloved by all for his frank and generous demeanor. He had a wife and two sons, who were also much respected by their white neighbors where they resided, near the falls of Paint Creek.

Waw-wil-a-way was frequently engaged in taking wild game and skins to Old Town, for the purpose of exchanging them for such articles as he needed. He had left home this morning on foot with his gun, for the purpose of visiting Frankfort, and meeting the company named, he approached them in that frank and friendly manner which always characterized his intercourse with his white brethren. After shaking hands with them most cordially, he inquired of the health of each and their families. The salutation being over, Wolf asked him to trade guns with him, and the chief assenting, an exchange was made for the purpose of examining previous to concluding the bargain. While this was going on, Wolf, being on horseback, unperceived by Waw-wil-a-way, opened the pan, and threw out the priming, and, handing it back, said he believed he would not trade with him.

Wolf and Williams then dismounted, and asked the chief whether the Indians had commenced war. He replied: "No, no! the Indians and white men are now all one, all brothers."

Wolf then asked whether he had heard that the Indians had killed Captain Herrod.

The chief, much surprised at the intelligence, replied that he had not heard it, and seemed to doubt its correctness. Wolf affirmed that it was true. Waw-wil-a-way remarked that perhaps some bad white man had done it, and after a few more words, the parties separated, each going his own way.

The chief had walked about ten steps, when Wolf, taking deliberate aim, shot him through the body. Waw-wil-a-way did not fall, although he felt his wound was mortal, nor did he consent to die as most men would have done under similar circumstances.

Bringing his unerring rifle to his shoulder, he leveled it at Williams, who, in his efforts to keep his horse between himself and the Indian, so frightened him that his body was exposed, and when the rifle was discharged, he dropped dead near his animal. Rendered desperate by his wounds, the Indian then clubbed his gun, and dealing Wolf a fearful blow, brought him to the earth. Recovering, and being strong and active, he closed upon the Indian, and made an effort to seize him by the long tuft of hair on the crown of his head. A shawl was tied around the Indian's head in the form of a turban, and this being seized by Wolf, instead of the hair, he gave a violent jerk for the purpose of bringing him to the ground. The shawl gave way, and Wolf fell upon his back. At this, the Indian drew his scalping-knife, and made a thrust at Wolf, who, seeing his danger, and throwing up his feet to ward off the blow, received the blade of the knife in his thigh. In the scuffle the handle broke off, and left the blade fast in the wound. At the same time, Wolf made a stroke at the Indian, the blade of his knife entering the breast-bone. Just then Ferguson came to Wolf's assistance; but the Indian, taking up Wolf's gun, struck him on the head a terrible blow, and brought him to the ground, laying bare his skull from the crown to the ear. Here the sanguinary conflict ended, and it all occurred in less time then it has taken the reader to peruse this acconnt of it.

When the deadly strife ended, the foes of Waw-wil-a-way were all lying at his feet, and had he been able to follow up his blows, he would have dispatched them, for they were completely within his power. But his strength failed him, and perhaps his sight, for he must have been in the agonies of death during the whole conflict. It may be that the poor Indian relented, and that forgiveness played like sunshine around his generous heart. He cast one glance upon his fallen foes; then turning away, he walked out into the grass, and fell upon his face amid the wild-flowers of the prairie, where his heart at once and forever was still.

During the entire engagement he never spoke a word. Silently he acted his part in the fearful drama, as though moved by an invisible agency. The course of Wolf and his comrades was most unwise indeed, and should never have been encouraged by any one.

They first attempted to disarm him by throwing the priming out of his gun, and then talking with him and parting under the mask of friendship. Had Wolf and his companions supposed him to be accessory to the death of Herrod in any way, he would have gone with them cheerfully to Old Town or Chilicothe, and given himself up to an investigation. But Wolf was determined on murder, and the blood of Waw-wil-a-way rests upon his head.*

Williams, when found, was stone dead, but Ferguson and Wolf subsequently recovered. The surgeon who examined Waw-wil-a-way stated that every one of his wounds was mortal, and those of the two whites were so severe that it was many months—and they underwent great suffering—before they were themselves again.

This occurrence added fuel to the excitement. The Indians fled in one direction and the whites in another, each party undecided what course to pursue. Several of the prominent citizens of Chilicothe went into the Indian country, where they found Tecumseh and a number of his people. These disavowed all connection with the murder of Herrod, and affirmed that it was their intention to remain true to the Greenville treaty. To quell the apprehension, Tecumseh returned with the deputation to give them personal assurance of his intentions. The people were called together, and through an interpreter, Tecumseh delivered a speech of which a listener said: "When he rose to speak, as he cast his gaze over the vast multitude, which the interesting occasion had drawn together, he appeared one of the most dignified men I ever beheld. While this orator of nature was speaking, the vast crowd preserved the most profound silence. From the confident manner in which he spoke of the intention of the Indians to adhere to the treaty of Greenville, and live in peace and friendship with their white brethren, he dispelled, as if by magic, the apprehensions of the whites—the settlers returned to their deserted farms, and business generally was resumed throughout that region." As Drake remarks, the declaration of no other Indian would have dissipated the fears of a border man which then pervaded the settlement.†

The maternal history of the Prophet and Tecumseh is, that their mother gave birth, about 1770, to three children at one time, who were subsequently named Tecumseh (meaning *a couger crouching for his prey*); Ellskwatawa, (*an open door*); and Rumskaka. The latter seems, however, never to have created any special attention among the tribes. During the early period of the life of the Prophet (Ellskwatawa), he is said to have given himself up almost wholly to a life of intoxication; and it was not until about 1804 that he began to abandon his old habit of drunkenness. A sudden change then came over him. One day, in his wigwam, while lighting his pipe, the account runs, "he fell back in a trance upon his bed, and continued a long time motionless, and without any signs of life." Supposing him to be dead, his friends immediately began to pre-

* J. B. Finley. † Life of Tecumseh, by Edward S. Ellis.

pare for his burial. Agreeably to Indian custom, the head men of the tribe at once gathered about the body, and were in the act of removing it, when, to their great astonishment, Ellskwatawa, (the Prophet) suddenly awoke, and began to address those about him as follows: "Be not alarmed," said he; "I have seen heaven. Call the tribe together, that I may reveal to them the whole of my vision." His request was readily complied with, and he at once began to speak. He said "two beautiful young men had been sent from Heaven by the Great Spirit," who spoke to him thus: "The Great Spirit is angry with you, and will destroy all the red men, unless you abandon drunkenness, lying, and stealing, If you will not do this, and turn yourselves to him, you shall never enter the beautiful place which we will now show you." Whereupon, he affirmed, he was "conducted to the gates of Heaven," and saw "all the glories, but was not permitted to enter. Thus viewing the beauties of the other world, without being permitted to enter, he was told to return to the earth again, and acquaint the Indians with what he had seen, and to persuade them to repent of their vices, saying that then "they would visit him again." After this. Ellskawatawa assumed the powers and title of "Prophet," establishing himself at Greenville, near the point where General Wayne had held the famous treaty with the tribes in 1795; and so famous did he become, that "immense throngs of men, women, and children from the tribes on the Upper Mississippi, and Lake Superior" visited him, and "the most extravagant tales were told and believed by the Indians of his power to perfom miracles." Indeed, "no fatigue or suffering was considered too great to be endured for a sight of him." Like the famous Delaware Prophet, at the period of Pontiac's movements, he proclaimed that "the Great Spirit who had made the red men, was not the same that made the white men;" and urged that the misfortunes of the Indians were owing to their having abandoned their old modes of living, and adopted many of the customs and usages of the pale faces, in the use of their guns, blankets, whisky, etc.—all of which must be thrown away, and the red men again return to their primitive customs, clothing themselves in skins, etc. His followers were now numerous, and the frontier settlements gradually became alarmed at his movements and those of his brother, Tecumseh.*

In 1805, the Shawanoes had wandered from their old hunting grounds and places of abode, and an effort was then made to bring the tribe together again. Tecumseh and his party had settled upon White river, and others of the tribe had begun to settle upon another tributary stream of the Wabash. Tecumseh and some others of the Shawanoes, from different points, having some time in 1805, started for the Auglaize towns, met at Greenville, the site of the old Wayne treaty ground, and there finding his brother, Ellskwatawa, the Prophet, Tecumseh and the other party, through the per-

* "Famous Indians," pages 255, 256, and 257.

suasions of the Prophet, concluded to proceed no farther, and at once began to establish themselves at the old treaty ground of Greenville.

Here, says Drake, the Prophet commenced the practice of those sorceries and incantations by which he gained such notoriety. In the autumn, he assembled a large number of Shawanoes, Delawares, Wyandotts, Pottawattamies, Ottawas, Kickapoos, Chippewas and Senecas, upon the Auglaize river, where he made known to them the sacred character he had taken upon himself. He harangued them at considerable length, denouncing, it is said, the belief and practice of witchcraft common among them, and declaiming against drunkenness with great eloquence and success. He advocated many practices which were really virtuous, and ended by affirming with great solemity that power was given him by the Great Spirit, to cure all diseases, to confound his enemies, and to stay the arm of death, in sickness, or on the battle-field.*

These assertions of the Prophet had great weight with the people —and so much confidence was placed in him, that he did not hesitate to put to death those who in the least disputed his peculiar claims. His plan, when he desired the death of any one, was to denounce him as guilty of witchcraft, and then to call in the help of others in putting him out of the way. Several prominent men of the tribe, who were unfortunate enough to possess more common sense then the others, were put to torture. Among these was a well known Delaware chief, named Teteboxti, who calmly assisted in making his own funeral pile. Others of his family were doomed to death, and the sacrifices at last grew so numerous that Governor Harrison sent a special messenger to the Delawares with the following speech:

"MY CHILDREN:—My heart is filled with grief, and my eyes are dissolved in tears, at the news which has reached me. You have been celebrated for your wisdom above all the tribes of red people who inhabit this great island Your fame as warriors has extended to the remotest nations, and the wisdom of your chiefs has gained for you the appellation of *grandfathers*, from all the neighboring tribes. From what cause, then, does it proceed, that you have departed from the wise counsel of your fathers, and covered yourselves with guilt? My children, tread back the steps you have taken, and endeavor to regain the straight road which you have abandoned. The dark, crooked and thorny one which you are now pursuing, will certainly lead to endless woe and misery. But who is this pretended prophet, who dares to speak in the name of the Great Creator? Examine him. Is he more wise or virtuous than you are yourselves, that he should be selected to convey to you the orders of your God? Demand of him some proofs at least, of his being the messenger of the Deity. If God has really employed him, he has doubtless authorized him to perform miracles, that he

* Drake.

may be known and received as a prophet. If he is really a prophet, ask of him to cause the sun to stand still—the moon to alter its course—the rivers to cease to flow—or the dead to rise from their graves. If he does these things, you may then believe that he has been sent from God. He tells you the Great Spirit commands you to punish with death those who deal in magic; and that he is authorized to point such out. Wretched delusion! Is then the Master of Life obliged to employ mortal man to punish those who offend him? Has he not the thunder and all the powers of nature at his command?—and could he not sweep away from the earth a whole nation with one motion of his arm? My children, do not believe that the great and good Creator of mankind has directed you to destroy your own flesh; and do not doubt but that, if you pursue this abominable wickedness, his vengeance will overtake and crush you.

"The above is addressed to you in the name of the Seventeen Fires.* I now speak to you from myself, as a friend who wishes nothing more sincerely than to see you prosperous and happy. Clear your eyes, I beseech you, from the mist which surrounds them. No longer be imposed upon by the arts of an impostor. Drive him from your town, and let peace and harmony once more prevail among you. Let your poor old men and women sleep in quietness, and banish from their minds the dreadful idea of being burnt alive by their own friends and countrymen. I charge you to stop your bloody career; and, if you value the friendship of your great father, the President—if you wish to preserve the good opinion of the Seventeen Fires, let me hear by the return of the bearer, that you have determined to follow my advice."

The effect of this speech was very great, both with the Delawares and the Shawanoes, for the governor was a man much beloved by the Indians of the northwest. For a time the influence of the prophet was greatly checked, though the Kickapoos, with some smaller tribes, who were still inclined to acknowledge and encourage the claims of the prophet, put the greatest trust in him. And it was about this period, that a Wyandott chief, from Lower Sandusky, a Christian preacher, licensed by the Methodist denomination, visited the Prophet, with a view of gaining some clue as to his noted power. After a year's sojourn with him, the Wyandott chief, returned to his people, fully persuaded that the Prophet was an impostor.

Hearing, sometime before its occurrence, that an eclipse of the sun was to take place at a certain time, during the year 1806, the Prophet announced to his people that, on a certain day, the sun would hide his face, and the earth be veiled in darkness for a time. Coming to pass, as he had told them, the occurrence of this phenomenon had the effect to greatly strengthen his influence again over the tribes. Nothing of special note, however, occurred until the spring of 1807, when it was made known that Tecumseh and

* The seventeen States then composing the Union.

his brother, the Prophet, had assembled several hundred of their people at Greenville, where, through their harangues, they had succeeded in working them up to the highest state of excitement, with a view to make their control the stronger, and to prepare the way for a confederacy of the Indian tribes of the northwest. At these demonstrations, the people of the west became alarmed, and soon began to make strenuous efforts to ascertain the meaning of such movement on the part of Tecumseh and the Prophet, but without success for a time.

Some time subsequent to the capture of this point by Wayne and the treaty of Greenville, Capt. Wells, with whom the reader is already acquainted, as having bid his old friend, Little Turtle, good bye, and left his old home here to join Wayne's army, then on its march thitherward, received the appointment by the government as Indian agent here, in which capacity he acted for several years after.

Having received a letter from the President, through the Secretary of War, addressed to the Indians, and reminding them that they were assembled within the government purchase, and desiring them to remove to some other point, where the government would render them all the aid they needed in settling anew upon territory not held by the government, Captain Wells sent one Anthony Shane, a half-breed Shawanoe, with a message to Tecumseh, inviting the latter, with his brother and two other chiefs, to visit him at Fort Wayne.

Shane had long been intimately acquainted with the Shawanoes, and they of course knew him well, but seem not to have regarded Shane very highly. Having made known the substance of the communication, Shane was met by Tecumseh with this reply: "Go back," said he, "to Fort Wayne, and tell Captain Wells that my fire is kindled on the spot appointed by the Great Spirit alone; and if he has anything to communicate to me, *he* must come *here*; and I shall expect him *six days* from this time."

But Wells did not comply with Tecumseh's request. He sent Shane again, instead, at the appointed time, with the letter of the President, through the Secretary of War, which was readily communicated to Tecumseh, who was by no means pleased that Wells himself had not complied with his desire in waiting upon him in person. Having delivered an eloquent and glowing speech to the council, he told Shane to return to Captain Wells and tell him he would hold no further communication with him; and further, that if the President of the Seventeen Fires had anything else to say to him, he must send it by a man of more importance than Shane. And thus, instead of dispersing, the Indians continued to assemble at Greenville. Fully fifteen hundred had passed and repassed Fort Wayne, in their visits to the Prophet, before the summer of this year (1807) had fairly set in. Messengers and runners passed from tribe to tribe, and were greatly aided by British agents in carrying out their plans, which were always carefully concealed from such as were known to be friendly to the United States.

At the close of summer, reliable witnesses bore testimony that about a thousand Indians, in possession of new rifles, were at Fort Wayne and Greenville, all under the control of the Prophet.

The alarm had now become so general, that the governor of Ohio, in the month of September, sent a deputation to Greenville to ascertain the meaning of the movement. Arriving at Greenville, the commissioners were well received by the Indians—a council was called, and the governor's message read to the assemblage; at the close of which, one of the commissioners addressed them in explanation of their relationship to the United States government, urging them to desist from all aggressions and remain neutral, should a war with England ensue. Having heard the commissioner attentively, according to Indian usage, they asked to be permitted to meditate upon the matter until the next day. In the meantime the famous chief, Blue Jacket, had been appointed to deliver to the commissioners the sentiments of the council; and at its re-assembling, Blue Jacket, through the interpreter, said:

"BRETHREN:—We are seated who heard you yesterday. You will get a true relation, so far as our connections can give it, who are as follows: Shawnees, Wyandots, Pottawatamies, Tawas, Chippewas, Winnepaus, Malominese, Malockese, Lecawgoes, and one more from the north of the Chippewas. Brethren, you see all these men sitting before you, who now speak to you.

"About eleven days ago we had a council, at which the tribe of Wyandots, (the elder brother of the red people) spoke and said God had kindled a fire, and all sat around it. In this council we talked over the treaties with the French and the Americans. The Wyandot said, the French formerly marked a line along the Alleghany mountains, southerly, to Charleston, (S. C.) No man was to pass it from either side. When the Americans came to settle over the line, the English told the Indians to unite and drive off the French, until the war came on between the British and the Americans, when it was told them that king George, by his officers, directed them to unite and drive the Americans back.

"After the treaty of peace between the English and the Americans, the summer before Wayne's army came out, the English held a council with the Indians, and told them if they would turn out and unite as one man, they might surround the Americans like deer in a ring of fire, and destroy them all. The Wyandot spoke further in the council. We see, said he, there is like to be war between the English and our white brethren, the Americans. Let us unite and consider the sufferings we have undergone, from interfereing in the wars of the English. They have often promised to help us, and at last, when we could not withstand the army that came against us, and went to the English fort for refuge, the English told us, 'I can not let you in; you are painted too much, my children.' It was then we saw the British deal treacherously with us. We now see them going to war again. We do not know what they are going to fight for. Let us, my brethren, not interfere, was the speech of the Wyandot.

"Further, the Wyandot said, I speak to you, my little brother, the Shawanoes at Greenville, and to you our little brothers all around. You appear to be at Greenville to serve the Supreme Ruler of the universe. Now send forth your speeches to all our brethren far around us, and let us unite to seek for that which shall be for our eternal welfare, and unite ourselves in a band of perpetual brotherhood. These, brethren, are the sentiments of all the men who sit around you; they all adhere to what the elder brother, the Wyandot, has said, and these are their sentiments. It is not that they are afraid of their white brothers, but that they desire peace and harmony, and not that their white brethren could put them to great necessity, for their former arms were bows and arrows, by which they get their living."

At the conclusion of this speech, the Commissioners made some explanation, whereupon the Prophet, who seemed determined to make every occasion advance his own importance, took upon himself the duty of informing the whites why his people had settled upon Greenville.

"About nine years since," said he, "I became convinced of the errors of my ways, and that I would be destroyed from the face of the earth if I did not amend them. Soon after I was told what I must do to be right. From that time I have continually preached to my red brethren, telling them the miserable situation they are in by nature, and striving to convince them that they must change their lives, live honestly and be just in all their dealings, kind to one other and also to their white brethren; affectionate in their families, put away lying and slandering, and serve the Great Spirit in the way I have pointed out; they must never think of war again; the tomahawk was not given them to go at war with one another. The Shawnees at Tawa town could not listen to me, but persecuted me. This made a division in the nation; those who adhered to me removed to this place, where I have constantly preached to them. They did not select this place because it looked fine or was valuable, for it was neither; but because it was revealed to me that this is the proper place where I must establish my doctrines. I mean to adhere to them while I live, for they are not mine but those of the Great Ruler of the world, and my future life shall prove to the whites the sincerity of my professions. In conclusion, my brethren, our six chiefs shall go with you to Chilicothe."

Tecumseh, Roundhead, Blue Jacket and Panther, returned with the Commissioners to Chilicothe, where a council was called, and in which they gave the governor positive assurances that they entertained none but peaceful intentions toward the whites. A speech which Tecumseh delivered at the time occupied between three and four hours in its delivery. It was eloquent and masterly, and showed that he possessed a thorough knowledge of all the treaties which had been made for years. While he expressed his pacific intentions if fairly treated, he told the governor to his face that every aggression or settlement upon their lands would be resisted, and that no pretended treaties would insure the squatter's safety. Stephen Ruddell (who, with Anthony Shane, has given to the world nearly all that has been learned of Tecumseh) acted as interpreter upon the occasion. Other of the chiefs spoke, but Tecumseh, it was evident, was the leader, and every word that he uttered was received with attention and its full importance attached to it.

The council terminated pleasantly, and the governor, convinced that no instant danger was threatened from the gatherings of the Indians at Greenville and Fort Wayne, disbanded the militia which he had called into service. The chiefs returned to their people, and for a short time the settlers were free from alarm and apprehension.*

Not long after this event the settlements were again thrown into still greater excitement by the murder of a man by the name of Myers, who was killed by the Indians, near where is now the town of Urbana, Ohio; and many of the settlers returned to Kentucky, where they had previously lived, where the alarm arose to such a height as to make it necessary to call into action a large body of militia. Being demanded to deliver up the murderers, Tecumseh and his brother, the Prophet, disclaimed any knowledge of them—said they were not of their people. A council being finally held at Springfield, Tecumseh, Blackfish, and other chiefs, with two separate and distinct parties of Indians, one from the North, the other from Fort Wayne, under Tecumseh, were in attendance. Being embittered against each other, each were quite anxious that the other should receive the blame for the murder. Says Drake, the party from the North, at the request of the Commissioners, left their arms a few miles behind them, but Tecumseh would not consent to attend unless his followers were allowed to keep theirs about them, adding that his tomahawk was his pipe, and he might wish to use it. At this a tall, lank-sided Pensylvanian, who was standing among the spectators, and who, perhaps, had no love for the glittering tomahawk of the self-willed chief, cautiously stepped up, and handed him a greasy, long-stemmed clay pipe, respectfully intimating that if he would only deliver up his dreadful tomahawk, he might use that article. The chief took it between his thumb and finger, held it up, looked at it a few seconds, then at the owner, who all the time was gradually backing away from him, and instantly threw it, with a contemptuous sneer, over his head into the bushes. The commissioners being compelled to wave the point, the council proceeded; and the result was, that the murder was an individual affair, sanctioned by neither party—which brought the

* Life of Tecumseh.

council to a close, with a reconciliation of both parties, and to the acceptance of the settlers.

But the air was still rife with trouble. The protestations of Tecumseh and the Prophet could not allay the uneasiness of the settlements; and before the end of the fall months of this year, (1807) Governor Harrison sent the following speech, by an Indian agent, to the Shawanoes:

"MY CHILDREN:—Listen to me; I speak in the name of your father, the great chief of the Seventeen Fires.

"My children, it is now twelve years since the tomahawk, which you had seized by the advice of your father, the king of Great Britain, was buried at Greenville, in the presence of that great warrior, General Wayne.

"My children, you then promised, and the Great Spirit heard it, that you would in future live in peace and friendship with your brothers, the Americans. You made a treaty with your father, and one that contained a number of good things, equally beneficial to all the tribes of the red people, who were parties to it.

"My children, you promised in that treaty to acknowledge no other father than the chief of the Seventeen Fires; and never to listen to the proposition of any foreign nation. You promised never to lift up the tomahawk against any of your father's children, and to give him notice of any other tribe that intended it; your father also promised to do something for you, particulary to deliver to you every year a certain quantity of goods; to prevent any white man from settling on your lands without your consent, or to do you any personal injury. He promised to run a line between your land and his, so that you might know your own; and you were to be permitted to live and hunt upon your father's land, as long as you behaved yourselves well. My children, which of these articles has your father broken? You know that he has observed them all with the utmost good faith. But, my children, have you done so? Have you not always had your ears open to receive bad advice from the white people beyond the lakes?

"My children, let us look back to times that are past. It has been a long time since you called the king of Great Britain father. You know that it is the duty of a father to watch over his children, to give them good advice, and to do every thing in his power to make them happy. What has this father of yours done for you, during the long time that you have looked up to him for protection and advice? Are you wiser and happier than you were before you knew him, or is your nation stronger or more respectable? No, my children, he took you by the hand when you were a powerful tribe; you held him fast, supposing he was your friend, and he conducted you through paths filled with thorns and briers, which tore your flesh and shed your blood. Your strength was exhausted, and you could no longer follow him. Did he stay by you in your distress, and assist and comfort you? No, he led you into danger and then abandoned you. He saw your blood flowing and he would give you no bandage to tie up your wounds. This was the conduct of the man who called himself your father. The Great Spirit opened your eyes; you heard the voice of the chief of the Seventeen Fires speaking the words of peace. He called you to follow him; you came to him, and he once more put you on the right way, on the broad, smooth road that would have led to happiness. But the voice of your deceiver is again heard; and, forgetful of your former sufferings, you are again listening to him. My children, shut your ears and mind him not, or he will lead you to ruin and misery.

"My children, I have heard bad news. The sacred spot where the great council-fire was kindled, around which the Seventeen Fires and ten tribes of their children smoked the pipe of peace—that very spot where the Great Spirit saw his red and white children encircle themselves with the chain of friendship—that place has been selected for dark and bloody councils. My children, this business must be stopped. You have called in a number of men from the most distant tribes, to listen to a fool, who spake not the words of the Great Spirit, but those of the devil, and of the British agents. My children, your conduct has much alarmed the white settlers near you. They desire that you will send away those people, and if they wish to have the impostor with them, they can carry him. Let him go to the lakes; he can hear the British more distinctly."

The Prophet's reply was, that evil birds had sung in the Governor's ears; and he denied any correspondence with the British, protesting that he had no intentions whatever of disturbing the adjoining settlements. It soon became evident, however, that the assemblages of the Prophet could not be dispersed without a resort to arms on the part of the government; and Gov. Harrison, strongly disposed to think that no harm was intended by the Indians towards the settlements, let the matter rest, and the assemblages continued, large bodies of Indians coming down from the lakes in the early part of the following year (1808), where, as their supply of provisions became reduced or exhausted, they received fresh supplies from Fort Wayne.

But a change of base was contemplated, and the Pottawattamies having granted them a portion of land, Tecumseh and the Prophet, in the spring of this year, removed with the tribe to Tippecanoe, where large bodies were soon collected, and, among other exercises, war-like sports became frequent among them. Again the settlements were in a high state of uneasiness, and many were ready to declare that they knew from the first that the Indians were but preparing for the consummation of some treacherous scheme. Many of the Indians among them were from the north. The Miamies and Delawares, being friendly to the whites, were greatly opposed to their coming, and even sent a delegation to the Prophet to stop them. But Tecumseh and his brother, the Prophet, in receiving them, said they were not to be thwarted in their purposes to ameliorate the condition of their brethren; and the Miami and Delaware delegation returned fully of the belief that the settlements were not without the strongest grounds for the apprehensions they had so long manifested.

August had come. The Prophet, accompanied by several of his followers, had visited Governor Harrison, at Vincennes, protesting, as formerly, that his purposes were peaceable. Said he, to Gov. Harrison:

"FATHER:—It is three years since I first began with that system of religion which I now practice. The white people and some of the Indians were against me; but I had no other intention but to introduce among the Indians, those good principles of religion which the white people profess. I was spoken badly of by the white people, who reproached me with misleading the Indians; but I defy them to say I did anything amiss.

"Father, I was told that you intended to hang me. When I heard this, I intended to remember it, and tell my father, when I went to see him, and relate the truth.

"I heard, when I settled on the Wabash, that my father, the Governor, had declared that all the land between Vincennes and Fort Wayne, was the property of the Seventeen Fires. I also heard that you wanted to know, my father, whether I was God or man; and that you said if I was the former, I should not steal horses. I heard this from Mr. Wells, but I believed it originated with himself.

"The Great Spirit told me to tell the Indians that he had made them, and made the world—that he had placed them on it to do good and not evil.

"I told all the red-skins, that the way they were in was not good, and that they ought to abandon it.

"That we ought to consider ourselves as one man; but we ought to live agreeably to our several customs, the red people after their mode, and the white people after theirs; particularly, that they should not drink whiskey; that it was not made for them, but the white people, who alone knew how to use it; and that it is the cause of all the mischiefs which the Indians suffer; and that they must always follow the directions of the Great Spirit, and we must listen to him, as it was He that made us; determine to listen to nothing that is bad; do not take up the tomahawk, should it be offered by the British, or by the Long-Knives; do not meddle with any thing that does not belong to you, but mind your own business, and cultivate the ground, that your women and your children may have enough to live on.

"I now inform you that it is our intention to live in peace with our father and his people forever.

"My father, I have informed you what we mean to do, and I call the Great Spirit to witness the truth of my declaration. The religion which I have established for the last three years, has been attended to by the different tribes of Indians in this part of the world. These Indians were once different people; they are now but one; they are all determined to practice what I have communicated to them, that has come immediately from the Great Spirit through me.

"Brother, I speak to you as a warrior. You are one. But let us lay aside this character, and attend to the care of our children, that they may live in comfort and peace. We desire that you will join us for the preservation of both red and white people. Formerly, when we lived in ignorance, we were foolish; but now, since we listen to the voice of the Great Spirit, we are happy.

"I have listened to what you have said to us. You have promised to assist us. I now request you, in behalf of all the red people, to use your exertions to prevent the sale of liquor to us. We are all well pleased to hear you say that you will endeavor to promote our happiness. We give you every assurance that we will follow the dictates of the Great Spirit.

"We are all well pleased with the attention you have showed us; also with the good intentions of our father, the President. If you give us a few articles, such as needles, flints, hoes, powder, etc., we will take the animals that afford us meat, with powder and ball."

Says Drake, to test the influence of the Prophet over his followers, Gov. Harrison held conversations with and offered them spirits, but they always refused, and he became almost convinced that he was really sincere in his professions, and had no higher ambition than to ameliorate the condition of his race.

Thus matters rested or rather continued; and during the following year Tecumseh and the Prophet sought quietly to add strength to their movement. Both were engaged in a deep game; and while the Prophet seemed the leading spirit, Tecumseh was yet the prime mover; and the Prophet attempted but little without first getting the advice of the former, if in reach, though it is evident he was most headstrong in much that he undertook.

In the spring of 1809, reports having reached the ear of Gov. Harrison that many of the Indians were leaving the Prophet because of his persistency in requiring them to become party to a scheme he had in view for the massacre of the inhabitants of Vincennes, he began the organization of two companies of volunteer militia, with a view to garrisoning a post some two miles from Vincennes. But the Prophet's followers having dispersed before the close of the summer, the alarm among the settlements became placid again, and so continued until the early part of 1810.

Up to 1809 Governor Harrison continued his efforts in the extinguishment of Indian claims to lands within the Indiana Territory; and on the 30th of September of that year concluded another treaty at Fort Wayne, in which the chiefs and head men of the Delaware, Pottawattamie, Miami, and Eel River tribes participated. According to the report of this treaty, the Indians sold and ceded to the

United States about two million nine hundred thousand acres of land, principally situated on the southeastern side of the river Wabash, and below the mouth of Raccoon Creek, a little stream which empties into the Wabash, near what is now the boundaries of Parke county, in this State. The chiefs and head men of the Wea tribe, in the following month, (26th of October) having met Gov. Harrison at Vincennes, acknowledged the legality of this treaty; and by a treaty held at Vincennes on the 9th of December following, the sachems and war-chiefs of the Kickapoo tribe also confirmed the treaty of Fort Wayne. Up to this time, the whole amount of land ceded to the United States by treaty stipulations between Governor Harrison and the different tribes of the Indiana Territory, according to the records, was 29,719,530 acres.

Having received, through what he believed a reliable source, certain facts regarding the conduct of Tecumseh and the Prophet in an effort to incite the Indians against the settlements of the west; and that those who had previously left the ranks of the Prophet had again returned to his support; and further, that the British had their agents quietly at work among the tribes thus banded; that the Indians were boasting to American traders that they were getting their ammunition—powder and balls—without cost; Gov. Harrison, through instructions from the Secretary of War, in July, 1810, began at once to prepare for the better safety of the frontier settlements.

CHAPTER XIV.

"At length Discord, the Fury, came,
Waving her murderous torch of flame,
And kindled that intestine fire,
* * * * * * *
Which, like the lightning-flame burns on,
More fierce for being rained upon."

———o———

Further movements of Tecumseh and the Prophet—The "Doomed Warrior"—Letter of Gov. Harrison—Death of Tarhe—Discovery of the plot to massacre Fort Wayne, &c.—Efforts of Tecumseh to obtain the aid of the tribes along the Mississippi—Influence of British agents—Agents are dispatched to Tecumseh and the Prophet—The Prophet complains that the Indians had been cheated—Gov. Harrison writes to the Secretary of War—He also sends an address to Tecumseh and the Prophet—Tecumseh's visit to Vincennes—The conference—Eloquence of Tecumseh—His contempt for the proffer of the government—Personal appearance of Tecumseh—His objections to the treaty of Fort Wayne—Sends wampum belts to the different tribes—Gov. Harrison's address to the legislature—Statement of a Kickapoo chief—Assurances of the Gov. of Missouri—Seizure of salt by the Prophet—Governor Harrison demands further aid from the government—Vincennes to be the first place of attack—Tecumseh again visits Gov. Harrison—His departure for the South—His efforts among the Creek Indians—His return northward—His charges to the Prophet—alarm of the settlers—Arrival of aid—Gov. Harrison determins to bring matters to a crisis—Peaceful protestations of the Prophet—Gov. Harrison grows more determined—Prepares for a march upon the Prophet's town—The army met by a deputation from the Prophet—A conference agreed upon—The army encamps for the night—An attack expected—The night dark and cloudy—Indians on the alert—Discovered by the sentry—An attack—The Prophet tells the Indians the bullets of the white men will not hurt them—Fierce struggle—Indians routed—The battle of Tippecanoe a success for the American arms—Anger of Tecumseh—He visits Fort Wayne; and the Prophet retires to the Missessinewa.

———o———

AS THE summer of 1810 advanced it became more and more evident to Gov. Harrison that the true purposes of Tecumseh and the Prophet were war upon the whites. Having accused a Wyandott chief, by the name of Leatherlips, known as the "Doomed Warrior," with witchcraft, it was thought that the Prophet and Tecumseh were instrumental in his subsequent murder; though it was asserted by a Mr. Thatcher that a Wyandott chief, of the Porcupine clan, known as Tarhe or Crane, was the principal agent in the deed. But Gov. Harrison, in a letter addressed to the editor of the "Hesperian," 1838, said of Tarhe: "I have often said I never knew a better man, and am confident he would not have been concerned in such a transaction as is ascribed to him. In support of this opinion I offer the following reasons: The execution of the 'Doomed Wyandott Chief' is attributed, and no doubt correctly, to the Shawnee Prophet and his brother Tecumseh. To my knowledge, Tarhe was always the opponent of these men, and could not have been their agent in the matter. The accusation of witchcraft was brought by these Shawnee brothers, and the accused were exclusively those who were friendly to the United States, and who had been parties to treaties by which the Indian titles to lands had been extinguished. In both these respects, Tarhe had rendered himself obnoxious to the former. Tarhe was not only the Grand Sachem of his tribe, but the acknowledged head of all the tribes who were engaged in the war with the United States, which was terminated by the treaty of Greenville; and in that character the duplicate of the original treaty, engrossed on parchment, was committed to his custody, as had been the grand calumet which was the symbol of peace. Tarhe united with his friend, Black-Hoof, the head chief of the Shawnees, in denying the rank of chief either to the Prophet or Tecumseh; and, of course, he would not have received it of them. If the 'Doomed Warrior' had been snetenced by a council of his own nation, Tarhe would not have directed the execution, but, as was invariably the custom, it would have been committed to one of the war-chiefs. The party sent to put the old chief to death, no doubt, came immediately from Tippecanoe; and if it was commanded by a Wyandot, the probability is that it was Round-Head, who was a Captain of the band of Wyandots who resided with the Prophet, and was, to a great extent, under his influence."

Rev. J. B. Finley, a missionary to the tribe of Tarhe, and for some years most intimately acquainted with Tarhe, said that Mr. Thatcher and his informant were wholly mistaken in the conclusions regarding the accusation against Tarhe; and added that a better and truer Indian than he never lived.

Finding the "Doomed Warrior" at his home, some twelve miles north of Columbus, he was made acquainted with the sentence passed upon him, and calmly prepared to meet the fate which he felt inevitable. A number of white men present, sought to interfere in his behalf, but without success; and when the fatal hour came, he is said to have "turned from his wigwam, and, with a voice of surpassing strength and melody, commenced the chant of his death-song. He was followed slowly by the Wyandott warriors, all timing, with their slow and measured march, the music of his wild and melancholy dirge. The whites were likewise all silent followers in that strange procession."

Having been led to his own grave, he knelt calmly, resolutely down, and offered a prayer to the Great Spirit, at the conclusion of which, still in a kneeling posture, one of the Wyandotts gave him a heavy blow upon the head with a tomahawk, breaking his skull.

After a few moments more, ceasing to stir, the unfortunate victim of the Shawanoe conspirators and revolutioners, with all his apparel and decorations, was consigned to the earth and hidden from view.

A few weeks later, and Gov. Harrison was made acquainted with a plot that was maturing for the surprise and massacre of Fort Wayne, Detroit, Chicago, Vincennes, and St. Louis. Tecumseh and the Prophet were moving as with the slow but sure action of a volcanoe; and the internal heat of their efforts was continually made the more apparent by the rising cinders cast up in the endeavor here and there secretly to draw the different tribes of the west and south within their circle, and by other means, equally wily and sereptitious, to bring their plans to bear for the overthrow of the whites of the northwest.

At the conclusion of the struggle for Independence, the opinion is said to have prevailed with many in England that the American colonies were not wholly lost to the mother country; and the hope was entertained by such, that, at some favorable hour the English government would be able to regain its former hold upon the country; in which anticipations, it was thought the British Ministry most earnestly and hopefully united. From anticipations and desires of this nature, together with the discomfiture felt at the failure of their arms, may have arisen the many hostile acts of interferance on the part of English agents, commandants, and others in their employ along the interior frontiers of the northwest, and also the bestowal of frequent large supplies of ammunition upon the various tribes within range of the Canadas.

After the discovery of the plot to massacre the forts, it was ascertained that strong efforts were being made to persuade the tribes along the Mississippi to unite with Tecumseh and the Prophet in their efforts, but up to the period in question, had met with no great degree of success; while the most influential chiefs among the Delawares, Miamies, and Shawanoes were much opposed to the reckless schemes and efforts of Tecumseh and the Prophet. Besides these facts, about this period, Governor Harrison learned from a friendly Indian that a British agent had recently visited the Prophet, who had encouraged the latter to continue in his efforts to unite the tribes, and to await a signal from the British authorities before carrying out their designs against the Americans.

Finding now that the most constant watchfulness was necessary, and being determined to obtain all the information possible regarding their plans, Governor Harrison dispatched two agents to Tecumseh and his brother with a view of ascertaining more fully and certainly, if possible, their real designs and plans. Receiving the agents very courteously, in reply to the inquiries made, the Prophet told the agents that the assembling of the Indians upon that spot was by the explicit command of the Great Spirit.

Having heard the Prophet, the agents told him that his movements had excited so much alarm that the troops of Kentucky and Indiana were being called out, and strong preparations were being made in anticipation of trouble with the tribes.

In answer to the questions of the agents as to the cause of his complaints against the United States, the Prophet replied that his people had been cheated of their lands. Insisting that his complaints would readily be listened to by laying them before Gov. Harrison, at Vincennes, the Prophet refused to go, saying that, while there, upon a former occasion, he was badly treated.

Receiving this information, the Governor at once wrote to the Secretary, stating the cause, and telling him that all this caviling was merely a pretext on the part of Tecumseh and the Prophet to gather strength in the furtherance of their designs; that he had been as liberal in the conclusion of treaties as his understanding of the views and opinions of the government would permit, and that none of the tribes had just cause for complaint.

Having heard, in the month of July, that the Sacs and Foxes had formed an alliance with the Prophet, and were ready and willing to strike the Americans at any time, Governor Harrison set about the preparation of the following address, which he forwarded to the Prophet by a confidential interpreter:

"William Henry Harrison, Governor and Commander-in-chief of the Territory of Indiana, to the Shawanoe chief and the Indians assembled at Tippecanoe:

"Nothwithstanding the improper language which you have used toward me, I will endeavor to open your eyes to your true interests. Notwithstanding what bad white men have told you, I am not your personal enemy. You ought to know this from the manner in which I received and treated you on your visit to this place.

"Although I must say, that you are an enemy to the Seventeen Fires, and that you have used the greatest exertions with other tribes to lead them astray. In this, you have been in some measure successful; as I am told they are ready to raise the tomahawk against their father; yet their father, notwithstanding his anger at their folly, is full of goodness, and is always ready to receive into his arms those of his children who are willing to repent, acknowledge their fault, and ask for his forgiveness.

"There is yet but little harm done, which may easily be repaired. The chain of friendship which united the whites with the Indians may be renewed, and be as strong as ever. A great deal of that work depends upon you—the destiny of those who are under you, depends upon the choice you may make of the two roads which are before you. The one is large, open and pleasant, and leads to peace, security and happiness; the other, on the contrary, is narrow and crooked, and leads to misery and ruin. Don't deceive yourselves; do not believe that all the nations of Indians united are able to resist the force of the Seventeen Fires. I know your warriors are brave, but ours are not less so; but what can a few brave warriors do against the innumerable warriors of the Seventeen Fires? Our blue-coats are more numerous than you can count; our hunters are like the leaves of the forest, or the grains of sand on the Wabash.

"Do not think that the red-coats can protect you; they are not able to protect themselves. They do not think of going to war with us. If they did, you would, in a few months, see our flag wave over all the forts of Canada.

"What reason have you to complain of the Seventeen Fires? Have they taken any thing from you? Have they ever violated the treaties made with the red-men? You say that they have purchased lands from them who had no right to sell them: show that this is true, and the land will be instantly restored. Show us the rightful owners of those lands which have been purchased—let them present themselves. The ears of your father will be opened to your complaints, and if the lands have been purchased of those who did not own them, they will be restored to their rightful owners. I have full power to arrange this business; but if you would rather carry your complaints before your great father, the President, you shall be indulged. I will immediately take means to send you, with those chiefs which you may choose, to the city where your father lives. Every thing necessary shall be prepared for your journey, and means taken for your safe return."

After hearing this speech, the Prophet told the interpreter that, as his brother intended to pay Governor Harrison a visit in a few weeks, he would let him carry the reply to the Governor's message. Receiving this information, Governor Harrison sent a message to Tecumseh, requesting him to bring but a small body of his followers, as it was inconvenient for him to receive many; to which Tecumseh paid little or no regard, and on the 12th of August, 1810, with four hundred warriors, all armed with tomahawks, war-clubs, and "painted in the most terrific manner," he began to descend the Wabash for Vincennes. Arriving near Vincennes, and encamping on the Wabash, on the morning of the 15th, attended by about fifteen or twenty of his warriors, Tecumseh approached the house of the Governor, who, in company with the judges of the Supreme Court, several army officers, a sergeant and a dozen men, besides a large number of citizens, waited upon the portico of his own house to receive the chief and his followers.*

During the milder season of the year, to hold a council other than in a grove or woody place, with logs or a clear, grassy spot of ground to set upon, was to invite the Indian to do an act very much to his distaste; and to the invitation to come forward and take seats upon the portico, he objected, signifying that it was not a fit place to hold a council, and expressed a desire that the meeting might be held beneath a grove of trees near, which was readily assented to, and soon the Governor, with his attendants was seated beneath a grove of trees in the open lawn, before the house.

* Ellis' Life of Tecumseh.

"With a firm and elastic step," says Judge Law,* and "with a proud and somewhat defiant look, he advanced to the place where the Governor and those who had been invited to attend the conferance were sitting. This place had been fenced in, with a view of preventing the crowd from encroaching upon the council during its deliberations. As he stepped forward, he seemed to scan the preparations which had been made for his reception, particularly the *military part* of it, with an eye of suspicion—by no means, however, with fear. As he came in front of the *dias*, an elevated portion of the place upon which the Governor and the officers of the Territory were seated, the Governor invited him, through the interpreter, to come forward and take a seat with him and his counsellors, premising the invitation by saying: That it was the wish of *their* 'GREAT FATHER,' the President of the United States, that he should do so." Pausing for a moment, at the utterance of these words by the interpreter, and extending his tall figure to its greatest height, he looked scanningly upon the troops and then upon the crowd about him. Thus, for a moment, with keen, piercing eyes fixed upon Governor Harrison, and then upward to the sky, and "his sinewy arm pointing towards the heaven," with a tone and gesture expressive of "supreme contempt for the paternity assigned him," in a clear, loud, full voice, which reverberated again upon the momentary stillness that his stolid demeanor had produced, with all eyes fixed upon him, he exclaimed:

"*My Father?*—The sun is *my* father—the earth is *my* mother—and on her bosom I will recline." Having finished, says Judge Law, he stretched himself with his warriors on the green sward; and the effect is said to have been electrical—for some moments there was a perfect silence throughout the assembly.

Governor Harrison having now begun to refer to the subject of the council, said to Tecumseh, through the interpreter, "that he had understood he had complaints to make, and redress to ask for certain wrongs which *he*, Tecumseh, supposed had been done his tribe, as well as the others; that he felt disposed to listen to the one, and make satisfaction for the other, if it was proper he should do so. That in all his intercourse and negotiations with the Indians, he had endeavored to act justly and honorably with them, and believed he had done so, and had heard of no complaint of his conduct until he learned that Tecumseh was endeavoring to create dissatisfaction towards the Government, not only among the Shawanoes, but among the other tribes dwelling on the Wabash and Illinois; and had, in so doing, produced a great deal of mischief and trouble between them and the whites, by averring that the tribes, whose land the Government had lately purchased, had no right ro sell, nor their chiefs any authority to convey. That he, the Governor, had invited him to attend the Council, with a view of learning from his own lips, whether there was any truth in the reports which he had heard,

*Judge Law's Address, page 83.

and to learn from himself whether he, or his tribe, had any cause of complaint against the whites; and if so, as a man and a warrior, openly and boldly to avow it. That, as between himself and as great a warrior as Tecumseh, there should be no concealment—all should be done by them under a clear sky, and in an open path, and with these feelings on his own part, he was glad to meet him in council."

In appearance, Tecumseh was accounted "one of the most splendid specimens of his tribe—celebrated for their physical proportions and fine forms, even among the nations surrounding the Shawanoes. Tall, athletic, and manly, dignified but graceful, he seemed the *beau ideal* of an Indian chieftain. In a voice, at first low, but with all its indistinctness,"* Tecumseh replied by "stating, at length, his objections to the treaty of Fort Wayne, made by Gov. Harrison in the previous year; and in the course of of his speech," says Benjamin Drake, "boldly avowed the principle of his party to be, that of resistance to every cession of land, unless made by all the tribes, who, he contended, formed but one nation. He admitted that he threatened to kill the chiefs who signed the treaty of Fort Wayne; and that it was his fixed determination not to permit the *village* chiefs, in future, to manage their affairs, but to place the power with which *they* had been heretofore invested, in the hands of the war-chiefs. The Americans, he said, had driven the Indians from the sea-coast, and would soon push them into the lakes; and, while he disclaimed all intention of making war upon the United States, he declared it to be his unalterable resolution to take a stand, and resolutely oppose the further intrusion of the whites upon the Indian lands. He concluded, by making a brief but impassioned recital of the various wrongs and aggressions inflicted upon the Indians by the white men, from the commencement of the Revolutionary war down to the period of that conncil; all of which was calculated to arouse and influence the minds of such of his followers as were present.

"The Governor rose in reply, and in examining the right of Tecumseh and his party to make objections to the treaty of Fort Wayne, took occasion to say, that the Indians were not one nation, having a common property in the lands. The Miamis, he contended, were the real owners of the tract on the Wabash, ceded by the late treaty, and the Shawnees had no right to interfere in the case; that upon the arrival of the whites on this continent, they had found the Miamis in possession of this land, the Shawnees being then residents of Georgia, from which they had been driven by the Creeks, and that it was ridiculous to assert that the red men constituted but one nation; for, if such had been the intention of the Great Spirit, he would not have put different tongues in their heads, but have taught them all to speak the same language.

"The Governor having taken his seat, the interpreter commenced

* Judge Law's Address, page 85.

explaining the speech to Tecumseh, who, after listening to a portion of it, sprung to his feet, and began to speak with great vehemence of manner.

"The Governor was surprised at his violent gestures, but as he did not understand him, thought he was making some explanation, and suffered his attention to be drawn toward Winnemac, a friendly Indian lying on the grass before him, who was renewing the priming of his pistol, which he had kept concealed from the other Indians, but in full view of the Governor. His attention, however, was again attracted toward Tecumseh, by hearing General Gibson, who was intimately acquainted with the Shawnee language, say to Lieutenant Jennings, 'Those fellows intend mischief; you had better bring up the guard.' At that moment, the followers of Tecumseh seized their tomahawks and war-clubs, and sprang upon their feet, their eyes turned upon the Governor. As soon as he could disengage himself from the arm-chair in which he sat, he rose, drew a small sword which he had by his side, and stood on the defensive. Captain G. R. Floyd, of the army, who stood near him, drew a dirk, and the chief Winnemac cocked his pistol. The citizens present were more numerous than the Indians, but were unarmed; some of them procured clubs and brick-bats, and also stood on the defensive. The Rev. Mr. Winans, of the Methodist church, ran to the Governor's house, got a gun, and posted himself at the door to defend the family. During this singular scene, no one spoke, until the guard came running up, and appearing to be in the act of firing, the Governor ordered them not to do so. He then demanded of the interpreter an explanation of what had happened, who replied that Tecumseh had interrupted him, declaring that all the Governor had said was *false*; and that he and the Seventeen Fires had cheated and imposed on the Indians.

"The Governor then told Tecumseh that he was a bad man, and that he would hold no further communication with him; that as he had come to Vincennes under the protection of a council-fire, he might return in safety, but he must immediately leave the village. Here the council terminated. During the night, two companies of militia were brought in from the country, and that belonging to the town was also embodied. Next morning Tecumseh requsted the Governor to afford him an opportunity of explaining his conduct on the previous day—declaring that he did not intend to attack the Governor, and that he had acted under the advice of some of the white people. The Governor consented to have another interview, it being understood that each party should have the same armed force as on the previous day. On this occasion the deportment of Tecumseh was respectful and dignified. He again denied having any intention to make an attack upon the Governor, and declared that he had been stimulated to the course he had taken, by two white men, who assured him that one half the citizens were opposed to the Governor, and willing to restore the land in question;

that the Governor would soon be put out of office, and a good man sent to fill his place, who would give up the land to the Indians. When asked by the Governor whether he intended to resist the survey of these lands, Tecumseh replied that he and his followers were resolutely determined to insist upon the old boundary. When he had taken his seat, chiefs from the Wyandots, Kickapoos, Pottawatamies, Ottawas and Winnebagoes, spoke in succession, and distinctly avowed that they had entered into the Shawnee confederacy, and were determined to support the principles laid down by their leader. The Governor, in conclusion, stated that he would make known to the President the claims of Tecumseh and his party, to the land in question; but that he was satisfied the Government would never admit that the lands on the Wabash were the property of any other tribes than those who occupied them when the white people first arrived in America; and, as the title to these lands had been derived by purchase from those tribes, he might rest assured that the right of the United States would be sustained by the sword. Here the council adjourned.

"On the following day, Governor Harrison visited Tecumseh in his camp, attended only by the interpreter, and was politely received. A long conversation ensued, in which Tecumseh again declared that his intentions were really such as he had avowed them to be in the council; that the policy which the United States pursued, of purchasing land from the Indians, he viewed as mighty water, ready to overflow his people; and that the confederacy which he was forming among the tribes to prevent any individual tribe from selling without the consent of the others, was the dam he was erecting to resist this mighty water. He stated further, that he should be reluctantly drawn into war with the United States; and that if he, the Governor, would induce the President to give up the lands lately purchased, and agree never to make another treaty without the consent of all the tribes, he would be their faithful ally, and assist them in the war, which he knew was about to take place with England; that he preferred being the ally of the Seventeen Fires, but if they did not comply with his request, he would be compelled to unite with the British. The Governor replied, that he would make known his views to the President, but that there was no probability of its being agreed to. 'Well,' said Tecumseh, 'as the great chief is to determine the matter, I hope the Great Spirit will put sense enough into his head to induce him to give up this land; it is true, he is so far off, he will not be injured by the war; he may sit still in his town and drink his wine, while you and I will have to fight it out.' This prophecy, it will be seen, was literally fulfilled; and the great chieftain who uttered it, attested that fulfillment with his blood. The governor, in conclusion, proposed to Tecumseh, that in the event of hostilities between the Indians and the United States, he should use his influence to put an end to the cruel mode of warfare which the Indians were accustomed to wage upon women and children, or upon prisoners. To this he cheerfully assented; and it is due to the memory of Tecumseh to add, that he faithfully kept his promise down to the period of his death."

Not long subsequent to the termination of this council, a Winnebago chief, who had been employed by Governor Harrison to watch the proceedings of Tecumseh, brought word to Gov. Harrison that the former was sending to each of the tribes a large wampum belt, with a view of uniting them in one great confederation; and that, upon a return of the belt, he saw a British agent fairly dance with joy—adding, with tears in his eyes, that he and all the village chiefs had been deprived of their power, and that the control of everything was in the hands of the warriors, who were greatly opposed to the United States.

Speaking of the Prophet, in his address to the legislature of this year, Gov. Harrison said: "His character as a Prophet would not, however, have given him any very dangerous influence, if he had not been assisted by the intrigues and advice of foreign agents, and other disaffected persons, who have for many years omitted no opportunity of counteracting the measures of the government with regard to the Indians, and filling their naturally jealous minds with suspicions of the justice and integrity of our views against them."

During the autumn of 1810, a Kickapoo chief visited Governor Harrison, and assured him that the peaceful assurances of the Prophet and Tecumseh were merely to cover up their real intentions against the United States; and about the same period, the Governor of Missouri sent word that the Sac Indians had allied themselves to the Tecumseh confederacy; that Tecumseh himself was then doing all in his power to induce the tribes west of the Mississippi to join him; to which were added the reports of different Indian agents, who were generally of opinion that the period for a war with the Indians would soon arrive. And thus passed the year 1810.

Early in 1811, as a part of the annuity to the Indians, Governor Harrison sent a boat load of salt up the Wabash, a portion of which was to be given to the Prophet for the Shawanoes and Kickapoos; but, upon the arrival of the boat at the point where the Prophet had his lodges, he made bold to seize the entire cargo, alleging for so doing that he had two thousand men to feed, who had been without that commodity for two years. Upon the receipt of this proceedure, Governor Harrison felt fully justified in demanding immediate aid from the government, and accordingly made application to the Secretary of War to have Colonel Boyd's regiment, then at Pittsburg, sent immediately to him, for the better safety of Vincennes, requesting, at the same time, to receive authority to act on the offensive as soon as it was known that the Indians were arrayed in actual hostility against the United States. The Governor's apprehensions were well founded, and it soon became an acknwoledged fact, that Vincennes was to be the first point of attack. The place was most accessible, and Tecumseh was fully aware of its situation. He could have made a descent upon it in a very short space of time, and then retreated into the unexplored country behind it, "where it would have been next to impossible for any cavalry to have penetrated" at that period. And so earnest was Governor Harrison upon the subject, that he notified the Secretary of War, that, should troops not be immediately sent to his relief, he would at once take the matter in his own hands.

Accompanied by three hundred warriors,* on the 27th of July of this year, Tecumseh again visited Vincennes; and on the 30th of this month, in an arbor near, attended by about two hundred of his warriors, another council was held. Opening the occasion by presenting the fact of several murders having been committed by Indians in Illinois, Governor Harrison expressed a desire that Tecumseh should pay a visit to the President with a view of laying before him what complaints he had to offer, assuring him that he should receive the fullest justice at the chief magistrate's hands; and concluded by demanding an explanation of the conduct of the Prophet in the seizure of the salt sent up the Wabash sometime before, to be devided among the tribes. Replying to the latter, Tecumseh remarked that he was not at home at the time of the seizure of the salt, and said nothing further than, that Governor Harrison seemed very hard to please, he having complained sometime before that they refused to take the salt, and that now he was not pleased because they had taken it. With but little further business of importance, the council adjourned to meet again on the following day.

Reassembling, says the account,† on the afternoon of the next day, the council was continued far into the night. There being a full moon and a clear sky, the members were distinctly revealed to each other. It must have been a picturesque scene—those one hundred and seventy warriors seated in grim silence, listening, spell-bound, to the eloquence of the wonderful Tecumseh, occasionally signifying their approbation by their odd grunts; or, taking in the words of the noble Harrison, as he strove by every means at his command to convince them that what he urged was for their own welfare and interest.

Still manifesting his well known self-will and independence, Tecumseh cooly admitted that he was still endeavoring to establish a union of the different tribes. And "why do *you* complain?" he enquired; "hav'nt *you* formed a confederacy of your different fires? We have raised no voice against that, and what right have *you* to prevent us doing the same? So soon as the council ends, I shall go south and seek to bring the Creeks and Choctaws into our confederacy;" repeating that his designs were peaceful, and that the whites were causelessly alarmed; while his reply regarding the Illinois murders is said to have been not only "justified by facts," but

* Ellis' Life of Tecumseh, page 48.

† As principally presented by Benjamin Drake.

was "cutting and pointed." Governor Harrison had previously stated, in a letter to the war department, "that it was impossible, in many instances, for the Indians to receive justice. Were one of their number murdered by a white man, no jury of settlers would convict him, and, many of the latter seemed to think the savage fit for nothing but insults and kicks." "As to the murderers, they are not in my town," was substantially Tecumseh's response; "and if they were, I would not give them up. We have set the whites an example of *forgiving* injuries, which they should follow;" and added that he wished no settlers to come upon the new purchase, near Tippecanoe before his return from the south, as the Indians would require it as a hunting ground, and that if they found cattle or hogs there, they would be apt to treat them as lawful game.*

In a brief but earnest response, Governor Harrison said "the moon above them should fall to the earth before the President would allow his people to be massacred with impunity; and that no land would be yielded which had been honorably and fairly bought of the Indians." And here the council terminated, from whence, as he had stated, with great pomp, accompanied by some twenty of his warriors, Tecumseh was soon rowing his canoe southward down the Ohio to arouse the Creeks for the overthrow of the whites.

Of his efforts and the result of his mission among the Creeks, the following graphic account† will be read with no little degree of interest. The Shawanoe chieftain and his followers had meet their friends, the Creeks of the south, and a council was at once proposed.

"Tecumseh led, the warriors followed, one in the footsteps of the other. The Creeks, in dense masses, stood on one side of the path, but the Shawanoes noticed no one; they marched into the center of the square, and then turned to the left. At each angle of the square, Tecumseh took from his pouch some tobacco and sumach, and dropped on the ground; his warriors performed the same ceremony. This they repeated three times as they marched around the square. Then they approached the flag-pole in the center, circled around it three times, and facing the north, threw tobacco and sumach on a small fire, burning, as usual, near the base of the pole. On this they emptied their pouches. They then marched in the same order to the council, or king's house, (as it was termed in ancient times,) and drew up before it. The Big Warrior and leading men were sitting there. The Shawnee chief sounded his war-whoop —a most diabolical yell—and each of his followers responded. Tecumseh then presented to the Big Warrior a wampum-belt of five different colored strands, which the Creek chief handed to his warriors, and it passed down the line. The Shawnee's pipe was then produced: it was large, long, and profusely decorated with shells, beads, and painted eagle and porcupine-quills. It was lighted from

* Ellis' Life of Tecumseh, pages 49 and 50.

† From "Claiborne's Life and Times of General Sam Dale."

the fire in the center, and slowly passed from the Big Warrior along the line.

"All this time not a word had been uttered, every thing was as still as death; even the winds slept, and there was only the gentle-falling leaves. At length Tecumseh spoke, at first slowly and in sonorous tones, but he grew impassioned and the words fell in avalanches from his lips, his eye burned with supernatural luster, and his whole frame trembled with emotion; his voice resounded over the multitude—now sinking in low and musical whispers, now rising to its highest key, hurling out his words like a succession of thunderbolts. His countenance varied with his speech; its prevalent expression was a sneer of hatred and defiance; sometimes a murderous smile; for a brief interval a sentiment of profound sorrow pervaded it, at the close of a look of concentrated vengeance, such, I suppose, as distinguishes the arch-enemy of mankind.

"I have heard many great orators, but I never saw one with the vocal powers of Tecumseh, or the same command of the face. Had I been deaf, the play of his countenance would have told me what he said. Its effect on that wild, superstitious, untutored, and war-like assemblage, may be conceived; not a word was said, but stern warriors, 'the stoics of the woods,' shook with emotion, and a thousand tomahawks were brandished in the air. Even Big Warrior, who had been true to the whites, and remained faithful during the war, was, for the moment, visibly affected, and more than once I saw his huge hand clutch spasmodically the handle of his knife. And this was the effect of his delivery—for, though the mother of Tecumseh was a Creek, and he was familiar with the language, he spoke in the northern dialect, and it was afterward interpreted by an Indian linguist to the assembly. His speech has been reported; but no one has done, or can do it justice. I think I can repeat the substance of what he said, and, indeed, his very words:

"'In defiance of the white men of Ohio and Kentucky, I have traveled through their settlements—once our favorite hunting-grounds. No war-whoop was sounded, but there is blood upon our knives. The pale-faces felt the blow, but knew not from whence it came. Accursed be the race that has seized on our country, and made women of our warriors. Our fathers, from their tombs, reproach us as slaves and cowards. I hear them now in the wailing winds. The Muscogee were once a mighty people. The Georgians trembled at our war-whoop; and the maidens of my tribe, in the distant lakes, sung the prowess of your warriors, and sighed for their embraces. Now, your very blood is white, your tomahawks have no edges, your bows and arrows were buried with your fathers. O Muscogees, brethren of my mother! brush from your eyelids the sleep of slavery; once more strike for vengeance—once more for your country. The spirits of the mighty dead complain. The tears drop from the skies. Let the white race perish! They seize your land, they corrupt your women, they trample on your dead! Back! whence they came, upon a trail of blood, they must be driven! Back! back—ay, into the great water whose accursed waves brought them to our shores! Burn their dwellings! Destroy their stock! Slay their wives and children! The red-man owns the country, and the pale-face must never enjoy it! War now! War forever! War upon the living! War upon the dead! Dig their very corpses from the graves! Our country must give no rest to a white man's bones. All the tribes of the North are dancing the war-dance. Two mighty warriors across the seas will send us arms.

"'Tecumseh will soon return to his country. My prophets shall tarry with you. They will stand between you and your enemies. When the white man approaches you the earth shall swallow him up. Soon shall you see my arm of fire stretched athwart the sky. I will stamp my foot at Tippecanoe,* and the very earth shall shake.'"

"Incredible as it may seem," says Ellis, in his life of Tecumseh, "the threat of Tecumseh, embodied in the last sentence of the foregoing speech, was fulfilled to the very letter. It was uttered by the chief when he saw the great reluctance of the Big Warrior and the Creeks to join him; and the confidence with which he made the threat had its effect upon them."

Moving northward again, Tecumseh and his followers, came by way of Missouri, rallied the tribes on the Des Moines, crossed the head-waters of the Illinois, and from thence to the Wabash and to Tippecanoe; and it was about this time that a heavy earthquake occurred.

Before quitting the mouth of the Tippecanoe river, Tecumseh had charged his brother, the Prophet, to be most careful in the preservation of peace with the whites during his absence, and especially until his arrangements were fully matured for the confederation of the tribes, north and south, as then advancing; to which the prophet gave his assent, and Tecumseh left him with the full belief that he would be true to his word.

But a short time elapsed, however, before the whites of the territory began to feel an increased alarm. Tecumseh's movement southward had spread among them, and many murders by the Indians in the region of the Prophet's town, at the mouth of the Tippecanoe, and other points, were now becoming more frequent, and it was evident that the Prophet was not wholly a stranger to these depredations, notwithstanding his promise to his brother, Tecumseh, to remain quiet and peacable with the whites during his absence.

In the meantime, the regiment under Col. Boyd, as desired by Gov. Harrison, had reached Vincennes, and the Governor was likewise ordered to add to this body a corps of militia, and to take immediate measures for the defence of the citizens, and, as a last resort, to remove the Prophet and his followers themselves.† And the Governor

*Other writers say that Detroit was mentioned in place of Tippecanoe, and in giving the exclamations of the astonished Indians, we have put that word in their mouth, in accordance with the authority quoted.—Life of Tecumseh.

†M'Afee.

was soon joined by a number of additional volunteers from Kentucky, many of whom were men of high standing as military, civil, and literary gentlemen.

Governor Harrison now began to take active measures to bring matters to a crisis, and wrote to his neighboring governors of Missouri and Illinois, asking their aid in an effort still to persuade the Indians to evade a recourse to arms; and also charged the Indian agents to do what they could in bringing the Indians to a sense of reason in the north; at the same time sending special messages to the different tribes, demanding that all who had been concerned in the recent murders of settlers, be at once given up, and from the Miamies a full disavowal of all alliance or connection with the Prophet; and concluded, says Drake, by saying that the United States, having manifested, through a series of years, the utmost justice and generosity toward their Indian neighbors, and having not only fulfilled the engagements which they entered into with them, but had spent considerable sums to civilize them and promote their happiness—that if, under these circumstances, any tribe should dare to raise the tomahawk against their fathers, they need not expect the same lenity that had been shown them at the close of the former war; but that *they would either be exterminated, or driven beyond the Mississippi.*

In reply to this, the Prophet assured Gov. Harrison that all his demands should be regarded, still insisting that his purposes were peaceable, though this response of the Prophet had hardly reached the hands of the governor, before he also received intelligence that a party of whites had been fired upon when in pursuit of some horses stolen by the Indians.

Gov. Harrison was now the more determined in his course, and the Prophet had already sent, upon learning of the Governor's course of action, word to the Delaware chiefs, inquiring as to what part they intended to play in the coming struggle—as to himself, it was his purpose not to lay down the hatchet until he was either killed or the grievances he complained of were repaired. In response to this, the Delaware chiefs at once set out for the Prophet's town, whither, upon their arrival, they used strong efforts to dissuade him from opening any hostilities with the United States. But they received only rebukes and insults for their efforts and advice; and finding it useless to tarry longer in their council with the Prophet, the Delaware chiefs, whose tribes had long been most friendly to the United States, left the Prophet's town, and made their way to the camp of Gov. Harrison, and at once informod him of the treatment they had received at the hands of the Prophet.

The Governor had already begun his preparations for a march upon the Prophet's town; and toward the latter part of the month of October, with some eight hundred men, embracing the Fourth U. S. regiment, commanded by the gallant Miller, moved forward toward the mouth of the Tippecanoe river, to bring the Prophet and his followers to terms or battle. Before quitting his camp, however, on the 29th, he sent twenty-four Miami chiefs forward to the Prophet, upon a similar errand to that for which the Delawares had visited him; but not having returned as he had expected, he concluded they had joined the Prophet's forces. Accordingly, on the 6th of November, at the head of about one thousand troops, Gov. Harrison took up his line of march for Tippecanoe. Desirous still to know whether the Prophet would come to terms, the Governor, when within a short distance ot the town, sent forward a captain and interpreter to learn what course the Prophet would pursue. But the Indians, on seeing these, only endeavored to take them prisoners, and they found it difficult to make their escape; and one of the sentinels of the army had been shot by the Indians. The Governor now determined to treat the Prophet and his followers as enemies, and again resumed his march upon them. But before he had gained the village, the army was met by a deputation from the Prophet, enquiring for what purpose they were thus advancing upon the town; insisting that they were anxious for peace, and that they had sent messages by the Miami and the Pottawattamie chiefs, stating to the Governor this desire.* At this a suspension of hostilities was agreed upon, and arrangements for a meeting submitted to take place the following day, the Governor telling them that he would move on with the army to the Wabash, and take up his encampment for the night. Having found a suitable place for rendezvous, near a creek, about three-fourths of a mile to the north of the town, and made all necessary arrangement for action, should an attack be made, the army took up its quarters for the night.

In approaching the town, the Indians, not being aware of the purposes of the commanding officers of the army to find a suitable place for encampment, ran out and cried to the advanced corps to halt, but the governor riding up, assured the Indians that his purpose was not to attack them, and, in response to questions, as to a favorable place for encampment, told the officers of a suitable one upon the creek they had, but a little time before, crossed, which point was soon after chosen for the encampment of the army.

The night proved dark and cloudy. The moon rose late, and a drizzling rain fell. Many of the men had anticipated a battle, and were not much pleased that they had not been permitted to engage the Indians in a fight, and were fearful that they might have to return without a "brush" with them; and, accordingly, had but little anticipation of an attack from them, although Colonel Daveiss had been heard to say that he had no doubt that an attack would be made before morning.† And true enough,—according to his habit, Governor Harrison being astir, getting his men under arms,—about four o'clock in the morning, it was discovered and made known that the Indians had stealthily "crept so near the sentries as to hear them challenge

*The Miami chiefs, in returning to the Governor, from their mission to the Prophet, had started on their return by way of the south side of the Wabash, and had accordingly lost sight of the army.

†M'Afee.

when relieved;" their aim being to rush upon the sentries before they could fire. But an Indian being observed by one of the guards, as the former crept through the grass, the latter fired upon the Indian, which was immediately followed by one of their fierce yells, and then a desperate charge upon the left flank of the encampment, which caused the guards to give way. The army was now all alive with excitement, but the men generally stood their ground and fought most bravely, and "the battle was soon maintained on all sides with desperate valor. The Indians advanced and retreated by a rattling noise made with deer-hoofs," and who also fought with great energy, as if "determined on victory or death." The Prophet had told them the bullets of the white men could not hurt them; that the Great Spirit would give them light, while the efforts of the army of the Americans would be "rendered unavailing," and "involved in thick darkness:" * and taking his position upon an eminence near, secure from the bullets whizzing in all directions, he employed his time in singing a war-song, and urging his followers "to fight on," that all would soon be as he had told them—singing the louder with each assurance.†

Soon after daylight, the Indians were put to flight in different directions, and the battle was ended—the power of the Prophet was broken, and the plans of Tecumseh forever frustrated and destroyed.

The force of the Indians was estimated at from six hundred to one thousand; whlie their killed was greater than ever known before. "It's certain," says M'Afee, "that no victory was ever before obtained over the northern Indians, where the numbers were anything like equal." It was "their custom," continues he, "always to avoid a close action, and from their dexterity in hiding themselves, but few of them could be killed, even when they are pouring destruction into the ranks of their enemies. It is believed that there were not ten of them killed at St. Clair's defeat, and still fewer at Braddock's. At Tippecanoe, they rushed up to the bayonets of our men, and, in one instance, related by Captain Snelling, an Indian adroitly put the bayonet of a soldier aside, and clove his head with his war-club, an instrument on which there is fixed a triangular piece of iron, broad enough to project several inches from the wood. Their conduct, on this occasion," continues M'Afee, "so different from what it usually is, was attributed to the confidence of succcess with which their Prophet had inspired them, and to the distinguished bravery of the Winnebago warriors." The loss of the Americans was sixty killed, and about one hundred and thirty wounded; among the killed was the distinguished Jo Daveiss, of Kentucky.‡ The Indians had not determined to attack the camp

*M'Afee.

†An uncle of John P. Hedges, Esq., of our city, who was in the engagement, and who was also badly wounded, avers that the Indians, under the inspiration and assurances of the Prophet, "went in," "cutting and slashing" most fearlessly and indifferently; but that they readily lost faith in him when they saw each other falling, pierced by the musket and rifle balls of the white men.

‡Says a note in Ellis' life of Tecumseh: "Jo Daveiss was, in many respects, one of the most remarkable men of his time. As a lawyer he had few equals—being considered the father of the Kentucky bar. He was very singular in his habits, traveling his circuit

until after night-fall. Their original plan was to meet the Governor in council the next day, and then for two Winnebagoe chiefs, "who had devoted themselves to certain death, to accomplish their design," were to loiter about the camp after the council had broken up, and, killing the Governor, a war-whoop from them was to be the signal of a general attack."

The Indians about the Wabash, after the battle of Tippecanoe, became very quiet, and most of them returned to their homes and villages.

Among the tribes engaged in this conflict, were the Shawanoes, Pottawattamies, Winnebagoes, Kickapoos, &c. After the burial of the dead, and caring for the wounded, the army began its return march on the 9th of November; and on the 18th Governor Harrison was welcomed to Vincennes by a body of some two hundred of her citizens; and in the following month a vote of thanks was tendered him by the Kentucky legislature.

While the Prophet was engaging the army of Gov. Harrison, Tecumseh was in the south rallying the tribes in behalf of his grand scheme of confederation, little dreaming that his brother had spoiled his plans and broken the chain of his wily efforts; and when he returned, he is said to have been so enraged at his brother, upon learning what he had done, that, in a feeling of great anger, he gathered hold of the hair of his head, and threatened to kill him.

Tecumseh now thought of peace; visited Gov. Harrison again, and wished to call upon the President, as the Governor had suggested, before his journey south; but upon Gov. Harrison not wishing him to take many of his warriors with him, he refused to visit Washington, and his conference with the Governor ended for the time, and soon after made his way to Ft. Wayne, while the Prophet took up his abode at a village on the Mississinnewa river, about seventy miles southwest of Fort. Wayne.

—which comprised his whole state—in the costume of a hunter, often entering the court room with his rifle in his hands, at the very moment his case was ready for hearing. His extraordinary life was ended at Tippecanoe. He assumed command of a troop of Kentucky horse, after having been defeated by Henry Clay, in the effort, as United States District Attorney to secure the conviction of Aaron Burr."

CHAPTER XVI.

As the dashing billows lave the beach,
And rush back again into the deep,
So the war element sought to reach
A frenzied height and keep
The West still unbless'd.

---o---

Assembling of the Indians at Fort Wayne to receive their annuities—Many of them fresh from the scene of the late battle of Tippecanoe—Col. John Johnson, Indian agent here—The old Council-House—Early scenes—Peaceful protestations of the Indians—Tecumseh visits Fort Wayne—Failing to obtain ammunition, he gives the war-whoop and leaves—Depredations begun again on the frontiers—The Ohio militia called out—Command of the army surrendered to Gen. Hull—Army under Hull reaches Urbana, Ohio—Triumphal arch erected—Further movements of the army—The British capture an American schooner—Col. Cass sent to demand its surrender—Gen. Hull proposes to invade Canada—issues a proclamation—Its effects—Reconnoitering expedition under Perry—Tecumseh joins the British—Hull retreats from Canada, and reaches Detroit again—His surrender to the British—Bitter feelings against Hull at this result—The British plan an expedition against Fort Wayne—Surrender of Mackinaw---Delay in notifying the Forts---Situation of Fort Dearborn (Chicago)---Maj. Stickney, Indian agent at Fort Wayne, sends an express to Chicago---Relief proposed for Capt. Heald, at Fort Dearborn---Capt. Wells chosen to carry out the designs of Maj. Stickney---Wells selects 30 Miami Indians, and leaves Ft. Wayne for Chicago---His arrival there---Situation of affairs---Wells sees danger ahead---The fort abandoned---With blackened face, Wells takes the lead---The Pottawattamies in ambush---An attack---Bravery of the troops---Death of Wells---The Miamies fly---The Indians demand a surrender, which is complied with---Their treachery---Bravery of Mrs. Heald---Division of the prisoners---Wells' heart cut out and eaten by the Indians---Escape of the prisoners and safe arrival within the U. S. lines.

---o---

SOME DAYS after the battle of Tippecanoe, (on the 22nd of Nov.,) the period for the annual meeting of the Indians to receive their annuities, having arrived, they began to assemble in great numbers to receive their allotted portions. John Johnson, Esq., was then Indian agent here.

Many of the chiefs in attendance were fresh from the scene of the recent hostilities at Tippecanoe, claiming their respective portions of the annuity equal with the most peaceful of the tribes—representing that the Prophet's followers had him in confinement, and purposed taking his life; that he was chargeable with all their troubles; together with many other stories of a similar character, all, more or less, in the main, untrue, especially as regarded the Prophet's confinement, for, at that time, he was at full liberty on the Mississinnewa. But the stories presented to Col. Johnson had the desired effect and he was induced thereby to inform the Government that the Indians were all favorable to peace, and "that no further hostilities should be committed against them;" and, "yet says M'Afee," in most of the nations here assembled, a British faction was boiling to the brim, and ready to flow on our devoted frontiers, wherever the British agents might think proper to increase the fire of their hostility."*

The old council-house was located about the spot now occupied by Michael Hedekin, Esq. It was a two-story log building, about sixty feet long, by about twenty wide; and stood but a short distance to the south-west of the fort. It was in this building the agent lived. And it was often an interesting as well as a painful sight to witness the tall red men, with their painted faces, gaily plumed with feathers and trinkets; their skins in some instances barely covering their loins, in others measurably dressed in skins, or with a blanket wrapped about them, sitting in groups here and there, or standing at some point recounting their adventures or misfortunes; or, having drank freely of "fire-water," were venting their savage ferocity upon each other in hard words or death-blows with the tomahawk or scalping-knife; the squaws wandering about with their pappooses to their backs, or sitting about with their Indian husbands, all awaiting their turns to receive their annuity, or in some way obtain some little favor, if only a pipe or loaf of wheat bread, at the hands of some pale face or friend. Such was life in the vicinity of the council-house and fort here during portions of many years subsequent to the treaty of Greenville.

The assemblage of the Indians, to receive their annuity at the hands of Col. Johnson, after the battle of Tippecanoe, consisted principally of chiefs and head men of the Miamies, the Delawares, the Pottawatamies, and Shawanoes. Col. Johnson, on this occasion, delivered them a speech, presenting the importance of an adherence to peaceable relations on the part of the tribes and the United States—telling them that the President was desirous of living in peace and friendship with them; and that pardon should be granted to any of the hostile tribes who would put away their arms and be peaceable. To which Black-Hoof, a Shawanoe chief, responded in behalf of all the tribes present, assuring the Col. that they all professed the strongest desire to lay hold of the chain of peace and friendship with the United States. It was believed that this expression was sincere on the part of the Shawanoes and a large number of the Delawares; but that the Miamies and Pottawattamies had little or no intention of being peaceable after receiving their annuities.† Says M'Afee, in his "History of the late war(1812) in the Western Country," page 40, "The Little Turtle of the Miamies, now in the decline of life and influence, was the strenuous advocate of

*Prior to the battle of Tippecanoe, the Governor-General of Canada had informed our Government that the Indians were hostile to the United States; but it was supposed that he had done so with a view only to remove suspicions as to the course of the British, and to render their intrigues with the Inians the more successful.

†M'Afee.

TECUMSEH

LITTLE TURTLE

peace, but the majority of his people followed the counsels of Tecumseh."*

The Indians now made many pretentions to peace. Stone-Eater, with others, visited Fort Harrison, and delivered a talk to Capt. Snelling, who, with a small detachment, had taken possession of that post after the battle of Tippecanoe. After professing much friendship, they visited Vincennes, and he told the Governor of their contrition at what had happened, and professed a strong desire for friendship, promising to punish the Prophet, or deliver him up to the United States, as soon as they could get hold of him; and soon after returned to their homes. Visits were now frequent to see the Governor at Vincennes;

*It was on the 14th of July of this year (1812) that the famous Little Turtle died in his lodge at the old orchard, a short distance north of the confluence of the St. Mary and St. Joseph, in the yard fronting the house of his brother-in-law, Capt. Wm. Wells. Turtle had suffered for many months previous with the gout, and came here from his place of residence, at Little Turtle village, on Eel river, about 20 miles north-west of Fort Wayne, to be treated by the U. S. Surgeon at the fort.

It was a solemn and interesting occasion. After the treaty of Greenville, Turtle had remained the true and faithful friend of the Americans and the U. S. Government, and was much beloved and respected by all who knew him. Tecumseh strove hard to gain his confidence and aid, but without effect, for nothing could move him from his purposes of peace and good-will towards the Americans.

In the language of one who was present at his burial: "His body was borne to the grave with the highest honors, by his great enemy, the white man. The muffled drum, the solemn march, the funeral salute, announced that a great soldier had fallen, and even enemies paid tribute to his memory."

His remains were interred about the center of the old orchard, with all his adornments, implements of war, a sword, presented to him by General Washington, together with a medal, with the likeness of Washington thereon,---all laid by the side of the body, and hidden beneath the sod in one common grave. The exact spot of his grave is still known to some of the early settlers of Fort Wayne, who still survive among us, Mr. J. P. Hedges among the number.

Turtle had a somewhat remarkable mind. Was, for many years, the leading spirit here,---unsurpassed for bravery and intelligence, perhaps, by none of his race. Of a very inquiring turn of mind, he never lost an opportunity to gain some valuable information, upon almost every subject or object that attracted his attention; and sought by every means in his power, during the latter days of his life, to relieve his people from every debasing habit---encouraging them only in the more peaceful, sober, and industrial relations of life.

In 1797, accompanied by Captain Wells, he visited Philadelphia, where he enjoyed the society of the distinguished Count Volney, and the Polish patriot, Kosciusko, and others. While in Philadelphia, at this period, he had his portrait taken, by order of the President. Stopping at the same house with Turtle, in Philadelpha, was an Irish gentleman, somewhat remarkable as a wit, who made it a point to "poke fun" at the Turtle whenever an occasion offered. The Irish gentleman and Turtle happening to meet one morning in the studio of Stewart, the artist engaged in painting each of their portraits, the Irishman, observing Turtle in a rather unusually thoughtful mood, began to rally him upon his sober demeanor, and suggested, through Captain Wells, that it was because of his inability to cope with him in the jocular contest. At this the Turtle brightened up. "He mistakes," said the Turtle, to Captain Wells, in reply; "I was just thinking of proposing to this man (the painter) to paint us both on one board, and here I would stand, face to face with him, and confound him to all eternity."

Little Turtle was of mixed origin—half Mohican and half Miami—and the son of a chief; born at his village, on Eel River, about the year 1747, and very early became the war-chief of the Miamies. In stature, he was short, well built, with symmetical form—prominent forehead, heavy eye brows, keen, black eyes, and a large chin.

Such was Little Turtle, (Me-che-kan-nah-quah)—the bravest among the brave, and wisest among the wise of the Indians of the Northwest of his day—leading an army of braves to sure victory one hour—cutting and slashing, as with the ferocity of a tiger, at one moment,—and as passive and gentle as a child the next. Ever may his gentler and better deeds be perpetuated by the American people.

but Tecumseh and the Prophet, who were known to be still hostile, kept away, and this readily led to the conclusion that but little reliance was to be placed upon what was said by many visiting the Governor, and others in authority, as agents and commandants.

Tecumseh made his appearance at Fort Wayne sometime during the month of December, soon after his return from the south. The result of his brother's efforts had effected him deeply. He seemed to know not which way to turn. His scheme was broken, but his great will still bore him aloft over the impediments that had accumulated in his path-way; and yet he was for war—for freedom—for the extermination of the white race that occupied the ancient hunting ground of his fathers. His air was haughty; and, says McAfee, he was still "obstinate in the opinions he had embraced. He made bitter reproaches against Harrison; and, at the same time, had the presumption to demand ammunition from the commandant (here), which was refused him. He then said he would go to his British father, who would not deny him. He appeared thoughtful a while, then gave the war-whoop, and went off."

Such was the spirit in which Tecumseh left Fort Wayne on this memorable occasion; and "early in the spring of 1812, he and his party began to put their threats into execution. Small parties began to commit depredations on the frontiers of the Indiana and Illinois Territories, and part of Ohio. Twenty scalps were taken in the Indiana Territory alone before the first of June; and the people were thus compelled to protect themselves by going into forts along the frontiers. Volunteer companies of militia were organized, and the Indians were frequently pursued, but generally without success, as they fled at once after committing their depredations. Governor Harrison asked permission of the war department to raise a mounted force to penetrate to their towns, with a view of chastising them. But this was refused, the government hesitating to disturb them in that way at that time, fearing least they would take a more active part with the British. Tippecanoe was again occupied, and there the Indians were again planting their corn. By vigorous measures," says M'Afee, "we might have beaten them into peaceable deportment and respect. Mr. Secretary Eustis, of the war department, thought differently; and while he was attempting to soothe them with good words, they were laughing at his credulity. To maintain peace with an Indian," continues the same writer, "it is necessary to adopt his own principles, and punish every aggression promptly, and thus convince him that you are a *man*, and not a *squaw*."

Thus stood affairs in the early part of June, 1812; and by the 18th of that month, matters had so far approached a war basis between Great Britain and the United States—an issue that had for some months prior been anticipated—that the American Government had announced a declaration of war against the English government. As early as the month of April an embargo was levied by Congress on all the shipping in ports of the U. S., and "an act authorizing the President to detach one hundred thousand militia for six months," was adopted and put into force; while several other acts, authorizing the recruiting of a regular army, were likewise passsd, and the masses were all astir with the feeling and anticipation of war.

During this month the President made a requisition on the State of Ohio for twelve hundred militia, and the famous 4th regiment, under command of Col. Miller, which had sometime before been ordered to the relief of Vincennes, was now ordered to Cincinnati, to join the militia. The Ohio militia had been soon raised, and were ordered by Governor Meigs, of that State, to rendezvous on the 29th of April, at Dayton, at the mouth of Mad river, on the Big Miami. As previously directed by the Secretary of War, on the 25th of May following, Gov. Meigs surrendered the command of the army to General Hull, for sometime previously Governor of Michigan Territory, but who, a short time previous to this period, had been appointed a Brigadier-general in the United States army. From Dayton the army under Hull took up its line of march for Staunton on the first of June. From Staunton they marched to Urbana. Here, on the 8th, says M'Afee, they were informed that they would be met that day on parade, by the governor, accompanied by many distinguished citizens and some Indian chiefs. On the following day, governor Meigs and general Hull held a council with twelve chiefs, of the Shawanoe, Mingoe, and Wyandot nations, to obtain leave from them to march the army through their territory, and to erect such forts as might be deemed necessary; which was promptly granted by them, and every assistance which they cold give the army in the wilderness was promised. Gov. Meigs had held a council with these Indians on the 6th, in which it was agreed to adhere to the treaty of Greenville.

On the 10th of June, the 4th regiment, under Col. Miller, made its appearance at Urbana, and were escorted into camp through a triumphal arch, adorned with an eagle, and inscribed with the words, "TIPPECANOE—GLORY."*

From Urbana the army, on the 16th, moved as far as King's Creek, and from this point opened a road as far as the Sciota, where they built two block-houses, which they called Fort M'Arthur, in honor of the officer whose regiment had opened the road. To this fort the whole army came on the 19th, and on the 21st Col. Findley was ordered to open the road as far as Blanchard's fork, on the Auglaize, whither the army, excepting a guard left at Fort M'Arthur, again followed on the 22d. Here, amid rain and mud, another block-house was erected, which was called Fort Necessity. From Fort Necessity the army soon after moved to Blanchard's fork, where Col. Findley had built a block-house, which was called in honor of that officer. A road was shortly after, under command of

*M'Afee.

Col. Cass, cut to the rapids, and the main army soon encamped on the banks of the Maumee, opposite the old battle ground of Gen. Wayne, in sight of the village then at the foot of the Rapids, which had the effect to greatly revive the feelings of the soldiers after their tedious march through the wilderness. From this point, after a day or two's rest, the army moved down just below the old British fort Miami, from which the Indians had been so long supplied with ammunition, etc., before their defeat in that quarter, in 1794.

From here, about the last of June, a small schooner was dispacthed to Detroit, with about thirty officers and privates, with the muster-rolls of the different companies, accompanied by an open boat, in which were a number of sick soldiers. Fears had previously been entertained that the boat would be captured, but General Hull insisted on its departure. In the meantime, the army had again taken up its march, and was to halt again at the river Raisin, whither, upon its arrival there, the army soon learned that the schooner, in attempting to pass Malden, had been captured by the British. The declaration of war was now generally known. From the river Raisin, the army proceeded to the River Huron, fifteen miles, over which narrow stream, on the 4th of July, they built a bridge. From this point, on the 5th, the army proceeded towards Detroit, and soon formed an encampment within view of the place. The northwestern posts were now informed of the declaration of war; and the commanding officers of Fort Wayne, Detroit, Michillimackinaw, and Chicago, were ordered by Gen. Hull to place their garrisons "in the best possible state of defence," without delay, and to "make a return to Brigade Major Jessup, at Detroit, of the quantity of provisions the contractor had on hand at their respective posts, the number of officers and men, ordnance, and military stores of every kind, and the public property of all kinds."*

On the 6th, Col. Cass was sent with a flag of truce to Malden to demand the prisoners and baggage of the captured schooner; but his demands were not respected, and, being blindfolded, soon after returned to camp with a British officer. The army now, with a view to safety, should the English commence a bombardment, removed to the rear of Detroit.

General Hull now conceived the plan of an invasion of Canada, and on the morning of the 12th of July, the British having moved from their former position towards Malden, in fear of loosing that point, the regiments of Cols. Miller and Cass, at a point about a mile above Detroit, successfully gained the Canadian shore, and soon after, followed by General Hull and others, the stars and stripes were run up from a brick dwelling on the farm of a British officer, by the name of Bambee, and on the same day, General Hull issued his noted proclamation to the inhabitants of Canada, in which he requested the Canadians to remain quiet; to pursue their usual voca-

* Order of General Hull.

tions, etc.; assuring them that he "came to find enemies, not to make them. I come to protect, not to injure you. Separated by an immense ocean and an extensive wilderness from great Britain," said he, "you have no participation in her councils, no interest in her conduct. You have felt her tyranny; you have seen her injustice; but I do not ask you to avenge the one or to redress the other."

The effect of the proclamation was most salutary for the time—many of the inhabitants of Sandwich returning to their dwellings again from the woods, whither they had fled on the approach of the American forces, having been told by the British officers, much like the inhabitants of Kaskaskia, at the time of Clark's movements in the west, that the Americans were an army of cannibals,—worse than savages.

With about forty men, on the 13th, Capt. Ulry was sent on a reconnoitering expedition in the direction of Malden, and, upon approaching a partially destroyed bridge extending over Turkey Creek, some nine miles from camp, he discovered a party of some two hundred Indians lying in ambush, intending, if possible, to cut off any detachment that might approach. A Canadian had informed Capt. Ulry that a great number of Indians were in the region, and being fearful that he might be encountered by a superior number, he at once returned to camp.

From the time of his abrupt departure from Fort Wayne, up to the breaking out of the war of 1812, Tecumseh had been most active against the Americans, spiriting up the Indians at various points; and, from the first hostile movements of the British, had allied himself to their cause, and begun to take a most active part with the enemy, who soon made him a brigadier-general in their army. In August, at the head of a party of Shawanoes, accompanied by a number of British soldiers, he made an attack upon a company of Ohio militia sent by General Hull to escort some volunteers engaged in bringing supplies for the army, which occurred at Brownstown, and was the first action that took place after the declaration of war had been made. Tecumseh and his party had succeeded in drawing the company in ambush, and the loss sustained by the company was considerable, and were resolutely followed by Tecumseh in their retreat towards the river De Corce. And it was about this time that General Hull retreated from Canada, and again took up his headquarters at Detroit. On the 16th of August, this post was surrendered by General Hull to a British force, consisting of some seven hundred troops, and about six hundred Indians, under command of General Brock, which placed not only the garrison at Detroit, but the whole territory, including all its forts and garrisons, in the hands of the British, which was a matter of as great astonishment to the British as the Americans. Said General Brock, in writing to his superior officer, after this event, "When I detail my good fortune, you will be astonished."

The feeling among the officers and privates at this result was very great, and brought down upon the head of Gen. Hull a shower of hard words from many directions; although General Hull, while Governor of Michigan, previous to his military appointment, had suggested to the war department the importance of having a superior naval force on Lake Erie, as an auxiliary in the capture of Upper Canada, stating that the object could not be effected without it, besides pointing out many obstacles that would necessarily attend a different course of action. And at another time advised, strongly, the erection of a navy on the lakes. At the time of the surrender, however, Hull's force was superior to that of the British.

Soon after the conclusion of the capitulation at Detroit, an expedition was planned by the British against Fort Wayne.

The garrison at Mackinaw not having received the order of Gen. Hull, as written about the 5th of July, relating to the declaration of war, putting the several forts mentioned in the best defence, etc., this post was surrendered on the 17th of that month, which had the effect to cut off all offensive operations in Upper Canada, and caused General Hull to feel much alarm, saying that "the whole northern hordes of Indians would be let loose upon them." The loss of Mackinaw was at once considered a great impediment to the American cause, for the surrender of which General Hull was greatly censured, because of his delay in forwarding the general order made out about the 5th of July. And Fort Dearborn, at Chicago, had suffered a similar neglect, and was in an equally hazzardous position to that of Mackinaw before its capture. Towards the last of July, General Hull began to think seriously of the situation of the Chicago Fort, and the relief of the garrison. Capt. Heald, its commandant, with his family, were now being surrounded by a furious party of Indians in communication with Tecumseh, who, though not yet attempting any acts of violence upon the inmates, were yet only awaiting the necessary encouragement from the enemy.

With this feeling upon him, General Hull, towards the latter part of July, sent an express to Fort Wayne with a view to the immediate relief of Captain Heald and his command at Chicago.

Major B. F. Stickney was then Indian agent at Fort Wayne, and the express sent here for the purpose of relief to the Chicago fort, brought a request from Gen. Hull that Major Stickney at once extend to Captain Heald all the information, assistance, and advice within his power, inclosing in his letter to Major Stickney "an order to Captain Heald to accept of such aid, and to conform to such instructions as he might receive from the Indian agent" at Fort Wayne.

Instructions were accordingly prepared by Major Stickney to accompany the order of General Hull, and an Indian agent dispatched to Chicago. Among the contents of the letter forwarded to Captain Heald, he was promised military aid as soon as it was possible to render it.

Captain William Wells, the brother-in-law of Little Turtle, was at this time sub-Indian agent here. He had lived among the Indians from his youth to an advanced age; was then, as before, a great favorite with the Miamies, and accounted a "perfect master of every thing pertaining to Indian life, both in peace and war, and withal a stranger to personal fear;"—was replete with a knowledge of Indian strategy; and, says Major Stickney, "if General Wayne desired a prisoner, to obtain information, Captain Wells could always furnish one."

Wells was the man for the work, and Major Stickney readily hit upon him to lead a party to the aid of Captain Heald. Having proposed the matter to Captain Wells, Major Stickney at once suggested the raising of thirty warriors to accompany him. With Wells, the Miamies were his favorites, and from among their tribe he selected the number required. The Pottawattamies were now known to be in the vicinity of Chicago, and the fact of Wells being a favorite with the Miamies, made the former tribe unfriendly towards him, there having long existed an unfriendly feeling between the Miamies and the Pottawattamies. So that Wells' position was at best,—should trouble arise upon their arrival at Fort Dearborn,—a most precarious one, a fact that he was by no means unacquainted with, but his fearless nature readily threw him into the opposite scale of undaunted determination, and on the 3d of August, with his braves well equipped by the agent, all in readiness, he set out, full of hope and courage, for the relief of the garrison at Chicago, whither they arrived on the 12th of the month.

Wells and his party had not been long at the fort before he discovered unmistakable evidences of coming trouble. For some days a large number of Pottawattamies and Winnebagoes, professing friendship, had been encamped about the fort; and for some time Tecumseh and the British, through their runners, had kept up a regular correspondence with the Indians in the locality, who had only been awaiting the result at Malden in order to join one side or the other. On the night of the 14th, a runner having arrived among the Indians there with the news from Tecumseh that Major Vanhorn had been defeated at Brownstown; that the army under Hull had returned to Detroit; and that there was every hope and prospect of success, the Indians about the region were at once decided to join the British, and resolved to remain no longer inactive.*

Wells was warmly attached to Captain Heald. The latter had married his niece, and she was with her husband, to share alike the dangers and vicissitudes that surrounded them.

On the arrival of Wells and his warriors at the fort, Capt. Heald told Wells that he had received the dispatch from the agent at Fort Wayne, with the order of General Hull; that, on its receipt he had called together all the Indian warriors in his neighborhood, and had entered into a treaty with them The leading terms were, that

* M'Afee.

he was to deliver up to the Indians, the Fort with all its contents, except arms, ammunition and provisions necessary for their march to Fort Wayne. The Indians on their part were to permit him to pass unmolested. Wells at once protested against the terms of the treaty. There was a large quantity of ammunition and whisky in the Fort. These, he declared, they should not have. He urged, that if the Indians had the whisky they would get drunk, and pay no regard to the treaty; and he was for throwing the ammunition and whisky into the Lake. The Indians learned what was going on in the Fort, and determined to attack Heald and his party, at the first convenient point, after they should leave the Fort. Wells understood Indian character so perfectly that he was aware of their intentions at a glance.

As soon as it was daybreak, Wells saw that the tomahawk was sharpening for them, and told Heald they must be off as quick as possible, hoping to move before the Indians were ready for them. No time was to be lost. To-pee-nee-bee, a chief of the St. Joseph's band, had, early in the morning, informed a Mr. Kinzie of the mischief that was intended by the Pottawattamies, who had engaged to escort the detachment; and urged him to relinquish his design of accompanying the troops by land, promising him that the boat containing himself and family should be permitted to pass in safety to the St. Joseph's, which was declined by Mr. K., on the ground that his presence might operate as a restraint upon the fury of the savages, so warmly were the greater part them attached to himself and family.*

As the troops marched out, on the morning of the 15th, the band struck up the Dead March, as if some invisible force had impressed upon them the inevitable fate many of them were soon to meet; and on they moved, solemn and thoughtful, in military array, Captain Wells taking the lead, at the head of his litle band of Miami warriors, his face blackened, "in token of his impending fate." Taking their route along the lake shore, as they gained a range of sand-hills lying between the prairie and the beach, the escort of Pottawattamies, some five hundred in number, instead of continuing along the beach with the Americans and Miamies, kept the level of the prairie, and had marched perhaps about a mile and a half, when Capt. Wells, who had rode a little in advance with the Miamies, suddenly came galloping back, exclaiming: "They are about to attack us; form instantly, and charge upon them," telling his niece not to be alarmed; that "they would not hurt her, but that he would be killed."† And no sooner had he ceased to speak, than a volley was fired from among the sand-hills. The troops being now hastily brought into line, they charged rapidly up the bank. A veteran, of some seventy years, was the first to fall. Capt. Wells soon fell, "pierced with many balls;" and in the words of one of the party, (Mrs. Kinzie), "Pee-so-tum * * held dangling in his

*"Wau-Bun, or Early day in the Northwest."

† Maj. B. F. Stickney.

hand a scalp, which, by the black ribbon around the queue, I recognized as that of Capt. Wells." Their leader now being killed, the Miamies fled; one of their chiefs, however, before leaving the scene of disaster, riding up to the Pottawattamies, and exclaiming to them in pretty strong terms: "You have deceived the Americans and us. You have done a bad action, and (brandishing his tomahawk), I will be the the first to head a party of Americans to return and punish your treachery;" and then galloped away over the prairie in pursuit of his companions, who were rapidly making their way back towards Fort Wayne.

"The troops," says Mrs. Kinzie,* "behaved most gallantly. They were but a handful; but they seemed resolved to sell their lives as dearly as posssible. Our horses pranced and bounded, and could hardly be restrained, as the balls whistled among them."

The Indians made several desperate attempts to rush upon and tomahawk the soldiers, but every such effort was bravely repulsed by them. Several women and children were killed; and the ranks at length became so reduced as not to exceed twenty effective men; yet they were undaunted and resolute, and remained united while able to fire. Having now withdrawn some distance from their former position, the Indians sent a small French boy to demand a surrender. The boy was Capt. Heald's interpreter, who had deserted to the side of the Indians in the early part of the engagement. Advancing very cautiously towards the Americans, a Mr. Griffith advanced to meet him, intending to kill him for his conduct in deserting; but the boy declaring that it was the only way he could save himself, and at the same time appearing quite sorry for having been obliged to act as he did, he was permitted to come forward. He said the Indians proposed to spare the lives of the Americans, if they would surrender. But the surviving soldiers all rejected it. Conveying their determination to the Indians, he soon returned, saying the Indians were very numerous, and strongly urged Mr. Griffith to use his endeavors to bring about a surrender, which was at length consented to, and the men having laid down their arms, the Indians at once came forward to receive them; when, in the face of their promise, they tomahawked three or four of the men; and one Indian, it is stated, with the fury of a demon, approached Mrs. Heald, with his tomahawk raised to strike her. Much accustomed to danger, and being well acquainted with Indian character, with remarkable presence of mind, she looked him earnestly in the face, and, smiling, said; "Surely you will not kill a squaw." Her "action, suited to the word," had the desired effect. The Indian's arm fell; his savage resolution was broken; and a moment more saw the heroic and thoughtful Mrs. Heald under the protection of the barbarous hand that was about to rob her of life. Mrs. Heald was the daughter of General Samuel Wells, of Kentucky, who fought most valliantly at the battle of Tippecanoe against

*"Early Day in the Northwest," pages 224 and 225.

the followers of the Prophet. Captain Wells' head was cut off and his heart taken out and eaten by the Indians."*

In accordance with their ancient custom, the Indians now devided the prisoners. Captain Heald, Mrs. Heald, and Mr. Griffith being selected by the Ottawas, were taken by this band on the lake, beyond the mouth of the river St. Joseph. Having been severely wounded, they considered their fate as inevitably sealed; but some angelic arm seem to have been stretched forth to aid them when least expected; and one day, Griffith's eye accidently fell upon a canoe, at a convenient point, sufficiently large to hold them all; and one night, soon after, they succeeded in making their escape, traversing the lake in this frail bark some two hundred miles to Mackinaw, where the British commandant enabled them to reach the United States in safety.

* As the character of Wells was unequalled for bravery, after his death the Indians took his heart from his body, cooked it, and divided it among themselves in very small pieces. They religiously belived, that each one who ate of it, would thereby become as brave as he from whom it was taken.—Stickney.

CHAPTER XVII.

What heroism! what perils then!
How true of heart and strong of hand;
How earnest, resolute those pioneer MEN!
* * * * * * *

—o—

The Indians greatly emboldened by their success at Chicago—The followers of Tecumseh threaten to exterminate the tribes refusing to aid their cause—Tecumseh's usefulness to the British—Tecumseh's scheme of the siege and massacre of Forts Wayne and Harrison—Renewal of the war—Ohio and Kentucky aroused—Col. John Allen—The Pottawattamies after the evacuation of Fort Dearborn—Preparations for the siege of Forts Wayne and Harrison—Antonie Bondie—The secret of the intended siege and massacre of Fort Wayne disclosed—Doubts as to its correctness—Major Stickney dispatches a messenger to Gov. Harrison—Active preparation for defense—Illness of Major Stickney—Indians prowling about the fort—Death of Stephen Johnston—A period of great peril—The siege begun—A stratagem—The Indians desire to gain an entrance into the fort—They ask for a signal—Thirteen of them admitted—Their plot frustrated—Winnemac and Captain Rhea—Two soldiers shot by the Indians—Perilous adventure of Wm. Oliver and some Indian guides—The garrison learns of the movements of Gov. Harrison—The army on its march for the relief of Fort Wayne—Gov. Harrison elected a Major-general—Ducking a soldier—The army at St. Mary's—Richard M. Johnson leads a corps of mounted volunteers to the relief of Fort Wayne—Logan, the half-breed, accepted as a spy—Incidents on the route of the army down the St. Mary—A court-martial—The halloos of the Indians taken as a signal of the approach of the army—Great rejoicing in the Fort—The "Key of the West" again unlocks the door of success.

—o—

THE SUCCESS of the Indians at Chicago, gave them great courage, and emboldened them for still greater efforts for the overthrow of the whites, or driving them beyond the Ohio. With few exceptions, the tribes were now, from the disasters at Detroit, in the capture there of the large army under Hull, and the previous surrender of Mackinaw, determined in their course, and were every where more or less inclined to the British interest. The few tribes continuing friendly to the United States, were soon threatened by the followers of Tecumseh with extermination, who was now fast bringing his great scheme to an issue, by the aid of the English. Possessing a most excellent memory, and being well acquainted with every important position in the northwest, he was readily enabled to point out to the British many important advantages. Before crossing to Detroit, at the time of Hull's surrender

General Brock took occasion to enquire of Tecumseh what sort of a country he should have to pass over, should he conclude to go beyond. Taking a roll of elm bark, and extending it on the ground by means of four stones, Tecumseh drew his scalping-knife, and at once began to etch upon the bark the position of the country, embracing its hills, roads, rivers, morasses, and woods, which, being a demonstration of talent quite unexpected in Tecumseh, had the effect to please General Brock very much, and readily won for him the confidence of the commanding-general. His position and influence—strengthened by the British, and joined by a numerous ally of his own blood—were now formidable, and he was determined to render them as potent as his strength and advantages would permit, destined, however, at last to fall.

His great plan was now the siege and massacre of Forts Wayne and Harrison. The Pottawattamies and Ottawas, as at Chicago, aided by the British, under Major Muir, were to be the leading spirits in the movement upon Fort Wayne, while the Winnebagoes, and a portion of the Miamies, who had been persuaded to join the Tecumseh party, were to surprise and capture Fort Harrison; and had appointed the first of September as the earliest period of attack.

The government, in the meantime, had begun most active measures for the renewal and prosecution of the war. From the first, the President had disapproved the armistice at Detroit, and the thought of an invasion of Canada, by the strait of Niagara, was soon upon the breeze of public expectation, and the British commander, General Brock, had early heard the rumor.

Ohio and Kentucky, upon the receipt of the news of Hull's situation at Detroit, were soon aroused to the highest sense of patriotic determination. The governor of Ohio at once ordered the remaining portion of the detached militia of his State, numbering some twelve hundred men, to be formed and marched to Urbana, under command of brigadier-general Tupper; while the Secretary of War had previously called on Governor Scott, of Kentucky, for a body of fifteen hundred men, embracing also the regulars previously enlisted in that State. In the early part of May, the governor of Kentucky, in accordance with instructions from the war department, had organized ten regiments, of some five thousand five hundred men, as the quota of that State. Among the many patriotic men who so eagerly joined the standard of their country, in Kentucky, was Colonel JOHN ALLEN, who took command of a rifle regiment. He was a lawyer of much distinction at the Kentucky bar, and combined many eminent and endearing qualities as a private citizen of that State. Allen county was so named after him.

After the massacre of Chicago, those Pottawattamies engaged in it spent some weeks about Fort Dearborn, and divided the spoils which had been given them at the time it was forsaken. They then retired to their villages on the St. Joseph of Lake Michigan, where they were assembled in council by British emissaries, and at their instigation determined upon a simultaneous movement to lay siege to Forts Wayne and Harrison. The British agents promised, that in case the Indians would besiege those forts, and prevent their evacuation by the garrisons, they should be joined, in one moon, by a large British force from Malden and Detroit, with artilery, who would be able to demolish the stockades, and would give up the garrison to massacre and spoil. Their success in these enterprises, it was but too evident, would have exposed the whole frontier to devastation, and the plans of Tecumseh were all looking to the consummation of this end. The siege was to be commenced in twenty days after the council adjourned.

At this time, there was an Indian trader residing near Fort Wayne, of French extraction, by the name of Antonie Bondie. He was about fifty years of age, and had lived among the Indians from the time he was twelve years old. He was an extraordinary character. At one time he would appear to be brave and generous, at another meanly selfish. He was recognized by the Miamies as one of their tribe—married one of their squaws, and conformed to their habits and mode of life. The hostile Pottawattamies, desirous of saving him from the destruction which they contemplated for the garrison, sent Metea, chief of their tribe, to inform him of their intentions and his danger. Metea went to his cabin in the night, and under an injunction of great secrecy, informed him of all that had transpired in relation to the contemplated siege of the two forts. He offered to come for Bondie and his family, before the siege was commenced, with a sufficient number of pack horses to remove them and their moveable property to a place of safety. Bondie did not decline the offer.

The morning after Metea had made this revelation, Bondie, accompanied by Charles Peltier, a French interpreter, went to the agent (Stickney) very early, and with many injunctions of secrecy, informed him of it all. The agent was thankful for their information; but doubtful whether to credit or reject it, as any mistake in a matter of so much importance, either way, would prove ruinous to his character, and cause his disgraceful ejection from the important office which he held. He had been but three months in office or in the country, and was acquainted with but few persons. The character of Bondie was not known to him, and the nature of his communication such as to require great secrecy, and if true, immediate preparation for the defence of the fort. Stickney sent a note to Rhea, the commanding officer of the garrison, desiring a meeting with him in the open esplanade of the fort, where there could be no one to overhear what might be said. This officer having been long in the country, had every opportunity of knowing Bondie. He met the agent, heard his communication, and dismissed it, by observing that Bondie was a trifling fellow, and no reliance could be placed upon what he said. This increased the perplexity of the agent. He sent for Bondie and his interpreter, to have a cross examination. This being completed, it remained for the agent either to pass the matter without notice, and incur the chances of the siege of the Indians against the two posts, to be followed by a regular force of British troops, with artillery, without any preparation for defence or relief from abroad, or to report the information, without attaching to it his official belief in its correctness, which would have no effect. In weighing and comparing chances and consequences, he determined that it was better that he should be ruined in his reputation, and the government suffer all sacrifices, consequent upon the falsity of the report, than that they should both suffer if it proved true. He, therefore, sent a second time to Capt. Rhea, and declared his intention to make the report, and give it the sanction of his belief in its correctness. He informed him that he had just received a dispatch from Governor Harrison, from Vincennes, saying that he was going to Cincinnati, where he must be addressed, if necessary, and that he should send "an express" to him, directed to that city, and another to Captain Taylor, the commanding officer at Fort Harrison. He then returned to his office and commenced making immediate preparations for acquainting Gov. Harrison with the information he had received regarding the contemplated siege of the fort. When nearly ready to dispatch his messenger, Capt. Rhea sent a note to him requesting that he would delay his express to Cincinnati, until he could write a letter to the governor of Ohio, informing him of the report. Stickney complied with this request, and the express was sent with letters to Governor Harrison and Governor Meigs. Active preparations were now commenced for defence. Such men as could be spared with teams were employed to send off ladies who were there, with children, to the frontier; and it was subsequently ascertained that within a few hours after the messengers had started, the Indians drew their lines of guard around the fort.

On the 5th of August, Major Stickney, the Indian agent, was prostrated by severe illness, from which he only became convalescent, after twelve days. He was then conveyed from the agency house to the fort for safety. It was now very plain that the statement of Bondie was no fiction. He, with his Indian family, moved into the fort. The Indian warriors, to the number of some five hundred, as then supposed, began to assemble in the neighborhood of the fort; and it was now evident that they had hopes of getting possession of it by stratagem. They would lie in wait near the fort, day after day,—a few near and in sight, but the majority of them would be scattered about, as much out of sight as possible. Those near were watching an opportunity to force the sentries. The sentinels were so faithful to their duty, that no chance was presented.

Stephen Johnston, who was a clerk in the United States factory store,* feeling very solicitous about the safety of his wife, who had

*Which had been erected near the fort, sometime subsequent to the erection of Fort Wayne, in 1794, for the purpose of supplying the Indians with agricultural implements.

been sent to the frontier in a delicate situation, accompanied by Peter Oliver, and a discharged militiaman, attempted to elude the vigilence of the Indians, and visit the place of her abode. They left at 10 o'clock at night. Johnston was fired upon by six Indians and killed instantly. Before the Indians could reload their pieces, the remaining two men made good their retreat to the fort; and for a reward of twenty dollars, an Indian was induced to bring in the body of Mr. Johnston.

The Indians now began to disclose their hostility and real purposes by violent and premature acts, showing most conclusively their full designs. On one occasion two soldiers were sent out on horseback, three or four miles, to drive in some cattle. One of them was taken prisoner, the other made his escape. The Indians obtained possession of both horses. They killed cattle and hogs near the fort, stole horses, and committed many other minor depredations.

Both parties wished to delay the final conflict—Major Stickney, to give time for Gen. Harrison to send the fort the necessary relief, in compliance with his dispatch; and the Indians, from a hope and expectation of the daily arrival of the British force, which had been promised them. The Indians, however, did not cease to employ many devices and stratagems, to accomplish their object, before the arrival of the British. An Indian would occasionally come near the fort, and hold conversation with an interpreter, who would be sent out for the purpose. The interpreter would be informed that the depredations had been committed by the young men, contrary to the wishes of the chiefs—that the chiefs wished for peace. At length the Indians expressed a desire to be admitted to see the commandant of the post, that they might agree upon some terms for a cessation of hostilities; and asked for a signal by which they might approach the fort and be permitted to talk with their white father. A white cloth was accordingly sent to them to be used as a flag of truce. For several days they delayed making use of the flag, and continued their depredations. The agent finally sent a message to them, by an Indian, that they had dirtied his flag, and he could not suffer them to retain it any longer; that they must return it immediately. The next day, the whole body of Indians moved up to the fort, bearing the white flag in front. The gates of the fort had been kept closed for a number of days. They were in hopes of obtaining the admission of a large number of their warriors. But the agent, who was still quite weak from his recent attack, was too well acquainted with Indian character to be deceived. Having, with difficulty, walked to the gate, he designated by name the chiefs to be admitted, who, upon their entrance into the fort, one by one, were disarmed by the guard, and examined very closely. Thirteen only were admitted, who at once followed the agent to his sleeping apartment. The officers in the garrison remained in their quarters. The agent now addressed a note to Capt. Rhea, desiring that the guard should be paraded and kept under arms during the continuance of the council. In accordance with the customs of such occasions, tobacco was presented to the chiefs that they might smoke.*

When the pipes began to go out, Winnemac, a Pottawattamie chief, rose and commenced a speech, which he addressed to the agent; the substance of which was, that the Pottawattamies had no hand in killing Johnston, and that the chiefs could not control their young men. The soldiers and horses had been taken without the knowledge or consent of the chiefs, in opposition to whose wishes the young men had committed all their depredations. "But," continued Winnemac, "if my father wishes for war, I am a man."† At this expression the chief struck his hand upon his knife, which he had concealed under his blanket. The agent at this time did not understand the language, but saw there was something serious. Bondie, who was present and understood the whole force of what was said, jumped upon his feet as quick as lightning, and striking his knife in a very emphatic manner, shouted in Pottawattamie, "I am a man too." At the same instant the interpreter turned quite pale, and Winnemac cast his eyes towards the principal chief present, whose name was An-ouk-sa, who was sitting at a window where he could see the guard under arms. He returned a look of disappointment, and the stratagem was brought to an abrupt termination; while the interpreter, having sufficiently recovered from his confusion, readily explained what had been said. Winnemac now finished his speech, and the agent returned for an answer, that in all that had been said, there appeared to be something concealed; and that if it was for war, he was ready for it. The Indians having been admitted under a flag of truce, were now permitted to depart. Winnemac, however, who was the last to leave the room, was invited by Capt. Rhea to his quarters, who soon sent to the agent for an interpreter, and remained in conversation with Winnemac, half or three quarters of an hour. The agent subsequently learned, from the interpreter, that Rhea professed great friendship for the chief, and invited him to take breakfast with him the next morning. Upon learning this, and with a view of dissuading him from such intimacy and want of discretion, at such a time, the agent with difficulty walked to the quarters of Capt. Rhea, whom he found in such a state of intoxication that it was useless to expostulate with him. Returning to his quarters again, he now sent for the two lieutenants, Ostrander and Curtis, and told them what had taken place,

* In the account of this siege the writer has mainly followed the statement of Major Stickney, the Indian agent here at the time of its occurrence.

† The whole plan of the Indians on this occasion was subsequently divulged. They were to obtain an entrance into the fort, for as many as possible. Winnemac was to be the speaker. When he should come to the expression, "I am a man," he was to dispatch the agent. Other chiefs were to rush to each of the officers' quarters, to massacre them, and others were to open the gates of the fort, to the force without. The work was then to be finished, by butchering every soul in the fort.

giving it as his opinion that an attack would be made the next morning; and urged upon them the necessity of all possible preparation.

The next morning, aroused by the firing of rifles, the agent stepped out upon a gallery that projected from the second story of his quarters, and saw two soldiers fall, mortally wounded, about fifty yards from the fort. It was now ascertained that no preparations had been made in anticipation of an attack. All was confusion in the garrison. The two men were taken into the fort, and died about one o'clock, that day.

About the first of September, a most interesting occurrence took place. A white man and four Indians arrived at the fort, on horseback, "in full yell." It was the Indian yell of triumph. The white man, who was foremost, proved to be William Oliver. He was accompanied by four friendly Shawanoe Indians, the brave Logan among the number. The garrison had been for more than a fortnight in a state of suspense; not knowing whether the express to Gov. Harrison had gotten through, or not, and every day, in expectation that the British force would arrive. All were on tiptoe to hear the news—William Oliver had arrived in defiance of five hundred Indians—had broken through their ranks and reached the fort in safety.

He reported that about two thousand volunteers had assembled in Kentucky for the relief of General Hull at Detroit, and had marched to Cincinnati. There they heard that Hull had surrendered, and deemed it unnecessary to march any further in that direction. Harrison having received the dispatch from the agent at Fort Wayne, had determined to march to its relief. Ohio was raising volunteers. Eight hundred were then assembled at St. Mary's, sixty miles south of Fort Wayne. They intended to march to the relief of the fort, in three or four days. At Cincinnati great fears were entertained that the fort had been captured, and its inmates massacred. When the question arose, as to how the condition of Fort Wayne was to be ascertained, the stoutest hearts in the army quailed.

William Oliver was then a young man of about twenty-three years of age. He possessed the true spirit; was at the time sutler to Fort Wayne. Previous to any knowledge of the hostile intentions of the Indians, Oliver had gone to Cincinnati on business. He went to Governor Harrison and made an offer of his services, individually, to obtain the necessary information. Harrison thought the danger too great, and endeavored to dissuade him from making the attempt; but he had determined to accomplish it, or loose his life in the effort. When Governor Harrison shook hands with him, he observed that he "should not see him again."

A man by the name of Worthington, an Indian commissioner of the time, embarked with Oliver in this adventurous undertaking, placing themselves at the head of about eighty whites, forty of whom, so perilous seemed the task before them, after a march of about three days, returned home. The balance, however, pursued their way to the Indian village of Waupaukonetta, where Oliver found friends and acquaintances among some friendly Shawanoes, and selected four of the bravest to accompany them through to Fort Wayne, Logan among the number.

Having pursued their course, with much care, until within some twenty-four miles of the fort, a council was called to consider the expediency of a further advance, when it was concluded best for all to remain behind except Oliver, Logan, and the other Indian attendants. On the following morning, with their horses, they continued their way "with the common wariness of Indians, and without any remarkable occurrence until they came within some four miles of the fort. Oliver had determined to enter the fort in broad daylight." They now began an examination of the ground with great precaution, determining to ascertain, if possible, what movement had taken place, and the exact locality of the Indians.

The keen eye of Logan now soon discovered that the enemy was concealed along the road, with a view to cut off any reinforcements that might attempt to reach the garrison.

Leaving the main road, they now moved cautiously across to the Maumee river, whither, leaving their horses in a thicket, they advanced on foot towards the fort, in order to get a view of it, and to ascertain, if possible, whether it still held out against the besiegers. Being fully satisfied on this point, they again repaired to the thicket where they had left their horses, remounted, and soon struck the main road again.

The moment of greatest peril and determination had now come. The fort was to be gained at the risk of life itself; and putting whip to their horses, Oliver and his faithful Shawanoe companions started in full speed for the fort.

What was most remarkable, the moment the scouts gained the fort proved to be the only safe one that had for some days presented itself, as though a kind providence had opened the way for the safe arrival of the party to cheer the inmates of the perilous garrison.

First reaching the gate of the esplanade, and finding it inaccessible, they descended the river bank, and were soon admitted by the northern gate.

Said one of the lieutenants of the fort: "The safe arrival of Oliver at that particular juncture may be considered miraculous. One hour sooner or one hour later, would no doubt have been inevitable destruction both to himself and his escort. It is generally believed by those acquainted with the circumstances, that not one hour, for eight days and nights preceding or following the hour which Mr. Oliver arrived, would have afforded an opportunity of any safety."

So close was their contact with the Indians, in this fearful ride, that they even saw the beds upon which they lay as they maintained their nightly guard.

Entering the general gateway, which was located about where now stands the residences of the late Jas. B. Hanna, or Martin Knoll, on Wayne street—the fort then, with several acres of ground, being enclosed by a substantial fence—a few moments more, and all was safety. The fort was gained, the north gate opened, and Oliver and his companions rode quickly in, to the great astonishment and joy of the little garrison, who eagerly gathered about the heroic riders to learn the news.

Oliver's story was soon told. When the volunteers of Ohio, assembled at St. Mary's, learned the extent of the Indian force about Fort Wayne, they deemed it imprudent to advance with so small a force, and concluded to await the arrival of the Kentuckians, thus subjecting the garrison to a still longer state of suspense. The anxiety was intense; and it was through extreme good fortune, and mere accident, that the fort was enabled to hold out, with so little good management—"the commanding officer had been drunk nearly all the time, and the two lieutenants inefficient men; entirely unfit to hold commissions of any grade." The non-commissioned officers and privates, eighty in number, behaved very well. The Indian agent was feeble and incapable of much exertion. Oliver, though a private citizen, was now the most efficient man in the fort.

Having prepared a letter, announcing to General Harrison his safe arrival at the fort, and its beleaguered situation, Oliver immediately started his Shawanoe companions back with the letter to Worthington, while he determined to take his chances with the occupants of the fort.

Seeking an opportune moment, Logan and his companions left the fort safely, but were soon observed, and pursued. Their exultant shouts, however, soon revealed to the inmates of the garrison that they had outstripped their pursuers and passed the lines unharmed.

The Indians now again begun a furious attack upon the fort, but the little garrison bravely met the assault, and were, in a few days more, enabled to hail the approach of the army.

The name of Oliver deserves to be enshrined in every heart. Such heroism is seldom met with, and who among us to-day can fail to cherish a kindly memory and regard for so valiant and self-devotional a spirit as the brave, determined WILLIAM OLIVER?

At Cincinnati, the Kentucky volunteers elected Gov. Harrison to command them as a major-general. When he received the information from Oliver that Fort Wayne was in existence, he took up the line of march for the scene of the beleagured garrison.

The faithful Shawanoes met the advancing army at Piqua, Ohio, where the message of Oliver was readily delivered to Gen. Harrison, who at once drew his men together, and made them a speech. Said he, in part: "If there is a man under my command who lacks the patriotism to rush to the rescue, he, by paying back the money received from the government, shall receive a discharge, as I do not wish to command such." But one man responded to the proposition. His name was Miller, of the Kentucky militia; and having obtained his discharge, on the morning of the 6th, his comrades not willing to let him return without some special manifestion of their appreciation of his course, put him on a rail, carried him around the lines to the music of the Rogue's March, and down to the Miami, where they took him off the rail and let him into the water and baptized him in the name of "King George, Aaron Burr, and the Devil." As he came out of the water the men stood on the bank and threw handsful of mud on him, then, forming into two lines in an adjacent lane, made him run the gauntlet, each one throwing a handful of dirt on him, and then let him go.

Soon after this event, on the morning of the 6th, the army began its march for Fort Wayne, encamping that evening in the woods, some twelve miles from Piqua. Early on the morning of the 7th, (Monday) the army resumed its march. This day, says one of their number,* "we made fifteen miles, and encamped on a branch, three and a half miles this side of St. Mary's river. Next morning a melancholy accident happened. In the act of receiving the guard a young man by the name of Thomas Polly, a sergeant in Captain Megowan's company, was shot by the accidental discharge of a gun in the hands of a sentinel by the name of Thos. Hamilton. The ball entered the left side, below the nipple, and passed out near the backbone, perforating the lungs. We carried him on a litter to St. Mary's, where he lingered till the next day. This was the first death that had occurred during our march. This day, Sept. 8th, we only marched to St. Mary's,† where we lay till next day. On this evening we were joined by two hundred mounted volunteers, under Col. Richard M. Johnson, who had volunteered for thirty days, on hearing that Fort Wayne was besieged. Wednesday, Sept. 9th, we marched eighteen miles, to what was called Shane's Crossing of St. Mary's. Here we overtook a regiment of eight hundred men from Ohio, under Cols. Adams and Hawkins, who had started on to the relief of Fort Wayne. On arriving at this place, an Indian, of the Shawanoe tribe, a half blood, by the name of Logan, (who had been taken when a small boy by Gen. Benjamin Logan, of Lincoln county, Kentucky, and raised by him, but who, after arriving at maturity, had gone back and joined his tribe) with four others, offered his services to Gen. Harrison as spies, which he accepted."

Logan was a remarkable Indian, and had early merited the esteem and confidence of the whites. Was some six feet in height, with robust form, broad shoulders, and prominent forehead. Was greatly attached to General Harrison, and a warm friend to the

*John D. White, of Lawrenceburgh, Ind.

† At this point some block-houses were built for the security of provisions and protection of the sick. This point had previously been known as Girty Town, doubtless after the famous Simon Girty.

American cause, for which he did much valuable service as a guide and spy.

Continues White: "Previous to our arrival, Logan had gone on in disguise, and passing through the camp of the besieging party, had ascertained their number to be about fifteen hundred. Logan also went to the fort, and encouraged the soldiers to hold on, as relief was at hand. On this night, (the 9th) the sentinels fired at what they imagined to be Indians, but, on examination, next morning, an old horse was found shot, having strayed outside the camp. Thursday morning we marched early. Cols. Adams and Hawkins having waited several days to come up, (after ascertaining the superiority of the enemy's forces) joined our army, and we all marched together. We now had about three thousand five hundred men. We marched ten miles and encamped. Nothing occurred of any interest. Friday morning we were under marching orders after early breakfast. It had rained, and the guns were damp. We were ordered to discharge them, and re-load, as we were then getting into the vicinity of the enemy, and knew not how soon we might be attacked. A strong detachment of spies under Captain James Sugget, of Scott county, marched considerably ahead of the army. Indications of the enemy having advanced from their position at Fort Wayne, for the purpose of watching the movements of our army, were manifest, and Captain Sugget came upon the trail of a large party, which he immediately pursued. After following the trail some distance he was fired on by an Indian, who had secreted himself in a clump of bushes, so near to Sugget that the powder burnt his clothes, but the ball missed him. The Indian jumped from his covert and attempted to escape, but Andrew Johnson, of Scott, shot him. At the crack of the gun, the Indian's gun and blanket fell. Supposing that he had killed him, and being eager in pursuit of the trail, they made no halt; but before they could overtake the Indians, they had to give up the pursuit, on account of the lateness of the hour and the distance they were ahead of the army. On returning to where the Indian was shot, they found the gun and blanket, but he had escaped. They followed the blood for some distance and found pieces of his handkerchief, which he had cut into plugs to stop the blood, but he had bleed so profusely that it had forced them out of the wound. On abandoning the pursuit of the wounded Indian, the party returned to the camp. We had marched about fifteen miles, and encamped an hour before Sugget's party arrived. Logan held up the bloody blanket and exhibited it as he rode along the line. Having repaired to Gen. Harrison's marque, orders were immediately issued for the troops to turn out and make a breastwork around the encampment, which order was promptly obeyed, and before dark the same was fortified by a breastwork, made by cutting down trees and piling them on each other. A strong picket guard was detailed and posted at a considerable distance from the line. After tattoo, at 9 o'clock, we lay down. After which the officer of the night came round to give us the watchword, which was 'fight on.' (The watchword is given to the sentinel as well as to the army, in order, that, in case of a night attack, and the sentinels having to run into camp, may be distinguished from the enemy by it.) Orders were given, that in case of two guns being fired in quick succession, the soldiers were to repair to the breastwork. From every indication we had strong reasons for believing that we would be attacked before day. We lay with our guns in our arms and cartridge boxes under our heads. About 10 o'clock, just as the soldiers were in the enjoyment of 'tired nature's sweet restorer,' they were aroused by the firing of two guns by the sentinels, and the drums beat the alarm. In a moment all were at the breastwork, ready to receive the enemy. Just about this time some fifty guns were fired by the sentinels, and some came running in hallooing at the top of their voices, 'fight on;' and, notwithstanding we had orders not to speak the watchword, the cry of 'fight on' went entirely around the lines. If there had been an attack, and the enemy had understood English, it would have afforded them the advantage of getting into the lines by giving the watchword.

"The Indians were around us, and we were in momentary expectation of an onset. At last all was calm again, and we were permitted to rest. But just as we were in the sweet embraces of sleep, we were again aroused by the firing of a number of guns, and again we were as prompt in repairing to our posts. We now stood a considerable time, and all became quiet again, when we were ordered to count off one, two, three, and every third man was made to stand at the breastwork, and the rest were permitted to retire to their tents. At length day dawned, and the guards were relieved. We ascertained afterward, from Indians taken prisoners, that they came from their encampment with the design of making a night attack on us, but on finding us so well prepared to receive them, they declined prosecuting their designs.

"Without being able to get round the entire encampment before daylight of the morning of the 9th, the Indians returned to their own lines with the word that '*Kentuck* was coming as numerous as the trees.'

"Lieut. Munday, of Kuley's company, of Madison county, Ky., and Ensign Herring, of Hart's company, of Lexington, being officers of the guard, both left their guard fires and ran in when the firing commenced.*

"Saturday, September 10th, we expected to reach Fort Wayne, but thought, in all probability, we should have to fight our way, for the Indians lay at what was called the Black Swamp, five miles on this side of the fort, immediately on our road. We started after

* Charges of cowardice having been preferred against these two officers, after the arrival of the army at Fort Wayne, a court martial was ordered for their trial. Munday resigned and went home. Herring proved that he stood his ground till the whole guard had left him, and was therefore acquitted.

early breakfast (if a few bare bones, boiled in water, could be called a breakfast) and marched with much caution. From St. Mary's we had moved in two lines, one on the right, and the other on the left of the road, at a distance of about one hundred yards therefrom, while the wagons kept the road. Sugget's spies went ahead, and on coming to where they had left the trail of the wounded Indian, they again took it, and after following it a short distance, found his dead body. When he found he could not survive, he broke bushes and covered himself over, and resigned to die. The Indians believe that if they lose their scalp, they will not be permitted to enter the favorite hunting ground which their tradition teaches them they are to inhabit after death. Hence they use every effort to prevent their enemies from getting the scalps of those slain in battle; and during an engagement a number are always employed in carrying off the dead. A short distance in advance of their camp, at the swamp, the spies returned with information that they were there, prepared to give us battle. A halt was made, and the line of battle formed. Col. Hawkins, of the Ohio mounted volunteers, had left the lines and gone some distance from the road. Being partly concealed by a clump of bushes, one of his men taking him for an Indian fired at him and shot him through. The ball entered between the shoulders and came out at the breast—which, however, did not prove mortal. We again took up the line of march, and in a short time came in sight of the smoke of the camp of the enemy."

At the first grey of the morning of the 10th of September, the distant halloos of the disappointed savages revealed to the anxious inmates of the fort the glorious news of the approach of the army. Great clouds of dust could be seen from the fort, rolling up in the distance, as the valiant soldiery, under General Harrison, moved forward to the rescue of the garrison; and soon after daybreak, the army stood before the fort. The Indians had beat a retreat to the northward and eastward, and the air about the old fort resounded with the glad shouts of welcome to Gen. Harrison and the brave boys of Ohio and Kentucky!

And again, as on former occasions, "the Key of the northwest" had unlocked the great door of success; and the country, though not yet through with its trials and conflicts with a wily and relentless foe, was safe, and destined soon to triumph over every obstacle. The prophetic words of Washington, years before, were again most fully realized; and the scene of the Miami village, more surely than ever, pointed to "a most important post for the Union."

CHAPTER XVIII.

All was flight, and for miles around,
No red man was to be found.

Flight of the Indians on the approach of the army—The Fort besieged ten or twelve days—Wooden cannon made by the Indians—The little village around the fort destroyed—The occupants of the houses about the fort seek safety in the fort—The fort able to hold out against the Indians still longer—The old well of the fort—Captain M'Afee's account—His prophecy and that of Captain Wells as to the future of Fort Wayne—Loss in the fort during the siege—Shooting an Indian in the St. Mary—Charges against Captain Rhea—Rhea permitted to resign—The army formed into two detachments to destroy the villages in the region of Fort Wayne—Destruction of corn and vegetables—The tomb of a chief—The village of Five Medals, near where Goshen, Ind., now stands—The tomb of an Indian sorceress—Evidences of British aid—Return of the divisions to the fort—Arrival of new recruits at Fort Wayne—A force sent to destroy Little Turtle Town—The ground now occupied by the city of Fort Wayne mainly cleared by order of Ganeral Harrison—An imposing scene—All approach cut off—Gen. Harrison's report—Arrival of Gen. Winchester at Fort Wayne—Popularity of Gen. Harrison—Winchester to take command of the army—Dissatisfaction among the soldiers at the proposed change of generals—A reconciliation—Gen. Harrison's return to Piqua—An expedition against Detroit—Movements of Gen. Winchester—Indians discovered—A party surprised, captured, and five killed.

THE INDIANS had mainly fled the evening before the arrival of the army. Some, however, were courageous enough to remain until within a few moments before the army reached the fort, who "were pursued by the Ohio horsemen, but without success." The fort had now been closely besieged for ten or twelve days; and the Indians, in their efforts to capture it, had made several pieces of wooden cannon, which they strengthened with iron hoops. Previous to the commencement of the siege, there were several dwellings near the fort, "forming," says M'Afee, "a handsome little village; but it was now (on the arrival of the army), in ruins, having been burnt down by the Indians, together with the United States' factory."

The occupants of the dwellings surrounding the fort, as the siege began, sought refuge within the garrison, where they remained in safety till the army arrived.

The fort, during the siege, was well supplied with provisions.

There was a good well* of water within the enclosure; and they had also four small field pieces. With these advantages, unless attacked by a formidable British force, they were well prepared to oppose the efforts of the Indians for several days longer.

Of the fort, at this period, which was the same built by order of Gen. Wayne, in 1794, in connection with other relations of this point, Captain M'Afee† said : "It is delightfully situated, on an eminence on the south bank of the Miami of the lakes, immediately below the formation of that river by the junction of the St. Mary's from the southwest with the St. Joseph's from the north. It is well constructed of block houses and picketing, but could not resist a British force, as there are several eminences on the south-side, from which it could be commanded by a six or nine pounder.

"This is the place where the Miami Indians formerly had their principal town; and here many an unfortunate prisoner suffered death by burning at the stake. It was here also, that Gen. Harmar suffered his army to be cut up and defeated in detachments after he had burnt the town in the fall of the year 1790. For more than a century before that time, it had been the principal place of rendezvous between the Indians of the lakes, and those of the Wabash and Illinois, and had been much resorted to about the year '56 and previously, by French traders from Canada. The Maumee is navigable for boats from this place to the lake, and the portage to the nearest navigable branch of the Wabash, is but seven or eight miles, through a level, marshy prairie, from which the water runs both to the Wabash and St. Marys. *A canal at some future day will unite these rivers, and thus render a town at Fort Wayne, as formerly, the most considerable place in that country.*

"The corn which had been cultivated in the fields, by the villagers, was nearly all destroyed by the Indians; the remains served as forage for the mounted corps. Captain Wells, who was massacred at Chicago, had a handsome farm in the forks of the river, with some good buildings, which were all destroyed in the general devastation."

During the siege, the garrison lost but three men. From subsequent information, it was believed that the Indian loss was about twenty-five. Eight were seen to fall. One Indian was killed at a distance of three hundred yards, while standing in the St. Mary's river. A soldier by the name of King, with a long heavy rifle, fired,

* The traces of this well are yet plainly to be seen. It was near the northwest end of the fort, now to be seen just at the edge of the south side of the canal.

† Author of the "History of the Late War in the Western Country," published in 1816. M'Afee was here in 1813. It is from this old volume that the writer has been enabled to draw many valuable and interesting facts relating to the early History of Fort Wayne. M'Afee's words in reference to the construction of a canal by this point and the subsequent growth of a "town at Fort Wayne," have been most conclusively realized. The writer also learned from early settlers that the unfortunate Capt. Wells, (killed at Chicago) some years before the war of 1812, had often told persons here that "a big ditch" would one day be dug from the lake to this locality, in which boats would run—and that there would also be a large town here some day—but he was not believed, in fact, thought very immoderate in his calculations. (15)

and the ball took effect in the back of the savage, between his shoulders, and he fell into the water. This feat was witnessed by the whole garrison.

Immediately after the arrival of Gen. Harrison, Lieutenants Ostrander and Curtis, preferred charges against Capt. Rhea, and called upon Major Stickney, the agent, as a witness. The General assembled his principal officers as a Board of Inquiry, and upon the testimony of the agent, that Rhea was drunk six days during the siege, the Board thought he ought no longer to hold a commission. Gen. Harrison, mainly because of his advanced age, granted Capt. Rhea the alternative of a resignation, (which he complied with,) to take effect the first day of January following.

The second day following the arrival of the army here, General Harrison formed his army into two detachments, with a view of destroying the Indian villages in the region of country lying some miles around Fort Wayne, the first division being composed of the regiments under Cols. Lewis and Allen, and Captain Garrard's troop of horse, under Gen. Payne, accompanied by Gen. Harrison. The second division, under Col. Wells, accompanied by a battalion of his own regiment, under Major Davenport, (Scott's regiment,) the mounted battalion under Johnson, and the mounted Ohio men under Adams.

In order that their means of subsistence might also be cut off, it was determined, while destroying the Indian villages in the region, to cut up and destroy their corn and other products.

After a march of a few miles, the troops under Payne came to the Miami villages, at the forks of the Wabash, where, finding the villages abandoned, the troops were ordered to cut up the corn and destroy the vegetables in the field adjacent. At this point, says M'Afee's account of the expedition, was observed "the tomb of a chief, built of logs, and bedaubed with clay." This chief "was laid on his blanket, with his gun and his pipe by his side, a small tin pan on his breast, containing a wooden spoon, and a number of ear-rings and brooches—all deemed necessary, no doubt, on his journey to the other world."

On the 16th of September, the body under Col. Wells had advanced to the Pottawattamie village, known as Five Medals, on the Elkhart river, in what is now Elkhart county, near the town of Goshen. Having crossed the river, about three miles above the village, and formed in order of battle, "in a plain, thinly timbered," the division advanced to the right and left of the village, and then surrounded it; but, to the regret of all, the place was found deserted, the Indians having abandoned it two days before, leaving behind considerable quantities of "corn, gathered and laid on scaffolds to dry, with abundance of beans, potatoes, and other vegetables, which furnished an ample store of provisions for the men and forage for the horses. This village was called Five Medals, from a chief of that name, who made it his residence. On a pole, before the door of that chief, a red flag was hung, with a broom tied above it; and on another pole at the tomb of an old women, a white flag was flying. The body of the old woman was entire, sitting upright, with her face towards the east, and a basket beside her, containing trinkets, such as owl and hawk bills and claws, a variety of bones, and bunches of roots tied together; all of which indicated that she had been revered as a sorceress. In one of the huts was found a morning report of one of Hull's Captains, also a *Liberty Hall* newspaper, printed at Cincinnati, containing an account of General Harrison's army. Several coarse bags, which appeared to have contained shot, and pieces of boxes with London and Malden printed on them, were also picked up in the cabin; which proved that these Indians were intimately connected with the British, and had been furnished with information by some one, perhaps, in our own country. This village, with some seventy acres of corn, was destroyed, and the same evening the army, on its return march, reached the Elkhart river; and after a most fatiguing march, for those on foot, and from the effects of which one man died soon after the return of the division, the army arrived again at the fort on the 18th, a few hours after the body under Payne had returned."*

On the day previous to the return of these divisions, (17th), Col. Simrall, with a regiment of dragoons, armed with muskets, and numbering some three hundred and twenty men; also a company of mounted riflemen, under Col. Farrow, from Montgomery county, Ky., had arrived at the fort; and on the same evening of the return of the divisions under Payne and Wells, Gen. Harrison sent them to destroy Little Turtle Town, some twenty miles northwest of the fort, with orders not to molest the buildings formerly erected by the United States, for the benefit of Little Turtle, whose friendship for the Americans had ever been firm after the treaty of Greenville.

Colonel Simrall most faithfully performed the task assigned him, and on the evening of the 19th, returned to the fort.

In addition to these movements, General Harrison took the precaution to remove all the undergrowth in the locality surrounding the fort, extending towards the confluence of the St. Joseph and St. Mary, to where now stands Budisill's mill, and westward as far as St. Mary, to the point where now stands the Fort Wayne College, thence south-east to about the point of the residence of the late Allen Hamilton, and to the east down the Maumee a short distance. And so well cleared was the ground, including a very large part of the entire limits of the present site of the city of Fort Wayne, that it was said by those who were here at that early day and to a later period, a sentinel " on the bastions of the fort, looking westward, could see a rabbitt running across the grounds as far as so small an object was discernable to the naked eye."

The seclusive points were thus cut off, and the Indians now had no longer any means of concealing their approach upon the fort;

*M'Afee.

and the scene thus presented by the destruction of the underbrush, including many trees, of some growth, was said to have been quite imposing indeed. Some thirty or forty acres, of what is now the Cole farm, extending to the junction of the rivers, and just opposite the Maumee, was then known as the Public Meadow, which, of course, was then, as it had long before been, a considerable open space.

The soldiers were thus readily enabled to observe the approach of any hostile movement against the fort, and to open the batteries, with formidable effect, upon any advance that might be made against the garrison, from any direction.

General Harrison now made an official report of transactions here to the War Department; and about the 19th of September, Brigadier-general James Winchester arrived at the Fort, with a view of taking command of the first division of Kentucky troops, which had early marched to reinforce the northwestern army.

General Winchester had seen service in the revolutionary struggle, as an officer of distinction, and at this period was somewhat advanced in years. Was a man of some wealth, and resided in the State of Tennessee, where he is said to have "lived many years in a degree of elegant luxury and ease, which was not calculated to season him for a northern campaign in the forest."

General Harrison was ever a favorite with the soldiers, and there was probably no man in the country at this period who could command a greater amount of esteem from the masses, or who could move at the head of an army with greater confidence and regard from the soldiers under him, both officers and privates, than he could; and when General Winchester arrived, it was soon understood that he was to take command of the forces. This produced much uneasiness among the troops, not that Winchester was by any means an inferior officer, but that Harrison was *the favorite*; and the *boys* wanted him to lead them. Indeed, so great was the aversion to the change, that many of the militia were disposed not to be under his command; and it was with much difficulty that General Harrison* and the field officers succeeded in reconciling them to the change of officers.

As it is a matter most essential that all raw troops should have the largest confidence in their commander, so the militia, at this particular juncture of affairs, needed the greatest confidence in their commanding-general, and much of this was unfortunately lost to the men by a change of general officers.

The men being at length prevailed on to march under General Winchester, with the confident belief that Gen. Harrison would sooner or later be reinstated, and again assume command of them,

* Says M'Afee: "The troops had confidently expected, that General Harrison would be confirmed in the command; and by this time he had completely secured the confidence of every soldier in the army. He was affable and courteous in his manners, and indefatigable in his attention to every branch of business. His soldiers seem to anticipate the wishes of the general; it was only necessary to be known that he wished something done, and all were anxious to risk their lives in its accomplishment."

on the 19th of September, the command of the troops, by a general order, at the fort, were transferred to General Winchester, placing "any part of the infantry which he might deem necessary to the extension of his plans, at his disposal."

The same evening, after the issuance of this order, Gen. Harrison started on his return, towards Piqua, to take command of the forces collecting in the rear; and to arrange for a mounted expedition against Detroit—intending thus to make a *coup de main* on that point, marching by way of a route but little known, from Fort Wayne, up the St. Joseph, from thence to the head waters of the river Raisin. These troops consisted of three regiments from Kentucky, under Barbee, Payne, and Jennings; three companies of mounted riflemen from the same State, under Captains Roper, Bacón, and Clarke; also a corps of mounted men from Ohio, who had rendezvoused at Dayton on the 15th, in obedience to a prior call by Governors Meigs and Harrison, which they had made early in September, intending to employ them against some Indian towns, the corps being commanded by Col. Findley, who had again entered the service since the surrender of General Hull at Detroit.

On the 20th General Harrison met the mounted men and the regiment of Jennings at St. Mary's (Girty Town), the remainder of the infantry being still further in the rear. The General having left word at the fort here for Johnson's battalion and Col. Simrall's dragoons, which were not included in General Winchester's command, to return to St. Mary's as early as possible, Major Johnson, on the morning of the 20th, in accordance therewith, took up his line of march, and after an advance of some twenty miles, was met by orders from General Harrison to return to Fort Wayne again, and there await further orders, with his dragoons, which was promptly complied with, excepting ensign Wm. Holton, with about twenty-five men of Captain Ward's company, who, refusing to obey orders, started to return home, to Kentucky. The next evening, the remainder of the corps under Johnson reached Fort Wayne again.

General Winchester had now removed his camp to the forks of the Maumee; and early on the 22d of September, he moved down the north side of that stream, over very nearly the same route as that by which General Wayne's army had reached the Miami villages in 1794, intending to go as far as Fort Defiance, at the mouth of the Auglaize, with a view of forming a junction there with the infantry in the rear, who were to come from the St. Marys, by way of the Auglaize,

Before leaving the forks of the Maumee, Winchester issued the following order:

"The front guard in three lines, two deep in the road, and in Indian files on the flanks at distances of fifty and one hundred yards, as the ground will admit. A fatigue party to consist of one captain, one ensign, two sergeants, and two corporals, with fifty men, will follow the front guard for the purpose of opening the road. The remainder of the infantry to march on the flanks in the following order: colonels Wells and Allen's regiments on the right, and Lewis and Scott's on the left. The general and brigade baggage, commissaries and quartermasters' stores, immediately in the rear of the fatigue party. The cavalry in the following order: captain Garrard and twenty of his men to precede the guard in front, and equally divided at the head of each line; a lieutenant and eighteen men in the rear of the whole army and baggage; the balance of the cavalry equally divided on the flanks or the flank lines. The regimental baggage wagons will fall according to the respective ranks of their commanding officers. The officers commanding corps previous to their marching will examine carefully the arms and ammunition of their respective corps, and see that they are in good order. They will also be particularly careful, that the men do not waste their cartridges. No loaded muskets are to be put in the wagons. One half of the fatigue party is to work at a time, and the others will carry their arms. The wagon master will attend to loading the wagons, and see that the various articles are put in, in good order, and that each wagon and team carry a reasonable load. The hour of march will be 9 o'clock this morning. The officer of the day is charged with this order. The line of battle will be the same as that of General Harrison in his last march to Fort Wayne."

The March down the Maumee was continued with great precaution, and the camp strongly fortified every night, advancing only about five and six miles each day. Not many miles had been gained before a party of Indians were discovered, and the signs were strong that there were many more in the region. A volunteer company of spies having previously been organized, under Captain Ballard, Lieutenant Harrison Munday, of the rifle regiment, and Ensign Liggett, of the 17th U. S. Infantry, they were usually kept in advance to reconnoiter the country. On the 25th, Ensign Liggett having obtained permission to proceed as far as Fort Defiance, he was accompanied by four men of McCracken's company, from Woodford, Kentucky. Late that evening, while preparing some food, they were discovered by a Frenchman and eight Indians, who surprised them, with a demand to surrender, being postively assured that they would not be hurt, and also be permitted to wear their arms till they entered the British camp. With these conditions, says M'Afee's account,* they surrendered; but the Indians and Frenchman, as they walked on, concocted, in their own language, and executed the following plan for their destruction: Five of the Indians, each having marked his victim, walked behind and on one side of the men, and, at a given signal, fired upon them. Four of them fell dead—Liggett only escaped the first fire—he sprung to a tree, but was shot also while raising his gun to his face. Next day, Captain Ballard, with a part of his company, being in advance, discovered the dead bodies, and a party of Indians watching near them. He formed his men for action, with the Maumee on his right; but not liking his position, and perceiving that the Indians were too strong for him, he fell back two hundred yards, and formed in a stronger position. The enemy supposing he had fled, filed off from their right flank, intending to surround him on his left, and cut off his retreat. He heard them pass by on his left without discovering him, and then filed off by the left in their rear, and by a circuitous route arrived safe at the camp.

Lieutenant Munday, with another part of the spies, presently happened at the same place, and discovering some Indians, who still

* "His. Late War in Western Country," page 135 to page 152.

remained there, formed his men and charged upon them, at the same time saluting them with their own yell. They fled precipitately, and Munday, on discovering their superior numbers, took advantage of their panic to retreat himself. Next morning, the 27th, Captain Ballard, with the spies and Captain Garrard's troop of horse, accompanied by Major Woolfork, aid to the general, and some other volunteers, went forward to bury the dead. The Indians were still in ambush; but Captain Ballard expecting it, approached them in a different direction, so as to disconcert their plans. He attacked them with a brisk fire, and Captain Garrard immediately ordered a charge, on which they fled in every direction, leaving trails of blood from their killed and wounded.

These Indians were the advance of an army destined to attack Fort Wayne, consisting of 200 regulars under Major Muir, with four pieces of artillery, and about 1000 Indians, commanded by Elliott. They had brought their baggage and artillery by water to old Fort Defiance, at the mouth of the Auglaize, where they had left their boats and were advancing up the south side of the Maumee towards Fort Wayne.

Upon the approach of Winchester, they threw their cannon into the river, together with their fixed ammunition, and retreated in great haste. Gen. Winchester did not pursue them.

And thus the original plan of the British authorities, at Detroit and Malden, to take the posts of Forts Wayne and Harrison, then to give them up to massacre, and to turn about 1500 Indians loose upon the frontier, to kill and lay waste, had now come to defeat.

CHAPTER XIX.

Again upon the march, 'mid scenes of renown—
On, with heroic valor, to bloody Frenchtown,
* * * * * * *
Where brave ALLEN fell.

———o———

Situation of Fort Harrison—The stratagem for its capture—The Indians, men, women, and children, gathered there in large numbers—They ask for food, and desire to be admitted into the fort—One of the block-houses fired—The Indians open fire upon the fort—A critical moment—Two men, of the fort, scale the picketing—One of them killed, the other wounded—Retreat of the Indians—The garrison repaired—Captain Taylor prepares for a siege—Scarcity of food—A messenger succeeds in passing the Indian lines at night—Capt. Taylor breveted for his bravery—His force but 50 men—Force of the Indians large—The Indians exasperated at their defeat—They leave the locality of Fort Harrison for the "Pigeon-Roost settlement"—Two men killed when within two miles of the settlement—The settlement surprised—The massacre—23 men, women, and children killed in a few minutes—A few only make their escape—The alarm given by those making their escape—A party reaches the scene of the massacre—The buildings burned, and the bodies mainly consumed by the flames—Burial, in one grave, of the remains—Trail of the Indians—Dangers and sufferings of the pioneers—Zebulun Collings' account—Regiments of Kentucky—Recruits of the regular army ordered to the frontier—Transportation of supplies—report of General Harrison—A movement against the British—Logan, the Shawanoe half-breed, sent to take observations—He and his party overpowered—Their retreat to the camp of Gen. Winchester—Logan suspected of being in complictity with the enemy—Logan's feelings greatly wounded—He resolves to prove himself true—Logan and his attendants move again—"A prisoner or a scalp"—They meet a superior party—Stratagem of Logan—A detachment sent against the Indians on the Mississiniwa—A sharp encounter—Loss and flight of the Indians—Tecumseh in the region—Return of the detachment—Privations of the army—The government and people restless—Advance of Gen. Winchester—Movement of troops under Lewis and Allen upon Frenchtown—The British prepare for an attack—Their advance and attack—The Americans overpowered—Terrible slaughter—Ferocity and barbarity of the Indians—Capture of Gen. Winchester—Bravery and death of Col. John Allen—Great valor of Majors Graves and Madison—Their refusal to surrender to Gen. Proctor—Horrible slaughter of the wounded by the Indians—Many burned alive—Movements of General Harrison for the relief of the sufferers at Frenchtown—Confinement of Gen. Winchester, Col. Lewis, and Major Madison at Quebec—Sad feeling of the country at the disaster of Frenchtown—Renewed efforts, and heavy reinforcements to the army of Harrison.

———o———

WHILE the garrison here is on the look-out for the wily foe that had now begun to prowl about again, occasionally visiting the fort in the guise of friendship, and the northwestern troops are engaged in active preparations for an advance on Detroit, the attention of the reader is turned again in the direction of the Wabash and Fort Harrison. Capt. Zachary Taylor was in command of this fort at this period. Sratagem, to the time of the siege here, had well-nigh assumed an epidemical form with the different tribes. It was an ancient artifice. It had often been resorted to as a means of success, and seldom failed in its operations, if cautiously engineered. Occasionally, however, a Gladwyn, a Harrison, or a Johnson was met by the Indians, in their purposes and plans, and then, after a desperate effort, they usually came to defeat.

On the 3d of September, a body of Winnebagoes and Kickapoos, men, women, and children, had gathered about Fort Harrison, and desired, as on many simiiar occasions, at other points, to be admitted into the fort, with the pretense of holding a council—insisting, also, that they were greatly in need of food.

Two men having been killed on the 2d, Capt. Taylor at once suspected their designs, and giving them something to eat, refused to admit them. But this did not suffice. They continued to loiter about the fort, still insisting upon their friendship. On the night of the 4th, their designs were made fully manifest. Setting fire to one of the block-houses, a large number of warriors, who had been concealed near by, now opened a brisk fire upon the fort, which was readily returned by the garrison. Several desperate charges were made by the Indians, in which an effort was made to fire the fort in several places, and then to enter by the breach; but they were bravely repulsed and entirely defeated at every side. "So critical and alarming was the situation of the garrison," says M'Afee, "that two of the men jumped over the picketing, preferring the chance of escape through the ranks of the enemy, to the prospect of being burnt or massacred in the fort; one of whom was killed, and the other retreated back to the walls of the fort after being wounded, and concealed himself behind some old barrels till the next morning, when the Indians retreated, though still hovering about within view of the fort for seven or eight days afterwards."

The garrison was now repaired and strengthened, and Captain Taylor prepared himself for a regular siege. The destruction of the block-house, in which were stored the provisions of the fort, was severely felt, as it exposed the men to the rigors of hunger in the lack of food. During the siege but three men had been killed, and about that number wounded. A small amount of corn, raised near the fort, was their only reliance for food for several days; while an effort to dispatch a messenger to Vincennes seemed out of the question, until, at length, a messenger succeeded in passing the Indian encampment at night.

For his valiant conduct in defending the fort, Captain Taylor received much praise, and was therefor soon after breveted a major. His force in the garrison did not exceed fifty men, many of whom were sick. The force of the enemy was quite large, comprising about all the Indians that could, at that time, be collected in that part of the country.

Greatly perplexed and exasperated at their failure, a large part of the Indians engaged against Fort Harrison, now soon started for a little settlement, known as "the Pigeon Roost settlement," at the fork of White river, in what is now Scott county, in this State. This settlement was founded in 1809; embraced an opening of about one square mile, and was about five miles distant from any other settlement. When within about two miles of the settlement, the Indians discovered two men of the same, who were hunting bee trees. These were killed, and then moving forward to the settlement, they surprised and massacred, in a few moments, twenty-three men, women, and children, a few only succeeding in making their escape. "The children," says M'Afee, "had their brains knocked out against trees," etc.

A large party now soon collected, and repaired to the scene of the massacre, where the bodies, many of them partially consumed in the flames of the ruined buildings, were collected together, and buried in one grave.

Many of the Indians engaged in this massacre, were Shawanoes, and their trail was followed for several miles, in the direction of the Delaware towns, at the head of White river, but without success.

A Mr. Zebulun Collings, who resided about six miles from the Pigeon-Roost settlement, thus relates the dangers and vicissitudes under which he proscuted his farm labors, and lived from day to day during much of those early times, which will doubtless also serve as an example of the hardships and dangers of most of the pioneers of those early days. Says he: "The manner in which I used to work, in those perilous times, was as follows: On all occasions I carried my rifle, tomahawk, and butcher-knife, with a loaded pistol in my belt. When I went to plow, I laid my gun on the plowed ground, and stuck up a stick by it, for a mark, so that I could get it quick in case it was wanted. I had two good dogs. I took one into the house, leaving the other out. The one outside was expected to give the alarm, which would cause the one inside to bark, by which I would be awakened, having my arms always loaded. I kept my horses in a stable, close to the house, having a port-hole, so that I could shoot to the stable door. During two years I never went from home with any certainty of returning—not knowing the minute I might receive a ball from an unknown hand; but in the midst of all these dangers, that God who never sleeps nor slumbers, has kept me."

The regiments of Colonels Wilcox, Miller, and Barbour, of the Kentucky militia, were now on their march to Vincennes, but they did not arrive in time to meet the Indians at Fort Harrison. Col. Russell being advised of its critical situation, collected some companies of rangers and Indiana militia, and, by forced marches, arrived there on the 13th, to the great joy of the garrison, who were in a starving condition. Several wagons with provisions were now ordered up to the fort, under an escort of 13 men, commanded by lieutenant Fairbanks, of the regulars. After Colonel Russell had met and passed this party on his return, they were surprised and literally cut to pieces by the Indians, two or three only escaping. Major M'Gary, with a battalion of Colonel Barbour's regiment, was at the same time on his way with provisions for the garrison; and being reinforced with some companies of Russell's rangers, they arrived in safety at the fort, having buried the mangled remains of the regulars on their way. In the Illinois and Missouri Territories, depredations had also been committed by the Indians. Governor Edwards, of the Illinois Territory, had been very attentive to these matters. He had sent spies into the Indian country, by whom he had ascertained, that they were greatly elated with their success and the prospect of driving the white people over the Ohio river, and were determined to carry on a desperate war against the frontiers in the month of September. To meet the emergency, he had called, under authority from the war department, on the governor of Kentucky for a regiment of men; and Colonel Barbour's regiment had been ordered by Governor Shelby to march to Kaskaskia; but General Gibson, the acting governor of Indiana, ordered it to Vincennes when Fort Harrison was in danger, conceiving that he was authorized to take such a step, as the lieutenant of Governor Harrison, who was commander-in-chief of all the forces in those Territories. Governor Edwards, though deprived of this aid, made vigorous exertions to defend his settlement. He embodied a portion of the militia, which he held in readiness to act whenever danger might present. Several companies of rangers were also encamped on the Mississippi, above St. Louis, and on the Illinois river. These troops served to keep the savages in check in those regions.*

General Harrison continued his headquarters at Franklinton and Delaware, for the most part employing himself in the superintendence of supplies, and early in October he ordered "all the recruits of the regular army in the western States to be marched to the frontiers.

For several months the army was now chiefly engaged in the transportation of supplies over the different routes they had, or were sooner or later to, march. In this relation many difficulties arose, which were most fully set forth by General Harrison at the time, in his report to the President and war department. On the 22d of October, he said: "I am not able to fix any period for the advance of the troops to Detroit. It is pretty evident, that it cannot be done, on proper principle, until the frost shall become so severe as to enable us to use the rivers and the margin of the lake, for the transportation of the baggage on the ice. To get supplies forward, through a swampy wilderness of near two hundred miles, in wagons or on packhorses, which are to carry their own provis-

* M'Afee.

ions, *is absolutely impossible*." The object, said he, "can be accomplished by using the margin of the lake as above mentioned, if the troops are provided with warm clothing, and the winter is such as it commonly is in this climate." "No species of supplies are calculated on being found in the Michigan Territory. The farms upon the river Raisin, which might have afforded a quantity of forage, are nearly all broken up and destroyed. This article, then, as well as the provisions for the men, is to be taken from this State —a circumstance which must at once put to rest every idea for a land conveyance at this season—since it would require at least two wagons with forage, for each one that is loaded with provisions and other articles."

The most important events, of a military character, that had transpired, up to the 22d of November, were a somewhat successful, though perilous movement upon a party of British and Indians at the Rapids, by a small body of troops under General Tupper, wherein the former were mainly put to flight, but after the retreat of the British and many of the Indians,—a few of Tupper's men having unthoughtedly given chase to a number of hogs for a distance of half a mile from the main body,—four of them were killed by the Indians. The British and Indians now fell back upon the river Raisin.

Soon after this movement, Capt. James Logan, the faithful Shawanoe chief, mentioned in a previous chapter, in connection with the army in its efforts to succor the fort here, in the early part of September, by orders from General Harrison, had proceeded with a small number of his tribe, to make observations in the direction of the Rapids. Having met and been closely pursued by a superior force, when near that point, he and his men were obliged to disperse and retreat; and Logan, with but two of his comrades—Capt. John and Bright-Horn—succeeded in reaching the camp of Gen. Winchester, where he faithfully recounted what had occurred. There were some persons in the camp, however, who suspected him of having been in complicity with the enemy, and so intimated, greatly to the displeasure and mortification of Logan, who at once determined to refute the charge by a still further manifestation of his fidelity to the American cause.

Accordingly, on the 22d of November, accompanied by Capt. John and Bright-Horn, he started a second time in the direction of the Rapids, resolved to bring in a prisoner or a scalp. Having proceeded down the north side of the Maumee, about ten miles, they met with a British officer, the eldest son of Col. Elliott, and five Indians. Four of them being on horseback, and too strong for them, and having no chance of escape, Logan at once determined to pass them under the pretense of friendship and a desire to communicate to the British certain information. With this determination, they confidently advanced to the party, one of whom proved to be Winnemac, the Pottawattamie chief, with whom the reader is already familiar, who unfortunately knew Logan well, and was fully aware of his regard for and adherance to the Ameriean cause. But, nevertheless, Logan persisted in his first course, telling them he was on his way to communicate with the British. After a conversation of some time with them, they moved toward the British lines, whereupon Winnemac and his companions turned and followed them, desiring to accompany them thither. As they traveled on together, says M'Afee, Winnemac and his party closely watched the others, and when they had proceeded about eight miles, he proposed to the British officer to seize and tie them. The officer replied that they were completely in his power; that if they attempted to run, they could be shot; or failing in that, the horses could easily run them down. This consultation was overheard by Logan; he had previously intended to go on peaceably till night, and then make his escape; but he now formed the bold design of extricating himself by a combat with double his number.

Having signified his resolution to his men, he commenced the attack by shooting down Winnemac himself. The action lasted till they had fired three rounds apiece, during which time, Logan and his brave companions drove the enemy some distance, and separated them from their horses. By the first fire, both Winnemac and Elliott fell; by the second a young Ottawa chief lost his life; and another of the enemy was mortally wounded about the conclusion of the combat, at which time Logan himself, as he was stooping down, received a ball just below the breast bone; it ranged downwards and lodged under the skin on his back. In the mean time, Bright-Horn was also wounded, by a ball which passed through his thigh. As soon as Logan was shot, he ordered a retreat; himself and Bright-Horn, wounded as they were, jumped on the horses of the enemy and rode to Winchester's camp, a distance of twenty miles in five hours. Captain John, after taking the scalp of the Ottawa chief, also retreated in safety and arrived at the camp next morning.

Logan had now rescued his character, as a brave and faithful soldier, from the obloquy which had unjustly been thrown upon him. But he preserved his honor at the expense of the next best gift of Heaven—his life. His wound proved mortal. He lived two days in agony, which he bore with uncommon fortitude, and died with the utmost composure and resignation. "More firmness and consummate bravery has seldom appeared on the military theatre," said Winchester, in his letter to the commanding general. "He was buried with all the honors due to his rank, and with sorrow as sincerely and generally displayed, as I ever witnessed," said Major Hardin, in a letter to Governor Shelby. His physiognomy was formed on the best model, and exhibited the strongest marks of courage, intelligence, good humor and sincerity. It was said by the Indians, that the British had offered one hundred and fifty dollars for his scalp. He had been very serviceable to our cause by acting as a guide and spy. He had gone with General Hull to Detroit, and with the first Kentucky troops, who marched to the relief of Fort Wayne.

Captain Logan, it will be remembered, had been taken prisoner by General Logan, of Kentucky, in the year 1786, when he was a youth. Before the treaty of Greenville, he had distinguished himself as a warrior, though still very young. His mother was a sister to the celebrated Tecumseh and the Prophet. He stated, that, in the summer preceding his death, he had talked one whole night with Tecumseh, and endeavored to persuade him to remain at peace, while Tecumseh, on the contrary, endeavored to engage him in the war on the side of the British. His wife, when she was young, had also been taken prisoner by Colonel Hardin, in 1789, and had remained in the family till the treaty of Greenville. In the army he had formed an attachment for Major Hardin, the son of the colonel, and son-in-law of General Logan, and now requested him to see that the money due for his services was faithfully paid to his family. He also requested, that his family might be removed immediately to Kentucky, and his children educated and brought up in the manner of the white people. He observed that he had killed a great chief; that the hostile Indians knew where his family lived, and that when he was gone, a few base fellows might creep up and destroy them.

Major Hardin having promised to do everything in his power to have the wishes of his friend fulfilled, immediately obtained permission from the general to proceed with Logan's little corps of Indians to the village of Wapoghconata, where his family resided. When they came near the village, the scalp of the Ottawa chief was tied to a pole, to be carried in triumph to the council house; and Captain John, when they came in sight of the town, ordered the guns of the party to be fired in quick succession, on account of the death of Logan. A council of the chiefs were presently held, in which, after consulting two or three days, they decided against sending the family of their departed hero to Kentucky. They appeared however to be fully sensible of the loss they had sustained, and were sincerely grieved for his death.

About the time that Tupper's expedition to the Rapids was in execution, General Harrison determined to send an expedition of horsemen against the Miamies, assembled in the towns on the Mississiniwa river, a branch of the Wabash. A deputation of chiefs from those Indians met General Harrison at St. Mary's, early in October, and sued for peace—they agreed to abide by the decision of the President, and in the meantime to send in five chiefs to be held as hostages. The President replied to the communication of the general on this subject, that, as the disposition of the several tribes would be known best by himself, he must treat them as their conduct and the public interest might, in his judgment, require. The hostages were never sent in, and further information of their intended hostility was obtained. At the time of their peace mission, they were alarmed by the successful movements which had been made against other tribes from Fort Wayne, and by the formidable expedition which was penetrating their country under General Hopkins. But the failure of that expedition was soon afterwards known to them, and they determined to continue hostile. A white man by the name of William Connor, who had resided many years with the Delawares, and had a wife among them, but who was firmly attached to the American cause in this war, was sent to the towns to watch the movements of the Miamies. He visited the villages on the Mississiniwa river, and was present at several of their councils. The question of war with the United States and union with the British was warmly debated, and there was much division among the chiefs, but the war party at last prevailed. The presence and intrigues of Tecumseh, and afterwards the retreat of General Hopkins, rendered them nearly unanimous for war.

To avert the evils of their hostility, was the object of the expedition against Mississiniwa. Said Harrison: "The situation of this town, as it regards one line of operations, even if the hostility of the inhabitants was less equivocal, would render a measure of this kind highly proper; but from the circumstance of General Hopkin's failure, it becomes indispensable. Relieved from the fears excited by the invasion of their country, the Indians from the upper part of the Illinois river, and to the south of Lake Michigan, will direct all their efforts against Fort Wayne and the convoys which are to follow the left wing of the army. Mississiniwa will be their rendezvous, where they will receive provisions and every assistance they may require for any hostile enterprise. From that place they can, by their runners, ascertain the period at which every convoy may set out from St. Mary's, and with certainty intercept it on its way to the Miami (Maumee) Rapids. But that place being broken up, and the provisions destroyed, there will be nothing to subsist any body of Indians, nearer than the Potawatamie towns on the waters of the St. Josephs of the Lake."

This detachment numbered about six hundred mounted men, armed with rifles. They left Franklinton on the 25th of November, by way of Dayton and Greenville; and reached the Indian towns on the Mississiniwa towards the middle of December, suffering much with the cold. In a rapid charge upon the first village, eight warriors were killed, and forty-two taken prisoners, consisting of men, women and children. About half an hour before day, the morning following this charge, the detachment was attacked by the Indians, and after a sharp but short encounter, with a loss of eight killed, and forty-eight wounded, several of whom afterwards died, the enemy, despairing of success, fled precipitately, with a heavy loss.

Learning from a prisoner that Tecumseh was within eighteen miles of them, with a body of six hundred warriors, with the number of wounded then to be cared for, it was deemed advisable to return, and the detachment, having previously destroyed the towns they had approached, together with all the property therein, started upon their return march, and reached Dayton during the early part of January.

"The good effect of the expedition was soon felt," says M'Afee. "It let us distinctly know who were our friends and who were our enemies among the Indians."

The winter being severe, and unfavorable to transportation, the army suffered many privations for the want of a sufficiency of provisions and clothing.

Though General Harrison had repeatedly presented the many difficulties attendant upon a movement, at this period, against Detroit and other points, the government and people were yet restless, and a continued anxiety was manifest for a forward march against the British.

On the 10th of January, 1813, General Winchester, having previously received orders to advance towards the British lines, reached the Rapids, preceded by a detachment of six hundred and seventy men, under General Payne, who had been ordered to attack a party of Indians gathered in an old fortification at Swan Creek.

A large stone house was now built within the encampment, at the Rapids, to secure the provisions and baggage. A considerable quantity of corn was also gathered in the fields, and apparatus for pounding and sifting it being made, it suppplied the troops with very wholesome bread.*

It now soon became apparent that an attack was meditated by the British upon the forces under Winchester, they having heard, through some Indians, of the advance of the army.

On the morning of the 17th, General Winchester detached Col. Lewis, with five hundred and fifty men, for the river Raisin; and a few hours later, Lewis' detachment was followed by one hundred and ten more under Col. Allen. On the morning of this day Gen. Winchester also sent a message to General Harrison, acquainting him with the movements made, and desiring a reinforcement, in case of opposition in an effort to possess and hold Frenchtown.† With this express was also sent word that four hundred Indians were at the river Raisin, and that Elliott was expected from Malden, with a detachment destined to attack the camp at the Rapids.

Early on the morning of the 19th, the messenger reached and acquainted General Harrison with the word sent by General Winchester; upon which he ordered another detachment to proceed at once to the Rapids, with which he also proceeded, whither he arrived on the morning of the 20th.

In the meantime, on the 18th, the troops under Lewis and Allen, who had proceeded towards the river Raisin, with a view of occu-

* M'Afee.

† Which was situated between Presque'Isle and Malden.

pying Frenchtown, had been attacked by the enemy, who were driven back with considerable loss, leaving the town in the possession of Allen and Lewis' troops.

This movement was soon communicated to Gen. Winchester, at the Rapids, who at once set out, with a small body of men, for the relief of the forces at Frenchtown, and arrived at the river Raisin on the 20th. The British, from Malden, were now preparing to renew the attack of the 18th, and, on the night of the 21st, had advanced, unobserved, to a point very near the lines of Lewis and Allen's forces, who had, since the former engagement, been joined by Gen. Winchester, with two hundred and fifty men.

Early on the morning of the 22d, the British, with a large body of Indians, having approached within about three hundred yards of the American lines, began to open a heavy charge of cannon and musketry upon them, and soon succeeded in nearly surrounding them.

The Americans fought bravely, but were soon overpowered, and an indiscriminate slaughter was begun by the Indians. "In their confusion and dismay," the Americans "attempted to pass a long narrow lane, through which the road passed from the village. The Indians were on both sides, and shot them down in every direction. A large party, which had gained the wood, on the right, were surrounded and massacred without distinction, nearly one hundred men being tomahawked within the distance of one hundred yards. The most horrible destruction overwhelmed the fugitives in every direction.

"Captain Simpson was shot and tomahawked at the edge of the woods, near the mouth of the lane. COLONEL ALLEN,* though wounded in his thigh, attempted to rally his men several times, entreating them to halt and sell their lives as dearly as possible. He had escaped about two miles, when, at length, wearied and exhausted, snd disdaining perhaps to survive the defeat, he sat down on a log, determined to meet his fate. An Indian chief, observing him to be an officer of distinction, was anxious to take him prisoner. As soon as he came near the Colonel, he threw his gun across his lap, and told him in the Indian language to surrender, and he should be safe. Another savage having, at the same time, advanced with a hostile appearance, Colonel ALLEN, by one stroke with his sword, laid him dead at his feet. A third Indian, who was near him, had then the honor of shooting one of the first and greatest citizens of Kentucky. Captain Mead, of the regular army, who had fought by the side of Colonel Daveiss, when he fell in the battle of Tippecanoe, was killed where the action commenced. Finding that the situation of the corps was rendered desperate by the approach of the enemy, he gave orders to his men—"My brave fellows," (cried he,) "charge upon them;" and a moment afterwards he was no more.

*Mentioned in a preceding chapter as the person after whom Allen County was named.

"A party with Lieutenant Garrett, consisting of fifteen or twenty men, after retreating about a mile and a half, were compelled to surrender, and were then all massacred, but the lieutenant himself. Another party of about thirty men had escaped near three miles, when they were overtaken by the savages, and having surrendered, about one-half of them were shot and tomahawked. In short, the greater part of those who were in the retreat, fell a sacrifice to the fury of the Indians. The snow was so deep, and the cold so intense, that they were soon exhausted, and unable to elude their pursuers. Gen. Winchester and Colonel Lewis, with a few more, were captured at a bridge, about three-quarters of a mile from the village. Their coats being taken from them, they were carried back to the British lines, where Colonel Proctor commanded."*

A small party, under Majors Graves and Madison, having placed themselves behind some picketing, where they maintained their position and fought bravely, until an order, reported as coming from General Winchester, was brought by Proctor, who was accompanied by one of his aids, desiring them to surrender. Major Madison remarked "that it had been customary for the Indians to massacre the wounded and prisoners after a surrender, and that he would not agree to any capitulation, which General Winchester might direct, unless the safety and protection of his men were stipulated." To which Proctor replied: "Sir, do you mean to dictate to me?" "No," said Madison; "I mean to dictate for myself, and we prefer selling our lives as dearly as possible, rather than be massacred in cold blood."

Terms, embodying positive protection to all, having at length been agreed upon, Madison surrendered, and his party reached Malden in safety. But the Indians soon returned to the scene of disaster, and began an unmerciful slaughter of the wounded, stripping them, and even setting fire to the houses in which many of them were sheltered, burning them with the buildings. About 300 Americans were in this way and in the struggle that preceded the burning of the bodies, killed, and 547 taken prisoners.

Such was the sad fate of this expedition. Such was the merciless spirit of British warfare at this period of our history. And the unwillingness of the troops to advance from Fort Wayne at the announcement of a change of general commanders, after the rescue of the garrison here from the wily efforts of the besiegers, would have seemed to have foreshadowed the terrible result of the engagement of Frenchtown.

General Harrison, on the morning of the 22d, (the news of Winchester's attack having reached him at the Rapids,) ordered Perkin's brigade to proceed to his relief, and soon followed himself, in the rear of some reinforcements under Payne, which he is said to have soon overtaken. But they had not proceeded far, when they were met by some men from the scene of defeat, who readily told

*M'Afee.

the sad story of the fate that had befallen their comrades in arms. But General Harrison was only nerved to push on with greater speed. Soon again, however, after proceeding some distance towards the scene of disaster, another party was met, and, after a council as to the wisdom and safety of proceeding further, it was deemed proper to venture no nearer the scene of conflict and disaster, feeling assured that no succor could be rendered the victims of the furious red men and merciless British opponents—that a further advancement would only tend to furnish more material for massacre and defeat; and so the main body returned to the Rapids.

General Winchester, Colonel Lewis, and Major Madison, were finally sent to Quebec, where, and at Beaufort, they were confined till the spring of 1814.

The gloom that had spread over the country at the receipt of the news of the sad disaster to the flower of the Kentucky troops at Frenchtown, was indeed great; but the people soon rallied again; and it was not long till large reinforcements began to swell the ranks of the regular army for a determined and vigorous effort for the overthrow of British rule and future safety from Indian atrocities.

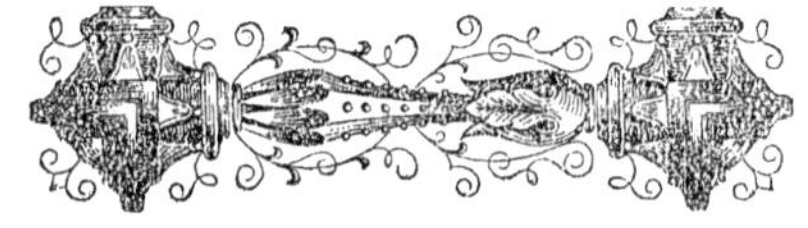

CHAPTER XX.

> "Upward, onward, in the battle,
> * * * * * *
> Never resting, never weary,
> Till victory crowns the fight."

—o—

Situation of affairs after the slaughter of Frenchtown—Heavy draft on Kentucky—Efforts of the British—The importance of placing the Kentucky militia at Fort Wayne—The British commander determines to march the American army to Montreal—Advance of the British and Indians on Fort Meigs—The British again occupy old Fort Miami, at the foot of the Rapids—Indians invest the American camp—Gen. Harrison's address—Bombardment of Fort Meigs by the British—Efforts of Tecumseh and the Prophet—Further movements of the British—Their batteries silenced by the Americans—Reinforcements under Gen. Green Clay—Order to Gen. Clay, and its execution—Capture of Fort Miami—The Americans overpowered, and many captured and killed—Orders not obeyed, and disaster the result—Removal of American prisoners—Success of Gen. Dearborn at Fort George, and evacuation of old Fort Miami by the British—Indians dissatisfied.

—o—

AFTER the terrible slaughter of Frenchtown, but little of great importance occurred until the latter part of April, 1813. On the 16th of February, of this year, the Governor of Kentucky, in compliance with a law that had been recently passed in that State, had ordered a draft of three thousand men, to be organized into four regiments, under Colonels Dudley, Boswell, Cox, and Caldwell, under the command of General Green Clay. As the season advanced, it became evident that the British would soon make an attack on the American lines at Fort Meigs; and this was made the more certain from the fact that the enemy had recently learned the situation of affairs in the American army from a prisoner they had taken.

This condition of affairs being communicated to the war department, "the propriety of calling out the balance of the Kentucky draft, to be placed at Fort Wayne to keep the Indians in check, was pressed on the attention of the government."*

Both the American and British armies now soon became active in their movements against each other; and the British commander made bold to assert that he would march the northwestern army, under Gen. Harrison, to Montreal by the first of June.

*M'Afee.

During the latter part of the month of April, the British had often been seen, in small bodies, near Fort Meigs, by scouts sent out by the commanding-general; and on the 26th of April, the enemy's advance was observed at the mouth of the bay, within a few miles of Fort Meigs. On the 28th of April, as Captain Hamilton was descending the Maumee, with a small reconnoitering party, he beheld the whole force of the British and Indians approaching within a few miles of the fort.

The British now soon drew up at old Fort Miami, just below the scene of Wayne's engagement with the Indians, in 1794, on the opposite side of the river, nearly fronting Fort Meigs, and began at once to land and mount their guns, the Indians being at once removed to the south-west side of the river, where they readily began to invest the American camp—yelling and firing their muskets.

General Harrison was now most attentive and energetic in his efforts; and on the following morning, he addressed the troops in language and feeling which had the effect to inspire all under him with the largest courage and determination. Said he: "Can the citizens of a free country, who have taken arms to defend its rights, think of submitting to an army composed of mercenary soldiers, reluctant Canadians, goaded to the field by the bayonet, and of wretched, naked savages? Can the breast of an American soldier, when he casts his eyes to the opposite shore, the scene of his country's triumphs over the same foe, be influenced by any other feelings than the hope of glory? Is not this army composed of the same materials with that which fought and conquered under the immortal Wayne? Yes, fellow-soldiers, your general sees your countenances beam with the same fire that he witnessed on that glorious occasion; and although it would be the height of presumption to compare himself to that hero, he boasts of being that hero's pupil. To your posts, then, fellow-citizens, and remember that the eyes of your country are upon you."

About the first of May, the British having completed their batteries, they commenced a heavy cannonading against fort Meigs, which was continued for five days, with but little effect. The American batteries returned the fire with good effect, but with no great amount of energy, not wishing to waste their balls and amunition.

Tecumseh and the Prophet, with a body of some six hundred Indians, since the fatal affair of Frenchtown, (Tecumseh not having been present at that engagement) had joined the British, and were now most active in their efforts against the Americans.

About the time of the opening of the British batteries, General Harrison had expected a reinforcement under General Green Clay; and when the movements of the British became fully apparent, Captain Oliver, accompanied by a white man and an Indian, was sent as a messenger to General Clay, with letters also for the Governors of Ohio and Kentucky.

Fears had been entertained that the enemy would at length make an effort to gain a nearer approach to the fort, from the opposite side of the river, and there erect a battery; which soon became evident, and on the 3d, three field pieces and a howitzer were opened upon the American camp from a clump of bushes on the left, but were soon hushed by a few eighteen pounders from the American batteries. Changing their position, their batteries were again opened upon the American camp, but with an air of mistrust and with but little effect. Says Colonel Wood, of the American forces: "With a plenty of ammunition, we should have been able to have blown John Bull almost from the Miami (Maumee.) * * * It was extremely diverting to see with what pleasure and delight the Indians would yell, whenever in their opinion considerable damage was done in camp by the bursting of a shell. Their hanging about the camp, and occasionally coming pretty near, kept our lines almost constantly in a blaze of fire; for nothing can please a Kentuckian better than to get a shot at an Indian—and he must be indulged."

With a reinforcement of some twelve hundred Kentuckians, General Clay soon drew near. Captain Oliver had met him at Fort Winchester. General Harrison immediately sent an order to General Clay, which was delivered by Captain Hamilton, requesting him to detach "about 800 men from his brigade, and to land them at a point he would direct, about a mile, or a mile and a half above camp Meigs. I will then conduct the detachment," continues General Harrison, in this order, "to the British batteries on the left bank of the river. The batteries must be taken, the cannon spiked, and carriages cut down; and the troops must then return to their boats and cross over to the fort. The balance of your men," said he, "must land on the fort side of the river, opposite the first landing, and fight their way into the fort (Miami) through the Indians."

This order was readily complied with. "Colonel Dudley being the oldest Colonel, led the van. As soon as Captain Hamilton had delivered the orders, General Clay, who was in the thirteenth boat from the front, directed him to go to Colonel Dudley, with orders to take the twelve front boats and execute the plans of General Harrison on the left bank, and to post the subaltern with the canoe on the right bank, as a beacon for his landing."*

Though somewhat "marred in the execution," yet the plans of General Harrison proved a success; and after some effort, with skillful manœuvering, the point of attack was gained, and the British flag cut down, to the infinite delight of the troops in the American garrison above.

General Harrison, who had been watching, with great concern, through his spy-glass, from a battery next to the river, the movements of the troops in the execution of this order, had discovered the enemy approaching the fort below (Miami) by a route that

*M'Afee.

would enable them to surprise the men under Dudley; and at once began to make signs for them to retreat to their boats, but without success. The General finally sent a messenger to warn them of their danger. Lieutenant Campbell undertook the mission; but he could not reach them in time. A party of Indians had fired upon the spies sent out, who were soon reinforced, by command of Colonel Dudley. Many of the men rushed rapidly forward in pursuit of the Indians. The left column still holding their position, were now soon encountered by the British artillerists, largely reinforced, who overpowered the Americans, capturing some at the battery, while others fled to the boats. The Indians had also been reinforced, and began their usual work of tomahawking, etc.

The greater part of the men were captured by the Indians or surrendered to the British. Colonel Dudley had received a wound, and was finally tomahawked by the savages. The number that escaped and regained the fort was less than two hundred. Had orders been strictly obeyed, which was not the case, says M'Afee, "the day would certainly have been an important one for the country."

"The prisoners," says Colonel Wood, "were taken down to head-quarters, put into fort Miami, and the Indians permitted to garnish the surrounding rampart, and to amuse themselves by loading and firing at the crowd, or at any particular individual. Those who preferred to inflict a still more cruel and savage death, selected their victims, led them to the gateway, and there *under the eye of general Proctor, and in the presence of the whole British army, tomahawked and scalped them!*"

For about two hours these acts of unmitigated ferocity and barbarity to prisoners of war was permitted and continued; "during which time, upwards of twenty prisoners, defenseless and confined, were massacred in the presence of the magnanimous Britons, to whom they had surrendered, and by the allies, too, with whom those Britons had voluntarily associated themselves, knowing and encouraging their mode of warfare. The chiefs, at the same time, were holding a council on the fate of the prisoners, in which the Pottawattamies, who were painted black, were for killing the whole, and by their warriors the murders were perpetrated. The Miamies and Wyandotts were on the side of humanity, and opposed the wishes of the others. The dispute between them had become serious, when Colonel Elliott and Tecumseh came down from the batteries to the scene of carnage. As soon as Tecumseh beheld it, he flourished his sword, and in a loud voice ordered them 'for shame to desist. It is a disgrace,' said he, 'to kill a defenseless prisoner.' His orders were obeyed, to the great joy of the prisoners, who had by this time lost all hopes of being preserved. In this single act, Tecumseh displayed more humanity, magnanimity, and civilization than Proctor, with all his British associates in command, displayed through the whole war on the northwestern frontiers."*

*M'Afee.

Retaining the prisoners in this place till night, many of the wounded for hours experiencing "the most excruciating torments," they were placed in "the British boats and carried down the river to the brig Hunter, and a schooner, where several hundred of them were stowed away in the hold of the brig, and kept there for two days and nights. Their sufferings in this situation," says Colonel M'Afee, "are not to be described by me: I leave them to be imagined by those who can feel for the wrongs of their country." Being finally liberated on parole, however, these prisoners were "landed at the mouth of Huron river, below the Sandusky bay."

At the conclusion of the disasterous movement at Fort Miami, but little of interest occurred while the British continued the siege; and having soon learned of the capture of Fort George, by General Dearborn, the British commander, on the 9th of May, evacuated the old Fort at the foot of the Rapids. Alarm had not only taken sudden possession of the British on receipt of the capture of Fort George, but the Indians, too, had snuffed the air of defeat, and had become much disaffected by the movements and success of the Americans against their British father; and before the evacuation of Fort Miami had been fully consummated, it was thought by many in the American army that they had measurably left the British standard.

The Prophet and his followers had been promised the Michigan Territory, and General Harrison was to be delivered up to Tecumseh. But all was now disaster to them, and their former hope of one day being able, by the aid of their British father, to drive the Americans beyond the Ohio, had vanished forever from their hearts.

CHAPTER XXI.

*   *   *   *   *   *
"And has the West no story
Of deathless deeds sublime?
Go ask you shining river."

——o——

Movements at Fort Wayne—Plan of Richard M. Johnson—Communication of the Secretary of War to Gen. Harrison—Mounted volnnteers under Col. Johnson—His address—Ordered to proceed to Fort Wayne, and to scour the northwestern frontier—Demand for more troops—Johnson's regiment—Indian guides—Anthony Shane—Johnson's march to Fort Wayne—Boat fired upon by the Indians, near the Fort—Pursuit of the Indians—An expedition—Anticipated attack from the British—Harrison's interview with the Indians—Movements towards Lower Sandusky—Re-investment of Fort Meigs by the British and Indians—Surprise of a picket-guard—Depredations by the Indians—Movements of Tecumseh—Heavy firing on the Sandusky road—Movements of the British—Council of war—Fort Stephenson—Bravery of the American troops—Valor of Major Croghan, and high appreciation of his course—A Wyandott scout.

——o——

DURING much of the time since the transfer of the theatre of strife and siege from Fort Wayne to points below, along the Maumee and elsewhere, but little had occurred here of marked interest. The garrison had been watchful; the Indians had been active in the region, but their attention had mainly been called away by the action and command of their British father below and about the Rapids of the Maumee.

The principal object of the expeditions against the Indians, from Fort Wayne and other points, as the reader will remember, was to destroy their provisions and means of subsistence, thereby effectually disabling them for renewed efforts in the following spring (1813); and Richard M. Johnson, who had witnessed the effect of these movements and the efficiency of the mounted riflemen, on his return to Congress, had laid before the war department a plan for a mounted expedition against the tribes, as already referred to, during the winter of 1812–'13.

The good effects of the expeditions were stated by him to be: "Security to the northwestern frontiers from Fort Wayne to the Mississippi—to the convoys of provisions for the northwestern army, when its force was diminished in the spring, and the neutrality of the savages in future, from the powerful impression that would be made on their fears; that the winter season would be most favorable for the movement—enabling the horsemen, while snow was on the ground, and the leaves off the bushes, to hunt out and destroy the Indians prowling about."

With this view, two regiments, consisting of about 1280 men, were proposed to be employed, which were then considered sufficient to traverse the entire Indian country, from Fort Wayne to the lower end of, and beyond, Lake Michigan, by way of the Illinois river, back to the river Ohio, near Louisville, Ky.; and "to disperse and destroy all the tribes of Indians and their resources to be found within that compass." Colonel Johnson also presented this subject to the Governor of Kentucky; and the same was finally submitted, by the Secretary of war, to General Harrison, on the 26th of December, 1812. Said the Secretary, in this communication: "The President has it in contemplation to set on foot an expedition from Kentucky of about 1000 mounted men, to pass by Fort Wayne, the lower end of lake Michigan, and round by the Illinois back to the Ohio near Louisville, for the purpose of scouring that country, destroying the provisions collected in the Indian villages, scourging the Indians themselves, and disabling them from interfering with your operations. It is expected that this expedition will commence in February (1813); and it will terminate in a few weeks. I give you the information, that you may take it into consideration in the estimate of those arrangements, you may find it necessary to make, for carrying into effect the objects of the government. I send you a copy of the proposed plan, on which I wish to hear from you without delay. You will particularly state, whether you can effect these objects in the manner which is suggested, by adequate portions of the force now in the field; and in that case, whether it will be better to suspend the movement of this force until the spring."

In the expedition under Colonel Campbell, in the middle of the winter, to the towns on the Mississinewa, as the reader will remember, General Harrison had already anticipated the plan of Colonel Johnson.

After having further considered the proposition of Colonel Johnson, General Harrison made the following response:

"I am sorry not to be able to agree with my friend, Colonel Johnson, upon the propriety of the contemplated mounted expedition. An expedition of this kind directed against a particular town will probably succeed. The Indian towns cannot be surprised in succession, as they give the alarm from one to the other with more rapidity than our troops can move. In the months of February, March, and April, the towns are all abandoned. The men are hunting, and the women and children, particularly to the north of the Wabash, are scattered about making sugar. The corn is in that season universally hid in small parcels in the earth, and could not be found. There are no considerable villages in that direction.

Those that are there are composed of bark huts, which the Indians do not care for, and which during the winter are entirely empty. The detachment might pass through the whole extent of country to be scoured, without seeing an Indian, except at the first town they struck, and it is more than probable, that they would find *it* empty. But the expedition is impracticable to the extent proposed. The horses, if not the men, would perish. The horses that are now to be found, are not like those of the early settlers, and such as the Indians and traders now have. They have been accustomed to corn, and must have it. Colonel Campbell went but 70 or 80 miles from the frontiers, and the greater part of his horses could scarcely be brought in. Such an expedition in the summer and fall would be highly advantageous, because the Indians are then at their towns, and their corn can be destroyed. An attack upon a particular town in the winter, when the inhabitants are at it, as we know they are at Mississiniway, and which is so near as to enable the detachment to reach it without killing their horses, is not only practicable, but if there is snow on the ground is perhaps the most favorable."

These practical suggestions of the General were sufficient. The plan was abandoned, and "the attention of government was directed to the organization of a mounted corps for the spring;" and Colonel Johnson was "authorized to organize, and hold in readiness, a regiment of mounted volunteers—which he readily complied with, on his return to Kentucky, at the close of the session of Congress, and soon moved towards the scene of action.

Addressing his men, he said: "The regiment of mounted volunteers was organized under the authority of the war department, to await its call, or to meet any crisis which might involve the honor, the rights and the safety of the country. That crisis has arrived. Fort Meigs is attacked. The northwestern army is surrounded by the enemy, and under the command of general Harrison is nobly defending the cause of the country against a combined enemy, the British and Indians. They will maintain their ground till relieved. The intermediate garrisons are also in imminent danger, and may fall a bleeding sacrifice to savage cruelty, unless timely reinforced. The frontiers may be deluged in blood. The mounted regiment will present a shield to the defenseless; and united with the forces now marching, and the Ohio volunteers for the same purpose, will drive the enemy from our soil. Therefore on Thursday, the 20th of May, the regiment will rendezvous at the Great Crossings in Scott county, except the companies, &c., which will rendezvous on the 22d at Newport; at which place, the whole corps wili draw arms, ammunition, &c."

Calling upon General Harrison, who, at this time, was at Cincinnati visiting his family, who then lived there, Colonel Johnson's regiment was accepted, and he was ordered by General Harrison to proceed immediately to Fort Wayne, to take command here and of the posts on the Auglaize; also "to make incursions into the country of the Indians; to scour the northwestern frontiers; and, if possible, to cut off small parties who might infest the forts, or be marching from the Illinois and Wabash towards Malden and Detroit —never to remain at one place more than three days."

An officer from each regiment was at once sent back to raise another body of men. The regiment under Johnson was composed as follows:

R. M. Johnson, Colonel; James Johnson, Lieutenant-colonel. First battalion—Duval Payne, Major; Robt. B. M'Afee,* Richard Matison, Jacob Elliston, Benjamin Warfield, John Payne, (cavalry) Elijah Craig, Captains.

Second battalion—David Thompson, Major; Jacob Stucker, Jas. Davidson, S. R. Combs, W. M. Price, James Coleman, captains.

Staff—Jeremiah Kertly, Adjutant; B. S. Chambers, Quartermaster; Samuel Theobalds, Judge-advocate; L. Dickinson, Sargeant-major.

James Sugget, Chaplain and Major of the spies; L. Sandford, Quartermaster-sargeant; subsequently added, Dr. Ewing, Surgeon, and Drs. Coburn and Richardson, surgeon's mates.

The regiment arrived at Fort Meigs on the first of June, 1813. From this point Colonel Johnson proceeded alone to the Indian village of Wapoghconata, on the Auglaize, "to procure some Shawanoe Indians to act as guides and spies;" and after a few days returned with thirteen Indians, among whom was the half-bred, Anthony Shane, whose father was a Frenchman, and in whom the largest confidence was placed by those who knew him in the northwestern army. Shane had been an active opponent of Wayne, in 1794, but after the treaty of Greenville, had been a most faithful friend of the United States.

On the 5th of June, the regiment under Johnson again took up its line of march for Fort Wayne. When the troops reached Shane's crossing of the St. Mary, about forty miles from Fort Wayne, they were halted and drilled for some time, and here remained over night. Heavy rains having but recently fallen, the St. Mary was found impassible; and on the following morning a rude bridge was formed over this stream by felling trees across it, upon which the army crossed with their baggage and guns, while their horses were gotten over by swimming them by the side of the fallen timber.

The remainder of the route to Fort Wayne proved very difficult; "all the flats and marshes being covered with water, and the roads very miry."†

Reaching the Fort on the evening of the 7th of June, it was found that the boats had all gained the common landing place, at the base of the hill, just below the garrison, in safety, but one, which had stranded on a sand-bar a short distance above, in sight of the fort; and while attempting to get the boat off, the boatmen

*Author of "History of the Late War in the Western Country." †M'Afee.

were fired upon by some Indians lurking near, and two of the men killed, while the third, in attempting to swim to the shore, was drowned.

Arriving a little in advance of the regiment, Colonel Johnson and staff, as soon as it was possible to get ready, mounted their horses and crossed to the boat. The Indians at once fired upon their advance, and then retreated.

The spies having now suggested that the Indians were considerably stronger than the party under Colonel Johnson, a pursuit was deferred until the arrival of the regiment, when a chase was immediately commenced and continued for some ten miles; but rain beginning to fall heavily, the party was compelled to return to the fort again, without having gained sight of the Indians.

But a further pursuit was at once determined upon; and the next day, (the 8th) after a council of officers, and some necessary preparation, an expedition was formed to proceed in the direction of the southeast end of Lake Michigan. With this view, the regiment, towards evening, deposited their heavy baggage in the fort; supplied themselves with ten days' provisions, and soon crossed the St. Mary, to encamp for the night in the forks, opposite the garrison, where the river had now just begun to rise; "though," says M'Afee, "on the evening of the 5th, it had been at the top of its banks at Shane's crossing, but forty miles from its mouth by land. Hence," continues he, "if we suppose the current to run three miles an hour, (which is near the truth), the distance by water would be two hundred miles, so extremely crooked is the course of the river."

Early on the following day, the regiment took the Indian trail again, leading towards the old Pottawattamie village of Five Medals, which had been destroyed, as the reader will remember, the previous year, but which was now thought to have been rebuilt. The regiment marched forty miles this day, before night. Stopping now to rest and permit the horses to graze, with a view to an attack upon the Indian village at daylight the next morning, a heavy rain came up, preventing the execution of the plan; but "after encountering many obstacles in crossing high waters and marshes, they arrived at the Elkhart river before it had risen so as to be impassable, and in half an hour afterwards the village of Five Medals was gained and surrounded;" but found unoccupied.

Determining now to visit a village on the other side of the St. Joseph of the Lake, known as Paravash, on the morning of the 11th, the regiment began its march for that point, but, upon arriving at the St. Joseph, and finding it impassable, further movement upon this village was abandoned. A rapid advance was now made upon the White Pigeon's town, arriving there in the afternoon of that day, meeting a few Indians on the way, who made their escape in a canoe across a stream on the route, which was also found impassable. The village of White Pigeon had long been the most extensive Indian town in that region; and the main trace of the

Indians, from Chicago and the Illinois country to Detroit, passed directly through this town, but appeared to have been but little traversed that spring. Here, near this village, the regiment encamped till the following day, when, having fulfilled his instructions to visit this trace, with a view to intercepting any movements of the enemy that might be making by this route, and finding also that the provisions of the troops had been considerably damaged by the rains encountered, Colonel Johnson determined to return to Fort Wayne; and, as there was an Indian path at that time leading direct from the White Pigeon town to Fort Wayne, the regiment now began its return march over this trail for the Fort, whither, after a march, in all, with heavy rains every day, of some two hundred miles, on the 14th, the troops again drew up at the Fort here, considerably fatigued, though as determined and earnest as ever in their patriotic efforts.

Though not encountering the Indians in his route, or finding them at either of the villages visited, yet the movements of the expedition under Colonel Johnson greatly increased his knowledge of the country; and it was now soon ascertained that all the Indians in the British service, and who had principally been engaged in the siege of Fort Meigs, were still mainly held and maintained in the vicinity of Malden.

After a few days' stay at Fort Wayne, and finding themselves much rested from their late fatiguing and most disagreeable march, the regiment under Johnson proceeded down the Maumee, with an escort of provisions, to Fort Winchester. The provisions were placed in boats, with a number of men to man them, while the troops continued their way along the road opened by General Winchester, on the north side of the Maumee, encamping every night with the boats. Arriving at Fort Winchester, Colonel Johnson received a dispatch from General Harrison, recommending him to make an attack on the enemy at Raisin and Browntown. To this suggestion, though by no means explicit, Colonel Johnson at once began to give his attention, feeling, from his high sense of patriotism and regard for General Harrison and any suggestion emanating from him, that the plan should be executed, if possible.

Having, just before this suggestion to Colonel Johnson, heard of the success of the American arms below Fort Meigs, and "that General Proctor was ordered in that direction to assist in repelling the invaders; and believing that Proctor had left Malden with a considerable portion of his force, the General supposed that an excellent opportunity had offered to attack his savage allies in the Michigan Territory, by a *coup de main* with the mounted regiment."

But Colonel Johnson, owing to the fact of his horses being much exhausted from the effects of their late expedition from Fort Wayne, as well as for lack of a sufficient number of men, a detachment of his regiment having been engaged in escorting provisions from St. Mary's, was unable to carry out immediately the plan proposed by

General Harrison. The execution of the plan proposed was considered most hazzardous indeed; and to have attempted a march of a "hundred miles, through swamps and marshes, and over difficult rivers, with guides not very well acquainted with the country," and with horses greatly worn down, "to attack a body of Indians who could, in a few hours, raise more than double the force of the regiment" of 700 men then under Johnson, required some consideration as well as time and preparation. "But fortunately for the regiment, on the next day an express arrived from General Clay, commanding at Fort Meigs, with information that the British and Indians threatened to invest that place again, and with a request that Colonel Johnson would march his regiment there immediately for its relief. Orders to march were given without delay; and such was the zeal and promptitude of both officers and men, that in half an hour they were all ready to march, and commenced crossing the Maumee, opposite the fort. * * * * * The heads of the column were then drawn up in close order, and the Colonel, in a short and impressive address, instructed them in their duties. If an enemy were discovered, the order of march was to be in two lines, one parallel to the river, and the other in front, stretching across from the head of the former to the river on the right. He concluded with saying: 'We must fight our way through any opposing force, let what will be the consequences, as no retreat could be justifiable. It is no time to flinch—we must reach the fort, or die in the attempt.' Every countenance, responsive to the sentiments of the speaker, indicated the same desperate determination. The ground on which the enemy had gained their barbarous triumph over Dudley was again to be traversed; and his allies woulddoubtless hope to realize another 5th of May, in another contest with Kentucky militia. The march was again resumed, and the regiment arrived at ten o'clock in the night, opposite Fort Meigs, without molestation, and encamped in the open plain between the river and the hill on which the British batteries had been erected."*

Apprehensions of an attack were now strong. Information, gained from a Frenchman and an American prisoner, who arrived at Fort Meigs on the 20th of June, was to the effect that the British were determined to renew the attack on the fort, and were to start for that purpose about that period. At this time, General Harrison was at Franklinton, where he was made acquainted with the determination of the British.

Before quitting Franklinton for other points in view, he held an important council with some chiefs of the friendly Indians of the Delaware, Shawanoe, Wyandott, and Seneca tribes; informing them "that a crisis had arrived, which required all the tribes who remained neutral, and who were willing to engage in the war, to take a decided stand either for the Americans or against them—that the President wanted no false friends—that the proposal of General Proctor to exchange the Kentucky militia for the tribes in our friend-

*M'Afee.

ship indicated that he had received some hint of their willingness to to take up the tomahawk against the Americans—and that to give the United States a proof of their disposition, they must either remove with their families into the interior, or the warriors must accompany him in the ensuing campaign and fight for the United States. To the latter condition, the chiefs and warriors unanimously agreed; and said they had long been anxious for an invitation to fight for the Americans. Tahe, the oldest Indian in the western country, who represented all the tribes, professed, in their name, the most indissoluable friendship for the United States. General Harrison then told them he would let them know when they would be wanted in the service—"but," said he, "you must conform to our mode of warfare. You must not kill defenseless prisoners, old men, women, or children." By their conduct, he also added, he would be able to tell whether the British could restrain their Indians from such horrible cruelty. For if the Indians fighting with him would forbear such conduct, it would prove that the British could also restrain theirs if they wished to do so—humerously telling them he had been informed that General Proctor had promised to deliver him into the hands of Tecumseh, if he succeeded against Fort Meigs, to be treated as that warrior might think proper. "Now," continued he, "if I can succeed in taking Proctor, you shall have him for your prisoner, provided you will agree to treat him *as a squaw*, and only put petticoats upon him; for he must be a coward who would kill a defenseless prisoner."

The subject being now strongly pressed upon the government, the Indians were soon reluctantly employed by the United States against the Indians in the employ of the British; and the movement, says M'Afee, "was perfectly justifiable, as a measure of self-defense; yet," continues he, "there is only one reason which reconciles me to it—we thus demonstrated that the north-American savage is not such a cruel and ferocious being that he cannot be restrained by civilized man within the bounds of civilized warfare. In several instances," he further remarks, "strong corps of Indians fought under the American standard, and were uniformly distinguished for their orderly and humane conduct."

On the first of July, General Harrison set out from Fort Meigs for Lower Sandusky, accompanied by seventy mounted men, under command of Captain M'Afee.

Soon after his departure, the Indians had begun again to invest the vicinity of Fort Meigs; and late on the evening of the 20th of July, the vessels of the British army were to be seen in the Maumee, some distance below the fort.

Early on the following morning, a picket-guard, of some eleven men, having been sent to a point about three hundred yards below the fort, were surprised by the Indians, and seven of them killed. At this time a large body of British and Indians were seen encamped below old Fort Miami, on the north side of the river;

and the woods in the rear of the fort was soon after possessed by the Indians, who began to commit some depredations, by occasionally firing into the fort, and capturing some horses and oxen.

General Harrison was at once apprised of the siege, while all in the garrison were attentively engaged in preparing for the movements against the fort; and General Clay was most vigilant in all his efforts.

On the 23d, with a body of some eight hundred Indians, Tecumseh was seen moving up the river, with a view, as was supposed, of attacking Fort Winchester. On the 25th, the enemy removed his camp to the south side of the river, which superinduced the belief that an attempt would be made by the British to take the fort by storm.

General Harrison was still kept advised of the movements of the British; but his force was not sufficient to enable him to reach the garrison as he had wished, though he continued to assure General Clay that all needed aid would reach him from Ohio and other points in good season. On the evening of the 26th, some hours after the arrival at the fort of the express from General Harrison, heavy firing was commenced on the Sandusky road, about the distance of a mile from Fort Meigs. The discharge of rifles and musketry, accompanied by the Indian yell, could be clearly distinguished; and by degrees the apparent contest approached towards the fort, though sometimes it appeared to recede. It lasted about an hour, and came in the end near the edge of the woods. The general pronounced it a sham battle, intended to draw out the garrison to relieve a supposed reinforcement. A few discharges of cannon at the fort, and a heavy shower of rain, at length put an end to the scheme, no doubt to the great mortification of its projectors. The express from General Harrison had providentially arrived in time to preserve the garrison from the possibility of being deluded by this artifice of the enemy. On the next day the British moved over to their old encampment, and on the 28th embarked in their vessels and abandoned the siege. The force which Proctor and Tecumseh brought against the fort in this instance was about 5000 strong. A greater number of Indians were collected by them for this expedition than ever were assembled in one body on any other occasion during the whole war.

Having raised the siege of Fort Meigs, the British sailed round into Sandusky Bay, while a competent number of their Indian allies moved across through the swamps of Portage river, to cooperate in a combined attack on Lower Sandusky, expecting, no doubt, that General Harrison's attention would be chiefly directed to forts Winchester and Meigs. The General, however, had calculated on their taking this course, and had been careful to keep patrols down the Bay, opposite the mouth of Portage river, where he supposed their forces would debark.*

General Clay now took care to acquaint General Harrison with

*M'Afee.

the movement of the British, and on the 29th of July, the messenger from Fort Meigs having reached him, he immediately called a council of war, consisting of M'Arthur, Cass, Ball, Paul, Wood, Hukill, Holmes, and Graham, which resulted in a determination to evacuate and destroy Fort Stephenson, if necessary.

By the 31st of July, the enemy had approached so near this fort as to be able to throw their shells about it; and a flag was soon seen approaching the garrison, which was promptly met by Ensign Shipp, by command of Major Croghan. The bearer of the flag had been instructed by Gen. Proctor, who accompanied the fleet, to demand a surrender of the fort, which was positively refused, Shipp replying that it was the determination of the commandant of the garrison to defend it to the last extremity, and to disappear amid the conflagration that should destroy it.

The Indians, as on former occasions, were not to be restrained, and the bearer of the flag thought it "a great pity that so fine a young man should fall into the hands of the savages."

"An Indian," says Captain M'Afee, "at this moment came out of an adjoining ravine, and advancing to the ensign, took hold of his sword and attempted to wrest it from him. Dickson interfered, and having restrained the Indian, affected great anxiety to get him safe into the fort.

"The enemy now," continues M'Afee, "opened their fire from their 6-pounders in the gunboats and the howitzer on shore, which they continued through the night with but little intermission, and with very little effect. The forces of the enemy consisted of 500 regulars, and about 800 Indians, commanded by Dickson, the whole being commanded by General Proctor in person. Tecumseh was stationed on the road to fort Meigs with a body of 2000 Indians, expecting to intercept a reinforcement on that route."

The enemy had directed their fire against the northwestern angle of the fort, which induced the commandant to believe that an attempt to storm his works would be made at that point. In the night Captain Hunter was directed to remove the six-pounder to a blockhouse from which it would rake that angle. By great industry and personal exertion, Captain Hunter soon accomplished this object in secrecy. The embrasure was masked, and the piece loaded with a half charge of powder, and double charge of slugs and grape shot.

Early on the morning of the 2d, the enemy opened their fire from their howitzer and three six-pounders, which they landed in the night and planted in a point of woods about two hundred and fifty yards from the fort. About 4 o'clock, p. m., that day, they concentrated the fire of all their guns on the northwest angle, which convinced Major Croghan that they would endeavor to make a breach and storm the works at that point.

Late in the evening, when the smoke of the firing had completely enveloped the fort, the enemy proceeded to make the assault. Two feints were made towards the southern angle, where Captain Hunter's lines were formed; and at the same time a column of 350 men were discovered advancing through the smoke within twenty paces of the northwestern angle. A heavy, galling fire of musketry was now opened upon them from the fort, which threw them into some confusion. Colonel Short, who headed the principal column, soon rallied his men, and led them with great bravery to the brink of a ditch near. After a momentary pause, he leaped into the ditch, calling to his men to follow him, and in a few minutes it was full. The masked port-hole was now opened, and the six-pounder, at the distance of thirty feet, poured such destruction among them, that but few who had entered the ditch were fortunate enough to escape. A precipitate and confused retreat was the immediate consequence, although some of the officers attempted to rally their men. The other column, which was led by Colonel Warburton and Major Chambers, was also routed in confusion by a destructive fire from the line commanded by Captain Hunter. The whole of them fled into the adjoining wood, beyond the reach of the small arms of the fort. During the assault, which lasted half an hour, the enemy kept up an incessant fire from their howitzer and five six-pounders. They left Colonel Short, a lieutenant, and twenty-five privates dead in the ditch; and the total number of prisoners taken, was twenty-six, most of them badly wounded. Major Muir was knocked down in the ditch, and lay among the dead till the darkness of the night enabled him to escape in safety. The loss of the garrison was one killed and one slightly wounded. The total loss of the enemy was calculated at about one hundred and fifty killed and wounded.

When night came on, which was soon after the assault, the wounded in the ditch were found to be in a desperate situation. Complete relief could not be brought to them by either side with any degree of safety. Major Croghan, however, relieved them as much as possible—conveying them water over the picketing in buckets, and a ditch was also opened under the picketing, by means of which, those who were able and willing, were encouraged to crawl into the fort.*

About 3 o'clock, on the morning of the 3d, the whole British and Indian force commenced a disorderly retreat. So great was their precipitation, says M'Afee's narration, that they left a sail boat behind, containing some clothing and a considerable quantity of military stores; and on the next day seventy stand of arms and some braces of pistols were picked up round the fort. Their hurry and confusion was caused by the apprehension of an attack from General Harrison, of whose position and force they had probably received an exagerated account.

At the council held with M'Arthur, Cass, and others, about the 1st of August, it was determined that Major Croghan should abandon Fort Stephenson as "untenable against heavy artillery;"

*M'Afee.

and as this fort was considered as of but little value as a military post, it was also concluded to destroy it at the moment of evacuation. To this end General Harrison immediately dispatched an order to Major Croghan, but which, owing to the messenger and his Indian guides having lost their way, failed to reach him in time, and deeming it then unsafe, in view of the near approach of the enemy, to attempt an evacuation and retreat, after a council with his officers, the most of whom readily coincided with him, Major Croghan at once started the messenger on his return to General Harrison with the following note:

"Sir, I have just received yours of yesterday, 10 o'clock P. M., ordering me to destroy this place and make good my retreat, which was received too late to be carried into execution. We have determined to maintain this place, and by heaevns we can."

His main reason for writing thus positively was, that he feared that the messenger might be captured, and the note fall into the hands of the British; and when received by General Harrison, without knowing fully the motive of Croghan in thus replying to his order of evacuation and retreat, presuming it to indicate a disobeyal of orders, on the following morning, Colonel Wells, with an escort, was sent to take his place, and Croghan at once ordered to repair to the post of General Harrison. Arriving at the headquarters of General Harrison, Major Croghan readily gave a satisfactory explanation of his course and the meaning of his note, which received the ready approval of Harrison, and Croghan was at once ordered to return to his post and resume its command, "with written orders similar to those he had received before."

In an official report of Croghan's course in this siege, General Harrison said: "It will not be among the least of General Proctor's mortifications, to find that he has been baffled by a youth, who has just passed his twenty-first year. He is, however, a hero worthy of his gallant uncle, George R. Clarke."

All under his command at this siege were highly praised by Major Croghan. "Never was there," said General Harrison, "a set of finer young fellows, viz: Lieutenants Johnson and Baylor of the 17th, Anthony of the 24th, Meeks of the 7th, and ensigns Shipp and Duncan of the 17th." Lieutenant Anderson, of the 24th, was also commended for marked good conduct on this memorable occasion; and soon after the siege of Fort Stephenson, Major Croghan was breveted a Lieutenant-Colonel by President Madison, then President of the United States; while the ladies of Chilicothe, Ohio, presented him with a splendid sword, accompanied by an appropriate address.

A little party of Wyandott Indians, after the retreat of the British from Fort Stephenson, were sent down the bay, with other scouts, for the purpose of intercepting the retreat of the enemy. Succeeding in capturing a few British soldiers, who had been left in the general retreat, the Indians "brought them to the camp, without doing them any injury; and, conscious," says M'Afee, "that they had done their duty, they were frequently seen telling the story to their brother warriors, and laughing at the terror which had been manifested by the soldiers, who, no doubt, expected to be massacred or carried off and destroyed by torture."

CHAPTER XXII.

" Come thou, old Erie, worthy of thy name,
Bearing the trophy of thy hero's fame—
*   *   *   *   *   *   *
Perry the young, Perry the bold and brave."

———o———

Ohio and Kentucky again aroused—Heavy reinforcements---Operations on the Lake—Commodore Perry in command of the Lake fleet---Activity of the British---Movement of troops from Ohio and Kentucky---Heavy engagement on the Lake, and victory of Commodore Perry---The British commander sends out a reconnoitering party---Evacuation and destruction of Malden---Arrival of the American forces at Malden---Retreat of the British towards Sandwich---Restless feeling of the Indians---Tecumseh proposes an abandonment of efforts against the Americans---He sees ruin ahead---His speech.

———o———

BOTH Ohio and Kentucky, from which points, at that time, and during some years previous, was derived the main support of the West in a military point of view, were now again aroused, and a large number of volunteers came forward at the call of Governors Meigs and Shelby.

The general attention of the country was now turned to operations on the Lake, of which the British then had the main control, with a considerable fleet afloat; and it became most important that the American government should begin to exercise the largest industry in naval affairs.

Two brigs and several schooners had been laid at Erie early in the month of March of this year, (1813) and Commodore Perry had been sent to superintend their construction and equipment. The enemy had also been most active in this relation, and had built a twenty-gun brig at Malden.

About the 2d of August, having completed his equipments and gotten his heaviest vessels over the bar at the mouth of the harbor, Perry "crossed the Lake to Long Point, and then proceeded up the British shore some distance without discovering their fleet, which had, in fact, returned to Malden for their new brig and additional reinforcements on discovering the force which Perry was able to bring against them."

About the 9th of September, volunteers began to quit Urbana,

Ohio, where they had assembled from different parts of that State and Kentucky, for Upper Sandusky—the Kentuckians headed by the venerable Governor Shelby.

In the meantime, (on the 10th) the vessels on the Lake had come to close quarters; and after an engagement of four hours, during which time it was most difficult to determine which would succeed, the British vessel at length surrendered, and very soon after, much as if the heroic spirit of Wayne had momentarily hovered about the mind of Perry, the following laconic note was addressed to General Harrison:

"*Dear General*—We have met the enemy and they are ours—two ships, two brigs, one schooner, and a sloop.

"Yours, with great respect and esteem,

"OLIVER HAZARD PERRY."

Immediately upon the receipt of the news of the loss of the British vessels, Proctor had sent spies to reconnoiter the forces of General Harrison; who soon obtained a distant view of the Kentuckians while encamped on the plains of Sandusky, at once reporting their number to the British commander at from ten to fifteen thousand.

Upon the receipt of this information, Proctor at once determined to burn Malden, and make good his retreat up the Detroit and Thames rivers, then to make his way to the lower parts of the province. Accordingly, on the 26th, Malden was evacuated and destroyed.

On the following day, (27th) agreeble to previous orders, the American army set sail from the Middle Sister Island for Malden, where the whole arrived in good order about three o'clock in the afternoon of that day, only to behold the ruins of the place. Proctor had retreated to Sandwich, "under the impression that there were at least ten thousand Kentuckians coming against him."

The Indians in the service of the British had now become very restless and uneasy. General Harrison had some time before these events sent some friendly Wyandotts among the Indians allied to the British with a view to neutrality with them. Tecumseh had previously urged an abandonment of the efforts of the Indians against the Americans, but without success; and the efforts of the friendly Wyandotts, sent by the General, had met with no better success. Some 15,000 rations had been daily issued to the Indians—warriors, women and children—by the British, for some time before the retreat of General Proctor, which was quite a weight upon the British government—too heavy to be borne long.

The impressive mind of Tecumseh saw ruin ahead. He did not like or approve of the course pursued by General Proctor in the destruction and evacuation of Malden. As early as the 18th of September, he had delivered a stirring speech to the British commander, in the name of all the chiefs and warriors in the employ of the British, which, by order of General Proctor, was written down and preserved by him until the defeat of the British at the battle of the Thames, when, among other papers left behind by the British in their retreat from the scene of the conflict there, it was found and brought away by the Americans. As the representative of their British father, the King of Great Britain, Tecumseh, in this speech, had appealed to General Proctor, who, doubtless, in view of the momentary approach upon his quarters at Malden of the American forces, was too much disturbed to hear the words of Tecumseh fully explained by the interpreter, or to read the speech himself, when written down. Said the Shawanoe chieftain:

"FATHER, listen to your children! You have them now all before you.

"The war before this, our British father gave the hatchet to his red children, when our old chiefs were alive. They are now dead. In the war, our father was thrown on his back by the Americans, and our father took them by the hand without our knowledge; and we are afraid that our father will do so again at this time.

"Summer before last, when I came forward with my red brethren, and was ready to take up the hatchet in favor of our British father, we were told not to be in a hurry, that he had not yet determined to fight the Americans.

"*Listen!* When war was declared, our father stood up and gave us the tomahawk and told us that he was then ready to strike the Americans; that he wanted our assistance; and that he would certainly get us our lands back, which the Americans had taken from us.

"*Listen!* You told us, at that time, to bring forward our families to this place; and we did so; and you promised to take care of them, and they should want for nothing; while the men would go and fight the enemy; that we need not trouble ourselves about the enemy's garrisons; that we know nothing about them, and that our father would attend to that part of the business. You also told your red children that you would take good care of your garrison here, which made our hearts glad.

"*Listen!* When we were last at the Rapids it is true we gave you little assistance. It is hard to fight people who live like groundhogs.

"*Father, listen!* Our fleet has gone out; we know they have fought; we have heard the great guns; but we know nothing of what has happened to our father with that arm. Our ships have gone one way, and we are much astonished to see our father tying up every thing and preparing to run away the other, without letting his red children know what his intentions are. You always told us to remain here and take care of our lands; it made our hearts glad to hear that was your wish. Our great father, the king, is the head, and you represent him. You always told us that you would never draw your foot off British ground; but now father, we see you are drawing back, and we are sorry to see our father doing so without seeing the enemy. We must compare our father's conduct to a fat dog, that carries its tail upon its back, but when afrighted, it drops it between its legs and runs off.

"*Father, listen!* The Americans have not yet defeated us by land; neither are we sure that they have done so by water; *we therefore wish to remain here and fight our enemy, should they make their appearance.* If they defeat us, we will *then* retreat with our father.

"At the battle of the Rapids, last war, the Americans certainly defeated us; and when we retreated to our father's fort at that place the gates were shut against us. We were afraid that it would now be the case; but instead of that, we now see our British father preparing to march out of his garrison.

"*Father!* You have got the arms and ammunition which our great father sent for his red children. If you have an idea of going away, give them to us, and you may go and welcome for us. Our lives are in the hands of the Great Spirit. We are determined to defend our lands, and if it be his will, we wish to leave our bones upon them."

CHAPTER XXIII.

> "The victory's lost and won"—
> "The battle's o'er! the din is past;
> Night's mantle on the field is cast."
> Long live those honored names—
> The valiant conquerors of the Thames.

—o—

Pursuit of the British from Malden---Harrison's letter to the War Department---Fright and flight of the Canadians---Capture of Tecumseh's chief counselor---His account to Colonel Johnson---Discovery of the bones of the massacred men of Frenchtown ---Excited feelings of the Kentuckians---Movement of the army in the pursuit of the British---Arrival at the mouth of the Thames---Capture of British dragoons--- An omen of victory---The bird of Liberty hovering over the army of Harrison---A sow-shoat follows the army from Kentucky to Bass Island---The army near the Moravian Towns---Capture of a British wagoner---The British army near, in order of battle, lying in wait---Near approach of Colonel Johnson to the British lines--- The great hour of defeat or victory at hand---Formidable position of the British and Indians---Preparations for an attack---Daring plan of Colonel Johnson---A sudden dash to be made upon the British lines---Advance of the American army Distant fire of the British---Intrepid charge of the cavalry under Johnson---Confusion and flight of the British---Contest with the Indians---Pursuit of Proctor---His sword and carriage captured---Loss sustained---Death of Tecumseh---Who killed him?---Estimates of the forces of the armies---The charge of the mounted infantry won the victory of the Thames---Order for the return of the troops---Manly and cheering address of Governor Shelby.

—o—

THE American forces having encamped about the ruins of Malden on the night of the 27th of September, with a view of pursuing the retreating army of Proctor the following morning, General Harrison, on the evening of the arrival of the army, in a letter to the war department, said: "I will pursue the enemy to-morrow, although there is no probability of overtaking him, as he has upwards of 1000 horses, and we have not one in the army. I shall think myself fortunate to collect a sufficiency to mount the general officers. It is supposed here, that general Proctor will establish himself upon the river Trench, or Thames, 40 miles from Malden."

Proctor had pressed into his service all the horses of the inhabitants, which they had not effectually concealed. One only, and that a very indifferent one, could be procured. On it the venerable Governor of Kentucky was mounted, and proceeded with the army towards Sandwich, where they arrived on the 29th, without meeting any obstruction from the enemy; except that the bridge over the Aux Canada river had been torn up, but was soon repaired again. There had been considerable expectation among the commanding officers that a formidable resistance would be made at this bridge, but no enemy was to be seen; and on arriving at Sandwich it was ascertained that General Proctor had retreated from that place early on the preceding day. The Indians, however, were in considerable force in the suburbs of Detroit, the inhabitants of which, who had already been very much plundered, were in great apprehension of an immediate massacre; but a few discharges of grape shot from the fleet, which had come up the river, soon compelled them to fly to the woods for safety. General M'Arthur went over with his brigade and took possession of the town; and on the same evening General Harrison issued his proclamation for re-establishing the civil government of the territory. All persons who had been in office at the time of the capitulation, were directed to resume their functions, and administer the laws which had then been in force.*

The Canadians, like the Kaskaskians, at the time of Clark's movement upon Kaskaskia, in 1778, had heard terrible accounts of the barbarity and ferocity of the Kentuckians, and on the approach of the American forces, had fled in the wildest consternation and fear, expecting to be massacred and plundered by the Long Knives, (the Kentuckians) but in this, they were destined to meet with agreeable disappointment.

On the 20th of September, Lieutenant Griffith having returned with a scouting party from the river Raisin, brought with him an Indian by the name of Misselewetaw, a chief counsellor to Tecumseh, and uncle to the famous Logan. He had led the Pigeon Roost massacre, as detailed in a former chapter. When captured, he was asleep in a house at the river Raisin. He told Col. Johnson, says M'Afee, that the Indians had been watching the movements of his army; had examined his encampments, and seen him arrive at fort Meigs; and that they estimated his forces to be at least 2400. He further stated that the Indians about Brownstown, amounting to 1750 warriors, had determined to give him battle at the river Huron—and that they were still ignorant of the fate of the British fleet. He was an Indian of excellent information, and had been the constant companion and friend of Tecumseh. Being under an impression that he would now certainly have to die, he gave Col. Johnson a long and apparently very candid account of past transactions, since the treaty of Greenville to that time. He said the British had supplied the Prophet's party with arms and amunition before the battle of Tippecanoe; that Tecumseh's plan for a common property in their lands had been strongly recommended and praised by Col. Elliott; and that the British had used every means in their power, since the year 1809, to secure the friendship and aid of the

*M'Afee.

Indians, in the event of a war with the United States—having often invited them to Malden and made them presents for that purpose; and having also represented to them that they should receive British aid to drive the Americans over the Ohio river, after which they should live in the houses of the inhabitants and have their daughters for wives. He said he was now convinced that the British had again deceived them, and that the Great Spirit had forsaken him in his old age for his cruelty and wickedness.

Since the massacre of the river Raisin, the bones of the Kentuckians had remained exposed until sometime in June, 1813, when Colonel R. M. Johnson had collected and buried a large number of them, which, after his departure, had again been dug up and scattered over the fields. On the evening of the 25th of September, orders having been received at Fort Meigs for the regiment under Colonel Johnson to march again for the river Raisin, on the following morning, after due preparation, the regiment moved forward, and on the second day after starting, reached the scene of massacre, where the bones of the slain were to be seen scattered about in every direction. Frenchtown was now generally deserted, and " the fine orchards of peach and apple trees were loaded with excellent fruit." " The sight of the bones," says Captain M'Afee, " had a powerful effect on the feelings of the men. The wounds inflicted by that barbarous transaction, were again torn open. The bleaching bones still appealed to heaven and called on Kentucky to avenge this outrage on humanity. We had heard the scene described before," says he,—" we now witnessed it in these impressive memorials. The feelings they excited cannot be described by me—but they will never be forgotten—nor while there is a recording angel in heaven, or a historian upon earth, will the tragedy of the river Raisin be suffered to sink into oblivion. Future generations will often ponder on this fatal field of blood; and the future inhabitants of Frenchtown will long point out to the curious travelor the garden where the intrepid Madison for several hours maintained the unequal contest of four to one, and repulsed the bloody Proctor in every charge. Yonder is the wood, where the gallant ALLEN fell! Here the accomplished Hart and Woolfolk were butchered! There the brave Hickman was tomahawked and thrown into the flames! That is the spot where the lofty Simpson breathed his last! And a little farther doctors Montgomery, Davis and M'Ilvain, amiable in their manners and profound in science, fell in youth and left the sick to mourn their loss! The gallant Meade fell on the bank in battle, but his magnanimous lieutenant, Graves, was reserved for massacre!"

At this point an express arrived from the main army, which the messenger had left on the Island of the Middle Sister on the morning of the 26th. He had been sent, while General Harrison was reconnoitering off Malden, by the attentive and watchful Governor of Kentucky, to apprize Colonel Johnson of the progress and prospects of the army, that he might regulate his march accordingly. Next morning, before the regiment marched, their faithful guide, Anthony Shane, the Shawanoe half-breed, observed that he knew the spot where Captain Simpson had been killed. The Colonels, with Captain M'Afee and Dr. Ewing, went with Shane to the place, and found the bones, which they buried. The frame of Captain Simpson was easily known from the others, by its length, the Captain having been upwards of six feet and a half high.*

On the 30th of September, the whole regiment under Colonel Johnson, had safely reached Detroit, where they soon crossed the river to Sandwich.

It was now concluded, in a council between General Harrison and Governor Shelby, that Proctor might be overtaken in three or four days' rapid marching; and the Governor was accordingly requested to collect his general officers at headquarters, with a view to arrangements for the plan of pursuit. Two courses were suggested—one, to follow up the Strait by land—the other, to embark and sail down Lake Erie to Long Point, then to move rapidly across by land, some twelve miles, to the road, and intercept the course of the enemy's retreat. Governor Shelby was of the opinion that the route by land, up the Strait, would be the best; which was unanimously agreed upon; and on the morning of the 2d of October, at sunrise, the army was in motion, the vessel troops moving some hours in advance of the brigade of General Cass, which was detained on account of their blankets and knapsacks having been left at the Island of the Middle Sister. The mounted regiments were also detained a short time in drawing provisions. But after a march of some twelve miles, the mounted troops overtook the advance corps.

It having been ascertained that the Indian chiefs, Five Medals and Mai-pock, with other chiefs, in connection with the Miamies, Pottawattamies, and other tribes, had remained on the west side of the Detroit river, General M'Arthur's brigade was left at Detroit to hold them in check.

Upon the arrival of the army at the mouth of the Thames, a small body of British dragoons was discovered by the spies, under Major Sugget, just below that point, who were pursued and captured, just after an effort, on their part, to destroy a bridge over a small stream near the place of capture. "This little affair, the first fruits of the pursuit," says Captain M'Afee, "had a very great effect in animating the pursuers."

As the army drew up at the mouth of the Thames, all eyes were turned upward. An omen of victory was hovering over the scene in the form of the glorious bird of Liberty—the American eagle! "A presage of success!" remarked General Harrison; "as it is our tutelary bird." A similar event had occurred to the fleet of Commodore Perry, before his victory, on the morning of the 10th of September.

*M'Afee.

And it may be remarked just here that another somewhat singular manifestation was presented for the thoughtful consideration and amusement of the army just prior to the appearance of the eagle at the mouth of the Thames. A sow-shoat had followed a company of mounted volunteers from the interior of Kentucky to the point where the army drew up for further orders at Lake Erie. Keeping "constantly with the army, she became generally known to the soldiers, who called her the governor's pig, and were careful to protect her, as they deemed her conduct an auspicious omen. At the margin of the lake," runs the account, "she embarked with the troops and went as far as Bass island." Being offered a passage into Canada from this point, she "obstinately refused to embark the second time;" and though her conduct was jocosely attributed "to constitutional scruples"—some of the men of the army humerously suggesting that "it was contrary to the constitution to force a *militia pig* over the line," yet she could not by any means be pursuaded to cross over to Canada, and was accordingly permitted to "return to the regiment at Portage."

Early on the morning of the 5th of October, the army was again in motion, and continued its march, without special interruption, until within a short distance of the Moravian Towns, some ninety miles northeast of Detroit, where, capturing a British wagoner, the army received the intelligence that "the enemy were lying in order of battle about three hundred yards before them," awaiting the approach of the American forces. Colonel Johnson, with Major Sugget and his spies, now advanced within view of the British lines, for the purpose of obtaining as much information as possible as to the position, &c., of the enemy, which was readily communicated to General Harrison.

The great hour that was to decide the triumph of American arms in the full establishment and maintenance of political rule over the vast territory of the Great West was now at hand; and the forces under General Harrison were halted and formed for the conflict!

The British commander had selected a formidable position for the prosecution of his plan of attack. The ground upon which the British forces had halted extended along near the margin of the river Thames, the ground being covered principally with beech, sugar-tree, and oak timber, with but little underbrush. Running nearly parallel with the river, for about two miles, was a somewhat extensive marsh, which grew narrower as one advanced up the stream. Where the British forces were stationed, there was a narrow swamp, some three hundred yards from the Thames, lying between which and the main swamp extending up the river, there appeared a spot of solid ground. In two lines, their left resting on the river, and their right extending to the first swamp, the British regulars were ranged, with their artillery planted in the road, near the bank of the river. The Indians, all ranged along the first swamp, their left at a point where Tecumseh commanded, occupying "the isthmus between the swamps, on which the undergrowth was tolerably thick; and their right extending a considerable distance down the main marsh, the margin of which, at this place, receding very fast from the river, formed a very obtuse angle with the lines" of the American forces.

At the out-set, in the order of arrangement for battle, the mountted regiment under Colonel Johnson occupied the space between the river and the first swamp. On approaching this regiment and learning of the discovery of the enemy, as well as satisfying himself as to the situation of the British forces, by personal observation, General Harrison at once directed Colonel Johnson, on the approach of the infantry, to assume a position at the left, from thence, if possible, to turn the right of the Indians.

The British regulars were drawn up in open order. A daring plan was now readily conceived by Colonel Johnson, and as quickly agreed upon. It was for the mounted infantry to make a sudden dash upon the British lines, confusing and breaking them at once; and the two mounted regiments were accordingly ordered to be formed "in two charging columns, in short lines, and, on receiving the enemy's fire, to charge through his ranks, form in his rear, and act as circumstances might require."

The rear and flanks being well secured against attacks, the foot troops, embracing five brigades, averaging some three hundred men each, were well arranged along the rear, the river, the swamp, the road, near the river, &c., and Governor Shelby was ordered to take his position—a very important one—at the angle between the swamps, while General Harrison took his position at the head of the front line, in order the better to observe the charge, and render ready and efficient support to the horsemen.

All was now readiness for the charge; and "the whole army advanced in the order" already presented, "until the front of the first battalion received a distant fire from the British lines," which "somewhat frightened the horses, and caused a little confusion at the heads of the columns; thus retarding the charge, and giving the enemy time to prepare for a second fire, which soon followed the first." But in a moment, the American columns "were completely in motion, and rushed upon the British with irresistable impetuosity," causing their front line to precipitately break away in every direction, and their second, also, some thirty paces in the rear of the front line, after a single fire, "was broken and thrown into confusion." The grand idea of the onset of the mounted troops under Colonel Johnson had now consummated its purpose; and sure victory at every point was already perching upon the American banner. The bird of Liberty had indeed proved "a presage of success;" and he had not yet ceased to spread his glorious pinions over the region of the scene of conflict! Such was the patriotic fervor and heroism of that eventful hour of our country's history—such the fierce contest between the receding monarchial element of the time, seeking dominion and control over the northwest, with a view to the overthrow of Republicanism, and the supplanting upon the ruins thereof the power and rule of of the British crown, on one hand, and the valiant pioneer soldiery and patriots of the West, striving to widen the avenues of free institutions, free government—to open the broad domain of the Great West for the cultivation of a boundles unity of goodness, order, truth, industry, and all the conditions and elements then and thereafter germanly pertaining to the welfare, general well-being, progressive education, and safety of a free people—the protection and perpetuation of a generous and progressive government, on the other. And the powerful will of the latter, intensified and impelled by a broad and glorious spirit and sense of freedom and hope of future governmental unity, charged upon the enemy with an undaunted and even reckless determination to achieve the end sought to be attained, viz: an unconditional victory over a common foe to republican institutions and a free, untrammeled government!

At this stage of the conflict, the American columns, having now passed through the broken lines of the enemy, "wheeled to the right and left, and began to pour a destructive fire on the rear of their disordered ranks;" but the contest was only momentary—for, says the narration of the very truthful and intelligent Captain M'Afee, a participant in this eventful struggle, "No sooner had our horsemen charged through their lines and gained their rear, than they began to surrender as fast as they could throw down their arms. And thus, in a moment, the whole British force, *upwards of eight hundred strong*, was totally vanquished, and the greater part of it captured by the first battalion of the mounted regiment under lieutenant-colonel James Johnson, before the front line of our infantry had got fairly in view of them. General Proctor, however, made his escape, escorted by a small party of dragoons and mounted Indians, who were immediately pursued as far as the Moravian town, by a party of the mounted regiment, consisting chiefly of officers.

"The contest with the Indians on the left," continues the narration of M'Afee, "was more obstinate. They reserved their fire till the heads of the columns and the front line on foot had approached within a few paces of their position. A very destructive fire was then commenced by them, about the time the firing ceased between the British and the first battalion. Colonel Johnson, finding his advanced guard, composing the head of his column, nearly all cut down by the first fire, and himself severely wounded, immediately ordered his column to dismount and come up in line before the enemy, the ground which they occupied being unfavorable for operations on horseback. The line was promptly formed on foot, and a fierce conflict was then maintained for seven or eight minutes, with considerable execution on both sides; but the Indians had not sufficient firmness to sustain very long a fire which was close and warm, and severely destructive. They gave way and fled through the brush into the outer swamp, not, however, before they had learnt the total discomfiture of their allies, and had lost, by the fall of Tecumseh, a chief in whom were united the prowess of Achilles and authority of Agamemnon.

"As soon as the firing commenced between the Indians and the second battalion, Governor Shelby, who was posted at the crotchet in its rear, immediately ordered that part of the front line of infantry which lay between the first swamp and the crotchet, being a part of Colonel Donelson's regiment, to march up briskly to the aid of the mounted men. They rushed up accordingly into Colonel Johnson's lines, and participated in the contest at that point. This was the only portion of the infantry which had an opportunity of engaging in any part of the battle. The Governor also dispatched General Adair, his aid-de-camp, to bring up the brigade of General King to the front line; but before this could be accomplished the enemy had fled from Colonel Johnson, and a scattering, running fire had commenced along the swamp, in front of General Desha's division, between the retiring Indians and the mounted men in pursuit, who were now commanded by Major Thompson alone, Colonel Johnson having retired in consequence of his wounds. This firing in the swamp continued, with occasional remissions, for nearly half an hour, during which time the contest was gallantly maintained by Major Thompson and his men, who were still pressing forward on the Indians. Governor Shelby in the meantime had rode down to the left of General Desha's division, and ordered the regiment of Colonel Simrall, which was posted on the extreme left, to march up on the right flank of the enemy in aid of Major Thompson; but before this reinforcement could reach the scene of action, the Indians had given up the contest.

"Soon after the British force had surrendered, and it was discovered that the Indians were yielding on the left, General Harrison ordered Major Payne to pursue General Proctor with a part of his battalion; which was promptly done, and the pursuit continued, by the greater part of the detachment, to the distance of six miles beyond the Moravian town, some Indians being killed, and a considerable number of prisoners, with a large quantity of plunder, captured in their progress. Majors Payne, Wood, Todd, and and Chambers; Captain Langham, and Lieutenants Scorgin Bell, with three privates, continued the pursuit several miles further, till night came upon them—but Proctor was not to be taken.

* * * * * * *

The pursuers, however, at last pressed him so closely, that he was obliged to abandon the road, and his carriage and sword were captured by the gallant Major Wood. The prisoners, about 50 in number, were brought back to the Moravian town, where they were left in charge of Captain M'Afee, with 100 mounted men, until Major Gano arrived, about midnight, with a reinforcement of 150 infantry. At the head of the town, six pieces of brass artillery were taken, three of which had been captured in the revolution, at Saratoga and York, and surrendered again by Hull in Detroit.

"The exact loss which either side sustained in this battle," continues Captain M'Afee, "has never been correctly known. According to the best information, however, which has been received, the total loss of the mounted regiment on that day, was 17 killed and 30 wounded. The loss of the infantry was much less, though considerable also, at the point where they reinforced Colonel Johnson, which was the principal theatre of our losses. The Indians left thirty-three dead on the battle ground, and had ten or twelve killed in different places by their pursuers. The British had 18 killed and 26 wounded, besides 600 prisoners captured, including 25 officers. Among our killed was Colonel Whitley, a veteran who had been a distinguished soldier in former Indian wars, and had been no less conspicuous and serviceable in the present campaign, in whcih the accompanied Colonel Johnson. Captain Craig and Lieutenant Logan died of their wounds a few days after the battle. Col. Johnson and Captains Davidson and Short were also wounded severely, but recovered. The Colonel was shot through his thigh and in his hip, by the first fire of the Indians; and shortly afterwards he was shot through his left hand, by a ball which ranged up his arm, but did not enter his body. He continued, however, in front of his men, gallantly fighting the enemy as long as the action lasted at that place. The white mare on which he rode was also shot so severely that she fell and expired soon after she had carried her rider within the lines of the infantry.

"Tecumseh was found among the dead at the point where Col. Johnson had charged upon the enemy in person; and it is generally believed that this celebrated chief fell by the hand of the Colonel.* It is certain that the latter killed the Indian with his pistol who shot him through his hand, at the very spot where Tecumseh lay; but another dead body lay at the same place, and Mr. King, a soldier in Captain Davidson's company, had the honor of killing one of them.

"From the best information that has been received, it appears that there was no material difference in the strength of the two armies in this battle. The troops under Harrison had been greatly reduced in number by detachments left as guards and for other purposes, and by those who were sick and otherwise unable to

* The question as to who killed Tecumseh? has never been decided. Drake, in his interesting life of this noted chief, devotes some twenty pages to the solution of this long unanswered question, but only to arrive at the sage conclusion, that somebody killed the Shawanoe Chieftain at the battle of the Thames.

While making a political speech at St. Louis, some years subsequent to the struggles of 1812-14, a voice in the crowd asked "who killed Tecumseh?" To which Col. Johnson replied: "I cannot tell; it is probable that I did, but equally probable that I didn't." One of our Western poets, the late Charles A. Jones, Esq., of Cincinnati, Ohio keep up on forced marches. The distance from Sandwich to the Moravian town is upwards of eighty miles, which our army marched in three days and a half, though frequently harrassed by skirmishing and forming in order of battle, and delayed by repairing bridges and procuring supplies. A body of undisciplined militia, urged along and regulated alone by their patriotism and military ardor, would necessarily be much reduced by such a journey. The whole of the regulars had been left behind, except the small fragment of a regiment under Colonel Paul. The brigade of General M'Arthur had been left at Detroit to protect the inhabitants against the Indians; and that of General Cass had been left at Sandwich, waiting for the baggage of the men, which delayed them so long that they were unable to come up with the army before the battle had been fought. The whole way from Sandwich to the battle ground was filled with scattering parties of the militia. Hence, our force at the place of action was believed to be less than 2500 men, which was very little more than the force actually engaged on the part of the enemy. The British part of that force appears to have been about 845 strong. Its loss in killed, wounded, and captured, was 645; and the adjutant-general of the British forces

some years ago, in the columns of the "HESPERIAN," paid the following beautiful tribute to the great warrior:

"TECUMSEH, THE LAST KING OF THE OHIO.

"Where rolls the dark and turbid Thames,
His consecrated wave along,
Sleeps one, than whose, few are the names
More worthy of the lyre and song;
Yet o'er whose spot of lone repose
No pilgrim eyes are seen to weep;
And no memorial marble throws
Its shadow where his ashes sleep.

"Stop, Stranger, there Tecumseh lies;
Behold the lowly resting place
Of all that of the hero dies;
The Cæsar—Tully—of his race,
Whose arm of strength and firey tongue,
Have won him an immortal name,
And from the mouths of millions wrung
Reluctant tribute to his fame.

"Stop—for 'tis glory claims thy tear,
True worth belongs to all mankind,
And he whose ashes slumber here,
Though man in form, was God in mind;
What matter he was not like thee,
In race or color?—'tis the soul
That marks man's true divinity—
Then let not shame they tears control.

"Art thou a patriot?—so was he—
His breast was Freedom's holiest shrine;
And as thou bendest there thy knee,
His spirit will unite with thine;
All that a man can give, he gave—
His life—the country of his sires
From the oppressor's grasp to save—
In vain—quenched are his nation's fires.

"Art thou a soldier?—dost thou not
O'er deeds chivalric love to muse?
Here stay thy steps—what holier spot
Couldst thou for contemplation choose
The earth beneath is holy ground,
It holds a thousand valiant braves;
Tread lightly o'er each little mound,
For they are no ignoble graves.

"Thermopylæ and Marathon,
Though classic earth, can boast no more
Of deeds heroic than yon sun
Once saw upon this lonely shore,
When in a gallant nation's last
And deadliest struggle, for its own,
Tecumseh's fiery spirit passed
In blood, and sought his father's throne.

"Oh, softly fall the summer dew,
The tears of Heaven upon his sod,
For he in life and death was true,
Both to his country and his god;
For oh, if God to man has given,
From his bright home beyond the skies
One feeling that's akin to Hoaven,
'Tis his who for his country dies.

Rest, warrior, rest—though not a dirge
Is thine beside the wailing blast;
Time cannot in oblivion merge
The light thy star of glory cast;
While heave yon high hills to the sky,
While rolls yon dark and turbid river,
Thy name and fame can never die—
Whom Freedom loves will live forever.

soon afterwards officially acknowledged that 204 of those who escaped had assembled at Ancaster on the 17th of October. This calculation is also confirmed by the official return of the troops at Malden on the 10th of September, which made them 944 in number—affording an excess of 100 above our estimate to meet the losses experienced on the retreat before the battle. As for the amount of their Indian force, when it is shown by their own official papers, captured with the army, that 15,000 rations were issued daily to the Indians before the retreat, and that the greater part of them accompanied Proctor up the Thames, it is certainly a reasonable calculation to estimate them at 15, 18, or even 20 hundred warriors in the battle. The whole force of the allies must hence have been at least considerably above 2000—yet a large portion of that force was captured, and the balance entirely driven off by the single regiment under Johnson, aided at one point only by a portion of the infantry, and making altogether, it is believed, much less than half the army. But had our force been greatly superior, the nature of the ground, and position of the enemy, would have rendered its superiority useless; for a larger force than his could not have been brought efficiently into action, had his resistance been so great as to render it necessary. The mounted regiment had but 950 men in the battle—hence the force of the battalion, which was led into action by Lieutenant-Colonel James Johnson, could not have been much more than half as great as the British force, which it shattered in a moment by its impetuous charge.

"Our important and glorious victory, it is evident, was principally achieved by the novel expedient of charging through the British lines with mounted infantry. 'The measure,' says General Harrison, who conceived it at the moment for its execution, 'was not sanctioned by anything I had seen or heard, but I was fully convinced that it would succeed. The American backwoodsmen ride better in the woods than any other people. A musket or rifle is no impediment to them, being accustomed to carry it on horseback from their earliest youth. I was pursuaded, too, that the enemy would be quite unprepared for the shock, and that they could not resist it.' The shock was indeed so unexpected and impetuous that all the resistance they were able to make amounted to nothing. Two or three killed, and a few more wounded, was all the execution done by upwards of eight hundred veterans, many of whom surrendered without giving a second fire. 'It is really a novel thing,' says Colonel Wood, 'that raw militia, stuck upon horses, with muskets in their hands, instead of sabres, should be able to pierce British lines with such complete effect, as did Johnson's men in the affair upon the Thames; and perhaps the only circumstance which could justify that deviation from the long established rules of the art military, is the complete success of the result. Great generals are authorized to step aside occasionally—

especially when they know that their errors will not be noticed by the adversary."

On the 6th the American troops continued to occupy the battle ground, and the Moravian town, about two miles above it, being employed in burying the dead and collecting the public property of the enemy, of which a considerable quantity was found in different places. In addition to the artillery already mentioned, and a great variety of military stores, there were at least 5000 stand of small arms captured by the American troops and destroyed by the enemy on this expedition. A large proportion of them had been taken at the surrender of Detroit, the massacre of the river Raisin, and the defeat of Colonel Dudley. Early on the 7th, Gen. Harrison left the army under the immediate command of Governor Shelby and returned to Detroit; and in the course of the same day the different corps commenced their return home, having embarked the greater part of the property they had captured in boats on the Thames, and set fire to the Moravian town, which was a very inconsiderable village, occupied chiefly by Delaware Indians, who professed to be of the Moravian sect of religion. On the 10th all the troops arrived with their prisoners at Sandwich. It now began to snow, and the weather was extremely cold and stormy. For two or three days the wind blew down the strait with such violence, that it was impracticable to cross it, and the vessels bringing down the public property, were greatly endangered, and much of it was lost.

In the meantime, an armistice was concluded by Gen. Harrison with the Indians. Before he marched in pursuit of the British, a deputation of Ottawas and Chippewas had sued for peace, which he had promised them on condition that they would bring in their families, and raise the tomahawk against the British. To these terms they had readily acceded; and before his return the Miamies and Pottawattamies had solicited a cessation of hostilities from General M'Artur on the same conditions. Even the ferocious and inveterate Mai-pock, of the Pottawattamies, now tendered his submission, and an armistice was concluded with seven of the hostile tribes, which was to continue till the pleasure of the President was known. They agreed to deliver up all their prisoners at Fort Wayne, and to leave hostages in security for their good behavior. Separated from their allies, by the American victories on the Lake and the Thames, from whom they had received subsistence and council, they were now glad to accept the American friendship on any terms, which would save them from extermination by famine and the sword.*

On the 12th the storm had so far abated, that the mounted regiment crossed over the strait to Spring Wells; and on the next day the Kentucky infantry crossed at the mouth of the river Rouge.

On the 20th of October, a general order having been issued for

*M'Afee.

the return of the troops to Kentucky, Governor Shelby said: "Although, in the course of this campaign, you necessarily encountered many difficulties and privations, yet they were met with that cheerfulness, and sustained with that manly fortitude which the occasion required. The uninterrupted good fortune which has attended us, is a source of the most pleasing reflection, and cannot fail to excite the warmest feelings of gratitude towards the Divine Being, who has been pleased in a peculiar manner to favor us, and to crown with success the exertions we have made for our country.

"In the course of the very active operations which we have performed, it is possible that expressions may have dropped, tending to irritate and wound the feelings of some who were engaged in them. The Commanding General hopes, that with the campaign will end every unpleasant sensation, which may have arisen from that source, and that we shall return home united as a band of brothers, with the sweet solace of having served our country from the purest motives, and with the best of our abilities."

In pursuance of this order, the troops returned to Kentucky, and were discharged by Major Trigg, at Limestone, on the 4th of November. The mounted regiment was detained a few days at Detroit, till the Indians had dispersed, after the armistice, and then returned home without any remarkable occurrence.

CHAPTER XXIV.

> "See! again, the smoke is curling
> From the friendly calumet,
> And the club of war is buried,
> And the star of slaughter set."

---o---

Further movements of the American Army—Holmes' expedition against the British near the old battle-ground—He posts his men on a height, and gives the enemy battle—The Americans again victorious—Movement against Mackinaw—Expedition of General M'Arthur—Resignation of General Harrison—The treaty of Greenville—Chief Pe-con—Durability of the old fort—Succession of commanders here—Destruction of the old fort and building of a new one—Peaceful attitude of the Indians after the war—Spirit of order and desire for peace among the Indians—Their close observation and intuition—New-comers—An incident—James Peltier, the interpreter, and the Indian.

---o---

ALTHOUGH the defeat of the British, at the battle of the Thames had virtually terminated the struggles in the northwest, yet there was a determinatiou to push the war still further. In February following, (1814,) an expedition was formed under Captain Holmes, to invade Canada, the enemy having, in the month of January, again taken a position at the point of Proctor's defeat, against which Holmes aimed to direct his expedition; but learning that the British were advancing with a superior force, he took his position upon an elevated point a few miles from the old battle ground, and at once proceeded to fortify himself. Here he was now soon attacked with much vigor, but after considerable loss, the British were again forced to retreat.

The next was a movement against Mackinaw, which had first been proposed soon after the battle of the Thames, but the unfavorable condition of the weather prevented the safe navigation of the lakes, and the purpose was abandoned. In the following April, however, the plan was again proposed, and put into execution for the double purpose of destroying some vessels the British were supposed to be building at Gloucester Bay, and to capture Mackinaw; which, through some misunderstanding, resulted in a fruitless effort, and was at length abandoned. It was again revived, late in the month of July following, from further information received relative to the building of vessels at Gloucester Bay. Failing at length to reach the point in question, the vessels sailed to St. Joseph's, where a trading house was destroyed, and the goods thereof seized. A portion of this fleet at once sailed for Mackinaw, and on the 4th of August made a landing upon the west side of the Island, where a rather spirited action occurred, in which Captain Holmes and 11 others were killed, which induced an abandonment of any further attempt to capture Mackinaw. The British were now somewhat successful in several efforts against the Americans.

M'Arthur, on the 26th of October, with seven hundred and twenty mounted men, left Detroit. Soon reaching Oxford, he proceeded to Burford, whence, instead of joining General Brown, at Fort Erie, as had been previously proposed, he moved towards the lake, by the Long Point road, and there defeated a body of militia, who had thought to stop his further march; destroyed also some five or six mills, and then made his retreat along the lake shore towards Sandwich, pursued by a body of regulars, nearly double his own number, arriving at Sandwich, on the 17th of November, with a loss of but one man; and this closed the struggles in the North-west.

General Harrison, feeling, for certain manifest reasons, that the Secretary of War entertained a dislike for him, resigned his position as commander-in-chief of the western forces, on the 11th of May, 1814. Prior to his resignation, however, he had arranged for a treaty at Greenville, where, on the 22d of July, with General Cass, on behalf of the United States, they had met the friendly Wyandotts, Delawares, Shawanoes, Senecas, and concluded a peace with the Miamies, Weas, and Eel River Indians, and certain of the Pottawattamies, Ottawas and Kickapoos; all of whom had engaged to join the Americans, should the war continue. On the 24th of December, the treaty of Ghent having been signed, by the representatives of the two governments, the difficulties ended, and the proffered aid of the Indians was no longer required.

The treaty of July, 1814, at Greenville, was one of the largest treaties that had ever been held with the tribes. Pe-con,* the successor of Little Turtle, as the representative of the Miamies, with one hundred and thirteen others, were signers to this treaty.

The old Fort, as originally built by order of General Wayne, in 1794, had withstood the ravages of time and the efforts of the Indians to destroy it, remarkably well. From the period of General Hamtramck's occupation of it, after the departure of General Wayne, to its final evacuation, in 1819, it had been in charge of many commandants. After the resignation of Captain Ray, in 1812, Captain Hugh Moore, assumed command, who, in 1813, was superseded by Jos. Jenkinson. In the spring of 1814, Major Whistler became its commandant, who in turn was superseded by Major

* Chief Pe-con died soon after this treaty, near the old residence of his successor, Chief Richardville, some four or five miles up the St. Mary's river.

Josiah H. Vose, in 1815, who continued in command until its final evacuation, 19th of April, 1819.

At the close of the struggles in 1814, soon after the arrival of Major Whistler, to assume command here, it was feared that the Indians might again make an effort to capture the post, and being much out of repair, and most uncomfortable for the garrison in many respects, Major Whistler applied to the War Department for permission to rebuild it, which was granted by General Armstrong, and *the main structure* was replaced by new pickets and other necessary timber for the rebuilding of the officers and other quarters within the enclosure.

Though many Indians continued, for several years after the war of 1812 to congregate here for purposes of trade; to receive their annuity; and also from a feeling of sympathy and attraction for the scene of their old home and gathering-place, aside from some petty quarrels among themselves, in which they would often kill each other, nothing of a war-like nature was ever again manifest between the Indians and the whites.

During 1818, a year remarkable for the congregation of many Indians here, the red man is referred to as presenting a general spirit of order and love of peace, not surpassed by many of the whites of the time, and well worthy of emulation in many instances. It was no uncommon thing in their visits to Ke-ki-on-ga, seeing a new hut, to enquire whether the new-comer was quiet—if he "make no trouble for Injun," &c. And their intuition and close observation were presented very often in the most striking and remarkable light.

On one occasion, about this period, an elderly Miamie had come to the village to trade a little. Soon meeting his old friend, Jas. Peltier, the interperter, his observing eye, in looking about the place, soon fell upon a hut near, that had but recently been built. "Ugh!" ejaculated the Indian; "new wigwam!" He now became most anxious to know if the white man was peaceable—whether he come to make trouble for Injun? The two now soon entered the hut of the new-comers, and shook hands with the inmates. The Indian at once began to look about him, and to enquire how many warriors (children) they had, &c. Eyeing the matron of the house or squaw, as the Indian called her, and observing that she was quite sad, the Indian became anxious to know what was the matter with her—he was sure she was sick. The woman averred that she was not sick. But the Indian knew she was. Turning to his old friend P. again, after looking at the woman and striking his hand upon his breast, exclaimed, "White squaw sick at heart;" and was anxious to know if she had not left something behind, at the settlement from which they came to Fort Wayne. In response to this, the woman quickly replied, that she had left her only son, by her first husband, at Piqua, and that she was anxious to have him with her, but her present husband did not want him to come. "Did'nt I tell you white squaw sick at heart!" replied the Indian, much elated; and he at once proposed to go to Piqua and bring her son to her, if Mr. P. would give him a blanket—which was readily agreed to. Receiving a note from the mother, the next morning early, with two Indian ponies, the generous red man was on the road to Piqua; and in five days from that time returned with the boy! The woman's heart was eased, and as the faithful Indian gazed upon the happy meeting of the mother and the son, his heart warmed within him, and turning to his friend Peltier, he exclaimed: "Is'nt that good medicine for the white squaw!"

The Indian now became the faithful protector and friend of the woman and her son, assuming the special guardianship of the latter—telling the husband that if he ever heard a word of complaint, either from the son or mother, as to ill treatment, "he would have his hide, if he had to lay in the Maumee river until the moss* had grown six inches on his back."

For six or seven years the Indian continued his visits to the hut of the new-comers, always bringing them supplies in the form of venison, and animals of different kinds; and the boy very often accompanied his kind benefactor to the forest in pursuit of game.†

*It was a custom with the Indians in warfare, when seeking to revenge themselves upon some one, often to cover their backs with moss or weeds, and thus to creep from point to point, surprising and killing their opponents.

†As related by Jas. Peltier to his son Louis Peltier, from whom the writer received the narration.

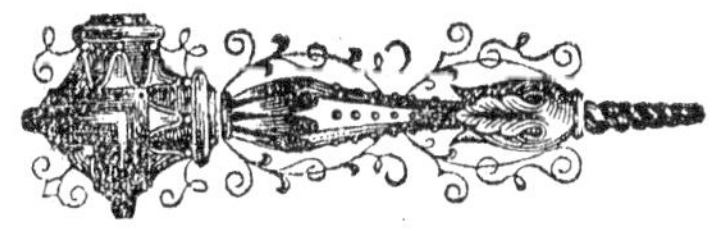

CHAPTER XXV.

"Broad plains—blue waters—hills and valleys,
That ring with anthems of the free!"

——o——

Fort Wayne regarded as an object of marked value to the country—Commanding officer's and soldiers' garden—Main road and general scenery from the fort—Burial grounds—Exhumation of Indian bones, &c.—Hospitality of the garrison—Early navigation of the St. Mary's and Maumee—The general landing-place—Dams and mills—The fur-trade—"Packs"—Richardville—His wealth—French traders—Treaties at St. Mary's, Ohio—Occupants of the fort in May, 1814—Return of chief Richardville to Fort Wayne in 1814—His refusal to attend the treaty of Greenville—Rebuilding of the fort—Early traces—The "Big Elm"—A fourth-of-July party—Arrival of the mail—Removal of Major Whistler, and appointment of Major J. H. Vosè and Lieutenant Clark—Abandonment of the garrison—Loneliness of the settlers—Captain James Riley's visit to and early impressions of Fort Wayne and vicinity—Early buildings—Settlers of 1815—Army contractors—Admission of Indiana as a State—The convention at Corydon—Vincennes the seat of government for the Indiana Territory—What is now Allen County, early formed a part of Randolph County on the south, of which Winchester was long the county-seat—Large gathering of Indians at Fort Wayne—How they drew their rations—The old Council-house and well—Letter of Major B. F. Stickney—Early traders—Visit here of General Cass and H. R. Schoolcraft—Formation of State Districts and election of Representatives.

——o——

AS WITH the heat of summer and the frost of winter, so the effects and agitated state of the war element only gradually disappeared, again leaving the atmosphere of the general mind in a state of comparative passivity and reconciliation.

Still remote from the "settlements," Fort Wayne continued as in former years, to exist as an object of special interest to the nation, not knowing what trials and conflicts might sooner or later call it into action again, in defence of the northwest; and for some years after the achievements of 1812-14, the soldier still continued to stand guard at its portals.

Attached to the fort, running west to about where the "Old Fort House" is located, and where David Comparet's warehouse stands, embracing about one acre of ground, was an excellent and well cultivated garden, belonging to the commanding officer, always filled, in season, with the choicest vegetation. Still to the west of this was the company's garden, extending to about where the Hedekin House now stands, which was also well tilled. The road then mainly used, extended westward from the fort along what is now the canal, to the corner of Barr and Columbia streets.

In general appearance, in the summer of 1814, looking out upon the surrounding scene from the fort, the country and vicinity was described as of the rarest beauty. Nature everywhere wore an aspect of grandeur. The surface, as cleared by order of General Harrison, in 1812, to thwart the efforts and designs of the Indians, was now formed, here and there, with beautiful lawns of tall blue grass, of the finest growth, undisturbed, from season to season, save by the tread and hunger of a few stray ponies.

Just to the south of the fort, in what is now "Taber's Addition," was located the burial-ground of the garrison; and where also were deposited others not immediately connected with the fort. Lieutenant Ostrander, mentioned in a former chapter, who had unthoughtedly fired upon a flock of birds passing over the fort, had been repremanded by Captain Ray, and because of his refusal to be tried by a court-martial, was confined in a small room in the garrison, where he subsequently died, was among the number buried in this old place of interment. Another place of burial, where also a number of Indians were interred, extended along the northwest corner of Columbia and Clinton streets, and to the adjoining block. Many bones were removed from this point some years ago, in digging cellars, and laying the foundations of buildings.

In 1846, in the progress of excavating for a foundation wall, immediately to the west of the northwest corner of Main and Calhoun streets, were dug up and "removed the remains of an Indian, who had long before that been buried, with a gun excellently mounted, some trinkets of silver, and a glass pint flask of whisky, which liquid was still preserved in at least as good a state as when buried. The hair was also in a fair state of preservation, though the skull was much decayed, as were the gun mountings carroded."*

Another burial ground, used principally by the Indians, within the recollection of some of the early settlers here, extended from about where Messrs. Hill & Orbison's warehouse stands, across the basin to the brewery, and beyond. And often had been seen, years ago, swinging from the bough of a tree, or in a hammock stretched between two trees, the infant of the Indian mother; or a few little log enclosures, where the bodies of adults sat upright, with all their former apparel wrapped about them, and their trinkets, tomahawks, &c., by their side, could be seen at any time for many years, by the few pale faces visting or sojourning here.

In those hospitable periods in the northwest, when it was the pride as well as pleasure of every one to freely help his neighbor, in any way that each could be serviceable to the other, the appearance of a stranger at the fort, from the settlements, or any part of the country, was a treat not to be lightly considered; and such an

*"Fort Wayne Times," 1858.

arrival was always hailed with unbounded pleasure by all, and entertained with the freest and most gratifying hospitality.

One of the principal ways by which Fort Wayne was reached at this period, was by water, either by way of the St. Mary's or Maumee rivers, usually in flat boats and what was then known as pirogues, embarking at St. Mary's, Ohio, when coming by way of the St. Mary's river. The boat landing was just below the fort, about where the Maumee bridge is, and in the bend of this river—a road leading obliquely down the embankment from the fort to the landing; and up to 1838, it was no uncommon thing to see pirogues and flatboats, laden with various articles of merchandise, whisky, flour, furs, &c., land and unload, and re-load, at this point. But many dams having been subsequently erected along the St. Mary's, with a view to the establishment of mills, navigation at length became impeded, and finally abandoned altogether. Among the early mills built along the St. Mary's and near Fort Wayne, was one erected by Captain James Riley, in 1822, at a point familiarly known as the "Devil's Race Ground," or what is now Willshire, Ohio; in 1824-5 Samuel Hanna and James Barnett built a mill some three miles from Fort Wayne, now known as "Beaver's mill."

Great quantities of hides and peltries arriving here on horses, familiarly called "packs," or by water, across by portage,* from the Wabash, &c., were placed in pirogues, and re-shipped to Detroit, and other points below. And this business was for many years the principal commerce of the place—in fact, the *coin* itself, by which notes and "promises to pay," were usually liquidated; and it was through these that goods of various kinds were generally

*This business of the portage or transporting of goods and furs to and from the waters of the Maumee and Wabash, had, before the erection of the fort, become of considerable importance. For some time previous to about the year 1800, it had been pretty much monopolized by the mother of the late chief Richardville, who usually employed a considerable number of men—Indians—and horses for that purpose. The extent and profit of the business was such, that the Indians, upon the grant of a tract of land on Little river, at the treaty of Greenville, endeavored to have reserved to themselves the exclusive right of transportation across the portage, a portion of which was included in the grant; and it was stated that as much as one hundred dollars had been yielded from this source in one day. It is quite certain that this woman amassed a considerable fortune at the business. Afterwards, Mr. Louis Bourie, of Detroit, who had a trading house here, principally carried on this business, from about the year 1803, to 1809. His clerk here, who usually employed a number of men and horses for the purpose, acted also as a kind of forwarding merchant for the traders. Upon the deposit of goods in their absence, he issued regular receipts for the same, and paid off the charges of freight and duties at the post of Miami. The traders would purchase their goods in Detroit or Canada, usually in the summer or fall; transport them in pirogues, in case of purchase from the former, to Detroit or Post Miami, where they paid duties; thence they ascended the Maumee river, by the same road to the portage at Fort Wayne; crossed the same by pack horses to the head waters of the Wabash, and down the same by pirogues to their respective establishments In the spring they returned, in the same manner with the furs they had collected in winter, to the marts of Detroit and Canada, whence they were sent to Europe. We can scarcely conceive, at this day, of the immense quantities of furs, consisting principally of beaver, bear, otter, deer, and coon, which were formerly collected on the Wabash and Illinois rivers, and nearly all of which passed over this portage. They were the principal staple of the country, and among the traders the only currency—when debts were contracted, or payments to be made, notes were usually drawn payable in furs. Such notes are found extending back in

obtained in exchange—such as dry goods, boots, shoes, hardware, &c—which were sold at exorbitant prices to the Indians, and others, and by which means, and the early purchase of lands, at a very low figure, many in after years became very wealthy. Richardville, the late chief of the Miamies, who was licensed as a trader with the Indians at this point, as early as 1815, amassed an immense fortune, mainly by this trade and the sale of lands. Schoolcraft estimated his wealth some years prior to his death at about $200,000 in specie; much of which he had had so long buried in the earth that the boxes in which the money was enclosed, had mainly decayed, and the silver itself greatly rusted and blackened.

In 1818, several French traders came here, but not meeting with such inducements as they had desired, passed on, after a few days, to the more remote regions of the West, where furs were supposed to be more abundant.

In this year there were also a number of treaties held with the Indians at St. Mary's, Ohio, on behalf of the United States, under the direction of Governor Jennings and Benjamin Parke, of Indiana, and General Lewis Cass, of Michigan; at one of which, on the 6th of October, a purchase of a considerable body of land lying south of the rivers St. Mary and Wabash, was effected.

When Major Whistler assumed command of the garrison, in May, 1814, aside from the little band of soldiers here, were the two daughters of the commandant, Mrs. Laura Suttenfield,* George and John E. Hunt; Lieutenant Curtiss, and William Suttenfield, husband of Mrs. L. Suttenfield. Soon after the war broke out, with many other members of the tribe, including his family, Chief Richardville, made his way to the British lines for protection, and with a view, doubtless, to render some aid to the enemy; for, as the reader already knows, but few among the tribes of the northwest remained neutral, or failed to give aid in some way to the British cause. At the close of the troubles in 1814, he again returned to this point, and soon passed on up the St. Mary's, about three miles from Fort Wayne, where he encamped.† Major Whistler, desiring to see him, at once sent an interpreter to him by the name of Crozier, requesting him to come immediately to the fort, with which he readily complied. The treaty of Greenville, already referred to, was now about to take place, and the Major desired that the chief should be present, and so requested him; but Richardville was very indifferent about the matter, hesitated, and soon returned to his camp again. A few days subsequently, however, he came back to the fort, where he was now held as a hostage for some ten days, when he at length consented to attend the treaty, and was soon after accompanied thither by Chief Chondonnai, of

date from 1810 to as early as 1738; at which latter period Kaskaskia was the emporium of the trade of the West.—C. B. Lasselle, from Fort Wayne Democrat, Feb. 20th 1867.

*See sketch of her in back part of this volume.

†It was not far from this point where the government, a few years later, built him a very neat brick house, in which he resided for several years afterwards.

one of the lower tribes, (who had been a party to the Chicago massacre,) Robert E. Forsyth, and Wm. Suttenfield.

Much of the season of 1815, was spent in rebuilding the fort; and when completed, as with the first erected in 1794, was a most substantial affair. The timber with which it had been built, was obtained principally from what is now the east end, about where stands the dwelling of H. B. Taylor, James Embry, and the late Samuel Hanna—the pickets consisting of timber, some twelve and a half feet in length, "in sets of six, with cross pieces, two feet from the top, let in and spiked, and a trench dug, two and a half feet deep, into which they were raised."* As the old pickets were removed, the new ones took their place.

At this early period, the roads leading from the fort were mere traces; one leading to Fort Recovery, and known as the "Wayne trace," passing through what is now Allen County, thence into Adams, to the north of Monmouth; from thence passing not far from Willshire to "Shane's Crossing," and so on. There was also a trace to Captain Well's place, on the banks of Spy Run; two traces led down the Maumee on either side; and one extended in the direction of Fort Dearborn, (Chicago;) between which point and Fort Wayne, no house was then visible, nor indeed, in any other direction, with, perhaps, one or two exceptions, short of the settlements in Ohio. The two common fording places at that time and for some years later, were above and below the Maumee bridge—the one below the bridge was better known as "Harmer's Ford," both of which are now most entirely obliterated.

It was below this latter ford, near a path leading towards Detroit, under the cheerful shade of what was then and long after known as the "Big Elm," on the 4th of July, 1810, that Captain Ray and a few others from the fort, were enjoying themselves most agreeably, partaking of a dinner, in honor of the glorious occasion, when an express came up the trace from Detroit, with the private mail and Government despatches. Here Captain Ray took possession of the "mail matter," all gathering around to receive their favors, which were then duly distributed by first Postmaster Ray; and the old Elm was thereafter known as "the Post Office." What has become of this "old familiar tree"—whose o'erhanging bows formed the shadow of the first post office in the region of Fort Wayne, is now unknown. Perhaps some unsparing axeman long since cut it down.

It was by way of Fort Wayne at this period and some years after that the troops at Chicago and Green Bay received their regular mail by military express.

Major Whistler, in 1817, being removed from this point to what is now St. Charles, Mo., was succeeded by Major J. H. Vose, of the 5th regiment of regulars, who held command until permanently evacuated, in April, 1819. The departure of the troops is

* "Fort Wayne Times," 1853.

said to have "left the little band of citizens" then here "extremely lonesome and unprotected. The cessation of the therefore daily music of the troops in the fort was supplied by the stillness of nature, almost overwhelming. The Indians were numerous, and their camp fires and rude music, the drum, made night more dreaded; but to this the inhabitants of Fort Wayne soon became familiarized." "The punctilio of military life was gradually infused into the social circle, and gave tone to the etiquette and moral habits of the citizens of" the fort.*

It was in this year, about the 24th of November, (1819,) that Captain James Riley, the surveyor, paid a visit to Fort Wayne. The following are some of his impressions as then dotted down.

"At every step, in this country," said he of General Wayne and the fort, "every unprejudiced mind will more and more admire the movements and achievements of the army, conducted by this veteran and truly wise and great commander, (General Wayne.) By occupying Fort Wayne, the communication between Lake Erie and the Ohio, through the channels of the Maumee and the Wabash (which is the shortest and most direct water route from Buffalo to the Missisippi river,) was cut off, or completely commanded." He also suggested the importance of a canal, by way of the portage, from St. Mary's to Little river, and said such "might very easily be cut six miles long, uniting the Wabash to the St. Mary's, a little above its junction; and from what I saw and learned from others," said he, "it is my opinion that the swamp might afford water sufficient for purposes of Canal navigation.

"The country around Fort Wayne," he continued, "is very fertile. The situation is commanding and healthy, and here will arise a town of great importance, which must become a depot of immense trade. The fort is now only a small stockade; no troops are stationed here, and less than thirty dwelling houses, occupied by French and American families, from the settlement. But soon as the land shall be surveyed and offered for sale, inhabitants will pour in from all quarters, to this future thoroughfare, between the East and the Mississippi river."

A year later, November, 1820, Captain Riley, writing to Hon. Edward Tiffin, surveyor-general, said he "was induced to visit this place for curiosity, to see the Indians receive their annuities, and to view the country." It was at this period that he levelled the portage ground, from the St. Mary's to Little river, and presented also some very practical suggestions, which, in after years, came to be highly serviceable. Every freshet at that time, brought many boats down the St. Mary's, which had, for some years, been quite common. This, (Fort Wayne,) said he, is "a central point, combining more natural advantages to build up and support a town of importance, as a place of deposit and trade, and a thoroughfare, than any point he had seen in the western country."

At this period, he remarked, there were about one thousand

* "Fort Wayne Times," 1858.

whites here from Ohio, Michigan, Indiana, and New York, trading with the Indians during the payment season, who had brought a great abundance of whisky with them, and which they dealt out to the Indians so freely as to keep them continually drunk, and unfit for business; horse-racing, drinking, gambling, debauchery, extravagance, and waste were the order of the day and night; and that the Indians were the least savage, and more christianized; that the examples of those whites were too indelicate to mention; all of which he thought could be remedied by a speedy survey of the lands, and then to dispose of them as soon as possible, from the mouth of the Maumee to Fort Wayne; and from thence down the Wabash, which would superinduce a rapid settlement, and give spur and energy to agriculture, commerce, and manufactures; and further suggested that the place should be laid out in lots, and sold, the money to be applied by the President, giving a place and lands on which to erect buildings of a public character for "*this future Emporium of Indiana.*" And he finally purchased, this year, at the Piqua Land Office, a number of tracts of land at the Rapids of the St. Mary's, (Willshire,) where he soon moved his family, laid off a town, and, two years later, (1822,) built a grist mill, and surveyed all the country, on both sides of the St. Mary's, embracing Fort Wayne, and also about twenty townships, of six miles square, between the St. Mary's and the Maumee.

Such were the prophetic words—such the spirit and energy of that stirling pioneer, Captain James Riley. And he will certainly long live in the memory of the people of Fort Wayne.

The trade with the Indians now constituted, for some years after the organization of the county, in 1824, the main life and business activity of the place, the principal features of which have been most fully presented in the foregoing, by Captain Riley.

As illustrative of what Captain Riley has said of the adventurous sptrit of the time, on one occasion, at a later period, in the history of this old carrying-place, an Indian had come to Fort Wayne, upon a very fair pony, and alighted in front of a little grocery and liquor store, which then stood on the west side of what is now Calhoun street, a little north of the north-west corner of Main and Calhoun streets. The Indian wanted money, and offered to sell his pony for a moderate sum, to a white man standing near the point at which he stopped. The man looked at the pony somewhat scrutinizingly, and said to the Indian that he would "like to ride him up the street a piece, and if he liked him, would buy the pony." The Indian assented, and the man sprang upon the animal and rode towards Wayne street. At that time, and for some years subsequent, the old jail, a rather substantial, though rough-looking log building, stood on the south-west corner of the the present enclosure of the court-house. Coming to this old edifice, the man turned the corner, eastward, passed the jail, and putting whip to the pony, was soon beyond the limits of the town! The pony was gone. None could tell him of the rider; and the Indian never saw him more.

In 1815, a few houses began to appear some distance from the fort, but usually in range of the bastions, so that, in case of attack, they might easily be destroyed, or the enemy driven away. One of these was built about the centre of what is now Barr street, near the corner of Columbia, which, some years afterwards, being removed from its former locality, formed a part of the old Washington Hall building, on the southwest corner of Columbia and Barr streets, destroyed by fire in 1858.

Among those who came to this point in 1815, were a Mr. Bourie, grandfather of L. T. Bourie; Dr. Turner, Dr. Samuel Smith, from Lancaster, Ohio, and John P. Hedges returned here from Cincinnati, whither, and to Bowling Green, Ky., he had gone after the battle of the Thames. The following year Dr. Trevitt came.

John H. Piatt, of Cincinnati, beginning with 1812, furnished supplies to the army here, with whom, in 1814, became associated Andrew Wallace. This contract was subsequently disposed of to Rob't Hugh Glenn and Jacob Fowles, who, in turn, disposed of it (in 1817,) to Major Wm. P. Rathbone, of New York City.

In 1816, Indiana having been admitted as a State, in compliance with an act of Congress, a Convention was held at Corydon, with a view to the formation of a State Constitution, in which body this part of the State, then a portion of Knox county, was represented by John Badolet, John Benefiel, John Johnson, Wm. Polk, and Benjamin Parke, all now deceased.

The seat of government of Knox county was at Vincennes, which had for several years been the seat of government for the Indiana Territory; and all judicial matters relating to the vicinity of Fort Wayne, were settled at Vincennes up to 1818, when this portion of the State, extending to Lake Michigan, was embraced in Randolph County, of which Winchester was the county seat, up to the formation of Allen County, in 1823.

During 1815, after the declaration of peace, the Indians began to gather here in large numbers, to receive their rations, &c., as per treaty stipulations, at Greenville.

Being admitted into the fort, on such occasions, in parties of six or eight, the Indians would present a little bundle of short sticks, to represent the number of rations they wished to draw. The council-house which had been destroyed by the siege of 1812, was rebuilt in 1816, upon the site of the old one, which was again occupied by the former Indian agent here, Major B. F. Stickney. The same well that was used at the time of its occupancy at this early period, is still used by Mr. Hedekin, whose residence now occupies the site of this old edifice.

The year following the rebuilding of the old council-house, (1817,) Major Stickney addressed the following letter to Thomas L. M'Kinney, then superintendent of Indian Affairs. This letter bears date "Fort Wayne, August 27th, 1817," and at once presents to the mind of the reader the true condition of the Indians here at that period. Said Mr. Stickney:

"I shall pay every attention to the subject of your letter, developing the exalted views of philanthropy of the Kentucky Baptist Society for propagating the gospel among the heathen. The civilization of the Indians is not a new subject to me. I have been, between five and six years, in the habit of daily and hourly intercourse with the Indians northwest of the Ohio, and the great question of the practicability of civilizing them ever before me. That I might have an opportunity of casting in my mite to the bettering of the condition of these uncultivated human beings, and the pleasure of observing the change that might be produced on them, were the principal inducements to my surrendering the comforts of civilized society.

"Upon my entering on my duties, I soon found that my speculative opinions were not reducible to practice. What I had viewed, at a distance, as flying clouds, proved, upon my nearer approach, to be impassable mountains. Notwithstanding these discouraging circumstances, I am ready to aid your views by all proper means within my power; and, in so doing, believe I embrace the views of the government of which I am agent. * * * It will be proper for me to be more particular, and give you something of my ideas of the nature and extent of the obstacle to be met.

"*First.*—The great, and, I fear, insurmountable obstacle is, THE INSATIABLE THIRST FOR INTOXICATING LIQUORS that appears to be born with all the yellow-skin inhabitants of America; and the *thirst for gain* of [some of] the citizens of the United States appears to be capable of eluding all the vigilance of the government to stop the distribution of liquor among them. When the Indians can not obtain the means of intoxication within their own limits, they will travel any distance to obtain it. There is no fatigue, risk, or expense, that is too great to obtain it. In some cases, it appears to be valued higher than life itself. If a change of habit in this can be effected, all other obstacles may yield. But if the whites can not be restrained from furnishing them spirituous liquors, nor they from the use of them, I fear all other efforts to extend to them the benefits of civilization will prove fruitless. The knowledge of letters serves as the medium of entering into secret arrangements with the whites, to supply the means of their own destruction, and, within the limits of my intercourse, the principal use of the knowledge of letters or civilized language has been for them to obtain liquor for themselves and others.

"*Secondly.*—The general aversion to the habits, manners, customs, and dress of civilized people; and, in many cases, an Indian is an object of jealousy for being acquainted with a civilized language, and it is made use of as a subject of reproach against him.

"*Thirdly.*—General indolence, connected with a firm conviction that the life of a civilized man is that of slavery, and that savage life is manhood, ease and independence.

"*Fourthly.*—The unfavorable light in which they view the character of the citizens of the United States—believing that their minds are so occupied in trade and speculation, that they never act from any other motives. * * * Their opinion of the government of the United States is, in some degree, more favorable; but secretly, they view all white people as their enemies, and are extremely suspicious of every thing coming from them.

"All the Miamies, and Eel river Miamies, are under my charge, about one thousand four hundred in number; and there are something more than two thousand Pottawattamies who come within my agency. The proportion of children can not be ascertained, but it must be less than among the white inhabitants of the United States. They have had no schools or missionaries among them since the time of the French Jesuits. They have places that are commonly called villages, but, perhaps not correctly, as they have no uniform place of residence. During the fall, winter, and part of the spring, they are scattered in the woods, hunting. The respective bands assemble in the spring at their several ordinary places of resort, where some have rude cabins, made of small logs, covered with bark; but more commonly, some poles stuck in the ground and tied together with pliant slips of bark, and covered with large sheets of bark, or a kind of mats, made of flags.

"Near these places of resort they plant some corn. There are eleven of these places of resort within my agency. The Miamies and Eel river Miamies reside, principaly, on the Wabash, Mississinewa and Eel river, and at the head of White river. The Pottawattamies [reside] on the Tippecanoe, Kankakee, Iroquois, Yellow river, St. Joseph of Lake Michigan, the Elkhart, Miami of the lake, the St. Joseph emptying into it, and the St. Mary's river. They all believe in a God, as creator and governor, but have no idea of his will being communicated to man, except as it appears in the creation, or as it appears, occasionally, from his providential government. Some of them had been told of other communications having been made to the white people a long time since, and that it was written and printed; but they neither have conception nor belief in relation to it. Their belief in a future existence is a kind of transubstantiation—a removal from this existence to one more happy, with similiar appetites and enjoyments. They talk of a bad spirit, but never express any apprehensions of his troubling them in their future existence."

Among those engaged in the Indian trade at this point and at what is now South Bend, in 1821, were Francis Comparet, with the Pottawattamies, at the latter place, and Alexis Coquillard, with the Miamies, at the former. Wm. G. and Geo. W. Ewing arrived here in 1822, and began to trade with the Indians.

En route for the Mississippi, General Lewis Cass and the historian, H. R. Schoolcraft, made a short stop at this point in June 1822, reaching here in a canoe by way of the Maumee, from Detroit, whence this little vessel was hauled across the portage to Little river, from whence they proceeded on their journey to the Father of Waters.

The following year, (1823,) the State being divided into two Congressionel Districts, John Test, of Dearborn county, was selected representative from the district, then embracing Allen, &c., at which period there were but about fifty votes polled in the whole north part of the State of Indiana.

CHAPTER XXVI.

Scenes varied—new life—
New acts in the drama ;
Still in the "forest deep and wild."

———o———

Establishment of a land office at Fort Wayne, and sale of lands—Purchase of Barr and McCorkle---The original plat---Donation of ground for burial purposes, and upon which to erect a meeting house and seminary---Purchase of Judge Hanna---The first school-house of Fort Wayne---Early school-teachers---Great abundance of fish in the Maumee---Manufacture of oil---What the Indians thought---Buildings and business of 1819---Store of Samuel Hanna and James Barnett---Appearance of the country in 1819---Scarcity of settlers---The Quaker trace---Settlers between Fort Wayne and Richmond, Ind.---Recollections of John Stratten---Early purchasers of land here---The Wells pre-emption---Organization of Allen County---First Masonic organization here---First plat of Fort Wayne recorded at Winchester---First election of county officers—First meeting of the County Board---County officers—First Justices of the peace---Early tavern rates---Taxation---Report on taxable property---Wolf-scalp certificates--First circuit court---First grand jury---First case on docket---First application for divorce---Tavern license---Application for citizenship---Pay of officers---Meeting of court---Attorney's device for seal---Miles C. Eggleston--Associate Judges---Report of Grand Jury---The county jail---Imprisonment for debt---Court sessions-- First will of Allen County---Murder by an Indian Chief, (Big Leg)---His trial---First restraining case---Term of 1831---County officers---Judge Hanna and John Right---Judge Right and Pat. McCarty---Daniel Worth---Organization of Delaware County---The three per cent fund---Grant of land by Congress for canal purposes-- Action of the land office--Cession of land to the State of Ohio --Canal stipulations---Canal commissioners---Hon. Oliver H. Smith---Trip to Fort Wayne, by Mr. Smith, Judge Eggleston, and James Rariden ---Election of John Test and Jonathan McCarty---Election of Mr. Worth, of Randolph County---Formation of Randolph, Allen, Delaware, and other territories, adjoining into a senatorial district--Re-election of Mr. Worth---Election of Mr. Holman---Allen, Randolph, St. Joseph, Elkhart, and Delaware counties formed into a senatorial district---Election of Messrs, Worth, Hanna, Crawford, and Colerick--County Board of commissioners---County addition---Taber's addition---First Probate Court---Letters of administration---Court terms---Estate of Chief La Gross---Appointment of W. G. Ewing-- Judge McCulloch---Lucien B. Ferry---Elections and appointments---Abolition of the Probate Court and organization of the Common Pleas Court---Election of Judge Borden---Organization of a Crimin-Court---Marriage records.

———o———

THROUGH an act of Congress, approved by the President of the United States, May 8th, 1822, a land office was established at Fort Wayne. By this act the district for the sale of lands at this point was also defined, and the President appointed Joseph Holman, of Wayne county, Register, and Captain Samuel C. Vance, of Dearborn county, Receiver. After the survey of the lands, the President issued a proclamation for their sale, to the highest bidder, the minimum price being $1.25 per acre ; and the sale began on the 22d of October, 1823, at the fort. Considerable rivalry having been awakened, touching that portion which embraced the town and immediate settlement—some forty acres, in the immediate locality of the fort, being reserved for the use of the Indian Agent—the most extensive purchasers thereof were Barr, of Baltimore, Md., and McCorkle of Piqua, Ohio. This portion of the city is marked on the city maps " Old Plat to Fort Wayne," and originally designated as "the north fraction of the south-east quarter of section two, township thirty, north of range twelve east ;" and it was on this that Messrs. Barr and McCorkle laid off the original plat of the " Town of Fort Wayne," as surveyed by Robert Young, of Piqua, Ohio. This plat was embraced in one hundred and eighteen lots.*

In this plat, Messrs. Barr and McCorkle set apart and donated, by deed, a body of ground, some four rods square, as a free place of burial, with the privilege to any denomination, that might form a first organization here, to build a Church thereon. They also set apart a lot, of similar dimensions, and adjoining the foregoing, upon which to erect an educational institute or seminary.

But all marks of these donations have long since been destroyed—the point† alone remaining to remind the reader of the thoughtful character of the donors.

In subsequent years, Judge Hanna having purchased all the Barr and McCorkle claims here, and the lots donated, as in the foregoing, being laid off by Mr. Hanna as a part of the place, for general building purposes, the dead of the grave-yard, were, in 1838–9, removed, at public expense or by loved friends, to the general cemetery, west of Fort Wayne.

Of the seminary or school-house erected on the donation of Barr and McCorkle, the " Fort Wayne Times," as late as 1858, in some sketches of the place by the editor, says: " In this old school-huose, many of those, then young, but now past middle life who yet live here, many dead, and others absent, had their early training for usefulness ; and many there experienced that joy only once to be enjoyed in a life-time ; while, perhaps, nearly every teacher, who there disciplined the youthful mind, has gone to his final account, and soon here to be entirely forgotten. * * * This old school-house was built of brick, in 1825, and was then quite

* Running north to Water street, on the bank of the slough, where the water from the City Mills now discharges, south to the alley south of the first Presbyterian Church, west to Calhoun street, and east to a line running just east of Barr street. The reason, for the peculiar direction of the streets, as variant from a north and south line, is this, that some buildings had been put up by the settle s and temporary streets thus adopted, which caused the proprietors to adopt the survey to the convenience of those squatters, who would, it was thought, buy the lots on which their improvements should happen to fall.—" Fort Wayne Times," 1858.

† Just west of the county jail, on Calhoun street, and north of what is now Water treet.

large enough for all needed purposes. * * * It was only one story in height, and served, for many years, not only as a school-house, but as the place of religious worship, town meetings, Masonic installations, political speeches, &c."

J. P. Hedges, who still survives as "one of the old ones of the old ones," of Fort Wayne, was among the first teachers in this old pioneer school-house. In the winter of 1826, he had it plastered at his own expense, that it might be the more comfortable and neat. A Mr. A. Aughinbaugh also taught in this old school-house at an early period. Mr. A., previous to 1833, had charge of the county seminary, at which latter period, it is presumed he took charge of a school in the old brick school-house. It will not be out of place here to remark that the old county jail, which, up to 1847, stood on the south-west corner of Calhoun and the court-house square, was used for some time as a school-room, in which Henry Cooper, Esq., taught; and Mr. Cooper is claimed as the first school-teacher of the place.

The Indians, perhaps for centuries, had been accustomed to look to the streams here for much of their food in the form of fish, so abundant were they from Lake Erie to this point, and for some distance up the St. Mary's and St. Joseph. During seasons of freshets, in great quantities, and some of them very large, they would find their way up the Maumee from the lake, and when the high water subsided, they were often so numerous, that it was difficult to ride a horse or drive a team across the streams here without the animals or the wheels of the vehicles running over some of the finny tribe; and some years ago, a company from Cincinnati began, and for several years carried on, the manufacture of oil from the fish caught here. Many boys and Indians made very good wages by catching the fish for the company. The Indians had always been of the belief that the Great Spirit had thus filled these streams with fish for their special benefit, and when, a few years subsequent to the period in question, a dam was built near the mouth of the Maumee, at the Lake, and the fish prevented from getting into this stream, as their number gradually diminished, and the company compelled to cease its operations thereby, the Indians expressed great displeasure, and considered it a direct encroachment upon their rights, and the designs of the Great Spirit.

Among the buildings erected here in 1819, was a log house, by Samuel Hanna, at the north-west corner of Barr and Columbia sts., where his brick block was some years ago erected, and still stands.* In this log edifice, he and James Barnett opened a considerable store, for wholesaleing to traders, in which business and building they continued for several years—their goods reaching here from the east, by way of Detroit, Toledo, and the Rapids of the Maumee, from which point they arrived here in pirogues, a kind of "dug-out," though usually quite long, and of one solid tree.

* See sketch of Mr. Hanna in latter part of this volume.

At this period, the north-west was yet a comparative wilderness. On the Wayne trace, already alluded to on a former page, not a house was to be met with between this and "twenty-four mile Creek." At this point, there resided a man by the name of George Ayres, near Willshire. By the St. Joseph trace, the nearest was the house of a Colonel Jackson, on Elk Hart Prairie; and it was not until a few years later, that a house appeared, in which Joel Bristols lived, about three miles south of Wolf Lake, in what is now Noble county. At a later period, about four miles north of Kendallville, a man by the name of Norris settled; where Lima is now located. On what was known, at an early day, as the "Quaker trace," a few miles this side of Richmond, Indiana, there was an occasional house to be seen; a man by the name of Robinson lived on the Wabash, about thirty miles south of Fort Wayne; and a few Quaker missionaries had a small settlement at the forks of the Wabash, where they gave the Indians instructions, as at Wa-pa-konnetta, Ohio, in the art of agriculture.*

At the sale of lands at the fort, as already mentioned, "the south half of the south-east quarter of the section referred to, and immediately south of that on which the original town was laid off, was also purchased by Barr and McCorkle, running to the section, line, and also the south-west quarter of section one, just on the east of the fort; while Alexander Ewing got the east half south-west quarter of section two—same on which Ewings' and Rockhill's addition were laid out afterwards. * * The section of land over in the forks of the St. Mary's and St. Joseph, known as the 'Wells pre-emption,' had been, by an act of Congress, May 18th, 1808, set apart as a pre-emption to Captain Wells, who was authorized to enter it, when adjacent lands should be offered at $1.25 per acre; but having lost his life, as the reader has already seen, in 1812, his heirs were thereafter authorized to, and entered it, at this land sale, at $1.25 per acre."†

By an act of the legislature of 1823,‡ the present county of Allen was organized, as then forming a part of Randolph and Delaware counties; and James Ray, of Indianapolis, W. M. Conner, of Hamilton county, and Abaithes Hathaway, were commissioned to deter-

* John Stratten, Esq., now residing some six miles north of Fort Wayne, came here about 1824-5, from Wayne county, near Richmond, mainly by way of the Robinson trace, with a load of boots and shoes, which he then sold to the Messrs. Ewing, trading here. At that time, he says, there were not more than six or eight houses to be seen between Fort Wayne and Richmond, and the best house to be seen here at that period was a hewed log house, one and a half stories high, kept as a tavern; besides which, he says, there were but about eight ordinary pole cabins. Besides the Ewings, he met Peter Kiser here at that time, who is still a goodly citizen of Fort Wayne, and, as for many years past, still engaged in the sale of Dry Goods, Groceries, &c.

† "Fort Wayne Times," 1858.

‡ The first Masonic organization here was formed in this year, (1823) and known as "Wayne Lodge, No. 25, F. A. M." The place of meeting was within the pickets of the fort, in the room of General John Tipton, at which place the order regularly met, until finally removed to the old Washington Hall building, on the southwest corner of Columbia and Barr streets.

mine upon the county seat, which they agreed upon in the early part of 1824.*

In the last week of May, in this year, the first election for county officers occurred; and the first session of the "County Board" was held on the 31st of May, the same month; the Board was constituted of the following persons: Wm. Rockhill, James Wyman, and Francis Comparet.

The county officers were: Anthony L. Davis, Clerk; Allen Hamilton, Sheriff; Samuel Hanna and Benjamin Cushman, Associate Judges; Joseph Holman, Treasurer; H. B. McKeen, first Assessor; Lambert Cushoois, first Constable of Wayne township, then embracing the entire county; W. T. Daviss, Overseer of the Poor; R. Hars, Inspector of Elections; Israel Taylor, Joseph Troutner, and Moses Scott, Fence Viewers; Samuel Hanna, Road Supervisor for the township.

At the first session of the Board, an election for three Justices of the Peace, for the township, was ordered, which resulted in the choice of Alexander Ewing, Wm. N. Hood, and Wm. Rockhill, who then assumed the position, *ex officio*, of the "Board of Justices," taking the place of County Commissioners. Their first session was held October 22d, 1824, at which time the commissioners gave notice of the location of a "State Road from Vernon, in Jennings county, by way of Greensburgh, Rushville, and New Castle, to Fort Wayne."

The following were the tavern rates at that early period: Keeping horse, night and day, 50 cts; Breakfast, Dinner and Supper, each 25 cts.; Lodging, per night, 12½ cts.; whisky, per quart, 12½ cts.; Brandy, per quart, 50 cts.; Gin, per quart, 37½ cts.; Porter, per bottle, 37½ cts.; Cider, per quart, 18¾ cts.

In matters of taxation, the rates were arranged as follows: For every male, over 21 years of age, 50 cts.; for a horse, gelding, or mare, over 3 years old, 37½ cts.; every work ox, 18¾ cts.; stallion, prices of the season; gold watch, $1.00; silver watch, 25 cts.; pinchback, 25 cts.; four-wheeled pleasure carriages, $1.00. The report of Mr. Holman on taxable property for 1824, was $112.62, embracing delinquents, errors, &c.

The State, at this period, and for some years later, granted certificates of bounty on all wolf scalps taken, which certificates were received by the collector for taxes. "So small was the tax," it is said, "that the State revenue due from this county, was nearly all paid off in these certificates, which were usually sent up to Indianapolis by the representatives." †

The first circuit court held in Allen county, was on the 9th of August, 1824, which then embraced what is now Adams, Wells,

* The original plat of Fort Wayne, as laid out in this year, was duly recorded at Winchester, in Randolph county, which, as the records of the Recorder's office here exhibit, were subsequently transferred to Allen.

† "Fort Wayne Times," 1858.

Huntington, and Whitley counties. C. W. Ewing, was at this time prosecuting Attorney. John Tipton was made foreman of the grand jury, which was composed as follows: Paul Taber, William Suttenfield Alexander Ewing, James W. Hackley, Chales Weeks, John Daviss, Wm. Probst, Horace Taylor, James Wyman, James Conner, Cyrus Taber, and W. N. Hood, Peter Felix being discharged. The first case found on the docket was that of Richard Swain, vs. Joseph Troutner, for trespass; and continued. At this time, W. G. Ewing was admitted to the bar as a practitioner at law.

The first application for a divorce in the county, occurred during the first session of this court. The names of the party were A. Canada and Nathaniel Canada; which was continued. The nearest paper at that time, in which such matters received publicity, was the Richmond, Ind., *Enquirer*, about one hundred miles from Fort Wayne.

Two applications for license, to open taverns here, were also made at this term of the court, by Wm. Suttenfield and Alexander Ewing—the former on the corner of Barr and Columbia streets; the latter on the southwest corner of Barr and Columbia. An application was also made for citizenship, during this term, by Francis Aveline, or St. Jule, as then known, father of Francis A Aveline; which was granted. The St. Jule family, (French) came from Vincennes to this place.

Some indictments were found against parties for selling liquor without license, &c., at this term of the court—each being fined $3 and cost. In one instance, for gambling, a man was fined $10. The first master in chancery of this Court, was Charles W. Ewing, then a young lawyer of much ability. "To show the difference, between the manner of allowances of that day and this, when six times as much service was rendered in a given time, * * * the records show that Rob't Hood,* (well remembered by our old citizens,) was allowed 75 cts. per day for three days' service as bailiff to the Circuit Court; Allen Hamilton $16.66 for four months service as Sheriff of Allen county; and Charles W Ewing, for his services as Prosecuting Attorney, for the term, $5. This court after a session of three days, adjourned on the 12th of August, 1824, to convene again as the Court in course."† The following year, 1825, the Board of Justices appointed W. G. Ewing county treasurer; and the second term of the circuit court was convened at the residence of Alexander Ewing, on the 6th of June—Hon. F. Morris, of the fifth judicial circuit, a resident of Indianapolis, presiding—Judge Hanna officiating in the capacity of Associate Justice. James Rariden, and Calvin Fletcher were admitted as practitioners of law at this term—both men of consid-

* A very kind-hearted man, always ready, in those early days, to entertain the stranger and aid the western mover, when ever occasion presented; and many were the interesting adventures and laughable stories he related to his old friends and the many strangers then often gathered about the big fire of the log-cabin in winter.

† "Fort Wayne Times," 1858.

erable distinction in after years. Henry Cooper, a man of many estimable qualities, long since deceased, was also admitted to the bar, at this term of the court, which continued only five days. The third term of this court was convened at the house of Wm. Suttenfield, on the 21st of November, 1825, Judges Hanna and Cushman presiding; and it was at this term that a device for a seal was reported by Charles W. Ewing. Calvin Fletcher having presented his commission, was also sworn as Prosecuting Attorney at this time.

The term which convened 13th February, the year following, 1826, was held at the residence of Alexander Ewing, Judges Hanna and Cushman presiding, Hiram Brown, of Indianapolis, and Moses Cox, being sworn in as attorneys, and Calvin Fletcher receiving the appointment of prosecuting attorney.

But two indictments were issued by the grand jury at this term —one against an Indian, known as Sa-ga-naugh, for murder, and the other against a man by the name of Elisha B. Harris,* familiarly known as "Yankee Harris," for larceny, neither of which, however, came to trial.

At the next regular sitting, August 13th, of this year, Hon. Miles C. Eggleston, of Madison, then pronounced one of the best *nisi prius* judges of the west, presented his commission at the court here, as president judge, was sworn in, and presided over the third term, Benjamin Cushman acting as Associate Judge, Cyrus Taber, (afterwards of Logansport, where he died some years ago,) sheriff, and Amos Lane, of Lawrenceburgh, father of Hon. James H. Lane, of Kansas, was sworn in as prosecuting attorney.

The report of the grand jury, at this session, of which John P. Hedges, now among the last of the *old* pioneer stock yet remaining, was foreman, relates to the county jail, and runs as follows:

"We, the grand jury, empannelled for the county of Allen, and State of Indiana, after examining the county jail, are of the opinion that the criminals' rooms are not a place of safety for persons committed thereto; that the debtors' room, upper department of said jail, is not in a suitable condition for the reception of debtors, from the want of locks, floor, and bedding. "JOHN P. HEDGES, Foreman."

As this report clearly attests, imprisonment for debt was a common custom at this period, and continued for some years after to be a common law in the land. At this session, Judge Eggleston presented a report relative to the mode of keeping a marriage record by the clerk. No marriage record having been previously kept, it was thereafter determined to keep such a register.

The next session met at Wm. Suttenfields', August 27th, 1827, Messrs. Eggleston, Hood and Cushman, presiding, Abner Gerrard, acting as sheriff, Oliver H. Smith, being sworn in as prosecuting

* Harris was a singular character. He lived on the St. Mary's, about seven miles from Fort Wayne. Had early adopted for his life's motto—"To be as honest as the nature of the circumstances would permit." He seems to have possessed a considerable amount of common sense, but his main failing was, to engage in as many law suits as possible, and in that way, in part, gained a very unenviable reputation.

attorney. At this time, Wm. Quarles, of Indianapolis, was licensed to practice as an attorney.

The next term began May 12th 1828, at the residence of Benjamin Archer, and was presided over by Judges Hood and Cushman, at which time, Charles H. Test, and Andrew Ingram were sworn in as attorneys, and Mr. Test, late Secretary of State, received the appointment of prosecuting attorney for the term.

It was at this session that the first will was recorded in Allen county. The party thus recording, was Abram Burnett.

At the next term, November 10th, 1828, Messrs. Hood and Cushman, presiding. David Wallace, subsequently Governor of the State, was sworn in and appointed special prosecutor. It was at this term that the first conviction of felony occurred—the State vs. Joseph Doane, who was sentenced to the penitentiary for three years.

The next term began May 11th, 1829, Judges Eggleston and Hood presiding; Martin M. Ray sworn in as prosecuting attorney. At this term Joseph Carville, for larceny, was sentenced for three years to the state's prison. During the vacation that followed, Anthony L. Davis having resigned the clerkship, on the 14th of October, 1829, the Associate Judge met and appointed Joseph Holman thereto, but to which position Robert Hood was subsequently elected, to assume the duties of the office from February 15th, 1830. On the 10th of May, of this year, C. H. Test, presenting his commission as President Judge, began the term of 1830, with Wm N. Hood, Associate Judge; Robert Hood as Clerk; James Perry as prosecuting attorney; Thomas J. Evans being sworn in as attorney, while David H. Colerick, Esq., was sworn in as attorney, *ex gratis*, for the term.

At this term a case of murder came up for trial. A Miami Indian, known as Ne-we-ling-gua, or (Big-Leg,) being the accused. A half Indian and negro woman, whom he claimed as his slave, had been in the habit of entering his cabin during his absence, and taking his meat. After repeatedly warning her to desist, he at length told her that if she disobeyed him again, he would kill her. From her residence among the clan, of which Big-Leg was chief, whose village was on the Wabash, a few miles from Fort Wayne, with a view to escape the fate that she knew must befall her, after a further disregard of the commands of the chief, the woman came to Fort Wayne, and was soon employed by some of the citizens.

Shortly after her departure, Big Leg came to town, too, and wandering about, he soon discovered her washing, at a house then standing about what is now the southeast corner of Clinton and Columbia streets. Stealing suddenly upon her, with his long knife ready for her destruction, he plunged it into her with such force, that it is said the blade passed through her body, and she fell dead at his feet; whereupon he proudly ejaculated, "was'nt that nice!" Though no uncommon thing, at that period, for the Indians visiting here to kill each other, and for which no redress* had ever been sought by the authorities, the citizens here, who were then largely outnumbered by the Indians of the region, were greatly incensed at this terrible procedure of Big-Leg, and the civil authorities at once had the chief arrested, and placed in the old county jail.

His main plea was that the woman belonged to him—was his property, and that he had a right to do what he pleased with her. When told that he was to be hanged for the offense, he could not comprehend it, but seemed to get the idea that it was some such operation as that he had often witnessed in the use of the old steel yards by the traders in weighing venison, &c., and concluded that he was to be *weighed until he was dead*; which fact soon became commonly understood among the Indians of his tribe and the region here; and as he was a chief much regarded by his clan, they early sought to exchange him for one of their number, whom they considered rather worthless; but without avail.

Having received some explanations as to his probable fate by hanging, or weighing, as he understood it, which he seemed to regard as fixed, he, with his friends, thought to have the experiment tried upon a dog, in order to see how the animal would act. Accordingly, while the chief was still confined in the jail, a number of his Indian friends collected about the outside of the prison, in view of a small opening, where the chief could look out and see the action of the canine as his Indian friends proceeded to execute him. Placing a rope around the animal's neck, and suspending him from a pole that had been arranged for the purpose, at the height of a few feet from the ground, by means of crossed stakes driven into the earth, the dog was soon dangling in the air. Observing the animal very closely through the grates of the jail, the violent throes and contortions of the dog at once gave him a great aversion to hanging, or being thus *weighed* till he was dead; and when the jailor again made his appearance, he urged that he might be shot, rather than be killed by such a process as that he had seen tried on the dog.†

When his trial came on, John B. Bourie and chief Richardville acted as interpreters. He was convicted, but being recommended to mercy by the jury, the governor subsequently granted him a pardon; and in 1848, with a body of Miamies, he removed to Kansas.

The first restraining case that came before the court of Allen county, was that of Maria Caswell, vs. Wm. Caswell, to prevent the latter from selling certain property during the pendency of a

* Indian usage guaranteed the right to kill one another, if they saw proper, as a matter of revenge, or for other reasons, without any other punishment than that often sought to be inflicted by way of common retaliation for the murder of friends.

† Recollections of T. W. Hood, 'Squire John Dubois, and others, then residing here.

suit for divorce. This case came up at the September term, 1830, Judges Hood and Cushman presiding.

But little was now done in court matters until the latter part of 1831, when Judges Test, Hood, and Lewis G. Thompson, (the latter of whom had then but recently been elected,) presided as Judges. Allen Hamilton was now clerk, and David Pickering, sheriff. As clerk, Mr. Hamilton had been commissioned for seven years, beginning with June 14th, 1831, all of which period he served. David H. Colerick was also again sworn in as attorney for the term.

The first case, that of H. Cooper, vs. J. Wheeler, sent down from the Supreme Court, occurred at this time. The case had been reversed.

The spring term of 1832 began April 9th, and was presided over by Judges Hood and Thompson, W. J. Brown acting as prosecuting attorney. Gustavus A. Everett, and John S. Newman appeared as attorneys, and David H. Colerick, Esq., having produced a license, signed by Judges Test and Morris, was then fully admitted as a practitioner at the bar.

In 1826, Samuel Hanna was elected a representative to the Legislature, the district then being composed of Randolph and Allen counties—Jay, Adams, Wells, and Delaware, having since been formed out of these, the limits of Allen then embracing the territory of about all of these latter counties, west to the Illinois line. Mr. Hanna's opponent, at this time, was John Right,* of Winchester, formerly a representative from Randolph, and the adjoining district. As representative Mr. Hanna now served but one term.

Daniel Worth, of Randolph county, was the successor to Mr. Hanna.

During this legislative term of Judge Hanna, Delaware county was organized; and a considerable region of country then lying between Randolph and Allen counties received the name of "Adams," but was not organized as a county until 1836. At that period the three per cent. fund, amounting to about $500 for each county, was appropriated by the State, to the use of the different counties, for the purpose of opening roads. The territory then

* In those Pioneer days, when log cabins of various dimensions, served for the general purposes of dwelling, court-room and tavern, wherein, in the latter case, many often slept in the same room, and not unfrequently, when very much crowded, two and three in a bed, Mr. Right, while attending court in this district, of which, at the time, he was Judge, the landlord of the house in which he was stopping, being very much crowded, requested the Judge to receive a bed-fellow for the night in question, that all might be accommodated. Being averse to "strange bed-fellows," the Judge was by no means favorable to the proposition of the landlord; but being assured that the man was a very clever fellow, a good-natured Irishman, by the name of McCarty, —the Judge at length consented, and the two were soon "in the one bed," with a FEW OTHER BEDS IN THE SAME ROOM, all as full as that occupied by the Judge and his friend McCarty. Awakening "bright and early" the next morning, the Judge began to quiz his Irish friend. "Pat," said the Judge, "I guess you'd have lived a long time in the old country before you'd have had the honor of sleeping with a Judge."

"Yes, be jabers," quickly replied Pat; "and if you'd lived in Ireland, it would have been a mighty long time before you'd uv had the honor of being a judge."

embraced within the boundaries of Allen, was so extensive, that the sum allowed her for road purposes, was considered of little value in carrying out the design of the appropriation; and Judge Hanna drew the amount coming to Allen county, and bestowed it upon what was afterwards called and organized as Adams county.

In the following year, (1827,) on the 2d of March, by an act of Congress, " every alternate section of land, equal to five miles in width," on both sides of what is now the Wabash and Erie canal, "was granted to the State of Indiana," for the purpose of constructing " a canal from the head of navigation on the Wabash, at the mouth of the Tippecanoe river, to the foot of the Maumee Rapids," the same to be commenced at the expiration of the five years following the passage of the act; " and to be completed within twenty years " from that time.

Soon after this grant, the Land Office Commissioners closed the sales and entry of all government lands lying along and embraced within the limits of said grant, until such time as "the State should select and locate her bounty under the grant," which, for a time, had the effect to retard, rather than superinduce and encourage settlement in the northern portion of the State, and along the region of the intended line of canal. A large body of this land, amounting to some two hundred and fifty thousand acres, lay in the State of Ohio, which were eventually ceded to that State, by an act of Congress and the consent of the State of Indiana, under certain stipulations, viz: "that the canal should be commenced and completed according to the original grant; and that it should be sixty feet wide on the surface of the water, and five feet deep, instead of forty feet wide, and four deep." To adjust this, Hon. Jeremiah Sullivan, during 1829, was commissioned to adjust and settle this matter.

"In the winter of 1826 and 1827, a Board of Canal Commissioners was created, whose duty it was to examine into the practicability of a canal route across from the Maumee to the Wabash, and of obtaining a supply of water therefor, from the St. Joseph, St. Mary's, Maumee, or Wabash, or all of them; for which purpose $500 were appropriated, and Samuel Hanna, of Fort Wayne, David Burr, of Jackson county, and Robert John, of Franklin county, were elected Commissioners. It was very difficult to get this Board together, but finally it was convened by Governor Ray, on the 14th of July, 1828, at Indianapolis, and there received from him, plats, maps, surveys, profiles, notes &c., of a report made by a corps of Government Engineers, under instructions of the Engineer's Department, from the mouth of Little river,—at which point a prior survey had been suspended in 1826—thence down the Wabash, and from the summit at Fort Wayne down the Maumee river. This Board of Commissioners met at Fort Wayne in the summer of that year, (1828,)and being without a level or any instrument to work with, and having no engineer, and the $500 of appropriation being insufficient for any practical purpose, Judge Hanna agreed to procure the instruments, and was thereupon dispatched to Detroit, which place he reached, on horse, in two days, then proceeding to N. York, procured the instruments, and returned in an extraordinary quick time for that day. The Board then proceeded, by the aid of John Smyth, of Miamisburgh, Ohio, (an engineer) early in September, to gauge the St. Joseph, St. Mary's, and Wabash, at the forks. During these observations, Smyth was taken sick, and left the Board (none of whom were engineers,) to carry on the work as best as they could. From the 10th to the 23d of September, they spent the time in examining the St. Joseph river, and the adjacent country, for the purpose of locating the Feeder for the canal, and finally succeeded in locating the dam and Feeder-line to the summits, making their own estimates of this, and adopting the estimates, &c., of Colonel Moore, under whose directions former surveys had been made, down the Wabash and Maumee rivers; which, in the meantime, had been received from the War Department, enabling the Commissioners, after the most diligent work, night and day, to present a report of their labor on the 26th of December, later than was intended by law creating the commission. So exhausted was Colonel Burr, by constant fatigue, in caluclation, &c., that for a time his mental powers were overcome, and hence it devolved on Juge Hanna to report; as he did—a report replete with liberal suggestions, and sound sense. This report was concurred in, and from that day went on a work which has proved so great a benefit to Indiana. In this capacity Judge Hanna served three years. The canal lands were located by commissioners, under act of January 25th, 1829, and platted, and a sale opened at Logansport, after some delay, in October, 1830, and an office opened in the first week of October, 1832, at Fort Wayne."*

The sale at Logansport was attended by a large number of persons, and much land was then sold in Cass and adjacent counties, which resulted in the attraction of quite an influx of emigrants to that section and contiguous parts of the State. "But," says C. B. Lasselle, Esq., "owing to the length of credit given on the purchase, availed but little in affording means for the prosecution of the construction of the canal. It was, therefore, found necessary to appeal to the means of the State. Accordingly a bill was introduced in the Legislature during the sessions of 1831–2, for effecting a loan upon the faith of the State, predicated upon the moneys arising from the sales, with interest thereon, together with the tolls and water rents of the canal. The bill met with fierce opposition upon the part of many prominent men in the Legislature; but it finally passed. Its success was duly celebrated by the citizens of Logansport."

The "Cass County Times," of March 2d, 1832, gave the following interesting account of the meeting of the commissioners, and commencement of the work on the canal at Fort Wayne:

* "Fort Wayne Times," December 16th, 1858.

"The Commissioners of the Wabash and Erie canal met at Fort Wayne on the 22d ult., for the purpose of carrying into effect the requisition of the late law of the Legislature of this State, providing for the commencement of said work, prior to the 2d day of March, 1832, whereupon the Commissioners appointed the anniversary of the birth of the Father of his country as the day on which the first excavation should be made on said canal, and by an order of the Board, J. Vigus, Esq., was authorized to procure the necessary tools and assistance, and repair to the most convenient point on the St. Joseph Feeder-line, at 2 o'clock, on said day, for the purpose aforesaid.

"The intention of the Commissioners having been made known, a large number of citizens of the town of Fort Wayne and its vicinity, together with a number of gentlemen from the valley of the Wabash, convened at the Masonic Hall, for the purpose of making arrangements for the celebration of this important undertaking; whereupon Henry Rudisill, Esq., was called to the chair, and David H. Colerick appointed secretary. * * * * *

"The procession, having been formed agreeably to order, proceeded across the St. Mary's river, to the point selected, when a circle was formed, in which the Commissioners and Orator took their stand. Charles W. Ewing, Esq., then rose, and in his usual happy, eloquent manner, delivered an appropriate address, which was received with acclamation. J. Vigus, Esq., one of the Canal Commissioners, and the only one present, addressed the company; explained the reason why his colleagues were absent—adverted to the difficulties and embarrassments which the friends of the canal had *encountered and overcome;* noticed the importance of the work, and the advantages which would ultimately be realized; and then concluded by saying, 'I am now about to commence the *Wabash and Erie canal* in the *name* and by the *authority* of the *State of Indiana.*' Having thus said, he '*struck the long suspended blow*' —broke ground—while the company hailed the event with three cheers. Judge Hanna and Capt. Murray, two of the able and consistent advocates of the canal, in the councils of the State, next approached and excavated the earth; and then commenced an indiscriminate digging and cutting. The procession then marched back to town in the manner it went forth, and dispersed in good order."

Hon. Oliver H. Smith, at the period in question, a resident of Connersville, Ind., in 1826, was elected a representative to Congress, and took his seat at the session of 1827. His opponent was Hon. John Test. Allen County then gave Mr. Smith but ten votes. In his "Early Indiana Trials," Mr. Smith presents the following interesting account of a trip to Fort Wayne, in company with Judge Eggleston and James Rariden, in 1825:

The fall term of the Circuit Courts, 1825, found Judge Eggleston and myself well mounted, once more on the Circuit. The Judge upon his pacing Indian pony: the same that I afterwards rode through an electioneering Congressional campaign; I then rode my gray "fox." We were joined at Centerville by James Rariden, mounted on "Old Gray," one of the finest animals I have ever seen. Our Court was to be held on the next Monday at Fort Wayne. We reached Winchester late in the evening and took lodgings at the hotel of Paul W. Way, but no newspaper heralded the arrival. How different was the circumstance that occurred when I was in the Senate of the United States. Silas Wright, Thomas H. Benton and James Buchanan, for recreation, ran up to Philadelphia; the next day the Pensylvanian announced that Senators Benton and Buchanan had arrived in that city, and taken lodgings at the United States Hotel. A few days after the three distinguished Senators were in their seats. I sat at the time in the next seat to Gov. Silas Wright; turning to the Gov., "I see by the papers that Mr. Benton and Mr. Buchanan have been in Philadelphia and taken lodgings at the United States Hotel; how did it happen that your name was not announced, as you were with them?" "I did not send *my* name to the printer." So it was with us.

After early breakfast we were once more upon our horses, with one hundred miles through the wilderness before us. There were two Indian paths that led to Fort Wayne, the one by Chief Francis Godfroy's on the Salamonia river, the other in a more easterly direction, crossing the Mississenewa higher up and striking the "Quaker Trace," from Richmond to Fort Wayne, south of the head waters of the Wabash river. After a moment's consultation, Mr. Rariden, who was our guide, turned the head of "Old Gray" to the eastern path, and off we started, at a brisk traveling gait, in high spirits. The day passed away; it was very hot, and there was no water to be had for ourselves or horses. About one o'clock we came to the Wabash river, nearly dried up, but there was grass upon the bank for our horses, and we dismounted, took off the saddles, blankets and saddle-bags, when the question arose, should we hold the horses while they grazed, tie them to bushes, spancel them, or turn them loose? We agreed that the latter was the best for the horses and easiest for us, but I raised the question of safety, and brought up the old adage, "Safe bind safe find." Mr. Rariden.—"You could not drive Old Gray away from me." Judge Eggleston.—"My Indian pony will never leave me." I made no promise for my "Grey Fox." The bridles were taken off, and the horses turned loose to graze. A moment after, Old Gray stuck up his head, turned to the path we had just come, and bounded off at a full gallop swarming with flies, followed by the pacing Indian pony of the Judge, at his highest speed. Fox lingered behind, but soon became infected with the bad example of his associates, and away they all went, leaving us sitting under the shade of a tree that stood for years afterwards on the bank of the Wabash. Our horses were, a week afterwards, taken up at Fort Defiance, in Ohio, and brought to us at Winchester on our return. It took us but a moment to decide what to do. Ten miles would take us up to Thompson's on Townsend's Prairie. Our saddles and blankets were hung up above the reach of the wolves. Each took his saddle-bags upon his back, and we started at a quick step—Rariden in the lead, Judge Eggleston in the centre, and I brought up the rear. The heat was intense. None of us had been much used to walking. I am satisfied we must all have broken down, but most fortunately there had fallen the night before a light rain, and the water lay in the shade in the horse tracks. We were soon on our knees, with our mouths to the water.—Tell me not of your Croton, ye New Yorkers, nor of your Fairmount, ye Philadelphians, here was water, "what *was* water." Near night we reached the prairie worn down with heat and fatigue. The thunders were roaring and the lightnings flashing from the black clouds in the west. A storm was coming up on the wings of a hurricane, and ten minutes after we arrived at Mr. Thompson's it broke upon us in all its fury, and continued raining in torrents during the night. We were in a low, one story log cabin, about twenty feet square, no floor above, with a clapboard roof. Supper, to us dinner, was soon ready. Three articles of diet only on the plain walnut table, corn-dodgers, boiled squirrels, and sassafras tea.—Epicures at the 5 o'clock table of the Astor, St. Nicholas, Metropolitan and Revere, how do you like the bill of fare? To us it was sumptuous and thankfully received. Supper over, we soon turned in, and such a night of sweet sleep I never had before or since. The next morning our saddles and blankets were brought to us from the Wabash. The landlord provided us with ponies and we set forward at full speed, arrived at Fort Wayne that night, and took lodgings at the hotel of William N. Hood. In the morning court met, Judge Eggleston, President, and side judges, Thompson and Cushman on the bench. Fort

Wayne contained about two hundred inhabitants, and the County of Allen some fifty voters. There were no cases on docket to try of a criminal character. Court adjourned early, and we all went up the St. Mary's river, to Chief Richardville's to see an Indian horse race.

The nags were brought to the ground, a gray pony, about twelve hands high, and a roan, rather larger, like Eclipse and Henry, to contest the superiority of stock between the bands of Miamies and Pottawattamies. Six Indians were selected as judges—two placed at the starting point, two at the quarter stake, and two at the coming-out place. "Riders up—clear the track," and away they went under whip and spur. The race over, the judges meet, the spokesman, a large Miami, says "Race even, Miami grey take first quarter, Pottawattamie roan take last quarter," and all are satisfied. In the evening the grand-jury brought in a bill against Elisha B. Harris far stealing an Indian pony. Judge Eggleston.—"Any more business before you, Mr. Foreman?" Gen. Tipton.—"None sir." "You are discharged."

JUDGE EGGLESTON.—"There is but one case on the docket for trial, an appeal case, damages claimed five dollars. I feel quite tired, and will be obliged to my associates to try the case." Judge Cushman.—"Certainly." The case was called. Henry Cooper for the plaintiff, and Hiram Brown for the defendant. Case submitted to the Court. The action was for damages, five dollars claimed, for killing the plaintiff's dog. The witness swore that he saw the defendant running with his rifle across his yard; saw him lay it on the fence; saw the smoke; heard the crack; saw the dog fall; went to where the dog lay, and saw the bullet-hole just behind the fore leg. Here Cooper rested with a triumphant air, and indeed, to a common eye, the case seemed beyond hope, but to the mind of the skillful advocate, capable of drawing the distinction between positive and circumstantial evidence, a different conclusion was come to.—Breckenridge's Miscellanies, and Phillip's Evidence, stating the danger of listening to circumstantial evidence, and enumerating many lamentable cases of convictions and executions for murder upon circumstantial evidence, when the convicts were afterwards proved to be entirely innocent, had been widely circulated and extensively read by courts and lawyers until the tendency of the courts was to reject circumstantial evidence. My friend, Mr. Brown, an ingenious attorney, of fine talents, and, by the way, rather waggish, said: "A single question, Mr. Witness—Can you swear you saw the bullet hit the dog!" "I can swear no such thing." "That's all, Mr. Cooper; a case of mere circumstantial evidence, your Honors." Cooper's countenance fell; defeat stared him in the face; the case was submitted to the Court without further evidence. Judge Cushman.—"This is a plain case of *circumstantial* evidence. Judgment for the defendant." Cooper, with great indignation, with his eye upon Brown:—"When I die I wish it engraved upon my tombstone, here lies Henry Cooper—an honest man." Brown, rising as quick as thought:—"Pope says an honest man is the noblest work of God. There have been Atheists in this world—Bolingbroke of England, Voltaire of France, and Tom Paine of America, with a host of other infidel writers who may be named: they have all done nothing against the Almighty. But let Henry Cooper be held up in the mid heavens, by an angel, for the whole race of man to look upon; and let Gabriel, with his trumpet, announce to gazing worlds, *this is God's noblest work*, and all the human race would become Atheists in a day." We returned to Winchester on our borrowed ponies, took our horses that had been brought from Defiance, and reached the Wayne Circuit Court in good time.

At the expiration of Mr. Smith's term, in 1828, Hon. John Test, then of Brookville, Ind., was elected from the same district, for the term of 1229–30, and was succeeded by Jonathan McCarty,* of Fort Wayne; the latter taking his seat in 1831.

Mr. Worth, of Randolph county, was elected State Senator, and Anthony L. Davis, of Allen, Representative, in 1829, during which year the counties of Allen, Randolph and Delaware, including also the territory north thereof, was formed into a senatorial district; while Allen, Cass, Randolph, and Delaware, were organized into a

* Mr. McCarty had previously been receiver of public money at the land office here, at which time Captain Robert Brackenridge was register in said office.

Representative District. In 1830,* Mr. Worth was again elected a Senator, and Joseph Holman chosen a Representative from the foregoing district, at which session, Allen, Randolph, St. Joseph, Elkhart and Delaware were formed into a senatorial district, from which, in the following year, (1831,†) Mr. Worth was again elected State Senator, and Samuel Hanna, from the district at this time formed out of Allen, Elkhart and St. Joseph, was chosen a Representative. The following year, (1832,) Samuel Hanna, of Allen county, was selected State Senator, and George Crawford, of Elkhart, Representative. The following year, Mr. Hanna was re-elected Senator, and David H. Colerick, Esq., chosen Representative.

The "Board of Justices" having, in 1829, been changed to that of "County Board of Commissioners," consisting of James Holman, Wm. Caswell, and N. Coleman, on the 29th of September of this year, it having been previously presented that two-thirds of the citizens of Fort Wayne were in favor of incorporating the place, the County Commissioners ordered an election of Trustees, the following gentlemen being chosen therefor: John S. Archer, W. G. Ewing, Hugh Hanna, Dr. L. G. Thompson and John P. Hedges. In the month of November following, the first meeting of this Board took place.

By an act of Congress of May 31st, 1830, the associate judges of Allen county were authorized to enter some twenty acres of land off the west side of the fort reserve, at $1.25 per acre, which was complied with and patented to them March 31st, 1831. Having previously been transferred to the agent, and for the use of Allen county, by order of the County Board, these twenty acres were laid off, platted, and filed Nov. 3d, 1830, and designated "County Addition."

The remains of the fort reservation, by an act of Congress, was set apart for the benefit of the canal, and, with other public lands, at Logansport, Ind., was subsequenty offered at public auction, and purchased by Cyrus Taber, who, April 15th, 1835, portioned it off into forty lots, which have since been known as "Taber's Addition."

*At this period there were but 252 males, over 21 years of age, in Allen county.

† The winter of this year, (1831,) was a most remarkable one. As early as the latter part of November, snow began to fall, and continued to lie upon the ground until the middle of March following; and the settlers, during this long season of snow, with their roughly-constructed pole "jumpers," together with frolicking upon the ice of the adjacent streams, sought to, and did enjoy themselves most freely and happily. So intense, much of the time, was the cold and great the depth of the snow during this long winter, that—though the settlers suffered but little from lack of food, and the general necessaries of life---the animals of the forest were brought to the greatest hunger; and the wolves, of which there were still vast numbers throughout the northwest, and which only disappeared from the country, as the red man receded---were brought to such a state of hunger, that their fierce howlings were nightly heard by the citizens of the place; and it was long unsafe for the settlers to venture far beyond the limits of the town. The Indians also suffered greatly this winter for food, and several of them were killed and eaten by the wolves. So reduced were the Indians, in some instances, that they actually ate dead carrions that had lain upon the ground for months. What was most peculiar with the wolves, during this long winter, which exhibited largely the native instinct of this animal, they would never make a direct attack upon man or beast, unless their numbers were sufficient to insure their success.

Previous to 1825, the associate judges of the different counties in the State also exercised probate jurisdiction, the clerk thereof acting also as clerk of the Circuit Court, while the sheriff acted for both.

It was in this year, (1825,) November 14th, that the organization of the first Court for Probate purposes occurred, which met at the Old Washington Hall, and was presided over by Samuel Hanna and Benjamin Cushman.

On the 23d of May, (1825,) in a small book, some six inches spuare, the first entry of letters of administration was made.

The next term of this court, February 12th, 1826, was opened at the residence of Alexander Ewing, and closed at that of Wm Suttenfield. The third term, August 13th, 1826, was presided over by Judge Hanna, and W. N. Hood, A. L. Davis, Esq., acting as clerk. At the term of 1828, May 5th, Samuel Hanna, executor of A. Burnett, received the first order for the sale of land made to him. This sale consisted of two sections reserved to Burnett at the Indian treaty of 1826—one lying at Winnemac prairie, on the northwest side of the Wabash, and the other just opposite the mouth of Deep Creek, or what is now Delphi, in Carroll county, Ind. At the next term, Nov. 1828, "letters of administration" were issued to Joseph Holman, upon the estate of the then late principal war chief of the Miamies, known as La Gross,* who had previously been poisoned and died at the fort here, near which he was buried. La Gross had exercised a very conspicious part among the Indians here as early as 1794, and was esteemed as a very good man.

At the next term of the Probate Court, May 3d, 1830, W. G. Ewing presided as Judge, having previously been commissioned to serve in this capacity for seven years, from September 10th, 1829, the duties of which office he is said to have discharged with marked ability, till 1833, when he resigned in favor of Hugh B. McCulloch, who became his successor, also to hold the office for seven years, from June 7th, 1834; but Mr. McCulloch resigned the position after one session, in 1835, to take charge of the Branch of the State Bank of Indiana; after which, Governor Noble appointed Thomas Johnson to fill the vacancy of Mr. McCulloch. Mr. Johnson presided as Probate Judge until August, 1836, when, by general election, Lucien P. Ferry † was commissioned to discharge the duties of the office for seven years, from 5th of October, 1836, but, having resigned, he was superseded, February 10th, 1840, by

* It was after this chief that the town of La Gross, in Wabash county, in this State, was named.

† During September, 1843, Mr. Ferry, accompanied by Thomas Johnson, Esq., said to have been a very estimable man and a good citizen, returning late one evening, from Bluffton, Wells county, in this State, whither they had been on court business, the night overtook them, and a heavy rain coming up, they mistook their way, and got very wet, from the effects of which Mr. Johnson died two days after. Mr. Ferry, who also bore the reputation of a most intelligent and worthy citizen, died in August of the following year, 1844, at the age of thirty-three. Judge George Johnson, esteemed as a

Reuben J. Dawson. Mr. Dawson continued but a few months, and was followed by Samuel Stophlet, November 9th, 1840, who held the position till 1844, when, resigning, he was followed by George Johnson, appointed by Governor Whitcomb, who held the position till the period of election, in August, 1844, when he was elected to the office, and held the judgeship till 1847, when he resigned, and was succeeded by Nelson McLain, April 12th, 1847, who was appointed to this position, but in the following August was elected to the office, and held the position until this court was abolished by provisions of the new constitution of 1853, when Hon. James W. Borden was elected Judge of what is now the District Court of Common Pleas, embracing Allen, Adams, Wells and Huntington counties, with probate jurisdiction, whose first term began November 3d, 1853. Since this period, the Courts have undergone no special change. In the early part of 1867, a Criminal Court was created here, to preside over which, in the month of April, of this year, Governor Baker appointed Hon. James H. Fay, Judge, R. S. Taylor, Prosecuting Attorney; and in the month of October following, by election, Hon. J. W. Borden assumed the judgeship of this court.

Of marriage records, previous to October, 1834, there had been no record of marriage licenses presented here, nor any return made of the solemnization thereof in the county of Allen. Up to 1824, while what is now Allen county still formed a part of Randolph, all such licenses had to be procured at the Clerk's office in Winchester, the county-seat of Randolph.

The first record of marriage here, occurring in 1834, was that of George Withmer to Eleanor Troutner. For some years prior to the issue of this first license here, it was a custom for officers of the army to solemnize marriage without license; some were also married upon license issued from the Clerk's office in Miami county, Ohio; while others were procured at Vincennes, in Knox county, Indiana; and many came together and lived very agreeable without any license at all.

most worthy and intelligent young man, while attending a course of theological studies at Gambier Ohio, in December, 1850, lost his life by the accidental discharge of a gun.

CHAPTER XXVII.

Still moving forward—onward ever!
* * * * * *
"The four first acts already past,
The fifth shall close the drama with the day;
Time's noblest offspring is her last."

———o———

The first court-house—Treasurer's, Auditor's, Clerk's, and Recorder's offices—The old jail—The present court-house—Post office and post-masters—Mails—The old pond—Shawanoe run—An incident—Sketch of Chief Richardville—The old sand-hill—Exhumation of Indian bones and relics—Steady improvement of the place—Population at different periods—Recollections of an early resident—Commanding position of the place—Roads—Buildings—General business—Manufacturing interests—The World's future great commercial city—Railroad interests—Arrival of the first locomotive—First printing office—Names and number of papers now published in Fort Wayne—Churches and educational relations—The Future.

———o———

THE FIRST edifice erected for court and general public purposes, was a two-story brick building, built by S. Edsall, in 1847. This edifice stood upon the site of the present substantial court building. The original court building was of slender build, and after a few years use, it became evident that its longer occupancy would be attended with danger, and a one-story building was subsequently erected on the south-east corner of court-square, with a side-room for jury and other purposes fronting on Berry street, which was also torn down a few years after its erection. At the time of the occupancy and use of this building, the Treasurer's and Auditor's offices were in a small edifice on the northeast corner of court-square; the Clerk's office on the northwest corner; and the Recorder's office on the southwest corner of the same.

At the time of the erection and during the occupancy and use of the first court-house, built by Mr. Edsall, the old county jail still stood on the southwest corner of the square. This old building was destroyed by fire in 1847.

During the period intervening between the destruction of the one-story brick court-house, on the southeast corner of the square, and the erection of the present substantial and commanding edifice in 1861, court was held in Colerick's Hall, on Columbia street. The cost of the present edifice was over $80.000. Its corner-stone was laid with Masonic honors, in 1861, and bears the following inscription on the northeast corner of the building:

"CORNER STONE, laid with Masonic ceremonies, May 1, A. D. 1861, A. L. 5861, by Sol. D. Bayless, P. G. M. Michael Crow, John Shafer, and Isaac Hall, County Commissioners. Contractors: S. Edsall and V. M. Kimball. Designed by Edwin May. Superintendent, Samuel McElfatrick. Builder, D. J. Silver."

Its architecture is a combination of Doric, Corinthian, etc. On the north side of the building appears the figure of General Wayne, on the west side, the figure of Washington, both in colonial uniform. In the general court-room, on either side of the judge's stand, are the figures of Columbus and the goddess of Liberty, in fresco.

As the postoffice is always an institution of interest and importance in every place, a little account of the establishment of postal relations in Fort Wayne will not be out of place here.

The first post master of the place, was the late Judge Hanna. He kept the office in his store, on Columbia street, near where Colerick's Hall now stands. The next postmaster was Henry Rudisill, father of the present County Auditor, H. J. Rudisill, Esq., who kept the office in a frame building, on the north side of Columbia street, between Calhoun and Clinton, near the place now occupied by Ash & McCulloch's hardware store. Mr. Rudisill was followed by Oliver Fairfield, (brother of Captain Asa Fairfield,) and Smallwood Noel, who kept the office in the same place till the appointment of Wm. Stewart, Esq., in 1845, when Mr. Stewart took it to his own lot, on Calhoun street, where his present building stands, in place of which was then a frame building, about 25 feet square. In 1849, Samuel Stophlet, Esq., succeeded Mr. Stewart, and took the office further down Calhoun street, to a frame building, near where Kline & Marsh's shoe store now stands, where he kept it till the burning of the Phœnix Block, on the opposite side of the street, when it was removed to the site now occupied by the drug store of Gratigny & Bro., corner of Main and Calhoun streets. Jno. G. Maier, Esq., followed Mr. Stophlet, in 1853, and held the office during the administrations of Presidents Pierce and Buchanan, keeping it first on the south side of Columbia near Clinton, and afterwards on Clinton street, near where the Mayor's office now is. In 1861, M. Drake, Esq., the present incumbent, received the appointment, still keeping the office for a time on Clinton street; then removing it to Robinson's block, on Harrison street, and subsequently to its present locality, on Court street, opposite the courthouse, which is considered one of the best arranged post offices in the western country.

The first regular mails began in 1822-3, which were brought here on horseback, from Maumee and Piqua, Ohio. Prior to that period, the news reached here, only through private and special messengers. The mail carriers usually had to camp out one night on the road from Piqua and Maumee, and made the trips regularly, not unfrequently coming through, however, with empty mail bags. The mail matter of Chicago often came by way of Fort Wayne, and it is remembered, that, for one trip, it was carried afoot, by Mr. Bird, a farmer, still living a few miles from Fort Wayne. After the opening of canal navigation, the Maumee mail was transferred to the packets, other mails still being carried by horses, and subsequently by stages, until the completion of the railroad from Pittsburgh to this point; and notwithstanding the march in railroads, &c., a few stage lines still continue to reach Fort Wayne from interior points.

It may here be interesting for the reader to know that just east of the court-house, about half a square, at a former period there was to be seen a large pond, extending from what is now the residence of Mr. Bowser, on Berry street, past the rear of Peter Kiser's store, to where now stands the store rooms of Messrs. Townley, DeWald, Bond & Co., corner of Calhoun and Columbia streets. Many of the early settlers frequently caught fish out of this pond. A little brook, the remains of which is still to be seen, just north of the canal, opposite the Robinson block, meandered to the west of this pond, and just north of the court-house, extending around the same and running through what is now the alley-way immediately west of and opposite the court-house, thence to about the rear of the Berry street M. E. Church, and across Harrison, thence towards the St. Mary's. At the point about where the Berry street M. E. Church is, it was some four or five feet deep, and was a favorite fishing place. This little stream was known as "Shawanoe Run," so called from an incident that occurred many years ago near its banks, at a point about half-way between what is now Harrison and Calhoun streets, the general surface of the locality, at that period being covered mainly with small trees, hazle-bushes, etc.; and where the Indians were much accustomed to idle about. On one occasion, a Shawanoe was asked by a Miamie to take a drink at the point referred to, to which the former readily assented, and as he proceded to do so, the Miamie plunged a knife into his breast, killing him on the spot. The deed was a barbarous and most treacherous one, at best; and it was not long before the Shawanoes—quite a large body of whom then resided a short distance to the southeast of Fort Wayne—were made acquainted with the revengeful procedure of the Miamie in killing their brother; and each and all were alike maddened at the event. The spirit of the slain member of their tribe was to be revenged ere he could be appeased, or presents sufficient to cover up the grave of the murdered warrior were to be proffered and accepted, before the living members of the clan could feel any sense of forgiveness towards the murderer and his tribe; and two days after the event came a considerable body of Shawanoes to the place, all painted and armed for a bloody conflict with the opposite tribe. And they are said to have presented a most ferocious and determined appearance, as they halted upon a little rise at what is now the corner of Washington and Clinton streets.

The matter had now become serious. The Shawanoes had come to settle the affair—to revenge the murder of their brother—and the Miamies knew at once that the case had to be met. Nothing short of "an eye for an eye," or an adjustment of some kind, would serve to quell or reconcile the determined will of the painted Shawanoes. Accordingly, Chief Richardville,* of the Miamies,

* With the birth-place of this distinguished chief, as referred to on page 22, Chapter II, in connection with the "old apple-tree," the reader is already familiar. His father, Druet de Richardville, was a French trader here for some years before and after the fated expedition of La Balme, in 1780. Among the many thrilling and interesting incidents and narrations, as frequently recited by the chief to the late Allen Hamilton, he gave, some years ago, an account of his ascendency to the chieftainship of his tribe. The occasion was not only thrilling and heroic, but, on the part of his famous mother and himself, will ever stand in history as one of the noblest and most humane acts known to any people, and would serve as a theme, both grand and eloquent, for the most gifted poet or dramatist of any land.

It was a wild, barbarous moment, now more than eighty years ago. Ke-ki-ong-a still occasionally echoed with the shrieks and groans of captive men; and the young warriors of the region still rejoiced in the barbaric custom of burning prisoners at the stake—a custom long in vogue with the Indians here. A white man had been captured and brought in by the warriors. A council had been convened, in which the question of his fate arose in debate and was soon settled. He was to be burned at the stake, and the braves and villagers generally were soon gathered about the scene of torture, making the very air to resound with their vociferations and triumphant shouts of pleasure and gratification at the prospect of soon enjoying another hour of fiendish merriment at the expense of a poor, miserable victim of torture. Already the man was lashed to the stake, and the torch that was to ignite the cumbustible material placed about the same and the victim of torture, was in the hands of the brave appointed to create the flame that was so soon to consume the victim of their cruelty. But the spirit of rescue was at hand. The man was destined to be saved from the terrible fate that surrounded him!

Young Richardville had for some time been singled out as the future chief of the tribe, and his heroic mother saw in this a propitious and glorious moment for the assertion of his chieftainship, by an act of great daring and bravery, in the rescue of the prisoner at the stake. All eyes were now fixed upon the captive. Young Richardville and his mother were some distance from the general scene, but sufficiently near to see the movements of the actors in the tragedy about to be enacted, and could plainly hear the coarse ejaculations and mingled shouts of triumph of the crowd. At that moment, just as the torch was about to be applied to the bark, as if touched by some angelic impulse of love and pity for the poor captive, the mother of young Richardville placed a knife in her son's hand, and bade him assert his chieftainship by the rescue of the prisoner. The magnetic force of the mother seemed instantly to have convulsed and inspired the young warrior, and he quickly bounded away to the scene, broke through the wild crowd, cut the cords that bound the man, and bid him be free! All was astonishment and surprise; and though by no means pleased at the loss of their prize, yet the young man, their favorite, for his heroic and daring conduct, was at once esteemed a god by the crowd, and then and thereafter became a chief of the first distinction and honor in the tribe!

The thoughtful and heroic mother of Richardville now took the man in charge, and soon quietly placing him in a canoe and covering him with hides and peltries, in charge of some friendly Indians, he was soon gliding safely down the placid current of the Maumee, beyond the scene of the turbulent warriors and villagers of Ke-ki-ong-a. The rescue was complete.

was at once called upon by the members of his tribe to adjust and reconcile the matter, which was only accomplished after a lengthy council between the tribes, wherein the Shawanoes finally agreed to a reconciliation upon the proffer and gift of several head of horses, and a quantity of trinkets and goods of various kinds. And thus the matter ended—and it was out of this incident—fierce and

At a later period in the life of the chief, some years subsequent to this event, being on his way to Washington City, he came to a town in Ohio, where, stopping for a little while, a man came up to him, and suddenly recognizing in the stranger the countenance of his benefactor and deliverer of years before, threw his arms about the chief's neck, and embraced him with all the warmth of filial affection and gratitude! He was indeed the rescued prisoner; and the meeting between the chief and the man was one of mingled pleasure and surprise.

In stature, the chief was about five feet ten inches, with broad shoulders, and weighed about one hundred and eighty pounds. His personal appearance was attractive; graceful in carriage and manner; and bore all the marks of a "finished gentleman." Exempt from any expression of levity---a simple child of nature---he is said to have "preserved his dignity under all circumstances." His eyes were of a lightish blue, and slightly protruding---"his upper lip firmly pressed upon his teeth, and the under one slightly projecting. His nose was roman, and the whole contour of his face was classic and attractive."

From the recollections of David H. Colerick, Esq., long intimate with the chief, and who served as his attorney, transacting much of his business for many years here, Richardville was computed the wisest and most sagacious chief of all the Indians of the entire northwest; and "was the successful head and ruler of the Miamie tribe for more than fifty years before and to the time of his death," in 1841.

His mother was a most remarkable woman. Her Indian name was Tau-cum-wa. Chief Richardville was an only son, and much beloved by her. Her reign as chiefess of the tribe, continued for a period of some thirty years, prior to the war of 1812, during which time, according to the traditions of the Indians, "she ruled the tribe with a sway, power, and success as woman never ruled before." After her reign, "she retired and passed the mace of power to her son," John B. Richardville, whose Indian name was Pe-she-wa (or Wild Cat,) by which he was always called by his people, and thus signed it at all the treaties he attended, to transact business for the tribe or tribes of which he was the representative or head. With a mind somewhat massive, a rather close observer, and apt in his business transactions, he was always extremely careful in what he undertook. A most patient listener, his reticense often almost assumed the form of extreme indifference; yet such was far from his nature, for he ever execised the warmest and most attentive regard for all of his people and mankind in general; and "the needy never called in vain---his kind and charitable hand was never withheld from the distressed of his own people or from the stranger; and he was beloved and esteemed by all who knew him."

So well and wisely did he manage the affairs of his tribe---with such wisdom and moderation did he adjust and settle all matters relating to his people—that he was not only held in the highest estimation by the Indians generally, throughout the northwest, but "honored and trusted as their law-giver with the most unsuspecting confidence and implicit obedience"---always adjusting affairs between his own people, as well as all inter-tribal relations, without resort to bloodshed. A patient and attentive listener ---prudent and deliberate in his action----when once his conclusions and determination were formed, "he rarely had occasion to change them." "Averse to bloodshed, except against armed resistance, he was ever the strong and consistent friend of peace and good-will.

Many were the vivid recollections he gave, years ago, to early settlers here. At the time of Harmar's movements and defeat at this point, he was a boy of some ten or twelve years of age. But his recollection of the way the Indians stole along the bank of the river, near to the point, long since known as "Harmar's ford," were most thrilling. Not a man among the Indians, said he, was to fire a gun until the white warriors under Harmar had gained the stream, and were about to cross. Then the red men in the bushes, with rifles levelled and ready for action, just as the detachment of Harmar began to near the centre of the Maumee, opened a sudden and deadly fire upon them; and horses and riders fell in the stream, one upon the other, until the river was literally strewn from bank to bank with the slain, both horses and men; and the water ran dark with the blood of the slain!

thrilling to those who remember* it—that grew the name of this little run.

In the extreme west end of the city there was formerly an extensive bluff, perhaps some fifteen or sixteen feet higher than any other point within the present limits of Fort Wayne, which covered originally some two squares. It was, indeed, an immense sand heap. When, and how long accumulating, the ages alone can determine. The sand is of a rather fine quality, and much of it has served well, doubtless, for mortar, in building and other purposes. It extended from Wayne street, fronting and within a few yards of the college, towards the river, a short distance below Berry street, and eastward perhaps about a square; somewhat sloping in its general character. Its highest point was at about the present terminus of Berry street. Over this knoll there extended but little vegetative life; a few indifferent bushes here and there over it and about its margin, formed, perhaps, the principal part of its productive growth, as is usually the case with sandy points.

*Among whom is D. H. Colerick, Esq., from whose recollections this account is given.

"There seemed, in the settling of this section of the country," says, Mr. Colerick "a rivalry between the settlers and the Indians, as to who should tender the chief the highest respect, for all admired who knew him."

At the treaty of St. Mary's, in 1818, a reserve of three sections of land was made to him, principally located some four or five miles from Fort Wayne, up the St. Mary's river, which, since his death, have been in the hands and keeping of his descendants, "and now owned and occupied by Archonge, (daughter of La Blonde, the first daughter of the chief,) wife of James R. Godfri, whose interesting family, with some three or four other persons, relatives of the same, living near, now constitute the only remnants of the once powerful Miamie tribe in this part of their old strong hold, each and all of whom have long since assumed the garb of civilization, and not only cultivate the arts of peace, but live upon, and annually and successfully till one of the finest bodies of land to be found in the northwest.

It was an ancient custom with the Indians never to council during cloudy weather. Open day, and a sun-light unobscured by the frowns of lowering clouds, were the only guarantees of a successful council among them. In 1832, at a treaty appointed to be held at the forks of the Wabash---where it is said the Government, through its agents, not only spent vast sums of money, but fed the Indians most sumptuously for some days, (which latter was a great source of pleasure and pride to the red men then and there assembled, for they always liked the white man's fare, and ate most lavishly of it, whenever occasion offered)---the principal agent of the treaty, through his interpreter, requested a council of the tribes on a certain day, and had assembled a number of the principal chiefs present, to make known the desire. Having concluded his remarks, which were principally addressed to chief Richardville, as the main representative of the tribes present, the chief, in an unusually dignified and resolute manner, arose to respond. The red men, said he, never council when the great Spirit frowns. Already he has shut his face from view, and dark clouds are spread over our heads. When he shall smile again, and the sun begin to allumine the earth, then will we council

No council was therefore convened; and the Indians are said to have continued to fare most sumptuously, much to their liking, for several days longer, on the choice food set before them, at this expensive gathering of the tribes, under the auspices of the United States Government.

Such was the famous chief--such was John B. Richardville, (Pe-she-wa,) for so many years the head and ruler of the Miamies of this ever memorable and ancient stronghold of Indian life in the northwest; and to-day, in the Catholic cemetery, just on the confines of his birth-place and early associations, is to be seen at any time, by the visitant to this city of the dead, a neat and imposing marble shaft, upon which may be clearly read, both when the sun shines and the clouds lower, the name of JOHN B. RICHARDVILLE, the beloved and famous chief of the Miamies.

The Indians are said to have had some huts upon it, some years ago. In removing this great sand heap, as in digging at other points, within the present limits of Fort Wayne, the Indians having deposited their dead here and there, many bones and skulls were exhumed and removed. On one occasion, some workmen thus engaged, among many others, dug up a most remarkable skull —with high forehead and general formation extremely large—indicating a giant form to the possessor.*

Somewhat to the south of this once great sand-hill, where there were also some open points, the Indians, for many years, cultivated small patches of corn and other products.

Since the incorporation of the "Town of Fort Wayne," in 1825, when the principal edifices were "substantial log buildings," there has been a steady improvement and increase of populaiton. More especially, during the last twenty years, has the place advanced in material wealth and general improvement.

The estimated population of the place and vicinity, in 1828, was about 500. Two years later, 1830, it had reached about 800; and in 1840, about 1200; in 1850, about 4200; in 1860, 10.300, while, at the present period, subburbial portions included, it has reached a population of upwards 29.000; and its material growth in building, manufacture, and general commercial pursuits, has kept pace with the advance in population.

A former resident of Fort Wayne, who visited the scenes of his boyhood, during 1867, thus writes:

"Nearly a third of a century ago, when the writer, then a boy, was residing half a mile from Fort Wayne, the place was known abroad chiefly as being the site of the fort, which gives it a part of its name, and as one of the villages on the line of the canal. Columbia street monopolized the business, being the focus of the village trade. The only church then built was the old Presbyterian, now an unsightly wreck. When the act of secession occurred, and the church became divided into Old School and New School, the court house served as a place of worship for the latter.

"By the laws common to humanity, most of those who were prominent in business at that day have since passed away, and their places have been filled by another generation. A few still remain, however, and I have had the pleasure of meeting and con-

* Mr. Daniel Kiser, some eighteen or twenty years ago, on the Cole farm, dug up the remains of an Indian woman, and also found in the grave a silver cup, a number of brooches, and a snuff box, on which was the portrait of Wm. Penn—the figure of an ordinary quill-pen being located near the portrait, as expressive of the name of this old Quaker philanthropist.

Mr. Charles M. Wells, also, some seventeen years ago, dug up a number of Indian bones—seemingly a man and woman. On the breast of the woman were a number of ear-drops, brooches and crosses. A beautiful piece of ribbon was also found near the ear-drops, &c., which seemed to have retained all its primitive elasticity and beauty, until touched, when it instantly crumbled to dust. A little son of N. P. Stockbridge, Esq., some months since, among a number of other Indian relics, found two little Indian bells. Many flints, tomahawks, &c., have also been dug up at different times during the past few years How long many of these bones and relics have thus been concealed in the earth, none can tell.

versing with several of the 'old residents.' Two teachers who taught my young ideas 'how to shoot,' a third of a century ago, are still residents of this city. The schools were then taught in the basement of the Presbyterian Church above referred to, and in a little brick building, located about where the jail stands. The former was then at the eastern extreme of the village, while the latter was beyond the western extreme. The Old Fort was then in the suburbs.

"During the interval of a third of a century the writer has visited Fort Wayne several times, and has been glad to notice, of late years, so commendable a spirit of enterprise exhibited by her business men. Without any natural advantages, the city has been and must be the architect of her own fortunes. That truly liberal and far-seeing policy which sacrifices the present for the future, and builds lines of railroads into and through new, thinly settled regions, will yet, I think, make Fort Wayne one of the foremost manufacturing cities of the West. If the last few years have done much, the next few years may be made to do far more for the growth and material prosperity of the place. Your numerous churches and your seats of learning show that the moral and intellectual advancement of your city have been cared for; and it is to be hoped that Fort Wayne will become celebrated for law and order, as well as for the enterprise and liberal spirit of its business men. I do not here allude to events of recent occurrence. With these I have nothing to do. I only claim, as one, a portion of whose boyhood was passed here, to feel a friendly interest in the growth and welfare of your city. Peace be within its walls, and prosperity within her gates. * * Show the outside world that Fort Wayne is up to all the requirements of the age in educational facilities; expend money liberally in Nicholson pavements; encourage the new lines of railroads by every private and public means; ornament and improve your public grounds and private residences, and in the next decade you may challenge comparison with any city in our borders. As a *permanent business investment*, eligible lots are worth more, foot for foot, than in any city in Indiana."*

"The causes that produced this rapid growth," says Mr. Williams, are apparent. The commanding situation of the town, in the centre of a large and fertile scope of country that sought this point for trade, with no competing town and the facilities for export and import, were important elements in its growth. The facilities for this commerce, resulted from the important internal improvements constructed so as to make this an important point on their routes."†

* Fort Wayne Gazette, April 4th, 1867.

† Referring to the canal and railroads. "By affording the means of shipping direct to the lake," says the same writer, "the canal drew the trade of a large region of country, north and south, immediately to this point. The water power resulting from this improvement, furnished facilities for the erection of mills and manufactories that were a great importance in its progress; and from this period it took a new start, and this impetus continued till the era of plank roads, in 1848. These roads," says he, "were constructed with much energy and rapidity to a great distance in every direction, attracting an increased trade from a large and fertile section of country."

During 1867, upwards of 200 dwellings, handsome and commodious storehouses, and other edifices, were built.

The general business relations of the city of Fort Wayne, at the present period, are of the first order; and it may be said of the business men of our city to-day, that they are among the most active, liberal, and enterprising of the land, with a credit and reputation for promptness unsurpassed by any place of equal size in the West. Of manufactories, of different kinds, there are few cities of similar size in the union that can equal her. The busy wheels and spindles of the machine shops and factories; the steady click of the hammer; and constant puffing of steam-pipes, at every hand, tell how active and how numerous—in "what a heat and what a forge"—the hardy yeomanry—the working-men—of Fort Wayne are employed. Such a scene of industry and civilization, could the ancient inhabitants of Ke-ki-ong-a suddenly step in upon their old familiar "stamping ground," would indeed "astonish the natives." Possessing, as this locality does, the many natural advantages of material for building purposes; the facilities for reaching, and nearness to, the principal markets of the country, with other important reasons and advantages, Fort Wayne—if keeping alive within her borders those finer feelings and relations of sociality, harmony, good-will, and fair dealing, so essential to the better growth and prosperity of every people, town, city, and county—is destined to become one of the most extensive and important MANUFACTURING cities of the country. And there is, perhaps, no material reason why the great central depot—the great mart of trade—of the American Central Railroad, soon to connect California with the East, may not at no distant period, find a seat at this point as the most central and important of all the points yet referred to by those who have given the matter candid and impartial consideration.*

The following list of manufacturing establishments, independ-

*The thought of a "COMING MAN," in whose organism would centre, as a grand exemplary model, all the more harmonious and exhalted conditions and attributes of mental and physical life, has long attracted the attention and earnest consideration of a large mass of the civilized world. So, also, among the more reflective and studious of mankind, has the idea of a great commercial centre on the American continent, located at some favorable point west of the Alleghany mountains, on the great "central plain," lying between the seaboard on the east and California on the west, taken deep root, beginning mainly with General Washington, De Witt Clinton, and others at an early period of our country's history, and of late years, and perhaps never more earnestly and thoughtfully than at the present time, has the subject been discussed and reflected upon. And still it will attract attention, until the end is attained.

Everything seems to gravitate towards a common centre. Water finds its level; and globes and men act and re-act continually, both magnetically and imperceptibly, upon each other, to the attainment and out-growth of the unity and better developement of the human race.

Everything serves some wise end in the great economy of existence; and Commerce, like the evolution and promulgation of the great principles and elements of science and philosophy, in its gravitative movements from point to point over the old world, has for ages contributed largely to this glorious "end and aim" of life---the unity of the human family-- the establishment of a natural relationship and common genealogy of the elements of the globe---organic and inorganic, as their general condition and structure may appear.

Unlike past ages, when the great centre of the commercial world sought to plant itent of the industrial relations of the railroad shops, will give the reader an extended view of the manufacturing enterprise of Fort Wayne and vicinity at the present period:

There are three large founderies, employing from forty-three to upwards of one hundred men each, with an average pay-roll of from two thousand five hundred to eight thousand dollars per month, and are unable to keep pace with the demand for their labor.

self at some favorable point upon the shores of the ocean, or at the mouth of some extensive stream, flowing oceanward, or through vast regions of territory, regardless of centralization, or nearness to the main body of the civilized inhabitants surrounding, sending out, annually, vast quantities of goods and commerce of various kinds through one mighty channel, as it were, here in America, to-day, and for years past, a great centre is being sought, wherein and without shall flow the vast commerce of the continent, and perhaps the world---penetrating in every direction to the most remote as well as the nearest points of trade, by railroad and navigable water courses, with ease and speed.

Let us for a moment look at Fort Wayne as one of the most favorable as well as most central (in view of the vast population to the east, north and south of us,) points for the establishment of such a centre. With her railroad advantages present and prospective, the reader will already have made himself familiar---penetrating as they will, in a few years more, in every direction, connecting her, in a few hours of travel, with every important seaboard and inland town and city on the continent---even to California itself. The streams that centre here, including the advantages long afforded by the Wabash and Erie canal, with proper attention and the outlay of a few thousand dollars, in clearing their channels, &c., may be made navigable for the largest steamboats, during the greater part of the year—the St. Joseph from Lake Michigan, and the Maumee, formed here by the junction of the St. Mary's and St. Joseph, flowing into Lake Erie---thus affording ready and easy transportation from the Lakes and all interior points, to the most advantageous centre of trade, to all adjacent points thereto, and to the fartherest limits beyond, where demand shall call for supply. While, as a grain and fruit-growing, wool-producing, and stock-raising district, in a few years, with the proper inducements for extensive scientific culture, in the use of the best mechanical appliances in the cultivation and chemical understanding of the soil, in planting, reaping, mowing, etc., etc., this, with the great scope of country lying for hundreds of miles in every direction around us, may become among the foremost of the land. Timber, for fire wood, manufacturing and building purposes, is to be had in great abundance, at every side; and as will already have been seen, the material and advantages, in other respects, for building, are inexhaustible. (See chapter I, page 2.) In point of health, there are few sections of the country, where the masses enjoy better general health than Fort Wayne and vicinity.

These, then, with many other important relations and advantages, that might be named, are of the first necessity and importance in the building and establishment of such a manufacturing centre of industry and commerce; and the rapid strides that have been made here, in building and general improvement during the past few years—the early location here of some of the most extensive railroad shops in the west, for the manufacture of cars, engines, etc.—point most clearly, if not absolutely, to this as the world's future manufacturing and commercial centre. And while, at the same time, the suggestion of such a result may awaken a smile of disbelief in some, yet, in after years, (for it will not be the growth of a day,) we may behold its fullest realization. Let the reader note the suggestion, and await results.

Toledo, Ohio, Chicago, Ill., and Omaha, Nebraska, are already named as this great commercial centre. It is not likely to settle down upon or gravitate towards all of these flourishing cities; and as Fort Wayne, with her many rare advantages, is most favorably located between the former, and an important point on the line of the Great Central American Railway from New York to San Francisco, Cal., which will touch neither Toledo or Chicago, the chances are largely in our favor. To this end, therefore, every citizen—every farmer of Allen county,—by a continuous due regard for order, honesty, truthfulness and fair dealing,—the better developement of the social, intellectual, manufacturing, horticultural, agricultural and general industrial relations of our city and county, may and should contribute something each day towards the consummation of this glorious end. "Ye know not what ye shall be." The

Two extensive file manufactories; one lock factory; three large steam tanneries; soap and candle factory; four saw mills; four large flooring and dressing mills; an extensive woolen factory; two spoke and hub factories; two shingle factories, one boiler factory; three sash and door factories; one box factory; two trunk factories; four candy factories; four saddle and harness manufactories; five wagon factories; three carriage factories; three undertakers and coffin makers; two plow manufactories; two potash manufactories; three cooper shops; and one large paper mill, all doing an extensive business, with heavy shipments, in some instances, as for east as Boston, Mass., south and west as far as New Orleans, St. Louis, &c.

The business-showing, in other relations, is equally fair and promising. Of dry goods, grocery, clothing, boot and shoe, china, hardware, tin and stove, variety, drug, book and periodical, millinery, music, and other stores, banking houses, hotels, &c., there are about two hundred and seventy; some of the larger business houses doing an annual business of from twenty, thirty, fifty, one hundred and seventy-five thousand, to a quarter of a million dollars.

Among the most extensive as well as most important adjuncts to the general manufacturing interest and business relations of the city of Fort Wayne, at the present period, are those presented by the Fort Wayne and Chicago Railroad, which was commenced in

conditions of this great superstructure are with us. Let us improve them, and wait.

"Westward, ho! the seat of empire takes its way!" rang out upon the still air of the continent during the colonial days of our Republic; and a steady influx of emigration—a continuous enlargement of our agricultural domain, in clearing, etc., have now continued for upwards of sixty years; until to-day, the west, in every material, as well as intellectual point of view, is mighty to look upon. Look, then, at her advancement, fifty years or less hence! She'll then, and before, demand such a commercial and manufacturing centre; and Fort Wayne is as likely to be that centre—perhaps MOST likely—than any other of the points already brought forward.

The past, in a commercial point of view, may be no special criterion for the Future. Presuming that the city of London, England, is now, and for years past has been, the world's great commercial centre, it is not fully presumable that this centre will, within a few score years, shift its locality to the city of New York, and there rest for an hundred years more, and then make its way westward. No; we shall long ere that period build up and most fully establish a commercial radius in the west, and from her extensive workshops and well-tilled agricultural districts, we shall be, as in no small degree, we are now, enabled to furnish the markets of the East and Europe with vast stores of grain and other of our productive wealth. The demand for such a centre is already apparent; already it is beginning to grow—to show the strongest signs of life, and to present the fullest and most substantial prospects of realization in future years.

Before the era of railroads, the lakes and navigable rivers were the principal courses of travel and trade; but latterly, for some years past, these channels have greatly diminished in importance as well as trade and travel; though by no means likely to be lost sight of entirely in this relation, as a means of commercial intercourse, yet, so long as the convenience and speed of the railroad is maintained,—which is likely for centuries to be the case, with the addition of many comforts, more safety, and greater cheapness of travel thereon—the navigable streams and lakes are not likely to gain any material ascendency in the future. So that it does not necessarily follow that the future great commercial and manufacturing city of the globe should be located on the shore of some extensive lake or river, or at some favorable point on the seaboard, at either extreme of the American continent, in order to be the more extensive and equable in its intercourse with, and relations to, other parts of the globe.

1854,* and completed in 1857. The Ohio and Indiana railroad was the first located here, which occurred in 1852, and completed in 1854. In 1856, the Ohio and Indiana and Fort Wayne and Chicago roads were consolidated with the Ohio and Pennsylvania road, and continued thereafter to constitute the "Pittsburgh, Fort Wayne, & Chicago Railroad Company," forming a line of some 550 miles in length, which is unequalled in general importance and successful business management by any road of similar length in the United States.

Being a central point on these extensive lines, the companies early selected this as most convenient for the location of the various machine shops necessary for the repair of machinery and building of rolling stock, such as cars, engines, &c. As now enlarged and faciliated, the shops of the Pittsburgh, Fort Wayne, and Chicago Company furnish employment for upwards of seven hundred mechanics and laborers, with a monthly pay-roll of over $50.000. Aside from these, the travel over the road and the freight receipts, have added immensely to the general commercial interest and wealth of the place. And already several new lines are centering here from different points—most prominent among which, are the Fort Wayne and Southern; the Grand Rapids and Indiana; Cincinnati, Richmond, and Fort Wayne; while the Great American Central Road will make this an important point in its route from New York to San Francisco.

The total earnings of the P., Ft. W., and C. road for 1866, were $7,467,217.56; expenditures, $5,147,686.54.

The shops of this road embrace a two-story brick depot, 190 feet long, by 70 feet wide; a freight-house, 200 by 60 feet; main building of the car shop, two stories, 220 by 75 feet, with two wings, one story, 188 by 75 feet each; machine and blacksmith shops, 327 by 65 feet, two stories, with two wings for engine and boiler shops, each 100 by 59 feet; a round-house, 60 feet deep by 308 feet in diameter, with stalls for forty engines. A new machine shop, 340 by 120 feet, was added to these in 1866; by which they are enabled to build one entirely new engine per month, besides keeping up all repairs on the western division of the roads. When it is necessary, one hundred freight and passenger cars can be built per month, besides keeping up repairs on rolling stock. The average amount of lumber used per month, is upwards 700,000 feet, at a cost of more than $12.000. Already further enlargements are contemplated, and a new paint shop and foundry will soon be built.

*The first locomotive that reached Fort Wayne, came by way of the canal, in charge of R. W. Wohlfort; and was landed near the warehouse of D. F. Comparet, Esq., June 4th, 1854. So great was the interest and curiosity upon its arrival, that hundreds of the citizens of Fort Wayne flocked near the place of landing to get a peep at the "iron horse." Mr. W. tells many amusing incidents, as well as "hair breadth escapes," as connected with his "voyage" thither, with this first engine for the western division of this road. At this time there was a temporary building near Mr. Comparet's warehouse, which served as a sort of "round-house" for the engines, and a track also extended from this point to the site of the present railroad buildings.

The general superintendent of the western division of the P., Ft. W., and C. R. R., C. E. Gorham, Esq., resides at Fort Wayne.

The Toledo and Western road was begun in 1854, and completed in 1856, which connects Lake Erie with the Mississippi river.

The buildings of this road embrace a round-house, 140 feet in diameter, with a capacity for 24 engines; a brick machine shop, 100 feet wide by 160 feet long; a blacksmith shop, 40 feet wide, and 160 feet long; a wood shop, 30 feet wide, and 200 feet long. There is also a passenger and freight depot. The shops of this road, as in the foregoing, give regular employment to about 300 workmen, with a pay-roll of $20.000 per month. Length of road, 520 miles. Earnings for 1866—$3,717,386; Expenditures for 1866, $2,811,186; with a constant increase of business. 40.000 tickets were sold at the Fort Wayne office of this road during the year 1866

The manufacturing interests of Fort Wayne, as the reader can well infer, from the facts and figures thus presented, form no small amount of interest in the general business-showing of the place, and have attracted hither many of the most efficient and exemplary workmen to be found in America, who receive good wages, and not a few of whom have bought property and built themselves neat dwellings, with a view to permanent residence in the place.

With such advantages—such a growth in manufacturing relations and facilities—what should impede the continued and rapid progress of our city in every noble and generous point of view—every unselfish, intelligent, and patriotic relation of life!

The year following the arrival here of the first railway engine, in 1854, the "Fort Wayne Gas Company" was incorporated, March, 1855, and works erected, whose pipes now extend throughout the largest portion of the city.

The first printing office established in Fort Wayne, was that of the "Fort Wayne *Sentinel*," by Thomas Tigar and S. V. B. Noel, Esqs., in June, 1833,* and located in the old Masonic Hall building, which then stood on the site of Messrs. Hill & Orbison's warehouse, on Columbia street.

At the present period, there are two Daily papers and three Weeklies issued in the place, viz: the Daily and Weekly Democrat, Daily and Weekly Gazette, and a German paper, the *Staats Zeitung*.

In a denominational and educational point of view, Fort Wayne has long borne a most favorable reputation, as a church-going and educational-loving people. Nearly every Christian denomination has its representative here, with fifteen churches, including the synagogue of the Hebrew denomination. Some of these edifices

*It was in the Spring of this year (1833) that quite a large, elegant steamboat, called the "PHENOMENON," commanded by Capt. DENIELE, and piloted by Capt. ISAAC WOODCOCK, of Antwerp, Ohio, came up the Maumee to Fort Wayne, and made a landing just opposite where now stands the woolen factory of French, Hanna & Co., on Water street. On behalf of the citizens of the place, David H. Colerick, Esq., gave the Captain and all on board a most cordial welcome, and a gay party of citizens, of both sexes, were soon gathered on board the vessel, who, with music, dancing, and social converse, spent several hours, and till far into the night, in the most agreeable manner.

are most handsome in their general architectural appearance, and quite commodious. In public as well as private schools, there are few places of equal size in America that can present a better showing in the number and regularity of pupils in attendance each week than Fort Wayne. The reader is already familiar with the locality and *status* of the first school and school-house in our city, as also the first schoolmaster. From these small beginnings, Fort Wayne has steadily advanced, until, at the present period, there are upwards of 2000 pupils in regular attendance in the two spacious public school buildings, known as the "East-end" and "West-end," with a corps of some 36 teachers, and a superintendent, whose efficiency and care in the disciplining and culture of the youthful mind, are only equalled by their earnestness and good-nature. Jas. H. Smart, Esq., is the present worthy superintendent of our public schools, and under his supervision, for the past three years, the schools have arisen to a point of excellence unequalled anywhere in the West or East.

Among the different denominations there are also several excellent schools, which are largely attended. There is also a thriving commercial college here, enabling the poorest to obtain a complete commercial and business education at a very small out-lay—a rare advantage in any place.

In a collegiate relation, aside from the commercial institute, we have two most excellent institutions, the "Concordia University," and the "Fort Wayne College," both of which are admirably conducted and well attended.

Such is the *City* of Fort Wayne at the present period. Let its march still be onward. Let us advance continually, not only in things physical, but in all that pertains to the mental and spiritual welfare of every soul within and without her walls. Let us move steadily on, with the Right ever in view, adding, day by day, to the strength and durability of the great edifice of Truth and Progress, in which we all hope to find an agreeable seat in that glorious Future when the "good-time" shall have *come*.

NOTE TO THE READER—ERRATA.–Since the main body of the work was printed, in looking over the volume, I discovered a few typographical errors, which had been overlooked in reading proof and by the printer in the correction of the proof-sheets; all of which, however, will be readily comprehended by the intelligent reader. The most important of these are as follows: In the "Sketch of the Life of General Anthony Wayne," first page, first line, for "not alone a valiant officer and soldier," read "not ONLY a valiant officer," &c. On page x. of same, 19th line from the top of the page, instead of "whither he soon returned," &c., read "WHENCE he soon returned," &c. In Chapter I, page 5, 21st line from top of page, first word, for "colonel," read colonial. Page 6th of same Chapter, 10th line from top of page, for "purported to have been," &c., read "reported to have been," &c. Chapter XXIII, page 273, 7th line from bottom of page, for "Lieutenants Scorgin Bell," &c., read "Lieutenants Scorgin and Bell," &c. At the bottom of page 22, Chapter I, in note two, (†) beginning at first of third line from the bottom of the page, read "throwing;" second line from bottom of same, first word, read "very;" bottom line, same page, first word, read "fort." In Chapter II, page 25, 17th line, in a part of the edition, the word "heroines" is printed heroes. In "Prefatory Remarks," second page, 2d line, "Dr. J B. Brown," should be Dr. S. B. Brown.

Biographical Sketches

OF

EARLY SETTLERS

OF

FORT WAYNE,

ETC.

Engraved by [illegible]

Yours Affectionately
Saml. Hanna

BIOGRAPHY

OF THE LATE

HON. SAMUEL HANNA.

———o———

It is the dictate of our nature, no less than of enlightened social policy, to honor the illustrious dead; to bedew with affectionate tears the silent urn of departed genius and virtue; to unburden the fulness of the surcharged heart in eulogium upon deceased benefactors; and to rehearse their noble deeds for the benefit of those who may come after us. It has been the commendable custom of all ages and all nations. Hence the following feeble tribute to one of nature's noblemen.

Samuel Hanna was born October 18th, 1797, in Scott county, Kentucky. His father, James Hanna, removed to Dayton, Ohio, in 1804, and settled on a new farm, lying contiguous to the southern boundary of that town. He was one of a numerous family, all of whom attained respectable, and most of them, distinguished positions in life. Samuel's early days were passed, like those of most boys in a new country, in assisting his father to clear up his farm, and in the enjoyment of such limited educational advantages as were attainable in the West at that early day. His earliest employment, away from the protection of the parental roof, was that of post-rider, as it was called; that is, taking newspapers from the publication office and delivering them to subscribers at their residences, located far and near over the country—an employment now obsolete, but extensively practiced fifty years ago, when post-offices were almost entirely limited to the county-seats. In this humble calling, the youthful Hanna passed considerable time, traversing, week after week, the then wilderness of western Ohio.

There is one incident connected with his first business enterprise well worthy of being recorded for the benefit of the young men who are ambitious to rise in the world.

It seems that in his nineteenth year, young Hanna occupied the position of clerk in a store in Piqua, Ohio. He and another young man, also a minor, bought out the proprietor, giving their notes for $3,000. Soon after, these notes were transferred to an innocent purchaser. About the same time, the goods which they had purchased were taken from them by writ of attachment, leaving the young men without means, and incumbered by a heavy indebtedness. Hanna's partner soon relieved himself of the liability by the plea of infancy. Not so young Hanna. Although his friends advised him to the same course, representing that he had been swindled, he nobly declined, declaring that he would pay the last dollar of the debt, should providence ever favor him with the means. It is but justice to the memory of Mr. Hanna to say that he subsequently redeemed this promise, and paid the debt, in full, principal and interest.

Integrity and uprightness thus early evinced, amidst strong inducements to a contrary course, characterized his long and useful career, and gave him immense influence over his fellow men. If young men would emulate his example in this respect, the word failure would seldom be written over their business lives.

Subsequently he engaged for some time in teaching a country school; and he is represented, no doubt, truly, as having been a vigorous disciplinarian—an exact, systematic, and thorough instructor. Indeed, he seems, at that early day, to have indicated his future eminence and usefulness, by adopting and acting upon, that honest but homely maxim that exerted an influence so marked and so beneficial on all his subsequent career, and extended up to the hour of his death: "Whatever you find to do, do it with all your might," or, "Whatever is worth doing, is worth doing well."

He attended the Indian treaty at St. Mary's, in 1818, in the character of a sutler, or purveyor, in connection with his brother Thomas, furnishing both food for men and provender for horses, all of which was hauled with an ox-team from Troy, Ohio; he, with his own hands, hewing out feed-troughs for the stock. By this operation he realized a small amount of money. This was his first substantial acquisition—the corner-stone upon which his subsequent colossal fortune was reared. Here, too, his purpose was formed of emigrating to Fort Wayne, where he was destined to act so conspicuous and important a part in developing the resorces of the country and building up a city.

He arrived here in 1819, when he was in his twenty-second year. He found the place a mere Indian trading-post, with very few white inhabitants, and those merely remnants of the old military establishment. Outside of the "Post" and its immediate vicinity, there were no white settlers, and the country in every direction, for hundreds of miles, was an unbroken wilderness, swarming with the red men of the forest. He immediately entered upon mercantile pursuits in a small way, at what is now the Northwest corner of Columbia and Barr streets. The town was not then laid out. His first store-house was a rude log cabin, erected, principally, with his own hands. This primitive structure was soon superseded by a story-and-a-half frame building, and that, in after years, by a substantial brick block of business houses. These are still retained by the family and belong to the sharer of his joys and his sorrows, his toils and his trials, the trusted and honored companion of his youth, his manhood, and his old age, and who yet survives. May her remaining days be many among the living.

Of course, at that early day, his chief customers were Indians. Indian trade has always been profitable, even when conducted honestly and justly, as is universally conceded it always was by this young trader. It may here be remarked that Indian traders, as a class, have mostly been regarded as about the worst specimens of the race; being chiefly intent, by the basest arts, upon defrauding the ignorant and simple-minded children of the forest out of their annuities, or whatever little property they might possess. But no such imputation attaches to the character of Mr. Hanna. By a course of fair and honorable dealing, first with his Indian customers, and then with the whites, as they came into the country and the Indians receded, he acquired a high degree of regard and consideration on the part of the people among whom he lived so many years. This regard and consideration went on increasing in volume and intensity while he lived, and only culminated when the portals of the tomb shut him from mortal sight forever.

SAMUEL HANNA'S splendid fortune was not acquired by defrauding his fellow-men, either white or red; but by great business sagacity, the most indomitable industry, and rigid economy. These three qualities he possessed in an eminent degree. He especially claimed credit for his economy during the early stages of his business career; and often declared that he never expended one dollar for any personal pleasure or luxury until he was worth over fifty thousand. How many young men of the present day will be able to say this when they are old?

From his first settlement at Fort Wayne, Mr. Hanna, at all times, and on all occasions, evinced a strong desire to build up the town, to advance its material interests in every way, and to improve and develope the resources of the country; and though not inattentive to his own individual interests, the cardinal purpose was kept steadily in view during his whole life. In all meetings of the people for the promotion of public improvements or public welfare, he was always a conspicuous and leading actor. He early perceived the indispensible necessity of opening and improving roads and other facilities for travel and intercommunication; but to fully appreciate his designs in this respect, it may be necessary to revert to the condition of things at that time.

As has already been remarked, Fort Wayne, as he found it, was situated in a wilderness, far removed from all improvements. The country around afforded no supplies, except the inconsiderable amount yielded by the chase, and a very small quantity of corn grown on the bottoms in the immediate vicinity by the occupants of the "Post," or Fort, themselves. The chief supply of provisions or provender, and almost every necessary of life, had to be brought from a distance; mostly from Miami county, Ohio, by way of St. Mary's; being transported by wagons to the latter place, thence to Fort Wayne by flat-boats, down the St. Mary's river. The dangers and difficulties that attended the shipment of supplies through this channel, can scarcely be conceived at the present day. Imagine men with loaded teams, struggling through swamps and interminable mud, day after day, lodging in the wilderness by night, then conceive the perils of boating on a crooked, narrow stream, through dense forests, beset with fallen timber and other obstructions in its whole course. Then think of the hardy boatmen, day after day, standing for hours waist deep in water, cutting away the fallen trees and removing them, exposed to wet and cold, with no protection but the scanty garments they wore, and they saturated with water for days in succession. Such was the severity of the service, that many persons engaged in it were brought to a premature grave.

The facilities for obtaining goods were little or no better. They were, mostly, purchased in New York or Boston, and brought up the Maumee in pirogues, a most laborious task; or packed through the wilderness from Detroit, on horses.

When it is considered that these were the best, and almost the only sources of supply, at that early day, the gigantic difficulties in the way of founding and building a city, may be faintly imagined but never described, nor even fully appreciated at the present time. Mr. Hanna, though he clearly saw and deeply felt them all in their fullest force, was by no means discouraged or disheartened. They only excited the ardor and enthusiasm of his indomitable nature, and nerved him to redoubled effort and determination. He and a few other public spirited men, who generally followed his lead, addressed themselves to the work of their removal with resolute and untiring energy.

The fruits of their noble efforts we this day largely enjoy. Pause for a moment and contrast the present Fort Wayne and its surroundings with the Fort Wayne of 1819. Then but few people, except Indians, no schools, no churches, no improved country, no town—not even a laid-out town plat. Now, a population rapidly approaching 30,000; a well cultivated, densely peopled, wealthy, productive and prosperous country in every direction; canals, turnpikes, railroads and other facilities for travel and transportation, abound, bringing to the city abundant supplies of produce, goods, building materials, and whatever may conduce to the comfort and convenience of the people (giving profitable employment to many of them), or add material prosperity to the place. New structures are springing up in all directions as if by magic. Temples of public worship, colleges and free schools, are being erected and beautified. Everything indicates thrift, enterprise, progress, and prosperity. Society is out of its infancy, and is rapidly assuming the proportions of a giant.

What has caused this wonderful transformation?—this bleak, desolate, and savage wilderness "to blossom as the rose," and become, in this short period of time, the habitation of a great, a free, a powerful, prosperous and magnanimous people? Such wonders are not visible everywhere. In many places, even in this favored land, instead of the rapid advances of improvement, we see evident signs of stagnation, of decay and dilapidation. Why this difference? In many instances the country lacked those enterprising men so indispensable to lead the masses, and inspire them with energetic effort, to direct those efforts, when aroused, to proper means and judicious ends—in short, to lend a powerful helping hand, and throw in the scale a heavy purse, when other resources fail. Society needs generals in civil life, as well as in war. SAMUEL HANNA was emphatically a general in civil life. His name is intimately associated and blended with every period in the history of Fort Wayne. No public enterpise of importance was ever undertaken by her citizens without his concurrence and aid. In truth, it would be impossible to write the history of Fort Wayne, without, at the same time, writing a large portion of the biography of SAMUEL HANNA. His vast and controling influence is visible everywhere, and was potential for good wherever it extended.

Soon after commencing operations at Fort Wayne, SAMUEL HANNA was appoined Agent of the American Fur Company, a responsible position, which he filled for a number of years to the entire satisfaction of the Company. He was, also, Associate

Judge of the Circuit Court, and was repeatedly elected, at that early period, and, in subsequent years, a member of the State Legislature. To the importance of some of his services in the latter capacity, allusion will, hereafter, be made. As his means accumulated he extended his mercantile operations to other places, particularly to Lafayette, where he was, for many years, concerned in a large house with his brother Joseph; and to Wabash, where he was connected in business with his brother Hugh, from both of which he realized large returns. He became an extensive land owner in the Wabash valley and elsewhere. The writer well remembers having heard him remark, upon setting out for Indianapolis, in 1843, that he could go by way of Lafayette and return by way of Andersontown, and feed his horse at his own corn crib every night during his journey.

The American people have been informed that a dim foreshadowing of a canal to connect Lake Erie with the Ohio river, was entertained by Gen. Washington, and other early patriots and statesmen, as one of the possibilities of the far future. But they are indebted to Judge HANNA for the first practical conception of tha, magnificent project. It was in a familiar conversation with the late David Burr in a little summer-house attached to his then residence, at the northwest corner of Barr and Berry streets, that he first broached the subject of a canal to connect Lake Erie with the Wabash river, to that gentleman. It struck Mr. Burr favorably. He was a scholarly gentleman, of ability and influence, well and respectfully remembered by the older citizens of the place. The two frequently consulted together in regard to this important matter, and partially matured a plan of operations. They opened correspondence with the Indiana Representatives and Senators in Congress, and secured their favor and influence for the great undertaking. These efforts resulted, in 1827, in a grant by Congress to the State of Indiana, of each alternate section of land for six miles on each side of the proposed line, through its whole length, to aid in the construction of the canal. Strange as it may seem at the present day, a powerful opposition to the acceptance of the grant by the State, was organized in some parts thereof, and Judge HANNA was elected to the Legislature as the especial champion of the canal policy. The contest was ardent and protracted, but resulted in the acceptance of the grant, and an appropriation of one thousand dollars to purchase the necessary engineering instruments and procure the survey and location of the summit level. Judge HANNA, David Burr, and a Mr. Jones were appointed Canal Commissioners. Judge HANNA went to New York, purchased the instruments, and, returning by way of Detroit, packed them on horseback from that city to Fort Wayne. Civil Engineers were scarce in the West at that day, but the commissioners procured one and immediately entered upon the survey, commencing on the St. Joseph river, six miles above Fort Wayne, where the feeder dam was afterwards built, Mr. Burr operating as rod-man and Judge HANNA as ax-man, both at ten dollars per month. The second day the engineer was taken sick and was compelled to abandon the work, Judge HANNA and Mr. Burr, alone, continuing and completing the survey of the summit feeder. They made their report to the succeeding session of the Legislature, and Judge HANNA, being again a member, secured its adoption, and the passage of an Act authorizing the construction of the Wabash and Erie Canal. Thus originated, and was inaugurated, almost, if not entirely, through the untiring energy, the indomitable perseverance of these two noble pioneers, HANNA and Burr, this stupendous work of Internal Improvement—the longest continuous line of artificial water communication on the American continent; if not in the world; and which was of such incalculable value to Fort Wayne and all Northern Indiana. They are far, very far, in advance of what they would have been, had there been no Wabash and Erie Canal. Indeed, it is no exaggeration to say that they would hardly yet have been out of the primeval wilderness without that great work.

Judge HANNA was Fund Commissioner for several years, and negotiated for most of the money with which the work was carried on.

In alluding to this subject, the American Railway *Review*, of September 1st, 1859, says:

"Probably no one contributed more to the success of the canal policy during the first and trying years of its progress, than SAMUEL HANNA of Fort Wayne. From 1828 to 1836, he was successively Canal Commissioner and Fund Commissioner, besides serving three years in the State Senate and one year in the House, representing, as Senator, perhaps one-third the entire area of the State, and filling, in each body, for a part of the time the post of Chairman of the Canal Committee. In these official stations he evinced the same judgment, tact and force of character which, nearly a quarter of a century afterwards, enabled him to render important service to the Northern section of Indiana, the enterprise of completing, under financial difficulties, such as would have discouraged men less courageous in assuming pecuniary responsibilities, that portion of the Pittsburg, Fort Wayne & Chicago Railway lying west of Crestline."

Perhaps the wisdom and ability of Judge HANNA were never more strikingly displayed in any single act of his life than in the establishment and organization of the State Bank of Indiana. When the derangement of the currency and financial embarrassment, consequent upon the veto of the United States Bank and other kindred measures occurred, he was a member of the Legislature. The President had recommended the creation of more State Banks to supply the circulation, retired by the closing of that institution. Accordingly, a charter was introduced into the Indiana Legislature of such a character that Judge HANNA and other judicious members thought it ought not to pass. He opposed its passage with great power and ability, and was principally instrumental in defeating it; but it was clearly seen that a charter of some kind would pass at the next session. A committee was appointed to prepare a proper charter during the vacation, to be presented when the Legislature again convened. Judge HANNA was made Chairman of that committee, and to him was confided the duty of drafting the proposed new charter. How well he performed the duty, may be inferred from the fact that it passed both houses of the Legislature almost precisely as it came from his hand, within a few days after their coming together, and was approved January 28th, 1834. Thus was created the State Bank of Indiana, by common consent, one of the best banking institutions that has ever existed in this country—an institution that continued in operation twenty years, affording the people a safe and sound currency, and yielding to the State a large accumulated fund at its close; an institution that exerted a marked influence on the subsequent Bank Legislation of many other states. No one ever lost a dollar by the State Bank of Indiana.

A branch was at once established at Fort Wayne, of which Judge HANNA was President much of the time, and Hon. Hugh McCulloch, present Secretary of the United States Treasury, Cashier, during the whole time of its continuance. The branches of this institution were generally well and discreetly managed, but according to a unanimous public sentiment, the Fort Wayne Branch was managed with pre-eminent skill and ability.

In 1836, Judge HANNA purchased the large remaining land interest of Barr and McCorkle, adjoining, and surrounding the then plat of Fort Wayne. This purchase, although it ultimately proved very profitable, for many years, involved him in serious financial embarrassments. He immediately commenced laying off and selling lots, but sales for some time were not rapid, money was exceedingly scarce, and most of those who did buy were unable to pay when their liabilities became due. Meanwhile, the interest on his large purchase had to be paid regularly. Moreover, such was his leniency towards his debtors, that he would, and did, for years, suffer every kind of inconvenience and pecuniary sacrifice, rather than press or distress them. Multitudes have comfortable homes to-day, in this city, who are indebted for them to the kindness and forbearance of Judge HANNA. It was a rule with him never to urge payment of any one who kept his interest paid up, and many were in arrears for even that for years together, without being disturbed.

In 1843, an outlet for produce and an inlet for people were opened by the opening of the canal to the Lake; the country began rapidly to settle, and the town to improve. The sale of lots was greatly augmented, money became more abundant, and payments more ready. Then Judge HANNA began to reap the benefits of his hazardous purchase—to enjoy the reward of his years of toil and embarrassments, and of his generous forbearance towards his poor debtors. "Hanna's Addition" is a very extensive and important part of the present city of Fort Wayne.

For several years succeeding 1836, Judge HANNA devoted himself, mainly, to the affairs of the Fort Wayne Branch Bank, to the management and improvement of his estate, and to the enjoyment of his domestic and social relations; accepting, occasionally, a seat in the Legislature of the State. During this period, his pet project, the Wabash and Erie Canal, was open to Toledo, working wonders in the developement of both town and country. But the roads leading to Fort Wayne were in a wretched condition much of the time, and their improvement became a subject of vital necessity. The question as to how the desired improvement could be effected was extensively agitated. About this time the building of plank roads was coming into practice in some of the eastern states and in Canada. A gentleman of this county, the late Jesse Vermilyea, visited and examined some of them, taking particular note of the manner of their construction and reported favorably. The idea was seized by Judge HANNA with avidity and acted upon with his accustomed promptness and energy. He and some other enterprising gentlemen, here and along the line, northward, immediately began to organize the Fort Wayne and Lima Plank Road Company and procure the stock subscriptions. The people were very solicitous for the road, but they were generally poor in money, and these subscriptions were almost entirely made in land, goods, labor, &c. About all the money used in building fifty miles of this road was borrowed of the Branch Bank, on the credit of the company; and this was expended in building the necessary steam saw-mills. The first attempt to let contracts proved a failure. In order to give the work a start, Judge HANNA took the first ten miles north of Fort Wayne and went, personally, into the work; superintending, directing, and with his own hands assisting in the most laborious operations. Others followed his example, and within about two years the road was completed to Ontario, a distance of fifty miles—the first improvement of the kind undertaken and completed in Northern Indiana. Other similar works followed in quick succession leading to Fort Wayne, among which was the Piqua Plank Road. In the construction of this, as in that of the Lima road, Judge HANNA was an active and leading participant. While others nobly did their whole duty, it cannot be denied that he was the Hercules, whose shoulder to the wheel propelled both of those works onward toward completion.

When the Pennsylvania and Ohio Railroad reached Crestline, and it was proposed to extend it to Fort Wayne, under the name of the Ohio and Indiana Railroad, Judge HANNA was ready with his powerful co-operation. He was largely instrumental in inducing the people of Allen county to vote a subscription of $100-000 to its capital stock. This was the turning point of the great enterprise at that time. Without this timely aid, the work would have been indefinitely postponed, if not entirely defeated. The project was strong in merit, but weak in funds. It was difficult to find responsible parties who were willing to undertake the construction of the work; but Judge HANNA, as in all else, was equal to the emergency. In 1852, he, in connection with our respected fellow citizen, Pliny Hoagland, Esq., and the late Hon. Wm. Mitchell, took the whole contract from Crestline to Fort Wayne, 132 miles, and immediately entered upon the prosecution of the work. After making some progress, the available means of the company became entirely exhausted, and the work was suddenly brought to a stand-still. A meeting of the directors was called at Bucyrus; but the prospect presented was all dark and dubious. No one could devise the ways and means to advance a step in the work. The case looked hopeless and desperate. Dr. Merriman, the President of the company, a most amiable and estimable gentleman, resigned in despair of rendering any further service. Judge HANNA was immediately elected to fill the vacancy occasioned by his resignation. In three days he was in the Eastern cities, pledging his individual credit and that of his coadjutors, Hoagland and Mitchell, for funds. This effected, without delay, he hastened to Montreal and Quebec, to redeem iron that had been forfeited for non payment of transportation. In this he was successful. The crisis was passed—light was ahead. Work was resumed. The Ohio and Indiana Railroad was again making progress, and in November, 1854, overcoming the most formidable obstacles, the cars from Pittsburg and Philadelphia, came rolling into Fort Wayne, waking the echoes of the wilderness as they came, and bringing hilarious joy and gladness to this hitherto isolated community. Then "was the town all a jubilee of feasts," festivity and exultation, such as it had never exhibited before, and possibly may never exhibit again. It was the initial line of a system of railroads that are destined, at no distant day, to radiate from Fort Wayne, "like the spokes from the hub of a wheel."

In the autumn of 1852, while incumbered with the building and financial embarrassments of the Ohio and Indiana Railroad, the Fort Wayne and Chicago Railroad company was organized, and Judge HANNA was elected President. "The means of this company to prosecute the work were to be derived, mainly, from the sale of the stock and bonds. The stock subscriptions which were paid in cash into the Treasury, were very small—amounting, perhaps, in all, to less than *three per cent.* on the final cost of building and equiping the road between Fort Wayne and Chicago. The stock subscriptions were paid, mostly, in uncultivated lands, farms, town-lots, and labor upon the road. A large portion of the real estate thus conveyed to the company in payment of subscriptions to stock, (over $1,000,000 in value,) was mortgaged by the company to obtain the necessary cash means to pay for grading the road-way." Other cash means had to be derived from the sale of bonds; and, as the company had been but recently organized, with but little or no work done on its line of road, of course, its securities met with no ready sale. In the face of these discouraging circumstances, which would have overwhelmed almost any other man, Judge HANNA went resolutely to work on the new line. He was thus, President and chief manager of two companies—both without money, except what his own exertions provided—whose united lines extended from Crestline to Chicago, a distance of 280 miles, and a leading contractor for the construction of one of them. Instead of being overcome or depressed by this immense responsibility; instead of fainting or faltering under the load that would have crushed most other men, he was fully up to the occasion. The difficulties that surrounded him only nerved him to the exertion of his great powers. The brightness of his true character never blazed out in fuller effulgence. The greater the pressure, the greater was always his resources, and the greater the elasticity of his nature.

Under such adverse circumstances, as above alluded to, it was not to be expected that the work would progress with great rapidity. The Pennsylvania Central Railroad Company extended a little assistance to the new enterprise, but not sufficient to effect any very decided result. In the beginning of 1856, however, the cars were running to Columbia City, and considerable grading had been done between that town and Plymouth, a distance of 45 miles further west.

During that year, it became apparent to many of the stockholders, as well as managers of the separate corporations, extending from Pittsburg to Chicago, and which, in fact, for all practical and business purposes, formed but one line, that the nterests and convenience of each, as well as of the public, would be promoted by merging their seperate existence into one great consolidated company. Judge HANNA early and earnestly espoused the cause of consolidation, and a meeting was called at Fort Wayne to consider and act upon the subject. Contrary to expectation, considerable opposition to the projected consolidation manifested itself at this meeting, headed and managed by the shrewd and talented Charles L. Boult, encouraged and assisted by others hardly less astute. The debate was animated and exciting. The best talent on both sides was warmly enlisted. The contest extended to considerable length, and its issue appeared doubtful. Before the debate closed, Judge HANNA rose for a final appeal No one who heard that brief effort will forget it. It was a condensed array of facts and arguments—a splendid out-burst of burning, earnest eloquence. The opposition was literally crushed out. The vote resulted in a large majority for consolidation—many who had opposed it in the beginning, voting in its favor. Thus, on the first day of August, 1856, the three minor corporations were obliterated on terms satisfactory to themselves, and the great Pittsburg, Fort Wayne, and Chicago Railroad Company succeeded to their franchises and liabilities.

The Hon. G. W. Cass was elected President, and Judge HANNA Vice President of the consolidated company; the former holding the position until the present day, and the latter until his decease. Out of respect to the memory of the late incumbent, the vacancy has never since been filled.

The new arrangement infused new life and energy into the work. Jesse L. Williams, Esq., was appointed Chief Engineer, and under his vigorous management, in November, a little over three months after the consolidation, the road was open to Plymouth, sixty-six miles west of Fort Wayne. That section of the Cincinnati, Peru, and Chicago Railroad, extending from Plymouth to La Porte, and there connecting with the Southern Michigan and Northern Indiana Railroad, was opened for business about the same time; thus giving, by the aid of two other lines, a through route from Pittsburg to Chicago. The idea was conceived, and gained some strength, of permitting the western terminus of the Pittsburg, Fort Wayne, and Chicago Road to rest at Plymouth for a while, perhaps indefinitely; and of reaching Chicago over the two other routes, by way of La Porte. This plan Judge HANNA opposed with even more than his usual vigor and ability, and was largely instrumental in defeating it. Nothing less than a direct, independent line—the company's *own line*—would satisfy him. As the round-about arrangement, upon trial, proved disadvantageous to the company, it was abandoned, and the direct line pushed forward to an early completion.

While Judge HANNA would never yield an iota of the interests of the company to any outside consideration, he was not unmindful of the interests of Fort Wayne, nor, perhaps, of his own individual interests. When those of the company could be as well, or better, subserved at Fort Wayne than elsewhere, he preferred Fort Wayne. Hence his untiring efforts for the establishment and building up, here, of the immense repair shops and manufactories that constitute so important a feature of Fort Wayne.

To him are we, mainly, if not entirely, indebted for the incalculable benefit derived from their location here. His sagacity foresaw their importance from the beginning, and he never, for a moment, lost sight of it. He had the aid and co-operation of other able and influential men, but he had to encounter the determined opposition of others equally able and influential. Those who are familiar with the proceedings of the Board of Directors, from the time of the consolidation, onward, know with what persistent industry and faithfulness he pursued this cherished object. Sometimes he advanced towards it by direct approaches—sometimes by strategy, or a "flank movement"—but he always advanced, never receded. Success was the work of years, but success was achieved at last, and the people of this city are now enjoying, and always will enjoy the fruits of those enduring, persevering, effective exertions for their benefit, that were silently, steadfastly prosecuted all those years, and of which few of them were aware until the work was consummated. Judge HANNA, by his wisdom, his moderation, his prudence, his conciliatory manners, possessed a standing, and exerted an influence in, the Board of Directors, equalled by few and surpassed by none; and now, that he has ceased from his labors and gone to his reward, it is no disparagement to the other distinguished gentlemen who composed that Board, nor evidence of undue partiality on the part of his friends, when they regard him as having been "the noblest Roman of them all."

On the 12th day of June, 1866, the day after the death of Judge HANNA, a meeting of condolence was held at the Court House by the citizens of Fort Wayne, and addressed by Hon. Joseph K. Edgerton. At the risk of some repetition, the following truthful and eloquent passages are extracted from his address on that occasion * * * * * * * * *

* * * * * * * * * * *

"When I first knew Judge HANNA, he was a large town proprietor in Fort Wayne, and a large Real Estate owner in Allen county—reputed rich in property, but poor in money—and all the powers of his mind and body seemed identified with and concentrated on the developement of his county, and the building up of Fort Wayne. He had before been an active coadjutor in the construction of the Wabash and Erie Canal, and,as one of the Fund Commissioners of Indiana, had in part borne well the heavy burden of managing the finances of the State, during the darkest period of its financial history.

The Wabash and Erie Canal, upon which great hopes had been based, had not realized those hopes. It had done much, but not all that was required, for the material developement of the Wabash Valley. It had helped Fort Wayne to grow from an Indian frontier trading post, to a thriving county town of some 2,000 or 3,000 people—but with the projection and construction of Railroads on the North and South of us, drawing to them the movement of men to the Northwest, Fort Wayne and Northern Indiana were passed by, and it plainly was not in the power of the Wabash and Erie Canal to save Fort Wayne from impending stagnation. No man more clearly saw this than did Judge HANNA, nor was more active and able in effort than he to avoid the impending evil.

A section of country so thinly peopled and so poor in money as ours was then, was not able to build railroads, and at first but little hope was felt, or effort made in that direction. Plank-roads, then a new and popular mode of public improvement—the materials and means for which were in our power—were first looked to, to supply the growing want of easy transportation, and to them, Judge HANNA, chief among our citizens, directed his energies. He was a projector and active and leading worker in the Fort Wayne and Lima Plank Road and in the Piqua Plank Road, two projects by which Fort Wayne sought to draw to itself a large Northern and Southern trade naturally belonging to it. Citizens of sixteen or eighteen years residence here, all know how faithfully Judge HANNA worked to build plank roads. With the efficient co-operation of Wm. Mitchell, Drusus Nichols and other public spirited citizens in and out of Fort Wayne, the Lima Plank Road, fifty miles long, was built, and this soon led to the construction of the Bluffton, and, in part, the Columbia, the Goshen and the Piqua plank roads, all of which did their part and much, to advance the growth and prosperity of Fort Wayne.

Judge HANNA not only planned and worked with his head, but with his hands also, in building the Lima Plank Road. He was one of the contractors on that work, and I well remember seeing him on one occasion, with ax in hand, superintending the work and showing the workmen how to lay the plank

Plank roads had their day—they were poor substitutes for the iron way, and the locomotive power o steam.

When that grand national line of railway, which is now the pride and strength of Fort Wayne, and with which his name is forever identified, the Pittsburg, Fort Wayne and Chicago Railway, was first projected,—beginning with the section from Pittsburg to Massillon, thence from Massillon to Crestline, thence from Crestline to Fort Wayne, and finally developing in the grand idea of a consolidated continuous line of railway from Pittsburg to Chicago—Judge HANNA was among the first to see, to appreciate, and to take hold of the golden enterprise, that was, in ten years time, to bring up Fort Wayne from the condition of an insignificant county town, to rank and dignity among the first commercial and manufacturing towns of Indiana; and not only to do that, but to make hundreds of miles of before wilderness country, to bear their golden grain, and to dot them over with thriving, busy towns and villages.

Judge HANNA early became identified with the Ohio and Indiana Railroad—the middle section between Crestline and Fort Wayne—of what is now the Pittsburg, Fort Wayne & Chicago road—on which work was commenced in the Spring of 1852. He was greatly instrumental in procuring the Indiana charter for this road, and the Allen County, Indiana, subscription of $100,000, and other county subscriptions in Ohio to aid in its construction. In 1852 he succeeded Dr. Merriman as President of the road, and became emphatically its leading spirit. In September, 1852, he was made first President of the Fort Wayne and Chicago Railroad Company, on its organization at Warsaw. From that time until the reorganization of the Pittsburg, Fort Wayne and Chicago Railway Company in 1861-62, no man held a more important position, or took a more active or influential part in the completion and management of that line of railway than did Judge HANNA. His labor and devotion in the work were unceasing.

It was my fortune to be intimately associated with Judge HANNA in active railroad management from 1854 to the close of 1860. I had abundant opportunity of knowing his zeal, his ability, his devotion, his untiring labor in the great work on which he had built his hopes of fortune and a public name. The powerful corporation, now so strong and prosperous, measuring its annual income, by well-nigh half a score of millions of dollars, knew in its early history, both before and after the consolidation, many dark and gloomy hours. From the Fall of 1854 to the close of 1860, it passed through a fearful struggle, not only for the completion of its work, but for its own corporate and financial life. The financial disasters of 1857 found the consolidated company with an incomplete road, with meagre revenues, and a broken credit. Many of its best friends, even among its own managers, were inclined to grow weary and to faint by the way. Through all this trying period no man worked more faithfully and hopefully, or was consulted more freely, or leaned upon with more confidence, than was Judge HANNA. He was a tower of strength to an almost ruined enterprise. He was at brief times gloomy and desponding, but he was a man of large hope, and a robust, physical organization, that eminently fittted him to stand up and toil on to a successful end. I think I may truly say, that no man who has ever been connected with the management of the Pittsburg, Fort Wayne and Chicago Railroad has had a larger share of confidence of all interested in it than Judge HANNA possessed. I have seen him in all phases of the company's affairs, and in the midst of negotiations involving the most vital interests in Chicago, Cleveland, Pittsburg, Philadelphia, and New York. Surrounded by the most sagacious financiers, and railway men of the country, such men as J. F. D. Lanier, Richard H. Winslow, John Ferguson, Charles Moran, J. Edgar Thomson, Wm. B. Ogden, George W. Cass, Amasa Stone, there was in Judge Hanna, a weight of character, a native sagacity and far-seeing judgment, and a fidelity of purpose to the public trust he represented, that commanded the respect of all, and made him the peer of the ablest of them.

If I were to attempt to define most clearly Judge Hanna's position and influence in the management of the Pittsburg, Fort Wayne and Chicago Railroad, I would say that he was especially the advocate and guardian of the local interests of the road. He was ever watchful for the home stock-holders, the local trade, the rights and interests of the towns and counties on the railway, and the rights and interests of the men who worked on the road. In those dark days, when the company could not, or did not, always pay its men, and suffering and strikes were impending, Judge Hanna sympathized with, and did all he could for, the men on the road who earned their daily bread by the work of their hands and the sweat of their brows.

Judge Hanna lived to see the Pittsburg, Fort Wayne and Chicago Railroad a completed and eminently successful public work. He lived to see Fort Wayne, the city of his love, to which he came when it was but a trading post, with no town or even post office between it and Chicago, grown to a large and prosperous city. He lived to reap, as he deserved, large pecuniary rewards for his years of toil and risk and self-denial. He died peacefully in his own home, surrounded by the evidences of the material prosperity he had aided to promote.

In our cemetery of Lindenwood, there is a beautiful monument, which Judge Hanna's own forecast and good taste have already erected to his memory. It will ever be looked on with interest, but Samuel Hanna has a grander and more lasting monument in Fort Wayne itself. Of him may well be said here what is inscribed upon a marble tablet over the entrance to the choir in St. Paul's Cathedral in London, to the memory of Sir Christopher Wren, its architect, '*Si Monumentum requiris circumspice.*'

One marked feature of Judge Hanna's character was his untiring energy. It was not in his nature to cease to work, until he ceased to live. We have evidence of this as well as other marked characteristics, his hopefulness and self-reliance, in the zeal and energy with which, just before his death, he was entering upon a new field of public labor, the building of the Grand Rapids and Indiana Railroad, a project second only in its public importance, and in its bearing upon the interests of Fort Wayne, to the Pittsburg, Fort Wayne and Chicago Railroad itself.

Knowing Judge Hanna, as I did, and of the influences he was able to bring to bear upon his new enterprise, I have but little doubt that if he had lived and retained his mental and physical strength, but few years would have elapsed before the iron rails of the Grand Rapids and Indiana Railway would have stretched from Fort Wayne to Mackinaw. But, like other greatly useful public men, it was his fate, under the will of God, to die ere he seemed to have rounded the full sphere of his usefulness.

It is perhaps not meet that I should say but a few words more as to the personal character and domestic habits of Judge Hanna. Most of you knew him well, for he went in and out before you for many years. Neither in person nor in mind was he what may be called a polished or educated man. He was a self-made man. He had received few advantages of early education. His was not a disciplined mind in the scholastic sense of the term. His teacher was the experience of an active and eventful life. He was eminently a man of affairs,—a practical man—not a man of minutiæ or detail—not a particularly orderly or systematic man, but one of a large, clear mind, and of indomitable purpose, grasping with great power the salient points and bearing and end of a public question, and moving towards it, if not always rapidly or gracefully, yet strongly and surely. While Judge Hanna was not a scholar, he was a great reader, and had learned much from books, as well as from men and things, and if without the aptitude or genius to produce what was elegant in literature or in art, he was an intelligent admirer and judge of both.

Judge Hanna belonged to the higher type of the pioneer class of men. He was a planter and builder, more than a legislator. He had the hope, the courage, the forethought, the fertility of resource, the unfaltering purpose and will that characterise the planters of colonies and founders of cities. He was a fine type of many of the unlearned, but nevertheless wise and able men who were the pioneers of the northwest. With high elements of statesmanship in his nature, he was not altogether adapted for legislative or even administrative statesmanship. He had rarely sought for or held political office. He was not a politician, he moved in a higher sphere of life. It has been said of Manasseh Cutler, one of the pioneers of Ohio, 'He was more than a statesman, he was the founder of a State. In the covered wagon in which he left his village home in Massachusetts to found Marietta, the imperial State of Ohio was wrapped up.' The same sentiment may be applied to Judge Hanna. He was more than a statesman, for he had in him the elements and powers of the men who build cities and found States.

With all his mental strength, and public usefulness, it was perhaps in his domestic life and social relations that Judge Hanna appeared to the best advantage. I have never heard a whisper against the purity of his private morals. He was a temperate, well controlled man. He was the idol of his family. He was of a genial, social nature, full at times of a quaint, homely, simple humor, that had about it the freshness of childhood. He loved his children and his grandchildren, and children and young folks generally. He was pleased to have them with him and around him. In the gallery of our accomplished young artist, Mr. J. A. Shoaff, I have lately seen the stereoscopic views of Judge Hanna's homestead, himself, and his household. They will remain as vivid pictures, not only of the person, but of the habits and character of the man. Among the pleasing mementoes that will remain of him, none can be more pleasing than these miniature scenes, portraying Judge Hanna, the strong and earnest worker through a life of public care, as a pleased spectator and actor in the scenes of his own home.

When such men as Judge Hanna die, not only the public heart is filled with sadness and an abiding sense of loss, but there is within the sanctuary of his own household a depth of sorrow that cannot be fathomed."

Judge HANNA accepted the Presidency of the Grand Rapids and Indiana Railroad Company, to which Mr. Edgerton alludes in the foregoing passages, with extreme reluctance. He seemed to have a foreboding that his life's work was drawing to a close. The position had been strongly urged upon him, but he had steadily declined it. When he was about leaving home to attend a meeting of the directors at Grand Rapids, less than two months before his decease, the remark was made to him that he would return President of the Company. He replied "No, that cannot be," and added with a mournful cadence, "the responsibility is too great, I can not accept it." The result showed, that although a man may be a ruler among men, he cannot always govern his own actions. He returned President of the Company. His desire for the success of the road, and the benefits its construction would confer upon a city whose interests he had cherished and fostered for a life-time, overcame any objections he had entertained to accept the laborious and responsible position. Judge HANNA's efforts for the improvement of both town and country, were not confined to those of a public nature, but his means were always freely advanced for the promotion and encouragement of private and individual enterprise. The Woolen Factory of French, Hanna & Co., the extensive Foundry and Machine Shops of Bass & Hanna, and the large Hub, Spoke and Bending Factory of Olds, Hanna & Co., may be cited as the later instances of the kind, and attest his liberality in this regard. They were all essentially aided in their earlier stages, by the use of his capital.

With the utmost charity and good-will towards all Christian denominations, Judge Hanna's "religious training was in the faith and spirit of the Presbyterian Church, of which his father was an elder for some fifty years." The organization of the first Presbyterian Church at Fort Wayne, in 1831, had his cordial co-operation and support, although he did not become a member until 1843; soon after which he was chosen a Ruling Elder, a position which he retained during the remainder of his life.

Upon the announcement of his death, in addition to the meeting of condolence, before alluded to, and other manifestations of public grief and sorrow, the Common Council of the City convened and unanimously adopted an appropriate preamble, and the following resolutions, as expressive of the universal bereavement that pervaded the whole community:

Resolved, That the Mayor and Common Council of the city of Fort Wayne have received, with the deepest sensibility, the announcement of the death of our great and good fellow-citizen, Hon. SAMUEL HANNA.

Resolved, That, as a mark of our respect and esteem to the memory of him we mourn, the Mayor, Common Council and officers of the city attend in a body the funeral obsequies, and that the municipal offices be closed for business during the funeral.

Resolved, That to the widow and family now borne down by the weight of this affliction, we tender our heartfelt sympathies and condolence, together with the assurance that we share with them their sorrow and their tears.

Resolved, That these proceedings be spread upon the minutes of the Common Council; that a copy of the same be furnished the daily papers of the city for publication, and the City Clerk be directed to transmit to the bereaved family a certified copy thereof, and that the citizens, in accordance with the proclamation of the Mayor be requested to close all places of business between the hours of two and four o'clock on to-morrow afternoon.

Resolved, That, as a further mark of respect to the memory of the lamented dead, the Council do now adjourn for one week.

The last illness of Judge HANNA was of brief duration. He was taken ill on Wednesday, June 6th, 1866; on Thursday his case was regarded as dangerous; on Friday he was partially relieved, and on Saturday he was decidedly better, so much so that he was up a portion of the day and walked about the house. But during Saturday night he was seized with a violent relapse, soon succeeded by unconsciousness which continued until Monday A. M., the 11th, when the community was startled and shocked by the intelligence, which flashed over the city with electric rapidity, that Judge HANNA was dead. No other event has caused so universal a gloom and sadness. Every one had lost a friend, and every one was in mourning.

The funeral took place on Wednesday, June 13th. The arrangements were under the charge and direction of the Masonic Fraternity, of which Judge HANNA had long been a consistent and honored member. A discourse was pronounced by the Rev. Mr. Wilson, of Warsaw. The attendance was, undoubtedly, by far the largest ever witnessed, on a funeral occasion, in Northern Indiana. It was, in fact, a spontaneous outpouring of the whole people. The procession extended from the Court House to the Cemetery, a distance of nearly two miles, while the street for almost the whole distance was lined with thousands of spectators. The bells of all the city churches tolled their sad notes simultaneously. All business was suspended in accordance with the resolution of the Common Council. Many houses were draped in mourning, and a deep sorrow pervaded the minds of the whole people. The Railroad shops and buildings, if not, literally, the works of his hands, the emanation of his fertile mind and effective purpose, were gracefully festooned with evergreens, wreathed into ingenious and tasteful devices, among which were inwrought, in large evergreen letters,

SAMUEL HANNA, THE WORKING-MAN'S FRIEND.

Every man in and about those shops and buildings knew him as a friend and loved him as a father.

In contemplating the many estimable qualities of Judge HANNA, integrity and industry appear as prominent characteristics—an integrity that no personal or other consideration could swerve, and an industry that knew no rest while anything remained undone. When a given task was accomplished, he would throw off all care and become cheerful, even mirthful—a rich vein of mirthfulness permeating his whole nature—or he would retire to his home and devote himself to domestic and social enjoyments, for which he had the keenest zest and relish. His temper was calm and equable, seldom aroused, even under severe provocation, but when it was aroused, it was swift and terrible. His manners were emphatically, those of the old school gentlemen—plain, simple, dignified—despising sham and pretense of all kinds. Passing the early part of his life on the frontiers, and his whole life in the rough experience of a new country, he possessed none of the sycophancy and false polish of the courtier. His devotion to every duty was intense, while his perception of truth and worth was almost intuitive. In his estimate of these he was seldom mistaken. His opinions were positive and strong; but he was always open to conviction, and when satisfied that they were erroneous, his concessions were graceful and unqualified.

Judge HANNA's mental endowments and reasoning powers were of a high order, and he had cultivated them through many years of close observation and intense thought. His far-seeing sagacity and prescience in the solution of great financial problems were remarkable. His experience in such questions had been extensive, and he had profited by it to the utmost. He stood among the great railroad managers of the country, and the great financiers of Wall street, the acknowledged peer of the ablest, and he was always listened to with deference.

Judge Hanna was a life-long student. His love of nature and of books, and his thirst for knowledge, were ardent. His mind was wonderfully retentive, and he had accumulated a fund of information on all the current topics of the day, that was rarely surpassed. Particularly in agriculture, horticulture, and pomology, which, for years, he had made a specialty, his knowledge was varied, extensive, and exact, as the many who have listened, with delight, to his discourses on these subjects, will remember. Though approaching the limit allotted to human life, his capacity for labor was undiminished; his mental acuteness, undimmed; his vigorous manhood, unabated. He was just entering upon a new and arduous field of labor and responsibility, when he was suddenly called from all earthly cares to a final account. Like one of America's greatest statesmen, he may be said, literally, to have "died in the harness."

Such is a brief and imperfect outline of the life and services of one of the pioneers of Fort Wayne; a bright exemplar, worthy the imitation of our young men, and whose fitting epitaph would be: "A Noble, Honorable Christian Gentleman."

GEN HYACINTH LASSELLE,

FIRST WHITE MAN BORN AT KE-KI-ONG'A.

GEN. HYACINTH LASSELLE.

THE FIRST WHITE PERSON BORN AT KE-KI-ONG-A.

—o—

The first white person born at Ke-ki-ong-a, or in this portion of the State, was the late Gen. Hyacinth Lasselle, of Logansport, Ind. His father, Col. James Lasselle, of Montreal, Canada, having been appointed an Indian Agent, for the tribes of this vicinity, removed with his family, to the village then, and for many years after, opposite the present site of Fort Wayne, in the fall of 1776. On the 25th of February following, the subject of this sketch was born at this point. He continued here with his parents until the fall of 1780, when the sudden assault upon the village by La Balme and his troops caused a very precipitate retreat by the few white, as well as all the Indian inhabitants. Col. Lasselle made his escape, with his family, down the Maumee by means of boats, with a loss of an only daughter, who, in the confusion of the flight, fell overboard and was drowned. He afterwards returned to Montreal, where he placed his son, Hyacinth, at school. The latter remained here at school until about sixteen years of age, when he was taken into the employ, as a clerk, of his older brothers, James and Francis Lasselle, who were then extensive traders at Detroit. After ascending the St. Lawrence, and crossing the Lakes, by means of battaux,—then the ordinary mode of travel—his party reached Detroit in the fall of 1793, after a journey of two months duration. Here he remained as a clerk in the establishment of his brothers for about a year.

The Indian war having been closed by the victory of Gen. Wayne, in 1794, and peace being fully restored, he was sent by his brothers to trade with the Indians at Fort Wayne, which had been erected in October following the battle at the rapids. He arrived here in the month of May, 1795, and continued to trade with the Miamies, and other tribes visiting the Fort, for about a year and a half. After this, he descended the Wabash, and traded at several points on that river, until the year 1804, when he removed his establishment to Vincennes, Ind., and located permanently at that place.

Upon the inauguration of Indian hostilities, by the battle of Tippecanoe, in 1811, he discontinued the Indian trade, and entered the military service. He served for a period of four years as a Lieutenant and Captain of a company of Mounted Riflemen, or Rangers,—a service of great hardship and danger,—and eventually attained the position of Major-General of the Militia. In the Spring of 1833, he removed from Vincennes to Logansport, and died at the latter place on the 23d of January, 1843, in the 66th year of his age.

In person, Gen. L. was about 5 feet 6 inches in height; erect, full-chested, and muscular. In his prime he was rather rotund and weighed about 160. His complexion was light, inclining to florid; his eyes of a light-grey color, and full; and hair dark. His features were regular, inclining to the Roman cast, and indicated intelligence, generosity and firmness. The accompanying portrait represents him as he appeared in 1812.

From the year 1795 until 1804 he was almost a constant resident or visitant of Fort Wayne in his character as a trader, and was very intimately acquainted with the various tribes visiting the Fort, and with their character, manners and customs. His relations of the many incidents connected with Indian life at the Fort here, would be highly entertaining; but their recital would necessarily occupy a very large space in this volume to detail all the interesting reminiscences of life here, as seen and often recounted by Gen. L. He was held in high esteem by the Indians, and especially by the Miamies, who, on account of his birth among them, always called him by the name of *Ke-ki-ah*, or the little Miami. He was very active and fleet of foot, and they took great pride in claiming him as their champion in that line; for, in early times athletic sports of all kinds, and especially foot-racing, were in great favor with the Indians and white pioneers here. It so happened, on one occasion, that the Miamies sent a challenge to all the neighboring tribes to meet him in the race. The Winnebagoes, of Lake Michigan, accepted the challenge, and sent a deputation with their champion to Fort Wayne to contest the palm. The race was run. But the Winnebagoes, exasperated at the prospect of defeat, let fly their arrows at him, just as he was in the act of winning the race, one of which pierced his thigh. This act of bad faith caused great excitement among the Miamies, who were about to proceed to acts of violence towards the Winnebagoes, that might have produced trouble between the tribes; but through the intercession of their favorite, the matter was finally dropped. His wound did not prove serious, and the arrow was readily extracted; but he beat the Indian.

---o---

HENRY RUDISILL.

---o---

One of the early pioneers of North-eastern Indiana, the subject of this brief memoir, was born in Lancaster, Pa., in 1801. His father subsequently moved to Franklin County, Pa., and, at the age of 14, Henry was placed in a mercantile establishment in Shippinsburg, Pa., to be thoroughly educated in all the different branches of that business. Three years afterward he removed to Chillicothe, Ohio, (then on the borders of Western civilization) as an employee of Messrs. Barr and Campbell, who were then largely engaged in the mercantile business at that and other points, east and west.

He remained with this firm till 1824, when he moved to Lancaster, Ohio, where he engaged in business on his own account, and was subsequently married to Miss Elizabeth Johns, who still survives him. In 1829 he moved to Fort Wayne, Ind., and, as the agent of Messrs. Barr and McCorkle, the original proprietors of Fort Wayne, had charge of their interests here until 1837; and while acting in that capacity, cleared and cultivated a large portion of what is now the "Old Plat" and "Hanna's addition" to Fort Wayne.

Mr. Rudisill was of active and energetic temperament, and a true representative of the men, who, under Providence, have made the Western country what it now is; and, with unselfish aim, always took an active and important part in every movement that tended to advance the interest of the county and city in which he lived. As early as 1836, he, in connection with his father-in-law, Mr. Johns, commenced the improvement of the Water Power of the St. Joseph river, at the point where the St. Joe Mills are now located, one mile north of Fort Wayne, and built there a saw mill and the first flouring mill capable of manufacturing merchantable flour in Northern Indiana. A few years later, he put in operation the first machine for carding wool that was ever used in Allen county; and, some years subsequent, in company with Mr. L. Wolkie, he started the first oil mill for making oil from flax seed; and also established the first woolen factory of North-eastern Indiana. So, too, in church and educational matters, and in such public improvements as tended to develope the resources of the county, he was always ready and willing to aid, and contributed freely to their support, according to his ability.

Being of German descent, and for a number of years the only one in the city who could speak both languages, he soon became the counsellor, friend, and helper of many who came from the Old World to make this portion of the New their home; and there are many in the county to-day who can date their first steps in their course of prosperity to his assistance and advice.

He was not a partisan in politics, though voting and acting with the Democratic party on all State and National questions, till 1854, when he began more especially to reserve the right to vote for men, on local questions, regardless of party caucuses or conventions. He served as Postmaster at this point eight years under Jackson's administration, and a term of three years a Commissioner of Allen county; and probably did more than any other man, through his personal influence with the Germans, to make the Democratic party the ruling power in the county.

Injured by a fall while superintending some work at one of his mills, his spine became affected, causing partial paralysis and subsequent death in February, 1858.

His uprightness, kindness, and affability in his intercourse with his fellow-citizens, early won for him a host of friends, who will ever cherish for him a kindly memory and regard.

In his more private, social intercourse, he was no less happy in winning the regard and esteem of every one with whom he came in contact, and we have the consolation of knowing that his true piety and earnest Christian faith have prepared for him a rich reward in that better world to which he has gone.

MRS. LAURA SUTTENFIELD.

But few of the pioneer mothers of Fort Wayne still survive among us to tell the adventures of the past, one of whom, is Mrs. Laura Suttenfield; who is now in her 73d year. Mrs. S. was born in the city of Boston, Mass., in 1795, and, as the reader will already have seen, came to Fort Wayne as early as 1814, by way of the St. Mary's river, then much navigated by "flats." It was soon after the arrival of herself and husband here, with some friends, that the old fort, built by order of Gen. Wayne, in 1794, was removed, and a new one erected on the site of the old one, by order of Major Whistler; in the building of which, her husband took an active part. From the time of her first arrival here, she, with others, made the fort their home, and continued to reside in the garrison several years after.

Ever attentive and amiable in her disposition, she early won the esteem not only of those within the garrison, but strangers visiting the post, then so famous in the northwest; and her recollections of the brave men who participated in the struggles peculiar to those early times are ever clear and interesting, as many can well attest among us to-day. Indeed, during many years past, if any question of special import came up for consideration, about which any doubts were entertained as to accuracy of date, name, etc., as one of the early pioneers of Fort Wayne once remarked to the writer, an appeal was at once had to the memory of Mrs. S.; and all felt confident and satisfied when she gave her decision on the point under consideration. Such was her memory in other days, and a few moments conversation with her upon early pioneer life in the west, at her present advanced age, will be sufficient evidence of her wonderful memory. Her husband, Col. Wm. Suttenfield, who has now been dead some years, was a most patriotic, kind-hearted man. For some time after his removal to this point, he was a non-commissioned officer of the fort here. At an early period of the struggles in the west he was engaged in the recruiting service, and for many months after his arrival here, he was mainly employed in bringing provisions and other articles needed by the garrison from Piqua and other points, on pack-horses, and usually had three or four men to accompany and aid him in his perilous and burdensome duties back and forth to the settlements. Being short and slender of form, and very active on foot, he would often say the Indians could'nt catch him, and that he was not afraid of them. And, as during the period of his recruiting service, in his labors as superintendent of "packs" and general provision contractor for the fort here, he was long and early a most serviceable man to his country and the little band of settlers and sojourners at Fort Wayne at the early period to which this sketch more especially refers. The first house (a substantial log edifice) that was built in what is now the "old plat," was erected by Colonel Suttenfield, at the northwest corner of Barr and Columbia streets, just opposite the grocery store of T. B. Hedekin, in which Mr. Suttenfield and family resided for many years after its erection, and were ever esteemed for their many kindly traits of character.

Mrs. S.'s recollections of Major B. F. Stickney, who often sat at the same table with them, are still quite fresh. Mr. Stickney was a sterling pioneer and soldier, and did much for the alleviation of his country during its infant struggles in the west, ever attentive to the wants and sufferings of the red children of this locality, as will have been seen elsewhere in this volume, who, in many instances, came to sad destitution and debasement through the use of intoxicating liquors, a few years after the struggles of 1812–14. Also of Colonel John Tipton and Colonel John Johnson, two most patriotic, intelligent, energetic, and serviceable pioneer, soldiers and citizens of the west—the former, for some years after the war of '12, a resident at this point, and more or less constantly in the society and at the residence of Mrs. S. and family; while the latter and family were long among her warmest and best friends, and at whose house she resided while living in Piqua, Ohio, before coming to Fort Wayne—of these and many others that might be mentioned, would the space allow, including also many interesting incidents of those early days, with some of which the reader is already familiar, her memory is yet most clear.

In view of the vast improvement that has taken place, within a few years, in what to her and others of the early pioneers here, was an uncultivated field, strewn with vast quantities of underbrush, with occasional heavy timber, knowing, and known by every one in the region, Mrs. Suttenfield now finds herself in the opposite extreme; and says she "knows no one now, and but few know her" among the great throng of new-comers in and about Fort Wayne; while the immense improvement in building, general culture, and industrial pursuits, have conspired to surround her with a busy air and tread that

> Tell no more of those primitive days,
> And cheery pioneer ways,

wherein, but a few years since, she mingled so hopefully and free.

With Gallagher, in his "Song of the Pioneers," how cheerfully can she, as, "with halting step," she moves forward, in view of

> "Another land more bright than this,"

join in the pleasing refrain—

> "A song for the early times out west,
> And our green old forest home,
> Whose pleasant memories freshly yet
> Across the bosom come:
> * * * *
> We shunn'd not labor: when t'was due
> We wrought with right good will;
> And for the homes we won for them,
> Our children bless us still.
> We lived not hermit lives, but oft
> In social converse met;
> And fires of love were kindled then,
> That burn on warmly yet.
> * * * *
> Our forest life was rough and rude
> And dangers closed us round;
> But here, amid the green old trees,
> Freedom was sought and found.
> * * * *
> Oh, merrily pass'd the time, despite
> Our wily Indian foe,
> In the days when we were pioneers,
> Fifty years ago."

ALLEN HAMILTON.

One of the early settlers of Fort Wayne, was the late Allen Hamilton. Mr. Hamilton was a native of Ireland, born in the county of Tyrone, in the year 1798. At the age of 18, meeting with a gentleman of some talent, who had but recently returned from a visit to America, young Hamilton listened with great attention to the glowing description of the New World—its free institutions, &c., and so thoroughly imbued was he with the excellence and beauty of the new country over the waters, that he returned home to his aunt's, with whom he was then living, with a full determination of seeking a home in America, and to emigrate thither just as soon as his means would admit; and, accordingly, in July, 1817, having acquired through his own exertions and by the aid of friends, sufficient means to bring him across the deep, with a small sum also to maintain him for a short period after his arrival in the Canadas, or until such time as he should be able to obtain employment, he set sail for Quebec, whither he arrived in due course of time, and soon presented himself to friends of his aunt, then residing there, who sought at once, through the commendation of his aunt, to obtain employment for him. But he seemed destined to meet with trouble and be deprived of the advantages presented by the recommendation of his aunt and efforts of his friends; for, but a few days had elapsed before he was taken sick with the ship fever, a disease that had prevailed on board the vessel that had brought him to Quebec. For six weeks young Hamilton lingered with this fatal malady. Beginning to show strong symptoms of recovery at the expiration of this time, through his physician's advice, he sought to reach a milder climate, and had only succeeded in reaching Montreal, when he was taken with a relapse of his recent attack of fever. His little means was now nearly exhausted, and upon his recovery from the fever that had greatly prostrated and enfeebled him, he found himself with but a small sum over and above his physician's fee; and desiring to reach Philadelphia, with no one to aid him in the procurance of money he sold some of his most valuable wardrobe in order to obtain the necessary means for his journey to the city of Brotherly Love.

After many vicissitudes and a long and tedious journey afoot, he at length reached Philadelphia. Without means and without friends, he wandered about the streets in pursuit of employment, almost despairing of obtaining anything to bring him a competency—still looking pale and haggard from his late illness. But at length his eyes fell upon a notice for laborers, tacked "on the door of an iron store." It was a moment of joy to him; yet the thought of his enfeebled situation flashed upon him, and fears soon arose in his mind as to the probability of his being able to obtain the position offered; for he had already, in his efforts and wanderings for a place, been refused a situation "as a common porter on account of his delicate appearance." From momentary distrust and fear, his feelings rose to the height of unwavering resolution and courage; and he at once entered the iron store. A benevolent Quaker chanced to be the proprietor of the establishment. Young Hamilton soon presented his claims, and having told his story, which was listened to attentively by his new acquaintance, the Quaker gentleman promised his assistance; and but about two days had elapsed before young Hamilton found himself, through the aid of his new benefactor, in "a clerkship, with a salary of one hundred dollars a year and board."

With "an increased salary," our young adventurer remained with his new employer till the spring of 1820, when he determined to visit the west, with a view to meeting a cousin of the name of James Dill, who had formerly been a general in the army. Learning that Mr. Dill resided in Lawrenceburgh, Ind., young Hamilton soon made his way to that point, and found his cousin in the position of Clerk of the Dearborn County Court. Desiring "to prepare himself for the bar," young Hamilton soon proposed to his cousin to enter his office, "agreeing to write six hours a day for his board and the use of his library;" which seems to have been readily agreed upon.

Here young Hamilton remained for some time, forming the acquaintance of many men of note, and, among others, made the acquaintance of Hon. Jesse L. Holman, then one of the Judges of the Supreme Court; and it was to the daughter of Judge Holman, (Miss Emeline J. Holman,) that Mr. Hamilton was subsequently united in wedlock,—a most amiable and intelligent woman, who still survives Mr. H.

Being induced, by Capt. Samuel C. Vance, to visit this famous military point in 1823, Mr. Hamilton was so much pleased with the general aspect of the country surrounding, and especially with the beauty of the scenery, about the confluence of the St. Mary and St. Joseph, besides perceiving many advantages of a desireable nature, he soon concluded to take up his abode here for the future. Captain Vance, a short time previous to his departure for Fort Wayne, having been appointed Register of the Land Office, then located here, Mr. Hamilton expressed to him his determination to remain here, and at once entered the land office as a deputy register, where he also "pursued his legal studies, with a view of being admitted to the bar as soon as the naturalization laws of the country would permit." But the country being yet very thinly populated, and thinking the law business would hardly prove remunerative, he abandoned further preparation as a lawyer, and subsequently turned his attention to that of merchandising—having, through "his good character, been enabled to purchase a small stock of goods on credit." This occurred about a year after his advent here with Capt. Vance. His stock was small, and the trade was principally with the Indians, who were then very numerous here—perhaps thirty to every white man in the region.

In his new enterprise, he was quite successful, and two years later, he was enabled to bring hither a very extensive stock of goods, with capital and credit largely increased.

Associating himself, at an early period of his business relations here, with Cyrus Taber, Esq., recently of Logansport, Ind., under the title of Hamilton & Taber, Mr. Hamilton now advanced rapidly in material wealth and influence; and the firm of Hamilton & Taber long enjoyed an extensive and enviable reputation and credit.

Possessing much of the tact and good nature of Sir Wm. Johnson, with whom the reader is already familiar, Mr. Hamilton early won the confidence and friendship of the Indians, and was especially liked and admired by the Miamies, who early and for years confided their business affairs to him. Chief Richardville, during several years prior to his demise, in 1841, had entrusted his affairs to the keeping of Mr. Hamilton, and never ventured upon any enterprise, legal transaction, or business affair of any kind, in his own behalf or that of his tribe, without first consulting his friend Hamilton; and the result was, that immense sums of money were not only placed in his charge by the Indians, but large amounts were often disbursed among them by him. Knowing the Indian character well, and their fondness for liquor, it often occurred, when they came to town, and desired to get "squabby," they would call upon Mr. Hamilton for *sho-nia;* but, instead of giving them money at such times, he would often persuade them to accept of something else, in order to discourage their thirst and desire for liquor; for which they would unhesitatingly spend all their money, if even, amounting to hundreds of dollars, in a few days. In this way, and for this reason he often induced them to take goods, and such articles that would serve them as clothing, &c., rather than see them throw their money away for liquor, and then lie about drunk, or, being maddened and bewildered by the liquor, kill or dangerously wound each other in the broils and petty animosities, sure to be awakened when intoxicated.

That Mr. Hamilton was largely indebted to the Indians for the major part of his wealth and business success, he often averred in his life time; but while this is true, it is clear that the Indians were long and largely in his debt for the great care and attention he always bestowed upon them, in transacting their business affairs, giving them much kindly advice, &c., during many years subsequent to their removal beyond the Mississippi, in 1846; and the Indians ever, to the time of their departure, for the west, and to the day of Mr. Hamilton's death, held him in high esteem.

In 1824, Mr. Hamilton received the appointment of Sheriff, for the purpose of organizing the county of Allen; which office, by a subsequent election by the people, he held for two years. In 1830, he was chosen county clerk, and remained in this position seven years. In 1824, commissioners having been chosen "to negotiate a treaty with the Miamies," Mr. Hamilton was chosen Secretary of the commissioners; and in 1838, being again tendered the secretaryship, he declined to accept it. In 1840, though politically opposed to the administration of Mr. Van Buren, who was then President of the U. S., Mr. Hamilton was appointed a commissioner with others, to treat with the Miamie Indians in the extinguishment of their land claims in Indiana, and to induce them to remove to Kansas; which terminated agreeably to the wishes of the government. In these latter relations, in view of his great influence with the Indians, Mr. Hamilton proved most servicable to the State and government. Constantly exposed, as they were here, to the whisky barrel and its debasing influences, Mr. Hamilton readily saw that they must soon be destroyed as a people, if they remained under its influence; and he humanely sought to induce their withdrawal to a point westward where they would see less of the traffic, and have a larger and more abundant field for the pursuit of their favorite mode of life—that of hunting and fishing; and readily succeeded in inducing a large mass of them to leave for the west.

During the administration of General Harrison, in 1841, Mr. Hamilton was appointed agent of the Miamies, which position he held till 1844, when he resigned. Some $300,000 or $400,000 were disbursed by Mr. Hamilton during the period of this agency, to the satisfaction of both the government and the Indians of the time.

Accustomed to frequent association with Chief Richardville, they enjoyed many a jocular contest. On one occasion, some years ago, Mr. Hamilton was riding a very spirited, fine-looking horse along Columbia street, and the Chief, who then had a trading house about where stands the store of Messrs. Heustis & Hamilton, in accordance with quite a prevalent custom with the Indians of the time, when they saw anything that pleased them very much, taking a fancy to the animal, cried out: "I strike on that horse, Mr. Hamilton." Seeing the Chief had the advantage of him in the "strike," Mr. Hamilton at once alighted and handed the horse over to the future care and keeping of the Chief, who, according to the custom, at once became the bona-fide owner of the horse. The next "strike" necessarily fell to Mr. Hamilton, and he was not long indifferent to the right now in his possession. So, some time subsequent to this "strike" of the Chief, he and Mr. Hamilton were riding together along the Wabash, where the Chief had several very fine reserves of land, one of which, particularly, drew the attention of Mr. Hamilton, and he at once exclaimed to Richardville: "Chief, I strike on this section." "Well," said the Chief, "I make you a deed for it, but we'll not strike any more." Mr. Hamilton got the land; and though the Chief had the *first* "strike," yet Mr. Hamilton certainly had the *largest*. But the matter ended in the greatest good feeling.

A convention for the revision of the Constitution of the State of Indiana being called in 1850, Mr. Hamilton was chosen a member, over a very popular Democratic competitor, by a large majority, which was a marked evidence of the esteem in which he was then held by the people. In the convention Mr. H. received the appointment of "Chairman of the committee on currency and banking." Among other important measures brought forward and adopted by this convention, was that of a provision for the establishment of free banking institutions, in which Mr. Hamilton wielded a most salutary influence; and the general proceedings of the convention were signalized by many wise and beneficial enactments, in all of which Mr. H. took an active part. Not possessed of great oratorical powers, he readily devoted himself to *work*—was an active *working* member—and made his points *tell*, whenever he presented them for consideration.

In the summer of 1857, Mr. Hamilton visited Europe—among other places the home of his boyhood, where he remained till the summer of the following year. Soon after his return home he was chosen, by a handsome majority, representative in the State legislature, which position he continued to hold during the whole term of election (four years), much to the satisfaction of the people generally of this section of the State--and here again, he was a *working* member,—striving on all occasions, where matters of general or special public interest came up for attention, to devote himself to the achievement of "the greatest good to the greatest number."

For some years after the expiration of his senatorial term, he continued to devote himself to his business relations in Fort Wayne; had been for some years President of the Branch Bank of Indiana, which was located at Fort Wayne some years previous to the convention already referred to; and the name of ALLEN HAMILTON is still familiarly associated with the banking interests of Fort Wayne—the old familiar banking-house of "Allen Hamilton & Co.," still retaining the name and title of the old firm.

Being now possessed of ample means, including a considerable amount of real estate,—a comfortable and beautiful home, with numerous advantages in almost every material point of view that might relate to business, political or social distinction—warm friends, and a commanding position as a man of marked integrity, intelligence, and good nature, he was enabled to look back upon his trying advent in the New World, and his first "small beginnings" at the *village* of Fort Wayne with no little interest. The

* * * "tide in the affairs of men,
Which, taken at the flood, leads on to fortune,"

had of late years signally favored him; and once fairly before the current of success, he seemed to have moved resolutely forward, gathering strength, at every turn—adding continually to his little fund still larger amounts, until at length he was able to count his hundreds of thousands, and, finally, in August, 1864, died a prosperous banker, and a most worthy citizen of a noble and worthy country.

---o---

MRS. EMELINE GRISWOLD.

---o---

This eldest of the few remaining pioneer mothers of Fort Wayne, who came to this point at a very early day, is now in her seventy-sixth year. She is of French origin, and was born in Detroit, Michigan, in 1792. As the reader will already have seen, she came to Fort Wayne as early as 1807, with her grandfather and grandmother, Batis Maloch and wife, the former being attracted hither in the capacity of a trader, this then being, as it had been for some years before, and so continued for many years after, a noted trading post with the Indians.

At the time of her advent here, she was a sprightly girl of sixteen. Her maiden name was Sheptaun. It was not the intention of her friends to remain permanently here when they came; but the scenery and everything in the region, though wild and uncultivated, proved so agreeable to them, and the trade that had called them hither so profitable, that they concluded to make their future home here; and at once located near the fort.

From an early period after their settlement here,—having sometime subsequently been united to a Mr. James Peltier, long a trader with the Indians of the northwest, and much liked by them,—the subject of this sketch became a great favorite with the Indians of this locality; and their warm regard for her enabled her to wield a most potent influence over their actions during many years of frontier life in this section of the northwest. Many of her narrations are indeed most thrilling and interesting.

Some time prior to the siege of 1812, some of the occupants of the garrison had received an invitation to join a pleasure party at the house of a French family, a short distance down the Maumee, and being somewhat fearful of the Indians then lurking about, and many of them by no means friendly towards the Americans, the young Miss Sheptaun, the subject of this sketch, was placed in the lead to shield the party from harm, should the Indians attempt to molest them. Leaving the fort, the party had not proceeded far in the direction of their place of destination, when some of the unfriendly Indians caught sight of them, and rushed suddenly upon them, intending to kill them. The Americans at once began to huddle about their leader and protectoress. Upon a near approach to the party, the Indians suddenly recognized their friend and favorite, Madamoselle S., who at once insisted that her friends must not be hurt or disturbed. The Indians now began to make some effort to sieze and strike the Americans, saying to her in their tongue, (for she could freely talk with them in their own language,) that if it were not for her they would kill the Americans. But she finally prevailed upon them to withdraw, and the party, much rejoiced, soon proceeded again on their way down the Maumee, arriving safely at the house of the French family they had started to visit and join in the festivities in view, enjoying themselves for several hours, and returning again in safety to the fort in the evening. Had the party thus ventured upon a pleasure excursion alone, or for any other purpose gone out of the garrison, at this period, it is not improbable that they would all have been killed by the Indians. Such was the young Miss Sheptaun's control over the savge men at Ke-ki-ong-a at the time.

Sometime subsequent to this event, some unfriendly Indians made an attack upon the fort. At this time she was alone in the hut occupied by herself and friends, the latter being then absent. Having made a sally upon the fort, a small party of Indians passed down the hill, to the northwest of the garrison a short distance, where the hut in which the subject of our sketch then resided, and stepped into the cabin, where they unexpectedly found their favorite alone. Instead of raising the tomahawk to kill her—as was then and formerly often the case when meeting a white male or female under similar circumstances—and would doubtless have been the result, in this instance, had any other than the family of their friend lived there,—they simply asked her for something to eat, which she freely and pleasantly gave them. Having partaken of the food set before them, the Indians signified that they were sleepy, and desired to lie down; and the savage party at once stretched themselves upon the floor of the cabin, where they soon fell asleep, and continued to snore heavily for some hours, when, fearing lest some of the garrison might come down, and see them thus quietly enjoying themselves, in her presence, she awoke them and told them they had better go away, as some of the men from the fort might come down and shoot them; to which they willingly assented, and soon passed out of the cabin-door, and strode away across the common and the St. Mary, toward the northwest, leaving their heroic friend and favorite again alone and unmolested.

Let the reader go back to those frontier times for a moment, and look about him. What a wild scene is presented about the point where now so much of life and civilization are want to be seen and enjoyed. What a contrast between the present and the Fort Wayne of that period,—a lonely garrison, with a few indifferent huts near it, far removed from the confines of civilized life; surrounded by a wily foe, daily seeking an opportunity to destroy the inmates of the Post, and make themselves masters again of this old rendezvous and scene of their early associations—what a contrast, I repeat, do we behold between the scenes through which the subject of this sketch so long ago passed, and the aspect presented to-day in the same locality and for miles around this old center of Indian life in the Northwest! Yet our pioneer mother, the once sprightly M'lle Sheptaun, has lived on through all the years of this great change, and, with a few others of "long ago," is with us to-day, to tell the story of the past—to tell the little ones, as well as the older folk, of those romantic days in the west, when the country was yet a vast wilderness, and the red man was lord of the forest—feared by day as well as by night.

But let us return to our story again. The Indians had not long been gone from the cabin of our heroine, before an officer of the fort, seeing none of the Indians about, ventured down to the little cabin to ascertain whether its inmates had been killed or not. Finding her still safe, and hearing her story of the manner in which she got rid of the warriors, he at once insisted that she must go into the fort, where she would be more secure, whither she went, and where, with her uncle, David Bourie, and other friends, she resided for some months, prior to and during the famous siege of Fort Wayne, in 1812.

Though now in the decline of life, her memory is yet quite acute, and when in a talkative mood, she readily and frequently details to her friends and acquaintances many interesting scenes and incidents of her early days at Fort Wayne.

———o———

THE EWINGS—W. G. AND G. W. EWING.

———o———

Most prominent among the early settlers of Fort Wayne, was the Ewing family; and having been favored with a manuscript account of the family, written as early as 1855, by Col. G. W. Ewing, deceased, while on a visit to Washington City, D. C., I here introduce a portion of the same, which will be read with no little interest by the many surviving friends of the Colonel and his esteemed brother, Wm. G. Ewing—while the stranger will find much to gratify his curiosity in its perusal.

"WASHINGTON CITY, D. C.,
"April 24th, 1855.

"Being the last and only remaining one of the four brothers, and in view of the uncertainty of life, I have thought that it would be but right, and that it was perhaps, a duty I owe to those who survive me, that I should make a statement of reminisences and facts within my knowledge, relative to the genealogy, rise, and progress of the family to which I belong.

"The absence of any record respecting my own parents, and of their fore-fathers, has always been a source of regret to me, as well as to my lamented brother.

"We could glean but a meager knowledge of them, only as it was gathered, incidentally, in conversation, from time to time, with our beloved parents. Even this, we failed and neglected to perpetuate, for my noble brothers were yet in the prime of manhood, and counted not on dying so soon.

"But they have all sunk to their final rest, and I am spared. I will not therefore longer defer, but will aim to make a plain statement from memory relative to the Ewing family.

"My father, Alexander Ewing, was born in the State of Pennsylvania, (the county not recollected,) about the year 1763, of Irish parentage—the third son—(his father's name was also Alexander) had two older brothers named William and Samuel.

"About the year 1769, my father, then a lad of some sixteen years of age, attracted by the spirit of patriotism, which, at that trying period, governed every true American, repaired to Philadelphia, and there enlisted in the continental army, and remained in service during the last three years of the glorious Revolutionary war. I often heard my brave sire speak of the incidents of that war, and of his love and veneration for Gen. Washington; but like many other young and thoughtless men who served in the Revolutionary war, he failed to preserve the written evidence of his discharge, or to leave behind him any statement showing what regiment he served in or the name of his commander.

"The next I remember of my father's history is, that some years after peace was restored, perhaps as late as the year 1787, he was engaged in a trading expedition, in what was then called 'the far west,' among the Six Nation Indian tribe. He erected a trading post on 'Buffalo Creek,' then an entire wilderness, and extended his winter trading expedition, after furs and peltries, into the country of the Alleghany mountains, encountering all the privations and hardships that are usual in a frontier life.

"Where once stood his humble trading cabin, now stands the great and growing commercial city of Buffalo.

"A few years later, and my father had settled down, prosperously, on a large and splendid farm, on the Genessee flats, near the village of 'Big Tree.' This is in the State of New York, on the Genessee river, some sixty miles above the city of Rochester. There he courted and married my mother, whose maiden name was Charlotte Griffith, the daughter of Wm. Griffith, a most excellent and moral man, of Welsh descent, and a farmer by vocation. The nuptials of my beloved parents, were celebrated at or near Avon Springs, not far from what is now known as Genesseeo. I cannot state the year that they were married, but think it must have been in 1795, or there abouts. An aunt of mine, my father's youngest sister, 'Katy,' or Catherine Ewing, was married, at the same time, to the Hon. John Jones. This uncle and aunt continued to reside on the Genessee flats, for many years; raised a large family of sons and daughters, and finally, both died there. These Jones are first cousins of mine—my mother had also several sisters and brothers; two of her sisters resided near Genesseeo, and do yet if not dead. One was married to a Mr. Squires—the other to Hon. John White. They have both raised large and highly respectable families.

"In the year 1802, my parents, in consequence of reverse fortune—my father having lost his splendid farm and residence, in consequence of security debts,—removed from the State of New York, and settled on the river Raisin, in the territory of Michigan, where now stands the village of Monroe, a beautiful and flourishing town. There my brothers, Wm. G. and Alex. H. Ewing, were born—and there too, I was born. In 1807, my parents moved to the State of Ohio, and settled in the small frontier town of 'Washington,' now known as Piqua—there, and at Troy, a town seven miles south of Piqua, we resided, until the year 1822. At Piqua, my sister Lovina was born, and at Troy, my sister Louisa.—(I forgot to state, in the proper place, that Sophia C., our elder sister, and the first born of our family,—and Charles W. Ewing, our eldest brother, were born in the State of New York, previous to our parents removing from the Genessee country.)

"In the war of 1812, my father volunteered and accompanied the Northwestern army, under command of Wm. H. Harrison. He was along in the fall campaign of 1813, when the great war chief, Tecumseh, and his British allies, were defeated at the celebrated battle of the Thames. My father attached himself, as a volunteer, to the spies, commanded by Capt. Wm. Griffith, my mother's eldest brother, a brave, and gallant officer. He received two balls, in the skirmish at the crossing of the river at the Moravian Towns, a few days before the final action, but they were not mortal. James Knaggs, another uncle of mine, by marriage, to one of my mother's sisters, and who is yet living near Monroe, Michigan, was also a spy, under Capt. Griffith.

"At the battle of the Thames, which, if my recollection is right, was fought on the 5th day of Oct., 1813—the great Shawnee war chief, Tecumseh, was killed. He was a brave, gallant, and noble Indian, and an implacable enemy of all the 'pale faces,' but not cruel, nor savage. He would not do a mean action. I saw him frequently, in 1810, and though then a lad only seven years old, still I recollect him well—heard him speak in council to Gen. Harrison, before the war of 1812 broke out. He was a native orator, a most graceful and elegant-looking Indian. My father and uncle Knagg found and recognized his body, very shortly after the battle of the Thames was over, for they both knew him well. In a short time afterwards, his person, being recognized and known, the Kentuckians cut all the skin off his body, to carry home as trophies, to be used, as they said, for 'razor straps.'

"My uncle, Capt. Wm. Griffith, was in the massacre at Chicago, in August, 1812, where Capt. Wells, and nearly the entire command, of two or three companies of infantry, were overpowered and nearly all massacred, by a very large force (supposed to have been three thousand) of Indians. They showed no quarters, except to a very few, whom they made prisoners. Capt. Griffith was among the latter, though he had fought gallantly during the whole fight. He was believed, by the Indians, to be a Frenchman—for he spoke the Canadian French language—and on this account his life was spared.

"The Northwestern Indians have always entertained a great friendship for the French, and call them their 'brothers.' Under this disguise, Capt. Griffith was spared from the tomahawk, and he soon after made his escape, and returned home in safety, but immediately again joined the army, and marched against the combined British and Indians, under Gen. Richard M. Johnson, of Kentucky. Capt. Griffith was a brave and gallant officer. He died in 1824, and was buried amid the ruins of old Fort Meigs. He left one daughther and two sons.

"In the spring of 1822, my parents moved from Troy, in the State of Ohio, to Fort Wayne, in the State of Indiana. On the first day of January, 1827, my father died, aged about sixty-three years. His disease was asthma, and other infirmities, produced by a life of hardship and adventure. He was a man of limited education, but possessed a strong will and indomitable energy; with him, to will was to do. He was a man of warm impulses—a true friend, and a bitter enemy. He was proud of his family, and delighted in the well doing of his children; was proud of his sons, and rejoiced in their prosperity. He was a Free Mason, and bore the title of 'Colonel.' His personal appearance was commanding. He was six feet high; straight, athletic, and active, when young. His complexion was rather light, his hair was auburn, and his eyes were blue. His weight, up to the age of forty years, did not exceed, perhaps, 170 lbs; but in after years, he became large, and somewhat corpulent, weighing over 200 lbs. His mortal remains were, by his own request, interred on a small mound, on the prairie, (his own land,) just west of what was then the village of Fort Wayne. This sacred spot is marked by a small oak tree, still standing—but in consequence of the construction of the Wabash and Erie Canal, in 1833, which passed very near to this spot, my brother, (Wm. G. Ewing,) and myself, thought it an unfit place for the final reposing of the remains of our father; so, in 1847, we erected a vault, known as the 'Ewing Vault,' situated in the public grave yard immediately south of the 'Ewing addition' to Fort Wayne, and there we caused to be deposited our father's mortal remains—enclosed in a zink coffin. The remains of our dear mother, and eldest brother, Charles W. Ewing, and of his little infant son, are also there—in zink coffins; and lastly, the remains of my last, and most lamented brother, Wm. G. Ewing, are there.

"I next proceed to speak of my most excellent and estimable mother, whose goodness I shall never forget. My mother, (Charlotte Ewing,) was many years younger than my father. She was, in all relations of life, a most worthy and excellent woman—a good neighbor, a kind mother, and possessed of great goodness of disposition, as well as energy of character. Her industry and solicitude for the success and happiness of her children, knew no bounds. It was the grand object of her honorable life. She clung to her children like a true mother, and no matter what the cold world said or did, she *never*, for a moment, withdrew from them, her love. She remained single, after the death of our father, and resided alternately among her children, each vieing with the other for her society.

"After my marriage, which was on the 10th of December, 1828, she resided much with me, and it was the happiest period of my life. She looked upon my wife, as if she had been her own daughter, and, for the love she bore me, took great interest in her. In return, my wife often, told me, that she loved my mother better than she loved her own mother.

"On the 18th day of March, 1843, my good mother departed this life, at the residence of her eldest daughter, Mrs. Sophia C. Hood—and within an hundred yards of where I then resided. She lingered for many weeks, and finally died,.from the effect of a large abscess, which had formed on her right side, internally. It was a mournful satisfaction to me, that I happened to be at home, and where I could, and did attend in person, on her, during all the time of her last sickness.

"She died, as she had lived—in peace, and with good-will to all. She was not, strictly speaking, a member of any christian denomination, at the time of her death, though she had, in former years, been a member of the Methodist church, and was always pious, and exceedingly moral in all her acts. She was a firm believer in the christian religion, and in a future existence, and I think she expressed her regrets to her daughter, Mrs. Hood, that she had not attached herself, formally, to some church and continued through life as a member—this was on her death-bed, during her last sickness. She died in March, 1843, at the age of sixty-three years, having survived my father, and remained a widow some sixteen years. Her remains were temporarily interred in the grave yard at Peru, Ind., adjoining Mrs. Hood's residence, where she died, but were afterwards removed to Fort Wayne and deposited in our family vault there. Her life had been a virtuous and well spent one, and she died without reproach, respected and esteemed by all who knew her.

"My parents left a valuable property, and the estate has been divided equally among the seven heirs—namely, their four sons and three daughters. * * * * * * * * The Ewing family are of Irish extraction—we are descended from Irish patriots who bore our name, and who were obliged to leave their native country because of their republican sentiments.

"Some of them settled in Pennsylvania—some in Kentucky—and some in Tennessee. The Hon. Thos. Ewing, of Ohio, is distantly related to us—so are most of the Ewings of Kentucky, Tennessee, and Missouri; and it is a remarkable circumstance, and fact, which I may here insert, without being guilty of egotism, that I never yet saw, or knew, a man of this family, of Ewings, (and I have seen and know very many of them), who was not a man of more than ordinary talents, and and ability, and many of them, were prominent, and distinguished men. The Hon. Thos. Ewing is one of the most distinguished lawyers and statesmen of this country; was Secretary of the Treasury, under Gen. Harrison's administration, in 1841, and again in 1853, was Secretary of the Interior, under Gen. Taylor. Has several times represented his State, (Ohio) in the U. S. Senate. Hon. Wm. Lee D. Ewing, one of the Kentucky branch, was also a prominent man—was once U. S. Senator from the State of Illinois, where he resided up to the time of his death. Hon. Andrew Ewing was a Representative in Congress, from Tennessee, and the Hon. Prebley Ewing was also a Representative in Congress, from Kentucky; and thus I might go on, speaking of others, of the name and kindred, who have filled, with signal ability, many places of honor and responsibility; but I will not enlarge—my object being simply to give, from memory, a simple and truthful family narrative, which may survive me, and be read with interest, by my children and their descendents,—and I cherish the fond hope that they will aim to emulate those who have preceded them, and *add to* our family name and reputation, rather than, by unworthy conduct, sink down, and detract from it. I wish that they would not only read and study the course and conduct of my lamented brother, Wm. G. Ewing, and of Alex. H. Ewing, and myself, but I want them to appreciate them, and aim to profit by our examples."

The names of the seven heirs mentioned in the foregoing, were Hon. Charles Wayne Ewing, some years ago President-Judge of the 8th Judicial Circuit of the State of Indiana; and ever esteemed, and yet extensively and kindly remembered, for his many excellent, intelligent traits of character; but who came to a very unhappy end, several years since, by destroying his own life in a fit of sorrow, brought on by an ill-advised marriage—a want of compatibility of temperaments; Wm. G. Ewing, formerly Judge of the Allen county Probate Court, also much beloved and regarded for his fine intellectual qualities and spirit of generosity; Alexander H. Ewing, for some years a very successful merchant at Cincinnati, Ohio; Geo. W. Ewing,* widely known for his fine business and general intellectual qualifications; Sophia C. Ewing, relict of Smallwood Noel, Esq; Lovina, deceased, some years ago married to the Hon. Geo. B. Walker, of Logansport, Ind.; Louisa, consort of Dr. Charles E. Sturgis, of Fort Wayne. Charles W. and Sophia C. were born at Big Tree; Lovina and Louisa Ewing at Troy, Ohio.

As early as 1827, Wm. G. and Geo. W. Ewing began their business operations, which have since become so extensive and widely known, under the title of "W. G. & G. W. Ewing;" and "by their articles of copartnership, all their estate, of any name and nature, became, and continued to be, the common property of the firm, until the 11th day of July, 1854, when the co-partnership ceased by the death of William." Ever reposing the largest confidence in each other, "no settlement of accounts ever took place between them."

In connection with their general business transactions, they established, at different times, a number of "side partnerships and branches," in Fort Wayne, Logansport, and La Gro, Ind.; in Michigan, Iowa, Kansas, Minnesota, Wisconsin; and it is said "their business extended from Europe to the Rocky mountains." With numerous and faithful employees, their name was long familiar "in every town and hamlet from the Alleghany to the Rocky mountains"—embracing extensive buildings and property in the cities of Chicago, Ills., and St. Louis, Mo.; also, under the firm of W. G. & G. W. Ewing, large business operations were carried on at Westport, Mo.

After the demise of Wm. G. Ewing, 11th of July, 1854, while on a visit to Lake Superior, Geo. W. gave much of his time to the winding up of the extensive business relations of the firm; and, aided by his agents and confidential friends, Mess. Miner & Lytle, by the 10th of October, 1865, made "a full, final, and complete settlement to the satisfaction of the administrators and legatees of his brother's estate," and which was "confirmed at the March Term (1866,) of the Common Pleas Court of the county of Allen," and the estate of Wm. G. Ewing closed."

At quite an early day, Col. Geo. W. Ewing was engaged in trade, and indeed began his first business operations among, the Shawanoe Indians, establishing a trading-post at the famous Indian village of Waughpocanata, Auglaize county, Ohio. In 1826, he attended the treaty of the Miamie Indians; and seems here to have laid the foundation of his subsequent business success. After this treaty, others were held at different points in Ohio, Michigan, Indiana, and Illinois, which he also attended, and "took a prominent part."

Being united in wedlock to Miss Harriet Bourie, in 1828, Col. Ewing now settled down at the village of Fort Wayne, where he remained till 1830, when he, with his family and a few others then living here, removed to the Wabash, at the mouth of Eel river, where they founded the present thriving city of Logansport, Ind. Quitting this point in 1839, with his family, he took up his residence at Peru, Ind., where he remained till October, 1846; when he removed to St. Louis, Mo. Here, in January, 1847, he lost his wife, and where he continued to reside till the death of his brother, William G. Ewing. It now became necessary that he should return

*The following, found among some of his papers after his decease, which refers, in part, to the MSS. from which the foregoing extracts are made, will show much of the finer feeling that imbued his *inner life*. "It is my intention," says he, "to complete this family sketch, (but he died, leaving it unfinished) if I can ever get time—and I will revise it, and divest it of all unkind expressions, for I would not transmit any thing of that kind to a future generation. It would be in bad taste. The good that men do lives after them, whilst their errors should be buried with them in their graves. To err is human, and where is that man who never errs? To forgive, when malice, and hatred, detraction, and ingratitude, have done their worst, is manly and noble."

to Fort Wayne, to attend to the business affairs of the firm here; and, in the latter part of December, 1865, he came back to his old home and the scenes of his early association; but his period of physical life now seemed destined to be of short duration. Upon his arrival in Fort Wayne, he found himself greatly afflicted with bilious pneumonia, from which he sometime after had only partially recovered, when heart disease took a severe hold upon him; and after a lingering and most painful illness of some five months, on the 29th day of May, 1866, his spirit passed quietly away to the brighter land beyond the grave

The estate of Wm. G. Ewing was quite extensive, amounting to some $750,000, 200,000 of which fell to his excellent wife, who still survives him; while the children of G. W. fell heir to the main bulk of his large fortune of about 1,225,000 dollars; and Messrs. Miner & Lytle, by certain provisions of the will left by the Colonel, are supervising the erection of many large and handsome buildings in Fort Wayne, Chicago, St. Louis, and elsewhere; the income from which, with other property of the estate of Geo. W., must reach a vast increase and value during the next half century.

But the scene has shifted; and these early pioneers have all passed away, leaving their stocks and bonds behind them, let us hope, wisely to be enjoyed, and judiciously, humanely employed and dispensed.

———o———

EARLY GERMAN SETTLERS OF FORT WAYNE.

———o———

What was written near a half century ago of the German, is equally true of him to-day: He is a "man of the world; he lives under every sky, and conquers every obstacle to his happiness. His industry is inexhaustible." Poland, Hungary, and Russia were years ago indebted to German emigrants; and the same may be said, in a great measure, of America—that almost universal characteristic of the German people, *rectitude*, united with an unswerving perseverance and industry, at an early period of our country's history, found their way to this land of promise in the continued influx of German emigrants; and while they, as a general rule, have prospered well, and in very many instances grown rich, the country has been greatly benefited and improved by this stable people.

Long noted for their liberal, philosophic sentiments, they are here, in America, as in the old world, extensive readers and apt thinkers. Sociable and talkative as a class, they know no fetters for the honest conscience of any man, and would as readily measure swords with the opponent of their national or individual freedom, as drink a glass of choice Rhine wine with a beloved countryman.

As in the Old World, the works which they produced and still produce there, "in watch and clock-making, in the arts of turnery, sculpture, painting, and architecture, are very wonderful," so in the New World of North-America, the German every where stands high in his profession, what ever it may be.

"The character of men," says Goldsmith, "depends much on the government under which they live. That of the Germans (of the Old World) has in general as little brilliancy in it as the constitution of the empire. * * * * There is one thing," continues he, "in the character of the Germans for which it is not easy to account; that is loquacity. The French themselves scarcely talk faster, or are more communicative, whether they are or are not strangers to each other, than these sons of the more northern regions." And "they write," he adds "with no less profusion than they talk, as their numerous authors and books can attest. The peculiar turn of the Germans," he further remarks, "seems to be for philosophy; they are distinguished from all the nations of Europe for a cool, and generally just judgement, united with extreme industry."

Everywhere in America, where there is population sufficient, you find the German newspaper; and books, in great quantities, are annually published in the German language in this country; while vast quantities, of every description, are being continually imported from the extensive publishing house of Leipzig, Stuttgard,

Bremen, Berlin, and Wien, in Germany, as the capacious shelves of our German fellow-citizens, Messrs. Siemon & Bro., of Fort Wayne, can well attest.

Here, as in the old German States, we have the two schools of religion, in many parts of the country quite extensive, and, perhaps, for the size of the place and settlement surrounding, none more so than Fort Wayne and vicinity; and while the German Protestants, as in the old country, are noted for their remarkable frugality, the German Catholics are here still distinguished for their frankness and good-heartedness.

Most conspicuous among the early settlers of Fort Wayne, many of whom still survive, are the familiar names of J. and B. Trentman, Jacob and J. M. Foelinger, A. Meyer, Geo. Meyer, H. Nierman, John Orff, H. R. Schwegman, Dr. C. Schmitz, Henry Baker, Jacob Fry, B. Phillips, C. Morrell, C. Nill, Louis Wolkie, S. Lau, H. Rudisill, A. Lintz. Rev. Dr. Sihler, Geo. Miller, E. Vodemark, C. Piepenbrink, D. Wehmer, Chas. and L. Baker, Chas. Muhler, and many others.

One of these early settlers gives an amusing account of his advent here. Having made his way up the Maumee with his family and what little household goods he then possessed, he at length drew up about the center of the village, which then consisted of a few indifferent log huts, scattered about the head of Columbia street and the old fort. The largest hospitality then (as, let us hope does now exist among the citizens of Fort Wayne) prevailed among every class of citizens here; ever anxious and ready, as they were, to attend to the wants of and entertain in their best and kindest way, the many emigrants and travelers seeking new homes in the west, regardless of race or sect; and scarcely had our German friend halted, before he was greeted with the words: "*Landsleute, wie gates*,' by a kind old Pennsylvania settler, Capt. Robt. Brackendridge, then register in the land office here, who at once pressed him to stop, saying they wanted more settlers, and that here was a good place to stop.

At this point, our new-comer enquired as to where Fort Wayne was, and how far it was to that place; saying that he wished to go there; to which Capt. B. replied that he was already in the place. Casting his eyes over the village, with both wonder and disappointment, at this announcement, he exclaimed, with no little emphasis, "*pshaw!*" But he stopped—is here to-day; and has seen, from year to year, with many others, the little village, with a few indifferent log huts, as presented on his advent here, between thirty and forty years ago, gradually expand into wonderful proportions, annually offering large inducements for the settlement here of men of industry, enterprise, and honesty of purpose.

Of this hardy, thrifty class of people, many of them but recently from the Old World, and others from Pennsylvania, Fort Wayne, at an early day, was made up. Early procuring small tracts of land, in some instances, and considerable sections in others, in and about the present limits of Fort Wayne, with their usual indomitable will and perseverance, they began to hew down the trees, clear away and burn the stumps and underbrush, until at length, in unison with other early settlers, of this section of the northwest, many beautiful and fertile gardens and farms began to appear on all sides; fruit trees were planted, and extensive orchards, in a few years more, began to gladden the new-comers with abundance of choice fruits; while, as the ground upon which our beautiful city stands to-day became gradually prepared and made free of stumps and other impediments, in the form of sand-hills, hazel-bushes, ponds, etc., new buildings began gradually to appear, and many comfortable dwellings, by the aid and energy of German labor, everywhere served to cheer the masses and encourage still greater efforts in building and general improvement. And so the place has moved steadily on to its present growth and prosperity of near thirty thousand inhabitants, the masses of our German fellow-citizens always busy with their hands, heads, and capital—aiding each other, planning new enterprises, erecting new edifices, and preparing the soil for the reception of seed and cultivation of plants and herbs. The result has been glorious; and at every side our improvements give promise of a still wider range of culture and general material advancement in the future. Many of the German settlers have now been here between thirty and forty years—some of them poling their way, at the period of their coming to this point, up the Maumee in pirogues to the then village of Fort Wayne—all quite poor in means, but able of hand and willing of heart, to *work*—to till the soil, and build themselves homes. Land being then quite cheap many made small purchases, while others worked at their trades or hired out as common day and monthly laborers, as was then common among nearly all classes of the early pioneer settlers of the west, for then all was new, and *work* was to be done by all, if a competency was to be gained, and the common necessities of life procured. And to-day it would be difficult indeed to enter any of the various machine and general workshops of Fort Wayne and fail to find the German unrepresented—indeed, in many of these extensive establishments a full score of these hardy yeomanry of the Old World are constantly employed from year to year; and are annually making purchases of lots in the city or its suburbs, and building thereon. and raising families; while many of the old German settlers have for years largely prospered in various ways; and to-day are variously engaged in extensive business pursuits, and greatly esteemed by the masses of Fort Wayne for their integrity, intelligence, and broad spirit of liberality and love of order.

Such are the Germans of Fort Wayne; and may their better sense of frugality, perseverance, integrity, and general spirit of industry and philanthropic liberality ever serve as worthy examples of emulation and regard for the generations yet to come.

———o———

These lines are appropriate here. They tell in rhythm of the brave and noble "PIONEERS OF THE WEST," who years ago sought homes in the western wilds, and, amid hardships and dangers, laid the foundation of future greatness. They are from the pen of Eliezer Williamson, of Ohio, and were written as early as 1842:

Where now, I ask, is that bold, daring band?
The honored fathers of this Western land;
They who first crossed Ohio's silvery wave,
And did unnumbered toils and dangers brave?
Though some of them did bid the world farewell,
Some still survive, their matchless deeds to tell.
Though fleeting years have passed forever by
Since first they trod beneath this Western sky;
Yet they remember well those early days,
And view our country NOW with great amaze.
The country THEN was an unbroken wild;
The "WESTERN WILDERNESS," it then was styled;
The Ohio *then* sent forth a wild-like roar,
And dark, dense forests waved upon the shore:
Along her strand the Indians then did dwell,
And oft was heard the wild and savage yell.
The mighty oak—proud monarch of the wood,
Upon these hills in stately grandeur stood.
Along these vales did ferocious panthers prowl,
And oft was heard the fierce wolf's frightful howl;
But all these savage beasts have pass'd away,
And the wild Indians too—where now are they?
They've disappeared—most of those tribes are gone,
Like night's dark shades before the rising dawn.
Can we forget that brave and hardy band
Who made their homes first in this Western land?
Their names should be enroll'd on history's page,
To be perused by each succeeding age:
They are the fathers of the mighty West;
Their arduous labors heaven above has bless'd.
Before them fell the forest of the plain,
And peace and plenty followed in the train,
In vain would I attempt to bring to view
The dangers which those pioneers pass'd through.
The wintry winds in wildness round them blow,
And o'er them often rolls the drifted snow.
Upon the cold damp earth their blankets spread,
There they reposed—this was their only bed.
They often crossed great rivers, deep and wide,
Their frail canoes they paddled o'er the tide.
Through pelting storms and the descending snow,

Though thinly clad, they still would onward go.
How many long and cheerless nights they pass'd
Unsheltered from the cold and chilly blast!
For many years those hardships they endured,
And they to arduous toil became inured.
What lasting gratitude to the them we owe!
'Tis from their toils our richest blessings flow.
Illustrious men! though slumbering in the dust,
You still are honored by the good and just!
Posterity will shed a conscious tear,
And, pointing, say, "THERE SLEEPS A PIONEER."

——o——

ALLEN COUNTY AGRICULTURAL SOCIETY.

——o——

This society was first organized in 1852 for the encouragement of agricultural interests and domestic manufactures. Under the management of Hon. Wm. Rockhill, I. D. G. Nelson, Lott S. Bayless, Wm. Hamilton, F. P. Randall, D. M. W. Huxford, H. C. Gray, and others, it continued, with varying fortunes, until 1860, when, owing to the disturbed condition of affairs throughout the country, meetings of members and annual exhibitions were discontinued. In 1859 a Horticultural Society was organized by some of the members of the Agricultural Society, and in 1863, the two societies were united, forming one sssociation, under the above title. The new Organization has been very successful, and, with weekly meetings, at their rooms, in the Court House, at Fort Wayne, aided by a fine Library, their discussions, are doing a good work in directing the attention of the public to the most improved system of agriculture and horticulture. The officers for the year 1868, are Adam Link, President; F. P. Randall, Secretary; S. J. Housh, Treasurer.

——o——

REMARKS.

In the compilation, writing, and arranging of the material throughout this volume, I have drawn freely from every available source, and have been most careful to accept of those facts only that are well substantiated by previously published records and persons yet living whose recollections of many of the scenes and accounts presented are still quite fresh and clear. I would gladly have continued the "Sketches of Early Settlers of Fort Wayne," had I been supplied with the necessary material with which to form the same, as I had frequently both publicly and privately expressed and desired at an early day in the preparation of this work. But a failure to comply with this desire is not to be attributed to neglect or indifference on the part surviving friends; and in view of a further issue of the work, it is still my wish to receive at any time such facts and reminisences of the early fathers and mothers of Fort Wayne as may be deemed interesting and valuable for this department of the volume.

The HISTORY OF FORT WAYNE could not perhaps have been prepared and sent forth at a more favorable or propitious period. Having attained a wonderful, and let us hope, a most valuable and lasting growth, with the prospects of, and earnest desire for, a still wider, more beautiful and benificent range of culture in the future, we are to-day the better enabled to look back upon the scenes and hardships of the Past, and to scan with a more scrutinizing vision the perils and vicissitudes that beset the pathway of the pioneers of the West; and the general connecting links of the work have been most carefully preserved throughout, rendering it thereby most vauable in a general as well as local point of view.

W. A. B.

INDEX.

* By an oversight of the printer, this Chapter is printed "VI," instead of V; and Chapter XV, by a similar mishap, is made to read, "Chapter XVI;" neither of which, however, otherwise interfere with the regular order or reading of the chapters throughout the book.

BIOGRAPHICAL SKETCHES OF EARLY SETTLERS OF FORT WAYNE, ETC.

www.ingramcontent.com/pod-product-compliance
Lightning Source LLC
LaVergne TN
LVHW020120110826
845151LV00001B/221